ETHICS FOR A
BRAVE NEW WORLD

ETHICS FOR A BRAVE NEW WORLD

John S. Feinberg & Paul D. Feinberg

CROSSWAY BOOKS

A PUBLISHING MINISTRY OF
GOOD NEWS PUBLISHERS
WHEATON, ILLINOIS

Ethics for a Brave New World.

Copyright © 1993 by John S. Feinberg and Paul D. Feinberg.

Published by Crossway Books
      a publishing ministry of Good News Publishers
      1300 Crescent Street
      Wheaton, Illinois 60187.

Art Direction/Design: Mark Schramm

First printing, 1993

Printed in the United States of America

Scripture is generally taken from *The Holy Bible: New International Version®*. Copyright © 1973, 1978, 1984 by International Bible Society. Used by permission of Zondervan Publishing House. All rights reserved.

The "NIV" and "New International Version" trademarks are registered in the United States Patent and Trademark Office by International Bible Society. Use of either trademark requires the permission of International Bible Society.

Library of Congress Cataloging-in-Publication Data
Feinberg, John S.
    Ethics for a Brave new world / John S. & Paul D. Feinberg.
      p.   cm.
    Includes bibliographical references and indexes.
    1. Social ethics. 2. Christian ethics. I. Feinberg, Paul D.
II. Huxley, Aldous, 1894-1963. Brave new world. III. Title.
HM216.F4 1993   170—dc20   93-4015
ISBN 13: 978-0-89107-736-7
ISBN 10: 0-89107-736-7

SH		15	14	13	12	11	10	09	08	07	06
23	22	21	20	19	18	17	16	15	14	13	12	11

To
our sister
Lois Anne Gonzenbach
with all our love
and appreciation

TABLE OF CONTENTS

Acad	*Academy*
Am Drug	*American Druggist*
Am J Hum Genet	*American Journal of Human Genetics*
Amer J Theol Phil	*American Journal of Theology and Philosophy*
Angl Th R	*Anglican Theological Review*
Asia J Th	*Asia Journal of Theology*
Bib Sac	*Bibliotheca Sacra*
Bib Th Bul	*Biblical Theology Bulletin*
Br Res	*Brain Research*
Breth Life	*Brethren Life and Thought*
Cal St Bar J	*California State Bar Journal*
Can J Theol	*Canadian Journal of Theology*
CBQ	*Catholic Biblical Quarterly*
Chi Trib	*Chicago Tribune*
Child Fam	*Child and Family*
Chmn	*Churchman*
Chr Cent	*The Christian Century*
Chr Cris	*Christianity and Crisis*
Chr Life	*Christian Life*
Chr Sch R	*Christian Scholar's Review*
Chr Soc Action	*Christian Social Action*
ChrT	*Christianity Today*
Chr TI	*Christianity Today Institute*
CL	*Campus Life*
Com	*Communio*

ConJ	*Concordia Journal*
Conrad Grebel R	*The Conrad Grebel Review*
Cov Q	*The Covenant Quarterly*
CTJ	*Calvin Theological Journal*
Curr Th Miss	*Currents in Theology and Mission*
DH	*Daily Herald*
Educ	*The Educator*
Ec R	*The Ecumenical Review*
Encount	*Encounter*
E/SA	*Engage/Social Action*
Etern	*Eternity*
ExposT	*Expository Times*
Faith Phil	*Faith and Philosophy*
Fort R	*Forthnightly Review*
FuJo	*Fundamentalist Journal*
GH	*Good Housekeeping*
GTJ	*Grace Theological Journal*
Hast Center Rep	*Hastings Center Report*
IBR	*IBR: A Review of Human Subjects Research*
Iliff R	*Iliff Review*
Int Her Trib	*International Herald Tribune*
Int J Phil Relig	*International Journal for Philosophy of Religion*
Interp	*Interpretation*
Ir Theol Q	*Irish Theological Quarterly*
JAAR	*Journal of American Academy of Religion*
JBL	*Journal of Biblical Literature*
J Ch St	*Journal of Church and State*
JES	*Journal of Ecumenical Studies*
JETS	*Journal of the Evangelical Theological Society*
J Fam Law	*Journal of Family Law*
J Law Rel	*The Journal of Law and Religion*
J Med Phil	*Journal of Medicine and Philosophy*
J Psych Th	*Journal of Psychology and Theology*
J Rel	*The Journal of Religion*

J Rel Aging	*Journal of Religion and Aging*
J Rel Health	*Journal of Religion and Health*
J Relig Ethics	*Journal of Religious Ethics*
JSNT	*Journal for the Study of the New Testament*
JSNTSupp	*Journal for the Study of the New Testament Supplement*
J Th So Africa	*Journal of Theology for Southern Africa*
Lode R	*The Lodestar Review*
Lon Q & Hol Rev	*London Quarterly and Holborn Review*
Luth F	*Lutheran Forum*
Luth Th J	*Lutheran Theological Journal*
Luth Wit	*Lutheran Witness*
McC Q	*McCormick Quarterly*
MenQR	*The Mennonite Quarterly Review*
Mod Ch	*The Modern Churchman*
Monist	*The Monist*
Morb Mort W Rep	*Morbidity and Mortality Weekly Report*
NEJM	*New England Journal of Medicine*
NTSt	*New Testament Studies*
NY Times	*New York Times*
NY Times Mag	*New York Times Magazine*
Other Side	*The Other Side*
Pacif	*Pacifica*
Par Mag	*Parade Magazine*
Past Psych	*Pastoral Psychology*
Perkins J	*Perkins Journal*
Per Rel St	*Perspectives in Religious Studies*
Per Sci Chr Faith	*Perspectives on Science and Christian Faith*
Phil Phenomenal Res	*Philosophy and Phenomenological Research*
Phil Pub Affairs	*Philosophy and Public Affairs*
Phil Quart	*Philosophical Quarterly*
Phil Stud	*Philosophical Studies*
Psych T	*Psychology Today*
Pub Int	*Public Interest*
Q Rev Biol	*Quarterly Review of Biology*

Ref J	*The Reformed Journal*
Rel in Life	*Religion in Life*
Rel Soc	*Religion and Society*
Relig Stud	*Religious Studies*
Rel St R	*Religious Studies Review*
RD	*Reader's Digest*
R Rel Res	*Review of Religious Research*
Rv Ex	*Review and Expositor*
St Luke J	*St. Luke's Journal of Theology*
Sci Chr Belief	*Science and Christian Belief*
Sec Opin	*Second Opinion*
Sev Mag	*Seventeen Magazine*
SJT	*Scottish Journal of Theology*
Sound	*Soundings*
Springf	*The Springfielder*
Stud Bib Theol	*Studia Biblica et Theologica*
St Vlad Th Q	*St. Vladimir's Theological Quarterly*
Them	*Themelios*
Th	*Theology*
Th St	*Theological Studies*
Th Today	*Theology Today*
Thomist	*The Thomist*
Tyndale Bul	*Tyndale Bulletin*
Un Ev Action	*United Evangelical Action*
USAT	*USA Today*
USNWR	*U.S. News and World Report*
VigChr	*Vigiliae Christianae*
Witness	*The Witness*
WJ Med	*Western Journal of Medicine*
Word World	*Word and World*
WSJ	*Wall Street Journal*
Zy	*Zygon*

P rospero, rightful Duke of Milan, was banished by his usurping brother Antonio to a deserted island. There Prospero lived and raised his daughter Miranda. As William Shakespeare's *The Tempest* opens, Prospero uses his powers to stir up a storm that shipwrecks a number of dignitaries from Italy, including Antonio and Alonso, the King of Naples. As the play progresses, Miranda, who has never seen a man other than her father, meets Ferdinand, son of the King of Naples, and falls in love. Near the play's end, Prospero confronts his brother Antonio along with the others who were shipwrecked in the tempest. Miranda, upon seeing this whole entourage of people, exclaims joyously, "O, wonder! How many goodly creatures are there here! O brave new world, that has such people in't!"[1] Miranda meant it seriously.

Several hundred years later Aldous Huxley entitled his vision of the future *Brave New World*. He meant those words ironically, because *Brave New World* is Huxley's frightening vision of a world in which freedom is dead and all concepts of morality are forgotten. Life is manufactured and controlled from beginning to end by modern technology. Huxley acquired his copyright for this book in 1932. It is incredible to see how similar our world is today to many things Huxley only imagined for literary impact.

Within our lifetime developments in technology have brought staggering changes to the way people can be conceived, born, healed, or die. And prospects for the future are as mind-boggling as what has already happened. Ethics intends to set forth what ought to be, not what is. But it should help us evaluate the rightness or wrongness of what is and tell us how to act in light of it. Unfortunately, changes in what "is" in modern life have far outdistanced reflection upon how we ought to live in such a time. This seems to be especially true among Christian ethicists, though even secular ethicists disagree about how we should live in this changing world.

So much is changing today in regard to the control of life and death and the understanding of human sexuality. Most of the developments in technology could not have been foreseen nor addressed by writers of Holy Scripture. Because of this, some may think it impossible to address these topics from a Christian perspective. We strongly disagree. Though Scripture never addresses directly many of the topics covered in this book, it sets forth enough principles about life and death, human sexuality and a citizen's relation to government that it is possible to evaluate contemporary practices in light of biblical teaching. Moreover, it is not only possible to address these matters biblically—it is *mandatory* to do so. In our pluralistic societies, Christians can no longer assume that others, our children included, will be exposed to and adopt Judeo-Christian morals or will know how to apply them to concrete situations. Hence, as Christians we must speak to these topics lest we find out too late, as in the case of abortion, that a morality foreign to Scripture has not only won the day, but has even been enacted as the law of the land.

The burden for this book grew over a period of years and through a set of developing circumstances. We both teach an introductory course in ethics at Trinity Evangelical Divinity School. Frustrated in attempts to find textbooks from an evangelical Christian perspective which cover more than one or two of the topics handled in this book, Paul suggested there was a need for a book like this and that we write it. Convinced of that need for the classroom, deeply disturbed by the moral drift of our nation, and convinced as well that this information needed exposure in the local church, we decided to write this book.

Though this book began out of academic and intellectual interest, three events in our lives turned it into a project that had direct implications for our life situations. We could no longer write this book as disinterested observers trying to discourse dispassionately about issues and decisions foreign to us. So, yes, we do have a vested interest in the way many of these topics are discussed and practices evaluated. However, we have attempted as best as possible to let our judgments, though influenced by our experiences, be determined by Scripture and its application through reason.

The first of these life-changing experiences came in November 1987 when John's wife was diagnosed as having Huntington's Chorea, a genetically transmitted disease. The disease is a slowly debilitating disease that has both physical and psychological components, and it is eventually fatal. It is controlled by a dominant gene, so that each of John's three children have a 50-50 chance of getting the disease. Symptoms do not begin to appear until around thirty years of age or later. Currently, there is no known cure for the disease.

The second event came in 1989. In April of that year, Paul's eldest daughter, then a single college freshman, informed Paul and his wife that she was pregnant. Though there was never a question raised about abortion, many agonizing hours were spent wrestling over whether his daughter should keep her baby or give him up for adoption. After struggling deeply with this question, his daughter decided to keep the baby. He was born in November 1989 and is a great joy and delight to his immediate and extended family. Still, the memory of the circumstances of his conception is troubling, and only time will tell how he will handle the news that his stepfather is not his genetic father.

In the midst of dealing with these events, we were overwhelmed by another set of events. In late spring of 1988, our mother suffered a stroke as a result of complications from diabetes. By the end of that year she had suffered another stroke and had to be moved to a nursing home. As a result of the stroke, she was unable to feed herself, so a feeding tube was inserted into her stomach. Though she was not continually comatose, she fundamentally did not interact with the external world. At the same time, the aging process in our father was having a rather dramatic impact. By early 1990 it became clear that he no longer could care for himself. A decision was made after considering Dad's wishes to move him and Mom to Northern California where they would be cared for by our sister. Mom's condition improved somewhat, but in January of 1992 she went to be with the Lord. Dad is still in a nursing home, but his condition continues to deteriorate as the aging process takes its toll.

As one can imagine, these events have dramatically impacted our lives. They have also delayed the completion of this book, though we feel that as a result of these experiences we can better identify and empathize with others who face difficult ethical dilemmas and agonize over hard decisions.

As we began to work on this book, we very quickly realized that with each new chapter and each new topic, we were in essence starting over on our research. Moreover, we also found that within the last fifteen to twenty years there has been a veritable explosion of literature on these topics. It is impossible to cover everything; decisions must be made at every turn. Any of the chapters could easily be expanded into a separate book. One of the early decisions made was that we would try to cover these topics as they relate to individuals facing ethical decisions. Even the chapter on the Christian and the secular state attempts to focus on the Christian's obligations to the state, not the state's handling of its citizens. Though it would be instructive to reflect on ethical conduct for larger groups (for example, one's community or nation), we simply could not get into matters of public policy. Such issues as whether the state should mandate and/or fund sterilizing the mentally retarded or should regulate (and how it should regulate) allocation of funds as well as procedures for genetic engineering really take the discussion into issues of social and political philosophy. These issues merit treatment, but they go beyond the focus of this book.

The writing of the chapters was divided between John and Paul. John wrote the chapters on decision-making, euthanasia, capital punishment, birth control, genetic engineering, divorce and remarriage, and the

Christian and the secular state. Paul wrote the chapters on abortion, sexual morality, homosexuality, and war, with John editing all of these and composing some of the first abortion chapter. Each of us read and commented on the chapters written by the other. Though we had not previously discussed our views on a number of the topics covered, we were pleased to find ourselves comfortable with the positions each espoused.

In order to complete a project like this, the help of many people is needed. We feel they should be acknowledged. First, our love and appreciation go to our families for their constant encouragement and their patience with us while we worked on this project. They have sacrificed time with us in order to allow us to write this book. We also want to express our appreciation to the administration and board of Trinity Evangelical Divinity School for granting us sabbatical time during which we worked on this project.

In addition, various student assistants have helped us. Some have gathered bibliography, others have proofread our chapters, and still others came to our rescue when there were computer problems. For all their help in these and many other ways, we express our gratitude to Gregg Allison, Matt Cook, Jim Dahl, Gary Nordick, Bruce Shauger, David Wegener and Steve Wellum. Then, a special word of appreciation is due to Crossway Books, and Jan Dennis, then editor-in-chief there, in particular. The Crossway personnel have been incredibly understanding and patient with us despite the delays in completing this book. In addition, Jan's friendship and encouragement amidst the difficult circumstances detailed has ministered tremendously to us both. We are deeply grateful to him and most appreciative to our Lord for such a friend.

Finally, a special expression of thanks and love is due to our sister Lois Anne Gonzenbach, to whom this volume is dedicated. Her tireless care of our parents has made it possible for us to have time to write this book and to carry on our other ministries. She has cared for their needs with exceptional expertise and diligence. Her life is a living example of what it means to honor one's father and mother. Our family is eternally indebted to her for her service to all of us in serving our parents. She has experienced firsthand many of the difficult situations of which we write, and she has handled them exceptionally well!

Ours is, indeed, a brave new world. Prospects of living in it are both frightening and exciting. May God be pleased to use this book to give guidance to those seeking to live Christianly in our times as they await the new world that our Lord himself will establish at his coming! And as a result, may the name of our Lord, who alone deserves praise, be magnified!

John S. Feinberg
Paul D. Feinberg
October 1992

CHAPTER ONE

Moral Decision-making and the Christian

W hat makes good acts good and evil acts evil? If German soldiers ask if I am hiding Jews in my attic, is it immoral to lie in order to safeguard those I am protecting? How do I know my moral rules are correct? How would I prove that Christian ethics are binding on non-Christians?

At one time or another most of us have wrestled with questions like these. One could easily study such issues for a lifetime, and yet they are only a sample of the many concerns facing moralists as they try to construct a theory of ethics which will guide daily decision-making.

In this chapter we want to isolate the major questions that arise in thinking about ethics and note various responses to them. Moreover, we want to set forth the theoretical framework for discussing the practical issues handled in the rest of the book. We turn first to definitions and distinctions used in discussions about decision-making.

FOUNDATIONAL DEFINITIONS AND DISTINCTIONS
ETHICS AND MORALITY

Terms like "ethics," "morals" and "morality" are often used synonymously. The same is true of "ethical" and "moral." In this chapter (and the book as a whole), we shall frequently do the same. Thus, to act ethically or morally means to act in accord with accepted rules of conduct which cover moral (as opposed to non-moral) matters. To have ethics or a morality is to hold a set of beliefs about that which is good and evil, commanded and forbidden. To "do" ethics or moral philosophy is to reflect on such issues as the meaning of terms such as "good" and "ought" and the method of justifying ethical rules.

On the other hand, "ethics," "morality," etc. are terms which are not always used interchangeably. For example, ethics is often defined as the branch of philosophy that reflects on such issues as the source of moral norms and how to justify one's rules for governing action in moral matters. Morals or morality may refer simply to the specific set of norms or rules by which people should live.[1]

Some define ethics as the study of morals, but that does not explain what morality is *per se*. Typically, the concept of morality is understood in one of two ways. For some, the point of morality is to note those things which are good (i.e., valuable or beneficial) and even to define "good" itself. Others maintain that the focus of morality is what is right (moral as opposed to immoral) and what ought to be done (i.e., one's duty). Each emphasis fits with a certain kind of ethical judgment that may be made. *Judgments of value* are judgments about what is good and bad, desirable or undesirable. *Judgments of obligation* focus on what is right and wrong and on what one must do or forego.

Taken together, the theory of value and the theory of obligation comprise the whole field of ethics. Some theories of ethics focus more on value than on obligation, though each ethical theory usually addresses both issues at least implicitly.[2] In this book, our focus will be more on matters of obligation than on matters of value. That is, our emphasis will be to answer what one is morally obligated to do or refrain from doing. Of course, as we address that question in regard to each topic, we shall frequently note the values that are upheld by fulfilling moral obligations. In fact, we shall often argue that a certain course of action is obligatory at least in part because it upholds a certain value (e.g., sanctity of life or justice).

NORMATIVE ETHICS AND META-ETHICS

A second way to divide the field of ethics is to split it between normative ethics and meta-ethics. Normative ethics deals with which actions are morally right and obligatory. Normative theories about what is right and obligatory presuppose some notion about the meaning of concepts such as right and good. Determining their meaning, however, falls within the domain of meta-ethics. Meta-ethics itself can be subdivided as follows: 1) discussions about the meaning of ethical terms and concepts such as right, ought and good; and 2) considerations of how ethical judgments (whether of value or of obligation) can be justified or established.

In this chapter we discuss both meta-ethical and normative concerns. In the book as a whole, we handle primarily normative questions as we try to delineate actions that are morally right and wrong in regard to the various topics discussed.

DESCRIPTIVE V. PRESCRIPTIVE LANGUAGE

Descriptive language tells what is the case and what is done. Prescriptive language commands what ought to be done; it sets forth moral obligation. Prescriptive language includes terms such as "must," "should," and "ought." Prescriptions are often stated in the imperative mood (e.g., "thou shalt not steal"). Descriptive language includes terms such as "is," "had," and "happened." When descriptive language is used, the intent is not normally to make moral judgments or commands.

The two kinds of language can be illustrated as follows: 1) John and Mary engaged in premarital sex; 2) John and Mary should not engage in premarital sex. Sentence 1) reports what John and Mary did. It makes no moral judgments about right or wrong, nor does it encourage or discourage any kind of action. On the other hand, sentence 2) states a moral duty (it prescribes a course of action), but it also implies an evaluation of a particular action. That is, whoever utters the sentence as a command presumably does so (at least in part) because he makes the judgment that premarital sex is not good (morally and/or otherwise).

We raise this distinction because sometimes it is assumed that an act is morally right and even obligatory just because it is being done. On the contrary, merely describing what is done does not in itself set forth moral obligation. In fact, ethicists debate whether it is possible to move from statements of fact to statements of value and vice versa. That is, can one derive statements of *ought* from statements of *is*?[3] A detailed examination of that issue is beyond the scope of this work. However, we raise these issues to remind readers to take seriously the distinction between descriptive and prescriptive language in ethics.

MORAL RESPONSIBILITY AND FREEDOM OF ACTION

Moral philosophers commonly agree that in assessing moral praise or blame for an action, one must consider whether the agent acted freely or not. The principle involved is: no one is morally guilty for failing to do what he could not do or for doing what he could not fail to do. That is, moral responsibility presupposes freedom of action. Moral "oughts" imply that the agent can do his duty. Thus, if someone points a gun at me and says he will shoot me if I do not rob a bank, I am likely to rob the bank. It is my duty not to steal, but presumably there is also a *prima facie* duty to preserve my life. In this case, I apparently cannot obey both duties. I disobey the duty not to steal, but I do so under constraint, not freely. In neither law nor morality am I held responsible as I would be if I had robbed the bank without compulsion.[4]

MORALLY PERMISSIBLE, MORALLY OBLIGATORY, MORALLY SUPEREROGATORY

These three concepts are very important in determining what may or may not or should or should not be done in particular situations. These notions are especially helpful when actions are not covered by explicit (or even implicit) moral absolutes. Many of the practical issues covered in this book involve such actions.

To say that an action is *morally permissible* means one may do it or refrain from it without incurring any moral guilt. Obviously, mandated acts are also permitted, and refraining is also allowed if the act is forbidden. However, the notion of morally permissible acts primarily refers to deeds neither mandated nor forbidden.

To say an action is *morally obligatory* means there is a moral command which mandates it or forbids it. The morally obligatory must be done (or avoided), and failure to fulfill moral obligation brings moral censure. While there is debate about which acts are morally required, it is agreed that moral duties may not be ignored without incurring moral rebuke.

Morally supererogatory deeds are not duties but are praiseworthy, because they produce good which goes beyond what duty demands. The concept may be illustrated as follows: it is a *prima facie* duty to preserve life, and that duty includes preserving one's own life. If I can save someone else's endangered life without jeopardizing my life, moral philosophers would usually say it is my duty to do so. On the other hand, if saving another's life endangers my life or would cause me to lose my life, I am not morally obligated to try to save the other person's life. If my life is endangered, but I try to rescue another person anyway, my attempt goes above and beyond the call of duty. My act is morally permissible but not morally obligatory. It is also a work of supererogation, an act beyond the call of duty. Suppose, then, that I do not know how to swim, but I see a child drowning in a river. If I try to save her, under those circumstances my act is not my duty but is an act of supererogation. Even if I fail to rescue her, my attempt (regardless of what happens to me) still goes beyond the call of duty (a supererogatory work). If I lose my life in the process (regardless of whether I save the drowning child), my sacrifice is supererogatory.

In this book our concern is to discover moral obligation in regard to each topic discussed. In some cases it will be difficult to specify a moral absolute that covers the issue. In those instances our goal will be to present as carefully and clearly as possible the kinds of acts that are morally permissible. In discovering the morally obligatory and permissible, acts which are morally supererogatory become evident.

WHAT MAKES AN AGENT MORAL IN DOING AN ACT?

How does one know if his actions are moral or immoral? Without an answer to this question, sinners may think they are saints, and saints may be tormented by doubts about their moral rectitude. The first step in addressing this issue is to distinguish it from the question of what makes an *act* a moral or immoral one (an issue for a later section). Even if one knows a particular act is morally good, it is still proper to ask if the one doing the act has acted morally.

Two answers, though often heard, are wrong. First, some answer that an agent is moral if he does an act that is morally good or refrains from doing a morally evil act. This answer does not emphasize motivations or intentions for doing an act, but merely notes that the agent did what the law demanded. If this sounds familiar, it should, for the Lord frequently rebuked the Pharisees for adopting this approach. They were very careful to conform their actions externally to the law, but Jesus was clear that mere external conformity to the law did not gain eternal reward, nor was it morally acceptable. Likewise, in the OT the Lord frequently stressed that he was not interested in mere outward conformity to the law; he wanted a proper heart attitude (cf. Hos 6:6). Scripture is not alone in rejecting mere external conformity to the law as the prerequisite for acting morally. Traditionally, philosophers and theologians have agreed that something else is required.

A second problematic answer is that one acts morally if good comes from what he does (consequences are the key). This may sound like utilitarianism, but it is not. For some utilitarians it is one's duty to act so as to maximize the greatest good for the greatest number. Thus, for them the results of an act determine whether the *act* is morally good or bad. However, even they would admit that what makes the *agent* moral in acting is not that good was maximized by his action, but that he *intended to do his duty* (in this case, the duty was to maximize good). Hence, for both utilitarians and non-utilitarians alike, consequences are not what makes the *agent* moral in his action.

Are consequences, then, the key for determining the morality of the agent? We think not. Our reasoning is best illustrated as follows. Suppose someone sees a child drowning in a swimming pool and tries to rescue him just because he needs help and because it is right to help. Suppose as well the attempt fails, and the boy drowns. On this theory of what it means to be moral, the would-be rescuer did not act morally, because the child died. Surely that conclusion is unacceptable. Likewise, suppose someone wants to rob a bank, but during the robbery he is apprehended before he gets the money. Because of the attempted robbery, the bank installs a better security system. As a result, everyone who comes to the bank will be safer, and money deposited in the bank will be better protected. On this theory of what it means to be moral when acting, the thief tried to do a harmful act, but because he was unsuccessful, he cannot be considered immoral. In fact, since good came from this incident, one might even say the thief acted morally. Examples like these should convince the reader that what makes an agent moral is not the results of his action.

What, then, does make an agent moral? We believe a combination of three factors is involved in assessing moral praise or blame. First, the agent must have acted freely, as already argued. If someone conforms to the moral law under compulsion, he is not considered moral. Likewise, if he disobeys the moral law, but is forced to do so, he should not be assessed moral blame. Moral responsibility involves freedom of action, so whether someone acts morally or immorally can only be determined when he acts freely.

Second, moral praise or blame depends heavily on the agent's motives for doing what he did. There are many possible motivations for action, but we follow Immanuel Kant's understanding of this matter. According to Kant, one may act from a desire to do one's duty, or one may act to further his own interests. Acting from a sense of duty (i.e., solely because the act is right to do and is one's obligation) is acting morally. Acting from self-interest is acting prudentially (wisely), but not morally. Consider the store owner who charges everyone the same price and does not overcharge an inexperienced customer. He may do so because it is right to do, but he might do it, because it is to his own advantage in the long run to be fair in his dealings. If he is not, word will get around that he takes advantage of unwitting customers, and business will suffer.[5] According to Kant, the merchant who charges fair prices out of a sense of duty acts morally. The one who has fair prices to achieve some further personal benefit acts prudentially (wisely), but not morally.[6]

Motivation, then, is crucial in determining whether someone acts morally, but finally, for an agent to act morally, he must do an act which is morally right to do. It is not enough to act from a sense of duty if one misjudges what is his duty. Even if an agent freely acts solely motivated by duty, his act is not moral if he does an immoral act. Depending on one's normative ethical theory, some acts will be prescribed as right and others forbidden as wrong. The list of right and wrong acts, obligatory and forbidden acts, may vary from theory to theory. Whatever deeds one's theory stipulates as right and wrong, the agent can only act morally if he does an act which is right to do.

In sum, an agent acts morally if he acts freely, does an act that is right to do, and does it with the sole motivation of doing his duty.

SURVEY OF ETHICAL SYSTEMS

Though ethical theories generally agree about the matters already discussed, nothing said so far presents an actual system. In this section we survey the basic kinds of theories available. Ethicists often like to group individual theories into broad categories. This can help understanding, but it can also be very frustrating. Frustration arises because authors categorize theories differently. Confusion begins to lift, however, once one recognizes that each category scheme is structured to respond to some critical question in ethics.

To illustrate this point, Edward Long (*A Survey of Christian Ethics*), William Frankena (*Ethics*), and Norman Geisler (*Ethics: Alternatives and Issues*) each discuss and classify a variety of theories. Each scheme differs, and that can be confusing. However, each scheme responds to a specific ethical question. Long's category scheme emphasizes answers to the question "What is the source of ethical norms?" Frankena's organization addresses more the issue of what makes good actions good and evil actions evil. Geisler's schema centers around how many ethical norms there are and how they relate. All three questions are very important, but they are not identical.[7]

Our desire is to discuss theories from the perspectives of the three questions mentioned. However, we must first note several other distinctions which form the bases for classifying ethical theories. The distinctions are between naturalistic and non-naturalistic theories and between cognitivist and non-cognitivist theories. Both distinctions relate to questions about meaning and justification of ethical terms and judgments.

NATURALISM AND NON-NATURALISM

Naturalistic ethical theories claim that ethical terms can be defined in terms of non-ethical ones and that ethical claims can be translated into factual ones. Thus, naturalistic theories hold that ethical sentences assert some fact (empirical or metaphysical, e.g.) and that the terms in them can be defined in non-ethical terms. For example, one theory may define "good" as "being conducive to harmonious happiness," while another understands "good" as referring to whatever God commands.[8] Thus, "murder is evil" may simply be a veiled assertion (for a divine command theory) that "God commands us not to commit murder" or (on a different definition of good) that "murder is not conducive to harmonious happiness." The claim about happiness is open to verification or falsification through empirical means, whereas the assertion about God's commands is open to justification through what might be called metaphysical reasoning. As to justifying ethical claims, according to naturalistic theories, one should be able to justify them the same way he justifies any other statement of fact (by empirical investigation or by *a priori* reasoning).

Non-naturalists think ethical terms such as "good" and "ought" are not definable in non-ethical terms. In fact, they hold that some of these terms are indefinable or simple and unanalyzable, just as yellowness or pleasantness are. G. E. Moore thought this about "good;" Henry Sidgwick thought it about "ought."[9] In addition, for non-naturalists, ethical and value judgments are true or false, but they are not justified as such by empirical observation or metaphysical reasoning. Typically, non-naturalists say that basic judgments are self-evident and can be known only by intuition. Non-naturalists, then, are often intuitionists.

COGNITIVISM AND NON-COGNITIVISM

The distinction between cognitivism and non-cognitivism in ethics concerns the meaning of ethical terms and judgments, but beyond that it emphasizes the difference between theories that claim moral judgments are matters of knowledge and those that say they are not. Cognitivists think ethical judgments state facts which may be verified or falsified. Hence, ethical judgments are items of knowledge. Since cognitivists believe this about purported facts which are natural or non-natural, both ethical naturalism and non-naturalism are cognitivist theories.

For non-cognitivists, ethical statements do not assert any kind of fact. They are meaningful, but not as raising items of knowledge. According to non-cognitivists, ethical judgments may be used in one of several ways. *Emotivists* hold that moral utterances merely vent an emotion or express an attitude. Thus, to say murder is wrong is to express a negative attitude toward murder ("I don't like murder"), but in so doing one is not asserting anything about whether murder really is or is not good or bad. *Prescriptivists* think ethical judgments do more than express emotions, but they do not regard them as statements of fact. Instead, they interpret them as expressing a command. Thus, "murder is wrong" means something like "you must not commit murder." Of course, this says nothing about justifying this prescription as proper. Prescriptivism does not even suggest whether commands are justifiable. It simply holds that moral utterances should be understood as merely giving a command.[10]

SOURCE OF ETHICAL NORMS

As already noted, ethical category schemes normally address some question in ethics. An initial schema focuses on the source of ethical norms. Both Christian and secular ethics address this issue in one of three ways: 1) reason, 2) prescription, and 3) relationship.

Reason-based Systems

Here the basic idea is that ethical norms are generated from and discernible by reason. For some theories, reason is also thought to justify the theory. Some Christian systems in this category also hold that revelation plays a role, but even if revelation provides some norms, reason alone could have generated those norms. In secular ethics one of the most famous reason-based systems is that of Immanuel Kant. Kant derived his categorical imperative ("act only according to that maxim by which you can at the same time will that it should become a universal law")[11] from reason alone. Though it is a prescription, it is not a demand that someone makes just because he has power to command others to obey. Rather, by reason Kant thought all should conclude it necessary to act in accord with this imperative.

Undoubtedly, the most significant Christian reason-based system is natural law ethics. Thomas Aquinas is the prime example of a Christian thinker who held this system. Stemming from him, natural law ethics has been especially associated with the Roman Catholic tradition. Though there are different forms of the theory, certain items typify natural law ethics generally. According to natural law theories, the end (the goal toward which it strives) of each thing in the natural order is built into the thing itself. Thus, by observing an object in nature, one can discern easily its intended purpose in the natural order. This end immediately indicates how the thing should act.

In addition, built into the structure of things is a set of laws governing conduct. Those laws will be closely related to each object's intended end or goal. Natural law theories also hold that such laws of conduct are universally known and that they are known by reason apart from special revelation. Moreover, since human nature and the natural order do not change, whatever ethical norms are derivable from nature do not change from time to time and place to place.

Finally, natural law theories typically claim that what reason discovers by reflecting on the natural order is consistent with what man intuitively knows through his conscience.[12] As one writer claims, essential to the notion of natural moral law are the "features of universality, unwrittenness and intuitively perceived or rationally discoverable moral knowledge of the divine will apart from special historical Biblical revelation."[13] Proponents of natural law ethics use various Scriptures to support their views, but the central passages are Rom 1:18-32 and 2:14-16. Natural law ethicists think biblical revelation of moral norms is important, but they hold that even without that revelation everyone can know by reason alone the basic principles of right and wrong. Consequently, one need not be a Christian or even a theist to know the moral law.[14]

Prescription-based Systems

For these theories, ethical norms originate from an authority figure who mandates them. This does not mean theories based on reason have no prescriptions, nor that theories based on prescription are irrational. The point is that commands in reason-based systems are determined by reason alone, whereas prescriptions in prescriptive theories come from an authority figure. That person may or may not choose rules on the basis of what seems rational, but that is not the key for prescriptive theories. The key is that someone or some group decides what is to be law and sets that forth.

Prescriptive theories often appeal to God as the prescriber, but not all theories do. For example, Brandt and Firth's ideal observer theory holds that calling an act right just means that any ideal observer would approve the act (and most likely prescribe it as well). But what defines an ideal observer? Brandt and Firth fill in the background conditions that make an observer an ideal one. Firth emphasizes procedures normally considered rational for decision-making. For example, one usually assumes that someone informed about the facts of a particular moral issue (for example, abortion) is better prepared to make a moral decision than someone not so informed. Hence, someone who qualifies as an ideal observer should be fully informed about all relevant facts for moral decision-making. Likewise, in moral decision-making, qualities such as impartiality are important; an ideal observer should have those qualities, too. By using this procedure, one can specify what would make an observer ideal. Then, one merely asks what moral norms that person would likely prescribe if he had the right to choose ethical rules. Those rules become prescriptive for all.[15]

Undoubtedly, the most influential prescriptive theories claim God as prescriber. Such theories are often labeled divine command theories, and there are varieties of them. The key, of course, is that God's will determines the norms. The basis of his choice, however, is understood differently depending on the theory. Divine command theories can be roughly divided on this matter in terms of the question raised pointedly in Plato's *Euthyphro*. That dialogue discusses whether an act is right *because God wills it*, or whether God wills it *because he knows it is right*. Divine command theories vary in their answer to Plato's question, but during the Middle Ages divine command theorists typically chose the former option. A prime example of such a theory from medieval times is William of Ockham's. According to Ockham, whatever God wills must be done simply because he says so.[16] If God had wanted, he could have ordered men to obey the opposite of the Ten Commandments. Even now he can rescind those laws and will their opposite.[17]

On the contemporary scene there are proponents of the divine command theory. Some give the impression that God chooses his commands completely arbitrarily; others hold that God's choices are not purely arbitrary, though they do not always explain God's rationale for his choices.

In addition, some ethicists hold a modified divine command theory. Robert M. Adams is a well-known proponent of such a view. He follows divine command theories in that he claims that ethical prescriptions say something about God's will and commands. On the other hand, Adams says every statement of ethical right and wrong presupposes that "certain conditions for the applicability of the believer's concepts of ethical right and wrong are satisfied."[18] Among those conditions is that God is love. Thus, Adams's theory amounts to the following: "x is ethically wrong" means "x is contrary to the commands of a *loving* God."[19] For Adams this implies that while it is logically possible for God to command cruelty for its own sake, it is unthinkable that he would do so.[20]

Relation-based Systems

Here the key idea is that actions are shaped either 1) by the sense of excitement or gratitude one feels as a result of a relationship with some person or group, or 2) by how some crucial principle relates to each new situation. In relation-based systems the emphasis may be responding to a person and/or because of one's relation to that person (God or Christ, e.g.), or the focus may be responding to a situation (e.g., what is the loving thing to do in this situation?), or both (e.g., what would Jesus do in this situation?). This broad category of systems includes such diverse approaches as those set forth in Thomas à Kempis' *The Imitation of Christ*, Karl Barth's notion that one must simply obey whatever God commands when God encounters him, and Joseph Fletcher's situation ethics which instructs us to calculate the most loving thing to do in any situation and to consider it one's duty. Each of these systems has a constant rule (do what Christ would do—à Kempis; do what God tells you to do—Barth; do whatever you calculate as the most loving thing to do—Fletcher). Nonetheless, the specific action following from this rule varies from situation to situation.

CRITERIA FOR GOOD AND BAD ACTIONS

A second category scheme for ethics addresses what makes good acts good and bad acts bad. Traditionally, there have been two main answers to this question and respectively two broad categories of theories. Those categories are teleological (consequentialist) theories and deontological (nonconsequentialist) theories. In more recent years, various ethicists have argued for theories that mix deontological and teleological concerns.

Teleological Theories

According to these theories, what is morally good or bad, right or wrong, obligatory or forbidden is determined by the non-moral value produced when the act is done. If the deed generates more non-moral good than evil, the *act* is considered *morally* good. Consequences (results), then, determine which acts are good and which evil. For a teleologist, what is good in the non-moral sense may vary. Many teleologists have been hedonists, identifying good with pleasure and evil with pain. Others have identified good with power, knowledge, self-realization, or other non-moral goods. Despite this variation, whatever non-moral good is the key for a given theory, those acts are *morally* good that produce the greatest amount of that *non-moral* good, and those actions are morally evil that remove or reduce such non-moral good. Teleological theories are generally of two sorts. The first kind focuses on producing the greatest good for oneself (ethical egoism). The second type emphasizes producing the greatest good for the greatest number (ethical universalism).

The most commonly held teleological theories are utilitarian. Utilitarian theories are of two kinds: 1) act utilitarian theories and 2) rule utilitarian theories. For act utilitarianism, an act is morally right and obligatory if it would produce the most utility (the best consequences) under prevailing conditions. Since this means one must calculate the effects of his action in each situation, no general rules such as "telling the truth produces the greatest general good" should be stated. Rule utilitarianism, on the other hand, claims that an act is right if it would be more beneficial to have a code of moral rules permitting that act than one which excluded it. Thus, rule utilitarianism looks for the rules that as a whole produce the greatest utility, and it prescribes them. On a rule utilitarian theory, like situations are handled in like ways, whereas with act utilitarianism, like situations are not necessarily treated the same way.[21]

Deontological Theories

Deontologists deny that morally good acts are determined by the non-moral consequences they produce. Other considerations make an act morally right or wrong, obligatory or forbidden. For example, an act is considered right because it keeps a promise, it is just, or God commands it. The key for deontological theories is that an act is right because it is one's duty to do it, and it is one's duty for some reason other than the consequences stemming from the act. Deontologists do not ignore consequences altogether. They only claim that consequences are not the basis for deciding the moral rightness or wrongness of an action. Examples of deontological theories include prescriptivist theories like divine command theories and reason-based systems like Kant's.

Mixed Theories

Some ethicists favor a theory which mixes deontological and teleological concerns. They believe that determining right and wrong must involve consulting rules. However, they are concerned that consulting rules alone might obligate one to do acts which are possibly arbitrarily chosen and may even have detrimental results for human well-being. For example, on a very strict divine command theory, what makes an act right or wrong is God's command. Nothing about the act itself commends it for prescription or prohibition. Theories like this give the impression that God may arbitrarily choose which norms we must obey. Likewise, depending on what God prescribes, the results could be harmful if those rules are obeyed. Think again of Ockham's claim that God could demand that we obey the opposite of the Ten Commandments. That would mean that murder, stealing, lying, etc. are morally good and our moral obligation, but obviously, the consequences of such acts could be ruinous for the victims. Concerns like these have led many ethicists to argue that the moral worth of an act must be determined by its ends and consequences at least as much as by deontological considerations.[22]

William Frankena offers an example of a mixed theory that he calls a mixed deontological theory. He says there are two basic principles of moral obligation: benevolence and justice. From the former stems principles such as the principle of utility, the principle of not injuring anyone, and the principle of not interfering with another's liberty. From justice follows principles such as equality before the law.[23] Now, his theory is deontological in that it tells us to decide on right and wrong by consulting rules normally associated with morality. It is teleological in that "it goes on to say that the best way to tell what rules we should live by is to see which rules best fulfill the joint requirements of utility and justice."[24]

THE NUMBER AND NATURE OF ETHICAL NORMS

How many ethical norms there are and whether those norms ever conflict are crucial concerns for people confronted with concrete decisions. If many norms supposedly have universal application, what should one do if several conflict in a given situation? Norman Geisler classifies theories according to their answers to this question.[25] He finds six answers. The first is *antinomianism*. According to this theory, there are no norms of any sort, so norms can never conflict. Of course, this theory gives no guidance on what to do in any situation.

The second possibility is *generalism*. According to this view, there are no *universal* norms but only general ones. Thus, ethical norms take the following form: "it is usually morally right (obligatory) to tell the truth." Such general norms allow exceptions. The exceptions provide a way to resolve conflicts between moral duties.

A third theory is *situationism*. It says there is only one norm, and it applies universally. Typically, that rule states the basic duty in each situation (do the loving thing, or do what brings the greatest good to the greatest number, e.g.), but it does not predict which act will fulfill the duty in any specific situation. The individual must decide that as he evaluates each situation. Obviously, with only one norm ethical rules can never conflict, but that does not mean one will always perform the same action even in similar situations. It only means that whatever one chooses to do will be governed by the one overarching principle.

Geisler labels a fourth approach *non-conflicting absolutism*. This view says there are many ethical norms that are all universal in nature. Though one might think those norms would frequently conflict, this theory claims otherwise. The norms never produce moral conflicts.

A fifth view is *ideal absolutism*. According to this theory, there are many ethical norms, they are universal, and they do conflict. Consequently, ethical dilemmas will arise where one must disobey one rule in order to obey another. Despite being put in situations where one is *forced* to break a rule, this theory says it is always wrong to break an ethical norm. One should be encouraged to act, however, for though there will be times when one must disobey a norm, there is forgiveness through Christ's blood.

A final theory is *hierarchicalism*. Geisler personally espouses this view which claims there are many norms that are all universal. Those norms are hierarchically ordered on the basis of their significance. When norms conflict (and they will), one must determine which is the higher rule and obey it. If one does this, he commits no sin by breaking the lower norm. Thus, if the rule to preserve life is higher than the rule to tell the truth, on this theory the one who lies about hiding Jews when asked by the German soldiers does what is morally right, and has no sin to repent.

Authors' Position

It is only fair to state our views on these various theories. We take our ethical norms from Scripture. Since we believe Scripture is God's word, we hold a form of the divine command theory. Contrary to some divine command theories, we think God's commands are neither arbitrary nor irrational, because we think they stem from and reflect his nature. Thus, because God is just, for example, he knows which acts are just and prescribes them; unjust acts are forbidden. On our view, certain acts are inherently right and others inherently wrong. They are so because they either reflect or do not reflect the character of the God who made the world and all in it. In sum, our view is a modified form of the divine command theory and comes closest to what Frankena calls metaphysical moralism.[26] Because we take our norms from Scripture and hold that Scripture is God's revealed word, the source of our norms is revelation, not reason. However, given our view that norms reflect God's character and that there are inherently right and wrong acts, we also hold that by reflecting on God's attributes and the world he made, reason can see the reasonableness of what God has prescribed. For the same reasons, we think reason on its own can reach some perception of what should and should not be done. At this point, we find some kinship with natural law theories.

Given this description, it should be clear that our theory is deontological. It is not that we think God is disinterested in consequences. In fact, we think his nature inclines him to act in his creatures' best interests. Moreover, we hold that if his commands are followed, the creature's best interests will be served. While some may think this makes us mixed deontologists, we think not. Being concerned about matters of benevolence and justice (to invoke Frankena's principles) does not mean our ultimate judgment of whether an act is right or wrong rests on those principles. We believe that assessment of the act rests on whether God has prescribed or forbidden it. Let us illustrate.

Christians are commanded to love their neighbors. In fulfilling that obligation one will undoubtedly consider whether a specific act in a particular situation is just and benevolent to the neighbor—to do so seems necessary in view of what it means to love someone. But what makes the loving act *morally good* is not that it is benevolent or just, but that God commanded it. To summarize: what makes an act an act of *love* is at least in part that it exemplifies benevolence and justice. What makes such a loving act *moral* is that it obeys God's command to love. We believe this approach to ethics is deontological, for it bases judgments of the morality of an act not on consequences, but on whether the act is governed by a rule (and in this case a rule prescribed by God). Obviously, however, it does not rule out concern over results of actions.[27]

As to moral conflicts, we think some form of hierarchicalism handles matters best. As W. D. Ross held, there are certain *prima facie* duties that we all have. A *prima facie* duty is a duty that arises out of a particular situation and obligates one to act in a certain way. For example, if one makes a promise, he obligates himself to keep the promise. When others help someone, the person helped is obligated to express gratitude. When one can help others, he is obligated to do so (a *prima facie* duty of beneficence).[28] When all things are equal, *prima facie* duties turn out to be actual duties. However, sometimes all things are not equal. When, for example, *prima facie* duties conflict, one cannot fulfill both. Failure to do both does not make one morally guilty.[29]

In this respect, Ross's position is like hierarchicalism. As to which duty becomes actual duty, Ross holds that one must use moral judgment. Sometimes the answer will be easy. For example, suppose someone promises to meet someone else at 10 A.M. However, while on his way he sees someone in danger whom he can help. If he stops to help, he cannot keep his promise to arrive at 10 A.M. Ross suggests that in such a case the duty to render aid is paramount, and the duty not to break a promise appears trivial. The right course of action becomes obvious.[30] In other cases, the actual duty will be harder to discern, but one must do so anyway.

Geisler's hierarchicalism has similarities to Ross's views. As with Ross, Geisler holds that when norms conflict, one is not guilty for failing to do both. Whereas Ross claims one must use moral judgment to discern actual duty, Geisler's position, though similar, argues that there will be a hierarchy of duties and one must obey the higher duty. Ross does not give the impression that one can construct such an absolute hierarchy.

As to our own view, we agree that there are *prima facie* duties and that sometimes they conflict. We agree with both Ross and Geisler that obeying one and disobeying or neglecting the other is not sin. One reason for holding this stems from an earlier point about being morally accountable only when one acts freely. If two duties mutually exclude one another, one cannot obey both when those duties conflict. No one is free to do the impossible. But if one cannot obey both duties, he cannot be held guilty for leaving one of them undone, for no one can be guilty for failing to do what he could not do.

Our belief that one is not guilty for failing to obey both duties also stems from an appeal to the example of Christ. As Geisler argues, it is unthinkable that while on earth Christ never confronted a situation where two duties conflicted so as to make it impossible to do both. In fact, Scripture says he was tempted in all points as we (Heb 4:15), and since we face such situations, he must have, too. However, the same verse says he was without sin; if that is so, it must be possible to confront such decisions, obey one duty, and not sin by neglecting or disobeying the other.[31]

The major point remaining is how to decide which duty has priority. Here we tend to follow Ross more than Geisler, for we are not sure it is possible to discover from Scripture or elsewhere an answer to how duties relate to one another in a hierarchy. Nor are we certain that if one did construct a hierarchy, it would be applicable to every situation, regardless of the factors involved in each case. Hence, we hold that one must evaluate each situation separately. In a given situation, one duty may clearly have priority. In that case, one must obey it. In other cases, both duties may appear to have equal priority. In those cases, the agent is free to do either one. So long as it can be shown that the duty chosen either counterbalances or overbalances the duty not chosen, the agent has acted morally. If, however, the duty chosen can be shown to have lesser priority than the one not chosen, the charge of moral impropriety is deserved.[32]

THE USE OF SCRIPTURE IN ETHICS

This topic raises two fundamental questions. First, can Scripture, written at different times and places from our day, be used at all in contemporary ethics, and if so, how? Second, how is the OT to be used, if at all, in Christian ethics?

THE BIBLE AND ETHICS

The Problems

This issue may appear to concern only non-evangelicals. Typically, they deny that Scripture can be used in ethics, for they see no single ethical system in Scripture, but rather conflicting ethical perspectives from the various authors. Moreover, some say we cannot even be sure about Jesus' thinking on ethical issues, since we only know Jesus as presented by the various Gospel writers. Those authors had their own purposes for what they presented and how they presented it, and they did not always offer a unified picture of Jesus' teaching (cf., e.g., Matthew and Mark on Jesus' teachings on divorce).[33]

Evangelicals often respond that the inspiration and inerrancy of Scripture guarantee unity in its teachings on every topic, despite the obvious diversity of perspectives of individual writers. When properly understood, no contradictions can be found.

Though evangelicals might think this ends the matter, it does not. Even granting an evangelical position on Scripture, can one directly apply every command to modern times? For example, must someone who believes OT law applies today keep OT dietary laws (Leviticus 11)? Are we required to build a parapet around our roof so no one will fall off and be killed (Deut 22:8)? As one writer aptly notes, one must distinguish between biblical ethics and the use of the Bible in ethics.[34] The Bible presents a perspective on ethics, but that does not mean every biblical teaching can be applied to modern times without any modification. The evangelical must decide which rules as stated in Scripture apply to our own day, and he must know how to decide which apply. The second task is more difficult, but it is foundational to the first.

Hermeneutical Principles

Rather than analyze each biblical command in order to discern which apply to today, we prefer to offer several principles for determining which commands pertain to our era. These principles must be used in conjunction with one another. First, one must distinguish between general principles or commands and specific applications of those commands. "General" and "specific" refer to the nature of the command, not the number of people the command covers. Is it a broad principle capable of covering many kinds of instances, or is it a rule covering a very specific type of occurrence? "Love your neighbor" is a general principle. It does not tell us how to express that love in a specific situation. It merely demands that whatever one does must exemplify love. On the other hand, "build a railing on your roof" commands a specific way to show concern for one's neighbor in a particular situation.

The key point here is that general principles normally apply to many situations, including those of our own day. Time and culture do not so qualify them as to make them irrelevant. Specific rules, on the other hand, often relate to particular circumstances of a culture different from our own and thus do not directly apply to us.

All of this may be illustrated by two examples. First, the command to love our neighbor is general enough to apply directly to today. A demand to build a railing on the roof is a particular application for a specific culture of the more general command to love one's neighbor. We should not take the specific command to mean that *we* must have houses with flat roofs and build a railing around them. However, the specific command rests on an underlying principle that loving one's neighbor means taking measures for his protection. That underlying, more general principle is applicable to our day. A legitimate application of it today would be to ensure that our friend wears a seat belt while riding in our car (an application totally irrelevant to Moses' day).

Consider a second illustration. Biblical injunctions about stealing are general enough to cover all times. However, Scripture nowhere explicitly outlaws videotaping a movie on television and charging others to see it. Nonetheless, doing so surely violates biblical principles, because it transgresses the general biblical teaching about stealing what rightly belongs to others. A rule about charging others to see a videotaped movie is irrelevant for biblical times, but it is a proper specific application today of an underlying general principle relevant for all times.

A second principle is that one must interpret the OT or NT command in light of its own social, political, and religious context. Before one can decide if and how a biblical rule applies to his day, he must first understand it in its own day. This may lead one to see that the rule was meant for a specific situation in another day, rather than being a general rule for all times.[35]

Third, one must discover, if possible, the reason for the command. Is the rationale theological or purely cultural? If the reason for a command is a theological principle that is always true, it is likely the rule will apply to our day. If the justification appeals to some point of culture peculiar to biblical times, the rule will not likely apply beyond those times.[36] Though not all agree, we believe (and will later argue) that Genesis 9 with its teaching about capital punishment illustrates the point. Genesis 9 demands capital punishment, because the killer has taken the life of someone made in God's image. God demanded that when that happens, the killer must forfeit his life. Since Scripture teaches that all people are created in God's image, it seems clear that capital punishment for murder must always be appropriate.

Fourth, one should decide how modern society relates to OT law altogether. Since we live during what may be called the NT era, NT principles pertain to today, but what about OT law, especially Mosaic Law? The question of the relevance of OT law for our day must be decided before one can decide how biblical ethics in general relate to our day. To that issue we now turn directly.

OT LAW AND THE NT ERA

Continuity Positions

These are views that see OT law continuing into the NT era. Some such as Greg Bahnsen say all of OT law applies today. Jesus came to fulfill it, not abolish it; none of it is irrelevant.[37] Bahnsen's basic hermeneutical principle for handling OT law is that unless Scripture shows change with respect to OT law, NT era believers should assume it is still in force.[38] For Bahnsen this means the moral law still applies, but it can be divided into two parts (general precepts of morality and specific applications of more general norms, i.e., case laws). General precepts apply without alteration, whereas one is not bound to keep case laws as worded (e.g., rules about railing one's roof), but are responsible only to obey the underlying princi-ple.[39] As to ceremonial law, Bahnsen argues that the ritual ordinances of the OT typified Christ and his sacrifice. "Christ does not abrogate their *meaning* and intention; rather, He makes their old manner of *observation* irrelevant, for circumstances have radically changed."[40] Those circum-stances center around the once-for-all death of Christ. That death does not abolish OT ceremonial law, but only reminds us that God in Christ has fulfilled the requirements of that law. Hence, observing it as in OT times is outmoded.

As to civil law, Bahnsen appeals to the Reformation notion of the three uses of the law. The second use is to drive sinners to Christ, and the third is to guide regenerated believers in living the Christian life. The first use of the law is known as its political use, its use in controlling government and society to curb the ungodliness of men.[41] Bahnsen argues that even in OT times the political use of the law was relevant to Gentiles, though they did not live under the Jewish theocracy. As to NT teaching, Bahnsen appeals to Romans 13 as teaching three principles also found in the OT: 1) rulers are not to be resisted, because God has appointed them; 2) rulers are avengers of divine wrath; and 3) "so rulers must deter evil by ruling according to God's law."[42] Since both testaments agree on these points, the political use of the law applies today.

A second more moderate continuity position holds that while OT law generally applies today, one must adjust it in view of changes in time. For example, we no longer live in a theocracy, so civil law does not apply, and the OT sacrificial system no longer applies today because of Christ's sac-rifice. Nonetheless, there is basic continuity between the law of Moses and the Law of Christ. The former generally applies today, even if one cannot always predict exactly how some laws (e.g., laws about fasting and dietary rules) apply.[43]

Discontinuity Positions

These views see more discontinuity than continuity between OT law and the NT era. One view (a moderate discontinuity view) holds that Christ fulfills OT law. Because of that fact of salvation history, one cannot assume that all OT law is operative precisely as it was in the OT era prior to Christ's coming. The NT elucidates the implications of Christ's coming for the believer's relation to God's law. In particular, the NT teaches that believers are bound to the Law of Christ as set forth in the NT. There is great overlap with OT injunctions, but of necessity, many OT commands no longer apply today.[44]

A final more radical discontinuity view is that Christ not only termi-nates Mosaic Law, but all law. This view sounds antinomian but is not, for the Christian is not left to do whatever he wants. Instead, he is to follow the direct leading of the Spirit. Practically speaking, this means that the believer usually obeys biblical precepts, but that is so because the Holy Spirit would not contradict Scripture's demands. The key point, however, is that the believer is not bound to any specific code but rather to the direct leading of the Holy Spirit. While we know of no proponents of this exact position, it seems to be a logical extension of the general discontinuity approach.

Authors' Position

We hold a moderate discontinuity position somewhat like the one described. In the NT we see neither OT ceremonial or civil law in force. Christ's sacrifice ended the need for ceremonial law, and civil law no longer pertains since NT life is not life under a theocracy. We hold this view in part because we think continuity positions have serious problems. For example, if all of OT law continues into the NT, then why do even proponents of that view admit that some parts no longer apply? One can say ceremonial law, for example, still applies though OT methods of observing it are irrelevant, and one can say OT law still applies, but the event of Christ transforms it in the NT era. However, when we hear such claims, we really wonder how it makes sense to say it is the *same* or *identical* law in the NT as in the OT. Is it not merely playing word games to call it the *same* law?

Even more perplexing is trying to discover hermeneutical principles that tell how to transform OT laws into NT precepts. For example, by what hermeneutical rules does one decide that OT fasting is "transformed" by Christ's coming but remains fasting in the NT, whereas dietary laws are transformed in the NT into a need to be separate from the things of the world?[45] Those who make such interpretive decisions neither delineate nor defend the hermeneutical rules they use to arrive at their conclusions. One wonders what those rules could possibly be.

In turning to our case for a discontinuity view, we begin by stating the basic hermeneutical principle we use in determining how the testaments relate. For us, since the OT is God's revelation of truth, whatever is true and binding during OT times still applies for the NT era, *unless the NT either explicitly or implicitly abrogates it*. Bahnsen agrees, but then argues that OT law is not canceled in the NT. We contend that both explicitly and implicitly the NT argues for the end of the Mosaic Law, though it does not abolish law altogether. Several points lead us to this conclusion.

First, both explicitly and implicitly the NT teaches that various aspects of the Mosaic Law are no longer binding. The epistle to the Hebrews, for example, makes it clear that OT ceremonial law, including the Mosaic sacrificial system, no longer applies in the NT era. In addition, the NT teaches that Jews and Gentiles are on equal footing spiritually before God and one another (Eph 2:1-15). Moreover, the NT assumes that believers will be under the political rule of non-believing rulers, and it explicitly commands believers to submit to such powers (Rom 13:1ff., 1 Pet 2:13-15). This all seems to us to imply that God is not dealing primarily with one ethnic group in the NT era, nor does he intend to govern his people under a theocracy. If this is so, then it follows that regulations that governed Israel as a theocracy bind neither believers nor non-believers today. It is surely true that Rom 13:1ff. teaches that the ruler is established by God, is the avenger of God's wrath, and deserves submission from his people. However, we fail to see how those facts logically entail a theocracy or anything like it. It is crucial to remember that Paul and Peter commanded believers to submit to the government of that day, the Roman Empire. Rome was neither a theocracy nor run by OT civil law. If God expects society to be a theocracy or to be run by OT civil law, then such a demand contradicts his demand through Paul and Peter that believers in their day submit to Rome, which was neither a theocracy nor run by OT civil law.

If neither Mosaic ceremonial nor civil law applies today, in what sense does it make sense to say we are under Mosaic Law? Additionally, as some have argued, the Mosaic Law cannot be detached from the Mosaic Covenant or vice versa. They are part and parcel of one another.[46] If this is so, then to say the Mosaic Code is still in force today is also to say the Mosaic Covenant is binding for today. However, continuity-oriented thinkers traditionally say the New Covenant of Jeremiah 31 governs the Church. Jeremiah 31 clearly distinguishes the New Covenant from the Mosaic Covenant. All of this raises the following dilemma for continuity positions: if the Mosaic Code is part and parcel of the Mosaic Covenant and inseparable from it, then to say we are under the Mosaic Code is to say we are under the Mosaic Covenant. But to hold that contradicts the belief that NT believers are governed by the New Covenant. It is inconsistent to say the Church is governed by the New Covenant when it comes to salvation, but by the Mosaic Code (and Covenant) when it comes to law. A discontinuity position avoids this problem by claiming that the Church is governed by the New Covenant as to salvation and by the Law of Christ as to law.

Second, those holding a continuity position on the law often raise Matt 5:17-19 as an objection to the discontinuity view. A detailed treatment of that passage is beyond the scope of this chapter, but suffice it to say that the crucial issue is the meaning of "fulfill." As many claim, the word does not mean "annul" but "bring to completion." However, to say the OT points to Christ who brings it to completion is not to say the OT still applies just as it did during the OT era. Rather, it means it must be interpreted and applied in light of its fulfillment by Christ. That means we must view it through Christ's teaching and ministry.[47] That teaching comes both from his mouth and from the mouths of his apostles (John 14; 15; 16).

What do they teach? As already noted, they teach that various aspects of Mosaic Law no longer apply today.[48]

Third, there are passages that, though debated, we believe entail that Mosaic Law has ended. In particular, we are thinking of passages such as Rom 10:4, Gal 3:21-25, Gal 5:18, and 1 Cor 9:20-21.[49] As to Rom 10:4 in particular, recent studies show that it is unlikely Paul means *only* that Christ ends the law in the sense of termination. Rather, the primary notion is culmination, completion, reaching the goal of the law.[50] However, as others note, it is dubious that the verse in no sense speaks of termination. Having reached its goal, it need no longer continue. Here again the teaching reminds us of Christ's comments in Matt 5:17ff. Christ is the law's fulfillment. He does not abolish it, but its application must always be viewed in light of its fulfillment in Christ.[51] We believe verses like these warrant concluding that believers are no longer subject to the Mosaic Code of law. However, that does not mean they are without law altogether; they have the Law of Christ.

Some will strongly object that Mosaic Law cannot be abrogated, for it is God's law, and since God does not change, his law does not. However, this confuses applicability of a particular expression of God's law (a particular code, like the Mosaic) with God's enduring ethical principles. The latter never change, because they are grounded in God's unchanging nature. But that does not mean those norms forever find expression in only one code of law, the Mosaic Code. Nor does it mean one has no divine law unless he has the Mosaic Code. On the contrary, in 1 Cor 9:20-21 and especially Rom 2:12, 14-15 Paul teaches that all people at all times have a form of God's law "written in their hearts," even if they do not have the Mosaic Code. Moreover, prior to the Mosaic Code, law was in the world. The book of Genesis shows that prior to the giving of the Mosaic Law people had some expression of God's law. If all this is true, why must this particular expression of God's law, the Mosaic Code, be so crucial?

In our day, non-believers are not under the Mosaic Code, but they still have a sense of God's law. Are they not like the Gentiles described in Rom 2:14-15? Are they not accountable to the law of God written in their hearts, even if they have never heard of the Mosaic Law? As for believers, passages such as 1 Cor 9:21 and Gal 6:2 teach that they are under the Law of Christ. We do not believe there is vast divergence between the Law of Christ and the law written in men's hearts any more than we think there is great divergence between the ethical norms of the Mosaic Code, the law written in men's hearts, and the Law of Christ. The same God is author of all three, and the norms in each are grounded in his character.

From the preceding we conclude that rejecting the Mosaic Code as binding today is not antinomianism. Whether one has only the law written in his heart or is under the Law of Christ, he is still accountable to some expression of divine law. Certain ethical principles are grounded in

God's nature and will always apply, though they find expression at different times in different codes. Just as driving laws for two U.S. states may contain many of the same laws and yet represent two separate codes (one for each state), so laws reflected in the law of Moses and the Law of Christ have much overlap while coming from two distinct codes.

A position like this seems the best way to avoid the dilemmas raised by having to specify hermeneutics for deciding which parts of OT law apply today and which do not and which parts are transformed in the NT era and what they become. Those problems (and others we have mentioned) that confront continuity positions are avoided by holding that none of OT law applies today, for believers are under the Law of Christ. Moreover, since the Law of Christ is quite similar to OT law (including the Mosaic Code) in regard to general ethical norms, nothing of significance is really lost.

Does the preceding mean the OT is useless for Christian ethics? We think not. Where the content of the Mosaic Law, for example, and the Law of Christ overlap, appeal to the OT is proper. In fact, appeal to the OT may give a fuller explanation of a principle and God's reasoning for it than one finds in the NT. For example, while we believe Rom 13:1-7 warrants capital punishment, we believe Gen 9:5-6 gives a much clearer statement of why God enjoins it. Second, even when OT and NT law do not exactly overlap, the OT can be very instructive in setting forth God's underlying attitude toward an ethical issue. For example, nowhere in the NT does one find the specific regulations of Exod 21:22-25 that protect pregnant women and their unborn children. Those ordinances are part of the Mosaic Code but are not part of the NT Law of Christ. On the other hand, as we shall argue when discussing abortion, proper understanding of that passage shows it to be one of the strongest passages in Scripture defending the rights of pregnant women and unborn children. Given that fact, it seems proper to appeal to it as indicating God's attitude toward any kind of harm to the unborn, including abortion. Since nothing in the NT suggests that God's attitude toward the unborn has changed, the OT passage is relevant for determining God's attitude toward the unborn and for demanding protection of them.

In discussing the use of Scripture in Christian ethics, James Gustafson outlines various ways Scripture may give guidance to contemporary ethical problems. We think at least three of his suggestions are helpful in answering how the OT is useful in Christian ethics. Gustafson says judgments can be made about contemporary situations on the basis of: 1) specific commands of Scripture about what is right and wrong; 2) moral ideals (such as love and peace) found in Scripture; and 3) analogies between biblical situations where moral pronouncements are made and contemporary situations.[52] So long as one joins these items with the two principles stated above (the norms in both codes must overlap or the OT must show God's underlying perspective on an issue even if the specific OT regulation is not in the Law of Christ), we believe one who holds that believers are under the Law of Christ and not the Mosaic Law has a good set of rules of procedure for using the OT in Christian ethics.

THE QUESTION OF JUSTIFICATION

This is an extremely difficult question, and it is important at the outset to clarify what is and what is not at stake. Some might think the source of ethical norms is also their justification, but this is wrong as a simple illustration shows. If a mother commands her child to do something, the child might ask why that rule is right. If the mother responds, "Because I said so," the perceptive (and perhaps "irreverent") child might reply, "That tells me why I must obey. You made the rule, and you are the boss. But it does not tell me why your rule is right." Similarly, to say one must obey because God or love commands us, or because reason says the best outcome will occur if we obey is not to justify the command as right. It only explains the source or origin of the rule. The crucial matter in justification is to present evidence (perhaps even proof) that the commands (wherever they came from) are correct.[53]

Just as one must distinguish the source of norms from their justification, so one must differentiate justification of norms from motivation for obeying them. Often the question "Why should I be moral?" is taken to be the question of justification. The question can be construed so as to raise that issue, but it actually raises the matter of motivation.[54] One's impetus for obeying a command may be fear of the consequences of disobeying, desire to do one's duty, love for the one commanding, or any other number of things. However, none of that explains why the rules obeyed are the right norms to obey.

APPROACHES TO JUSTIFICATION

There are four main approaches to justification. The first two seem inconsistent with Christianity, but the latter two are not.

Relativism

According to relativism, ethical systems vary from one culture to another (and even from one person to another), and there is no ultimate way to justify one ethical system over any other. This does not mean relativistic systems are chosen arbitrarily without reason. It only means relativists do not believe anyone can show his system to be right for all cultures and all times. While each system has its own advantages for those who hold it, none can be proved worthy of universal acceptance.

Relativism is obviously an inadequate approach to *justification,* but it is also an objectionable ethic on other grounds. With relativism, no system is right, but none is wrong either. Everyone is left to do what is right in his own eyes, even if it contradicts what others see as right or removes their rights. If everyone lived by such a morality, law and society would collapse. Moreover, if everyone's morality is right, there cannot be any refutation of the ethics that sanctioned the Holocaust or would justify any other atrocity. Anyone repulsed by such ideas can see the bankruptcy of ethical relativism.[55]

Non-cognitivism

According to non-cognitivist theories, ethical claims are in no sense assertions of fact. Instead, they merely vent one's emotions, show his intention to act a certain way, or whatever. Since ethical claims are not statements of fact, they cannot be justified. Thus, there is nothing to argue about as to which ethical norms are right or wrong, for non-cognitivists do not think ethical statements are claims about what is right or wrong. For example, if "murder is wrong" means nothing more than "I do not like murder," the only matter open to proof or disproof is whether I really do not like murder, but that is in no respect a question about justification of any ethical norms.

Intuitionism

Intuitionists believe ethical judgments are about matters of fact. According to them, one intuitively knows those facts to be true. Consequently, there is no need for justification, since justification is self-evident. Proponents of this kind of theory believe their norms are the right ones and that all people should intuitively see that.

Intuitionist theories appear compatible with Christianity, for at least they claim that moral statements assert facts about the world and hold that one set of norms is justifiable. One might even argue that the basic idea of intuitively knowing right and wrong is supportable from Romans 1 and 2 (though this is indeed a debatable understanding of those chapters). Nonetheless, we reject intuitionism for reasons that traditionally have been raised against it. Intuitionist theories entail belief in simple, non-natural properties that adhere in things, properties that are intuitively recognized and in virtue of which acts and objects are immediately recommended. We find it hard to prove there are such properties. Moreover, in view of widespread relativism in ethics, we wonder if it is true that everyone intuitively knows these moral principles. One might argue that everyone intuitively knows but many stubbornly reject what they know in favor of other notions of right and wrong, but that would be very difficult to prove. To prove so, one would at least need to know what each person knows about ethical norms, how each came to it (intuitively or otherwise), and why each accepts or rejects it. It is dubious that one could ascertain these psychological facts about one person, let alone all.[56]

Definism

According to these theories (often called definist theories because ethical notions may be defined in terms of factual ones), ethical and value judgments are disguised assertions of fact of some kind. In other words, ethical norms, for example, assert facts about the world and rest on some ultimate kind of fact.[57] For definist theories, ethical pronouncements not only rest on factual statements but are justified by them. One of the fundamental differences between definist and intuitionist theories is that intuitionists claim the connection between fact and value and the recognition of which acts are right and wrong is intuitively known, whereas definists say the tie is rationally demonstrable, but not intuitively known. As Frankena notes, naturalistic definist theories usually are justifiable by empirical inquiry (as with ordinary scientific factual claims), and metaphysical or theological theories can be justified by means typically used to justify metaphysical and theological propositions.[58]

Anyone holding a form of the divine command theory will likely handle justification this fourth way. In fact, most Christian ethical systems, whether generated by reason, prescription, or relation, will likely justify themselves by holding that ethical norms ultimately rest on theological principles about the nature of God and man and their relation to one another. Since we hold a modified form of the divine command theory, we classify ourselves as metaphysical moralists. However, this is not the end of the matter of justification. The last element in justification appears in response to the key objection to definist theories.

G. E. Moore raised the fundamental complaint against definist theories. He accused them of committing the naturalistic fallacy—namely, the error of identifying or defining an ethical or value judgment with a factual one. Suppose "right" is taken to mean "having the property q" and the property q is "being conducive to the greatest general happiness." Then to say it is right to do action x means that x has the property q. The problem with this, according to Moore, is that it still makes abundant sense to say: "action x has property q, but is it right?" For example, the following makes abundant sense: "Telling the truth is commanded by God [being commanded by God is the factual property], but is it right to tell the truth?"[59]

In response, many answers have been offered to this objection,[60] but suffice it to say that the objection need not be seen as refuting definist theories. Rather, the objection basically indicates that if one wants an ultimate justification of an ethical norm, a sufficient answer will not simply be something like "the norm is right because God commands it." Instead, one must specify why God would command it, i.e., what is it about the act and about God that would lead him to command it? However, even more must be done. To justify the norm as correct, once one answers what it is about

God and the act that causes him to command it, one must offer evidence that this understanding of God is correct. In other words, in order to justify a divine command theory, for example, one must establish as correct the worldview on which it rests. This may seem like an intolerable burden for a Christian ethical system, but a similar burden falls on proponents of all other ethical systems. Even a relativist in ethics must ultimately justify his views by producing evidence that his relativistic conception of reality is correct. From our perspective, the only kind of theory which has much chance of succeeding at this ultimate form of justification is one based on a Christian perception of reality. The reasons that is so (and the actual justifying of that worldview) fall within the domain of apologetics, and hence go beyond the scope of this book.[61]

We conclude, then, that though intuitionist and definist theories are both possible options for a Christian, a definist theory is preferable for one who hopes to justify his theory. All approaches to justification face objections, but the definist approach seems to us to be most in line with biblical revelation and the most supportable apologetically.

CHRISTIAN LIBERTY

Christian liberty involves practices not covered in Scripture by a moral absolute that either commands or forbids them. Such activities, scripturally speaking, are morally indifferent. Still, because of social and cultural background, individuals may find such practices offensive.

Examples help to understand what is at stake. Scripture prohibits drunkenness (Eph 5:18), and while some think even an occasional drink of alcoholic beverage is also forbidden, others cite Paul's advice to Timothy (1 Tim 5:23) as evidence that an occasional drink is morally indifferent. Many American Christians consider card playing morally indifferent as long as gambling is not involved. Likewise, many think social dancing is acceptable if the intent of the dancers is not to arouse lust and impure thoughts. Despite a lack of moral absolutes to cover these practices, some believers find them offensive. Should Christians do these things? How should they decide whether to indulge or refrain? These are the issues at stake when discussing Christian liberty.

Paul discusses this whole question at great length in Romans 14–15. The *practices* under question are eating meat offered to idols and observing one day as special above another, but the *principles* Paul teaches cover morally indifferent practices in general. Paul's fundamental point is that no one has a right to impose his scruples on others in these matters. Those who indulge must not despise those who do not, and those who refrain must not judge those who indulge (Rom 14:3). If there is any judging at all, it must be done by each individual concerning himself and by Christ who judges (Rom 14:4, 10-13). Each person should decide with the Spirit's help which practices are right for him and which are not.

In view of the preceding, one might think the discussion over. However, it is not, for Paul teaches that although all things are clean in themselves (and thus morally indifferent), they are wrong for those who think them wrong (Rom 14:14). That is, something morally neutral becomes a sin if one thinks it is wrong but does it anyway (Rom 14:22-23). Each person must decide for himself before God whether to indulge or refrain, but since a wrong decision turns a morally neutral practice into sin, one must make right decisions. How can one know which practices are acceptable for him? Paul offers guidelines that can help Christians decide which activities are acceptable for them. These guidelines may be stated as eight questions (tests) that each Christian must face when deciding whether or not to indulge in a given activity. If one answers any negatively, he should not do it. Each person must ask and answer for himself alone before the Lord.

The first question is *Am I fully persuaded that it is right?* Paul says (Rom 14:5, 14, 23) that whatever we do in these areas, we must be persuaded it is acceptable before God. If we are not, we doubt rather than believe we can do this and stand acceptably before God. If there is doubt, though, Paul says there is sin. So if there is any doubt, regardless of the reason for doubt, one should refrain. In the future, doubt might be removed so one could indulge; but while there is doubt, he must refrain.

Second, *Can I do it as unto the Lord?* Whatever we do, Paul says we must do as unto the Lord (Rom 14:6-8). To do something as unto the Lord is to do it as serving him. If one cannot serve the Lord (for whatever reason) in the doing of the activity, he should refrain.

Third, *Can I do it without being a stumbling block to my brother or sister in Christ?* Much of Romans 14 (vv. 13, 15, 20-21) concerns watching out for the other brother's or sister's walk with the Lord. We may be able to indulge, but he or she may not have faith to see that the activity is morally indifferent. If he or she sees us participate, he or she may be offended. As much as possible, we must avoid giving offense in these areas. This, however, does not mean one must always refrain. Paul's advice in 14:22 is helpful. For one who believes he can indulge, his faith is right, but let him have it before God. In other words, he need not flaunt his liberty before others. It is enough for him and the Lord to know he can partake of these practices. In sum, if one truly cares about his brother's or sister's walk, sometimes he will refrain, and at other times he will exercise his liberty privately.

Fourth, *Does it bring peace?* In Rom 14:17-18 Paul says the kingdom of God is not about things such as the meat we eat or what we drink. Instead, it is about righteousness, peace, and joy in the Holy Spirit. Thus, believers should handle these matters so as to serve Christ. How would one do that? Paul instructs us (v. 19) to do what brings peace. Certain practices may be acceptable for one person, but if others saw him indulge, it might stir up strife between them. Hence, one must do what brings peace.

Fifth, *Does it edify my brother?* The command to do what edifies is in the same verse as the charge to do what brings peace (14:19). By juxtaposing the two demands, Paul makes an important point. Some activities may not create strife with another Christian, but they may not edify him either. One must choose activities which both bring peace and edify.

Sixth, *Is it profitable?* In 1 Cor 6:12 Paul addresses the issue of Christian liberty, and he reminds believers that morally indifferent practices are all lawful, but they may not all be profitable. They may be unprofitable for us or for our brother. For example, no law prohibits playing cards, but if my card playing causes a brother to stumble, it is unprofitable for me to indulge. If the act is unprofitable, I must refuse to do it.

Seventh, *Does it enslave me?* (1 Cor 6:12). Many activities, wholesome and valuable in themselves, become unprofitable if they master us more than Christ does. As John warns, Christians must not love the world, but are to love God instead (1 John 2:15ff.). It is not that everything in the world is evil and worthless. Rather, our devotion and affections must be focused first and foremost on God. If we are to be enslaved to anything or anyone, it must be Christ.

A final test is *Does it bring glory to God?* Paul discusses Christian liberty in 1 Corinthians 10, and in verse 31 he sums up his discussion by saying that whatever we do in these areas should bring glory to God. How does one know if his actions bring God glory? We would say at the least that if one answers any of the other seven questions negatively in regard to a particular activity, he can be sure he will not bring God glory if he indulges. Conversely, if the activity is acceptable on those other grounds, it should be acceptable on this ground as well.

In sum, Scripture distinguishes actions covered by moral absolutes and those that are not. Believers must make up their own minds (under the Holy Spirit's leading) on what to do in matters of Christian liberty. Personal preferences must not be imposed on others. In deciding what to do, one should use these eight tests taught by Paul. Each one must answer those questions honestly before God. Whatever decision stems from that process of questioning, each must have the integrity to obey.

CHAPTER TWO

Abortion

One of the most pressing moral problems of our day is abortion. It is the second most common surgical procedure in the U.S., circumcision being the first. Since the historic *Roe v. Wade* decision on January 22, 1973, in the United States abortions have risen from about 775,000 in 1973 to about 1.6 million annually.[1] Statistics in the U.S. from 1983 through 1988 suggest that about 30 percent of the pregnancies of married women were unintended. Of those that were unintended, about 30 percent were unwanted, while the other 70 percent were mistimed (i.e., they were wanted, but wanted at another time).[2] U.S. figures that include both married and unmarried women suggest that one of every two pregnancies is unintended. Of those that are unintended, one out of every two is aborted. This means that in the U.S. approximately one in every four pregnancies ends in an abortion.[3]

Who is having these abortions? Statistics here are also interesting. In 1987, for example, it was estimated that the largest group of women having abortions were in the twenty- to twenty-four-year-old group (33.1 percent of U.S. abortions), while the second largest group ranged from twenty-five to twenty-nine years of age (22.3 percent of U.S. abortions). Moreover, the largest portion of abortions (63.3 percent) were among those never married, while only 18.5 percent of abortions involved married women. Twice as many white women were responsible for abortions (67 percent of all abortions) as nonwhites (33 percent of all abortions). Income seemed not to be a major factor, as 33 percent of abortions were obtained by women whose family income was less than $11,000, 34 percent by those in the $11,000 to $24,999 range, and 33 percent in the group making $25,000 or over.[4]

Worldwide abortion is rather prevalent and is quite frequently seen as an appropriate method of birth control. In Red China—approximately one out of every four persons in the world today lives in China—the government felt that population control was a necessity. As a result, in 1979 it introduced a policy that no family is allowed to have more than one child. This policy has led to infanticide (usually of female babies) and massive numbers of abortions. Abortions can range as high as 800,000 a year in a single province of China.[5] Those who refuse face significant pressures to comply one way or another, as the government can impose severe financial penalties for failure to comply. In other parts of the world, especially developing countries, women are having a significant number of abortions as well. It is estimated that about thirty million to forty-five million women in those countries have abortions *annually*, and about 125,000 to 250,000 of them die from botched procedures.[6]

Though many countries in the world seem relatively comfortable with the numbers of abortions that occur, the abortion debate in the U.S. is one of the most divisive issues confronting the country. Hence, we believe that before turning to the argumentation surrounding this issue, it would be helpful to sketch major developments in the U.S. with respect to abortion.

Prior to 1973, there were abortions in the U.S., but the *Roe* decision in essence legalized abortion on demand.[7] That decision struck down existing laws against abortion, but did agree that the government still has a legitimate interest in protecting fetal life. Still, the way the decision was written and interpreted essentially abrogated any governmental ability to stop abortion.

The Justices divided pregnancy into three trimesters (a trimester is approximately thirteen weeks). They ruled that within the first trimester, abortion was a decision between the woman and her doctor alone. The state cannot intervene. During the second and third trimesters, the Court said abortion could be reasonably regulated by the states and even prohibited once the child reached viability (the ability to exist outside the mother's womb). However, the right to prohibit abortion could be overturned in order to save the woman's life or simply to protect her health. Moreover, *Doe v. Bolton* defined the health of the mother in the broadest terms to include psychological, emotional, and familial factors. In essence, so long as a doctor certifies that an abortion is necessary to protect the mother's "health," abortion is thoroughly legal well into the ninth month of pregnancy.[8] Still, it is estimated that 90 percent of abortions in the U.S. are performed much earlier than the twentieth week,[9] and only about 2 percent after the fetus is viable.[10]

In the years after the *Roe* decision, anti-abortion groups have organized and mobilized in an attempt somehow to overturn or at least restrict *Roe*. At one point there was talk of a right-to-life amendment to the Constitution, but that seemed like an unlikely avenue for success since such an amendment would have to pass both houses of Congress and be ratified by the states. A better hope seemed to rest in the judiciary. Various members of the Supreme Court were coming to retirement, and with the election of Ronald Reagan there was hope that the texture of the Court could be changed so as ultimately to overturn *Roe*. Reagan, and Bush after him, have used appointments to the Supreme Court to change the direction of that Court. So far, however, gains for the pro-life side have been somewhat slim.

What pro-life forces hoped would be a major breakthrough came on July 3, 1989 with the Supreme Court's ruling in the *Webster v. Reproductive Health Services* case. This case, which involved Missouri's abortion laws, did not overturn *Roe*, but it gave states more leverage to rewrite their statutes so as to restrict abortions. The ruling upheld three basic points of Missouri law. It agreed that Missouri's public hospitals and public employees could not perform abortions except in a case where it was necessary to save a mother's life. In addition, the ruling refused public funds for abortion counseling and made it illegal for public officials to encourage a woman to have an abortion unnecessary to save her life. Finally, and most significant, in cases where women have been pregnant for twenty weeks or more, it is now mandatory that doctors perform tests to determine if the fetus can exist outside the womb. If the fetus can survive, the doctor cannot carry out the abortion.[11]

While the decision in *Webster* restricted abortion rights in Missouri, it also sent the message that individual states could go back and rewrite their laws concerning the handling of abortion. At the time of the *Webster* decision, there were some 140 anti-abortion bills before state legislatures nationwide.[12] Previously, states might pass anti-abortion legislation and the governor sign it, but there was little concern about negative political fallout from pro-choice groups, because it was assumed the law would be appealed to the Supreme Court and struck down. Now the political implications of voting for these bills has changed, because an anti-abortion law passed in a given state might not only be upheld by the Supreme Court; it might serve as the occasion for the Court to overturn *Roe* altogether.

After the *Webster* decision, pro-life forces were very optimistic about the prospects of restricting abortion rights. Unfortunately, that optimism has not been matched with much change.[13] One of the few victories came on May 23, 1991 when the Supreme Court upheld federal rules that prohibit family planning centers which receive government funds from counseling women about abortion or telling them where they can get one. The controversy surrounds Title X of the Public Health Services Act of 1970. That act provides $140 million annually to family planning clinics. The law bars federal funding of abortions as a method of family planning, but until the Reagan Administration in 1988 drafted more restrictions, such clinics could inform women about abortion and refer them to clinics that performed abortions. The restrictions, known as the "gag rule," were challenged as a breach of the First Amendment, but the Court ruled to

uphold the restrictions.[14] Since this decision, Congress has passed legislation to overturn the gag rule, but President Bush vetoed the bill, and
Congress was unable to muster enough votes to override the veto.[15]
Restrictions eased slightly, allowing doctors but no one else at these clinics to discuss abortion with patients. Many clinics responded to the gag
rule by simply refusing federal funds in order to continue counseling
women about abortion. Of course, now the issue seems to be dead, since
President Clinton threw out the "gag rule."

These events are discouraging, especially in light of the number of lives
of unborn babies who are at stake. Pro-choice advocates have found
renewed hope of keeping abortion rights intact with the election of a pro-
choice U. S. President. Pro-life forces are reorganizing, but are less hope-
ful than before that the demise of *Roe* will come soon.

A DEFINITION OF ABORTION

While most know the term *"abortion,"* few realize the variety of uses it
has. Abortions can be divided into those that are *spontaneous* and those
that are *induced*.[16] Spontaneous abortions are not usually thought of as
abortions. What characterizes this class of abortions is that there is *no*
outside or external intervention. There are two basic kinds of spontaneous abortions. On the one hand, there are a surprisingly high number
of cases where an egg is fertilized by sperm, but never implants in the
woman's womb. Instead, it simply passes out of her body in her monthly
period. J. N. D. Anderson in *Issues of Life and Death* says it is estimated
that 30 percent, and perhaps as many as 50 percent, of the eggs fertilized
are lost before they implant in the mother's womb.[17] Second, there are
miscarriages. In this case a developing fetus is expelled from the mother's
body before the baby is able to live outside the womb. Anderson thinks
that as high as 30 percent of the fertilized and implanted eggs may miscarry.

Induced abortions are commonly what we think of when we hear people talk about abortions. This class of abortions is characterized by outside or external intervention into the reproductive process with a view to
terminating pregnancy. There are several kinds of induced abortions.
Therapeutic abortions are performed to save the mother's life. Because of
the present state of medicine, such abortions are rare. *Ectopic* or *tubal*
pregnancies are examples. In this kind of pregnancy the fertilized egg does
not implant in the uterus but in the fallopian tube.[18] Only two options are
open to the doctor. Either he intervenes to take the baby's life in order to
save the mother's life, or both baby and mother die. Another potential
cause of therapeutic abortion is maternal heart disease. At one time
women with heart disease were at risk in full-term pregnancies. However,
that is almost never the case today. The most common candidates for ther-

apeutic abortions are pregnant women with cancer (especially uterine cancer). If treatment of the cancer requires either radiation or chemotherapy, that will likely kill the baby. Hence, it must be decided whether to delay treatment until the birth of the baby, or begin it immediately and risk losing the child.

Eugenic abortions are a second category of induced abortions. They are performed to abort a fetus that has or is at risk for some physical and/or mental handicap such as Down's syndrome. The most typical method of determining such problems is a procedure called *amniocentesis.*[19] Amniocentesis cannot be performed until around the fourth month of pregnancy, since it requires the development of the placental sac and its fluid. A needle is inserted into the sac, and fluid is removed and examined to determine any abnormalities. Amniocentesis is very good at determining problems such as Down's, but it has two limitations. There is a very small group of diseases that it can detect, and it cannot be performed until relatively late in the pregnancy. However, as other techniques for detecting problems are developed for the first trimester, eugenic abortions will probably increase, particularly since some doctors pressure parents to abort a child where there is the slightest risk of any handicap. For instance, some diseases are gender specific. Sickle-cell anemia is a disease only males get. So, if a family is at risk and the baby is a male, there will be great pressure to abort this child on eugenic grounds.

Finally, *elective* abortions complete the category of induced abortions. Here the mother's life is not threatened, and there is no known risk of physical and/or mental handicap for the child. The reason for abortion is simply the convenience of the parents (e.g., control of family size, physical and/or mental strain on the parents, or financial hardship on the family). Moreover, as it becomes easier to choose the sex of a child, families can choose a gender specific child and abort those of the "wrong" sex.

TECHNIQUES OF ABORTION

Several different methods are used in performing abortions. One is *dilation and curettage (D & C).*[20] This is one of the two preferred methods for aborting a fetus during the first trimester of pregnancy. The mother's cervix is dilated, and the surgeon inserts an instrument to scrape the wall of the uterus, cutting the baby's body to pieces and removing the placenta from its place in the uterine wall.

Suction[21] is the other preferred method of abortion during the first trimester of pregnancy. According to some estimates, it is used in 80 percent of these abortions. It is often used in conjunction with D & C. The cervix is dilated, and a suction tube is inserted into the womb. The suction tears both the baby and his or her placenta from the uterus, sucking them into a jar. The force of the suction is twenty-eight times stronger than a normal vacuum cleaner. With both methods mentioned so far, it is possible to identify human arms, hands and legs.

Saline injection is the most commonly practiced method of abortion during the second trimester. Neither D & C nor suction can be practiced during the second trimester because of the danger of hemorrhaging. By the fourth month of pregnancy the water bag or placenta has developed. A long needle is inserted through the mother's abdomen into this sac surrounding the baby, and some of the fluid is removed and replaced with a solution of concentrated salt. The baby breathes in and swallows the salt, and is poisoned by it. Often the outer layer of skin is burned off. With saline injection there are osmotic pressure changes in the fetus, causing brain hemorrhages. It takes about an hour for the solution to slowly kill the baby. About a day later the mother goes into labor and delivers a dead, shriveled baby.[22]

Hysterotomy is the technique that must be practiced in the final trimester of pregnancy, because the baby is simply too large to use the other methods. In light of the *Roe* decision, it is legal in the U.S. to have an abortion into the ninth month of pregnancy. Hysterotomy is typically the technique used, and medically it is exactly the same procedure as a cesarean section. However, a C-section is done to save the life of the child; a hysterotomy is done to take it. Though the aborted fetus is alive, he or she is allowed to die of neglect or through some deliberate action. In a case where the latter was done, a Boston jury found the doctor guilty of manslaughter. However, with the Supreme Court decision *Planned Parenthood v. Danforth*, July 1, 1976, physicians have been given the right to do whatever they want with the fetus![23]

A final method of abortion is *prostaglandin*. It may be used at any stage of pregnancy. The drug prostaglandin is taken in some form, and it induces labor. The result may be the delivery of a live infant who is allowed to die, or prostaglandin may be used in conjunction with a saline solution to assure the birth of a dead fetus.[24]

Not infrequently we hear that abortion is a simple, painless medical procedure. But painless for whom? The mother? Not necessarily. Abortion is not always as safe and painless as we are led to believe, even when the abortion is legally performed by a doctor. One must be careful in using maternal complications statistics, since medical techniques have improved dramatically in all health care. Furthermore, it is difficult to get exact figures because even these will be influenced by one's point of view on abortion. Also, medical complications vary widely based on age, social class and the number of previous pregnancies.[25]

Despite these notes of caution, we can offer specifics. For example, there are cases of maternal deaths from legal abortions ranging from 1.2 to 75 per 100,000 abortions.[26] There are, however, much more common complications. The most immediate problems are infection and bleeding. Bleeding is related to the difficulty in getting the cervix to dilate in the first pregnancies of young girls. Thus, in the very cases where abortion may appear to have the strongest argument, likelihood of injury is greatest.[27] The long term complications are equally as problematic. If an infection is severe enough, it may result in infertility. Even a legal abortion may hinder a woman's ability to carry a child in future pregnancies. The most difficult damage to assess is the psychological damage to the mother and the father. Both parents of an aborted fetus often experience severe depression over what has been done.[28]

What about the baby? Does the fetus feel pain? The best way to answer is to set forth the particulars of the physiology of a developing baby and then compare those data with what has been said about the different abortion techniques and the stages of pregnancy when they are used. This is a matter of no small import, since some claim that abortion is not cruel to the baby since it feels no pain.

THE PHYSIOLOGY OF HUMAN DEVELOPMENT[29]

To understand the seriousness of abortion, one must know the physiology of human development. Ignorance of these facts is in no small measure responsible for the willingness of mothers to have an abortion and for the general public to allow abortions on demand.

CONCEPTION	Father's sperm penetrates mother's egg cell. Genetic instructions from both parents interact to begin a new and unique individual who is no bigger than a grain of sugar.
DAY 1	The first cell divides into two, the two into four, and so on.
DAYS 5–9	The new individual implants in the mother's womb. The baby's sex can already be determined.
DAY 14	Mother's normal menstrual period is suppressed by a hormone produced by her child.
DAY 18	The heart is forming. Soon the eyes start to develop.
DAY 20	The beginnings of the brain, spinal cord, and nervous system are laid.
DAY 24	The heart begins to beat.
DAY 28	Muscles are developing along the future spine.

DAY 30 — The child *in utero* has grown 10,000 times to 6-7 mm (1/4 inch) long. The brain has human proportions. Blood flows in the veins and is separate from the mother's blood supply.

DAY 35 — The pituitary gland in the brain is forming. Mouth, ears and nose are taking shape.

DAY 40 — The heart's energy output is 20 percent of the adult output.

DAY 42 — The skeleton is formed. The brain coordinates movement of the muscles and organs. Reflex responses have begun. The penis has begun to form in male infants. **The mother misses her second period.**

DAY 43
(1 1/2 months) — Brain waves can be recorded.

DAY 45 — Spontaneous movements have begun, and the teeth are developing.

7 WEEKS — Lips are sensitive to touch, and the ears may already be taking on the family shape.

8 WEEKS — The child is well-proportioned, a small-scale baby: 3 cm (1 1/8 inches) sitting up, and a gram (1/30 oz) in weight. Every organ is present. The heart beats sturdily; the stomach produces digestive juices; the liver makes blood cells; the kidneys begin to function; the taste buds are forming.

8 1/2 WEEKS — Fingerprints are being engraved. They will grow larger, but they are unique and will never change. The eyelids and palms of the hands are sensitive to touch.

9 WEEKS — The child will bend fingers around an object placed in the palm. Thumb-sucking begins. Fingernails are forming.

10 WEEKS — The body is sensitive to touch. The child squints, swallows, furrows his or her brow, and frowns.

11 WEEKS — The baby urinates and makes complex facial expressions, even smiling.

12 WEEKS	The baby is capable of vigorous activity. He or she can kick, turn feet, curl and fan toes, make a fist, move thumbs, bend wrists, turn the head, open the mouth, and press the lips tightly together. Breathing has begun.
13 WEEKS (End of the First Trimester)	The baby is prettier, and the facial expression resembles the parents'. Movements are graceful, reflexes vigorous. The vocal cords are formed, although without air the baby cannot cry. The sex organs are apparent.
4 MONTHS	The baby can grasp with his or her hands, swim, and turn somersaults.
4–5 MONTHS	**The mother first feels the baby move.**
5 MONTHS	Sleeping habits are noticeable. A slammed door will result in activity. The child responds to sounds in frequencies too high or low for adults to hear.
6 MONTHS (End of the Second Trimester)	Fine hair grows on the eyebrows and head. Eyelash fringe appears. The baby's weight is about 640 g (1 lb, 6 oz), and height is 23 cm (9 inches). **Babies born at this age have survived.**
7 MONTHS	Eyeteeth are present. Eyelids open and close. Eyes look around. Hands grip strongly. The mother's voice is heard and recognized.
8 MONTHS	Weight increases by 1 kg (over 2 lbs), and the baby's quarters get very cramped.
9 MONTHS	The child triggers labor, and birth occurs, usually 255-275 days after conception. Of the 45 generations of cell divisions before adulthood, 41 have taken place. Four more will come during the rest of childhood and adolescence.

We are now prepared to answer the question about whether the baby undergoing abortion feels any pain. Certain conditions necessary for the existence of pain are known to exist in the developing fetus. They are 1) functioning neurological structures to sense pain; 2) overt behavior expressive of pain; and 3) a cause for pain.[30] Dr. A. W. Liley, a respected professor of fetal psychology at the National Women's Hospital in Auckland, New Zealand, has demonstrated that an eleven-week-old fetus can experience pain and responds to touch, light, heat and noise. Liley has shown through the use of closed-circuit television cameras that such a child will feel pain when pricked with a needle. Moreover, if a beep is used before the prick several times, the baby will recoil at the beep alone.[31] But this is within the first trimester of pregnancy, and during that time D & C and suction are the methods of abortion most commonly used. Moreover, though this is late in the first trimester of pregnancy, it must be remembered that most women do not even know they are pregnant until the second month of pregnancy, and once they know, they are not likely to get an abortion immediately. They will consider it for a while. All of this, of course, gives the fetus more time to develop and only helps to ensure that it will likely feel pain if it undergoes an abortion.

If the baby can respond to pain during the first trimester of development, it is obvious that it feels pain during the second. But during that second trimester saline injection is used for abortion. Undoubtedly, the baby feels very vividly the pain from that procedure. By the final trimester of pregnancy, the baby's nervous system and ability to experience sensations is not much different, if at all, from a newborn baby. If it would hurt a newborn to starve it or kill it by some other deliberate action, then surely the baby aborted during this period feels significant pain. So, contrary to what proponents of abortion claim, when a mother aborts her baby, most likely the baby feels great pain.

THE DEBATE OVER ABORTION

Though in some countries abortion is an accepted practice with little debate about its morality, that is not so in other countries such as the U.S. The abortion question is one of the most morally, socially, and politically sensitive issues confronting America as it approaches the end of the twentieth century. Rhetoric is often loud and reason thin on both sides of the debate, and for some this is an issue that demands protest not only in word but in deed.

Typically, each side portrays the other as uncaring and unfeeling about rights it feels are crucial. Pro-life advocates cannot understand why abortionists are insensitive to the baby's right to life. After all, they reason, this baby is a human being. If there is no right to kill a person after birth, why should there be a right to kill one before birth? Can't abortionists see that this is murder?

On the other side of the question, advocates of abortion rights cannot understand why pro-lifers want to abridge a woman's right to exercise freedom of choice and apparently control what she can do with her body. In this vein, they remind us that they are really not pro-abortion. They decry it as much as pro-lifers do, and they believe they are not insensitive to the rights and needs of the developing fetus. But they feel that a woman's right to choose what to do with her body must be paramount. Hence, they prefer to refer to themselves as pro-choice.

This fundamental difference in perception of the key right involved in the abortion debate colors the way the two sides support their respective positions. Invariably the two sides begin their defense and focus it around either the baby's right to life as a person or the woman's right to freedom of choice. In what follows we offer the main arguments that are raised in the abortion debate. We begin with the question of personhood, not because we are unaware of or uncaring about a woman's right to control her body, but because we believe that right cannot outweigh a person's right to life.

THE FUNDAMENTAL ISSUE: PERSONHOOD

Is the beginning of life or the beginning of personhood the key issue in the abortion debate? Pro-choice advocates who opt for the former often say no one really knows when human life begins. That is a religious, philosophical or metaphysical question. But if the beginning of life is the key, and it is impossible to know when it begins, then when and whether to abort are decisions between the mother and her physician.[32]

Pro-life proponents respond that we in fact do know when human life begins, because that is a scientific or biological question, and we are in a position to answer that question. The embryo is alive. Once sperm penetrates the egg and fertilizes it, the cells begin to replicate. That is life, isn't it? And, not just any life, but human life.

A recent study by Norman Ford challenges such claims. Ford's concern is when human life begins. He does not relate his findings to the question of when personhood begins, but only considers the issue of the start of human life. As he says, we do not know the exact time sequence in natural reproduction, but our knowledge of that sequence with *in vitro* fertilization gives us good estimates. Soon after the sperm penetrates the egg, the egg is activated. There is no question that the new cell is alive, but it is not yet human life. Once the egg is activated, "the paternal chromosomes decondense within a new envelope to form the male pronucleus, while a membrane also develops around the remaining twenty-three female chromosomes to form the female pronucleus."[33] During the next six to ten hours, the two pronuclei move towards each other. Approximately twenty-two hours after insemination in a case of *in vitro* fertilization, syngamy occurs when membranes of the two pronuclei break down, allowing male and female chromosomes to mingle. The union of male and female chromosomes at syngamy "gives rise to a single cell with a set of twenty-three pairs of maternal and paternal homologous chromosomes, in all forty-six chromosomes. This cell is called a zygote because it yokes or brings together the maternal and paternal chromosomes into one genetically new individual cell."[34] This process is completed approximately twenty-four hours after fertilization, and yields a cell that is ready to replicate itself. As Ford argues, though the fertilized egg is alive before syngamy, it is really not until syngamy that there is human life. This is so because only at that point is there a human cell, i.e., a cell containing twenty-three pairs of chromosomes that have fused male and female components into a cell that represents the genetic makeup of a human life. Since in human beings male and female chromosomes have fused to form the genetic makeup of a particular human, a cell which merely contains *unfused* male and female elements (as is the case with the fertilized egg before syngamy) is not yet a human cell.[35]

The implications of this for abortion are significant. If one claims that abortion is permissible until there is human life, then these findings would allow abortion up to approximately one day after sperm penetrates the egg, or roughly within twenty-four hours of sexual intercourse. One might respond to Ford's claims in one of two ways. On the one hand, one might agree that there is not actually a human life until syngamy, but claim that the fertilized egg before that has all the potential for human life. Though some might say that is true of sperm and eggs that are completely separated from one another, it is not true in the same sense that it is true of sperm that has already penetrated the egg. Sperm and egg that have not united might never unite to begin the process of fertilization. However, the fertilized egg, though not human life until syngamy, has already begun the process of forming human life. That process should not be interrupted. Hence, abortion even during the first twenty-four hours is wrong.

Another possible response to Ford is to grant that syngamy marks the beginning of human life and to grant that abortion prior to syngamy would be acceptable. However, it is virtually impossible to know that one is pregnant within twenty-four hours after sexual intercourse, so an abortion would not likely occur during that time period anyway. Moreover, methods of birth control that involve aborting a fertilized egg do not begin to function until after the twenty-four hour period.[36] Thus, one would not likely decide on or have an abortion until well after syngamy, and by then it would be ruled out since human life certainly is present. The practical result would be the same as claiming life is present at fertilization. No abortions that could be morally acceptable would occur.

Though the issue is sometimes argued in terms of when life begins, more often in recent years the key question is when personhood begins. Harold O. J. Brown rightly observes that in the present discussion, a biological term, *life*, has been exchanged for a legal term, *person*. It is further argued that only persons have rights, one of which is the right to life, with corresponding obligations to others not to take one's rights. This switch is not insignificant, as rights no longer are grounded in natural law or biological considerations, but are granted by the state. Of course, what the state grants, it may take away.[37]

Paul Ramsey, formerly a moral theologian at Princeton, concurs. He has argued that the debate has taken a new turn. Previously, while there might be disagreement as to the beginning of human life, it was agreed that whenever it did begin, there was a person with rights. Now there is an attempt to divorce human life and personhood. No longer is personhood grounded in the possession of biological human life.[38]

Pro-life advocates argue that personhood begins at conception, because at that point the DNA strands are species-specific. That is, if the newly fertilized egg is examined under a microscope, one can determine that the DNA strands are those of human beings. Moreover, it is argued that though the fetus is dependent upon the mother, he or she is an independent individual.[39] This view can be called the biological, genetic view of personhood.

Usually, pro-choice advocates attack the claim that the developing egg is a distinct person. Because of the problems associated with segmentation discussed below, it is argued that such a criterion of personhood cannot be met.[40] A different attack on the pro-life claim, however, has been made by Charles A. Gardner, a doctoral candidate at the University of Michigan Medical School in the Department of Anatomy and Cell Biology. He questions whether a person's constitution is completely determined by the genetic material in the fertilized ovum. He argues that there is not one and only one path the egg must follow on its way to full gestation. Rather, as cell division continues, the way in which the embryo progresses toward greater complexity and differentiation is the result not only of the forty-six chromosomes, but also of the pattern of cells and molecules in the preceding cell division. He says that the information for the formation of an eye or finger does *not* exist in the fertilized egg. On the contrary, it is a product of the positions and interaction of the cells and molecules immediately before their development. So, in Gardner's view any individual is a mix of "chance and planning." There is no prepackaged human being waiting to emerge. Therefore, if something as simple as a fingerprint is not "genuinely present" in the fertilized egg, how can something as complex and unique as an individual human brain or personality be said to be present from conception?[41]

In our opinion arguments such as Gardner's should make pro-life claims about the fetus at conception having everything it will be *as a unique person* more moderate. However, his claims still miss the fundamental point. Even if exact characteristics depend on a mixture of genetics and the positions and interaction of the cells, the genetics of the developing embryo demand that this will be a human being, not a dog or a cat. Regardless of the exact characteristics of the developing eye, brain, etc., there can be no question as to whether the eye, brain, etc. will be those of a human being. Gardner's claims do not allow limitless possibilities for the developing egg. Hence, our point about the DNA strands being species-specific still stands. Therefore, unless there is some overriding reason for terminating that life, abortion is *prima facie* wrong.

Views on the Commencement of Personhood

Since the fundamental issue in the abortion controversy is not now when human life begins but when a human person is present and when we begin to value human life, it would serve us well to examine various answers to those questions. A number of places along the gestation cycle are suggested for the commencement of personhood: conception or fertilization; implantation or blastocyst; the attainment of a recognizable human form; animation or the movement of the baby (fourth to fifth month); viability or the ability of the baby to survive outside the womb (about the sixth month); birth; and the attainment of the ability to interact with his/her environment (one to one and a half years).[42] Where one places the commencement of personhood on this spectrum is not unimportant in its implications for the permissibility of abortion.

Views on the Nature of Personhood

Not only is the timing of the commencement of personhood debated, but so is the very nature of personhood. In fact, at the heart of the timing question is the issue of a proper definition of personhood. This is really the crux of the present debate over personhood, and there are two competing answers to what it means to be a person.

Biological, Genetic or Structural View of Personhood

This is the view that when human life is present, there is a person with rights, one of which is the right to life. Personhood is grounded in biological considerations. Since species-specific DNA strands, identifying the fertilized egg as human, are present at conception, a human person with rights is present at conception. Since personhood begins at conception, abortion is *prima facie* wrong.

This position is supported by several arguments. First, because of the species-specific character of the DNA strands, it is argued that a living human being exists in the mother's womb.[43] Second, the Aristotelian theory of substantial change supports the personhood of the fetus. Before fertilization, both the egg and the sperm can be said to belong to the mother and the father respectively. However, after conception a new cell exists. It is not identical to either parent. In the union a distinct entity is produced.[44] Finally, there is substantial identity between the fertilized egg, the viable fetus, the infant, the child, the adult and the elderly person.[45] If from infancy to old age there is personhood, genetic identity throughout life guarantees personhood in the fertilized egg and viable fetus.

Several objections to the genetic view of personhood are raised. First, some argue that if we ground personhood in the genetic code (DNA strands), we have rooted personhood in chemical values only. That seems a shaky foundation upon which to erect the varied human values that society has traditionally revered.

In response, we believe the argument is misguided. Our concern is not chemicals alone, but the specific combination of chemicals in humans. Granted, DNA is present in all animals, but not in the specific configuration found in humans. Moreover, it is our claim that any other basis for determining personhood (such as those mentioned below) offers too subjective a basis for deciding this important issue. The genetic code is an objective basis open to all for determining who qualifies as a person.

A second objection claims that since so many conceptions result in spontaneous abortions, and since a human individual is believed to have a soul, this means that a large percentage of souls are never born. We reply that this objection apparently rests on two assumptions, both of which we find dubious. The first is that there can be no person where there is a large number of deaths, and the second is that 20 to 30 percent mortality is a large portion of the population. It should be remembered that throughout most of human history 70 percent of the babies born died in infancy. Should we say that they had no souls and were not persons? Beyond these considerations, we fail to see how the objection disproves the genetic concept of personhood. Even if the argument were correct, it does not prove that the babies spontaneously aborted were not persons. It only shows that those persons were not born. Those who offer this argument may respond that unless the baby is born, it cannot be a person. However, that answer simply begs the question of what it takes to qualify as a person.

By far the most formidable objection relates to twinning and mosaics. Twinning involves the splitting of the developing zygote into two zygotes. This usually occurs between the seventh and the fourteenth day. What results are identical twins. If there is really a unique person prior to this, it is difficult to understand how one person could split and become two persons. Hence, there must not be an individual person until the fourteenth day. Some see this as the decisive objection to the biological view of personhood. Ramsey calls this problem of segmentation the "rebuttal argument" to the genetic school. If one were to ask parents of identical twins when their individual lives began, in light of modern genetics, they would not likely say before segmentation.

Mosaics present a similar problem. In mosaics two eggs are fertilized, but one is absorbed and only one person is born. Thus, there appears to be a certain fluidity or indeterminacy in either direction during the first few days of life.

Because of the phenomena of twinning and mosaics, Ramsey holds that it is not until after blastocyst that there is an individual human person. He thinks this modification to when personhood begins is really of no consequence since most women are not even aware that they are pregnant during the first couple of weeks of a pregnancy. However, such a concession does allow for eventualities that are clearly unacceptable to the anti-abortionist. For instance, abortive mechanisms such as an intrauterine device would be permissible, as would "morning after" pills.

In response to this objection, we think it has some merit but does not prove what it claims to prove. The argument does not in fact prove that what is developing inside the mother is anything less than human. Check the DNA strands. They are species-specific at the point of conception. The most the argument shows is that until after blastocyst we do not know *how many* persons are present, but that is clearly a different question than whether personhood is present. On the genetic view of personhood, personhood can be determined from the point of conception. How many persons are present is technically not decidable until after blastocyst. Hence, we disagree that this objection refutes the genetic concept of personhood.[46]

Developmental, Sociological, Psychological and Interactive View of Personhood

Fundamental to this position is the belief that human value is "an achievement rather than an endowment." Attainment of personhood is a process. Many grant that human life begins at conception. However, there is agreement that human value or personhood does not begin at conception. At best there is a potential person. Value is achieved in social interaction.

As Fowler points out, criteria for personhood on this view may emphasize the physical, the social, the mental, or some combination of these. A good example of criteria that are suggested for personhood appears in the writings of Mary Anne Warren who gives five that are most central to the idea of personhood. They are roughly the following: consciousness of things external and internal to oneself, and especially the ability to feel pain; reasoning; self-motivated activity, activity that is independent of genetic or external control; the ability to communicate with an indefinite number of contents and topics; and the presence of self-concepts and self-awareness. Warren also claims that these criteria must be possessed, not merely potential.[47]

It should be clear that a fetus does not and cannot meet these criteria. Hence, the fetus cannot be considered a person. Since only persons can be members of moral communities and thus possess rights, the fetus has no rights, or at least very minimal rights, which may upon the wishes of the mother be overridden.

Various objections seem appropriate. First, this view of personhood involves a stipulative definition of personhood and value. This means that one simply stipulates what will count as personhood. The right to stipulate one's definition really does not help the case for this view of personhood. If one can stipulate any definition whatsoever, then why not alternative definitions that grant personhood to the fetus or at least take a more sympathetic view toward it. Proponents of the developmental view will obviously object, but if one may choose whatever definition one wants, the complaint must be rejected.

Of more concern to us, however, are the implications if one accepts this procedure for determining personhood. If one is allowed to choose a definition to one's liking, then one can (as some have) so define value that Jews, Blacks, Asians, and American Indians no longer count as persons. Moreover, because the definition is stipulative, any criteria that demarcate the commencement of personhood will be arbitrary. Thus, there will be nothing to commend those criteria more than other choices one might make (unless, of course, one chooses genetic criteria).

We are also troubled by the ambiguity of criteria such as Warren's. Take, for example, the criterion of being able to discourse on an indefinite number of contents and topics. Since the number is indefinite, no matter how educated any of us is, we could always be excluded on grounds that we cannot yet discourse on enough topics. It is clear that criteria such as Warren's (and they are typical of criteria used to determine personhood on this view) are sufficiently ambiguous as to warrant some interpretation that would eliminate every person. That alone should demonstrate that this is not at all a just or helpful way to determine who is a person.

By far the most serious objection to this view is that it is a classic example of a slippery slope argument. This means that if the argument proves anything, it proves too much. The same argument would support infanticide, euthanasia and destruction of the severely mentally handicapped, since they cannot achieve functions that are necessary for human value under this view. Moreover, those disqualified as persons and open to elimination are just the ones we would think merit the most protection by the law, since they are the most unable to protect themselves. In light of all of these arguments we cannot see the developmental view of personhood as an adequate account of personhood.[48]

Exodus 21:22–25—A Special Case?

This is an important text, thought by some to support the view that a fetus in the womb is not a person. If that is so, it would seriously damage the case for the genetic view of personhood and help the case for the developmental view. In our judgment, this passage is a "special case," but one that, properly understood, is an unusually strong argument for the pro-life position. To see this, we need to examine various interpretations of this passage.

The interpretation that would support the view that the fetus has a lesser status (or no status) of personhood can be called the *miscarriage interpretation*. According to this understanding of the text, verse 22 deals with a case where two men are fighting near a pregnant woman and accidentally strike her so that she miscarries the child. On this view, though she loses the child, she herself sustains no injury. The penalty prescribed by law is a fine as the woman's husband demands and the court will allow. Verses 23-25 tell of a case where not only does the baby miscarry, but injury comes to the mother. More severe punishment is commanded, even the death penalty for the death of the mother. If the mother is hurt, *lex talionis* (the law of retaliation) is required. The men shall give life for life, eye for eye, tooth for tooth, hand for hand, foot for foot, burning for burning and wound for wound. Because the penalty is more severe for harm to the mother, it is concluded that Scripture makes a distinction between the mother's personhood and the non- or limited personhood of the fetus, or a distinction between the mother's value and the baby's.

We believe this understanding of the text is incorrect. In fact, it is open to criticism from two perspectives. Even if one assumes that the interpretation is correct, the passage still would not authorize abortion. But as one examines alternate interpretations, one realizes that the miscarriage interpretation is incorrect and that this passage is an exceptionally strong one for protection of both pregnant women and unborn children.

Let us first assume that the miscarriage interpretation is correct. That interpretation would not justify abortion of a fetus for several reasons. For one thing, the death that occurs in verse 22 is accidental, not intentional. Abortion is intentional intervention into pregnancy with the express purpose of terminating a life. Second, the fact that a penalty is required shows that the death of the unborn is an evil. If the baby did not matter at all, why require any fine? Third, the fact that the fetus' death does not require the death penalty is quite in keeping with the Mosaic exception to the death penalty in cases of accidental death (Exod 21:13-14, 20-21; Num 35:10-34; Deut 19:1-13). Hence, a mere fine does not necessarily suggest less value of the fetus. Finally, while Exodus 21 specifies a variety of penalties for the killing of different individuals, these differences can hardly be explained in terms of personhood. For instance, the one who kills a slave unintentionally escapes without any penalty (vv. 20-21). Surely, no one today would say that penalty stems from the slave's reduced or lack of personhood.

We conclude that even if one grants the miscarriage interpretation of this passage, the passage does not teach that developing babies have reduced or no personhood, and it surely does not sanction abortion. However, we are not at all convinced that this passage is about miscarriage. Instead, we prefer the interpretation that this passage speaks of *premature live childbirth*.[49] Let us explain.

According to this interpretation, verse 22 describes a case where two men are fighting and strike a pregnant woman. She delivers a healthy premature baby, and is not harmed herself. In fact, there is no injury to anyone. Still, the men are to be fined, but only as the husband demands and the court allows. However, verses 23-25 tell what is to be done if any harm comes to either the fetus or the mother. If either is injured, the law of retaliation is to be invoked—life for life, eye for eye, foot for foot, etc.

What evidence supports such an interpretation? As a matter of fact, quite a bit. First, *yeled* is used for what issues from the womb. This word is never used elsewhere for a child who lacks recognizable human form or cannot exist outside the womb. If such was desired here, two other Hebrew words would have been more likely. *Gōlem* means fetus and is found once in the OT Scriptures (Ps 139:16). On the other hand, the commonly used noun to express the death of an unborn was *nephel*. It speaks of "an untimely birth" in Job 3:16; Ps 58:8; and Ecc 6:3. The use of *yeled*, therefore, is unlikely to refer to the product of a miscarriage, at least in the absence of some decisive evidence. Moreover, it is the usual word used to designate a normal child.

We note, secondly, that the verb *yātzā'* is the verb used to speak about what happens to the baby when the mother is accidentally struck. But this is the word used ordinarily of normal births (Gen 25:26; 38:28-30; Job 3:11; 10:18; Jer 1:5; 20:18), not for the death of a child. With the possible exception of Num 12:12, which most likely refers to a stillbirth, this verb never refers to a miscarriage. Moreover, the OT term normally used for a miscarriage or spontaneous abortion, both in humans and in animals, is *shākōl*. It is found in Gen 31:38; Exod 23:26; Job 2:10; Hos 9:14; cf. 2 Kgs 2:19, 21; Mal 3:11. Its use in Genesis 31 and Exodus 23 shows that Moses knew the word. Therefore, the most likely meaning of the phrase "and her child comes forth" is that an induced premature birth occurred. The child arrives alive, but ahead of the anticipated time.

Finally, the noun *'āsōn* is indefinite in both verses 22 and 23, indicating that the harm that is avoided in verse 22 and that is to be punished in verse 23 is to *either* the mother or the child. If only the mother was in view in verse 23 (as the miscarriage interpretation suggests), we would expect the harm to be restricted by the use of the pronoun "to her." Hence, if there is harm to either mother or child, *lex talionis* takes effect.

In sum, given this interpretation, this passage, rather than demonstrating that the value of an unborn fetus is less than that of his or her mother, shows that God places the highest value on the developing life. When the baby is born prematurely but unharmed, a fine is assessed. When there is harm to either mother or baby, the law of retaliation is required. And both stipulations apply in a case where what happens is *accidental*! In fact, this is the only place in Scripture where the death penalty is required for *accidental* homicide! The obvious condition of the woman should have been a signal for caution on the part of the men, and when they were negligent, the most severe penalty was required. This passage is a special case, but not one that downgrades or devalues developing babies or pregnant women. On the contrary, it shows the extreme importance God places on both.[50]

CONFLICT OF RIGHTS ARGUMENTS

Not all arguments in support of abortion are based on the claim that the fetus is not a person. Many arguments focus, instead, on a conflict of rights. Some of these even accept the personhood of the fetus, but claim that some right conflicts with the fetus' right to life and supersedes it. On this view, the right to life is not an absolute right. Proponents of this view even note that while the right to life is a fundamental right that is generally to be honored, not even all pro-lifers think it is absolute, for there are cases where even they allow the taking of life. A prime example of this is the approval of taking the fetus' life to save the life of the mother. In this section we want to look at the most common arguments favoring abortion based on conflict of rights thinking.

Right to Life v. Right to Control One's Body

Undoubtedly, the most commonly raised case of conflicting rights is the conflict between the fetus' right to life and the mother's right to control her own body. According to this argument, the baby does have a right to life, but the mother has a right to bodily self-determination. In this case the right of the mother is preferred over that of the baby.

A classic and widely anthologized form of this argument is found in Judith Jarvis Thomson's "A Defense of Abortion."[51] She asks the reader to imagine awakening to find that he or she is in bed with a famous violinist who is unconscious. The violinist has a fatal kidney ailment, and only you have the right blood type to help. Therefore, while you slept, his blood was passed through your system to cleanse it. To unplug him would kill him. You express your displeasure with the set-up, but are advised that it will only take nine months to complete your task. Thus, the question you are faced with is simple. Since all persons have a right to life, are you morally obligated to spend the next nine months of your life keeping this world-famous violinist alive? Thomson's answer is no.

Thomson next applies this illustration to the case of the pregnant mother. She claims that even if the fetus has a right to life, the mother's right to control her own body outweighs the right of the child. The mother and child are not seeking control of a body that has unfortunately been rented to both of them. Rather, the mother owns the house. The child is the intruder.

Why, though, should the rights of the mother be preferred over those of the child? Thomson answers in terms of a distinction between a minimally decent Samaritan and a good Samaritan. The good Samaritan goes out of his or her way to help one in need, even at great cost to oneself (e.g., the loss of one's rights). On the other hand, the minimally decent Samaritan helps when it involves no cost to him or her. From our discussion in Chapter 1, it follows that a minimally decent Samaritan acts in accord with duty, whereas a good Samaritan is someone who does a work of supererogation (above and beyond the call of duty).

How does this apply to the question of abortion? To function as a good Samaritan would be to grant the fetus continued use of the mother's body. Being a minimally decent Samaritan does not require that, since to give the fetus use of the mother's body helps the baby at great cost to the mother, i.e., it is a work of supererogation. Since all that is required is that one be a minimally decent Samaritan, the fetus has no right to use the mother's body unless she grants it. As Thomson claims, "I am arguing only that the right to life does not guarantee having either a right to be given the use of or a right to be allowed continued use of another person's body—even if one needs it for life itself."[52]

Is Thomson correct in saying that women have a right to non-interference and a right to choose to do with their body as they please? Her argument seems to show that at least in some cases they do. Nonetheless, we believe there are a number of problems with her argument in particular and this argument in general. The major assumption of the argument is that a woman has the right to do with her own body what she pleases. This is true to a point for both men and women, but that right is not unlimited. This can be seen in existing laws against self-maiming or the restricted access to harmful drugs.

But specifically, are the cases of the violinist and the pregnant mother sufficiently analogous to be instructive on the abortion issue? Wennberg does not think quite so. He lists five dissimilarities. First, the violinist is a stranger, where fetuses are not. They are blood-relatives of the mother. Second, the woman is bedridden for nine months, something that is not true of the typical pregnancy. Third, the woman and the violinist are linked against her will, whereas pregnancy generally has not been forced on a woman. Fourth, the violinist's need for the woman's body is not something she is responsible for, but in pregnancy the woman usually has some sort of responsibility. Finally, in Thomson's example, presumably the woman can simply unhook herself. An abortion, however, normally requires assistance of a second party to remove the fetus.[53]

Wennberg, however, thinks he can qualify the violinist's story sufficiently to make it analogous to pregnancy. Make the violinist the woman's son or daughter. Then, require the mother only to be linked to him at night during sleep, not continuously for nine months, twenty-four hours a day. Third, have the woman agree to the hook-up voluntarily and with full knowledge of what is required. Without this qualification Wennberg thinks Thomson's story is more applicable to pregnancies that result from rape than to anything else. Fourth, Wennberg tries to avoid the woman becoming involuntarily responsible for the violinist by imagining that the violinist has only a few hours to live and the woman finds an antidote that saves him but makes him dependent on her body periodically for nine months. Finally, Wennberg thinks that if one has a right to control one's body, there is also a right to any reasonable assistance to have that control.[54]

It should be clear from Wennberg's suggested changes that Thomson's original illustration is too dissimilar to pregnancy to help the pro-choice case. Moreover, even if one grants the changes Wennberg makes in the story, that in no way grants the violinist's mother or the baby's mother the right to refuse access to her body. Having granted permission for that access, it would be wrong to withdraw it, especially when withdrawal would mean death. That is, even if the woman's right to control her body is paramount, once she has chosen to grant use of her body, changing her mind is wrong, especially since this change would result in the death of the violinist/baby.

Returning to Thomson's example of the violinist, it is clear that it is not parallel to pregnancy, and thus, it does not uphold the pro-choice argument. The violinist's use of the body was without that person's consent. The mother's pregnancy is usually with her implied or explicit consent through engaging in intercourse. That is, whenever a woman consents to sexual intercourse, she must understand that she is consenting, explicitly or implicitly, to becoming pregnant if that should eventuate. Adult privileges and pleasures include adult responsibilities! In the next chapter we discuss what happens when there is no consent to intercourse (i.e., rape occurs), but whatever rules apply to that case cannot overturn rules that apply when a woman grants consent to intercourse.

Another problem with Thomson's illustration and this argument in general is that the claim to the ownership of one's body is at best a feeble excuse to kill. In the U.S. and many other countries there is a right to own property, but that right does not give the owner the right to kill innocent trespassers, especially when they are present at the invitation of the owner! On the contrary, one is likely to be held legally responsible if such persons are hurt while on that property. What is true of owning property in general is also true of a woman's ownership of her body.[55] She has no right to kill "trespassers," especially when they are present at her implied or explicit consent.

Finally, Baruch Brody's discussion[56] of Thomson's argument is especially insightful. As he argues, a major problem with Thomson's argument (and the right to control one's body argument more generally) is that it fails to distinguish between two duties one might have. On the one hand, there is the duty to save or preserve another's life. Here Thomson's distinction between the good Samaritan and the minimally good Samaritan is applicable. One has a moral duty to help save a life only if it does not endanger or cost the life of the helper. For instance, one is not morally obligated to save a patient with a malfunctioning kidney if that help would result in loss of the donor's life. To help out in such a case would be an act of supererogation, i.e., in Thomson's terminology, to act as a good Samaritan. Clearly, one is only required to act as a minimally decent Samaritan.

If the case of a mother granting use of her body to the baby was simply a matter relating to a duty to preserve life, then Thomson's case might well be sound. However, there is another duty that is far more relevant to the matter of abortion, and it is significantly different from the duty to preserve life. In addition to the duty to preserve life, Brody notes that there is a duty not to take a person's life. This duty is simply the requirement not to murder. Brody argues that this is really the right of significance in abortion cases, not the right to preserve life. But now consider this right in light of the minimally decent and good Samaritan distinction. A minimally good Samaritan will do his/her duty, according to Thomson, unless doing so would endanger his/her own life. If doing one's duty (not taking a life) means forfeiting one's life, then that would be to act as a good Samaritan. As Thomson says, one is not obligated to be a good Samaritan. On the other hand, if doing one's duty does not endanger one's life, and if the duty is not to take a life, then that means the mother's duty is not to take the life of the baby. Even on Thomson's terms, this asks the mother only to act as a minimally decent Samaritan, and Thomson has said the mother is obligated to do that. The upshot of Brody's point is that once one recognizes the real duty that confronts the mother in this case, the duty not to take a life, Thomson's argument actually becomes an argument against the mother choosing to abort her baby.

Right to Life v. Right to Free Choice or Freedom.
Most other arguments for abortion based on conflict of rights focus in some way on the conflict between the baby's right to life and the mother's right of free choice. In what follows we present and critique three of the most common of these arguments.

Right to Life v. Unwanted Children
According to this argument, it is morally wrong to bring any child into the world who is unwanted. Unwanted pregnancies lead to unwanted children, and unwanted children result in abused children. Therefore, if a woman does not want a child, she should be free to choose to abort that fetus.

Though many find this argument compelling, there are numerous difficulties with it. First, it is very difficult to see how freedom of choice is a right that supersedes the right to life. Second, it is extremely difficult to know whether an unwanted pregnancy will lead to an unwanted child who as a result will be unloved and abused. Many parents who do not plan to have a child, find that the wife is pregnant. By the time the birth occurs, the child is loved and wanted. Once a child is born, few would be so cruel as to abuse a child just because his or her conception was unplanned. Third, one might ask, unwanted by whom? Given the large number of abortions, the acceptability of keeping a child conceived out of wedlock, and increasing infertility, there is a large number of childless couples who desperately want to adopt but are unable to do so. Hence, a child unwanted by its birth mother is not necessarily unwanted altogether. Finally, the way this argument is stated hides the real source of the problem. The description makes it appear that there is some deficiency in the child for which he or she is responsible, when in fact the deficiency is in the parents. There are, to be sure, cases of reasonable hardship. Such circumstances may justify putting up the child for adoption, but cannot excuse killing the fetus. The real problem, however, in the vast majority of these cases is that the parents are heartless, selfish cowards. The baby, then, is asked to give its life not for the sake of the parents' freedom of choice, but to accommodate their selfishness.

Right to Life v. Right to Be Loved

Closely related to the unwanted child argument is the claim that every child born into the world has the right to be loved. The implication seems to be that if a child will not be loved, then the mother is justified in seeking an abortion.

Careful examination of this argument shows that it too is faulty. If one would be better off with something than without it, it does not follow that he or she has a right to that thing. Clearly, every child would be better off with a $10,000 trust fund established at birth, but that does not mean the child has a right to it. Analogously, a newborn child is better off loved, but does this constitute a right? If so, this is a heavy weight to hang around the neck of the fetus, especially if the fetus can be killed because of it! Such a right, if there is one, can in no way supersede the child's right to life. In fact, if rights and duties are correlative, the right of the fetus to be loved implies a correlative duty on the parents' part to love that child.

Remember, too, that the person deciding whether the child is loved is seldom disinterested. That is, the person who decides if the baby will be loved and whether it should be aborted is its mother, but she is hardly disinterested. If for personal reasons she decides she will not likely love the child, she may seek an abortion. It seems, however, much fairer to all parties concerned if the decision about the baby's fate is made by someone who has no personal interests at stake in the case.

Finally, this argument is troublesome because a similar argument would justify killing fussy infants, as well as retarded, elderly, and paraplegic persons. That, of course, would be outrageous, but so is using this argument to justify killing the unborn.

Right to Life v. Right to Choose One's Morality

This argument is often given in support of one's right to choose abortion. It claims that it is not right for pro-lifers to impose their morality on someone else. In its strongest form, the argument says imposing one's morality on another is wrong, especially when Christians do not all agree on the issue of abortion. Since there is not agreement on this matter, why deny someone the right to choose what he or she will do?

Like so many arguments, this seems to have an initial plausibility, but in the end must be rejected. What must be seen is that unless one is willing to grant moral anarchy (everyone decides for themselves what they will and will not do), someone's morality is imposed on someone else all the time. Unquestionably, *Roe* imposed someone's morality on the U.S. Not only that, it makes all of us pay for that morality through federally funded abortions that use our tax money! The issue, then, is not whether a morality should be imposed, but whether the one being imposed is the correct one. We are not embarrassed to impose a morality on society that requires us not to kill another human being on whim. Why, if abortion is wrong, should we be afraid to impose on society a ban against it?

CONCLUSION

In assessing the relative merits and demerits for the pro-life and pro-choice positions, we must conclude that the pro-life position makes the better case. As a result, we believe that elective abortions in general are immoral. Obviously, that judgment does not handle hard cases such as the morality of abortion when pregnancy results from rape or incest. In the next chapter we discuss those and other special cases.

In concluding the discussion of this chapter, we return to something written almost fifteen years ago. It seemed correct then, and we still stand by it today: "While it is difficult, and perhaps impossible, to convince a pro-abortionist of the personhood of the fetus, nevertheless from a purely ethical point of view it still makes sense to demand that human life should not be arbitrarily terminated, particularly when less drastic solutions exist. Such solutions should be sought on the side of both the fetus and the mother. Having once been conceived, the fetus has no choice but to grow, just as it had no choice in its conception or its blond hair or blue eyes. Hence, the fetus is without recourse and remedy. The same is not true of the mother, who has at least three alternatives other than abortion. She can exercise initial will power by abstinence, which is grossly out of fashion today. She has the option to use contraception to prevent the unwanted child. And finally, given the birth of the child, the mother can allow the living but unwanted infant to be put up for adoption. While this approach does not entirely resolve the confrontation between the two sides in the debate, it does make it clear that it is the fetus who is the innocent victim,

and it is the mother who controls, at least in some human sense, the beginning of life and thus should take the necessary precautions to prevent the
conception and subsequent destruction of it."[57]

CHAPTER THREE

Abortion and Special Problems

In Chapter 2 we argued that there are many good reasons, biblical and philosophical, for thinking abortion is *prima facie* morally wrong. Hence, there must be some morally compelling reason to permit an abortion. Certainly, abortion for reasons of convenience is immoral.

Though a Judeo-Christian view of life addresses many moral questions, there are some questions that, as Holmes observes, it does not answer by itself.[1] Some of those issues are special problems relating to the question of abortion. Included among those problems are the hard cases—threat to the life of the mother, a handicapped child, rape and incest, RU-486, fetal tissue research, and civil disobedience in protest of abortion.

Important ethical issues typically have hard cases. We intentionally did not discuss abortion's hard cases in the last chapter. The reasons are twofold. First, these cases never should be the basis for developing normative ethical principles. As the saying goes, hard cases make bad laws. That is true in law, and it is equally true in ethics. Second, consensus on these issues will be harder to reach since what is ethically right is more difficult to decide. Still, they must be addressed, for it is often in these matters that we need the most direction.

ABORTION TO SAVE A MOTHER'S LIFE

Is abortion ever justified when the developing fetus is a threat to the very life of the mother? We begin by noting a view that is not very popular today, but once was defended particularly in certain Roman Catholic ethical circles. It is the view that one is never justified in taking a life. There is a difference, so the argument goes, between taking a life and letting one die. The former is never a moral option; the latter may be. If one simply does nothing in a case where mother and/or baby are endangered, and one or both die, one has simply let them die. This was the best that could be done in this case, and at least no life was taken. It is not hard to see why this view is unpopular today. One runs the risk of losing two lives, when it seems quite clear that one could be saved.

If one rejects the position just mentioned, where does that leave us? We think a lot depends on the nature of the mother's problem as well as when in the pregnancy it occurs. However, we believe that whatever one decides, one must remember that both the mother's life and that of the unborn child are precious to God. Thus, every effort should be made to save both lives. This is also why it is important to have a pro-life doctor who will not counsel abortion at the first sign of difficulty in a pregnancy.

As to specifics, if the problem occurs late in the pregnancy, the child can likely be taken prematurely without dying, i.e., probably both lives can be saved. If the mother's illness is diagnosed early in pregnancy, treatment should be delayed as long as possible and the baby taken prematurely. Of course, a lot depends on the nature of the illness. In some cases both lives cannot be saved. However, with advances in medical technology the number of times one life must be lost is rare indeed. As mentioned in the previous chapter, ectopic or tubal pregnancies and cancer are the most common cases where a life will be lost. With ectopic pregnancies, the baby's life must be taken, for the baby is developing outside the uterus, and without intervention both mother and baby will die. Intervention must come so early in the pregnancy that even if a mother wanted to save the baby, the baby would be too premature to survive. In cancer cases where treatment for cancer or the removal of the cancer would terminate pregnancy (as, e.g., with cancer of the uterus), we think commencement of treatment for the mother is morally permissible.[2]

This has been defended in a number of ways. Some have argued that there are important similarities to self-defense, and if that is morally justifiable, so is an abortion of this kind. However, we believe there are important enough differences from self-defense to reject this argument. Others defend taking the child's life on the ground that the mother is an actual person and the child is only a potential person, and the rights of actual persons outweigh those of potential persons. We find this argument quite unconvincing as well. A person is a person, or he or she is not. Furthermore, if the unborn baby's rights as a potential person are outweighed by those of actual persons, this seems to reopen the door to abortion for any reason, including convenience. We find that thoroughly objectionable.

Still, we believe there are principles that justify taking the baby's life in this case. One is that if it is possible to do good to someone else without endangering or harming oneself, one is obligated to do so. Otherwise, one is not so obligated. As applied to this case, this rule means the mother is not morally required to give up her life to save that of the baby. The other principle mentioned in our first chapter is that one is not morally responsible for failing to do what could not be done or for doing what one could not fail to do. That is, one is not guilty for failing to do something if one is not free to do it. In this case, it is not possible for the mother to save both her life and that of the baby. But then, she is not morally culpable if she doesn't do both. Granted that she cannot do both, the first principle shows that she need not save the baby's life instead of her own. Of course, it is also morally permissible for her to decide to put off treatment until the baby is born, even if that course of action shortens her life. As noted in the previous chapter, this would be an act of supererogation (beyond the call of duty). Such an act of courage and love is morally praiseworthy and certainly morally permissible, but it is not her moral obligation.[3]

Before leaving this issue, two words of caution are in order. First, we repeat that in light of advances in medical technology, the actual number of cases where the life of either mother or baby must be sacrificed is very small indeed. Second, abortion to save the mother's life has been called therapeutic abortion. In the current discussions on abortion the meaning of "therapeutic" has been expanded to cover anything that affects the well-being of the mother. This now includes whether she is depressed at the thought of having another child or whether having a child fits in with her career goals. That is not what we are advocating here. The only therapeutic abortions we are sanctioning are those where the mother's life is genuinely endangered, and it is impossible to save both her life and the life of the baby.[4]

ABORTION AND THE HANDICAPPED CHILD

A commonly heard argument for abortion is that we should not allow "nature's anomalies" to be born. Where possible, we ought to abort children who will be born with some handicap, particularly if it is severe.

In response, we have a number of things to say. First, society in general and family and friends in particular must deal compassionately with any parent called upon to take up the added burden of caring for a handicapped child. Even when that burden is accepted, it is not easy. It often requires enormous sacrifice. It takes emotional energy, finances, and possibly a rearranging of one's goals and priorities. Self-sacrifice for the good of another is not very popular today. Those willing to do it should be applauded, encouraged, and helped as much as possible.

Second, it is easy to forget that there are at least two parties to be considered in this matter, the parents and the handicapped child. It is important not to pit the parents' needs against the child's. Put another way, the child's right to life should not be bartered for freedom from care for the parents. It is hard to imagine a parent asking God for a handicapped child. However, many testify that just such a child has been an incredible blessing, even drawing the family closer together and to the Lord.[5] We should not forget Christ's attitude toward those who were sick and infirm (e. g., John 9:3). It was God who said to Moses: "Who makes [man] deaf or dumb? Who gives him sight or makes him blind? Is it not I, the Lord?" (Exod 4:11).

Third, handicaps cover a wide range of disabilities. Some children are born with mild handicaps, others with moderate, and still others with severe disabilities. To summarily condemn them all as a group to death is cruel indeed. Moreover, while some persons are born with disabilities, others develop them along life's way. If one is justified in terminating the life of an unborn child merely on the suspicion that he or she may have some disability, does it not follow that those whom we know have some handicap should be put to death postnatally? The desire to cure or avoid disease should not so consume us that we destroy those among us who have disabilities. A utopian society is a tricky one. It immediately raises the question, whose utopia? One must be careful not to ticket oneself for termination in the process.

Fourth, while methods for detecting disabilities in unborn infants are constantly improving, there are still cases of false positives and false negatives. The former lead to the abortion of perfectly healthy infants, while the latter raise the question as to whether those who escape detection prenatally ought to be euthanized postnatally. If expectant parents tried to determine whether their unborn child had some handicap and the tests failed to reveal the difficulty, why should they be burdened with a child they did not want? If detected handicaps or defects warrant destroying the child, then it seems to follow that parents have a right to kill the child, regardless of when the handicap becomes known. The logic follows, but the result (sanctioning infanticide) cannot be morally tolerated.

Someone may, however, respond that we are addressing the easy cases, cases where the child will survive and live at least a moderately normal human existence. There are, on the other hand, far more severe cases which we have not handled. There are children who will be so severely handicapped that they will live a life that can only be characterized as subhuman. They may need skilled care all their life and still live in a vegetative state. Or, in the most extreme cases, unborn children are diagnosed as having a disease that will cause them to die at birth or shortly thereafter. Should not abortion be available at least in these extreme cases? Why prolong death? Why try to avoid the inevitable? Is not the anguish of the parents to be considered?

Our answer will not satisfy everyone. Yet, it is not given out of a callous disregard for the pain of the parents and possibly even the child. Still, we must respond that even in these extreme cases eugenic abortions are not moral. We think not for two reasons. Even where death is inevitable, we have no right to take someone's life. Life and death are in God's hands, not man's. Moreover, how we treat those in this state will influence our attitude more generally to the sanctity of life. A society that permits the abortion of handicapped children prenatally can easily become a society that finds reasons to terminate the lives of others who are undesirable for some other reason. The taking of innocent life is forbidden by God's word. Obeying that prohibition is right, and it also seems a reasonable price to pay even in these cases in order to uphold the broader goal of respect for life.

ABORTION AND RAPE OR INCEST

In rape and incest we again confront extreme examples. Rape and incest are some of the most horrible sexual crimes imaginable. They often result in great physical and psychological harm to the victim. Add to that the fact that in incest there is the possibility for a severely handicapped baby, because the parents are so closely related genetically. Are we to add to the already enormous burdens rape or incest places on a victim the responsibility to bear a child from this union and to care for him or her until maturity?

Before offering moral guidance on these matters, we must acknowledge facts that cannot help but enter into our judgment. We have never been involved in rape or incest, and as men we cannot fully appreciate the utterly devastating character of these crimes. Nonetheless, those facts need not invalidate our moral evaluation of this issue. The reader must evaluate what we say on its own merits, apart from one's assessment of those who offer it. Having said this, we suggest that the place to begin discussing this issue is with the arguments for both sides.

As to arguments against abortion in cases of rape and incest, an initial argument is that it is never right to do evil to achieve good. Put another way, two wrongs do not make a right. While rape and incest are horrible acts, so is abortion. Second, while rape and incest are acts of violence against the mother, so is abortion. As argued in the previous chapter, abortion is not without possible complications for the mother. Third, aborting a fetus conceived by rape or incest makes the baby a victim of the crime as well. The mother is already a victim of this crime; abortion only adds another. Fourth, it is never right to commit murder to alleviate suffering. Abortion is murder, like it or not, and in this case it is committed to alleviate the pain of the mother. Fifth, to demand that the mother bear the child is not to lack compassion. Harm, both physical and psychological, may come to the mother who aborts in the situation, so there is concern for her. However, to terminate the life of an unborn child certainly shows no compassion for him or her. We have a right, so it is argued, to require the mother to give birth to the child, and if she cannot bear to care for it, she should give it up for adoption. Sixth, it is wrong to force someone to do something they have no duty to do. No one is obligated to lay his or her life down for another's life, much less for some lesser benefit. Therefore, it is wrong to force someone to do so. But that is exactly what the baby is asked to do. We are asking the unborn child, conceived by rape or incest, to forfeit life in order to ameliorate the mother's pain. To refuse abortion is an example of the no duty-non-forcing principle.[6] Finally, conception in cases of rape is very rare. The reasons are many. The emotional trauma of the act may prevent ovulation, the offender may experience impotence, or the woman may use contraceptives or be in her infertile period of the month. It is estimated that .06 of 1 percent of all abortions are for rape. Undoubtedly, the numbers are low because some who become pregnant from rape decide not to abort. Still, it is safe to say that the main reason figures are low is that most rape victims don't get pregnant.[7]

In turning to the case for permitting a woman to have an abortion in cases of rape or incest, one finds few arguments. Some claim that abortion must be permissible as the woman has already suffered enough. Rape and incest are horrible, violent acts, and we should not add to the woman's already heavy burdens by requiring her to carry the child. Second, in cases where the act is particularly heinous, the child will be a constant reminder of the crime. That crime may even result in severe psychological damage and death (suicide) to the mother. Finally, the most important argument for allowing abortion in these cases is that there is a morally significant difference in cases of rape and incest as opposed to other abortions. The difference is that with rape and incest, the mother did not consent, implicitly or explicitly, to sexual intercourse. Instead, she was forced into an act that resulted in conception of an unwanted pregnancy.[8]

In evaluating these arguments, we think some are not as weighty as they first seem. On the side of prohibiting abortion, the claims that we should never do evil to achieve good and that two wrongs never make a right assume that abortion in this case is immoral. But that is just the point in question, and to use this argument seems to beg that question. Moreover, the claim that it is wrong to commit murder just to prevent suffering is another example of the same problem. If murder is defined minimally as the taking of innocent life without just cause, then that assumes rape and incest are not just causes, which is, of course, the whole point of the debate.

On the side of permitting abortion in these cases, there are similar problems. There is the assumption that a child who is the product of rape or incest will be an unwanted child. This argument bears some similarities to the more general unwanted child argument. The child could be carried to term, and then adopted by someone who very much wants a baby. Furthermore, while the child is certainly unwanted at conception, that does not mean the child will always be unwanted. In fact, it is entirely possible that this child could be a factor in healing the wound opened by rape or incest. With respect to the most important argument, we can agree that there is a morally significant difference in cases of rape and incest, but that does not entitle the victim to an abortion. The reason is that the argument assumes that if one is *unjustly* denied her freedom of choice, that gives her the right to take a life. That seems clearly to be a faulty assumption.

Our position is that although we acknowledge the horror of rape and incest and have genuine compassion for victims of such crimes, we think the weight of argument goes against permitting abortions even in these hard cases. We hold this view for several reasons. First, we do not think it is morally right for someone to give up his or her life without consent merely to alleviate someone else's suffering. That is what the fetus in these cases is asked to do.

Second, we are unconvinced that abortion in such cases ends or even lessens the suffering of the mother. David Reardon's book, *Aborted Women: Silent No More*, is the most extensive study of the long term effects on women of their decision to have an abortion.[9] This book is the result of extensive research and of a detailed survey of 252 women who had abortions and are now members of WEBA (Women Exploited by Abortion). From this research Reardon found that over 95 percent would not now have chosen abortion, and that 66 percent feel they are now worse off than they would have been had they not had an abortion. These are truly surprising findings, but they should be tempered a bit because of two factors. First, it is not clear that these women had abortions for rape or incest. Second, the fact that they are members of WEBA makes them an atypical sample of all women who have had abortions. Still, the findings do underscore our general point that it is not clear that an abortion solves all the problems for a woman. It may solve some, but engenders others.

Finally, we think it is possible even in cases of rape or incest to prevent conception, and believe this is the course of action that should be taken. There is a period of time between intercourse and conception, and, if estrogen treatment is given, conception can be prevented.[10] In a Minnesota hospital 3,500 rape victims received treatment without one becoming pregnant. In Buffalo, New York, there was not one pregnancy from rape in thirty years, and in Washington, D. C., a study of over three hundred rapes showed only one pregnancy.[11] Hence, it seems possible to reduce dramatically the number of rape and incest cases where the question of abortion would even arise. In those cases where it does arise, however, we see no morally acceptable reason for demanding the forfeiture of the baby's life.

ABORTION AND RU-486

RU-486 is the name of a drug that has been called the pill that will revo-lutionize the abortion issue worldwide and end the abortion debate. It is hailed by some as one of the greatest medical discoveries of all time. We want to discuss the pill's development, its use, its so-called advantages, and finally its acceptability.

THE DEVELOPMENT OF RU-486

RU-486 was first discovered in 1980 by a biochemist, Georges Teutsch, who worked for the Paris-based pharmaceutical company Roussel-Uclaf. RU-486 stands for the laboratory name and molecule number for the com-pound in the pill. Etienne-Emile Baulieu, a doctor at the Bicetre Hospital outside of Paris, heard of the pill and got Dr. Gilbert Schaison, an endocri-nologist and university professor, to supervise a study that began in 1983 on a selected number of non-pregnant women to ensure that the drug was safe. He observed that the pill does indeed have an antihormonal effect. RU-486 functions by blocking the action of the hormone progesterone, a hormone that is needed at every stage of pregnancy. This prevents the fer-tilized egg from implanting in the uterus, or if it has, it causes the uterine lining to break down, triggering menstrual bleeding that ultimately ends the pregnancy.[12]

Schaison, who alone conducted the medical tests, then gave the drug to a gynecologist at Bicetre, Beatrice Couzinet, to use on women who wanted to terminate pregnancies in the early stages. Of one hundred women test-ing the pill, eighty-five aborted. From the test it was concluded that RU-486 was a safe and effective means for early termination of pregnancy. It has few side effects, because it passes through the body within forty-eight hours, does not affect fertility, and can be used only when a woman is sex-ually active.[13]

In 1988 the French health minister approved the drug's use on a restricted, prescription-only basis. Almost immediately there was an out-cry of public opinion in France and abroad. Anti-abortion groups threat-ened to organize boycotts of Roussel-Uclaf and its parent conglomerate, Hoechst AG of Frankfurt, Germany. Opposition was so intense that Roussel withdrew the pill one month after it was approved for distribu-tion. The French government immediately ordered its distribution, citing as reasons "concern for the public health and what this pill means for women."[14]

At present the pill is available in France and England under very strict procedures. Some 110,000 women have used the drug in France.[15] The drug has been copied and is used widely in China. It is thought that it will be available more widely throughout Europe quite soon. As to the U.S., the AMA has recommended its testing, but the Food and Drug

Administration has put RU-486 on its "import alert" list that prevents individuals from bringing it into the country. On July 1, 1992 this was challenged by a California woman, Leona Benton, who was six and a half weeks pregnant. Twelve RU-486 pills were seized from the woman on her return to New York's Kennedy Airport from London, where the drug is legal. The seizure was appealed to the Supreme Court where the ban on the drug was upheld by a 7-2 vote.[16]

USE OF RU-486

Originally, RU-486 pills were thought to be once a month pills or an early abortion pill. That is, the pill would be taken for four days at the end of a woman's monthly cycle, and within forty-eight hours menstruation would begin. If this prevented the need to take pills throughout most of the cycle, and if a woman had been sexually active, she had no further need for the drug.[17] That procedure has changed, because it only had a 60 percent success rate. However, when RU-486 is combined with prostaglandin thirty-six to forty-eight hours after taking RU-486, the success rate jumps to 96 or 97 percent.[18]

Thus, there has developed in France a regimen which requires four visits to a clinic (not a doctor's office) where a patient receives rigorous supervision. On the first visit the woman is given a full physical exam, often including a vaginal sonogram to establish the fact that she is pregnant. The second visit is then scheduled about a week later, at which time three RU-486 pills are swallowed so that the action of the hormone progesterone is blocked. On the third visit, two days later, the woman is given prostaglandin, which induces contractions to help expel the uterine lining and the embryo. During this visit the patient is monitored for about four hours for any side effects. Three out of four women abort while at the clinic. The rest are sent home to wait. A fourth visit is scheduled a week later so the doctor can be sure the embryo has been expelled from the mother and that there is no excessive bleeding. To ensure that the drug is effective, RU-486 is not used after forty-nine days from the beginning of a woman's last period. When this procedure is unsuccessful, there is the need for a surgical abortion.[19]

ADVANTAGES OF RU-486

Many advantages have been claimed for this drug. Some relate to abortion, while others do not. Advantages often cited are the following: first, RU-486 is a safe and effective way to terminate pregnancy in its early stages. It requires no surgery, and as such is non-invasive. Dr. Etienne-Emile Baulieu has argued that it is a way to prevent the estimated death of about two hundred thousand women worldwide from botched abortions. For many, that alone justifies its use. Second, because it requires no surgery, it is a cheaper way to get an abortion.

Third, it allows a woman to abort in relative privacy. At present in France she must make four visits to a clinic, but it is possible that the drug could be made available from regular doctors and taken in their office or even at home. This would eliminate the traumatic march past protesters at abortion clinics. In fact, some suggest that a woman could take the pill without having to know whether she was pregnant or not. The pill could be used as a combination of contraceptive and/or abortifacient. This would allow the process to take place in the most ideal psychological circumstances.

Fourth, since the drug is not used after forty-nine days from the beginning of a woman's last menstrual period, it has been suggested that if the pill were widely available, the need for later term abortions would decrease dramatically. Moreover, this pill places women in control of their own bodies. If given easy access to the pill, women would then have greater control over the reproductive functions of their bodies.

Sixth, present studies show that RU-486 has *not* increased the number of abortions. It is argued that women who used RU-486 would have had an abortion anyway. Therefore, the central concern ought to be the safety of the procedure. Since RU-486 is safer than surgery, it is wrong to withhold it from women who want it.

Finally, there are many benefits of RU-486 unrelated to abortion. As already mentioned, it could be used as a contraceptive. Moreover, it has shown promise in treating other diseases and physical conditions. Included among these are brain tumors, cancers of the breast and pituitary gland, Cushing's syndrome (a life-threatening adrenal-gland disorder), the easier removal of ectopic embryos and abnormal fetuses by softening and dilating the cervix (which would possibly reduce the number of cesarean sections needed), and endometriosis. Some argue that the testing and use of the drug should not be prohibited for these considerations alone.[20]

ACCEPTABILITY OF RU-486

Having set out the so-called advantages of RU-486, it still makes sense to ask if we ought to make this drug available to women generally. We believe the answer is quite clearly no. We offer two reasons, the first moral and the second medical. The place to start in assessing the acceptability of RU-486 is with the morality of abortion. It is interesting that RU-486's most ardent defenders are those who support a woman's right to an abortion. They assume, either because of the legality of abortion in many parts of the world or for other reasons, that abortion is moral. However, this simply does not follow. Because something is legal does not make it moral. As already argued, we see abortion as immoral except when a mother's life is clearly threatened. If this is so, then questions of cost, safety and invasiveness are inconsequential. There is no obligation to make it easier to perform immoral acts.

But might one not argue that since abortion is legal and since the use of RU-486 does not increase the number of abortions, we should not prevent its use because it does not worsen the moral climate? We find this argument unconvincing. Again, if abortion is immoral, then the aforementioned considerations have no bearing on the question. However, it is not clear that *widespread* availability and use of RU-486 would not increase the number of abortions. In France where the best data are available, RU-486 is administered under very strict control. Moreover, because four visits to a clinic are required, the cost of terminating a pregnancy chemically is no less than ending it surgically. But no one can say whether there would be a dramatic rise in the number of abortions if the drug were available worldwide and without the need of a prescription in some countries.[21]

However, what we find most ironic about this whole matter is that this drug threatens to remove the element of choice in an abortion. Those who want to retain the legality of abortion argue that a women ought to have a choice about continuing a pregnancy. This choice is so intimate and personal that it should only be made between a doctor and patient. But if RU-486 is readily available, it could be taken at the end of the monthly cycle of sexually active women without ever having to know whether they are pregnant and aborting a fetus. As Joan Beck says, a woman can tell herself that she is simply facilitating late menstruation.

In addition, there is a further medical question about the pill. Is it safe? Despite talk of the pill's safety and a lack of side effects, there is evidence that calls this into question. One wonders whether the euphoria about the so-called advantages of the drug have not blinded its advocates to its genuine dangers. For one thing, this abortion process is painful and can lead to excessive or severe bleeding which can last as long as thirty-five days.

Second, the present procedure for using RU-486 requires taking prostaglandin, a drug that has long been known to have possible severe side effects. In 1991 the French Health Ministry announced that a thirty-one-year-old who was a heavy smoker died of heart failure after taking prostaglandin sulprostone. In 1990 two other French women, also known to be heavy smokers, had serious heart complications from the procedure. All of this prompted the French government to prohibit women who were heavy smokers or over thirty-five years old from using the drug. However, this seems to be just the tip of the iceberg. Roussel-Uclaf warns that women who have had a recent cesarean section, cardiovascular problems, hypertension or bronchial asthma should not use the drug. Furthermore, in clinical tests around the world women with complaints about liver or gastrointestinal disorders, blood clotting difficulties, anemia, pelvic inflammatory disease, irregular menstrual periods and obesity have been excluded. Thus, the side effects of RU-486 and prostaglandin may be far more severe and widespread than the public has been led to believe. A study was completed in March 1991 in which the pill Cytotec (misoprostol), a pill marketed by Searle as an ulcer drug, was taken in conjunction with RU-486. Baulieu says the use of Cytotec made the process less painful, possibly safer, and as successful as the original formula. Cytotec is nevertheless a prostaglandin, and as such has many of the same side effects. The cramps are not as severe, but the bleeding is. The average duration of bleeding for both drugs was 20.5 days. Cytotec commonly produced nausea, vomiting, diarrhea, abnormal heart rhythm and low blood pressure. No one can predict how these side effects will affect maternal health if there is the relaxation of the four clinic visit requirement.

Third, there is no study of the possible long term effects of exposure to RU-486 and prostaglandin. This should cause some pause about the safety of the procedure, given what occurred with the use of DES, a drug used to prevent morning sickness and miscarriage that later was shown to produce cancer in the offspring.

Finally, while no abnormal babies have been reported from RU-486 use in France, there are studies where rabbits were given RU-486, and deformities in the skulls of some of the fetuses were reported. There were also two reports in 1983 and 1986 of babies born with hydrocephalus after unsuccessful abortion attempts using prostaglandin. Thus, we have two very powerful chemicals combined whose long term effects are unknown, and also test data about those effects that are limited and rather troubling.[22]

Having cited moral and medical reasons against the use of RU-486, one question remains. Is it not morally wrong to ban the testing and use of RU-486 for purposes other than contraception and abortion? For instance, should it not be used in treating Cushing's disease? We have no objection to using RU-486 for purposes other than contraception and abortion. It seems that the most troubling side effects occur when it is used in conjunction with prostaglandin. If the drug itself or in conjunction with some other pill shows promise in the treatment of non-abortion related conditions, we think its use is acceptable. However, we do not say this without some concern. At present the pill is administered under very strict guidelines. The pills are numbered. They are given by prescription only. And they are taken in a clinic. Incidents such as the one involving Leona Benton cause us to wonder about the medical community's ability to police itself.

ABORTION AND FETAL TISSUE

Fetal tissue implantation is at least as old as the late 1880s. First attempts centered around transplanting tissue from the bodies of fetal animals into those of adult animals. Research, however, really did not pick up momentum until the 1970s.[23] A Swedish and American medical team used this technique to treat animals that had a chemically-induced form of

Parkinson's disease. This procedure showed some promise. However, they decided to cease experimentation because it would be ethically impossible to test their findings on human subjects. The reason for the ethical problem was that such tests would require human fetal brain tissue. Other research teams did, nevertheless, continue experimentation in both animals and humans.[24]

By 1985 two Denver researchers, Dr. Everett Spees and Kevin Lafferty, used fetal tissue from aborted fetuses in treating diabetes in humans. And in 1987 a transplant team in Mexico used fetal brain tissue from a fetus that reportedly had miscarried to treat a patient with Parkinson's disease. The fetal tissue was transplanted into the brain of the patient, causing significant improvement in the sufferer. By April 1988 reports of fetal tissue transplantation came from Sweden, England and Cuba.[25]

In March 1988 President Reagan formed a panel on fetal tissue research and transplantation after he rejected a request from the National Institute of Health for permission to transplant tissue into the brain of a patient with Parkinson's disease. Along with the establishment of this panel, all federal funding for research was stopped, and this panel, comprised of ethicists, scientists and lawyers, was given ten specific questions to consider, one specifically asking whether fetal tissue research could be divorced from the question of the morality of abortion.[26]

On September 16 of the same year, the panel voted 19-0 with two abstentions that use of fetal tissue taken from legal abortions is acceptable. This conclusion was preliminary and non-binding, but it did not consider the question of the morality of abortion. A month later a second vote was taken, at which time two panel members insisted that the morality of abortion had to be addressed. However, the panel rejected a proposal to deal with the morality of abortion by an 11-4 vote. Kenneth Ryan, the NIH's scientific chairman, argued that a fertilized egg (a single cell) should be invested with all the rights of a human being in the world.[27]

The interest in fetal tissue grows out of the promise that it may offer hope in treating a number of neural and endocrinal diseases, Parkinson's disease and diabetes in particular. This promise seems to rest in the unusual regenerative powers of this tissue, which some researchers claim permits it to continue to develop after transplantation and to grow quickly. The cells are soft and pliable, making them much easier to work with than those taken from an adult cadaver. Fetal tissue adapts well to new environments and is easy to freeze and store. Moreover, since the fetal immune system is not well developed, fetal tissue is less likely to be rejected by its recipient.[28]

DISTINCTIONS

Before turning to the arguments on this issue, some distinctions are helpful. First, it is important to see that human fetal tissue has a number of uses. It is a medium for research. Cells have been implanted into neural and endocrine systems. Transfusions of blood and its derivatives have been used. Organs such as kidneys, eye parts, hearts and lungs have been transplanted, and immunization has been achieved by the introduction of pathogens, antigens or antibodies.[29] Second, there is a distinction between tissue procured from what are called family planning abortions as contrasted with tissue gotten from abortions performed for the express purpose of having tissue to transplant. Third, there is a significant difference between taking tissue from living fetuses as opposed to dead. And finally, it is important to distinguish between experimentation that has therapeutic value for the fetus and that which does not. In the latter case we do not mean to suggest that the experimentation has benefit for no one, just none for the fetus. For instance, if cells are taken from a fetus and implanted in the brain of a patient suffering from Parkinson's disease, there may be benefit to the recipient, but there is none to the fetus.[30]

Having set out these distinctions, we are now able to state quite precisely the central focus of our discussion. We want to determine whether fetal tissue taken from dead, family planning aborted fetuses can be used morally for research and experimentation, implantation for treating disease, or transplantation where the procedure has no therapeutic value or benefit to the fetus. In what follows we present arguments used for allowing such research, as well as our reasons for thinking this kind of research should not be practiced.[31]

ARGUMENTS FOR USING TISSUE FROM ABORTED FETUSES

By far the most commonly offered and compelling argument for using fetal tissue is the benefits for its recipient.[32] Take, for example, its use in treating Parkinson's disease. This is a degenerative brain disease that affects more than a million and a half Americans over the age of fifty. As the disease progresses, it produces body tremors, rigid muscles, and in some cases impaired thought due to lack of the hormone dopamine. This disease has been treated by implanting cells from the patient's adrenal glands, but fetal tissue seems to be more promising. Therefore, advocates of using fetal tissue ask if it is not immoral to permit the continued suffering of Parkinson's patients when there is some promise of relief.

According to a second argument, the question of fetal tissue research and implantation can be divorced from the morality of abortion. Family planning abortions are legal and will take place regardless of what is decided about fetal tissue use. Fetal tissue will be available, and its use implies neither approval nor disapproval of abortion. The use of this tissue to benefit others at least rescues some good from a tragic circumstance.[33]

Third, the use of aborted fetal tissue need not increase the number of abortions. Obviously, a consequence that would concern pro-lifers is the possibility that more abortions might take place on the grounds that some good would come out of the act. However, it is argued that safeguards could be put in place to minimize this possibility. For example, mothers contemplating an abortion need not be informed that they can donate tissue until after the abortion. At present there are enough abortions worldwide to meet the demand for fetal tissue, so there would be no need for pregnancies having the express purpose of providing tissue. One could separate the procurer and the researcher or user. Restrictions could also be put in place so fetal tissue could not be sold for a profit, removing that motive for abortion. That is, reimbursement would only cover the cost of the procurement and delivery of the tissue, but the cost of the abortion could not be paid.[34]

ARGUMENTS AGAINST USING TISSUE FROM ABORTED FETUSES

While we feel great compassion for those with a debilitating disease and hope for the day when effective treatment and even cure is possible, we do not feel that this should include the use of aborted fetal tissue. First, we seriously doubt that the widespread use of fetal tissue in medical therapy will not increase the number and timing of abortions. While it is true that at present there is sufficient fetal tissue from the number of aborted fetuses worldwide, there is no certainty that will always be the case. There are relatively few therapies that require its use at present. Its use is not permitted worldwide. Who can say what would happen if its use were shown to have beneficial effect for a much broader assortment of ills and its use was not banned anywhere. Would there still be enough tissue? Beside that, if fetal tissue becomes a permitted therapy, how can one be sure that babies might not be conceived solely for the purpose of achieving a better tissue match? One might argue that a mother would not calculate the donation of her fetus' tissue in her decision to abort or not. That might be so where tissue experimentation and implantation is a relatively new and restricted procedure. But who can say such considerations would not weigh on a woman's decision to abort or not if it were widely known that tissue from these aborted fetuses had beneficial medical uses? Prospects of eliminating the profit motive are probably somewhat better. No doubt some will sell tissue for profit just as some sell babies, but one can place strict guidelines on its procurement and require severe penalties for those who transgress.

Moreover, it is not clear that the timing of abortions would not be affected by the uninhibited use of aborted fetal tissue. Nearly 80 percent of induced abortions occur between the sixth and eleventh weeks of pregnancy. By that time tissue in the brain and elsewhere is sufficiently developed so it can be transplanted. Abortions performed in the fourteenth to sixteenth weeks yield fetal tissue that is usable in pancreatic transplantation. The significance of this is that the later the abortion occurs in the gestation process, the more useful the tissue is. For instance, fetal organs are best taken from anencephalic babies, babies who are full or near full term but who lack an upper brain.[35] All of this seems to raise the possibility that abortions would be performed later in pregnancy, causing even greater moral consternation to those who find abortion immoral. Even those who think abortion is acceptable early in pregnancy but not later would be troubled.

Second, there is the problem of moral complicity. At the heart of the argument for using aborted fetal tissue is the claim that its use can and must be separated from the morality or immorality of abortion. As a matter of fact, it is even claimed that one can be against abortion and for aborted fetal tissue research and implantation. The argument from moral complicity denies that claim. A fine summary of that argument is given by James Burtchaell in his article setting forth the course of reasoning that led the University of Notre Dame to oppose aborted fetal tissue experimentation.[36]

Burtchaell cites four types of moral complicity in evil, complicity which makes one a party to the act. First, there is active involvement in the evil, as when one drives the getaway car in a bank robbery. Second, there is indirect association with an act that implies approval. One does not join in the evil itself but enters a supportive role. The difference between neutrality or opposition and complicity is in the way one does or does not hold oneself apart from the enterprise. Burtchaell cites the difference between infiltrating a gang for the purpose of being an informant as opposed to a sociologist coming to some agreement with child pornographers in order to study the effects of its use on its subjects. In this latter case informed consent is not with the victims but their victimizers. Third, there is complicity from culpable negligence. Such occurs, for example, when parents fail to give their children proper supervision and the children practice vandalism. And fourth, complicity may occur through actions aimed at curbing wrong which in fact legitimize or stimulate it. An example of this type of complicity is found in agencies who single-mindedly try to stem the tide of adolescent pregnancies by offering contraceptives and abortions (the consequences) rather than coming to terms with the problem itself (inappropriate sex).[37] The unifying thread throughout each form of complicity is that one aligns oneself with another's act. One may either further or endorse it by collaborating in it, by looking the other way, or by shielding the victimizer from the consequences of the act. However, the end result is that one is put in the same moral stance the other person assumes by direct action.

It is Burtchaell's contention that experimentation on or use of fetal tissue derived from elective abortions puts one in moral complicity with the abortionist. One is corrupted by association with the principal agent, and is a comrade with the abortionist by resorting to him or her for a steady supply of tissue from unborn humans who have been purposely destroyed.[38] If this argument is correct, and we think it is, it shows that one cannot remove the moral stain of a wrong action by simply covering it with a moral, beneficial act. Thus, a partnership in which one benefits from injurious behavior, even after the fact, puts that one in clear alliance with the one doing wrong. The morality of abortion and the use of aborted fetal tissue cannot be divorced.[39]

John A. Robertson, an advocate of using aborted fetal tissue, objects to Burtchaell's argument. He says that even proponents of the complicity argument recognize that subsequent benefit from an action does not make one morally complicitous in it. He points out that opposition, neutrality and approval (even help) are all relationships that one can have to an evil act according to Burtchaell. Robertson thinks Burtchaell's argument must assume that the researcher applauds the act of abortion. However, we disagree. Burtchaell's argument is that anything but opposition to the act of abortion has the consequence of making one an ally of the act, particularly where one benefits from the act. Robertson offers an analogy for the use of fetal tissue in the use of the organs and tissue of a homicide victim. We do not hold that the doctor who transplants the organs or the one who receives them is morally complicitous with the prior evil act.[40]

However, Robertson's analogy breaks down at too many points to be convincing. The doctor who harvests and transplants the organs does not approve of the taking of the life. He would most certainly deplore it. But could not one deplore abortion and yet at the same make steady use of fetal tissue for such acts? Surely one could do that, but would not one's actions call into question the sincerity of the protestation? We think so. The most fundamental problem with Robertson's analogy is that while medical personnel are used to try to save the homicide victim, they intervene to kill the fetus. While both may die, in one case intervention is to save a life and in the other to take it. This means that the implanter or researcher is tied to one or the other of these acts, and that act casts a moral shadow over his or her act.[41]

A third problem is that informed consent is impossible in the case of fetal tissue research. Who could give informed consent for the use of aborted fetal remains? The most likely candidate is the mother, because the tissue is from her body. However, this is false since the tissue is carried within her body, but it has a distinct genotype, blood, and gender, and the body is that of another. But might not the mother have this right anyway as guardian of her offspring? The problem with this view is the growing conviction that she has forfeited the office of guardian in resolving to destroy her fetus. Another possibility might grant the right of disposal to the abortionist. There is, however, no reason to think that medical personnel acquire the right to dispose of the bodies of their patients. This seems all the more true when the patient dies as the result of the non-therapeutic intervention of the doctor without consent of the victim. Still another possibility is the state. But while the state may acquire a legal right to dispense with fetal remains, it has no more *moral* right to do so than does the medical profession. Moreover, if the state were to consign to research only the remains of those fetuses who have suffered the ultimate abuse, the state would then be placed in a position of patronage toward their destruction. Like the aborting mother, the state would be irresponsible in the use of its protective powers, thus forfeiting them. The net result of this whole discussion is that there is no one to give the needed informed consent.[42]

Robertson objects to this argument as well. He argues that the mother retains the right to determine how the fetal tissue is to be used if her choice is informed and free, and if the decision to abort the fetus and to donate the tissue are separate decisions so that one does not influence the other.[43]

As we see it, Robertson misses the point. The right to dispose of the aborted fetal tissue rests on the office of guardian. That office has been forfeited by the decision to abort the fetus. To change the conditions related to the right of disposal does not address this central issue of who is rightfully the child's guardian. One might, of course, appeal to the right to privacy mentioned in *Roe v. Wade* as justification for a woman's right to abort her unborn fetus. However, the right to privacy is irrelevant to aborted fetal tissue. Even if one grants for the sake of argument that right to privacy insures a right to abortion, right to privacy certainly does not apply in aborted fetal tissue questions. When a woman decides to have an abortion, the fetus is inside her and depends on her. When the decision is made about the disposal of the aborted fetus, it is not a part, within, or dependent upon the mother. Deciding what to do with the aborted fetus in no way invades the mother's privacy or attempts to control *her* body! Under any interpretation of privacy, a right to privacy no longer pertains to the situation.[44]

Finally, using deliberately aborted fetuses for research and transplantation is objectionable, because there are alternative sources of research material, cell lines. We object to using fetal material related to induced abortions. We have no objection to using the remains of unborn or newborn children who die as the result of a spontaneous abortion (miscarriage) or trauma, so long as the parents of the child grant permission. In these cases, we believe as well that the parents do have a right to grant permission, since they have not forfeited their right of guardianship by any deliberate act of killing.

Obviously, there are two difficulties with using such children that make it *difficult* but not necessarily *impossible* to do so. But the problems are scientific and emotional, not ethical. The scientific problem relates to spontaneous abortions, since they often occur as a result of genetic abnormalities in the baby. Any research conducted on them might be compromised by this fact. The second problem is emotional. It is the difficulty of asking traumatized parents for the remains of their stillborn or newly deceased child for research. This is not easy, but it is no more difficult than asking the family of a motorcycle accident victim for the right to transplant his heart. If a concerted effort was made to collect tissue from such children, there is reason to think it would meet present needs for fetal tissue since certain tissues in a stable, controlled environment are capable of reproducing, metabolizing and proliferating. Some tissues can even last through as many as fifty cycles of replication.[45]

ABORTION AND CIVIL DISOBEDIENCE

Since the *Roe* decision in 1973, concerned Christians have tried to prevent destruction of innocent human life in a variety of ways. In attempts to gain its goals, the pro-life movement has been rendered virtually impotent by the federal courts, legislatures and the media. After failing to get redress through the normal channels available in a democratic society, some have taken to civil disobedience in support of their views. The most visible and popular of these groups is Operation Rescue.[46] They advocate peaceful violation of trespassing and other property laws in order to preserve the civil rights of the unborn. In this section we will examine their position to see if it is justified.

Before turning to argumentation pro and con, we must distinguish several questions and clarify which are under discussion. The first question asks whether it is *morally obligatory* to break the law to protest abortion. Operation Rescue's position has been that it is. A second question is whether it is *morally permissible* to break the law to protest abortion. Though it might not be obligatory to do so, it still might be permissible. A final question asks whether it is *prudentially advisable* to break the law in protest of this evil. Only the first two questions are questions about morality. However, we want to address all three in what follows. Our primary focus, however, is the first issue, since Operation Rescue does claim that Christians are morally obligated to protest abortion through civil disobedience.

IS CIVIL DISOBEDIENCE *OBLIGATORY*?

The Case for Obligation

Most of the arguments offered in favor of an obligation to civil disobedience are ethical or philosophical in nature. However, the position is also argued on biblical grounds. We present both kinds of arguments.

The Argument for the Law Above the Law[47]

This argument says there is a higher law, divine law, or some universal, absolute moral law that stands over any expression of positive law. Any law passed by any state may be judged to see if it accords with this higher law. If government passes a law that conflicts with this higher law, the citizen is permitted, even obligated, to disobey that law. Another way to put this is that just because one has a legal right to do something, it does not follow that he or she has a moral right to do it. Therefore, though *Roe* gave a woman a legal right to an abortion, it does not follow that she has a moral right to it. In fact, the higher moral law against murder supersedes her legal right. So opponents of abortion are obligated to engage in civil disobedience in light of this higher law.

The Argument from the Good Samaritan Principle[48]
This argument claims that intervention is necessary (with the use of minimum force) to save an innocent baby's life. While abortion may be outlawed or limited in the long run by working within the law, this affords no hope for the baby who is to be aborted *today*. All legal means of redress for that baby have been exhausted. Therefore, we have a right and duty as good Samaritans to intervene to save the baby's life.

The Argument from Self-defense
This argument says the Bible expressly permits self-defense. This biblical right is extendable to the defense of others. That is, one has a right to defend oneself against unjustified attack. One also has a right, even if it is not an obligation, to defend others whose lives are threatened unjustly. If there ever was a paradigm case of defending the defenseless, abortion is that case.

The Argument from the "Necessity Defense"[49]
The necessity defense is used, for instance, to justify the breaking of a window in a burning house to free someone who is trapped. The necessity defense protects the rescuer against the charge of breaking and entering. Thus, while the act of breaking a window and entering a home would normally be a case of breaking the law, the necessity defense excuses one from following the law in that case. She is *not* a lawbreaker. In a similar way, breaking the law to stop an abortion is permissible, because it is necessary to protect the life of the endangered. In fact, given the other considerations already mentioned, it is obligatory.

The Biblical Argument
Scripture is used in support of Operation Rescue's program. The primary passage used to support this civil disobedience is Prov 24:10-12.[50] It is claimed that this passage demands that we intervene on behalf of those who are being taken off to death. If we fail to do so, we will be guilty of their death.

The Case Against Obligation
In setting forth the case against moral obligation to civil disobedience in protest of abortion, we shall interact with the arguments offered in favor

of it. We begin by saying that we believe there are instances where one is justified and even obligated in disobeying a state's law or laws. Thus, we agree that the Christian is not obligated to do *anything whatsoever* the state might demand.[51] The question now is whether abortion is one of those cases where civil disobedience is mandated. Here we limit our discussion of civil disobedience to non-violent action. If non-violent action cannot be required, then the stronger position that even violent action is mandatory fails.

We have serious doubts that current U.S. laws on abortion mandate civil disobedience generally or the actions of Operation Rescue in particular. At the heart of our reservations is the distinction between direct and indirect civil disobedience.[52] Direct disobedience occurs when a law that demands or forbids something is *directly* violated. An example of direct disobedience is the eighteen-year-old who violates the Selective Service Act and fails to register for the draft because he believes God has forbidden Christians to fight in any war. On the other hand, indirect civil disobedience involves breaking some law which is only indirectly related to the problem involved. A common example of this kind of civil disobedience is practiced by nuclear pacifists. They trespass on government property to protest the arms race and a government's possession of nuclear weapons. As Norman Geisler explains this distinction, direct disobedience involves breaking the law when it compels *me* to sin or do evil. Indirect civil disobedience occurs when the law allows someone else to sin, and we break a law to protest what they are doing.[53]

It should be clear that this distinction applies to abortion. There are no laws in the U.S. which require anyone to have an abortion. If a Christian were commanded to have an abortion, she would be morally obligated to refuse. If a doctor were mandated to perform an abortion, he or she should refuse. But if doctors were compelled to perform abortions, those of us not in the medical profession would not be in a position to violate that law directly. And if women were compelled to have an abortion, those not pregnant could not directly disobey. Civil disobedience is morally obligatory, we believe, in cases where one is directly compelled to do what is evil or a sin, but not when the law simply permits someone else's sin.

Some might object that the direct/indirect distinction fails in the abortion case. First, we *do* support abortions as tax paying Americans as millions of dollars from both the federal and state budgets go each year to fund abortion on demand. Second, the Supreme Court in *Roe* specifically commands us to allow abortions which result in the destruction of 1.6 million innocent babies a year. In other words, the Court prevents us from stopping the murder of innocent life by another.

We believe this objection is incorrect. If the direct/indirect distinction is correct, then the appropriate response to the public funding of abortions is to refuse to pay one's taxes or at least a portion of one's taxes, not to block someone else's entrance to an abortion clinic. Blocking a woman's entrance to an abortion clinic in no way addresses the question of whether I should pay tax money to fund abortions. As to the complaint that the Court prevents me from rescuing innocent victims, that simply reasserts the Operation Rescue position. It does not explain the basis of my moral obligation (if I have one) to break the law in protest of *someone* else's evil. While it may stop me from legally preventing abortion, the law does not command me or anyone else to have an abortion. Only if the law commands me to do something immoral am I morally obligated to disobey.

Our second main problem with the Operation Rescue position again focuses on indirect civil disobedience (and this is really where we disagree with Operation Rescue in that we agree with them that one is obligated to disobey when directly commanded to do evil). Our concern is that indirect civil disobedience involves breaking *good* laws to protest bad ones. Laws protecting property rights are good ones. Most would not generally want to see laws against trespassing or even destroying property struck down. Yet in this case it is possible that such laws might be violated. We think it morally significant that direct civil disobedience involves breaking bad laws, while indirect civil disobedience requires breaking good laws to protest bad ones. Might not disrespect for these good laws lead others to disrespect good laws indirectly related to other laws they think unjust? In fact, might it not even more generally lead to disrespect of a law-governed society?

Some may again object that the necessity defense makes the violation of trespass laws no crime. We do not see that the cases are parallel. Breaking a window to save someone trapped in a burning house would in a court of law legitimately be an example of the necessity defense. Hence, the person who broke the window would not be considered guilty of a crime. Moreover, moral law would also say it is acceptable. One has a duty not to break a window, but one also has a duty to preserve life if one is in a position to do so without endangering one's own life. In this case the two duties conflict, but it seems clear that the duty to preserve life has precedence over the duty not to break a window. As argued in our chapter on decision-making, when duties conflict, failure to fulfill one is not morally reprehensible, for no one is guilty for failing to do what cannot be done.

As to the case of abortion, the necessity defense has been used in courts of law and rejected. Therefore, the necessity defense is not a *legally* acceptable defense. But is it *morally* defensible? We think not, because as argued, there is no moral obligation or right to break any laws (much less good laws) to keep others from doing what is wrong.[54]

In sum, while we think certain of these ethical arguments apply when one is *commanded* to do something immoral, we do not see that they apply when someone else is *allowed* to do evil. Hence, we do not see that any of these ethical/philosophical arguments make it morally obligatory to intervene to stop others from having abortions.

But perhaps the biblical argument mandates such intervention. Specifically, does Prov 24:10-12 mandate intervention?[55] We think questions about using this passage to demand intervention may be raised at two levels. First, assuming that this text does teach generally intervening to save those who are perishing, that will not settle the matter in regard to abortion, for these verses do not explain how to apply the general rule in every situation where one might intervene to save the perishing. Moreover, the context of the passage does not consider how this demand would relate to a believer's relationship to civil government and its laws. In light of what Scripture says about obeying and being subject to civil authority (Rom 13:1-4; Acts 4:19-20; 5:29), we think one should withhold judgment on whether to obey the Proverbs passage in regard to the abortion question, at least until all relevant evidence is considered. As we shall frequently note in this book, general rules do have exceptions. Whether the general rule in Prov 24:10-12 has exceptions in regard to abortion cannot be decided on the basis of that passage alone. Simply lifting a passage from Scripture without seeing it in conjunction with other biblical teaching relevant to the topic seems to be a serious example of prooftexting.

But even more fundamentally, one may ask about the interpretation of this text. It is found in the book of Proverbs. Are we justified in taking a proverb and universalizing it into a moral law or obligation? Moreover, beyond the question of universalization is the question of whether rescue (in the Operation Rescue sense) is meant by this text at all. This text was given to Israel. Temples were erected in the land for the worship of Baal. At some point that worship included making children walk through the fire and sacrificing them. It is to that situation Proverbs speaks. But rescuing these children in no way would defy the government or break its laws unless one could show that Baal worship was mandated by the government, and it wasn't. Unless rescuing these children would have constituted an act of civil disobedience, the Proverbs passage does not speak to the situation Operation Rescue uses it to address.[56]

In sum, there are times when civil disobedience is not only morally justified but obligatory. These are instances where laws that compel *me* to do evil can be *directly* broken. The law permitting abortion is not such a case, for permission and compulsion are not the same, and abortion is an action taken by another, not by me. Hence, in this case the only kind of civil disobedience one can do must be done indirectly. But as we have argued, in such cases there is no moral obligation to disobey, and beyond that no Scripture explicitly demands civil disobedience in such circumstances. These considerations show, we think, that intervention to save the unborn is *not* morally obligatory.

One must not misunderstand what this means. On the one hand, it does not mean it is wrong to protest the evil of abortion that government permits. We are merely saying that so far we have seen nothing that warrants such protest to include breaking laws. Moreover, our conclusion that civil disobedience in this situation is not morally obligated does not answer whether it might be morally permissible. We turn now to that question.

IS CIVIL DISOBEDIENCE MORALLY *PERMISSIBLE?*

Though civil disobedience to protest others having an abortion is not morally obligatory, it might still be morally permissible. If so, one would not be obligated or required to break laws, but neither would one be prohibited from protesting abortion by breaking the law. Others might not take the same course of action, but at least those who feel so led could do it.

In addressing this question we refer initially to our explanation in the moral decision-making chapter of what makes an act morally permissible. As stated there, to say that an act is morally permissible means that one may do it or refrain without incurring any guilt. While mandated acts are also permitted, moral permission usually refers to cases where there is no moral obligation either commanding or forbidding an act.

As this matter of moral permission applies to civil disobedience to protest abortion, we have already seen that there is no moral rule that mandates indirect civil disobedience. That being the case, indirect civil disobedience will be permissible unless there is something that forbids it. But it is here where the problem arises. Given what we have said about why it is not right to break the law to protest others' doing of evil, we believe this means that breaking the law to protest others having abortions is forbidden. And if that is the case, then *indirect* civil disobedience is not morally permissible.

Though we are sympathetic with the goals of Operation Rescue, and though we know they and others will disagree with our position, if one accepts our argument about the propriety of indirect civil disobedience, we do not see how it is possible to escape the conclusion that indirect civil disobedience in this instance is not morally permissible. This conclusion may seem counterintuitive to some, but we think its accuracy can be illustrated by the following example.

Suppose I see someone about to kill someone else. It seems clear that I am morally *obligated* to do what I can to help the intended victim so long as my life is not endangered by so doing. But it also seems clear that this obligation does not obligate or even permit me to break the law in trying to stop the would-be murderer. That is, I certainly have no moral obligation to stop the murderer by killing him first (an act of mine that would also break the law). To say that I do would mean I am immoral if I don't stop the would-be murderer by murdering him! Obviously, that is absurd, but then we submit that thinking one is obligated to stop other evils about to be inflicted on others *by breaking the law* is equally problematic. In addition, in the case imagined it does not seem that one can even reasonably argue that I have a *right* to stop the would-be murderer by killing him. If I am a policeman, I may have such a right invested in me by the state, but if I am an ordinary citizen, I have no such right. Even a policeman will try to stop the murderer by some means other than an action that would cause the policeman to violate a law.

From this example, it should be clear that there is no obligation or right to disobey the law in order to prevent others from doing evil. Moreover, we believe this example is particularly germane to the issue at hand, since Operation Rescue's point is that it is simply trying to prevent others from committing murder. Obviously, Operation Rescue does not advocate stopping abortions by killing those who would have one, but they do urge stopping abortions *by breaking the law.* Hence, our example is analogous to indirect civil disobedience to stop abortion, because in both cases one tries to stop murder and because in both cases one tries to do so by breaking a law.

IS CIVIL DISOBEDIENCE *PRUDENTIALLY* ADVISABLE?

Not everyone will agree with our answers to the questions about moral obligation and permission. To those who disagree, our last avenue of appeal is prudential in nature. That is, some things that are morally permissible may not in fact be wise to do. On the other hand, some will agree with us, and of course, if something is morally forbidden, it is unwise to do it. But we believe that apart from the morality of the matter it is important to see whether a prudential case can be made for or against indirect civil disobedience to protest abortion. Hence, it is appropriate from both perspectives (agreement or disagreement with our answers to the first two questions) to raise the question of this section.

Does indirect civil disobedience to protest abortion attain the desired goal? Will action such as that of Operation Rescue result in saving the lives of unborn babies? Those in Operation Rescue think it does and will. First, interventions do save babies *now.* As mentioned earlier, even if pro-life forces are ultimately successful in the courts, this offers no hope for babies who are to be aborted *today.* When the entrances to abortion clinics are blocked, the abortion clinic is shut down at least for that day to avoid problems and possible violence. It is further argued that abortion rates go down in that area for some reasonable period of time. Thus, minimally, babies are granted another day of life. And if figures about decreases in abortions are correct, some babies who would be aborted are saved.

It is further argued that in the long run such actions will bring about the pro-lifers' goals. Intervention will bring the issue of abortion to the attention of the public, and the arrest of numbers of rescuers will force the courts to deal with the question of abortion. All of this will lead to the limitation or elimination of abortion on demand.

Despite these claims, we are unconvinced. It is true that anyone who comes to get an abortion at a picketed clinic will not get an abortion at that clinic while there is picketing. But the other points are not so clearly true. Will closing a clinic or even a group of clinics prevent abortion of the aforementioned baby or other babies? It is difficult to say. Is it really true that abortions suffer a decline? Even if there is a decline, is that decline due to the civil disobedience of Operation Rescue or is it due to some other cause?

In addition, there is a further question about whether civil disobedience will ultimately result in limiting or eliminating abortion on demand. On this point one can only conjecture. We do think civil disobedience will bring the issue of abortion up for public debate. However, will the perception of pro-lifers and their tactics allow a favorable conclusion to the debate? Given the pro-abortion inclination of the media, those who are for life are pictured as fanatic zealots. Such actions only reinforce these stereotypes.

We are also concerned about further implications of the proposed civil disobedience. The more there is civil disobedience to protest abortion, the greater the number of arrests of pro-lifers. How will the courts handle the overload of cases, if it should come to that? We fear that the courts' solution will not be in the best interests of the pro-life movement. Pro-lifers can be and already have been dealt with according to the *full* extent of the law. Leaders of civil disobedience will likely be given maximum sentences, and their assets may be seized. Furthermore, potential overcrowding of prisons at least raises the genuine possibility that someone guilty of a more serious crime and capable of further crimes will be put on the streets to make room for a "rescuer." Is it wise to pursue a course of action (civil disobedience) that could lead to this? Moreover, our concern at the deepest level is that disobedience to the law, even when justified, carries with it the genuine possibility that respect for law, even good laws, may be undermined.

Thus, we think that prudence counsels against indirect civil disobedience. Moreover, we believe it commits a serious tactical error. There are many who have no strong feelings either way on this issue. We fear that a confrontational approach like Operation Rescue's could push a goodly number of these people into the pro-choice camp.

CHAPTER FOUR

Euthanasia

On August 26, 1981 Clarence Herbert had a routine operation to remove a colostomy bag. During the first hour in the recovery room, he suffered a massive loss of oxygen to his brain, became comatose, and was put on a respirator. Though the brain still performed some lower brain functions, his wife was told he was brain dead, and she agreed to remove him from the respirator. On August 29 he was removed from the respirator, but he did not die. On August 31 the doctor ordered removal of all intravenous feeding. On September 6 he died from dehydration and pneumonia.[1]

Was this mercy or murder? In October 1983 the California Court of Appeals decided that the doctors did not commit murder. The court claimed that Herbert's comatose condition was "terminal illness," and argued that intravenous nutrition and water is "medicine" that can be withdrawn or denied if it does not cure the patient's disease or even make him better.[2]

Janet Adkins was fifty-four years old, but she was diagnosed with Alzheimer's disease. Informed about the course of this disease, she decided she did not want to live for years in this progressively deteriorating condition. She decided to kill herself, but she wanted a quick, painless death. She enlisted the aid of Dr. Jack Kevorkian of Michigan, inventor of the infamous suicide machine. On June 4, 1990 Dr. Kevorkian hooked her up to a heart monitor and intravenous tube. She pushed a button that released chemicals which killed her in five minutes. A murder charge was filed against Kevorkian, but it was dismissed, because Michigan's law against assisted suicide is vague. However, the court ordered Kevorkian not to use the device again or assist any more suicides. Despite warnings, Kevorkian later revealed that on October 23, 1991 he helped Shery Miller, forty-three, and Marjorie Wantz, fifty-eight, commit suicide. These incidents raised even greater complaint than the Adkins case, because neither Miller nor Wantz was suffering from a terminal disease. Miller had multiple sclerosis, and Wantz had a painful pelvic disease that was not terminal.[3]

In the U.S. twenty-seven states ban assisted suicide, and four ban suicide or assisted suicide. A new law in Michigan which outlaws what Kevorkian is doing was due to be in force March 30, 1993. In the meantime, Kevorkian continued to help others commit suicide. As a result, on February 25, 1993, the Michigan legislature voted to enforce the law immediately.

Should Kevorkian be charged with murder? Is it immoral to seek Kevorkian's help to commit suicide? What about those who "do it themselves" with instructions from the recent best-seller *Final Exit*?

These cases raise a whole series of questions that in contemporary discussions relate to the issue of euthanasia. Questions involved include the following: is mercy killing ever morally permissible or justifiable? If euthanasia is morally justifiable, are there cases where it would be morally obligatory to remove a patient's suffering? Is requesting a lethal dose of a drug equivalent to asking for help in committing suicide? If voluntary euthanasia is suicide, is suicide ever morally justifiable? Is there any moral difference between killing and letting someone die?

Advancements in medical technology that allow doctors to prolong life have raised these and many more ethical and legal problems. The problems are exacerbated not just by cases such as the Karen Ann Quinlan case, for which neither the medical nor legal profession was prepared.[6] Problems are heightened by the rapidly increasing numbers of people living well beyond sixty-five into their eighties and nineties. Statistics from the Census Bureau tell the story in America. In 1940, 365,000 Americans were eighty-five or over (.3 percent of the population). In 1982, 2.5 million (1.1 percent) were in that category. The bureau predicts that by the end of the twentieth century this group will top 5.1 million (almost 2 percent), and by 2050 more than sixteen million men and women will be eighty-five or over (5.2 percent of the population).[7] It is estimated that one fourth of all people who have ever reached sixty-five were alive as of 1975.[8] Since 1900, average life expectancy has increased more than 50 percent, from forty-nine to almost seventy today.[9]

Just because Americans are living longer does not mean they always remain in good health.[10] Increase in medical expenses as one grows older suggests a decline in health. It is estimated that per-capita hospital spending of the sixty-five-and-over group is more than 250 percent higher than that of the under-sixty-fives, and the eighty-five-or-over group is 77 percent higher again.[11] All of these factors contribute to a climate in which many are calling for legislation to legalize and regulate various forms of euthanasia.

Debates over euthanasia are not of modern invention. In the ancient world Pythagoreans opposed euthanasia, whereas Stoics favored it, especially in cases of incurable disease.[12] Plato approved it in cases of terminal illness.[13] Under the influence of Christianity, the Western attitude toward euthanasia and suicide has been negative, though some have advocated it.[14] Moreover, euthanasia is not unique to the Western World. For example, Indian sacrifices of the incurably ill to the Ganges and the Balinese practice of burning widows for the benefit of a dead chief are all well-documented.[15]

In more modern times debate over euthanasia has been quite lively.[16] In 1935 the Euthanasia Society of England was formed to convince the public that adults suffering severely from incurable fatal illnesses should be allowed a painless death if they requested it. The society's other goal was to promote legislation to that end. Despite the society's efforts, both in 1936 and 1969 bills to legalize euthanasia were defeated in the British House of Lords. In 1969 the British Medical Association passed a resolution that the medical profession has a duty to preserve life and relieve pain, but it condemned euthanasia.[17]

Holland has one of the most liberal attitudes toward euthanasia. Though the Netherlands has had a specific law against euthanasia that dates from the nineteenth century,[18] euthanasia was basically a dead issue until the early 1970s when a Dutch doctor killed her terminally ill mother with a lethal injection. The doctor was convicted, but the court suspended sentence and ruled that in cases where death is imminent and the patient has requested death, the physician could commit euthanasia.[19] Prior to 1993, euthanasia was still illegal in Holland, but Dutch courts were favorable to doctors who practiced it so long as they met the following guidelines: 1) the patient must be terminally ill, suffering unbearably, and must request it; 2) it must be a case in which no other treatment is possible; 3) the patient must consider the decision at length; and 4) only a physician in consultation with another physician can perform the act.[20] It is estimated that in Holland as many as six thousand people per year are put to death by euthanasia. Opinion polls show that about 60 percent of the Dutch population approve and only 12 percent of Dutch doctors oppose it. Moreover, surveys show that 80 percent of the doctors have been involved in euthanasia cases. One of the most telling facts about Dutch acceptance of euthanasia is that in Holland no surviving relative has filed a lawsuit against a doctor for performing euthanasia.[21]

In February 1993 the Dutch parliament voted to legalize doctor-assisted suicide and active euthanasia of terminally ill patients who request it. The guidelines governing these practices fundamentally follow those that were in use prior to the Dutch parliament's decision.

In the U.S., the Euthanasia Society of America was formed in 1938. Public opinion and American law have generally reflected opposition to any form of euthanasia, but in more recent years the trend has been shifting.[22] For example, in 1973 a Gallup Poll asked if in cases of incurable disease, doctors should be allowed to end the patient's life by some painless means if the patient and his family request it. Of those responding, 53 percent said yes. When the same question was posed in 1950, only 30 percent had answered yes.[23] A Harris Poll (1981) found that 78 percent of all polled would prefer not to suffer pointless life prolongation. That is, the majority preferred to reject life-prolonging care when there was no hope of recovery.[24]

Several events in recent years have really captured the attention of Americans, polarized views on the euthanasia question, and galvanized many to action. One is Dr. Kevorkian's suicide machine, and another is the book *Final Exit*. But undoubtedly the right-to-die case of Nancy Cruzan has been the most significant factor in raising people's awareness and "temperature" on this issue. Because of its importance, we briefly sketch the details of this case.

On January 11, 1983 twenty-five-year-old Nancy Cruzan was in an automobile accident in the Ozarks in southwestern Missouri. Paramedics arrived and restarted her breathing, but she had been without oxygen for so long that she never regained consciousness. On February 5, 1983 doctors implanted a feeding tube in Nancy's stomach. Apart from this apparatus, she was not on life support systems. Over the next years Nancy did not die, but she did not improve. She seemed to be in what is called a permanent vegetative state. As a result, in October 1987 Nancy's parents went to court to get permission to remove the feeding tube and let her die as they believed she would want. On July 27, 1988 the Jasper County (Missouri) Judge granted them permission to remove the tube. However, the case was appealed to the Missouri Supreme Court, and on November 16, 1988 the court in a 4-3 decision overturned the lower court ruling, claiming there was no legal authority to grant the Cruzans' request.

The Cruzans appealed the case to the U.S. Supreme Court. It was the first time the Supreme Court ruled on a right-to-die case. In a 5-4 decision on June 25, 1990 the Court ruled to deny the Cruzans' request. However, the decision was not based on a belief that food and water could not be removed because they are basics of patient care and are not medicine. Nor was it based on a belief that patients do not have a right to choose to die. Instead, the ruling came because there was no "clear and convincing evidence" that Nancy would have wanted to stop artificial nutrition.[25] Had she signed a living will to that effect or granted power of attorney to her family to make decisions on her health care, the petition would have been granted. But she had done neither, and once comatose she obviously couldn't. Though the Cruzans' request was rejected, the Supreme Court in essence affirmed a patient's right to die under certain circumstances so long as there is a living will specifying those situations or a power of attorney granting decision-making power to a surrogate.

On August 30, 1990 the Cruzans went back to the Missouri Judge and asked for another hearing, claiming they had new evidence that their daughter had once told three people she would rather die than live in a persistent vegetative state. In light of the Supreme Court's ruling that clear evidence of her desire to die was necessary to remove the tube, and in view of the new testimony to that effect, on December 14, 1990 the Judge ruled that Cruzan's parents could remove her feeding tube. Shortly thereafter, that was done, and Nancy Cruzan finally died.[26]

As a result of cases like the Cruzan case, many are resorting to a living will. The first U.S. state to enact a Natural Death Act (living will legislation) was California (1976). As of 1990, forty-one states and the District of Columbia had living will laws.[27] The document, signed while a person is in good health and spirits, states that if a time comes when the individual cannot take part in decisions about his/her future, and if there is no reasonable expectation of recovery from physical, mental, or spiritual disability, he/she asks to be allowed to die rather than to be kept alive by artificial means or heroic measures.[28] In some states living wills are not legally binding, but those who sign them hope friends and family will feel morally bound to honor them. In addition, by 1990 some thirteen states had power of attorney laws that allow individuals to name a proxy to make health-care decisions if the individual becomes incapacitated.[29]

Further developments have also occurred since the Cruzan case. For example, on September 26, 1991 Governor Jim Edgar of Illinois signed a right-to-die law. This law calls for naming a surrogate from a list of relatives and friends who will have the right "to decide when to end life-sustaining treatment for patients who are comatose, terminally ill or unable to decide for themselves, instead of leaving the matter to strangers in the legal system."[30] This law is considered especially important because two years earlier the Illinois Supreme Court had ruled that "without further direction from the legislature, such matters needed to be decided in court."[31] Of no small import in the drafting and passage of this law was the case of Rudy Linares. Linares's fifteen-month-old son was on life support systems at Chicago's Rush-Presbyterian St. Luke's Medical Center. The child was not going to get better, so Linares sought permission to withdraw life support. When the hospital denied permission because of legal concerns, in April 1989 Linares got a gun and unhooked his comatose son's respirator while holding police at bay. Linares was charged with murder, but a Cook County grand jury would not indict him. The right-to-die law should eliminate such problems in the future, since it provides medical workers legal immunity if they are strictly following the surrogate's decisions.

Permission to withdraw life-support systems from a terminally ill patient is one thing. Permission to help a terminally ill patient commit suicide is another. In California there was an attempt to get on the November 1988 ballot the Humane and Dignified Death Act. The measure would allow a patient to ask a doctor for help in committing suicide. The bill defined aid in dying as "any medical procedure that will terminate the life of the qualified patient, swiftly, painlessly, and humanely."[32] The bill would require two physicians to certify that the patient's death would occur within six months. Helping a patient under these conditions would protect doctors from any legal liability. The urgency of the bill stems from the increasing number of AIDS patients who choose to commit suicide and want help from a doctor to perform a successful suicide. Sponsors of the bill failed to get enough signatures to put the measure on the ballot, but they said public opinion polls showed nearly 60 percent approval of the measure, and they intended to get the measure on the ballot in 1990.[33] They were not successful in 1990, but a similar measure was on the November 1992 ballot in California. The previous bill would have allowed a surrogate to make the decision for someone who is mentally incompetent. The new bill removed that provision and stipulated that the person making the request must be a mentally competent adult (eighteen years or older), and must ask for this action on at least two consultation visits with the physician. Thankfully, that bill was defeated, but it will likely appear again, since forces favoring it are very persistent.

A similar aid in dying bill was voted on in the state of Washington on November 5, 1991. The bill was defeated there, but only by a close margin. Reflecting on the import of this proposed legislation, as well as the recent decision by the Dutch parliament to legalize doctor-assisted suicide, one is struck by how far medicine has strayed from the foundational principle incorporated in the Hippocratic Oath that a doctor will not use medicine to harm his patients.[34]

CLARIFICATION OF TERMINOLOGY

The term *"euthanasia"* is derived from two Greek words—*eu* meaning "well" or "good," and *thanatos* meaning "death." In contemporary discussions, it stands for a wide variety of practices. Terminology in regard to euthanasia can be divided into four different categories, each adding another dimension to the discussion.

VOLUNTARY/INVOLUNTARY

This distinction focuses on whether or not the patient requests death. *Voluntary euthanasia* refers to cases where a patient requests death or grants permission to be put to death. It is often considered equivalent to suicide. Euthanasia is *involuntary* when someone is put to death without requesting it or granting permission. This distinction is crucial to many doctors and ethicists who think euthanasia can be morally justified if requested (voluntary), but not otherwise.

ACTIVE/PASSIVE

These terms focus on the kind of action taken to bring about death.[35] *Active euthanasia* refers to taking some purposeful action to end a life, whereas *passive euthanasia* refers to the withholding or refusal of treatment to sustain life.[36] Passive euthanasia may also involve withdrawing treatment already begun.[37] The distinction is often equated with the ideas of commission (active) and omission (passive), and some see it as the difference between killing (active) and letting someone die (passive). Giving a lethal dose of drugs to someone diagnosed with AIDS is active euthanasia. Removal of Clarence Herbert's feeding tube is an example of passive euthanasia.

Upon minimal reflection, one can see that both active and passive euthanasia can be either voluntary or involuntary. What ethicists often debate is whether there is any morally significant difference between killing and letting die.

DIRECT/INDIRECT

These terms denote the role played by the person who dies when his life is taken. *Direct euthanasia* refers to cases where the individual himself carries out the decision to die. *Indirect* refers to situations where someone else carries out the decision. These terms are not equal to *voluntary/involuntary*. Those terms refer to whether the individual requests or permits the act, but not to the actual doing of the act. *Direct/indirect* refers to whether the individual does the act himself or not.

DEATH WITH DIGNITY, MERCY KILLING, AND
DEATH SELECTION[38]

These terms focus on the ultimate intended goal to be achieved through the act of euthanasia. *Death with dignity* refers to allowing the patient to die a truly human death. Rather than using extraordinary means (such as hooking him up to a machine) to forestall death (which is said to dehumanize him), the patient is allowed to die "naturally." Basic needs such as food and drink are met, but there is an attempt to avoid the dehumanizing effects of isolating a dying patient from family while making him little more than a body hooked up to a machine. Though this kind of euthanasia is often voluntary, rarely is it equated with suicide, since the patient is incurably ill and no medical procedure would heal him.

In *mercy killing*, the intent is to release someone who is suffering excruciating pain and has no other way of escape but death. It is seen as an act of mercy.[39] Mercy killing may involve using medical technology to hasten or cause death, or it may involve using ordinary means to bring death. The case of Janet Adkins is an example of mercy killing. Shooting someone who is trapped in a burning car, cannot escape, and is in terrible pain is another example. Often voluntary mercy killing is equated with suicide.

Whereas the goal with mercy killing is ostensibly the removal of individual pain and suffering, the goal with *death selection* is the deliberate removal of persons whose lives are no longer considered socially useful. People in this category need not be ill; they need only be deemed useless, a bother to society, expendable. This kind of euthanasia might fall on groups such as "hardened" criminals, the mentally retarded, or (as in Hitler's Germany) whole ethnic or racial groups.[40]

CONTEMPORARY DEBATE OVER EUTHANASIA

Arguments in the debate about euthanasia can be divided into broad categories. For example, some attempt to justify euthanasia generally without focusing on a specific form. Others attempt to justify both active and passive euthanasia, and still others focus on involuntary euthanasia. From these perspectives we shall present the case for euthanasia and then offer what we believe is an appropriate Christian response. We reject euthanasia in general, but we think there are some cases where euthanasia may be permissible. After considering arguments on both sides of the question, we shall turn to the difficult issue of decision-making in specific cases.

IN FAVOR OF EUTHANASIA

For Euthanasia Generally

Personhood

The issue of personhood is crucial to the abortion debate, and it is equally important in debates over euthanasia. We have already noted contemporary criteria for determining personhood (criteria used in both the abortion and euthanasia debates), so we need not repeat them here.[41] Those who use the argument to support euthanasia argue that an individual once possessed personhood, does not as his life nears its end, and has no potential of regaining it. Thus, someone in an irreversible coma, for example, is no longer a person but only a biological organism. There is no need to maintain biological life that does not sustain personal life. "Pulling the plug" on a comatose person neither increases nor relieves his suffering, since he feels nothing anyway. However, pulling the plug may relieve the agony of those who grieve over their relative and friend.[42] The obvious decision should be to pull the plug.

Several points become clear from this line of argument. For one thing, the mere possession of biological life is not enough to warrant one's continued existence. However, without personal life, life may be disposed of whether by abortion, infanticide, suicide, or any form of euthanasia. Unfortunately, as already noted in our discussion of abortion, the criteria of personhood are extremely ambiguous, and on some interpretations of them none of us qualifies as a person. Nonetheless, proponents of euthanasia believe the criteria are specific enough and use this line of argument to justify euthanasia.

Quality of Life Ethic

Preserving life at all costs, no matter what the condition of that life, is what Joseph Fletcher has called the "vitalist fallacy," the fallacy that all life is valuable and is to be maintained no matter what. Instead, a certain quality of life (as defined by criteria of personhood) is necessary to warrant continued existence.

Proponents of euthanasia further argue that the question of euthanasia is not always clear-cut even for those espousing a sanctity of life ethic. For example, if a person in an irreversible coma continues biological life without artificial means (e.g., Clarence Herbert and Karen Quinlan once the respirator was unplugged), does the sanctity of life principle require that such life go on? In cases of unrelenting and unrelievable suffering with no chance of recovery, does a sanctity of life ethic stand in the way of removing such pain by death? In other words, regardless of one's ethic, is there not a time when enough is enough, or must life always be preserved at all costs?[43] Those holding a quality of life ethic say that when sanctity of life proponents agree that sometimes enough is enough, they at least implicitly recognize that quality of life does matter. Of course, medical technology can prolong biological life way beyond a time when there is any significant quality of life. In virtue of that fact, and since the sanctity of life proponent agrees that sometimes enough is enough, must we not after all make decisions on the basis of quality, not sanctity, of life?[44]

Perception of God

Atheists and theists alike are using their views about God as a basis for supporting euthanasia. For example, the *Humanist Manifesto*, which presupposes atheism, sees man as the measure of all things and in control of decisions about life and death. If there is no God, all arguments against euthanasia on grounds that God is the owner of life are automatically ruled out.[45] Moreover, if one believes as atheists do that there is no life beyond the grave, that everything happens by pure chance, and that all creatures are subject to the whims of blind fate, then all men can do is treat one another with sympathy and kindness. That means, of course, that if someone faces hopeless suffering and unbearable pain, we should do what we would do to an animal, have pity on him and remove the pain by helping him die.[46]

As for some theists, a changed perception of God underlies their advocacy of euthanasia. For example, Joseph Fletcher still believes in God, but not the traditional one. Fletcher knows that many think modern medicine is "playing God" with the new technology. Fletcher admits this is true, but claims the real question is "which or whose God are we playing?"[47] Man used to believe in a God who was in charge of birth and death, believing that man had no responsibility and no right to tamper in these areas. When man did not understand matters relating to life and death, he appealed to this God who knew all and was in control. Now men have grown up spiritually as their knowledge of life and death has increased, and they are turning to a God who "is the creative principle behind things, who is behind the test tube as much as the earthquake and volcano."[48] Fletcher says this God can be believed in, not a God who prohibits freedom to choose our manner of birth and death or inhibits our research. According to Fletcher, the traditional God who allowed no tampering with matters of life and death is dead.[49]

Utilitarian Concerns

Invariably, proponents of euthanasia argue their case on consequentialist (usually utilitarian) grounds. Joseph Fletcher blatantly admits holding this ethic and sees it as a support for euthanasia. Fletcher asks whether we should ever hasten someone's death out of compassion or mercy. One's answer depends on whether he thinks the end justifies the means. Fletcher adamantly asserts that the end does justify the means. In fact, he asks what else could.[50] However, the key question in Fletcher's mind is what justifies the end. Fletcher responds "that human happiness and well-being is the highest good or *summum bonum*, that therefore any ends or purposes which that standard or ideal validates are just, right, good. This is what humanistic medicine is all about; it is what the concepts of loving concern and social justice are built upon."[51] This is unabashed consequentialism. If the consequences are acceptable, the means to those ends are morally justified.

Not only is utilitarianism often the underlying ethic, but frequently euthanasia is justified in virtue of utilitarian concerns. For example, some ask whether a family can afford the expense of "heroic" means of medical care. Others note that medical resources generally are limited, and some medical procedures (e.g., an artificial heart operation) are extremely expensive. The real dilemma arises when more than one person needs the expensive care. Paul Brand, former missionary to India, argues that we must ask whether $100,000 for a single operation is the best use of that money. Moreover, if more than one person needs special care, but there is only money or hospital resources for one, how does one decide who gets the medical attention?[52] A decision to let some die would be necessary, and who dies might be decided on the utilitarian ground of who is perceived to be of most use to society.

Freedom of Choice, Cruelty, and Euthanasia

Some argue that those who qualify as persons should be free to choose the kind of death they want. Submitting to "whatever God brings" even though it may involve the depersonalizing hooking of oneself up to a machine is not to act as a person.[53] For this reason the "living will" is favored. Removing choices about the end of life from the free control of the individual is dehumanizing.[54]

Anthony Flew agrees that freedom of choice *per se* is crucial, but he supports it as well on other grounds. Flew notes that some people suffering unbearably want to die quickly. He thinks it immoral to refuse legal grounds for them to do so. Any law which prevents them from doing so, and "usually thereby forces other people who care for them to watch their pointless pain helplessly, is a very cruel law."[55] We extend mercy to animals to put them out of their misery. Why be less merciful to humans?[56] Flew appeals here to the principle that it is immoral to be cruel, and he thinks that in the cases mentioned, denying requests to die is cruel.

Marvin Kohl goes even further. Some might *reject* euthanasia on the ground that *it* is cruel. Kohl says the difference between the two sides centers on what constitutes cruelty and whether or not avoiding cruelty is morally sufficient. Opponents of euthanasia define cruelty narrowly to refer to *causing* unnecessary pain or harm deliberately. They overlook the broader sense which means to cause or *allow* harm or pain deliberately. The narrower sense of cruelty tolerates human misery. However, this is contrary to the ideal of the good Samaritan, who not only avoided cruelty, but actively went out of his way to help the suffering person. Merely taking care not to cause cruelty is insufficient. That tells us what not to do, but not what to do. Only a notion of cruelty broad enough to include the obligation to help remove the suffering is adequate.[57]

Euthanasia and Abortion
Joseph Fletcher argues that if abortion can be morally justified, so can euthanasia. Fletcher has in mind cases where the individual no longer qualifies as a person. He says, "It is ridiculous to give ethical approval to the positive ending of subhuman life *in utero*, as we do in therapeutic abortions for reasons of mercy and compassion, but refuse to approve of positively ending a subhuman life *in extremis*."[58] This in itself does not prove that either eugenic abortion or mercy killing is morally right, but it does demand consistency in one's position. Fletcher, of course, thinks eugenic abortion is moral, and argues that termination of the lives of those suffering unbearably follows with logical inevitability.

Other Concerns
Three other considerations are raised to legitimize euthanasia generally. One appeals to the doctor/patient relationship. Normally, a patient expects his doctor to act in accord with his duty to preserve life. Of course, the doctor's duty is also to alleviate suffering. Sometimes those duties con-

flict, and such conflicts underscore the fact that a doctor's fundamental obligation is to his patient, not to a principle of preserving life. Thus, the morality of voluntary euthanasia becomes a question of whether a patient can expect a doctor to honor the patient's requests to end life.[59] If it is morally permissible for the patient to request euthanasia, then given the doctor's obligation to the patient, the doctor can also morally grant the request.

Another argument rests on a distinction between ordinary and extraordinary means of prolonging life. Even Roman Catholic thinking, for example, holds that when a patient faces imminent death from incurable disease, he must prolong life by ordinary means, but in good conscience may refuse treatment that is extraordinary.[60] Despite the fact that one generation's extraordinary means may be another generation's ordinary means, many ethicists still think the distinction is legitimate, even if category boundaries cannot be perfectly drawn.[61]

A final argument supporting euthanasia in certain circumstances appeals to the double effect doctrine. When a patient is terminally ill, will not recover, and is in terrible pain, many hold that giving that person medication to relieve pain is morally acceptable, even if the medication will also speed death.[62] The argument is that the directly intended effect of relieving pain is a good; the coincident effect of shortening life is only an inescapable, but unintended effect of the action.[63] Thus, such instances of hastening death are morally justifiable.

Biblical and Theological Considerations
Sixth Commandment Not Absolute
An initial biblical consideration used to support euthanasia appeals to the Sixth Commandment (Exod 20:13), "Thou shalt not kill." Many use this as a prohibition against all forms of euthanasia, but others question its validity. Ought this commandment be absolutized? Some think it wrong to do so, because the absolutizing of biblical commands is inconsistent. For example, Das and Mabry note that in India there is a tendency to absolutize this commandment but not to absolutize Jesus' teaching in Matt 6:2-4 about giving to those who beg from you. How does one decide which teachings to absolutize and which not?[64]

Moreover, the command against killing cannot be absolute, for those who invoke it against euthanasia typically favor capital punishment, war and killing in self-defense. The prohibition in the Sixth Commandment seems to be against vengeful killing, not all killing. If so, then clearly some forms of voluntary and even involuntary euthanasia are permissible if no other considerations rule them out. Erickson and Bowers note that OT teaching on killing reveals that there was condemnable killing (murder), excusable killing, and even mandatory killing (capital punishment). Murder is characterized as intentional, premeditated, malicious, contrary to the desire or intention of the victim, and against someone who has done nothing deserving of death. Voluntary euthanasia fits the first two and the last criteria, but does not always fit the third and fourth.[65] Even involuntary euthanasia would not always meet all these criteria, for in many cases no malice is intended. Patient benefit is the aim. Thus, euthanasia in general cannot be excluded by appeal to the Sixth Commandment.

Perspective on Death and the Afterlife

Scripture portrays death as the natural and appointed end of everyone (Heb 9:27). It should be accepted as a good gift from God, not an enemy. Through death man enters into the fullness of God's glory.[66] Paul's words summarize things for believers: "For to me, to live is Christ and to die is gain" (Phil 1:21). Clearly, death is not an enemy to avoid at all costs.

Some agree that death benefits those who go to heaven, but it does not make things better for those who wind up in hell. For example, Antony Flew claims that the strongest argument against euthanasia would be the existence of hell, if there were one.[67] Robert Wennberg disagrees. Christians usually portray hell as a place of horrible torment. Wennberg says we need not assume this is so. Symbolic imagery characterizes many biblical descriptions of heaven and hell, so the punitive aspect of hell need not include literal physical suffering. We cannot conclude that no matter how much one has suffered in this life, hell will be worse. Moreover, if one rejects euthanasia on the ground that a person will be worse off in hell no matter how much he suffers in life, one must also endorse prolonging life as long as possible regardless of the patient's condition in order to keep people from slipping into hell. Most would be uncomfortable with that position.[68]

Suffering as Valueless

Many think the book of Job illustrates that God often uses affliction to mature people spiritually. Thus, it should be accepted. On the contrary, Das and Mabry claim Job did not willingly accept suffering, nor did he ever understand why he suffered. If Job teaches anything, it is not confident acceptance of suffering, but the refusal of a pious man to yield to the temptation to reject God. "Thus we do not see in Job, nor in the Bible generally, a counsel to passively accept suffering. Rather, the general course of the Bible is in the other direction—to relieve suffering, to show mercy, to help the helpless."[69] Though one can learn through affliction, Scripture never guarantees that sufferers will respond properly. Suffering cannot justify continuing life at all costs, especially when suffering is solely for the sake of suffering. Scripture never sanctions that kind of suffering.[70]

Self-Sacrifice

Self-sacrifice for others is a value of the highest order. Jesus' death illustrates it, and his words (John 15:13) commend it as the highest form of love. When a patient suffers unbearably from an incurable disease, others suffer emotionally and even physically as they view their loved one. Depending on the cost of medical care, the family may also suffer financial hardship. In such cases some argue that the principle of self-sacrifice on others' behalf warrants the voluntary ending of the patient's life. In fact, if done to relieve the pain inflicted on family and friends, the act qualifies as a praiseworthy act of self-sacrifice.[71]

Voluntary Euthanasia and Suicide

Many think that most, if not all, cases of voluntary euthanasia (whether direct or indirect) are tantamount to suicide. Thus, for them to justify voluntary euthanasia, they must also justify suicide.[72] Historically, one of the best-known defenses of suicide comes from David Hume. For Hume the crucial issue was whether suicide violates one or more of the following obligations humans normally have: obligations to self, others, and God. As to God, Hume argued that life is not God's property just because he created it. Life and death are governed by natural causes, so one need not appeal to God to explain life and death. Moreover, if causal laws collectively constitute the divine order, then we should never do anything to control the natural order. Of course, that would be absurd, for unless we resisted some natural events (like extreme heat and cold), life could not exist. Thus, just as one may divert the course of a river to avoid a flood, so one may, for example, rightly divert the flow of blood from its normal course to prevent the evils of shame, dishonor, or constant suffering. Some might reply that since God has sovereign control over whatever happens, deserting one's position in the universe by suicide is rebellion against God. However, Hume thought this a worthless objection to suicide, for if God is so in control of life that nothing happens without divine consent, then neither does suicide happen without God's consent. When someone prefers death to life because of pain and anguish, that person must conclude that God is recalling him from his station in life.[73]

As to responsibility to society, Hume reasoned that committing suicide might actually better fulfill one's obligations than staying alive. If one cannot promote the interests of society and instead is a burden to it or at least to those who care for him rather than meeting societal needs, then suicide would better fulfill one's obligations to society than not.[74]

In regard to self-love, some assert that suicide, rather than deserting obligations to oneself, indulges one's own wishes. In fact, some suicides are condemned as supreme acts of selfishness. Thus, it can hardly be maintained that someone who commits suicide has no concern for his own well-being.

As to scriptural considerations, Erickson and Bowers (though not advocating suicide) question whether Scripture really rules out suicide so clearly as one might think. Citing the cases of Abimelech (Judg 9:50-57),

Saul (1 Samuel 31), Samson (Judg 16:28-30), and Judas Iscariot (Matt 27:5), they note that Scripture merely reports these suicides but does not evaluate them. David grieved over Saul's death, but the reason offered (2 Samuel 14–16) is that God's anointed had died, not that suicide was involved. Erickson and Bowers conclude that the morality of euthanasia cannot be determined simply by treating it as suicide and arguing that Scripture clearly prohibits suicide.[75]

Active/Passive—Killing/Letting Die

James Rachels has argued that there is no moral difference between active and passive euthanasia (killing and letting die). For one thing, sometimes active euthanasia is more humane than passive. For example, if it is morally right not to operate on a Down's syndrome child with intestinal obstruction, it is actually preferable to kill the child directly rather than allowing a slow death. The key issue is Down's syndrome, not the intestines (which could be repaired by surgery); so the moral justification for the child's death will have to come in regard to the Down's. But then the more rapid death is more humane.[76]

Rachels's other line of argument rests on two cases that show there is no moral difference between killing and letting die. Smith and Jones who have six-year-old cousins will each receive a large inheritance if those cousins die. Smith drowns his cousin while his cousin is bathing. Jones plans the same fate for his cousin, but as Jones enters the bathroom, his cousin slips, hits his head and falls facedown in the water. Jones stands by and lets the child drown. We are not inclined to think Jones more praiseworthy than Smith. Rachels argues that this shows there is no difference morally between killing and letting die.[77]

Gerald Hughes claims that even when no ill intent is involved, there is no significant distinction between killing and letting die. He offers two cases, one involving a patient on life-support systems without which he will die, and the other involving a terminally ill person who will die in a few days. In the first case, the doctor can switch off the machine and "allow the patient to die." In the second, the doctor can give a lethal injection which will work as quickly as pulling the plug ends the first patient's life. Since the intentions are the same, in these cases there is no difference between killing and letting die.[78]

For one who accepts this line of argument, active and passive euthanasia can be equally justified, because there is no morally significant difference between killing and letting die.

Involuntary Euthanasia

Several lines of argument can be used to justify involuntary euthanasia. The first appeals to arguments favoring euthanasia generally. Arguments about extending mercy and avoiding cruelty apply whether a person requests death or not. Moreover, on consequentialist views of ethics such as utilitarianism, one can justify any form of involuntary euthanasia, including death selection.

Second, the Jones/Smith cases can be used to support both active and passive involuntary euthanasia, because both cases are instances of involuntary killing. Anyone who agrees with the Jones/Smith argumentation can agree that there is no moral difference between active and passive involuntary euthanasia.

A final argument stems from Richard McCormick and Robert Veatch's discussion of Joseph Fox. Fox was put on a respirator after going into a coma during an operation. McCormick and Veatch note the reasoning behind the decision to remove the respirator. Judge Robert Meade granted permission because Fox had made his wishes known previously. In discussing the Quinlan case, Fox stated that if he were in a similar condition, he would not want to be kept alive artificially. The judge granted permission to uphold what he claimed was Fox's right to self-determination.

McCormick and Veatch disagree. They note that many people never express their wishes about such a situation. If one were forced to adopt Meade's reasoning, such people would have to remain indefinitely on a respirator. That would be unacceptable. Moreover, McCormick and Veatch note that some people even from birth are incompetent to render a decision on this issue. McCormick and Veatch suggest another set of principles for cases where the person is incompetent or has never expressed his wishes. The first and major principle is patient benefit. Someone must make a decision about the patient's best interests. The second principle is that the "someone" should be a family member or family surrogate. Thus, they claim that when the individual does not or cannot express his wishes (involuntary), the matter of patient benefit as determined by a family member can be used not only to decide what to do for the patient but to justify morally what is done, even if what is done brings about the death of the individual.[79]

A CHRISTIAN RESPONSE TO EUTHANASIA

Against Euthanasia Generally

Sanctity of Life Ethic

Opponents of euthanasia argue that life is so valuable that it should be terminated only when unusual considerations dictate an exception. Some exceptions such as a just war and self-defense are enumerated in the Bible. Scripture does not say the list is complete, but with no clear indication of other exceptions, one should not look for others, but should rather uphold the sanctity of life principle. In cases where life is less than most would call human, the person involved seldom can maintain life on his own anyway. No active means are needed to end his life; refusal of unusual means of care will suffice.[80] Some might think this approach too liberal, but what actually is being urged rules out active euthanasia in favor of the sanctity of life principle while ruling in passive euthanasia *only* in cases where the person would die anyway with ordinary care.

Biblically speaking, human life is sacred. It is sacred because man is made in God's image (Gen 1:26-27; 5:1). As we have argued in our discussion of personhood,[81] even someone severely deformed or wracked with pain from a terminal illness so that he cannot interact with his environment still bears the image of God. That alone suggests care in decision-making concerning such people.[82]

Life is sacred as well because God has given it and sustains it. Because it is his gift, we must treat it with care and not discard it. To treat it lightly is a supreme act of ingratitude, but it also suggests that we think we own our life, when in fact God gave it and owns it.[83] Christians have traditionally used this argument against suicide. It seems relevant as well to euthanasia in general.

Finally, a further biblical indication of the sanctity of life is the prohibition against life-taking. Killing is condemned both in the OT (Exod 20:13) and the NT (Matt 5:21; 19:18; Mark 10:19; Luke 18:20; Rom 13:9). While there are exceptions to the rule (e.g., killing in self-defense, capital punishment, just war), what is unexceptional is the prohibition against the deliberate, intentional taking of innocent life. In most cases, euthanasia is the deliberate taking of innocent life. Biblical teaching renders those cases morally unacceptable.[84]

Anti-Consequentialism

As already noted, much argumentation for euthanasia rests on consequentialist concerns. Deontologists respond that ends do not justify means. Some who espouse biblically-based ethics claim that scriptural precepts are deontological, grounded in the nature of God, and not consequentialist, grounded in the ends sought.[85] Moreover, some note that consequentialism also undercuts the difference between acts and omissions, a very important distinction in any case of letting die. Since the consequence in cases of killing and letting die is the same, consequentialism generally sees no moral difference between the two. This is unacceptable to anyone who sees a legitimate distinction between killing and letting die.[86] In our thinking, all of these considerations and more are serious problems with consequentialism. Once consequentialism is rejected, justification for many instances of euthanasia evaporates.

The Wedge Argument

Sometimes referred to as the slippery slope argument, this argument warns against opening the door even to the seemingly most innocuous instances of euthanasia. Appeal is often made to what happened under the Nazis. They began with mercy killing in limited cases to relieve suffering, but later genocide eventuated. Once a country starts down the slope of killing, it gradually becomes more comfortable with euthanasia, and it becomes much easier to accustom people to even more inhumane and unwarranted killing.

We believe Arthur Dyck states the wedge argument most convincingly. He notes that a wedge argument need not predict that certain practices will follow from others. The key to a wedge argument is the form or logic of moral justifications for actions.[87] One might want to limit the breadth of the category of people who qualify for euthanasia, but once it is decided that certain people are to die, it is hard to find any logical grounds for keeping others alive. For example, if the category includes those lacking the dignity of human beings, this can include many not terminally ill, nor in pain, nor desirous of death. They may simply fail to meet some ambiguous standard of what it means to be human. Proponents of euthanasia invariably guarantee that it will be used only in rather narrowly defined cases. The wedge argument says that "there is no logical or easily agreed upon reason why the range of cases should be restricted"[88] to what might appear at first sight as paradigm cases. The wedge argument assumes that killing is wrong generally and that there should be as few exceptions as possible to the command to preserve life. Realizing where it could lead, why make a wedge in the door for any euthanasia?

Medical Concerns

Several medical considerations cause many to hesitate before encouraging euthanasia. First, a request to execute a natural-death directive may be based more on fear or misinformation than anything else. The patient may think his situation far worse than it actually is and ask to die. Once the patient dies, the mistake cannot be undone.

Second, a cure for a supposedly incurable disease may be found. Medical history is filled with examples of people thought to have an incurable disease who were later healed when medicine progressed.[89] Medical science advances very rapidly, but new cures cannot be offered to a dead person.

Third, those who think patients must choose between terrible suffering and relief through death have overlooked a third option. Even in terminal cases, modern medicine can provide measures sufficient to reduce pain to a bearable level or even remove it altogether.[90] In most cases one need not choose death as the sole release from pain.

A final medical matter relates to a doctor's involvement in euthanasia. Many note that when a doctor takes the Hippocratic Oath, he promises to use medicine to help the sick and never to injure or wrong them. The doctor also promises never to give poison to anyone, even if asked to do so.[91] Some claim the Oath no longer applies in our times, but those who think otherwise have serious problems in squaring the Oath with aiding euthanasia.

Additional Biblical and Theological Concerns

Value in Suffering

Though suffering is neither enjoyable nor to be sought, that does not mean it cannot have any positive function in a person's life. Rom 5:3-5, 1 Pet 1:6-9, 2 Cor 4:17, 12:10 and the book of Job, for example, speak of the potential benefits to be gained from suffering. While afflictions are evils, God can and does use them to work good in our lives. Suffering need not be seen as valueless, something to be escaped at all costs.

Perspective on Life, Death and the Afterlife

Initially, we must underscore biblical teaching that God is in control of life and death. The humanist may dislike it, but passages such as Job 14:5, Ecc 3:2, and Jas 4:13-15 teach that no one can add or detract even one second from his life beyond what God has decided. Moreover, those who try to extend life endlessly, regardless of the patient's condition, are reminded by Ecc 3:2 that there is a time to be born and a time to die. Man's manipulations cannot overturn God's control.

As to the biblical portrayal of death, we agree with those who claim it is quite different from views that "glorify death" as a beautiful friend of man, greatly to be desired when suffering intensely. The biblical perspective is that death is not natural; it entered the world as a result of sin (Gen 3:14-19; Rom 5:12). Moreover, the process of dying is itself often very painful, and Scripture does not portray it otherwise. Death is not a friend; it is the last enemy to be overcome (1 Cor 15:26). As Paul Ramsey aptly states, we should not talk of the beauty of death or even of death with dignity. Death is the final indignity to man, and Scripture presents it that way.[92]

Douglas Stuart contends that the biblical perspective on life and death is seen in part by how biblical saints considered death. Those who asked God for a "good death" (e.g., Balaam, Num 23:10; Simeon, Luke 2:26, 29) showed no desire for an early death. In cases where someone is in agony or near death (e.g., Ps 22:19-21; 88), death is not welcomed or desired. Instead, the plea is for deliverance and restoration to a full active life.[93] All these facts suggest the preciousness of life and the disdain with which Scripture views death and dying.

Some think Paul forbids sorrow over death (1 Thess 4:13). However, he is not suggesting we should rejoice when someone dies. He only mandates that as believers grieve, they should not grieve *as those who have no hope*. This is hardly an endorsement of death. In fact, Paul sees the Christian's hope not as a death which releases from suffering, but as resurrection to life which occurs at Christ's return (1 Thess 4:13-18).

Proponents of euthanasia may reply that our portrayal of scriptural teaching on death contradicts the biblical teaching that dying is gain for the believer (e.g., Phil 1:21). However, the contradiction is apparent, not real, as can be seen by properly distinguishing 1) the cause and nature of dying from 2) what happens after death. From the perspective of 1), death is negative, as our immediately preceding comments indicate. As to 2), the outcome of death is negative for the non-believer, for he is consigned to eternal punishment. For the believer, the outcome is positive (2 Cor 5:8; Phil 1:21, 23). However, nowhere does Scripture encourage the believer to do something to "speed up" his entry into the Lord's presence. The time of his departure is in God's hands.

The biblical perspective on life, death, and the afterlife is incomplete without the teaching of the resurrection of the body. Scripture does not teach that death ends it all. Rather, it tells us that for believers and non-believers alike, following death there is disembodied conscious existence and eventually resurrection of the body (Luke 16:19ff.; Rom 8:18ff.; 1 Cor 15:20-23; 2 Cor 5:8; Rev 20:4-5, 11-15). Among other things, this means for the Christian that his ultimate hope for escaping pain and suffering is not physical death, but resurrection of the body.[94]

Other Concerns

Two other considerations are noteworthy. Some emphasize that learning from affliction is not the only biblical alternative to euthanasia. The other is healing. There are even cases of dead people being resurrected (e.g., 1 Kgs 17:22; John 11; Acts 20:10). This does not mean anyone has a right to miraculous healing or that he should expect it. It does mean that we have a right to ask God to heal and then wait to see what he does. Biblically, this is acceptable, whereas taking matters into our own hands and deciding in favor of euthanasia is not.[95]

Finally, what about biblical teaching to extend mercy to those in need? Many reply that mercy to the sick and dying does not include granting their wish to die. However, it does include proper care for their needs. Proper care involves giving drugs to relieve pain. Kerby Anderson appeals to Prov 31:6 as a moral justification for giving pain-relieving drugs. He also cites Gal 6:2 to urge believers to provide counsel and spiritual care for dying patients.[96]

Suicide

There are various biblical and common-sense arguments against suicide. Despite the fact that Scripture simply records the occurrence of suicides without offering an evaluation of them, it is safe to conclude that the biblical perspective on suicide is negative. Scripture directly forbids taking the innocent life of creatures made in God's image. This regulation applies whether the life is someone else's or one's own.

An additional biblical consideration is that Christians are commanded not only to love others but to love themselves (Matt 22:39; Eph 5:28-29,

33). However, suicide is not an act of self-love but of self-hatred. As such, it disobeys biblical commands.[97]

Those who claim to the contrary that the suicide of someone suffering greatly is an act of self-indulgence, not an act of self-hate, confuse issues. One must distinguish between response to a particular situation and over-all evaluation of one's life. There are many stop-gap solutions that one can apply at the moment that in the long run will have very negative effects on the person's overall well-being. Though suicide may bring immediate relief in difficult circumstances, it cannot help but communicate a low view of the worth of the life (one's own) taken.

In light of these moral principles that rule out suicide, we find especially troublesome talk of a patient's right to die. Granted, a government may legislate such a right, but that does not mean there is a *moral* right to die. In fact, given moral principles against taking life, we cannot see how there could be a moral right to die, if by "right to die" is meant a right to commit suicide. Undoubtedly, some who speak of this right are really asserting a right to have control over their own body via the right to privacy. However, as already argued in the abortion chapters, the right to do what one wants with one's body cannot be an absolute right, especially if so doing breaks moral rules.

We suspect that those who speak of a right to die are not thinking of voluntary euthanasia and suicide so much as they are thinking of cases such as that of Nancy Cruzan. But what was really at stake there was not a right to die (and there is no moral right to do so anyway), but rather a right not to be kept alive indefinitely by artificial means in a permanent vegetative state. The Cruzan family wanted natural processes to run their course, since attempts to forestall those processes could not have cured their daughter or even enhanced her ability to interact with the environment. While we are sympathetic with such desires, they have nothing to do with a right to die construed as a right to voluntary active euthanasia or suicide. They relate to passive euthanasia and hence have nothing to do with a right to take one's life.

Several common-sense objections to suicide are also noteworthy. Some contend that committing suicide is an act of cowardice. Of course, in some cases the motives are not cowardly, but when they are and when one is obligated to act bravely in the midst of affliction, suicide is wrong.[98] Second, some think about suicide but later regain their zest for living and are thankful they did not commit the irrevocable act of suicide. What seems insufferable today may dissipate tomorrow. Common sense suggests hoping for a better day rather than doing what cannot be undone.[99] P. F. Baelz thinks the most compelling common-sense argument against suicide is that it injures others. He admits that the amount of harm may vary from case to case. He also grants that on a utilitarian ethic some acts of suicide would be morally obligatory because they are acts of self-sacrifice that benefit those who are left. However, the utilitarian principle has limits. In human relationships there are what Baelz calls "canons of loyalty" which should guide our moral decisions, and these are more fundamental than utilitarians are willing to admit. These canons that govern relationships with one another and God must be considered when contemplating suicide.[100]

Finally, Hauerwas and Bondi reject both euthanasia and suicide on the ground that it involves the erosion of community. Suicide is the final sign of abandonment both by the individual and the society. The individual refuses any longer to fulfill his duties to society and expresses his feeling of being abandoned by it. As for voluntary euthanasia, it is akin to suicide. Involuntary euthanasia signals society's abandonment of its responsibility for the patient.[101] In ancient and medieval cultures the key issue was how people collectively could realize the true human good. In modern society the key matter is to ensure that individuals are safeguarded from interference by others as they pursue their own concerns. The problem is that this modern concern involves concern with individual rights (including the "right" to commit suicide), and an overemphasis on such individual rights has seriously damaged the concepts of community and obligation to others.[102]

Active/Passive—Killing and Letting Die

Some claim that for a consequentialist, the distinction between killing and letting die is not morally significant. For consequentialism, what matters is the end envisioned. Since both Jones and Smith intended the same end and since the same end was achieved, there is essentially no moral difference between the two cases.[103] On the other hand, deontologists, who are more likely to be concerned about means, might think there is a morally significant difference between the two cases.

From our perspective, this issue is not so simple as just suggested. In fact, we believe the consequentialist and the deontologist could agree on whether there is any moral difference between killing and letting die, despite their different ethical theories. Let us explain.

We begin by noting that headway can be made if one remembers what makes an act and an agent moral or immoral, and also recalls the principle that moral accountability presupposes acting freely. With those matters in mind, we believe we can show that in some cases there is not and in others there is a moral difference between active and passive euthanasia. Consider cases where I could refuse to kill or let die without harming myself (i.e., I am free to reject euthanasia), but I *choose* to kill/let die anyway. Whether my intention is to disobey a moral rule I am obliged to obey (deontology) or to achieve a certain end (teleology), the death of my friend, whether I kill him or let him die, makes no moral difference. In both cases I choose the same thing and carry it out. The Jones/Smith cases are good examples. Jones and Smith were free to preserve life or kill. They chose death even though they knew it was morally wrong. In cases like these, despite the different means, the acts are immoral acts, and the agents were immoral because their motives were wrong.

Consider, however, a different set of cases where the difference between active and passive does make a moral difference. Suppose I desire to but cannot save a dying individual through medicine or medical technology. My failure to use such means is not morally reprehensible. I do not preserve life, but since I am not free to do so, I am not guilty for letting someone die. On the other hand, if I know a patient is incurable and I freely decide to kill him, I am guilty. In this case I could avoid killing him, but I kill him anyway, even though this breaks a moral command. The fact that I break the command out of compassion for the sufferer does not overturn the fact that I freely broke the command. I am guilty. In sum, in the first case I cannot avoid breaking the command to preserve life, but in the second I am free to refuse to kill, but I kill anyway. The act of killing (active) is immoral, whereas the letting die (passive) is not. This analysis would fit whether one held a teleological or deontological ethic. The reason is that the moral difference stems not from one's ethical theory, nor from different means used in an attempt to reach ends, nor from different intentions in the two cases. The difference is the freedom to act in the latter case as opposed to the inability to act in the former.

The upshot of this discussion is that in some instances passive euthanasia is not as morally condemnable as active euthanasia. The key in assessing cases such as those sketched is the intent behind what the physician, family, or friends do or do not do and their ability to do otherwise. Each case of killing or letting die must be evaluated individually.[104]

Voluntary/Involuntary Euthanasia

Most who favor euthanasia argue for voluntary euthanasia alone. The implicit assumption is that it is morally permissible to take someone's life so long as he grants permission. Despite how entrenched this idea is in the thinking of so many, we disagree. If it is wrong to take innocent life, it is wrong whether the individual in question grants permission or not.

In elaborating our position, several things must be said. First, that moral evaluation of acts of euthanasia does not depend on the voluntary/involuntary distinction is evident from our discussion about what makes an *act* right or wrong (Chapter 1).[105] How one determines whether an act is moral depends on one's overall ethical theory, not on the voluntary/involuntary distinction. For consequentialists, the rightness or wrongness of an act depends upon the results. Thus, if euthanasia benefits the one who dies (and/or others as well), the act is right, regardless of whether the deceased asked to be killed or not. Non-consequentialism holds that the morality of an act depends on something other than consequences, but not on whether people affected by the act did or did not request it. Whether one is a consequentialist or non-consequentialist, his justification or condemnation of acts of euthanasia will not depend on the voluntary/involuntary distinction.[106]

Is the voluntary/involuntary distinction, then, irrelevant to ethics generally and euthanasia in particular? We think it is relevant, but not so as to justify voluntary euthanasia. The distinction is significant, because some acts cannot even be done unless they are done *without* permission. The classic example is theft. The very notion of stealing involves the victim's desire that his possessions *not* be taken. Thus, if I want you to take $100 of mine and you take it whether I am looking or not, it is dubious that I could rightly accuse you of stealing. Stealing is wrong not just because someone takes something that is not theirs, but because permission is not granted to take it. If I grant permission to take something of mine, that is gift giving, not theft.

Is murder like theft in this respect? That is, can it only be committed when the victim does not ask or consent to be killed? We think not. Murder involves the intentional taking of the innocent life of someone made in God's image. If that is the definition of murder, obviously murder can be committed whether the victim asks to be killed or not. Murder, unlike stealing, can be committed with or without the victim's permission. Thus, the voluntary/involuntary distinction matters in the way suggested to some acts like theft but not to others like murder.

There is another way voluntary and involuntary euthanasia differ, but again not so as to justify the former and condemn the latter. Both forms of euthanasia are wrong, because they ignore the obligation to preserve life. In addition, involuntary euthanasia is wrong, because it ignores the freedom of choice of the one killed (obviously, this comment pertains to cases where an individual can choose). So, involuntary euthanasia is wrong because it ignores two rights. However, voluntary euthanasia is still wrong. The difference is only that with voluntary euthanasia one less right has been abridged.

From the preceding, we conclude that when acts of euthanasia are wrong, they are wrong whether done voluntarily or involuntarily. In cases of death with dignity, for example, we might feel better about pulling the plug if the comatose patient left a living will, but the living will *per se* cannot determine whether pulling the plug is morally right or not. That evaluation must be made on other grounds.

MORAL DECISION-MAKING AND FORMS OF EUTHANASIA

Up to this point we have argued that euthanasia is generally unacceptable. However, how does one decide which cases are the exceptions? In what follows we shall note items that must be considered when making a decision in specific cases. Then we shall apply those guidelines as much as possible to death with dignity, mercy killing, and death selection.

CONSIDERATIONS IN DECISION-MAKING

In addition to all the preceding argumentation, we suggest that as one confronts individual situations five items will help in making decisions. They do not solve all problems but are helpful in many cases. The first is the proper understanding of death. Frequently, death is thought to be an event that occurs at a particular moment and involves separation of man's immaterial from his material part.[107] This sounds good, but modern medicine has shown that death is really a *process*. Moreover, doctors demand some kind of empirical evidence of the soul's departure from the body.

In our opinion, at present the best one can do is invoke criteria set forth by an Ad Hoc Committee of the Harvard Medical School. The committee defined brain death—irreversible coma—by four criteria. They are 1) unreceptivity and unresponsivity (no stimuli of any sort evoke any kind of response); 2) no movements or spontaneous breathing for at least an hour; 3) no reflexes, and fixed dilated pupils; 4) flat brain wave (flat EEG) for at least ten minutes, preferably twenty. All four must apply, and they must still be true of the patient twenty-four hours after first tested.[108]

A second consideration in decisions about euthanasia is one's overall ethical stance. Consequentialists will give greatest weight to arguments that emphasize the outcome of actions or omissions. Non-consequentialists will determine what is right on other grounds. For non-consequentialists like us, relevant divine commands will be paramount in decision-making.

Third, one's understanding of personhood is critical. We have espoused a view of personhood defined in biological terms, not in quality of life terms. Whatever is or potentially is genetically a person counts as a person and has a person's rights. This does not solve all problems in all cases, but it offers criteria far more objective than those proposed by those who hold a quality of life view of personhood.

Fourth, in assessing moral praise or blame for what is done with a patient, one must remember that only actions done (or omitted) freely are morally accountable. Finally (and related to the freedom point), there is the double effect doctrine. We are obliged both to preserve life and to relieve pain.[109] Sometimes it may be impossible to do both. If it is impossible to preserve the life of the terminally ill, we are not immoral if we do not. Of course, there is still the obligation to relieve pain and suffering. If we do what we can to relieve pain and in the process hasten death, there is still no moral blame, since we could not preserve life.

THE MORALITY OF DEATH WITH DIGNITY, MERCY KILLING, DEATH SELECTION

Is euthanasia ever moral? We have rejected euthanasia in general, but are there exceptions? From the preceding study we conclude that anyone holding an ethical theory such as ours cannot morally justify any cases of death selection. In cases of death selection, the individual does not deserve to die and is not suffering from a disease that warrants ending his life. The only considerations are matters of social, etc. utility. For a non-consequentialist, such concerns can never outweigh the prohibition against taking innocent life.

With mercy killing and mercy dying, matters are more difficult, but some general guidelines are possible. For example, when someone is not brain dead, and there is no evidence that death will come within hours or even days, but he is suffering intensely, we have a dual obligation—to preserve life and do everything possible to relieve pain. If some known medical procedure would improve his situation (even cure him), and we know he could undergo it without it killing him, it seems morally obligatory to use it. Likewise, the patient should not refuse treatment. On the other hand, if it is unclear that the medical procedure would improve the patient's condition, and it might harm him instead, there is no moral obligation to undertake the new treatment. For each person there is a time to die, and that must be accepted. Use of such procedures (extraordinary or otherwise) is certainly morally permissible, but not obligatory.

From these guidelines, we suggest the following for someone suffering terribly with a terminal illness: do whatever is possible to relieve pain, and do not force the patient to undergo procedures or take medicines already proven ineffective or that have no foreseeable benefit. However, because of the commandment not to take life, do not kill or aid the patient in committing suicide. If painkillers hasten death, but the intent is to relieve pain, giving pain medicine is morally acceptable. The principle of double effect applies.

Death with dignity cases are especially difficult, and part of the problem is evident when one understands what happens physiologically as someone dies. Traditionally, death was thought to involve cessation of heart beat and respiration. Today it is common knowledge within medicine that the heart continues beating for a few minutes after breathing ceases. Thus, artificial respiration can sometimes restore life. Respiration depends on reflex nervous activity which is governed from a center in the brain stem. Reflex action stops quickly if the oxygen supply to the brain fails. This information became especially important when techniques of mechanical respiration were invented. The respirator allows oxygenation of the brain to continue even if the reflex center or its connecting nerves are irreparably damaged. As a result, one may be kept biologically alive by means of a respirator. If the reflex center will not function autonomously and one pulls the plug on the respirator, oxygen will not reach the brain, and the person will die.[110]

This is not the end of the story, however. Superimposed on the brain stem is the cerebral cortex, which gives rise to consciousness and thought. As long as there is evidence of no more than minor cortical damage, doctors normally try to keep a person alive by whatever means are possible. What complicates matters is that there are cases where the heart-lung-brain stem complex can be maintained while cortical functions are so terribly damaged that evidence of personhood is hardly apparent.[111] Writing in 1976, James Mathers explained that in practice doctors tend to "accept responsibility for caring for the life of such 'cortical cripples' so long as the heart-lung-brain stem complex continues to function autonomously. It is when the complex can only be maintained artificially, while the cortex appears to be severely and irrecoverably damaged, that the dilemma of whether to turn off the switch appears in its most acute form."[112]

Mathers describes three situations which illustrate the problems in determining death and knowing what to do with a patient. In the first, circulation is maintained by a machine, but there is no evidence of brain activity (flat EEG). In the second, breathing and circulation continue without artificial help, but the cortex is severely damaged and the patient deeply unconscious. In the third, there is prolonged unconsciousness, evidence of great cortical damage, and circulation can only be maintained by machine. In the first case, the patient is presumed dead, in the second alive, and in the third, it is debatable whether the organism is a *person*, even though biologically there is life.[113] In the first case where a flat EEG indicates death, a decision to unplug the machine poses no moral predicament. The latter two cases involve obvious moral dilemmas. There is biological life, and the criteria for death are not met, but could the individual ever regain consciousness? Is cortical damage too severe to know? In either of those cases, who really knows if the immaterial part has left the body?

Though cases of death with dignity are very difficult, we offer the following generalizations: if a person is terminally ill (even hooked up to a machine), but according to the best medical opinion would not die within hours or even days, the obligation to preserve life takes precedence.[114] This does not obligate the use of means whose benefit to the patient is dubious. It does mandate not leaving the person to die without any care and not deliberately killing him. On the other hand, if the patient is terminal, and according to the best medical judgment will die within hours regardless of what is done, attempts to maintain life at all costs seem tantamount to refusing to accept the fact that it is that person's time to die. In those cases, allowing the person to die is morally acceptable.

CONCLUSION

We close this chapter with three final comments. First, in all potential cases of death with dignity and mercy killing, it is crucial to consult the best medical opinion of a pro-life doctor and make decisions in light of his advice and the Holy Spirit's leading. Second, despite the advances of modern medicine and regardless of how pro-life a doctor is, there will be cases where it is impossible to predict when a patient will die or what the outcome of a medical procedure will be. In such cases, our obligation is to do what is reasonable and moral to preserve life and relieve pain, and then leave the outcome in the hands of him who ultimately controls matters of life and death. Finally, though we believe the most acceptable view is that euthanasia is wrong in general, we grant that some forms in some instances may be acceptable. It has been said that hard cases make for bad rules. The problem in decisions about euthanasia is that so many cases are hard cases. We must solicit divine guidance!

CHAPTER FIVE

Capital Punishment

Prior to 1972 some 5,707 people were legally executed for capital crimes in the U.S.[1] Then, in 1972 came a landmark decision in *Furman v. Georgia.* By a 5-4 margin the Supreme Court ruled that the death laws of Georgia and Texas violated the Eighth Amendment by involving cruel and unusual punishment. The decisive issue for some of the Justices was that among all "eligible" for the most extreme punishment, the few chosen were selected by no clear standard.

Between 1972 and 1976 thirty-five states rewrote their laws to conform to the Supreme Court's decision. On July 2, 1976, by a 7-2 margin the Court declared most of the new statutes acceptable. The death penalty was legal again, and in 1977 executions resumed. Many predicted a flood of executions, but that has not happened. In fact, seldom is anyone executed in the U.S., and only after a lengthy battle in the courts. As a result, the numbers on death row continue to grow. As of 1992, thirty-six states plus the U.S. government and military had the death penalty, but the total number of prisoners on death row in the U.S. swelled to 2,616.[2]

With the death penalty legal, why are so many on death row? Opposition to the death penalty has not gone away. The appeals process in our court system successfully produces the current logjam. One of the newer delay tactics is a "proportionality" review. Several years ago convicted California killer Robert Harris demanded that the state supreme court review his sentence to ensure that it was not out of line with those imposed on other criminals. In 1976 when the death penalty was reinstated by the Supreme Court, the lower courts had made proportionality reviews before making their decisions. Since then, proportionality reviews have become a standard part of the judicial procedure. As of 1983, thirty-seven states had some form of proportionality review built into their sentencing procedure. Such reviews delay execution, but failure to include a review could be grounds for overturning the sentences of even convicted murderers.[3]

The battle rages on. One of the more recent chapters was written by the Supreme Court on April 22, 1987. In a 5-4 decision, the Court ruled that racial bias in imposing the death penalty is insufficient grounds for challenging the constitutionality of capital punishment laws. Statistics demonstrate that blacks are much more likely to be convicted and sentenced to death than whites, especially when the victim was white and the murderer black. Those least likely to be convicted are blacks when the victim is black. The Court ruled that such disparities do not invalidate capital punishment statutes.

Because of continued concern over discriminatory application of the death penalty and the Supreme Court's ruling in 1987, the Racial Justice Act (S.1696) was formulated. The legislation proposes to "prohibit any state from imposing the death penalty if the defendant could show statistical evidence of racial disparities in the pattern of death sentences with that state."[4] The intent is not to rule out all capital sentences, but to make certain that when evidence warrants the death penalty for both a white and a black, both will be executed. Likewise, in similar cases when a white is not convicted or given the death penalty, a black should not be either. Though the intent of the bill sounds admirable, one has to wonder if it would not in fact lead to more attempts to delay executions while court decisions are being challenged on the basis of whether they discriminatorily apply the death sentence.

To date progress has been slow in moving this legislation through Congress. In the Senate, the bill was changed to the Racial Justice/Fairness in Death Sentencing Act, but was attached to the Senate's Omnibus Crime Bill. That bill has been held up in the Senate over issues such as gun control, and it did not pass during 1992, an election year. In the House of Representatives, the bill has fared no better. It has been debated, and a substitute amendment called the Fairness in Death Sentencing Act was introduced.[5] Still, that legislation was not passed by the 1992 Congress.[6]

In addition to debates over the legality and moral propriety of the death penalty, there are discussions about proper methods of execution. Execution by electrocution was introduced in 1888 and lethal gas in 1924. In 1983 nine states decided to use lethal injection.[7] The new procedure has brought mixed reactions. Some claim it is far too humane, especially for those who brutally murder multiple victims. On the other hand, at its 1981 annual meeting the American Medical Association considered the following resolution: "[A] physician, as a member of a profession dedicated to preserving life when there is hope of doing so, should not be participant in a legally authorized execution." Doctors passed the resolution, claiming that they could not perform lethal injections and remain consistent with the Hippocratic Oath they had taken.[8]

Worldwide there is an increasing trend to outlaw the death penalty. For example, in England, as recently as 1800 over two hundred crimes were considered capital offenses. However, in the twentieth century Britain outlawed the death penalty. Between 1970 and 1980 six Western European countries did the same. Worldwide, by 1980 twenty countries had outlawed the death penalty for all crimes.[9] Some 134 countries retained it, though in twelve of those countries so-called ordinary crimes were ruled out as capital crimes. By 1992 the number of countries and territories retaining the penalty had reduced to 106. Some forty-six had abolished it for all crimes. Another sixteen had abolished it for ordinary crimes so that they only use it in exceptional cases such as in the military or during wartime. In addition, another twenty-one countries were abolitionist *de facto*. That is, they have the death penalty for ordinary crimes but have not executed anyone in the past ten or more years.[10]

Despite the number of nations that retain the death penalty, in December 1977 approximately two hundred delegates from fifty-five countries on all continents met in Stockholm, Sweden for the International Conference on the Abolition of the Death Penalty. That conference overwhelmingly passed a declaration imploring all governments to outlaw the death penalty and asking the UN to declare it contrary to international law.[11]

Capital punishment is a major issue worldwide, but debate about it is especially intense in Western countries. Argumentation surrounding capital punishment involves a series of issues. They are: 1) Is capital punishment permissible? 2) Is capital punishment mandatory? 3) If capital punishment is either allowable or mandatory, which crimes are punishable by a capital sentence? 4) If capital punishment is to be practiced, what methods are acceptable?

In this chapter our primary focus will be on the first two questions. We want to consider those issues from a moral standpoint, not a legal one. That is, our concern is not what countries' laws say, but what is morally right. Though the issues are complex, we think the best case can be made for mandating capital punishment. However, in our opinion the number of crimes punishable by capital sentence is quite limited, and the regulations for convicting someone of a capital offense should be very stringent.

Non-scriptural Arguments
Against Capital Punishment

Deterrence

Often capital punishment is rejected on a variety of grounds as an ineffective deterrent to crime. Consider, for example, statistical evidence. Records from 1967-68 in the U.S. show that abolitionist states had a lower first-degree murder rate than retentionist states. From 1920-1955,

Michigan, the first state to abolish the death penalty, had a lower homicide rate than Ohio and Indiana which both had the death penalty. Furthermore, Missouri abolished the death penalty from 1917 to 1919. Prior to abolition and after reinstatement, the number of homicides rose steadily; during the period of abolition homicide steadily decreased.[12] Similar findings have been reported in other countries. For example, in 1967 Canada abolished the death penalty for five years. Results of the experiment indicated no increase in violent crimes attributable to abolition. Consequently, Canada permanently banned the death penalty.[13]

In addition to statistical arguments, some maintain that the crucial issue is not whether capital punishment is an effective deterrent to crime, but whether it is more effective than life imprisonment.[14] Opponents of the death penalty claim either that life imprisonment is more effective or that it is impossible to prove capital punishment is a better deterrent.

Third, others note that the efficacy of a deterrent depends more on the certainty of being caught than on the severity of the penalty. Thus, a fine or imprisonment when apprehension and punishment are certain are just as effective or more so than capital punishment. Of course, this suggests that capital punishment *per se* is not what deters the criminal.[15]

Fourth, usually murder is a crime of passion committed in the heat of anger without premeditation.[16] The murderer does not think about consequences; he merely acts. Since the threat of the death penalty is hardly on his mind, it cannot deter him.

Finally, some argue that even if capital punishment effectively deters crime, there is no way to demonstrate that. Statistics always include the number of homicides committed, but think of how many murders do not occur. What keeps those who did not murder from it? No one has figured out how to determine how many are deterred from homicide by the death penalty.[17] However, if it cannot be shown that those who do not kill were deterred by fear of capital punishment, we must drop talk of capital punishment as a deterrent.

Retribution

A second major line of objection to capital punishment focuses on retribution. Either deterrence or retribution might serve as a basis for a penal system and thereby justify capital punishment. Deterrence is rejected for reasons just presented. Retribution is rejected on a variety of grounds. For example, many object that retribution is really nothing more than legalized vengeance. Christians are strongly warned against acting from revenge (Rom 12:17-21; 1 Pet 3:9). Moreover, even non-Christians think punishment based on retribution is inappropriate, for it lowers society to the level of the criminal who has acted in anger and without self-control. In fact, some claim that the death penalty contradicts what the retributivist hopes to accomplish. By enforcing the death penalty, he hopes to show the dignity of life. By taking another life, the retributivist actually contradicts his desire to instill respect for life.

Objections to retribution rest on even more fundamental concerns. Retributivists assume that the morally guilty should suffer. That means two key points underlay retributive justice: 1) it is only permissible to punish those who voluntarily do moral wrong; and 2) punishment must not exceed what is commensurate with the penalty incurred by the criminal.[18] The first point ensures that those forced to do wrong and those who break the law unintentionally (perhaps even in ignorance) will not become victims themselves. The second point concerns the need to make punishment fit the crime. If these two principles are foundational to retributive justice, many think there are serious problems. For example, how could any judge or jury be absolutely sure about the intentions behind the act of the accused person? Even if the accused states his intentions, there is no guarantee he is telling the truth or that he even knows what he intended in the heat of committing the crime. How, then, can we be sure about the guilt or innocence of any accused person?

Even more problematic is the second principle. How could anyone know which punishment is proper for each crime? For example, does grand theft merit five years, ten years, or what? Moreover, how do we determine answers to such questions? Some may reply that as long as like cases receive the same punishment, the demands of principle 2) are met. But that is not necessarily so, for one must still decide what is just punishment for the crime in question. If handling like cases alike is the rule, one could justify gross inhumanity by torturing *all* who commit the same crime.

Others say that if justice is derived from God, then we know the punishment fits the crime. However, God's justice is perfect, as Augustine argued, but the state's is not. For many crimes God has not stated a punishment. In many cases man simply cannot know if a punishment is too severe or even if an accused criminal is guilty.[19] Moreover, many ask whether some of *God's* standards are not too severe. Is not capital punishment for adultery (Lev 20:10), rape (Deut 22:25), striking or reviling a parent (Exod 21:15, 17), or incest (Lev 20:11-13) excessive? On the other hand, if God and religion are eliminated as justifying man's concepts of justice, it is moot as to whether one can know true justice. This is especially so if one refuses to define justice in terms of some social good that is produced (retributivists refuse to do so).[20] If retributivists must define justice apart from appeal either to some social value or religion, it is difficult to see how they can say what penalties are just.

In light of such arguments, retribution is rejected as the purpose of penal systems. Moreover, deterrence is also ruled out. The only other possible purposes are rehabilitation and restitution, but neither is possible with capital punishment. Consequently, capital punishment is unacceptable.

Cruel and Unusual Punishment

A third line of argument relates to the Supreme Court's ruling in 1972. The Court concluded that capital punishment as then practiced violated the Eighth Amendment to the Constitution, because it was cruel and unusual punishment. Opponents of the death penalty claim that despite reinstatement of the penalty in the U.S. and despite so-called more humane ways of killing, the death penalty is always cruel and unusual.

Some respond that the number of executions for capital crimes over the years shows that the death penalty is not unusual. Moreover, so long as the criminal is not tortured, the penalty is not necessarily cruel. Death by injection is viewed as relatively painless.

Opponents of the death penalty reply that the normal meaning of "cruel" includes deliberate causing of pain or injury. In that sense, the death penalty is cruel. It is also cruel in view of the emotional grief brought on the family of the condemned prisoner. Moreover, if by "cruel" punishment is meant unjustifiable punishment, then certainly the death penalty is cruel.[21]

This really raises a crucial issue. Is the death penalty cruel and unusual in the sense that it is unjustifiable? Many claim so, for they think neither deterrence nor retribution justify it. Moreover, whereas for many centuries public opinion viewed the death penalty as proper for certain crimes, standards of decency change. In contemporary society there is a certain moral offensiveness to taking life in response to crime. From that standpoint the death penalty is considered excessive.[22]

Other Concerns

Two other concerns are frequently raised. First, statistics show that in the U.S. capital punishment is unduly discriminatory against minorities and the poor. From 1930 to 1957 in the U.S. more than half the executions for murder involved non-whites (1,554 of 3,096), and in the South more than twice as many blacks as whites were executed.[23] Of all people legally executed in the U.S. between 1930 and 1980, about 53.3 percent were black, even though U.S. population during that period was only about 10 percent black.[24] Statistics also show that wealthy people accused of capital crimes are unlikely to be convicted, for they can afford good legal counsel. The poor get inferior legal representation and are much more likely to be sentenced to death, even when they are not guilty.[25] Such discriminatory imposition of the death penalty argues for its abolition.

Second, opponents cite the proneness of judge and jury to error. Humans are not infallible in their judgments. They may make decisions on too little evidence or inconclusive evidence. Cases are too plentiful where criminals were wrongly convicted, sentenced, and executed. Unfortunately, in a capital case there is no way to redress the wrong when evidence shows the executed person really was innocent. How much wiser, then, to make life imprisonment the maximum penalty! At least then the prisoner can be released if the court later learns that it erred.

A PRO-CAPITAL PUNISHMENT RESPONSE

Capital Punishment and Deterrence

Though many think capital punishment is not an effective deterrent to crime, others insist this is because criminals in the U.S. know they are not likely to be convicted of a capital crime and even less likely to be executed. However, if punishment were sure to be applied and fell swiftly, the figures would be much different.[26] Moreover, some contend that whether or not capital punishment deters potential criminals is not the entire issue. It surely does deter the person who already committed a capital crime. In that respect (and this is quite important to the safety of society), the death penalty is quite an effective deterrent.

In addition, those who think capital punishment deters note that opponents have never demonstrated that the death penalty does not deter. As Steven Goldberg argues, the crucial issue is what deterred all of us who never commit a capital crime. Opponents of capital punishment rarely address that question, but until they offer an alternate explanation of what deters, it is hard to accept their claims against capital punishment as a deterrent.[27] Opponents of the death penalty cite statistics that show a higher murder rate in countries with a death penalty and a lower one in countries without it. However, such statistics do not explain why those who did not commit the crime refrained. It seems virtually impossible to show that they refrained just because there was no death penalty. Moreover, as Goldberg argues, even if a society with the death penalty has twice the murder rate of one without it, that does not disprove capital punishment as a deterrent. Without the death penalty, the country might have a murder rate four times that of the other country.[28] Clearly, statistics do not disprove capital punishment as a deterrent, and opponents of the death penalty offer no other viable explanation as to why those deterred refrained.

In assessing the arguments pro and con, our conclusion is that the evidence is inconclusive. Goldberg's arguments undercut the claim that capital punishment does not deter, but neither do they prove it does deter. Moreover, it is probably not possible to prove or disprove the notion that capital punishment is a more effective deterrent than life imprisonment. How could one derive conclusive evidence in regard to which of two potential punishments would have the greater psychological deterrent value in the case of even a small sampling of criminals, let alone in the majority of cases?

If the evidence is ultimately inconclusive, one cannot expect to prove the rightness or wrongness of capital punishment on the grounds of the deterrence issue. We do not think this matters, because we believe capital punishment can be justified on other grounds. The deterrence issue is especially critical for those who think the purpose of a penal system is deterrence. For those such as us who see justice as the purpose of a penal system, retribution, not deterrence, is ultimately the crucial issue in punishment.

Capital Punishment and Retribution

Justifying retribution is no small task, but some objections are more easily met than others. For example, retribution may be vengeful in some cases, but vengeance and retribution are not identical. One may repay from a desire to get even or go beyond the crime committed, or one may repay out of a sense of rendering the criminal his just deserts. Moreover, proponents of the death penalty argue that requiring the death penalty for murder upholds rather than denigrates the importance of life. If life is so unimportant that one can snuff it out with only minimal punishment, life is trivialized. However, if the criminal's life is taken when he kills someone, the seriousness of the crime and the import of life are underscored.

In addition to responding to objections, there are positive arguments for retributive justice. An initial argument appeals to the benefits of participating in society. According to this argument, for someone to enjoy the benefits of a legal system, he must be willing to make a sacrifice. He must obey the system's laws even if he does not want to. Part of the arrangement, though, is that those who disobey laws cannot gain unfair advantage over those who obey. Punishing the disobedient accomplishes this goal. The net result is that retributive justice must operate in societies.[29]

A second argument deals with an even more fundamental issue. Specifically, how does one determine which acts should be punishable by law? That is, what is the basis of law and punishment altogether? We think that ultimately law and punishment reflect morality. That is, in general, laws are made to prohibit actions that societies consider immoral. Thus, when the state's laws are broken, the moral law supporting the law is also broken. We believe that those who break the moral law should be punished. All of this, however, is further justification for the state to practice retributive justice when its laws are broken.[30]

Two key questions still need an answer if retribution is to be justified: 1) whose morality is to be the basis for societal laws? and, 2) after determining which acts are to be punished, how does one know that punishments envisioned are fair for the crime?[31] Ethicists answer from the perspective of their general ethical theory. That suggests that in our pluralistic societies, hope of reaching a general agreement on these issues is minimal. Given our modified divine command theory of ethics, we respond that unless retributive justice is grounded in religion and theology, there is no ultimate hope of justifying it. That is, the commands of God (based ultimately in his nature as God) reveal which acts are to be prohibited and punished. As to the second question, God has not prescribed the precise punishment for every command that is broken, but he has in some cases. If God establishes the punishment, it is legitimate to call it just, because God is just. As we shall demonstrate, Scripture does reveal God's assessment of murder, and it also prescribes God's punishment for it. The net result is that one can justify capital punishment for murder, since God prescribes that penalty.

Cruel and Unusual Punishment

"Cruel and unusual punishment" is open to a variety of interpretations. One can so define "cruel and unusual" that any punishment would fail on that ground. On the other hand, it does seem possible to make headway on this issue. Thomas Long's discussion is especially helpful here.

Long notes that the basic issue behind the Eighth Amendment is the matter of the decency of a punishment. The key question is whether the death penalty is contrary to contemporary perceptions of moral decency.[32] Certain punishments such as torture undoubtedly would be deemed cruel. Executing someone for a crime committed under someone else's compulsion would be cruel punishment. Finally, if execution apparently exacted a greater penalty than the crime deserved (e.g., executing someone for lying to his parents), that would also be considered cruel.

Despite these examples of cruel punishments, unless one automatically rules out all punishments as cruel, some punishments would not be cruel. For example, in cases of first-degree murder many think execution by lethal injection is not a cruel method of punishment. The key point in this discussion, however, is that if penal and judicial systems should mete out justice, punishment is necessary to do so. In capital cases punishment is also required. We maintain that the burden of proof falls on the *opponent* of capital punishment to show that it is cruel punishment at least as much as on the proponent to show that it is not. Demonstrating that all methods of capital punishment are morally indecent for all cases of murder seems a hopeless task.

What about capital punishment as unusual? If "unusual" means seldom done, then capital punishment is not unusual. Of course, such a simplistic rendering of "unusual" allows for continual torture so long as it is the usual treatment of criminals. That cannot be morally justified. On the other hand, another sense of "unusual" (i.e., "irrational") is more germane to the discussion. Thomas Long argues that if capital punishment fails to serve a rational end, then it is unusual. Moreover, if it is unusual ("irrational"), it is also cruel.[33]

What might serve as rational ends for capital punishment? Deterrence is a rational end, but since it cannot be demonstrated that capital punishment accomplishes that end, the death penalty appears irrational on that ground.[34] Moreover, neither rehabilitation nor restitution are ends accomplishable through capital punishment, so it is irrational if those are the ends sought.

For someone committed to the notion that capital punishment is rational, one of two lines of argument are open. First, one could argue that the end envisioned is retribution. Capital punishment accomplishes that goal, so it is rational according to Long's definition. The only other question is whether retribution can be justified, and we have shown how to do so.

Second, one might reject the notion that the way to prove the death penalty rational is to show that it produces an intended end, because such a strategy tries to justify capital punishment on consequentialist grounds. Someone committed, for example, to some form of divine command theory would argue that capital punishment is rational, because God prescribes it, not because of any results produced when it is implemented. In fact, anyone committed to some form of non-consequentialism should be unimpressed by the notion that capital punishment is rational only if it accomplishes some intended end.

The net result of this discussion on capital punishment as unusual is twofold: 1) if one adopts a consequentialist ethic according to which the death penalty is rational only if it produces some valuable end, then capital punishment is not unusual, for it accomplishes retribution. On the other hand, 2) non-consequentialists can argue that the death penalty is rational, for example, because it obeys God's command, and it is always rational to obey a divine command. In either case, capital punishment is rational and thus qualifies as usual.

Other Concerns

The other objections presented actually focus on how the death penalty is implemented, not on whether it is right or wrong *per se*. Statistics about discrimination against the poor and minorities are deeply regrettable. However, discrimination does not show capital punishment to be morally wrong. Instead, it suggests a need to change the judicial system in order to administer the death penalty fairly. The proper or improper manner in which any penalty is implemented says nothing whatsoever about moral rightness or wrongness of the penalty *per se*.

Likewise, cases where convicted killers were later found innocent do not demonstrate that the death penalty *per se* is wrong. They only show that demands for proof of guilt must be much more stringent than current judicial procedures require. As we shall see, OT demands were more stringent than contemporary demands. If those standards (where applicable) were followed today, probably few people would be convicted of a capital crime. So be it. Better to have few convictions where the accused is shown guilty beyond doubt than to have many questionable convictions. The key point, though, is that the rightness or wrongness of capital punishment cannot be argued on the grounds of potential or actual human error.

SCRIPTURAL ARGUMENTS
AGAINST CAPITAL PUNISHMENT

Hermeneutical Considerations

John Yoder claims that those who favor capital punishment frequently employ an inconsistent hermeneutic in their interpretation of Scripture. They affirm the finality of Christ and the New Covenant, but they still appeal to the OT when it comes to issues of civil order such as capital punishment. Moreover, use of the OT itself is inconsistent. Proponents of capital punishment accept OT laws about executing murderers, but reject laws which prescribe execution of animals (Gen 9:5; Exod 21:28), witches, adulterers, and disobedient children (Exod 22:18; Lev 20:10; Exod 21:15, 17). Moreover, they ignore rules about cities of refuge for unintentional killers, and they do not require the executioner in cases of manslaughter to be the victim's next of kin (Gen 9:5). If the Mosaic Law is to be obeyed, why not mandate its injunctions on the sabbath, the cure for leprosy, slavery, or not wearing wool and linen garments together (Deut 22:11)?[35] If none of these injunctions are for today, why single out capital punishment from the OT? Defenders of capital punishment have no clear hermeneutic for determining which parts of the OT apply today and which parts do not.

Second, in interpreting the OT's relevance for today, one must remember that there is no theocracy in the NT era. In OT Israel ethnic, civil, geographic and religious communities were one. Today the people of God are from many ethnic groups, and government is in the hands of pagan authorities. The whole context of social and ethical thought has so changed that a simple transposition of OT laws is both impossible and illegitimate.[36]

Finally, Yoder claims that the function of capital punishment as stated in a passage such as Genesis 9 is not defense of society but expiation of a sin against the image of God. Of course, in the NT era Christ's sacrifice abolished all expiatory sacrifices. There is no further need for any blood sacrifices to expiate sin, including the sacrifice of one who has committed a murder.[37]

Capital Punishment and the Law of Christ

Even though the NT supersedes the OT, capital punishment should be practiced if the NT explicitly enjoins it. Some think that in the NT era, the Mosaic Law is abrogated in favor of the Law of Christ, for Christ is the end (completion and goal) of the law (Rom 10:4). Opponents of the death penalty emphasize the fact that the Law of Christ is love. Scripture requires believers to love and serve their neighbors (cf. Matt 22:37-40; 25:31-46; 1 John 3:18; 4:12, 20). Moreover, believers must love their enemies, not execute them (Matt 5:43-44). Revenge is forbidden (Rom 12:17-19; 1 Pet 3:8-9). Forgiveness of those who offend us is enjoined. In responding to *lex talionis*, Jesus explicitly replaced retribution with the principle of reconciliation (Matt 5:23-24). These considerations totally rule out capital punishment.[38]

The Biblical Emphasis on Mercy

Another objection appeals to biblical examples of mercy. Cain, David, and Moses murdered intentionally, not accidentally, but God extended them mercy. David and Moses went on to live fruitful and productive lives of service for the Lord. Given these examples of divine mercy and human rehabilitation, how can we withhold mercy to those convicted of capital crimes? At minimum, these biblical examples show that even if capital punishment is permissible, it is not mandatory.

In the NT, mercy is also present. The best-known case is recorded in John 8:1-11. A woman caught in the very act of adultery was brought to Jesus. The law demanded her execution (Lev 20:10; Deut 22:21, 24). However, Jesus instructed those without sin to cast the first stone. When the accusers left, Jesus told her he did not condemn her; she should go and sin no more. Opponents of the death penalty stress the importance of this passage. It is the one case where Jesus spoke to the applicability of the death penalty, and he did not demand it.[39]

OT Regulation of Capital Punishment

Another biblical argument against the death penalty invokes OT judicial procedure. David Llewellyn notes five key aspects of the Mosaic application of the death penalty. These procedures were meant to prevent the miscarriage of justice. If Mosaic standards were used today, the death penalty as currently practiced would be outlawed.

The five procedural items are: 1) Absolute certainty of guilt was required for conviction (Deut 17:4). This is stronger than the American rule of proof beyond reasonable doubt. 2) Conviction required the testimony of more than one witness (Deut 19:15; Num 35:30). Given the need for certain proof, most likely those witnesses were to be eyewitnesses. Moreover, since stoning to death was to be done by the witnesses (Deut 17:7), one might suspect reticence to cast the first stone unless one was an eyewitness. 3) To discourage attempts to "frame" someone for a crime, witnesses who committed perjury in capital cases were themselves to be executed (Deut 19:16, 19). 4) In difficult cases the verdict was deferred to judicial experts (Deut 17:8, 9). This differs from the American system in which jurors who often do not understand law must decide anyway. 5) If the verdict was "guilty," the death penalty was mandatory (Lev 27:29; Num 35:31). Lighter sentences could not be adopted. This made discriminatory application of the death penalty impossible; i.e., all people, regardless of social standing, etc., were treated equal if deemed guilty.[40]

With these regulations, undoubtedly fewer people were convicted under the Mosaic system than under others like the American system. Opponents of the death penalty maintain that if God really wants the death penalty enforced, it ought to be administered as God required. Until then, it should be outlawed.

Handling of Key Biblical Passages

Opponents of the death penalty know that the preceding arguments cannot negate clear biblical prescriptions to enforce the death penalty. Genesis 9 and Romans 13 are often understood to provide that mandate, but opponents think those passages do not prove the case.

As to Genesis 9, opponents complain that supporters of the death penalty focus on verse 6, but ignore the injunctions in verses 4-5. Verse 4 apparently prohibits eating rare meat, and verse 5 requires the execution of animals who kill humans. No one demands enforcement of those injunctions, but, then, consistency dictates ignoring the commands about capital punishment.[41]

Second, the statements in Gen 9:5-6 may be predictive, not prescriptive. That is, rather than demanding the execution of murderers, the passage may merely predict that those who take life can expect to be killed in return. The Hebrew does not decide the issue, for the verbal form in verses 5-6 could be either imperative or indicative. Because of the implications of taking this passage as a mandate, there must be clearer evidence that it is a command than this.[42]

Finally, both Genesis 9 and the Mosaic Law require that execution of murderers be done by a blood relative of the victim. In fact, Gen 9:5 designates the victim's brother to do it. This is surely a far cry from the state having the right of capital punishment. Thus, Genesis 9 cannot apply to today.[43]

What about Romans 13? Opponents of the death penalty think it neither mandates nor warrants the death penalty. The key phrase is, "it does not bear the sword for nothing" (v. 4). Does this reference to the state bearing the sword mandate or even allow capital punishment? Opponents deny that it does. They argue that while the sword clearly refers to the state's authority to punish evildoers, it does not demand that the state punish by execution. Under the Roman Empire most crimes were not punishable by death, but the sword was still an appropriate symbol for Rome's authority to punish criminals.[44] Also, Rome did not execute by the sword; capital offenses were punished by crucifixion.[45]

Finally, the issue under discussion in Romans 13 was whether Christians had to submit to governmental regulations about payment of taxes and custom fees (vv. 6-7). Paul argued that governments have authority over citizens both to punish criminals and to keep an orderly society. Christians must submit to the state, and that includes paying taxes. Of course, payment of taxes does not relate to the death penalty. So, reference to the sword in this context cannot invoke capital punishment; it merely underscores government's authority over its citizens.[46] Moreover, Paul does not say how the sword is to be used in enforcing governmental authority.

A PRO-CAPITAL PUNISHMENT RESPONSE

Hermeneutical Considerations

How one answers the hermeneutical issues raised by thinkers such as Yoder ultimately depends on one's understanding of the relation of OT law to the NT era. For example, someone seeing primarily continuity between the two might handle questions about Genesis 9 by noting that only the injunction about capital punishment rests on a theological justification. According to the passage, one must require life because the murderer has killed someone made in the image of God. So long as man is made in God's image, the injunction is applicable. As to Genesis 9's other commands, no such theological justification is offered. Moreover, in the NT neither Jesus nor the apostles say those commands still apply. Only the command about capital punishment is repeated. Even proponents of much continuity between OT and NT Law may think some OT injunctions cannot apply (unless repeated) because of changes in cultural and historical setting.

For those such as us espousing a discontinuity view, the response to the objections is different. Neither the injunctions of Genesis 9 nor regulations in the Mosaic Law covering capital crimes are *per se* part of the Law of Christ. Of course, any injunctions repeated as part of the Law of Christ are applicable today. Appeal to the OT for such rules is not illegitimate, if they are clearly part of the Law of Christ. We believe Romans 13 does repeat the demand for capital punishment, so it is part of the Law of Christ. However, it does not explain why God views this as just punishment for murder. Appeals to Genesis 9 are appropriate, for it offers that information. On the other hand, the other commands in Genesis 9 are nowhere repeated in the NT and thus are not operative today. The same is true of legislation about other crimes considered capital offenses in the Mosaic Law.

Capital Punishment and the Law of Christ

Christ's teachings about treatment of enemies are often thought to eliminate the death penalty. For example, in Matt 5:38-45 the Lord says we must love our enemies. Instead of demanding an eye for an eye, we should turn the other cheek. Thus, the Law of Christ calls for love of enemies, not execution.

Several things should be noted in response. Earlier in Matthew 5 (vv. 21-22) Jesus did address murder. He taught that not only murderers but anyone angry with his brother would be judged. Jesus did not say judgment would come in the form of capital punishment, but if his intent were to rule it out, we might expect such a comment. If nothing else, this passage shows that Jesus considers murder and anger serious issues and that he intends to mete out eternal punishment in retribution to anyone who breaks these commands and refuses to repent. Thus, though this portion of the passage does not explicitly sanction capital punishment, it does not rule it out either, and it demonstrates that God will practice retributive justice against unrepentant murderers.

Some would respond that 5:38ff., which commands Christians to turn the other cheek and love and pray for enemies, rules out the death penalty. On the contrary, those passages (and other often-cited NT passages such as 1 Pet 3:8-11) speak about the Christian's interpersonal relationships. The verses say nothing about how a government should respond to those who break the laws of the state. If one demands that these passages be applied to criminal justice, then the logical result would be to rule out all punishment for all crimes. Obviously, that would mean the collapse of orderly society and would negate biblical teaching that governments are instituted of God to reward the just and to punish evildoers (Rom 13:1-4). Finally, as to Matt 5:38ff., it should be noted that as part of the Sermon on the Mount, it is addressed to Christians about their behavior in regard to others. It is not a regulation for mankind in general meant to be adopted into societal penal codes.

Capital Punishment and Mercy

As to the cases of Cain, Moses, and David, they are exceptional cases where *God* extended his grace. There are many OT examples where God did not extend grace, but punished the evildoer; so these cases cannot be the norm, nor do they overturn the injunction of Genesis 9. Moreover, the decision to extend mercy in these cases was *God's*, not society's. Unless told otherwise, the state is to follow the general rule to mete out retributive justice.

The case of the woman taken in adultery (John 8) is more complex and worthy of further comment. The Scribes and Pharisees tried to trap Jesus on a matter of the law. They brought a woman caught in the act of adultery. Under Mosaic Law adultery was punishable by stoning to death, and eyewitnesses were to be the executioners. Jesus responded (v. 7) that those among her accusers without guilt should cast the first stone. After all the accusers had gone, Jesus told the woman he did not condemn her either.

She should go and sin no more. Opponents of the death penalty claim this is the one time Jesus spoke about the death penalty, and he waived it. He forgave the woman.[47] As John Yoder argues, Christ focused on two items: the moral authority of judge and executioner ("Let him who is without sin cast the first stone") and Christ's right to forgive sin and free the woman in a civil offense.[48]

An initial response is that it is always risky business to take one instance as a basis for a general principle. Inductive generalizations based on a small sampling of cases are always suspect.[49] Moreover, in John 8 Jesus *prescribed* nothing about capital punishment generally or even (as we shall see) about particular cases such as the one presented to him. Thus, it is hard to see how this passage can serve as normative for understanding biblical teaching on capital punishment.

In addition to the preceding, we would do well to see if Jesus really did overturn Mosaic teaching on capital punishment in this case. Careful examination of the passage shows that Jesus' actions strictly conformed to the law. Jesus questioned the moral fitness of the accusers (v. 7). Critics of capital punishment argue that the phrase "without sin" (*anamartētos*) means that no one who is a sinner has a right to judge or execute anyone else. However, if this is correct, all criminal justice goes, since no mere human is sinlessly perfect. Of course, then John 8 would contradict Paul's teaching in Rom 13:4 that the state should punish evildoers. Thus, it is better to understand *anamartētos* in its basic sense of "without fault" and to see Jesus' challenge as relating to this specific case. Christ told the woman's accusers that if they were without fault in this case, they should cast the first stone.[50]

Weren't the Scribes and Pharisees without fault in this case? Had they committed adultery? This last question misses the point. Jesus challenged whether they met the Mosaic qualifications for witnesses in this case. The Law demanded that guilt be established by two or three eyewitnesses (Deut 17:6-7). Perjurers were to suffer the penalty that would have been inflicted on the accused (Deut 19:16-19). The Law required that both persons guilty of adultery be tried and executed (Deut 22:22-24), but the woman's partner was absent on this occasion. Finally, the law demanded that the witnesses' motives be pure (Exod 23:1-8).[51] While the regulation about eyewitnesses was met, others, including the one about the integrity of the witnesses' motives, were not. Jesus knew these men had not brought the woman out of concern to uphold the Mosaic Law. Thus, it is most likely that by asking who was "without sin," Jesus was asking whether their motives in this case met Mosaic standards and left them without fault in that sense. No one knows the exact reason each accuser felt himself disqualified, but each did disqualify himself and left. Note, though, that Jesus never told them the woman should not be executed for her sin. Instead, he told them to cast the first stone if they qualified under Mosaic regulation as witnesses, judges, and executioners. They did not, so they left; but Jesus' comments strictly conformed to Mosaic procedures for such cases.

Despite these considerations, some will reply that Jesus forgave her, and that is the crucial point. However, the text does not say that. As Stephen James explains, the Greek word for "condemn" is a legal term and must be understood in the context of this dispute about the law. The Scribes and Pharisees had no right to condemn her because of their impure motives, so in the eyes of the law, she was not condemned. Jesus could not condemn her, for to do so would have grossly violated Mosaic regulation. He was not an eyewitness, and the law required more than one eyewitness, anyway.[52] Thus, even though as the divine Son of God he knew whether she was guilty, given Mosaic regulation, he had no right to condemn or execute her. Moreover, his admonition to "Go and sin no more" is not only excellent advice but a direct command in conformity with the law's demands. However, it implies nothing about whether Jesus forgave her, nor does it suggest anything about whether she was at all repentant.

The upshot of this discussion is that John 8 does not give a new teaching about capital punishment generally. Moreover, on the specific matter of adultery, it shows that while Israel was still under the Mosaic Code, Jesus strictly conformed to it. Finally, properly understood, the incident is not even an example of extending mercy; it is an instance of rigorous adherence to Mosaic standards.

OT Regulations on Capital Punishment

There is a simple response to this issue, regardless of whether or not one thinks Mosaic legislation applies today. Those regulations can never eliminate capital punishment as morally wrong. They do not even address that issue. The most such rules could mandate, if applied today, is a change in legal procedures in capital cases. OT regulations would probably result in fewer convictions, but could not rule out the death penalty altogether. These rules are ultimately beside the point of whether capital punishment *per se* is morally right or wrong, permissible or even mandatory.

Key Biblical Passages

In our opinion, one's decision about the moral rectitude of capital punishment ultimately depends on his understanding of some key biblical passages. The first is Gen 9:5-6. We believe that appeal to this passage is proper, even though we hold that OT law codes are inoperative today. Since the Law of Christ contains the same injunction, this OT passage cannot be off-limits for a proper understanding of the issue.

Though we think this passage mandates capital punishment, several questions must be addressed. For example, is the phrase "by man shall his blood be shed" (v. 6) prescriptive or predictive? That is, is God demanding capital punishment, or is he stating how things will be ordered so the criminal is punished?[53] The Hebrew is not determinative, for it could be understood either way. Several things, however, suggest that the phrase is prescriptive. According to the last phrase of verse 5 ("and from each man, too, I will demand an accounting for the life of his fellow man"), God will demand retribution upon the murderer by another. It seems most natural, then, that verse 6 states God's command to execute the murderer on the basis of the demand of verse 5. Second, the last phrase of verse 6 explains why the stipulation of verse 5 is to be carried out. It shows why capital punishment is neither arbitrary nor optional. If verse 6 offered merely a prediction of what is likely to happen to murderers, then why add the explanation at the end of verse 6? That explanation offers justification for a *command* to execute murderers, but it is irrelevant to a prediction. Finally, even if one still questions whether this passage is a command, later provisions of the Pentateuch (cf. Num 35:16-21) require the murderer to be executed at the hand of the avenger.

A second issue raised in regard to this passage is that it focuses on retribution by a family member (one referred to as a "brother"). It nowhere enjoins the state to punish. However, one must remember the context of Genesis 9. Only eight people who were blood relatives (Noah and his family) were alive. Therefore, the language is proper, and it did relate in that instance to all of society. Moreover, the OT notion of kinmanship extends to more than just those in the immediate family (cf. Deut 15:2; 19:15-21, and especially Leviticus 25). The command in Genesis 9 is thus properly related to all society.

Another common objection to using Genesis 9 is that the prohibition is too general. It apparently covers all instances of murder, but cannot be so applied. The Pentateuch gives instructions for cities of refuge for those who murder unintentionally. Moreover, even in cases of intentional murder, the death penalty is not uniformly enforced (cf. Cain, Moses, and David).

In response, suffice it to say that exceptions to a general rule do not nullify the rule. They only limit its applicability. Gen 9:5-6 gives the general rule. The cities of refuge give a qualification for one type of murder, but not for all cases. We have already spoken to the exceptional cases of Cain, David, and Moses. They cannot invalidate the general rule.

A second key passage is Rom 13:1-7. Verse 1 teaches that all governments, even bad ones, are divinely ordained and that all people must be subject to them (v. 1). Those who disobey the government ultimately disobey God's ordinance (v. 2). Verses 3-4 are crucial. Paul asserts that governments, as God's ministers, are divinely authorized to reward those who do good and to punish evildoers. Verse 4 states that government is a minister of God, an avenger of wrath. Commentators agree that the sword

(v. 4) is the symbol of authority given to government to execute retributive justice.

Despite this teaching, Smedes thinks the passage does not necessarily teach capital punishment. He agrees that the sword symbolizes the state's right to punish evildoers, but nowhere does the passage explain how the sword is to be used. It could be used to execute, but it could be used otherwise. Thus, the passage neither mandates nor even permits capital punishment.[54]

Though we appreciate Smedes's concerns, on several grounds we think Romans 13 sanctions capital punishment. Obviously, Romans 13 speaks to government's general authority to punish wrongdoers, and in non-capital cases Paul is not likely using the sword to symbolize execution. However, Smedes thinks that even in capital cases the sword should not be understood to symbolize execution. On the contrary, commentators uniformly agree that the symbolism of the sword points to death. If the sword merely points to governmental authority, other symbols could convey that notion just as well. Why the sword? Moreover, Paul states that government is divinely empowered to dispense retribution. If it is to be retributive *justice*, the punishment must equal the crime. Given Paul's background, what was he likely to think would be just retribution for murder? Raised as a Hebrew of the Hebrews and a Pharisee of the Pharisees, would he not think of Mosaic teaching and Genesis 9? If that is so, it seems fairly obvious what Paul meant by the symbolism of the sword, at least as it would apply to capital cases. Finally, the Roman Empire in which Paul lived practiced capital punishment. Granted, the form was crucifixion, but given the wording of verse 4, it makes more sense to say the state "does not bear the sword in vain" than to say it "does not bear the cross in vain." Thus, Paul's historical context suggests the most likely understanding of the symbolism of sword. We conclude that Romans 13 (and Genesis 9) not only permit but mandate capital punishment.

A CASE FOR CAPITAL PUNISHMENT

Much of what we have already argued supports capital punishment, but it is also possible to gather several items from that material to make a brief positive case. We begin by reaffirming that justice is the issue at stake in capital punishment. The purpose of any penal and judicial system should be to distribute justice. Of course, that means retribution must fall on the disobedient. Moreover, Scripture authorizes the state to punish those who break laws (Rom 13:1-7). God's word speaks against vengeance, but as already noted, those passages speak about interpersonal relationships, not cases where individuals transgress the laws of God or the state. Then, as also noted, retribution and vengeance are not equivalent.

Second, man is a free moral agent and is thus responsible for his actions.

Regardless of how one understands freedom, the consensus of most theologians and philosophers and the scriptural teaching as well is that man
is free.[55] This is an important point, because a commonly accepted principle of morality is that no one is guilty for failing to do what he could not
do or guilty for doing what he could not fail to do. Put simply, no one is
morally responsible for an act unless he does it freely. Thus, if someone
commits a crime freely, he is morally responsible. Retribution cannot be
deemed unjust on the grounds that the criminal was forced against his will
to commit the crime.

Third, some reject retribution on the ground that the NT portrays God
as a God of love, mercy, and forgiveness. However, God practiced retribution in both OT and NT times. In fact, sometimes, as in the cases of
Ananias and Sapphira (Acts 5) and Herod (Acts 12:20-23), God directly
killed people in response to crimes we would not consider capital offenses.
Moreover, if God did not practice retribution, no one would suffer eternal punishment for rejecting Christ, but of course, that contradicts biblical teaching (see, e.g., Rev 20:11-15).

The preceding line of argument suggests that God practices retribution
and that the state may do the same in response to agents who freely break
its laws. In fact, given the state's intended purpose to uphold justice, it
must practice retribution. Of course, none of this *per se* demands capital
punishment as the particular punishment for murder or any other crime.
In order to establish the death penalty as appropriate for murder, appeal
must be made to scriptural teaching in Gen 9:5-6 and Rom 13:1-7. As
argued, those passages not only permit but mandate capital punishment
in cases of murder.

In sum, having assessed both non-biblical and scriptural arguments,
and in view of the line of argument offered in this section, we conclude
that the best evidence supports capital punishment as not only permissible but mandatory in cases of premeditated murder. Mercy can always be
extended by God when he wants, but man cannot presume to know when
that is. Moreover, abuses associated with capital punishment as practiced
today suggest a need for revision of its application, not elimination of it
altogether. For example, errors in conviction underscore a need for more
stringent regulations governing convictions in capital cases.
Discrimination against the poor and minorities argues for revamping our
judicial systems so as to remove those abuses as well. None of this, however, nullifies the need or the warrant to practice the death penalty.[56]

CAPITAL PUNISHMENT AND A PRO-LIFE ETHIC

Can one consistently argue against abortion and euthanasia and espouse
capital punishment? We think so on at least three grounds: a sanctity of
life ethic, a demand to treat all persons justly, and a commitment to non-

consequentialist ethics. Given a sanctity of life ethic, human life is sacred and must be protected. Hence, abortion and euthanasia are ruled out. Execution of murderers underscores the sanctity of life and the seriousness of taking the life of others. As to justice, the unborn, the aged, and the infirm have done nothing deserving of death. The convicted murderer has. Justice demands rejecting abortion and euthanasia and executing murderers. Finally, on a non-consequentialist theory of ethics such as ours, God prescribes the protection of the innocent and the punishment of those who take life. If one follows those divine commands, he will have to reject abortion and euthanasia and favor capital punishment.[57]

Before leaving this issue of consistency, we should note that one can also consistently favor abortion and euthanasia and reject capital punishment. Such a position could be held consistently on at least two grounds: a quality of life ethic and a commitment to utilitarianism. With a quality of life ethic, the unborn, aged and infirm can be considered non-persons and thus expendable, whereas the convicted murderer qualifies as a person and has a right to life. Likewise, as noted in previous chapters, on utilitarian grounds one can also justify abortion and euthanasia while ruling out capital punishment.

The net result is that on these three matters of life and death one may hold either combination of views without contradicting oneself. Since that is so, neither should be rejected on the grounds that the ethicist contradicts himself. A decision on which set of positions should be held ultimately rests on which views are supported by the best arguments. Our conclusion is that the best biblical and non-biblical arguments favor the death penalty and oppose abortion and euthanasia.

CHAPTER SIX

Sexual Morality

We hardly need to be reminded in Western culture that we live in a sex-charged society. Everything from automobiles and underwear to vacations and wine is sold on its sex appeal. Sometimes the solicitation is explicit, but more often than not the appeal is implicit, hidden and quite subtle. People too often do not realize that they desire and buy objects because of their sexual attraction. The media contributes greatly to this situation. Michael A. Carrera, who teaches at Hunter College in New York and is director of Adolescent Sexuality Programs for The Children's Aid Society, says there are about twenty thousand scenes on television each year that suggest sexual acts, all of them without regard to the outcome. Such programming suggests that this is what "real" men are all about.[1]

Ed Pitts, director of Health and Environmental Services for the National Urban League, points out that parents are also major factors in making sex such a prominent element in the lives of their children. They encourage their sons in particular to "get involved." He says, "In most homes, both fathers and mothers seem to be concerned about their sons' appeal to girls. Covertly, they *want* their sons to be sexually active—to be 'manly.' So, besides peer pressure, there is a kind of unspoken pressure at home."[2] While not all parents encourage sexual experimentation, Pitts is right in pointing out that at least some do.

One reason human sexuality has such a prominent place in modern life is its importance. Christians have often been portrayed as viewing sexual activity even within marriage as at best necessary and at worst intrinsically evil. Though some Christians may feel this way, none should. Human sexuality is a good gift from God. And the church has a great stake in sexual morality. Strong relationships between husbands and wives and between parents and children are an important part of the fabric of society. When the church and individuals are unsuccessful in directing this powerful human drive, the state often feels it must step in because of the social consequences. On the other hand, there are those who oppose any intervention into the realm of personal morality by either church or state, contending that one ought to maximize one's pleasure without any restrictions, as long as those actions harm no one else. As long as participants are consenting adults and children are not involved, some feel they should be free to do as they please.

In light of this bewildering array of voices, we think it important to discuss sexual morality. In this chapter we shall discuss sexual morality before marriage, within marriage and the issue of masturbation. Various positions will be examined along with their justification. Each will be critically analyzed from a Christian perspective. Before turning directly to discuss sexual morality before marriage, it might be helpful to note some key changes that have contributed to contemporary attitudes about premarital and extramarital sex.

CHANGING ATTITUDES ON SEX

The value system of any culture lends structure and organization to it, and a major element in any culture's value system is its understanding of human sexuality. For the first half of this century, there was a general consensus in Western culture on this matter. This is not to deny that moral norms were often broken or that elements of the consensus underwent change. However, the central constituents (rejection of incest, adultery, and divorce, as well as the approval of lifelong, monogamous marriage) remained reasonably the same. As many note, the value system was not too dissimilar from the one found in the NT, though for many the values were not derived from the Scriptures. To this rough approximation of the NT view of human sexuality two unbiblical elements were often added. First, a double standard was practiced that tolerated a man who broke the rules but condemned a woman who did the same. Second, the sexual impulse was often attributed to the lower aspects of human nature. What resulted was a negative or "degraded" view of human sexuality.[3]

The decade between 1945 and 1955 saw the traditional consensus on sexuality erode. The Sexual Revolution began in this period. Monogamy was not universally praised; penicillin and the pill removed three of the most undesirable consequences of promiscuity: infection, detection and conception.

Over the last half of this century at least six factors have influenced a striking shift in our culture's attitude toward sexuality. The first is *secularism*. This is the view that God must be removed from all areas of human thought and activity. One of the outworkings of this belief has been a move to value-free sex education in our schools. Biblical and theological reasons for moral behavior have been removed from this teaching, and that has had an important impact on sexual attitudes. Without divine absolutes governing sexuality, one is left to personal preferences.

A second factor is *privatization*. It is commonly held that many areas of life, especially one's sexual preferences, are one's own business. Neither the state nor the church should interfere. Third, there is the matter of *scientific frankness*. Freud taught that the sex impulse is fundamental to our nature as human beings, that sexuality is open to enormous repression, and that by examining our unconscious we can neutralize our obsessions. To many this meant that any attempt to limit sexual expression is psychologically harmful, and even capable of making one insane. Thus, it was thought to be healthy to throw off restraint. Moreover, this scientific approach made sex appear to be a "thing" that could be studied, analyzed and modified. It seemed less mysterious.

Media exposure is a fourth factor. With the rise of modern technology the forms of public communication have multiplied. They reach us in our homes, cars, and in the workplace. And seldom do we encounter these media without some appeal to sex. So common is this experience that we are barely aware of it. This constant bombardment of depersonalized, seductive sex seems normal.

Part of the media exposure of sex includes the explosion of pornography, which glorifies all forms of sexual expression. It is not just the increasingly more explicit pictures that are so influential in contemporary attitudes and activities. It is the philosophy that accompanies these pictures that has been tremendously detrimental. Whereas earlier in this century certain forms of sexual permissiveness were unthinkable, the Playboy philosophy relentlessly expounded by Hugh Hefner and others has anesthetized modern society to the idea that any of this might be wrong.

A fifth factor can be called *existential schizophrenia*. Reality and personal meaning have been divorced. The real is what is scientifically quantifiable and verifiable. Emotions such as love and purpose are not quantifiable. Therefore, they are not real, but they have personal meaning. What results is a distinction between values and behavior. Values such as "love" and "community" are praised, while their application is left up to the individual. In the case of sexual ethics, the divorce between value and behavior often leads to sex simply for personal gratification without any thought for the other person.

Therapeutic values are a final factor. Values that govern the counselor in his or her work are becoming the values of society as a whole. The counselor must be accepting, sympathetic and understanding if the client is to be helped. Hence, there is reluctance to condemn any expression of one's feelings and needs as wrong. While these methods of dealing with people

have great pastoral worth, they should not be isolated from moral obligation. If they are, one becomes accepting of any behavior whether it is
right or wrong.[4]

SEXUAL MORALITY BEFORE MARRIAGE
ATTITUDES TOWARD PREMARITAL SEX

As the values of modern culture changed, so did the behavior of those living in it. This has been especially noticeable in regard to premarital sex,
as evidenced in a number of recent surveys that asked about attitudes
toward and practice of sex before marriage. Consider the following
examples.

U.S. News & World Report included a special report on ethics in its
December 9, 1985 edition. One question asked, "Is it wrong for a man
and a woman to have sexual relations before marriage?" Thirty-six percent said it was wrong, but 61 percent thought it was morally acceptable.
In the youngest age group questioned, the favorable response was even
higher, with 78 percent approving.[5]

A Parade survey of eleven million teenage boys in 1988 found that two-
thirds of them claimed to have had sex with a girl, most of them by the
time they were fifteen. About half thought that one should wait until sixteen to have sex, two-thirds of them calling sex under fourteen "risky."
Each year Planned Parenthood reports that 1.1 million girls aged fifteen
to nineteen become pregnant. Typically, boys go as far as girls will let
them.[6]

During 1989 the Gallup Organization took a survey for the Christian
Broadcasting Network. Sixty-nine percent of the students surveyed said
they believe premarital sex is not wrong, and 56 percent approved of living together in trial marriages. Furthermore, half said they had more than
one sex partner, 24 percent reporting five or more. Half said they had sex
at least occasionally, while 26 percent claimed they engaged in the practice "regularly."[7]

Finally, in a Seventeen Magazine survey, 44 percent of the girls and 54
percent of the boys thought there was nothing wrong with premarital sex.
Moreover, by age fifteen 24 percent of both boys and girls reported having had sex. This percentage goes up dramatically as they get older. By
eighteen 60 percent have engaged in sex, and by twenty-one 82 percent
have. In this survey only 39 percent of the girls and 32 percent of the boys
said people should wait until marriage for sex.[8]

VIEWS ON PREMARITAL SEX

In contemporary thinking, three views on premarital sex are significant,
and they deserve our attention. We have called them the natural impulse
view, the affection view, and the abstinence view.

The Natural Impulse View

This position is extremely liberal. One common form of it is the Playboy morality. This view says sex is a natural human impulse or instinct. Now that contraceptives are easily available and extremely reliable, sex should be seen as a purely pleasurable physical experience. Just as good food can be enjoyed in a variety of settings, so one can enjoy a casual sexual encounter with someone without deep feelings of love and affection. Fulfillment of one's sexual desire need not be limited to a single partner nor accompanied with feelings of love. Many who hold this view admit that love does tend to enhance sex with greater meaning, but they believe that most people at some time in their lives find themselves sexually attracted to an individual for whom they have little or no affection. Thus, greater human happiness is attained if people can take whatever pleasure they can get from sex without the burden of moral guilt, as long as they do not satisfy their sexual urges by using a partner involuntarily, hurtfully or deceitfully.[9]

Supports

Commonly offered arguments for this position are as follows. First, sex is a natural impulse or instinct, and, it is argued, it ought to be followed. Jean Jacques Rousseau thought humanity in the wild state was naturally good and happy. Mankind had been spoiled by society. Thus, one ought to return to the wild state.[10] A second argument claims sexual repression is bad. Christianity and Victorian ethics are the primary culprits. They have given sex a bad name and are responsible for most of the sexual repression. This repression has resulted in a variety of neuroses, even insanity. Thus, free sexual expression is healthy and ought to be pursued.[11] Third, mankind has an obligation to maximize pleasure. Some, though not all, defend free love on the basis of hedonistic utilitarianism (the view that we ought to act to maximize pleasure). Thus, any act that would increase pleasure ought to be performed, or at least it should not be prohibited. Finally, it is also argued that the burden of proof rests on those who would limit our behavior. *Prima facie*, any act is right. The burden of moral persuasion rests with those who would interfere or condemn what we can do. In the absence of such arguments, we are free to do whatever we want and whatever gives us pleasure.[12]

Objections

Clearly, from a Christian perspective this approach to human sexuality in general and premarital sex in particular is unacceptable. Moreover, there are also good reasons for rejecting this philosophy that have nothing to do with Christian belief. Some objections we shall raise question the morality of this view, while others question its wisdom. As a result, we reject this view as both immoral and imprudent. We also note that most of the objections to the affection view apply equally here and vice versa. For the sake of brevity, we offer each set of objections only once.

An initial objection questions whether hedonistic utilitarianism is an appropriate justification for moral commands. Anyone who rejects such a theory of ethics, as we do, will not find this understanding of premarital sex morally acceptable. Put another way, are we obligated to act to maximize pleasure? While there is certainly nothing wrong with pleasure, we may question whether it is the highest human good and whether all ways of pursuing it are moral, even if it is the highest good. Moreover, sometimes we are obligated to perform acts that are painful, and we are not morally justified in avoiding those acts just because we would like to pursue pleasure instead. For example, we are obligated to pay a debt rather than spend the money on a vacation, though that act may not bring us pleasure. All of these considerations lead us to believe that this view of premarital sex and the underlying ethical theory that supports it are unacceptable.

Second, is what is wild or natural naturally good? Rousseau advanced his theory two hundred years ago, but no happy "natural" humanity, unspoiled by society, has been located. Instead, men and women seem inevitably to form societies, and societies set limits on sexual behavior. Moreover, humans are not without restraints even in the so-called wild. God has written his moral law on their hearts, even if they have no written revelation (Rom 2:14-16).[13]

Third, even if one grants for the sake of argument that hedonistic utilitarianism is correct, there are still some aspects of sex for pleasure that raise questions about whether it is moral when considered against the background of that moral theory. That is, given a hedonistic utilitarian approach, one is obligated to do (and it is moral to do) whatever brings the most pleasure. But, then, casual sex cannot in all circumstances be morally right, for certain factors are likely to reduce its pleasure. For example, it is not unlikely that the couple, especially teenagers, will lack a suitable and completely private place, making it necessary to perform the sex act hurriedly and uncomfortably. While this problem does not confront all who engage in casual sex, for those who experience it, it lowers the pleasure value of the act and, hence, on a hedonistic approach lowers the morality of the act. Moreover, regardless of what they say about feeling no guilt, couples who engage in casual sex are likely to sense some anxiety in performing an act which is still generally socially forbidden. While one might respond that even reduced pleasure is pleasure, it is worth noting that almost always in the case of casual premarital sex it is trivial pleasure at best.[14] Moreover, if one uses hedonism to justify the act, one is obligated by that ethical theory to do what brings the most pleasure, not just what brings some enjoyment.

Fourth, the possibility of unwanted pregnancy is always present, and that raises questions about the wisdom of following this view. As already noted, Planned Parenthood reports that 1.1 million American girls between fifteen and nineteen become pregnant every year. The fact that we possess modern contraceptive devices makes it too easy to forget that *no* device is 100 percent effective. The fact that the largest percentage of abortions are obtained by unwed women (see Chapter 2) is a vivid reminder that many who aren't expecting to get pregnant (or never think about it at all) become pregnant, anyway. Unwanted pregnancies occur not just because people use contraceptives that fail. A major reason stems from the fact that contraceptives may be used improperly or not at all. Such an eventuality is increased when partners are engaged in casual sex. Since there is no established relationship or genuine love between them, neither may care enough about the other to take the necessary precautions. Moreover, both the strength of one's sexual drive and the lure of spontaneous lovemaking tempt casual sex partners to throw caution out the window.[15] A number of social problems have resulted from the rising number of unwanted pregnancies: the feminization of poverty, the increase in single-parent families, and, as noted, the alarming number of abortions.

Fifth, sexually transmitted diseases such as AIDS are at epidemic proportions and are strong objections against this view as imprudent. Those engaged in casual sex are most at risk for several reasons. For one thing, they are the most likely to engage in sex without adequate protection. Moreover, surveys show that they tend to have multiple partners. Some of these partners are casual acquaintances at best, and their sexual habits and history are unknown. That this is a real problem can be seen from the surveys mentioned earlier. Figures from those surveys indicate that a majority of those responding did not think premarital sex was wrong, but 42 percent of the girls and 43 percent of the boys from this same group worried that they might get AIDS someday.[16]

Sixth, casual or recreational sex, as it is sometimes called, lacks full meaning or significance for the partners. This is an important objection. The act of sexual intercourse lacks full meaning for casual partners, because it does not grow out of a life context "of past shared activities, present joint life, and future commitment that marriage can give. . . ."[17] In 1 Cor 6:12-20 Paul says emphatically that even the casual act of sex makes the couple "one flesh."[18] Sexual unchastity is not an act external to the partners; it affects one to the very core of his or her being. Paul teaches that the sex act does not have a certain meaning to one partner and something else to the other. It is not something we give meaning to by our choice or circumstances. Rather, it is already filled with meaning, and we disregard this to our own harm. In becoming "one flesh" with another, one has less to give to the love of his or her life. He or she "has memories, expectations, lessons from his [or her] experience; and these lessons go to the root of his [or her] character."[19] Those who took part in the Playboy experiment eventually found that they wanted love more than sex, a relationship more than pleasure.

Finally, the Bible explicitly prohibits sex before marriage.[20] In the OT era, if a man had intercourse with a virgin, he was required to marry her and to pay the bride price to her father (Deut 22:28-29). Men were also warned against sex with prostitutes (Prov 5; 7:5, 25-27). In the NT Paul rejects all forms of sexual immorality (1 Cor 5:9; 6:12-20; Eph 5:3-5; 1 Thess 4:1-8) and warns against becoming one with a prostitute (1 Cor 6:15-16).

The Affection View

Over the last twenty-five years a new ethic has emerged. It might be called the affection view or the ethic of intimacy. At first, this position seems not substantially different from the previous view, because those who hold it expect to have a number of sexual partners during their lifetime. However, it is quite different. Proponents of this view are at least moderately positive toward marriage. Less is said about the repression of sex in modern society. Sexual freedom is praised, but it is not an end in itself. Rather, it is to be guided by the ideal of intimacy. Intimacy is not identical with love. It is a feeling that two people may have for one another for a night, for a year, or for a lifetime. Intimacy is not something that can be planned; it just happens. And when it does, you will know it. There are no ethical absolutes to guide behavior, but only attitudinal ones such as openness and caring. Whereas traditionally marriage was required for sex, those who hold the affection view see couples going in and out of relationships. They go together, sleep together, live together, and then, if things work out, ratify their relationship by marriage.[21]

Supports

It is easier to give an outline of this view than to offer arguments for it. That is because so much is assumed about sexuality and personal freedom. The justification for the ethic of intimacy, however, can be described. It begins by claiming that sex is good. It is not related to our lower nature. Sex is inherently and completely good as long as it is done with someone you love. Casual sexual experiences will occur. They are excusable, but they are not to be taken as the ideal. Sexual intercourse is an expression of a loving and caring relationship.[22]

Second, each partner must retain his or her independence. Anything else would be stifling. Even in an ongoing and stable relationship each member must retain independence. Each has his or her own needs, and those needs are paramount. One partner never has the right to control the other. A covenant that binds one individual to another is to be rejected; one's primary obligation is to oneself.[23]

Third, the right to intimacy is created by compatibility, not covenant.

Compatibility is not primarily sexual compatibility, but affinity in personality and psychology. Compatibility just "happens." You "click," "receive good vibes," or "are attracted to your partner." As should be easily seen, one's personality and psychology change over time. Thus, someday you may find that you and your lover are no longer compatible, and for you, divorce is morally right, or at least not wrong.[24]

Fourth, sex is a private matter. Under the old consensus, society felt it had the right, even the obligation, to protect itself and to punish those who violated its norms. However, what you do and with whom is entirely up to you.[25]

Fifth, sex can be engaged in with no "strings attached." The idea that passage from virginity to experience involves a profound personal change is wrong. Today people make less of individual sexual encounters. One is expected to have many experiences with sex and with partners. Some will be good, and others not so good. Each new partner is a chance to start afresh.[26]

Sixth, there is no double standard in matters of sex. Women are to be treated exactly like men in sexual ethics. If indiscretion is excusable for one, it is also for the other.[27]

Finally, sex demands maturity. Since there are no absolute principles to guide one sexually, a number of variables in any situation must be weighed to determine if sexual intercourse is acceptable. This requires maturity. Though proponents of this position do not like to say this, they think that children under sixteen are too young for sex and ought to be told so.[28]

Objections

While the affection or intimacy view is an improvement over the natural impulse view, it too is open to serious objections. First, affection, love and intimacy as defined in this view are too weak to deal with the impulses that make up human sexuality. As Stafford says, "It is like walking a lion on a leash. Sometimes he goes where you want him to. Sometimes he will not. Sometimes he turns around and devours you."[29] In the passion of the moment, one can convince himself or herself that anything is love. Moreover, there is a certain passivity and fatalism connected with this ethic. Compatibility is something that strikes a relationship like lightning strikes a building. In contrast, a Christian ethic places one's will, not emotions, at the heart of human behavior. Love is seen in and fostered by action. True intimacy is developed through persistent self-sacrifice.[30]

Second, sex involves the expression of the total person. It grows out of lives that are fully shared. Even in stable relationships based on love but without commitment, sexual activities are emphasized at the expense of other activities. This can be true for married couples, as some share little of their lives except for the sex act itself. However, it is not as likely in marriage where the sex partners have opportunity over an extended period of time to grow as persons and to learn to share their lives together and where they must of necessity participate in many joint endeavors related to home and family.[31]

Third, the sex act may overcommit the couple to each other. We have previously spoken of the bonding effect of sexual intercourse. Where bonding is thought to be based on love, it may in fact intensify emotional involvement and lead a couple to make a commitment too quickly. Because a couple has great sex does not mean they will have a great marriage. Sexual compatibility may lead a couple who are badly mismatched in other areas to get married. This lack of general compatibility will in time affect their sexual affinity, and the relationship will not survive.[32]

Fourth, premarital sex destroys the possibility of sharing something unique to that marriage. On the other hand, if sexual intercourse is reserved for marriage, marital sex gains added significance.[33]

Thus, while a stable and loving sexual partnership avoids some of the most damaging consequences of casual sex (less meaningful sexual acts, anxiety about the circumstances surrounding the sex act, and danger of disease), this position in the end is not in keeping with biblical teaching.

The Abstinence View

This is the most conservative view. It has often been justified from Scripture and the examples of personal and social behavior that are thought to be ordained therein. God has spoken and has prohibited certain sexual practices as immoral. Not all, however, who advocate this position do so on the basis of divine revelation. There are those who justify the conservative view on the basis of a utilitarian interest in the maximization of human happiness. Certain practices about sexual behavior, however arbitrary, are essential to the maintenance of a sense of community and, in turn, to human happiness.

C. S. Lewis states the abstinence view succinctly: "Either marriage, with complete faithfulness to your partner, or else total abstinence."[34] He also goes on to note that chastity is the most unpopular of the Christian virtues. It is recognized that sex is both natural and enjoyable, but it should never be used merely for physical gratification. Rather, it should be the expression of deep love and affection. Moreover, it should have procreation as one of its ultimate purposes. The limitation of sex to marriage is necessary for the forming and maintaining of family units. The restriction of sex to marriage will encourage people to get married and stay married. The prohibition of sex outside of marriage will tend to strengthen marriages.[35]

Supports
Arguments for the abstinence position have served in a number of instances as objections to the previous positions. Nevertheless, we briefly

review them here. First, those who think the Bible is the revealed word of God believe that abstinence is clearly taught both in the OT and the NT. Premarital sex and prostitution are condemned in both testaments. For example, in the OT, the following verses teach that premarital sex and adultery are wrong: Exod 20:14; 22:16, 17; Lev 18:20; 20:10, 14; 21:13; Deut 22:15, 17, 20-21; Prov 23:27. NT teaching to the same effect is found in 1 Cor 5:1; 6:9, 13, 18; Eph 5:3; 1 Thess 4:3-8. Moreover, the following verses from both testaments teach that harlotry or prostitution is wrong: Lev 19:29; 20:5, 6 (here in connection with idols); Deut 23:18; Prov 23:27; 1 Cor 6:13-18.

Second, it is argued that the sex act involves the whole person, bonding physically and psychologically two individuals in a unique way. Therefore, while sex may bring gratification to two uncommitted partners, in at least some cases that pleasure is trivial and fleeting. Moreover, limiting sex to marriage encourages individuals to get married and stay married. The development of solid family units makes for a stable society and for human happiness. Conversely, where all the benefits of marriage are available without any of its responsibilities, society, and particularly children, will suffer.

Third, in a marriage where both partners are absolutely faithful to one another, the likelihood of contracting a sexually transmitted disease is almost nonexistent. With sexually transmitted diseases on the rise and with the threat of spreading AIDS by heterosexual promiscuity, this consideration is of growing importance.

Finally, while abstinence does not entirely eliminate the problem of unwanted pregnancies, it greatly reduces it. Young women who are sexually active before marriage have the most abortions.[36] If abortion is morally wrong, as has been argued earlier in this book, then this is a powerful reason for abstinence.

Objections and Answers

A number of objections can be imagined, but we believe they are answerable. For example, some object to the abstinence view by noting that problem and unwanted pregnancies do occur among married couples, and this is not taken as an argument against sex within marriage. Moreover, not all pregnancies that occur as the result of premarital sex are problematic or unwanted. A couple planning to get married might be quite happy with the birth of a child. Similarly, a single parent who is willing, even happy, to raise such a child would not be creating a problem or unwanted pregnancy. Finally, if the couples who are sexually active before marriage are willing to put any child conceived up for adoption, then the problem of abortion could be avoided, and a childless couple would be given a most desired and priceless possession, a baby.[37]

Several responses are in order at this point. First, since God condemns such practices, they are wrong or immoral. Second, one's mitigating some of the unhappy consequences of an immoral act does not make that act morally permissible. Utilitarian justifications of certain actions lead to just these kinds of moral dilemmas. Third, at the time of the sex act one cannot possibly know that all of the mitigating circumstances will follow without any of the problematic ones. We do know that premarital sex allows too many victims.

Finally, common experience teaches us that promises of lovers made in private are rarely reliable. Society has always required that lovers make their promises public. They should commit themselves to one another before church, state, family and *creator*. This public commitment strengthens personal commitments that may be weak or unstable. While public promises are no panacea, they do lend support to the relationship. Too often couples who thought they were committed to each other for life have found out only a few months later that they were not. Even in cases where a couple lives together for a long period of time, their relationship falls short of marital commitment. Living together, even at its best, is an experiment. The door out of the relationship is always left open.[38]

SEXUAL MORALITY WITHIN MARRIAGE

Both the OT and NT teach procreative, monogamous marriage as normative. God made human beings male and female in his own image (Gen 1:27). Human sexual differences or human sexuality are a part of God's design and are said to be good (Gen 1:31), not irreligious or immoral. Sexuality was ordained by God not only for reproduction (Gen 1:26-28), but also for social and personal enrichment (Gen 2:18-25). The fact that Adam was alone was not good, so God created Eve. Adam's response was one of delight. Scripture emphasizes their oneness: "For this reason a man will leave his father and mother and be united to his wife, and they will become *one flesh*." Marriage requires a separation from all other family ties. And finally, the original relationship between man and woman is an eloquent description of intimacy: "The man and his wife were both naked, and they felt no shame." God's original purpose was that husband and wife should be together in shameless nakedness. There was complete freedom; it was natural.

The OT also shows that God's ideal was not always practiced. Marriage in Israel was often polygamous until the time of the monarchy in the tenth century B.C. (cf. Gen 29:21-30; 2 Sam 5:13-16; 1 Kgs 11:1, 3). However, this was not God's ideal, as can be ascertained from the creation account and the many instances where many wives were a source of difficulty, even leading to idolatry. Concubinage (Gen 16:1-4; 30:1-13) was practiced, and levirate marriage was commanded to raise up heirs for a deceased family member (Gen 38:8; Deut 25:5-10). Divorce was permitted (Deut 24:1-4; cf. Mal 2:14-16) but was surely not God's wish.

That sex within the bonds of marriage is good can be seen in the Song of Solomon. The Song of Solomon or Song of Songs is a book extolling the virtues of married love between a husband and a wife. It portrays the tender, passionate eroticism of lovers without reference to procreation.

The NT reaffirms much that is said in the OT. Marriage is a one flesh relationship (Matt 19:3-8; Mark 10:2-9). Divorce, while permitted, is discouraged, practices at that time being very lax (Matt 19:9-11). Marital fidelity was commanded for both wife and husband.

The one extended treatment of sexual ethics in the NT is found in 1 Corinthians 7. There Paul says that sexual desire is a legitimate reason for marrying (vv. 2, 9, 36-37). Both husband and wife have a sexual duty to each other (v. 3). Each partner's body does not belong to himself or herself *alone* (v. 4). Therefore, neither is to deprive the other from the performance of that sexual duty *except* by mutual consent for a time in order to give oneself to prayer (v. 5).

As to adultery, both the OT and NT condemn it. In the OT theocracy it was punishable by death (Lev 20:10; Deut 22:22; cf. Exod 20:14; Lev 18:20; Deut 5:18). Note that there is no double standard. Both parties to adultery were to be put to death. In the NT, adultery is condemned by Jesus in his teachings (Matt 5:27-28; John 8:3-11) and by Paul as a part of a vice list (1 Cor 6:9). It has been noted that two sexual commands dominate both Testaments: "Do not commit adultery," and "Do not covet . . . your neighbor's wife."[39]

Jesus also taught about lust, "adultery of the heart." There is disagreement as to whether Jesus was strengthening the OT teaching or simply explaining its true intent. Whatever the case, he was teaching that the adulterous thought was as wrong as the adulterous act. Adultery of the heart violates the command not to covet one's neighbor's wife. Jesus was as concerned about the thought as he was about the act. While the act harms the marriage, lust harms the one lusting by confusing and distorting the shape of his desire. The idea that adultery of the heart will never bring harm is wrong. It has already. Desire has gone astray.

Commands against lust appear throughout the NT (e.g., Matt 5:28; Eph 2:3; 1 Thess 4:3-8, particularly v. 5; 2 Tim 2:22; Tit 3:3; 1 Pet 2:11; 4:2, 3; 1 John 2:16). These commands warn us that we live in a fallen world and that we must constantly guard against wrong desires. Desire for one's spouse is good; lust for someone who is not is wrong. God has given us his Holy Spirit to enable us to obey his commands and to receive his forgiveness when we fail.[40]

Objections to fidelity in marriage are few. Not many are so bold as to encourage adultery, even though it is on the increase in our society. A chief argument offered in favor of adultery is that marriage need not be conceived of as a lifelong covenant. Some argue that even if adulterous relationships take place behind a cloak of deceit or the breaking of a covenant, they might be justifiable on some other utilitarian grounds (e.g., an affair might actually help a marriage). Still others hold that even if adultery might be harmful to the institution of marriage, that assumes that the Western, Judeo-Christian views of marriage and childbearing are good and deserving of preservation, and that need not be the case.[41]

None of these objections is very convincing. Marriage is commanded by God to be a lifelong relationship, and therefore, vows should promise fidelity to death. It is difficult to see how even a utilitarian justification of adultery would be possible in most cases of adultery in that one may question how such a relationship really helps a marriage. Some people say it helps, but we doubt that even in cases where it may seem to help in the short run, it is positive for a marriage in the long run. Moreover, we have argued that utilitarianism is not the way for a Christian to make ethical decisions. And finally, we are not simply talking about a Western view of sex and marriage. We are defending God's view of marriage as set forth in creation. This is binding not simply on those who accept the Judeo-Christian faith or live in Western cultures, but on all people.

MASTURBATION

One of the most difficult and controversial questions in the area of sexual ethics or morality is the question of masturbation or autostimulation. Not only are secular psychologists disagreed on this issue, but so are Christians. Thus, we realize that not everyone will agree with our conclusions on this matter. However, to help the discussion we shall treat the extent of the problem, present a variety of Christian views on the subject, and finally offer our own thinking.

THE EXTENT OF THE PROBLEM OR PRACTICE

Social scientists estimate that perhaps as many as 90 percent of males have masturbated. However, this is not simply a male practice. While the figures are a bit lower for females, a majority of them have masturbated. This sexual practice, along with the self-loathing that often accompanies it, frequently dominates adolescence. But, again, this is not simply a problem of adolescence. Surveys show that it is practiced by many within a happy marriage that is sexually satisfying. Even more adults, male and female, practice autostimulation after divorce or death of a mate and the return to singleness. Thus, one simply cannot avoid addressing the practice.

In addition to the widespread practice of masturbation, the lack of consensus about its rightness or wrongness makes this a difficult problem. In a recent *Christianity Today* survey, 31 percent of laypersons and 30 percent of pastors thought it was right; 32 percent of laypersons and 35 percent of pastors thought it was wrong; and 37 percent of laypersons and 35 percent of pastors thought it depends on the individual situation.[42]

CHRISTIAN VIEWS ON MASTURBATION

Where there is lack of clarity about a practice, there is usually a variety of views. For many years the dominant, if not exclusive, view within the Christian church was that masturbation was always morally wrong. Arguments used to support this view were as follows: since masturbation is always accompanied by lust, usually for someone that is not one's spouse, it is forbidden. Second, it is done for self-gratification, but that end has not had much respect among Christians throughout church history. Finally, at one time it was claimed, even on the basis of scientific evidence, that it led to insanity, sterility and a whole host of mental and physical disorders.[43]

Modern science has shown that whether masturbation is right or wrong morally, it is not the cause of insanity, sterility, birth defects, and so forth. It is possible for one to be so consumed by sexual desire and to practice masturbation so regularly that he or she may become so guilt ridden that psychological disorders may appear. However, these disorders are not attributable to the practice alone. Thus, some Christians have taken a more tolerant view toward the practice.

Miles is such an example.[44] He argues that if masturbation is used sparingly and within certain limits by teenage boys (though not by girls) until marriage, it is morally permissible. His thinking can be summarized as follows. The practice is widespread, indicating a need. Sexual desire is strong in young boys and must have some outlet, as can be seen in nocturnal emissions. Girls do not experience similar emissions. Masturbation, however, must be practiced sparingly so that it does not become an obsession. Lust is not to be a part of the experience, as one is to focus on the goodness of God in granting such a gift and thank God for providing a partner at some later time in life to fulfill this need. Finally, the practice must cease upon marriage.

A third view is that of Tim Stafford.[45] He has written widely about sex to adolescents. In a *Campus Life* column dealing with the issue, he neither condemns nor condones the practice. He gives the impression that the decision is left within reason to the individual.

AUTHORS' VIEWS

Recognizing that this is a controversial and difficult issue, we realize that we must avoid as much as possible concluding more than Scripture and reason allow. However, we believe some things can and should be said. First, we note that Scripture never directly addresses masturbation. Therefore, any decision on this matter must grow out of the application of biblical principles. Second, where masturbation includes lust or desire for someone other than one's spouse, Scripture passages already cited against lust clearly condemn it. Third, 1 Cor 7:3-5 says that the only acceptable reason for failing in one's duty to one's spouse is abstinence for the purpose of prayer (and that only for a designated time). If, on the other hand, *masturbation* prevents one from performing one's duty to one's mate, it disobeys the teaching of this passage and is wrong.

Fourth, much depends on how one defines masturbation. In contemporary discussion, the term has been used not only for self-stimulation, but also for mutual arousal and climax by one's spouse apart from intercourse.[46] When defined this broadly, there are, we think, some cases where masturbation is not wrong. For example, if the husband's sperm count is low and must be collected to impregnate his wife, we think it is morally permissible for his wife to stimulate him to climax.[47] Moreover, where there is no sexual intercourse for reasons such as impotence or a wife's menstrual period, we think that stimulation between a married couple leading to climax is not wrong.

Finally, are any other instances of masturbation morally permissible? Without knowledge of the specifics of a case, it is hard to say that all other cases are definitely wrong. Where the act includes elements such as lust and failure to perform one's sexual duty to one's mate, the act is contrary to scriptural teaching, and we condemn it. Where the act becomes such a habit that it enslaves one, again it is immoral. Moreover, we cannot agree with Miles's double standard that says it may be morally permissible for teenage boys, but not for girls. If it is wrong for one, it is wrong for the other, and vice versa. But beyond these general guidelines, there may be other instances that are permissible. It is just difficult to make such judgments in abstraction from particular cases.

CHAPTER SEVEN

Birth Control

Duning the last half of the twentieth century there has been a steady increase in the use of birth control devices. This is true of Christians and non-Christians alike. Despite a long tradition of hesitation in regard to birth control, both pragmatic and biblical considerations have led many Christians to conclude that birth control is morally acceptable.

From a pragmatic standpoint, advocates of birth control emphasize three main issues. First, some cite population growth and apparent depletion of natural resources as warrant for population control. Recent literature has called into question the validity of such concerns.[1] We cannot here address the question of whether there is a genuine crisis because of population figures, but it is instructive to see some of the figures that have led many to conclude there is a crisis. For example, it is estimated that it took until around 1750 to produce the first billion people who had ever lived. Within the next hundred years (by the 1850s) a second billion were born. By the mid-1970s more than four billion had been born, and in the 1980s world population topped the five billion mark.[2] As of 1990, the population had reached 5,292,000,000.[3] This means there are now more people alive than the total of people born from the dawn of history to at least 1900. Writing in 1973, one writer stated that world population was increasing at the rate of 1.8 percent a year. At that rate it would take thirty-seven years to double.[4] Between 1980 and 1990 world population was still increasing at 1.7 percent.[5] The World Population Congress that met in Hungary in 1974 corroborated these figures. It estimated that if population continues to grow at the rate of 2 percent (and it was growing that fast every year between 1950 and 1974), world population would double every thirty-five years.[6] Population figures in Far Eastern, Latin American, and other developing nations are especially enormous.[7]

Historically, the three main checks to population growth have been war, hunger, and disease. Wars and starvation still abound, and yet population growth continues. The reason is undoubtedly due in part to medicine's growing ability to control disease and prolong life. In our chapter on euthanasia we cited figures on increasing life expectancy. In addition, reduction in infant mortality and the number of mothers who die in childbirth increases population. Though figures in the U.S. are surely better than in lesser developed countries, they seem suggestive of the trend. For example, in 1930 among U.S. whites, maternal mortality was 670 per 100,000 live births, but as late as the early 1970s it was down to 20 in 100,000.[8] As of 1988, maternal mortality was down to 8.4 in 100,000 in the U.S.[9] Worldwide, it is estimated that until about 1630 the world probably had a birth rate of about 45 per 1000 and a death rate of about 43 or 44 per 1000. By the early 1970s there was a birth rate of 40 per 1000, but the world death rate had slipped to 19 per 1000.[10] Between 1980 and 1985 the world average birth rate was 27, but the death rate slipped to 11 per 1000.[11] Between 1985 and 1990 the average birth rate remained the same, but the death rate was only 10 per every 1000.[12]

As to depletion of natural resources, countries such as the U.S. are among the worst at overconsumption. A U.S. Senate report found that Americans consumed in the decade of 1959-68 more of the world's resources than had previously been consumed by all the people who had ever lived. It is estimated that if the whole world consumed at the American rate, it would take approximately six years to deplete all known petroleum reserves.[13] At current rates of consumption such resources as coal, copper and aluminum would not last through the twenty-first century.[14] In addition to overconsumption there is the problem of overpollution. We are all familiar with such problems as the hole in the ozone layer, toxic waste disposal, and the garbage explosion.

A second pragmatic item influencing many to favor birth control methods stems from a change in sexual mores. Part of the shift in sexual mores involves a change in attitudes toward premarital sex. In the U.S. a 1971 survey of teenage women living in metropolitan areas showed that 30 percent of them had sexual intercourse before age nineteen. In 1976 the percentage rose to 43 percent. A survey conducted in 1979 put the figure at 50 percent.[15] In 1984-85, U.S. News and World Report surveyed a thousand Americans eighteen and older. Thirty-six percent of all people polled thought premarital sex was wrong, while 61 percent thought it was not. In the age bracket from eighteen to twenty-nine, only 20 percent said it was wrong, while 78 percent thought it permissible.[16] A Gallup Poll taken in 1968 showed that American opinion at that time was quite different. Sixty-eight percent of the total polled, and 49 percent of young adults, thought premarital sex was wrong.[17]

Since attitudes toward premarital sex are changing so that people are becoming sexually active at younger ages, many think there must be protection from unwanted pregnancies. Given the epidemic proportions of teenage pregnancies, many complain that birth control devices are not used enough. Despite outcries from many, Chicago's DuSable High School established a free clinic in 1985 to dispense birth control devices to those who had parental permission. The decision was made because of a childbirth rate of 30 percent among the thousand female students at the school. In other cases where parents have demanded parental permission and notification in order to dispense birth control devices to teenagers, courts have ruled that the devices may be dispensed without parental knowledge.[18]

While many plead for greater availability of birth control devices, statistics about contraceptive use demonstrate the growing general acceptance of it. In 1978 the World Health Organization estimated that between fifty and eighty million people worldwide were using birth control pills. It was estimated that in the U.S. about half of all married women practicing contraception (not including sterilization) used the pill. In the age group of thirty-five to forty-four, of the 49.9 percent of the fertile women at this age, 72 percent used contraceptives in their marriage, though only one out of five used the pill. It is assumed that the smaller number of women over thirty-five using the pill is attributable to health risks.[19] Though the official Roman Catholic position rejects artificial means of contraception, Catholic women do not necessarily practice what their Church preaches. For example, at the Synod of Bishops in Rome in 1980, statistics presented showed that 76.5 percent of American Catholic women used some form of contraception, and 94 percent of those women were using means condemned by the Pope.[20] Recent studies suggest that the small difference between Catholics and Protestants in the use of contraceptive sterilization is not attributable to doctrinal reasons.[21]

A third pragmatic concern involves family finances. Increasingly more married couples fear they will reproduce themselves into poverty if they do not control their own birth rate. Many wonder if it is morally right to potentially deprive existing children financially just to increase the size of their family. Moreover, given the need in many societies for both husband and wife to work, it becomes impractical to have a large family.

Pragmatic concerns are important, but they cannot be determinative for the Christian. Nonetheless, attitudes toward birth control among Christians have changed because of a belief that Scripture does not forbid it. That is not to say that Christians think all ways of controlling population growth generally and individual family size in particular are morally acceptable. Ruling out nuclear war and euthanasia as either morally or prudentially acceptable ways to control population size, one must control the birth rate. That can be accomplished by abortion, continence, contraception by either artificial devices or "natural" methods, and sterilization.

Having discussed abortion already, this chapter is devoted to the other means.

In this chapter our main concern is whether birth control is biblically and morally acceptable. If it is, which methods are morally acceptable? We believe contraception is morally permissible, though not all means of birth control can be justified. We must add that the moral propriety of birth control methods for the unmarried or for extramarital sex is not under discussion here. Premarital and extramarital sex relations are prohibited by Scripture. The use of birth control devices when involved in those forbidden relations does not somehow morally legitimize them. Nor do we accept the pragmatic reasoning of parents who would rather have their sexually active youngsters safe than pregnant. The biblical answer to that problem is not protection but total abstinence until marriage. Prudence may dictate the pill. Biblical morality demands abstinence.

ROMAN CATHOLICISM AND BIRTH CONTROL

Within Christianity the major opponent of birth control has been the Roman Catholic Church. Therefore, a brief summary of Catholic thinking would help to set the framework for our discussion. Roman Catholic thinking on this issue goes back at least to St. Augustine. Early Christians wrestled against two extremes in regard to sexual intercourse. On the one hand, there was a desire to avoid the promiscuity sanctioned by antinomians. On the other hand, various forms of gnosticism condemned all sexual intercourse. Christians felt that was wrong, but offered little answer as to why. Neither pleasure and satisfaction of sexual desire nor sex as an expression of a mutually supportive relationship between husband and wife were thought to be good enough justification for intercourse. Eventually, exclusive emphasis was placed on procreation as the purpose and justification. Augustine adopted this solution, though his basic opinion was that sexual union in marriage threatened spiritual freedom, for it turned the mind from reflection on spiritual truth to attention on the physical body.[22] Marital intercourse could be justified (using categories of a later period) as an example of the principle of double effect. Intercourse involves the satisfaction of sexual desire, which Augustine did not treat as a good, but it also served the purpose of procreation which was a good. When done with the purpose of procreation marital intercourse was morally justifiable, despite the "negative" result of satisfying sexual desire.[23] As to contraception, Augustine understood the story of Onan (who practiced *coitus interruptus* and was slain by God—Genesis 38) to teach that contraception is forbidden.

The next major development came from Thomas Aquinas. While Aquinas rejected Augustine's suspicion of the physical, his basic position on birth control amounted to the same thing. Coupling the Aristotelian notion of causes with natural law ethics in a way to be explained shortly, Aquinas concluded that contraception was outlawed, for it thwarted the natural purpose of the sex act, which is procreation. Engaging in sexual intercourse without the intent of procreation was, therefore, considered sinful. This meant, of course, that intercourse with one's pregnant wife or with a sterile woman was sinful, because intent to procreate was impossible. In the Middle Ages there was even debate about whether intercourse with one's wife was lawful if the sole purpose was to satisfy sexual desire so that one would not be tempted to commit adultery. Many thought such a motive made it unlawful.[24] The net result of all these considerations was to associate contraception with prostitution and perversion. For someone seeking to limit family size, the only legitimate option was complete abstinence.[25]

Little further change in the Catholic position occurred until the twentieth century. In 1930 Pope Pius XI published the encyclical *Casti Conubii*. In it he affirmed the purposes of marriage as procreation and the education of offspring. Sexual intercourse is by its very nature designed to produce offspring. Therefore, those who practice contraception do something contrary to nature and commit a sin. Using Augustinian and Thomistic reasoning and interpretation of Scripture, he condemned contraception. However, he claimed that it does not follow that sexual intercourse is sinful in marriages where, through natural causes, procreation is impossible. Moreover, he stated that though procreation is the primary purpose of marriage, sexual intercourse in marriage also serves such secondary ends as the fostering of mutual love and the abatement of lust.[26]

In 1932 the Ogino-Knaus theory was published. According to it, it is possible to calculate the exact days on which a woman could or could not conceive (the rhythm method). Roman Catholics were quite enthusiastic about the method, for they reasoned that it was "natural" and thus legitimate. In 1951 Pope Pius XII officially sanctioned the use of the rhythm method, though all other methods of contraception, except abstinence, were still outlawed.[27]

Unfortunately, for many women the rhythm method does not work, for their cycles are not as precise as needed. With the development of the birth control pill, again hopes were raised that the Church would change its stance. However, in 1968 Pope Paul VI issued another encyclical, *Humanae Vitae*. The historic position of the Catholic Church was reaffirmed. All forms of birth control except the rhythm method and abstinence were condemned as unnatural.[28] Statistics cited earlier about Catholics' use of birth control devices show that many Catholics disobey the hierarchy on this issue. However, despite the use of birth control devices by Protestants and Catholics alike, it is surprising to see how much both attitudes toward marriage and sexuality and the understanding of various scriptural passages is still colored by a line of thinking that goes back at least to Augustine.

METHODS OF BIRTH CONTROL

Apart from abortion or sterilization, birth control methods can be divided into two general categories: natural and artificial. Natural methods include continence, *coitus interruptus*, the calendar method (rhythm method), the temperature method, and the ovulation method. The rhythm method is based on some fundamental assumptions about the menstrual cycle. Ovulation is supposed to occur fourteen (plus or minus two) days before the onset of menstruation. Sperm survival is said to be three days and ovum survival two days. If a woman knows the length of her last six to twelve cycles and knows the longest and shortest, she should be able to calculate when she will be fertile or infertile. The temperature method is based on the fact that a woman's basal body temperature rises following ovulation. The infertile period is supposed to begin on the evening of the third day of the temperature shift. One of the newer natural methods is the ovulation method. Before a woman ovulates, there is a special secretion of mucus from the glands of the cervix which can be seen at the vaginal opening. This mucus itself goes through a cycle. The last day on which the mucus is clear, stretchy, and slippery is referred to as the "peak symptom." From the time the mucus first appears to four days after the peak symptom is considered the fertile period. From the evening of that fourth day until the beginning of the next period is the infertile period.[29]

Artificial devices are of various kinds. There are intrauterine devices (IUDs) such as the Brinberg bow and the Hall-Stone stainless steel ring. There are mechanical devices such as the diaphragm, cervical cap, and condom. Chemical contraceptive products such as foams, creams and jellies, and vaginal suppositories are meant to kill sperm. In addition, there are oral hormonal controls (birth control pills).[30] The typical birth control pill inhibits ovulation, but others can be used as a morning-after pill that causes the woman to abort any egg that was fertilized. In Chapter 3 we also discussed RU-486. One final contraceptive is the drug Depo-Provera. Originally used to prevent premature labor, doctors noticed that the drug has a side effect. Women who used it did not become pregnant for as long as a year after receiving the drug. The drug, administered by injection, is still not licensed in America by the FDA but has widespread use, particularly in Third World countries.

Artificial means of contraception generally work in one of three ways. Either they prevent fertilization of the ovum by the sperm altogether, or they prevent a fertilized egg from attaching to the wall of the uterus, or they destroy the embryo after implantation.

THE MORALITY OF CONTINENCE

There is no doubt that continence is an effective means of birth control. On the other hand, it is dubious that continuous abstinence is acceptable biblically. No passage of Scripture directly relates to continence, and only a few indirectly are relevant. Some appeal to Exod 21:10 to show that regular intercourse is a duty of marriage,[31] but that interpretation is questionable. The verse speaks of conjugal rights, but rights are not duties, nor do they necessarily entail them. (For example, I have a right to own property in the U.S. but no duty to do so.) Moreover, the verse says nothing about how often those conjugal rights are to be exercised. Theoretically, the verse could allow for some rather extended periods of abstinence, though in Jewish thinking regular intercourse was to be practiced, frequency even being prescribed in the Talmud.[32]

Others appeal to various OT regulations that are taken to justify abstinence. For example, sexual intercourse was to be avoided during menstruation (Lev 15:19-28; 18:19; 20:18) and after childbirth (Lev 12:1-8), and by men for religious reasons (Exod 19:15; 1 Sam 21:4-5). Though the Leviticus passages do forbid intercourse, they do not sanction such limitation *per se* as *a form of birth control*. In fact, the restrictions on menstruation increase fertility, for after her period a woman would be more likely to conceive and more desirous of sex relations because of abstinence. To use the Exodus and Samuel passages in regard to birth control is objectionable, because the passages say nothing about birth control, and the Samuel passage says nothing about a time frame. Even the Exodus passage merely commands one to be ready for the third day and not to go near a woman. The context of those passages has absolutely nothing to do with the marital relation or sex within marriage.

In the NT, teaching about continence is more explicit. Continence is allowed but only for limited periods. The key passage is 1 Cor 7:1-7 where Paul explicitly tells husbands and wives to perform their marital duty to one another (v. 3). In the context of verse 4, "marital duty" is clearly a reference to sexual intercourse. In verse 5 Paul tells them to stop depriving one another. However, there is an exception to this general rule. Paul allows continence for a time so that both may devote themselves to prayer. Once the time is over, they are to resume normal sexual relations. The explicit reason for regular sexual relations is offered in both verses 2 and 5. Nothing is mentioned about sexual intercourse for the purpose of procreation, but rather it is an aid in quelling the temptation to commit adultery. Paul, then, is teaching that one of the purposes of sexual intercourse among married couples is to curb the temptation to engage in immorality. *Total* abstinence runs counter to that end.

In sum, continence as a means of birth control is not ruled out completely, but the periods of continence are to be limited and for the specific purpose of devoting oneself to prayer. The general biblical expectation (as well as Paul's specific command) is that married couples are to engage in regular sexual intercourse. Absolute abstinence is contrary to Scripture and cannot be a morally justifiable means of birth control.

THE MORALITY OF OTHER CONTRACEPTIVE MEANS
AGAINST CONTRACEPTION
Natural Law and Final Causes

Traditionally, the major argument against birth control combines natural law ethics and the Aristotelian notion of causes. According to Aristotle, every object in the universe has a final cause. An object's final cause is the end, goal or purpose toward which it aims. When something is used according to its end, it is acting naturally. When it is used contrary to its purpose, it acts unnaturally.[33] When this notion of final cause was joined to natural law ethics, many concluded that by the light of pure reason alone as applied to the natural world, one could see that birth control is wrong. The reasoning was as follows: by mere reflection on the natural order, one can see that the intended purpose of sex organs is reproduction. God has created sex for procreation, and any other use of it is unnatural and contrary to God's intended design. Moreover, anything which prohibits the sex organs from performing their appointed role is sinful and thus prohibited. In view of this line of argument, one might wonder if sexual intercourse is sinful whenever the wife does not become pregnant. Catholic tradition answers that so long as the intention of the act is procreation, there is no sin, even if pregnancy does not result. The net result is that all *artificial* means of contraception are ruled out, and certain *natural* forms such as *coitus interruptus* are sinful.

Biblical Arguments

The passage used most frequently against birth control is Gen 38:1-10, the story of Onan. After Onan's brother died, Onan was commanded to have sexual relations with his brother's wife to raise up seed to his brother. Onan disobeyed by spilling his seed on the ground (i.e., he practiced *coitus interruptus*). God was displeased with him and slew him. Opponents of contraception argue that this incident is a clear case of practicing contraception, and God's response showed his displeasure with Onan's act of contraception. God's displeasure with this act is then generalized to other forms of birth control. The conclusion is that birth control is contrary to God's will.

Others point to Gen 1:28 ("Be fruitful and multiply") as a command which shows the purpose of sexuality. Of course, that command is deliberately disobeyed when contraceptive means are employed. It is argued that even if an act of intercourse does not result in pregnancy, it should not be performed in such a way as to make impossible the fulfillment of the purpose of sex and so disobey God's command.

Finally, appeal is made to OT passages like Deut 23:1 that do not allow eunuchs access to the congregation of the Lord in Israel. Opponents of birth control argue that this prohibition demonstrates God's displeasure with any means of birth control.

Contraception and Other Issues of Sexual Morality

The whole issue of contraception raises two further issues involved in sexual morality. First, many have argued that the use of birth control devices (especially those such as the pill that are quite effective) will encourage promiscuity among both married and unmarried persons. Opponents of the use of contraceptive means remind us that the sexual revolution of the 1960s and 1970s coincided with the increasing use of birth control pills. It is dubious that those two events were purely coincidental rather than being causally related. With the removal of fear of pregnancy, one can be moderately or even greatly promiscuous without fear of the consequences. Since birth control devices encourage sexual immorality, contraception should be discouraged.

Second, various artificial forms of birth control seem equivalent to abortion. Any device that prevents the fertilized egg from attaching to the uterine wall or forces the mother's body to abort the embryo once implanted is just another form of abortion. Morning-after pills and IUDs, for example, fall into this category. Of course, if abortion is immoral, then these forms of birth control must also be immoral and rejected.

Contraception and Health Concerns

Some reject artificial contraceptive devices on the ground that many of them have negative side effects for health. For example, IUDs facilitate pelvic infections and occasionally perforate the uterus. They are also associated with ectopic pregnancies and spontaneous abortions. Birth control pills can cause such problems as breakthrough bleeding, nausea, breast tenderness and weight gain. They can also cause even more serious problems such as blood clots. The likelihood of these problems occurring increases for women over thirty-five. While these risks are generally low enough that many women consider the advantages to outweigh them, some feminist groups view the risks as unnecessary. Other forms of contraception do not have such adverse side effects and do not put such a burden on women.[34]

It is also argued that the increase in birth control devices (especially the pill) may be tied to the rise of venereal disease. Some claim that in the mid-1950s there was a general feeling that VD was no longer a problem in the U.S. Later in that decade reported cases of infectious syphilis and gonorrhea began to rise. By the 1970s gonorrhea had become the number one reportable communicable disease in the U.S. Similar problems were reported in other countries such as England, Canada, Australia, and Denmark. In the last decade or so we have seen the onset of herpes and AIDS. Many contraceptive devices offer no protection against the spread of these diseases. Condoms provide better protection than other devices, but there can still be "accidents," even with condoms. The seriousness of this matter is that now the "accidents" may produce more than unwanted pregnancies; the result may be life-threatening diseases.[35]

Contraception, Love, and Sex

A final line of objection to birth control stems from the claim that artificial contraceptive means have altered negatively our concept of one another. Prior to the development of modern forms of birth control that are extremely effective, entering into a sexual relation always meant running the risk of conception. That fact gave the act a seriousness and importance that is lost when conception is so certainly forestalled. The level of love and commitment of the partners to one another was invariably high because of the risk they were taking. Now the gravity of the matter is obscured, because the risk is gone. Sex can mean anything or nothing. It can be mechanical; it can be casual. As a result, in many cases the act has lost the sense of intimacy it once had, and that loss of intimacy along with the ability now to treat one another as objects for personal gratification without any need of commitment or any fear of accountability represents a significant negative result of modern contraceptive means.[36]

IN FAVOR OF CONTRACEPTION

Although the preceding arguments may appear compelling, we think there are stronger arguments favoring birth control. In this section, we want to answer arguments against birth control and add other considerations in favor of contraception.

Natural Law, the Purpose of Sex, and Birth Control

The argument about natural law and the purpose of the sex act deserves serious attention. As noted, the argument rests on the Aristotelian notion of causes, but philosophically, there are no conclusive arguments that Aristotle's doctrine is correct. Nor is there any evidence that objects geared to perform a particular end may not also serve other ends just as well and "naturally." Moreover, unless one adopts a natural law ethic, the whole line of argument loses much of its force, and of course, there are reasons to have reservations about natural law ethics.

In addition, the argument is suspect even if one accepts natural law ethics. The problem is that the natural order of things in human beings negates the argument. No woman is fertile each day of the month, nor is she capable of bearing children all her life. A woman is likely to conceive only a few days each month. This is possible from the time she reaches puberty until menopause. Nonetheless, nature also shows that a woman still has sexual passion at times during the month when she is infertile and at times in life when she cannot conceive. If the sole purpose of sexual intercourse is procreation, then why did God give women the desire for sexual intercourse at times when they cannot become pregnant? Does not the natural order of things, then, demonstrate that procreation is not the only purpose of sex?

In response, one might argue that our objection undercuts the natural law aspect of the argument, but does not prove that the purpose of marriage (and the sex act) is anything other than procreation. Our answer is to point to biblical teaching on the purpose of marriage.

From a scriptural point of view, there are at least six purposes for sex within marriage. The first (though not necessarily the most important) is *procreation* (Gen 1:28; 9:1, 7). Some read these verses as a command, but the Hebrew can be just as easily interpreted as a blessing. Common sense suggests that if it is a command, it is not universally applicable, because any couple unable to have children because of some physical problem over which they have no control would be disobedient to God. Some note as well the context of these verses. The first passage records what is said to the first man and woman, and the second is said to Noah and his family after the flood. In those contexts, commands (if the verses are commands) to multiply and replenish the earth make great sense, whereas their direct applicability to a world of over five billion people is harder to see.

The second purpose for marriage is *companionship*. According to Gen 2:18, marriage is God's idea, and God raised the idea because he saw that man was alone. Nothing in the verse mentions the purpose of marriage or sex as procreation. Everything points to God in his goodness giving man a companion suitable to his needs.

Both the OT and the NT speak of *unity* as a third purpose of marriage. Gen 2:24 speaks of male and female becoming one flesh. In Matt 19:4-6 Jesus quotes from Genesis 2 and reaffirms that God unites husband and wife so they shall be one flesh. In addition, in Ephesians 5 Paul portrays the union of husband and wife as analogous to the union between Christ and his Church. The particulars of the passages suggest that the union is not merely a unity of mind and spirit, but also involves sexual relations as the physical expression of the marital unity God creates between husband and wife.

Fourth, *pleasure* is a purpose of marriage and sexual relations. Apart from all the allegory and typology that may or may not be present in the Song of Solomon, the underlying point of the book is to extol the beauties and pleasures of human sexuality. Moreover, in Ecc 9:9 readers are encouraged to "enjoy life with the wife whom you love." Undoubtedly, more than the pleasures of sex are meant, but surely such pleasures are part of the meaning.

Fifth, for the believer, one of the purposes of marriage is to *raise up a godly seed*. Obviously, this relates to procreation, but it is a more particular point. Sometimes Christians rue the thought of bringing any children into a world in which there is so much evil. But if believers who are able to have children do not do so, will not evil triumph even more in future generations? Granted, some children of non-believers will accept Christ, and there is no guarantee that children of godly parents will accept Christ. Nevertheless, the rearing of a godly seed is certainly a worthy goal of a married couple.

A final purpose of marriage and sex within marriage is the matter of *curbing fornication and adultery*. This point has already been made in our discussion of 1 Corinthians 7 (cf. 1 Thess 4:3ff.) in regard to continence, so we need not belabor it here.

The upshot of this discussion on the biblical purposes of marriage is that procreation is not the only purpose of sex within marriage. Since that is so, it must be permissible to use sex for the other purposes mentioned. There seems to be no reason to mandate that procreation also be intended when one of these other purposes is in view. However, in order to avoid pregnancy while fulfilling one of the other purposes, a birth control device may be necessary. Given the many purposes of marital sex, that seems morally permissible. If birth control is wrong, it cannot be because couples must intend to use sex for procreation.

Biblical Arguments

As to the passages used against birth control, Gen 1:28 has already been handled. Deut 23:1 is another matter. Scholars have speculated about the reasoning behind this injunction against eunuchs, but have reached no consensus. However, several points are noteworthy. Deut 23:1 speaks of those who are castrated. Nothing is said about how or why they were castrated. Nor can it be used to prohibit castration *per se*, for the text neither forbids it nor calls it morally wrong. The verse says only that anyone in that condition could not enter the assembly of the Lord. Moreover, simple logic demands that this injunction about castration alone cannot legitimately be generalized to cover all forms of contraception. It is even dubious that the passage is relevant to what modern society means by sterilization (vasectomy and tubal ligation). Finally, one must also remember that this command seems to be part of the ceremonial aspect of the Mosaic Code, and is not repeated in the NT. On the other hand, the NT contains Jesus' apparently positive comments about eunuchs (Matt 19:12) and a positive assessment of the Ethiopian eunuch led to the Lord by Philip (Acts 8:26-40). However one understands Deut 23:1, it must be consistent with these NT passages.

Historically, the Onan story has been of great significance. Here, however, it appears that traditional arguments against birth control rest on a mistaken interpretation. The Lord actually judged Onan for perverting the institution of levirate marriage in favor of self-gratification. Onan was willing enough to marry his brother's wife and have sex relations with her as the law demanded. However, by practicing *coitus interruptus* he showed his displeasure with the idea of raising up seed to his brother, seed for whom he would be personally responsible. He showed no concern for his brother or his brother's wife. His only concern was his own pleasure. In response to this perversion of the levirate institution, God killed him.[37] This condemns neither *coitus interruptus* nor any other form of birth control. Moreover, passages where one might expect a prohibition say nothing. For example, Lev 20:10-21 presents a list of specific sexual crimes punishable by death under the Mosaic Code. If *coitus interruptus* is a sexual abuse, one would expect to see it in this list, but neither it nor any other form of birth control appears.

Responses to Other Objections to Contraception

Many of the other arguments raised against birth control deal with negative consequences that may result from the availability and use of contraceptive devices. However, objectionable consequences do not *per se* necessarily rule out contraceptive measures as immoral. For example, using birth control methods to treat sex casually and remove intimacy from the act does not alone make contraception morally wrong. Casual sex is most likely to occur when sex partners are not married to one another and are merely seeking their own pleasure. However, fornication and adultery are wrong not because one can use a birth control device and thereby avoid genuine intimacy. They are wrong because God's word prohibits them. Adultery and fornication would not suddenly become right just because the couple did not use contraceptive devices, experienced great intimacy, and risked pregnancy. Clearly, the morality of such acts does not depend on the use of contraceptive devices. As to married couples, where there is genuine love and respect for one another, there will be appropriate intimacy even if contraception is used. On the other hand, in a marriage where there is little or no mutual love and respect, refusal to use contraceptive devices is not likely to have anything to do with increasing intimacy.

The arguments that birth control devices result in greater promiscuity and help to increase venereal diseases point again to consequences of birth control use. Those arguments are probably correct in drawing such causal connections, but that in itself does not mean birth control devices are morally wrong. It means (in cases of promiscuity) that they can be used to encourage fornication and adultery, which are morally wrong. However, to say all contraception is morally wrong because contraceptives have sometimes been used for immoral purposes is obviously erroneous. Such thinking fails to distinguish between the object (contraceptives) and the use to which the object may be applied (fornication and adultery *or* avoidance of pregnancy by a loving married couple). The error here is tantamount to thinking that automobiles are morally wrong because people have used them to escape apprehension after committing murder or burglary. The mere existence of things such as automobiles and birth control devices is neither moral nor immoral. Both can be used for immoral purposes, but those immoral acts do not prove that all acts involving those objects are immoral.

As to birth control devices that have negative side effects for a woman's health, they do seem morally improper (as well as practically imprudent) for someone who takes seriously biblical teaching about the importance of the body and the need to care for it. Moreover, we agree that any birth control method that is equivalent to abortion is morally objectionable. If abortion is wrong, and we believe it is, it is morally wrong whether the method is an IUD or a saline injection. However, this consideration rules out certain birth control methods, not all.

Final Considerations

Two final arguments suggest the moral acceptability of birth control methods that neither harm the mother nor abort a fertilized egg. The first appeals to Paul's comment in 1 Tim 5:8 that if anyone does not provide for the needs of the members of his own household, he has denied the faith and is worse than an unbeliever. Paul is not addressing the question of birth control, but his comments are not irrelevant to the issue. Each member of a family has financial, physical, emotional and spiritual needs. Parents should know whether those needs are being met, and they should also know whether the introduction of another life into that home would make it difficult or even impossible to meet the needs of all members. If a couple perceives that adding to the family size would hamper or even remove their ability to meet the needs mentioned, it is both irresponsible and improper to continue having more children. Under such circumstances, continuing to reproduce places one in jeopardy of falling under the condemnation of 1 Tim 5:8. In such cases, it is both prudentially necessary and morally right to use some morally acceptable form of birth control to limit family size.

A final argument appeals to a practical point. Since nothing discussed (biblical or otherwise) mandates or prohibits birth control *per se*, it is not wrong to entertain practical concerns in decision-making. The practical point here is as follows: if the medical history of the husband or wife indicates incidence of a genetically transmitted disease, it is both wise and morally permissible to practice birth control, even if it means the couple must refrain from having any of their own biological descendants. While it is certainly morally permissible for the couple to have children and take the chance that the disease will not be transmitted, nothing biblical or otherwise morally obligates the couple to have children.

In sum, nothing scriptural or otherwise prohibits all forms of birth control. In various circumstances (e.g., when there is the potential of transmitting a genetic disease or when the purpose of sex is something other than procreation) birth control is morally *permissible*. Contraception is seldom morally *obligatory*, though one might argue to mandate it in some instances in order to avoid the condemnation of 1 Tim 5:8. On the other hand, contraceptive methods that are equivalent to abortion are not permissible. Finally, there are cases where failure to have children seems wrong. For example, when a couple has no children, no medical reason to avoid children, and is fully capable of conceiving and raising children, but for purely selfish reasons (perhaps unwillingness to give up their freedom and take on the responsibility of children) or for fear of bringing children into such an evil world as ours refuses to have children, the practice of birth control is improperly motivated. Such couples should be encouraged to have children.[38]

THE MORALITY OF STERILIZATION

Sterilization raises a series of social and political questions as well as moral ones. The fundamental distinction made in current literature is between voluntary and involuntary sterilization. Most of the social and political issues arise in regard to the latter.

Sterilization poses a significant issue if only because of how many people are resorting to it. Studies done in the 1970s show sterilization is the most frequently used form of contraception in the world, and as of 1979, the second most frequently used among Americans. By 1976, 30 percent of all widowed, divorced and separated women and single mothers aged fifteen to forty-four in the U.S. had been surgically sterilized. Nearly the same percent among all U.S. married couples had at least one partner sterilized. By 1977 nearly ten million persons in the U.S. had been sterilized. Those figures include an average of one million per year from 1974 to 1977.[39] One further point should be noted before turning to the argumentation. In 1942 in the U.S., in *Skinner v. Oklahoma*, the Supreme Court ruled that the right to procreate is a constitutional right. Sterilization "forever deprived" an individual of this right.[40] This decision did not outlaw sterilization in the U.S., but it set a legal precedent for demanding that sterilizations be performed with informed consent. That is, sterilization against a person's will or voluntary sterilization without proper information about the procedure deprives individuals of their constitutional right to procreate. On March 8, 1979 the Department of Health, Education and Welfare implemented rules governing federally financed sterilization. Needless to say, the 1942 decision and the 1979 guidelines have not eliminated sterilization abuse, but they are legal ways to recognize individual rights and to attempt to minimize abuse.

Sterilization raises a number of questions, including the following: 1) is voluntary sterilization a morally acceptable means of birth control under any circumstances? 2) Should the state require the sterilization of citizens whose family has reached a certain size in order to control population growth? 3) Should sterilization be required for classes of individuals such as the mentally retarded and incompetent, low-income people, and habitual criminals? 4) Should parents be given the right to authorize the sterilization of mentally retarded children? 5) Should the state fund sterilization operations of mentally retarded and low-income individuals? 6) Should sterilization procedures (voluntarily or involuntarily sought) be subject to federal guidelines that include rules such as informed consent?

Most of these questions focus on involuntary sterilization. Many involve legal and political issues about the role of the state in personal lives. Such questions go beyond the focus of this chapter and this book, and invoke some fundamental issues in social and political philosophy. In this section we want to address voluntary sterilization in general. There will also be a discussion of the sterilization of the mentally retarded, and that will involve some discussion of involuntary sterilization.

VOLUNTARY STERILIZATION

In turning to the issue of voluntary sterilization, one finds that arguments raised against it on biblical and theological grounds typically follow the line offered by the Catholic Church in regard to birth control as a whole. As noted, those arguments are problematic, and applying them to the issue of sterilization does not make them any better. Of course, some, following the logic of the natural law/purpose of sexual intercourse argument, might claim that sterilization is objectionable because it not only removes the possibility of procreation but negates the other purposes of marriage as well. However, this confuses fertility with sexuality. They are not the same, because men and women who have been surgically sterilized can still participate in sexual intercourse, even though they cannot procreate.

Sterilization, as we think of it today, is really not addressed in Scripture. The closest one comes are the statements about eunuchs, but they are few and inconclusive. The first is the Deuteronomy 23 passage, but we have shown why that passage is inconclusive for this issue and for birth control generally. Acts 8 records the story of the Ethiopian eunuch, but it makes no value judgment whatsoever on his being a eunuch. Moreover, it gives no prescriptions about sterilization or being a eunuch. The fact that the Ethiopian is a eunuch seems incidental to Luke's story. Thus, Acts 8 offers no help on this moral issue.

The longest comment about eunuchs comes from our Lord in Matt

19:10-12, and its meaning is exceedingly difficult. After hearing Jesus' teaching on divorce, the disciples replied that in view of Jesus' rules it would be better not to marry. Jesus addresses the idea of not marrying and says that only those to whom it is given can receive this precept. While Jesus might be referring to his precept about divorce, it seems more likely contextually that "this" refers to the disciples' comment about remaining unmarried. Jesus then (v. 12) speaks of three classes of eunuchs and says that whoever can receive this teaching about remaining as a eunuch (i.e., celibate) should do so. The three classes of eunuchs mentioned are: eunuchs from birth, eunuchs made so by men (i.e., those castrated for whatever reason), and eunuchs made so themselves for the sake of the kingdom of heaven.[41]

We do not think this passage can be used to teach anything about the morality of sterilization for several reasons. First, as noted, Jesus' answer responds to the disciples' claims about marrying or not marrying. As such, it comments about the wisdom of marrying or remaining single; it says nothing about practicing any particular method of contraception once one is married. Second, Jesus says only those to whom it is given can receive his teaching about remaining celibate. Those who can, should. Jesus makes no comment whatsoever about the morality or immorality of those who cannot receive it, nor does he suggest that those who can receive it are morally superior to those who cannot. Moreover, since the "it" is the matter of *marrying or staying single,* it is dubious that one could use the passage to argue for the moral superiority or inferiority of people who are *surgically sterilized.* We conclude, then, that when properly understood, the passage is really not about sterilization. Even if it were, since Jesus makes no comments about the moral praise or blame of those who are eunuchs (i.e., "sterilized") or those who are not, the passage surely says nothing about the *morality* of sterilization as a contraceptive method.

A further biblical argument claims that the command of Gen 1:28 cannot be fulfilled by a sterilized person. However, as already noted, it is debatable as to whether that verse is a command or a blessing. If it is a command at all, remember the historical context, and remember also that the whole command includes the statement "replenish the earth." This alone suggests the historical particularity of the statement. Moreover, if the verse is a command, it is not universally applicable, for it cannot be a legitimate request of women who have reached menopause, had a hysterectomy for medical reasons, or are infertile. All of these considerations raise serious doubts about whether this passage is universally applicable in a way that could be at all helpful to the issue of sterilization in particular or birth control in general.

Others might appeal to biblical teaching on care for the body and argue that sterilization is improper care of the body, for it "mutilates" it or at least does not allow the body to function according to its intended purpose. Those acquainted with vasectomy and tubal ligation know that neither involves mutilation. As to the body's intended function, this invokes again the specter of Aristotelian final causes, and we have already seen the problem with that line of argument. On the other hand, the whole argument in some cases can be turned on its head and used in favor of sterilization. For example, if a woman has several children and has had difficult pregnancies and deliveries, it might be medically advisable not to force her body to undergo the physical strain of another pregnancy. Proper care for the body would apparently warrant use of some highly effective means of birth control (and sterilization surely qualifies here) to ensure no further pregnancies. The net result is that appeal to biblical concerns about caring for the body cannot rule out sterilization.

From the preceding discussion, we conclude that no scriptural or logical point rules out voluntary sterilization. In cases where birth control devices are morally acceptable, voluntary sterilization is also acceptable.

STERILIZATION AND THE MENTALLY RETARDED

This is a very difficult issue, in part because there is no general rule that can cover all cases of mental retardation and incompetence. Some decisions must be made in light of the retarded person himself and others in view of potential offspring from a retarded person. As to the retarded person, there are differing degrees of retardation and mental competence which allow for different levels of functioning. It is especially difficult in the case of a mentally retarded child to know the degree to which he might overcome the effects of retardation. Sterilizing the child on the assumption that he will never develop enough to cope with children may prove to be unwarranted. As to future offspring of mentally retarded people, it is known that a retarded individual will not necessarily give birth to a retarded child, even if his own retardation is genetically caused. Moreover, even if anticipated children would be retarded, there is no way prior to conception and birth to know how severe the retardation would be. Thus, one cannot legitimately mandate sterilizing retarded people on the ground that their children will be retarded.

The preceding suggests that each case of sterilization involving a retarded or mentally incompetent person should be considered separately. Nevertheless, we think there is a guideline relevant to the distinction between voluntary and involuntary sterilization. We have argued that sterilization *per se* need not be morally evil. On the other hand, sterilization is immoral if performed on a person against his will or without his decision. That would abridge his freedom and treat him as a victim rather than a moral agent. But what if one is dealing with a mentally retarded or incompetent individual? Here the basic guideline would be to determine whether the level of retardation/incompetence makes it impossible for the person to understand the procedure. That is, is he mentally capable of giving informed consent? If he can understand the procedure and its implications so that he could make an informed decision, then unless he is allowed to make the decision, his freedom of decision is abridged. Involuntary sterilization in that case would be immoral, for it treats someone who could make a moral decision as a victim, not an agent.

If, on the other hand, the person cannot understand the procedure and/or its implications, that raises a different set of problems. Inability to understand the procedure may or may not indicate inability to raise a child, depending on the level of the person's retardation. Whatever decision is made, it obviously will not be voluntary on the part of the person sterilized. Is there any way to justify sterilizing a person who cannot make the decision for himself? The answer seems to be the same as one might offer in regard to how the general needs of an incompetent person are to be met. Typically, someone who is a family member and in a position to know what is in the best interests of the incompetent individual is expected to care for his needs. Since sterilization is morally permissible in cases where other contraceptive means are permissible, the decision to sterilize an incompetent or retarded person will be morally acceptable, if other means of contraception would be acceptable and if it can be shown that sterilization is in the incompetent person's best interests.

CONCLUSION

For various reasons a married couple might want to limit the size of their family. Some means of doing so such as abortion and euthanasia are not morally acceptable ways. However, some birth control devices are permissible and in some cases advisable. Though the use of birth control devices would rarely be mandatory, each family should responsibly confront the question of the appropriate number of children for whom it can provide. Thankfully, God has allowed us to live at a time when quite effective, morally acceptable means for limiting family size are available. In all of this, however, we must affirm the great joy, privilege and blessing from God of parenting. Considerations about the appropriate number of children for each home must include those matters, too.

CHAPTER EIGHT

Homosexuality

Homosexuals have come out of the closet. Though many are still uneasy about going public, there are equally as many or more who are not embarrassed about their sexual preference. They tell us that homosexuality is gay, an alternative sexual orientation, a genetically inherited characteristic, and even compatible with the teaching of Scripture.

It is difficult to estimate accurately how many adults are homosexuals, since that depends a great deal on how one defines homosexuality. John Money of Johns Hopkins University, a well-known sex researcher, defined a homosexual as one who had six or more sexual experiences with members of the same sex. Using this as the definition, he found that 13 percent of adult males were gay and about 7 percent of adult females were lesbians.[1]

A more recent study published in 1989 using data gathered from adult men in the U.S. in 1970 and 1989 suggests lower estimates. Charles F. Turner, a coauthor of the study, said that the estimates made about homosexuals were the most conservative possible, since they took the lowest possible numbers that could be drawn from the data. There was also a lack of information from which one might establish the true number, which could be higher. Some of the estimates were as follows. At least 20.3 percent of American males had had a same-gender sex experience by the age of twenty-one, and 6.7 percent had that encounter by the age of twenty. The study further suggests that after the age of twenty, perhaps as few as 1.8 percent *rarely* had a sexual encounter with the same sex, 1.9 percent *occasionally*, and 1.4 percent fairly often.[2]

It is clear that homosexual men have traditionally been quite active sexually. In 1982 a study of fifty AIDS victims done by the Center for Disease Control in Atlanta discovered that the median number of lifetime sexual partners for these men was 1,100, some claiming as many as twenty thousand. The median number for a control group without the disease was 550. This study's findings are consistent with those of a 1978 survey of 685 gay men living in San Francisco. Psychologist Alan P. Bell and sociologist Martin S. Weinberg of the Kinsey Institute for Sex Research headed a study that showed that 15 percent of these men reported sex with between five hundred and one thousand partners, while more than 25 percent claimed more than a thousand partners. Lesbians showed a relatively lower rate of sexual activity. Better than 70 percent reported fewer than nine lifetime partners, 3 percent claimed to have had more than a hundred, and none more than five hundred.[3] There is no question that AIDS has reduced promiscuity, but how much is not yet determined.

GENETICS AND HOMOSEXUALITY

Homosexuals have long claimed they are different not just in their behavior but constitutionally. That is, they feel their sexual orientation is not a matter of choice or even formed through interaction with their social environment, but something they were born with.[4] Recently, there have been two studies that seem to confirm that claim, one by Swaab and Hofman[5] and another by Simon LeVay.[6] While both studies dealt with the hypothalamus of homosexual men, they were somewhat different. The Swaab and Hofman research studied the volume of the suprachiasmatic nucleus (hereafter referred to as SCN) in homosexual men. The SCN is a cell group located in the basal part of the brains of mammalians. It has been thought to be a principal component of the biological clock that generates and coordinates hormonal, physiological and behavioral body rhythms. Thus, it has been thought to have involvement in sex because of the varying body rhythms in sexual desire as well as the sexual changes that come with aging. The study observed the brains of thirty-four subjects. There was a reference group of eighteen male subjects who died of a variety of causes. There was a second group of ten homosexual men who died of AIDS and a third group of six heterosexuals who died of AIDS. This last group consisted of four males and two females.[7] The conclusion of this study is that ". . . the human hypothalamus revealed that the volume of the . . . SCN in homosexual men is 1.7 times as large as that of the reference group of male subjects and contains 2.1 times as many cells."[8]

    Simon LeVay examined the anterior hypothalamus in the area that regulates male-type sexual behavior. Four cell groups, called INAH 1, 2, 3, 4, were studied. Postmortem tissue was measured from three subject groups: women, men presumed to be heterosexual, and homosexual men.[9] LeVay found there were no differences in the volumes of INAH 1, 2 or 4. The INAH 3, however, was more than twice as large in heterosexual men as in women *and* homosexual men. Thus, LeVay concluded that there is a significant difference in the hypothalamus of heterosexual and homosexual men. He does caution that his results should be considered speculative. Moreover, the results of his study do not allow one to decide if the changes in the hypothalamus are the cause or consequences of an individual's sexual orientation.[10]

The caution expressed by LeVay was not exhibited by all. Many have concluded there is a genetic reason for homosexuality. Of course, this claim is extremely important to homosexuals for at least two reasons. First, if homosexuality is something innate or constitutional, then homosexuals are no more responsible for their sexual orientation than for eye color or height. Attempts to get homosexuals to change their sexual orientation will also be useless. Second, this claim has political ramifications. If there is a biological basis for homosexuality, then there will be pressure to grant them minority-rights status. This is a special civil rights status that would protect them from discrimination on the basis of their sexual orientation.[11]

We must be cautious about what we conclude from these studies. It is wrong to conclude from these and other studies that *no* genetic factors go into the homosexual's sexual orientation. On the other hand, it also concludes too much to think that these and similar studies show that homosexuality is constitutional and beyond change. Let us set forth our views on these studies and the broader issue of the biological basis for homosexuality.

First, LeVay's study seems more significant than Swaab and Hofman's. Both study the hypothalamus, a gland that is important both hormonally and sexually. However, LeVay's research dealt with an area that is directly related to sexual response.[12] Having said that, we would not simply dismiss the Swaab/Hofman research, for it constitutes some collaborating evidence.

Second, in both studies the number of subjects studied was very small. The Swaab/Hofman study was based on thirty-four subjects, while LeVay examined forty-one patients. Of the thirty-four subjects in the Swaab/Hofman research, only ten were homosexuals.[13] There were nineteen homosexuals in LeVay's study.[14] Thus, the two studies examined the brains of only twenty-nine homosexual men. This is hardly the kind of sample from which to make global pronouncements.

Third, in both studies an important group of subjects were *presumed* to be heterosexual. In the Swaab/Hofman research there was a reference group of eighteen subjects. As to their sexual orientation, Swaab and Hofman write: "Sexual preference of the subjects of the reference group was generally not known."[15] In LeVay's study, he called the second group of subjects "men who were presumed to be heterosexual."[16] Thus, in both studies the hypothalamus of homosexuals was compared with subjects from groups presumed to be heterosexual. Obviously, that could be wrong, and if it is, any conclusions from these studies become extremely dubious.

Fourth, it is not clear that the differences observed in the hypothalamus are not due to some factor other than the sexual orientation of these men. All homosexual males studied in both sets of research had AIDS. Could the differences in hypothalamus be the results of that disease rather than the cause of sexual orientation? Indeed, it could. Furthermore, it is possible that the observed differences in the hypothalamus result from some as yet unknown cause or causes.[17]

Fifth, even if it could be shown with certainty that the size of the hypothalamus and homosexuality are related, that would not settle the question as to whether size of the gland was the *cause* of the sexual orientation or a *consequence* of it. In other words, it would not tell us whether there is simply a correlation between hypothalamus size and homosexuality or a causal relationship.[18]

Finally, there is the need for more study in order to confirm the conclusions of the two mentioned. Research of sexual dimorphism, which both of these studies are, has a history of controversy and contradiction. The structures on the slides are difficult to see. Researchers disagree as to whether the most reliable way to determine size of the hypothalamus is volume measurement or actual cell count. Swaab and Hofman used both, LeVay only the volume measurement. And there is always the disturbing possibility that observed differences are influenced by factors not observed or tested for.[19] Thus, we suggest that it goes far beyond the scientific evidence we presently possess to conclude that homosexuality is constitutional and cannot be changed.[20]

CAUSES OF HOMOSEXUALITY

If homosexuality is not simply a genetic or constitutional condition, what are its causes?[21] That is a difficult and hotly debated question, even among those who do not appeal to Scripture for help on this matter. Some have suggested that homosexuality is traceable to an imbalance in sex hormones. G. Dorner's research on rats indicated that hormonal irregularities during the fourth to the seventh month of prenatal development might predispose them toward homosexuality. Male homosexuality, however, has been treated with the injection of male hormones with very limited success.[22] Lack of success, however, may be related to the fact that the treatment is after the fact. It has also been pointed out that while sex hormones are needed for the physiological development of sex organs, psychological factors determine the choice of a sex partner and the intensity of sexual pleasure.[23] Moreover, Dorner's studies have not been confirmed by those of other scientists.[24]

There is some evidence that family pathology at least contributes to homosexuality.[25] About 67 percent of male homosexuals come from a home where the mother is a domineering man-hater and the father is weak, detached and often uninvolved in the family. However, it seems clear that this family structure is neither a necessary nor a sufficient condition for homosexuality. Thus, Evelyn Hooker is most likely correct. Homosexuality is the result of a variety of causes, none of which decisively determines sexual preference. There may be some biological factors which either predispose or contribute to homosexuality, and the home environment is also a significant factor. Still, in cases where all of these elements are present, one will not necessarily become a homosexual.[26]

SCRIPTURE AND HOMOSEXUALITY

Christians have been among the most ardent opponents of homosexuality, because they believe it is contrary to the explicit teaching of the Bible. One might think gays would not really care what the Bible says about their lifestyle, because they do not view Scripture as their authority, and think it is wrong on this matter anyway. However, there are many homosexuals who not only care about scriptural teaching, but think it does not condemn their practice.[27] As Walter Barnett writes: "Some theologians and a number of Gay Christians, working from a growing understanding of the biblical texts, have come to the conclusion that the Bible does not exclude homosexual people from the Christian fellowship. . . ."[28] John J. McNeill's opinion is more extreme as he cites favorably what he calls the opinion of scholars that "nowhere in the Scripture is there a clear condemnation of a loving sexual relationship between two gay persons."[29]

Can these claims be right when at least six passages of Scripture (Gen 19:1-11; Lev 18:22; 20:13; Rom 1:26-27; 1 Cor 6:9-11; 1 Tim 1:8-10) appear to condemn the practice of homosexuality? In what follows we shall set forth recent homosexual interpretations of these texts and evaluate these interpretations to see if the traditional understanding of the biblical teaching on this subject has been in error.

GENESIS 19:1-11

The sin of Sodom and Gomorrah has traditionally been taken to be homosexuality. In fact, another name for homosexuality is "sodomy." The grossness of this sin was thought to be seen in the character of the judgment that God brought on these cities.

The traditional interpretation of this passage has been challenged in at least two ways by homosexuals. First, some have argued that if the sin of Sodom and Gomorrah was sexual, it was not simply homosexuality but homosexual *rape*.[30] Lot's pleas to the townspeople were not to rape the visitors (gang rape at that). If this is so, then condemning homosexuality because of homosexual rape is no more justified than condemning heterosexuality because of instances of heterosexual rape. Anyway, the sinfulness of any rape lies not in the fact that it is homosexual or heterosexual in character, but in the fact that it victimizes a nonconsenting partner.[31]

While it is true that the men of Sodom desired to rape the angelic visitors to their city, this interpretation is certainly wrong. Nowhere does the text even slightly hint that what the men of Sodom wanted to do would be permissible if only Lot's guests had consented. Moreover, this interpretation does not account for the fact that God's judgment fell upon two entire cities. Was homosexual rape a common practice and thus brought the judgment of God? It could have been, but such is not stated in the text. What is more damaging is that God's judgment on homosexuality in Sodom and Gomorrah is quite in harmony with his prohibition and denunciation of this sin in other Scriptures properly interpreted. It is not as though this is the only time homosexuality is denounced and judged.

A second reinterpretation of Genesis 19 is even bolder, for it claims the passage is not about homosexuality at all.[32] Rather, the sin of Sodom and Gomorrah related to a gross violation of the hospitality code. Sodom and Gomorrah were exceedingly wicked cities. God determined to find out the truth about their reputation, so he sent two angels to investigate. They came to the city one evening and were met at the gate by Lot who invited them to his home for hospitality. Before the visitors retired for the night, the inhabitants of the city demanded to meet and get acquainted with the visitors. This demand to meet the angelic visitors grew out of Lot's serious breach of hospitality rules. Lot was a resident alien, a sojourner. In return for the protection and toleration of the city, he had certain obligations, some of which pertained to visitors. This incident arose in regard to those obligations. Lot, either ignorantly or intentionally, exceeded the rights of an alien resident in receiving and entertaining two "foreigners." The visitors might have hostile intentions, so it was not unreasonable to require that their credentials be examined. The visitors should have been received first by the Sodomites. Moreover, the men of Sodom's suspicion of these visitors may have been heightened because Lot does not seem to have been a man of pleasing character, for Genesis says that though he was a sojourner, he acted as a judge among them.[33]

This interpretation is supported by three lines of argument. First, the Hebrew word *yada'* is found 943 times in the OT. It is used only ten times without qualification (excluding this text and its derivative, Judg 19:22) to refer to sexual relations, and always of heterosexual relations. Had homosexual relations been in view, then the Hebrew word *shakab* would be expected. *Shakab* is used some fifty times in the OT for sexual intercourse, relations between men and women, men and men, and even humans and animals. Thus, *yada'* must be taken in its common meaning of "to know" or "to get acquainted with." The men of Sodom and Gomorrah were simply interested in getting to know the angelic visitors.[34]

The offer of Lot's daughters is understood in two quite different ways. Some think there is no sexual overtone to it. Lot's daughters are offered to the men of the city simply as the most convenient bribe to get them to be hospitable in their actions.[35] Others are less convinced about the nonsexual nature of the verb "to know" when used of Lot's daughters. However, in their opinion this does not prevent the hospitality interpretation of Sodom's sin.[36]

The hospitality breach interpretation is also supported by the way other biblical texts refer to Sodom and Gomorrah. That is, it is argued, the interpretation of Sodom's sin as homosexuality is not supported by intrabiblical exegesis. Examine Isa 1:10, Jer 23:14, Ezek 16:48, 49, Matt 10:14, 15, and Luke 10:10-12. These passages use Sodom and Gomorrah as symbols of utter destruction, and their sin is said to be so great that it deserves exemplary punishment. These passages, however, make no mention of sexual sin. They either mention the arrogance of the cities or their lack of hospitality.[37]

Finally, proponents of this interpretation say the understanding of Genesis 19 as referring to homosexuality arose in the intertestamental period primarily as the result of the books of Jubilees and Josephus.[38] There are even some who try to connect this story with other ancient myths about hospitality.[39] 2 Peter and Jude are a reflection of this apocryphal attitude.

Careful examination of this interpretation leaves us unconvinced. For one thing, we disagree that *yāda'* simply means "to know" or "to get acquainted with." Statistics alone can never determine the meaning of a word, but even here statistics suggest something other than what Bailey claims. Of the fifty or so uses of *yāda'* in Genesis, five uncontestedly are sexual in nature (Gen 4:1, 17, 25; 24:16; 38:26).[40] In addition, there are two other passages in Genesis where sexual connotation is contested (Gen 19:5 and 19:8, the passage about Lot and Sodom). Bailey says there are only ten uncontested uses of *yāda'* with a sexual meaning in the *whole OT* (if Gen 19:5, 8 are added, that would make twelve instances of sexual connotation). Now, even if we rule out the two verses in Genesis 19, that still means that half of the ten sexual uses in the whole OT appear in Genesis. That seems rather overwhelming evidence that Moses did use the term with sexual connotation, and it seems clear that the way the writer in question (Moses) uses the term is more significant than the way other writers (the rest of the OT) use it. Moreover, both sides in this debate agree that Judg 19:22 is a clear parallel use of the verb and that no sense but the sexual sense makes sense there.[41]

Despite these considerations, statistics alone can never determine the meaning of a word in a specific passage. Context must decide which meaning of several is to be preferred. The sexual understanding of *yāda'* in Gen 19:5 is supported by its use in the immediate context of the Sodom story

(v. 8). In verse 8 the same verb has to mean "to have sexual relations with," for it makes no sense to say Lot's daughters were not acquainted with any men. If nothing else, they knew Lot, and he was surely a man! Even Bailey's claim that Lot's offer of his daughters was just the most attractive bribe available does not avoid the sexual use of the verb. He was offering his daughters for sexual use to the men of the city. The verb in verse 8 clearly has a sexual meaning, and it is very unlikely that the same verb in a single narrative (19:1-11) should have two different meanings without some indication in the text, particularly when the uses of the verb occur so close together.[42] Finally, if all the men of Sodom wanted was to investigate the visitors' credentials, Lot's offer of daughters for sexual pleasure makes no sense. Why did not Lot just introduce his guests and demonstrate their good intentions?

As to the way other Scriptures refer to Sodom and Gomorrah, it is true that not every reference to them condemns their sexual sins. But neither do those texts exclude homosexuality as at least part of the cause of divine judgment. The two cities were exceedingly wicked, and their utter destruction is graphic evidence of that. Even those who defend a non-sexual interpretation of the text recognize that Sodom was so wicked that she was destroyed for many reasons.[43] Furthermore, the sins mentioned in the texts cited are quite in keeping with the kinds of sins Romans 1 describes, of which sexual sins are only a part.[44]

We are also unconvinced by Mollenkott and Scanzoni's suggestion that the men of Sodom were not constitutional homosexuals but bisexuals. That is why Lot offered his daughters to them, and their *bisexuality* is why they were judged.[45] In response, we note that the text says *all* the men of Sodom wanted to have homosexual relations with the angels. Though we doubt there is such a person as a constitutional homosexual, if there is, there should have been some among *all* the men of Sodom. Hence, to say the judgment fell on them *because they were all bisexuals* is highly unlikely. What Scripture portrays instead is a culture that was so desirous of pleasure that it rejected any sexual restraints.[46]

In addition, those who believe in the inspiration and inerrancy of Scripture will be unpersuaded by the attempt to deny the genuineness of the 2 Peter and Jude passages. Jude gives a striking commentary on the sin of Sodom. It is called "going after strange or different flesh" (*sarkos heteras*), which is a way of describing unnatural sex acts. Jude uses the verb *porneuō* with the preposition *ek*, which means they gave themselves up to sexual immorality completely and utterly! This is an extremely strong statement.[47] These kinds of sin make the complete destruction of the two cities understandable. We realize that arrogance and inhospitality are terrible sins, but they cannot explain the judgment of God in the destruction of two entire cities.

Finally, we reject the breach of hospitality interpretation because it seems unjust. If the problem at Sodom was that the hospitality code was broken, it was Lot who broke it, not the inhabitants of Sodom. But then, Lot should have been the one judged. Instead, Lot and his family are the only ones who escape while Sodom and Gomorrah are destroyed. That is clearly unjust!

For all these reasons, we find this interpretation of Genesis 19 unacceptable. It is a novel interpretation, but not one that squares with the text or with other passages of Scripture that condemn homosexuality.

LEVITICUS 18:22 AND 20:13

The next major statement in the OT about homosexuality is found in the Holiness Code, Lev 18:22 and 20:13. This Code contains God's demands for ordering the life of his covenant people, Israel. This order had as its goal the setting apart of Israel from the immoral and idolatrous practices of her neighbors so that she might be acceptable to worship the true and living God (cf. Lev 18:3). In this Code are what appear to be two definite and direct prohibitions against homosexual acts. Lev 18:22 stands amidst legislation against all impermissible and unnatural sexual relationships. Lev 20:13 restates 18:22, and adds the death penalty for the practice. Both call the homosexual act an abomination (*tō'ebah*, in Hebrew). These commands expand the Seventh Commandment. Their purpose is not exhaustive regulation of sexual activity, but prohibition of the grossest offenses.[48]

Homosexuals have advanced a number of explanations for these texts. These explanations are sometimes offered by themselves and sometimes in combination. We present the most common ones.

D. S. Bailey thinks the prohibitions against homosexuality in the OT simply reflect the attitudes of the peoples of Canaan and Egypt. However, he thinks there is very little available information about these nations' attitudes, most likely because homosexuality was not as common among them as often thought. Most likely the Egyptians regarded homosexual practices with a degree of contempt, but such practices were not common among them.

Bailey thinks the Assyrian and Babylonian views on the matter are no clearer. While the Code of Hammurabi seems to show that homosexuality was practiced in Assyria, no extant portion of the Code expressly mentions that fact, and in Bailey's judgment, nothing can be construed as implying a reference to it. Two Middle Assyrian Laws which go back to the fifteenth century B.C. make homosexual acts indictable. If convicted, the man's penalty was castration and submission to the very act he had performed on others. There is no indication, however, how common such practices were.

The Hittites, whose culture is now thought to have had significant influence on the Hebrews, have a reference that calls homosexuality an abomination. However, it is Bailey's view that we are not able to tell from this the attitude of the people to such practices or how common they were. This leads him to conclude that it goes beyond the evidence to suppose that the homosexual practices of Israel's neighbors endangered her morals.[49] He says: "We can only judge from these two laws that the Hebrew attitude to homosexual practices differed but little from that of the Egyptians and Assyrians. . . ."[50]

Bailey's views do not reflect the majority opinion on this issue and seem quite clearly to be false. The compelling reason is that homosexual practices were often associated with the rites of pagan religion, a topic to which we now turn.[51]

A second understanding of the Holiness Code laws says homosexuality is condemned not because it is inherently wrong, but because it was practiced in the OT world in connection with idolatrous, pagan rites. This view is expressed by almost every pro-homosexual writer. Homosexuality, it is argued, is associated in the Jewish mind with idolatry, as can be seen in a passage such as Deut 23:17. This grows out of the fact that Israel's neighbors practiced fertility rites in their temple worship. God was understood as sexual, so worship included overt sexual acts. It is in this context that whenever homosexual acts are mentioned in the OT, the writer has in mind the use that male worshipers made of male prostitutes.

Support for this position is found in the word "abomination" (*tō'ēbah*), which, on this view, does not signify something that is inherently evil such as rape or theft, but something that is ritually unclean like the eating of pork or engaging in sexual intercourse during menstruation, both of which are prohibited in this context. Temple prostitution is called an abomination and is condemned in 1 Kgs 16:3, while prostitution in general is called "wickedness" (*zimmāh*) and is prohibited in Lev 19:29. Sometimes the word "abomination" refers to an idol, as in Isa 44:19, Jer 16:18 and Ezek 7:20. Specifically, it is claimed that Leviticus 18 has the purpose of distinguishing Israel from her pagan neighbors (18:3), and the prohibition of homosexuality follows directly after the condemnation of idolatrous sexuality (18:21). The same is true of chapter 20, which begins with a prohibition of sexual practice in connection with idolatry.[52]

Unquestionably, pagan religious rites included sexual activities among which was male homosexuality. Participation in the idolatrous worship of the pagans was certainly forbidden and punished by God. His people Israel were not to be like their neighbors. However, that does not end the matter. Nothing in Leviticus explicitly states why the prohibited practices are condemned. The Leviticus texts just naturally assume the practices are condemned because they are inherently wrong, not because they were part of the idolatrous worship of the Egyptians and Canaanites. In the Leviticus Code incest, adultery, child sacrifice, bestiality, spiritism and the cursing of one's parents are all prohibited. Only one act condemned in the Code has cultic or symbolic significance—child sacrifice, and it is condemned whether associated with religious worship or not. Child sacrifice was practiced in pagan religious rites, but it was wrong on two counts—in itself and because of its association with idolatry. As a matter of fact, that the surrounding nations practiced both child sacrifice and the other prohibited acts only serves to confirm the corruption of these cultures in the mind of the Israelite.[53] Moreover, homosexuality is condemned in the context of adultery, bestiality, and incest. Clearly, those practices were not prohibited simply because of their association with idolatry or Egyptian and Canaanite cultures.

A third handling of the Leviticus Holiness Code claims that the Mosaic Law or at least parts of it are irrelevant for the Christian today. In its most extreme form, this view argues that the Mosaic Law has *no* relevance for us today. All of it reflects folk ways of an ancient culture. We live in the enlightened twentieth century. Others say that since Christ is the end of the law for the Christian (Rom 10:4), even the Ten Commandments are no longer binding (2 Cor 3:7-11). The Law has been superseded (Heb 7:11).

A weaker version of this position is used far more commonly. It distinguishes between the moral and ceremonial elements within the law. The former are still binding, but the latter have ended. Just as we need not feel obligated to follow the prohibitions in the law against eating rabbit (Lev 11:26), oysters, clams, shrimp and lobster (Lev 11:10ff.) or rare steaks (Lev 17:10), there is no need to adhere to prohibitions against homosexuality, since they, too, are a part of the ceremonial element of the law and so are not binding today.[54]

This position in some forms contains an element of truth, but as argued in our chapter on moral decision-making, OT law does not become irrelevant even for those holding a discontinuity position on the relation of the testaments. In fact, we believe this is a classic example of a case where the OT prohibition is clearly relevant, since the NT repeats the same command.

As to the matter of the ceremonial versus the moral elements of the law, we can again agree that there are differences. The problem is that the distinction is irrelevant to the question of homosexuality. While there are ceremonial elements in the law that we may safely disregard today, most Christians as well as Jews have always recognized that there are commands within the law that are of continuing ethical significance. Exodus 20–40 and Leviticus contain much of that material. Even Boswell admits that these prohibitions are in chapters that seem to stem from moral absolutes, not ceremonial concerns.[55]

A fourth approach to these texts claims that the prohibitions against homosexuality are related to male dignity and the sacred character of the semen or "seed" of life. The Hebrews, like other ancient peoples, had no accurate knowledge of the biology of conception. They did not know that women produce eggs which in turn are fertilized by male sperm. They thought the seed for new life comes solely from the man. It was "sowed" in a woman and grew into a new being in the same way that a plant sprouts and grows when sown in the ground. Moreover, they did not know that matings between certain species were infertile. Thus, men ought not to sow their seed where it would be unproductive (as would happen in homosexual relations) or in animals where it might result in "confusion" as in a centaur. This ignorance also explains why women are prohibited from receiving seed from an animal, but are free to do among themselves what they please. That is, the OT does not prohibit lesbianism.[56]

Moreover, in the patriarchal society of the Hebrews the position of the male was inviolable. It was not uncommon for the victors in war to rape conquered kings or soldiers as a mark of utter contempt and submission. In a male-dominated society it is not unreasonable to think that homosexuality could be associated with effeminacy. At least one of the partners in male homosexual acts had to assume the position normally taken by a woman.[57] All of these things, then, would undermine the status and dignity of the male. Therefore, it is not that homosexuality is morally wrong in itself, but that it is prohibited because of an ignorance about conception and a desire to maintain the dominance of the male in a patriarchal society.

This proposal is as unsatisfactory as the preceding. The texts give no indication that these are the reasons for the prohibition, so the view is purely speculative at best. Moreover, we cannot be sure that ancient peoples were as ignorant as suggested. Certainly, they did not know what we know today, but one can fairly question whether they were totally ignorant of the biology of conception. Finally, this argument totally ignores the inspiration of the Scriptures and the divine source of these commands. These commands are not the result of human speculation and superstition, but are from God and are inscripturated in the Bible.

ROMANS 1:26-27

When we turn to the NT, we find that it too condemns homosexuality. A passage that immediately comes to mind is Rom 1:26-27, as it seems to be the strongest condemnation of such actions. Rom 1:26 deals with lesbianism (homosexual relationships between women), while 1:27 treats male homosexuality. This is the only text in Scripture that mentions female homosexuality. This passage teaches that homosexual practices are evidences of God's judgment on those who reject his revelation.

As we might expect, this interpretation of Paul's teaching has been challenged. A variety of alternative interpretations have been suggested. An initial one says homosexuality per se is not condemned, but only such acts in connection with idolatry.[58] Paul knew of the pagan rites associated with

Roman religion, and he took this opportunity to warn the Romans against them. That these verses are found in the context of condemning superstitious beliefs adds credence to this view. Moreover, this theory has possible echoes of OT attitudes on this matter, so it is argued.

Much of what has already been said about the connection of homosexual practice with idolatry applies here. As a matter of fact, it is even rejected by the pro-homosexual writer Boswell for the following reasons. He thinks the temple rites of the Romans included heterosexual as well as homosexual practices. Thus, if Paul was referring to such rites, there is no reason to think he would not have condemned both. It is also clear that the sexual practices themselves are objectionable, not simply their associations. More importantly, Paul is not condemning dispassionate acts done in the worship of a god, but those that grow out of lust or passion.[59]

By far the most common reinterpretation of the passage is that Paul is condemning *unnatural* homosexual actions. This view was first argued by Bailey,[60] but has been accepted widely by others.[61] The argument is sometimes called the "abuse argument" and is as follows.[62] Paul is condemning certain homosexual *acts*, not homosexuality, or the homosexual, or the responsible practice of homosexual behavior. Whether he knew it or not, we now know that some people constitutionally prefer members of the same sex. They experience no attraction to members of the opposite sex. Therefore, we must distinguish between the *invert* and the *pervert*, between *inversion* and *perversion*. Perverts are not genuinely homosexual. They engage in homosexual practices although they are heterosexuals, or they commit heterosexual acts though homosexuals. Inverts, on the other hand, are constitutionally gay. Their sexual orientation is the inverse of heterosexuals, and for them, engaging in homosexual acts is normal. In Romans 1 Paul condemns perversion, not inversion.

Support for this view is adduced from Paul's claim that those he discusses changed or left the natural use of their sexuality for that which was unnatural or against nature. Thus, Paul only condemns homosexual acts committed by apparently heterosexual persons.[63] This, so it is claimed, is in keeping with the point of Romans 1, which has as its purpose the stigmatization of those who reject their calling.

For those who reject this view and appeal to Paul's claim that homosexuality goes "against nature," Barnett disagrees. He says that "against nature" is difficult to interpret, but it must mean a variation from what is usual or normal. The homosexual is not desirous that everyone should be like him or her in sexual preference. Homosexuality is a variation from what is normal, i.e., heterosexuality. It is not, however, a sin or disorder. Nature is full of variations from its overall design. Some people are midgets, others are albinos, still others are left-handed. These, like homosexuals, are and always will be minority variations from the majority. These differences are not unique to our culture and time. They have always existed and will continue to do so. They evidence neither sin nor the fallen condition of humanity, but merely the lack of uniformity in nature. Rather than condemn them, he argues, we should affirm them and rejoice that they exist.[64]

Despite these claims, careful exegesis of the text does not support this view. As already argued, there is no proof that there is a constitutional homosexual for whom homosexual acts follow from a genetic condition, but this interpretation clearly requires that. Moreover, there is no reason to believe that even if such a condition exists, Paul knew of it and refers to it here. Even Boswell admits this,[65] but then, why conclude Paul is teaching what this interpretation asserts?

Furthermore, it is most unlikely that when Paul says they gave up the natural use of their sexuality and did that which was against nature (*para phusin*), he is referring to homosexual acts by heterosexuals or heterosexual acts by homosexuals, acts that would be against their natural inclinations. Nor is it likely that Paul asserts, as Barnett claims, that some people are just different from the norm, but there is no penalty for such variation. Instead, these verses teach that homosexual acts are against the order of sexuality established in nature (an order clearly revealed in Genesis 1 and 2)[66] and are an evidence that God has judicially given over those who practice these acts to their own lusts.[67]

Barnett's final judgment is that even if Paul does condemn homosexuality *per se*, he is simply stating his own opinions. At other places in Paul's writings, he offers his opinions about marriage, bodily pleasure, the status of women, slavery, and civil authority. Since all of these are his views, not God's, we are free to reject them.[68] However, Paul never claims that these words about homosexuality are his private opinions, and the OT passages already discussed show they are God's views as well.[69]

A third main line of interpretation of this passage claims that it does not condemn homosexuality *per se*, but only homosexual acts growing out of lust which is a wrong motive. Paul's comment in 1:27 that they burned in their lust for one another is the key to understanding what he condemns. Lust is wrong. Any sexual activity produced by lust is immoral, whether it is homosexual or heterosexual. The only moral sexual activity is that which grows out of love and devotion. Therefore, if homosexual acts are motivated by a sense of love, devotion and commitment, they are part of God's design for human sexuality.[70]

The problem with this interpretation is twofold. First, in view of what we noted about how many partners male homosexuals typically have, promiscuity seems to be a usual part of male homosexuality. And it is highly dubious that those who are sexually promiscuous with hundreds of partners (as the figures show) act out of love, devotion and commitment to all of them! Second, the text does not say lustful homosexual acts are condemned by God. It says that *because of* homosexual acts God has given them over to this lust for one another. The lustful desire is a consequence of their sinful homosexual acts.

A final approach to Rom 1:26-27 says that it really condemns false righteousness, not homosexuality. Hence, Paul's mention of homosexuality in Romans 1 is quite incidental to the real object of his attack—false religion (Romans 2). His real concern is those Jews who thought they were keeping the law and were thereby righteous. In Romans 1 he simply adopts a common catalog of vices from extrabiblical sources without endorsing its judgments in order to portray the sins of the Gentiles.[71] But this list is incidental to his main attack on the religious complacency of pharisaism.

On the contrary, however, this interpretation overlooks the fact that the argument of Romans 1 and 2 leads to a ringing condemnation of both Gentiles and Jews in chapter 3 that takes quite seriously the sins of both Gentiles and Jews.[72] Moreover, if Paul's actual attack is on Jewish self-righteousness, Romans 1 adds nothing to that topic. What function does it serve in the book?

From this analysis of alternate interpretations, we conclude that the traditional understanding of the passage is correct. Homosexuality and lesbianism are condemned. Moreover, Paul states very clearly that homosexuality is God's judgment (v. 26), a judgment that punishes those who reject the truth of God's revelation about himself (vv. 25-26). In essence, Paul is saying that homosexuals are made, not born!

1 CORINTHIANS 6:9–11 AND 1 TIMOTHY 1:8–10

These two passages from Paul complete our study of the major biblical texts on this subject. We group 1 Cor 6:9-11 and 1 Tim 1:8-10 together because they both contain vice lists which include a similar word that bears on our present discussion. In 1 Cor 6:9-11 Paul talks about who will inherit the kingdom of God. He gives a list of vices and says that anyone who persists in these sins will not inherit the kingdom of God. In 1 Tim 1:8-10 the law is the subject, and Paul says it is good if used wisely. It is not for the righteous man but for the ungodly and sinners. He then describes in a vice list sins that the ungodly and sinners commit.

In the 1 Corinthians passage Paul includes in his list the Greek words *malakoi* and *arsenokoitai*. The 1 Timothy list also includes *arsenokoitai*. These Greek words have been translated variously in English versions of the Bible. The KJV renders them "effeminate" and "abusers of themselves with mankind." The NASB retains "effeminate" but prefers "homosexual" for the second word, while the NIV uses "male prostitute" and "homosexual offender." As we shall see, there is some uncertainty about the precise meaning of the these Greek terms. But the majority opinion has been that the first term refers to the passive partner in a homosexual relationship and the second to the active member.[73]

The first response to these verses by pro-homosexual interpreters is that these actions are not singled out in these lists as being especially wicked, and if we were to take vice lists seriously, no one would enter into the kingdom of God, since we are all covetous.[74] Interpretations of this sort are really unsatisfactory. To say that a sin in a long list does not draw special condemnation does not mean Scripture approves the action. A vice list is still a *vice* list. Moreover, there is a failure to make a biblical distinction between a repentant sinner who seeks with God's help to be free of some sin but who may at some time fail and an unrepentant sinner who follows a planned and uninterrupted course of disobedience. The vice lists refer to the latter, not the former. There is grace and forgiveness for the former, but not for the latter.[75]

A more serious objection to the majority opinion on these texts stresses that the meaning of the two Greek words is uncertain and concludes that it is unwise, therefore, to use them in a blanket condemnation of homosexuality and homosexuals. There are some typical arguments offered in support of this approach.[76] Proponents claim there is no Greek word that perfectly corresponds to the English word "homosexual." Most likely this is because homosexuals in ancient Greek culture were married and therefore bisexual. There are, however, a number of Greek terms that refer to people who engage in homosexual intercourse: *paiderastia*, *pallakos*, *kinaidos*, *arrenomanēs* and *paidophthoros*. Thus, if Paul wanted to refer to these people, he most likely would have used one of these words. Instead, he used two terms whose precise meaning is a matter of debate. The word *malakoi* is the plural of a root that means "soft" (see, e. g., Matt 11:8; Luke 7:25). In moral contexts it is used of those who are loose, weak or lacking in self-control. Moreover, 1 Cor 6:9-11 and 1 Tim 1:8-10 are never used by patristic Greek writers as a reason for condemning homosexuals or homosexual behavior. On the contrary, they are used of generally dissolute behavior and occasionally of specific sexual acts such as masturbation.

The meaning of *arsenokoitai* is even more uncertain. It is a compound of *koitē*, which means "those who engage in sexual intercourse," and *arsen*, which means "male" or "masculine." Thus, it may mean that the male is the subject or object of the intercourse. If he is the subject, then the word refers to male prostitutes. If the object, it means those who have had sexual intercourse with males. For this reason many modern lexicons understand the term to refer to those who are the active partners in anal intercourse with males. Yet if either of these meanings is correct, it is surprising, so it is argued, that early Greek fathers such as John Chrysostom did not interpret the 1 Corinthians and 1 Timothy passages as referring to homosexual behavior.

In evaluating this position it is only fair to note that there is some difference of opinion about the meaning of these terms, but their meaning is not nearly as unclear as pro-homosexual writers want us to believe. In classical Greek, *malakos* is used of boys and men who allow themselves to be used homosexually and of those who play the part of the passive partner in homosexual intercourse.[77] In *Roman Antiquities*, written about 7 B.C. by Dionysius of Halicarnassus, Aristodemus of Cumae is called *malakos* because he had been "effeminate" (*thēludrias*) as a child, having undergone things associated with women.[78] Thus, while there is some ambiguity about *malakos*, there is evidence in supporting the view that it refers to the passive partner in homosexual intercourse. Moreover, this view is further supported by its use with *arsenokoitēs*, a term for the active member in such acts. Aristotle in *Problems* has a lengthy discussion on the origins of homosexual passivity, and he uses the word *malakos*.[79]

The second of these terms, *arsenokoitēs*, is used by Paul in both 1 Cor 6:9 and 1 Tim 1:10.[80] Boswell claims it has only tangential relationship to homosexuality.[81] His point seems to be that it is found in a list of sexual sins, sexual immorality (*pornos*), adultery (which is referred to in the passage by referring to adulterers, *moichoi*), and effeminacy (*malakos*). However, rather than strengthening Boswell's position, his point seems to weaken it. *Arsenokoitēs* is related to sexual sin. It is among sexual sins in Paul's list, and as Ukleja says, "It could have easily become a euphemism for homosexuality."[82] Further, Boswell's case is weakened by the fact that both *malakos* and *arsenokoitēs* follow *pornos* in Paul's vice lists. *Pornos* is a general term for sexual sin and is often, as in the texts under consideration, followed by specific examples.[83] Finally, much of Boswell's evidence for his views on these terms is based upon post-first century A.D. usage, but what we need to know is how the terms were used when Paul wrote, not several centuries later.[84]

In summing up our discussion of biblical teaching on homosexuality, we note that Scripture does not say a lot about homosexuality. Possibly this is because it was not widespread in Jewish culture. However, we cannot escape the clear conviction that when Scripture does speak of it, it prohibits and condemns it. Thus, we must conclude that pro-homosexual writers seem to escape the text's meaning, not explain it.

HOMOSEXUALITY AND AIDS

One cannot conclude a discussion of homosexuality in our day without saying something about AIDS. This is not to suggest that only homosexuals have AIDS, because others do as well. We discuss it, instead, because the vast majority of those suffering from this disease in the Western World are homosexuals.

AIDS—WHAT IS IT?

AIDS stands for acquired immunodeficiency syndrome. It is a relatively new disease. It was first recognized in 1981 when an unusual form of pneumonia due to a protozoan parasite killed five young men.[85] They all lived in Los Angeles and were all homosexual. In that same year a number of young gay men died of an extremely rare form of cancer (Kaposi's sarcoma). In all of these cases, during the final phases of these diseases these men exhibited a profound impairment of their immune defense systems. Since they had been healthy most of their lives, it was reasonable to think that they were immunologically normal until the terminal disease. Thus, it appeared that their condition was "acquired," and that it was secondary to something else.[86]

By examining these and other cases, it was discovered that this condition involves a lack of certain lymphocytes or white blood cells called T4 lymphocytes. These white blood cells are helper and regulatory cells necessary to mounting proper immune responses. Lacking these cells, a number of diseases, called "opportunistic," would attack the body, ultimately killing the person.[87] By the middle of 1985, twelve thousand cases of the disease had been diagnosed in the U.S. alone. In 1991, ten years after discovery, AIDS had killed 126,159 Americans, and 196,000 in the U.S. were known to have the disease. It was estimated as well that 1.5 million are infected, though exact figures are not easy to come by.[88]

We now know that AIDS is a secondary condition to the HIV virus. Moreover, the stages through which those infected pass are also fairly well known. The final stage or two stages (as some specialists count them) are AIDS. Upon infection with the HIV virus there may be a fever and rash, but they may be so slight as to go unnoticed. About four weeks later the person becomes infectious. Tests for detecting the virus are not effective until the twelfth week, and some infected may not discover their condition until three years have passed. During this time the victim may unwittingly infect many others. The period from onset of infection until full-blown AIDS may be as short as two years or as long as fifteen. Once one has AIDS, it is fatal in one to four years. At present there is no known cure for AIDS, though some drugs such as AZT slow its onset as well as its progress.

AIDS—HOW IS IT PASSED?

It is now believed that AIDS is only passed through intimate contact with someone who is infected. The two most common ways this happens are sexual intercourse and the mingling of one's blood with that of an HIV positive person. Semen and blood are two very effective vehicles for transmitting the virus. The two most common means of mingling one's blood with that of an HIV positive person are by sharing needles when using drugs and by passing the virus from infected pregnant mothers to their babies. Before the precise nature of AIDS was known, the blood supplies of the U.S. and a number of Western nations were contaminated with the virus. As a result, it is estimated that about 70 percent of all hemophiliacs are now infected, and many (such as the recently deceased Arthur Ashe) who had major surgery requiring blood transfusions are infected as well. Today it is very unlikely that AIDS would be passed through the blood supply in the West. However, that is not so in many Third World countries, particularly in Africa.

At times some have feared infection from mosquito bites or the saliva, sweat or tears of someone who has the disease. None of these has been shown to be very effective vehicles for transmitting the disease.

However, while there are various ways of becoming infected with the HIV virus, quite clearly the most common is through homosexual intercourse. It is estimated that 70 percent of those suffering from the HIV virus are practicing homosexuals. The reasons are not certain, but the most likely is that the membranes in the anal passage are not designed for sexual intercourse. Thus, when this type of sexual contact takes place, there is the greater probability that membranes will tear. The combination of bleeding and semen are a very hospitable environment for the virus and its transmission.

AIDS—IS IT GOD'S JUDGMENT?

Before answering this question, we believe one must distinguish between three questions. First, are AIDS victims responsible and thus blameworthy for their disease? Second, is AIDS the judgment of God? And, third, should we show compassion to those who have AIDS? These questions must be distinguished, because some think that if the answer to either of the first two questions is yes, there is no room for compassion. Not uncommonly, they try to avoid assigning any responsibility for their condition to those who are infected.

We think this is misguided. Even if one is responsible for becoming infected with AIDS, and even if AIDS is God's judgment, the appropriate Christian response is still compassion. In fact, these might be the best reasons for compassion. God himself does not delight in sending judgment. Just as parents on occasion must punish children for their actions and yet genuinely grieve that they must punish them, so it is with God. We make this point because however one answers the first two questions, we are truly sorry for those who have this disease. It is hard to know what they experience, but we do sympathize with them as much as is humanly possible.

But is AIDS the judgment of God?[89] The answer is more complex than it may initially seem. The answer depends on exactly what one means by the question. One may mean, is AIDS God's judgment for some personal, immoral acts that each person infected with the virus has done? If so, then everyone with the disease would be blameworthy because of what they did. If this is what the question means, then the answer is surely no. Many with AIDS did nothing blameworthy. We would not add, for example, to the burden already borne by those infected in their mother's womb or by those who received contaminated blood through a transfusion by saying they did something to warrant the disease. They are total victims of this disease.

There is a second way this question can be understood—is God judging innocent people by allowing them to receive the HIV virus? If that is what is meant, that appears to contradict God's justice. For persons to be judged, it seems that they must be responsible or blameworthy for their action. If God dispenses judgment indiscriminately, how are we to understand his justice and goodness? Some try to protect God against such claims by positing a God with limited power and (possibly) wisdom. He is doing the best he can, but evil comes to good people anyway. There is a certain attractiveness to this view, but in the end the problems it creates and the fact that it is contrary to the teaching of Scripture make it untenable.

What seems a better response begins by noting that while some AIDS victims are guilty of no direct action for which the disease is the just penalty, they do live in a fallen, sinful world. As a result of sin, Scripture teaches that there is death (Rom 5:12). And if there is death, there must be diseases that cause death. Scripture also teaches that we all sinned in Adam, and thus we all are responsible for what has befallen our world (Rom 5:12-21). In this sense, no one can claim complete innocence for the presence of AIDS or any other disease in the world.

Some may still question how it is fair for those who committed no specific act that brings AIDS to get it anyway. Moreover, even granting our corporate guilt in Adam, many have received God's forgiveness for sin by accepting Christ. Why should AIDS fall even on such as these? Here we respond that sin not only has eternal consequences but temporal ones as well. While God guarantees that repented sin will correct our standing before him and assures us of eternal life with him, God does not guarantee freedom from all earthly consequences of sin. All of us are sinners, and that sin seldom affects only the sinner. Hence, in war innocent people die. In a divorce the innocent suffer. In the AIDS epidemic people innocent of immoral acts, even people who know Christ as savior, can get the disease. Sin is a serious matter. Even when repented and forgiven, its social consequences can victimize us and others as well.[90]

We still must face the most common form of the question—is AIDS God's judgment on those who are guilty of committing homosexual acts? We think it is. This does not make many people happy, but it seems a proper conclusion from scriptural teaching. Scripture clearly shows that homosexual behavior is sinful. And since AIDS is transmitted through homosexual acts, it is hard to escape the conclusion that AIDS is recompense for that sin. To say anything else would give false hope to those who get AIDS as a result of these acts. This, of course, does not mean that everyone who practices homosexual behavior will get AIDS, but only that those who get it from such behavior, get it as God's judgment. That some homosexuals do not get AIDS neither disproves it to be God's judgment nor shows God to be unjust to those who do get it. Rather, it demonstrates his mercy and grace to those who escape.

Having said these things, we must remember several points as we reflect on this matter. First, this is a moral universe. We are not free to do whatever we want without any consequences. We break God's commands at our own risk. Some seem to think God is obligated to make us happy at any cost. That is simply not so. As Carson puts it, God is more concerned about our holiness than our health.[91] God loves us so much that he is willing to go to any extreme to make us the kind of people we should be, people who can go to live eternally with him. Second, we should not fail to see God's grace even in his judgment. As noted, many who are guilty of this sin do not get the HIV virus. Many others have been infected only after repeated instances of disobedience. God has been patient, hoping that the sinner would repent. Even when infected, God's presence is promised to those who desire it and repent. God can bless the afflicted even amidst the affliction. Moreover, Christ's death paid for the eternal consequences of this sin, so there is forgiveness. Finally, God's judgment on homosexuality is quite in keeping with his judgment on all sin. We may be tempted to single out homosexuality because of a distaste for the sin and the enormity of AIDS, but we should not forget that God's judgment rests on all forms of wickedness. That should drive all of us to our knees in repentance, asking for forgiveness for our own sins.

CHAPTER NINE

Genetic Engineering— Reproductive Technologies

J unior Davis and his wife Mary Sue had five unsuccessful pregnancies during their nine-year marriage. Then, they turned for help to *in vitro* fertilization. More eggs were taken and fertilized than were implanted. The two that were implanted failed to produce a pregnancy. The rest of the embryos were frozen. Later the couple filed for divorce. Who gets custody of the seven frozen embryos? Both parents want them, and neither wants the other to have custody.[1] On June 1, 1992 the Tennessee Supreme Court ruled that Mary Sue could not use the embryos to become pregnant, for so doing would force her former husband into fatherhood. Based on privacy rights and the "procreational autonomy" of each person, the court reasoned that the father's right to avoid procreation should not be abridged. Moreover, there were other ways his former wife could have a child.[2] Is *in vitro* fertilization morally right? What about freezing unused fertilized eggs? These things are being done, but should they be done?

If you could choose your child's sex, would it be morally right to do so? Through amniocentesis it is possible to determine the sex of a baby while in its mother's womb. Some, because the sex was not what the family wanted, have aborted the child. While many think this morally appalling, it may soon be possible to avoid this moral dilemma and still choose the sex of one's child. Researchers have discovered a way to separate X from Y sperm. Depending on whether a couple wants a boy or girl, the mother can be impregnated by artificial insemination with the appropriate sperm.[3] Though this avoids aborting an unwanted baby, is such tampering with reproductive processes morally acceptable? Is a refusal to accept whatever "the genetic lottery" brings an unwillingness to accept what God has willed for the family? If the sex of a child can be predetermined, are we far from producing babies with genes designed for just those traits we think make perfect babies?

Welcome to the brave new world of genetic engineering! Talk of test-tube babies, gene-splicing, cloning, and the like used to be part of science fiction. Within the last twenty-five years the field of genetic engineering has literally exploded on the scene. Technology available now and in the foreseeable future presents options for manipulating human reproduction and man's very genetic makeup. The prospects are at once exciting and terrifying. Unfortunately, as often happens, the new technology presents moral dilemmas that go well beyond anything scriptural morality envisions. Though the ethics of these procedures are under discussion, relatively few evangelicals have entered the debate. That needs to change before legal and moral decisions are made that we find unacceptable.

In surveying the field of genetic engineering, one sees quickly that many diverse procedures fall under this broad rubric. Generally, however, one can divide the field of genetic engineering into two broad categories: 1) procedures involving the manipulation of human reproduction and 2) procedures involving the manipulation of the genetic makeup of living beings. In this chapter we cover the former category and in the next the latter group.[4]

GENETIC ENGINEERING AND HUMAN REPRODUCTION
ARTIFICIAL INSEMINATION

Artificial insemination is used mainly to combat male infertility. It is not a new procedure, though it has gained popularity in the second half of the twentieth century. In 1785 John Hunter, a British physician, was the first to use the technique with humans. It was later developed and used primarily with animals.[5] Because of legal and social ramifications of the procedure (we will explain more about this later), detailed records have not been kept on the frequency of this practice. However, as of 1979 estimates were that over twenty thousand babies per year are conceived this way.[6]

Two kinds of artificial insemination are available, insemination using the husband's semen (AIH) and insemination using a donor's sperm (AID). The procedure itself is relatively simple. Sperm is collected, usually through masturbation, and then deposited by use of a syringe in or near the cervix of the woman's uterus. If all goes well, the woman conceives, carries the baby to term, and delivers a normal healthy baby.

AIH

AIH is much less problematic than AID. Since all the ethical concerns with AIH also arise with AID, our coverage of AIH will be brief. AIH is normally used for one of several reasons. First, the husband may be fertile, but for some physical or psychological reason cannot participate in normal sex relations. Second, the husband may have a low sperm count. This procedure allows sperm to be collected periodically and stored in order to increase its volume, so that chances of fertilization upon insemination increase. Finally, in some cases a husband may be planning a vasectomy or may need to have prostate surgery. Since he may wish later to have more children with his wife or by a second wife (e.g., if his first wife dies and he remarries), a husband may store sperm for possible future use.[7]

AIH and Practical Concerns
AIH presents few, if any, legal, social, or psychological problems. There can be no question about the legitimacy or the inheritance rights of the child, for its biological parents are husband and wife. Attempts to create the "perfect baby" by inseminating the wife with sperm from "superior donors"[8] do not arise. Moreover, unlike AID, AIH cannot be used to give lesbians, homosexuals, or other single parents children, practices of dubious social worth. From a psychological perspective, the child cannot be unwanted because unrelated to the father. Nor is the existence of the child a constant reminder of the husband's inability to father a child (as may happen with an AID baby). For some men, that realization would be a blow to their sense of masculinity.

AIH and Ethical Concerns
There are few ethical concerns with AIH, but they are worthy of note. Initially, there is the question of masturbation. Some do not consider this a moral problem, but for others it is immoral. We believe it need not be a problem, because for those opposed to masturbation, there are simple alternatives. Husband and wife could collect sperm during sex relations. Preferred methods of collection would be *coitus interruptus*, retrieval of sperm from the vagina, or the use of a condom.[9] Such methods are also usable with AID, *in vitro* fertilization, and surrogate mothering, and hence the issue of masturbation need not arise in regard to any of those practices. Of course, for those opposed to artificial methods of birth control, collecting sperm by these means will be problematic. But those who believe contraception is morally permissible will not likely deem these methods problematic. Regardless of one's views on contraception, the three methods of collecting sperm do avoid the problem of masturbation.

Two other ethical issues arise for both AIH and AID. One is whether it is morally right to tamper with and interrupt the natural order of procreation. This, of course, is the traditional Roman Catholic objection based on natural law theory. In the Church's statement "Instruction on Respect for Human Life in Its Origin and on the Dignity of Procreation," artificial insemination, *in vitro* fertilization, and surrogate mothering are all condemned as unnatural means of conceiving a child. According to the statement, any act of procreation through means other than those natural to the conjugal union is illicit and immoral.[10]

By way of response, we note that anyone unconvinced by natural law theory is unlikely to find this a compelling argument. Moreover, as we argued in our discussion of birth control, natural law itself can cut both ways (for and against) birth control. Likewise, strictly carrying out the implications of natural law thinking appears also to rule out such "unnatural" interventions in the birth process as taking fertility drugs to increase the likelihood of conception or delivery of a baby by cesarean section. Hence, we are unconvinced by arguments based on natural law, but even if we held natural law theory, it is not immediately clear what it would proscribe.

Our further response to the charge that this is unnatural is that we grant that these procedures are unnatural, but so is most medical intervention into the natural order. How can that alone make it immoral? Moreover, because of sin we live in a fallen world where things do not always work as they should. God has commissioned man to subdue the created order and has given him a certain dominion over it (Gen 1:28). While this does not allow man to harm or exploit the natural order, permission to subdue a natural order which does not always function as God intended because of sin's disruptive influence seems to necessitate man's intervention into natural processes. If this is not so, God has commanded man to do something (subdue the natural order) that, if man obeys, will be immoral, and that seems odd. Of course, this does not make absolutely any form of intervention into the natural order moral. It only means that if a medical, reproductive, etc. procedure is immoral, it is not immoral *solely because it is unnatural.*

A final ethical issue that arises with both AIH and AID is the matter of disjoining the sexual act and the procreative act. The complaint is not the unnaturalness of the procedure, but that whereas God so designed the sexual act as to tie it to the procreative act, AIH and AID sever the two. Though the sperm and egg in AIH are those of husband and wife, still, it is argued, God intended children to be conceived amidst the act that expresses the parents' love and commitment to one another.[11] We consider this a significant issue, though one which can be answered. However, because it is most complicated in cases of AID where a third party enters the equation, we shall discuss it under our handling of AID.

AID

AID raises many more questions than does AIH. Despite potential problems, there are significant reasons why people have used it. First, the husband may be sterile as a result of disease or accident. Second, the husband may carry a genetic disease and not want to risk passing it to a child.

Third, AID may be considered when the husband is Rh positive and the mother Rh negative, and there is concern over the results for the baby. However, injections of anti-Rh antibodies into the mother will prevent damage to any Rh positive child. Finally, AID allows a single woman to have children.[12] For some, AID is preferable to adoption in these cases, because it allows a couple to have a child who is genetically related to at least one of the parents.

When a couple decides to use AID, the physician normally tries to match the characteristics of the donor with those of the husband. Moreover, it is also possible to mix the husband's sperm with the donor's so as to raise the overall sperm count. In such cases, it may even happen that the sperm that fertilizes the egg is the husband's. In addition, AID is much more preferable than asking someone else to impregnate one's wife through natural means. If AID constitutes adultery, it does not do so in the same way as having one's wife have sex relations with another man.

Practical Legal Concerns

A major legal concern with AID is the legitimacy of the child. Legitimacy becomes important in several key respects. It is crucial with respect to inheritance. Specifically, does an AID child have a right to inherit from its mother's husband, or are its rights only related to its biological father, whoever that is? The Uniform Parentage Act holds that a husband who consents to AID of his wife is the child's legal father, and many U.S. states have enacted laws in conformity with this rule.[13] Nevertheless, that cannot preclude the possibility of an AID child trying to inherit from its genetic father or the possibility of the husband whose wife used AID trying to avoid legal responsibilities to the AID child. Moreover, legitimacy becomes very important when a couple divorces. Does the divorced husband owe child support to the AID offspring or not? What if he did not agree to the AID procedure? Generally, when husbands have consented to AID, the courts have held them liable for child support when husband and wife separate.[14] Though some U.S. states have adopted legislation to protect the rights of an AID child, not all have.[15] Then, does the divorced husband have visitation and custody rights to an AID child?

A second legal issue focuses on whether AID is adultery. Early cases in the U.S., Canada and England ruled that AID was adultery and thus sufficed as grounds for divorce. While the question is a moral one, it has obvious legal implications for divorce.[16]

Finally, there is the issue of legal liability of the doctor and even the donor in AID cases. Suppose the baby has a genetic defect that most likely comes from the donor. Is the doctor liable for failing to detect the genetically defective sperm?[17] Could the donor, if known, be legally liable for the defective sperm? Since presumably he was paid for the sperm donation, could he be sued for fraud? These are not easy legal questions, but they are potential complications that arise with AID.

Practical Social and Psychological Concerns

Psychologically AID can have advantages over adoption. The child may more likely be accepted by its family since both husband and wife can be involved in the pregnancy from conception onward and because the child, being biologically related to the mother and her other biological children, may likely resemble them more than an adopted child would. Likewise, AID rules out fears of the birth mother suddenly appearing, as might happen with an adopted child. Since very few records are kept about AID donors, the chances of the donor finding "his child" and disrupting the family are quite slim.[18]

On the other hand, potential psychological problems can arise with AID. The wife may think less of her husband's masculinity when she learns he cannot give her a child, or she may just feel that the child she carries has nothing to do with the love she has for her husband. However, most of the psychological problems are likely to arise in regard to the husband and child. The husband's masculinity may be threatened not only by his infertility, but by feeling that some donor was more "man" than he. Moreover, AID clearly marks the husband as infertile, whereas with adoption outsiders need not know whether husband, wife, or both are infertile.

From the child's perspective, there are disadvantages as well. The husband might love and care less for the child, for example, than he would if he/she were his biological child. If the child does not know the truth about his/her lineage, it may be very troublesome to sense alienation from his/her father and have no clue as to why that is so. Then, there is the dilemma of whether and when to tell the child the truth about his/her genetic identity, especially when there is little chance of his/her learning the actual identity of his/her biological father.[19] Moreover, while the child may resemble his/her mother, he/she may resemble neither husband or wife, and this may create significant problems in explaining why the child looks like neither, especially when friends of the family know the child is not adopted.[20]

Social problems also abound with AID. For example, because a husband knows his daughter is not genetically related to him, he may be more prone to consider sexual abuse and even incest with her. Even with a male child, the husband may be more open to abusing him than with his genetic descendant. Second, the matter of incest arises in another way. Studies show that some doctors use the same donor repeatedly. A study done by Curie-Cohen *et al.* showed that some doctors use one donor for more than six conceptions and that 10.3 percent of the doctors responding used the same donor for nine or more pregnancies.[21] It is possible that later in life people who are half-brothers and half-sisters would unwittingly marry and commit incest, especially since semen from one donor is likely to be used by people living in a given geographical locale.

A third social problem is that AID is used to give single women children. In fact, the Curie-Cohen study showed that at least 9.5 percent of the doctors responding to the poll had used AID for single women.[22] Not only is it disturbing to see children brought into a home with no father,[23] but it is even more troubling to see this as a means for lesbian couples to have children. Concerns here are not just ethical. It is dubious that it will be psychologically or socially healthy for these children to discover that their "parents" are both female, especially when other children each have male and female parents.

Fourth, AID encourages surrogate mothering (as can *in vitro* fertilization). While there are many variations on the surrogate theme, one is that the host mother contracts to being artificially inseminated and carrying a childless couple's baby to birth.[24]

Finally, AID also raises the specter of eugenics. As practiced, AID is detrimental from both a negative and positive eugenic stance. As to negative eugenics, attempts to prevent the birth of potentially genetically defective children seems a noble goal. However, as some have shown, record keeping by doctors who use AID is very poor. For example, the Curie-Cohen survey showed that while "93 percent of physicians kept records on recipients, only 37 percent kept permanent records on children born after AID and only 30 percent kept any permanent records on donors."[25] This makes it very hard to determine a child's genetic heritage, despite the importance of knowing this when a genetically controlled disease is involved. Moreover, when careful records are not kept, doctors will not likely stop using sperm from a given donor, despite the fact that his sperm may be the source of many genetically defective and diseased children (present and future). What is even more troublesome is that Curie-Cohen found that 32 percent of the physicians surveyed used sperm from multiple donors in a single cycle so as to obscure the identity of the genetic father.[26] That practice is hardly in the child's best interests, genetically speaking.

As to "positive" eugenics, if some want to attempt to build perfect babies or even a master race, the means are available with AID. There are sperm banks and egg banks with deposits from Nobel prize winners, for example. Moreover, Curie-Cohen showed that 80 percent of physicians surveyed used medical students and hospital residents all or most of the time.[27] Would lawyers likely choose lawyers, teachers choose teachers, and military personnel choose from their ranks? One comes to see that regardless of motivation, doctors who use AID make judgments all the time about which genes are superior (if they bother at all to screen donors). This plays right into the hands of those who would remake man in their image of the "ideal man."

Ethical Concerns

Many of the practical issues also have ethical implications. The question of masturbation is one ethical concern. Moreover, many would complain that AID is contrary to the natural order. The fact that AID can lead to single-parent and lesbian families is most troublesome, as is the possibility of incest that comes with AID. Then, existence of sperm and egg banks and their relation to attempts to design superior people pose real ethical questions. Also, many find ethically disturbing the fact that AID divides the unitive aspect of sexual intercourse from its procreative aspect.

In addition, three other ethical matters are noteworthy. First, does AID constitute adultery? AID removes procreation from within the marriage bond by involving a third party, but does that involvement of a third party constitute adultery? Some think so, for it grants someone other than the husband control over his wife's person and body, even though the married couple committed themselves only to one another.[28] Indeed, if AID is adulterous, it is ruled out for the Christian automatically.

Second, there is the question of the biblical and moral concept of parenthood. Some argue that God ordained marriage as the union of two people who would give birth to children genetically related to them. Though adoption is an exception, the divine ideal of children genetically related to parents married to one another is the standard by which AID must be judged. Initially, this means that AID should not be used outside the bounds of marriage, i.e., by single parents, lesbians, or those making surrogate arrangements.[29] On the other hand, even within a marriage, AID does not meet the divine ideal for parenthood.[30]

Though some think AID contrary to God's pattern for parenthood, others are not so sure. Some have argued that Christian attitudes toward parenthood have typically rested on four assumptions, but those assumptions need reexamining. Those assumptions are: 1) babies are God's gift to those who have the equipment and luck to beget them; 2) those not so blessed were intended by God not to have children; 3) the person bearing the child is naturally its best parent; 4) once a child is conceived, it belongs to its biological parents, especially its mother, and cannot be taken away even in the most difficult circumstances, i.e., blood relation is a stronger factor in establishing parenthood than love.[31]

Though it is normal to think of parenthood in these terms, critics claim these assumptions are not necessarily accurate. Does parenthood consist in mere biological relation, or in establishing a loving, nurturing atmosphere in which to rear the children? If biological relation is the only criterion for parenthood, then couples who adopt a child could never qualify as its parents, and that seems strange. Likewise, a man who marries a widow with children or a woman who marries a widower with children could never be parents to those children, but that also seems absurd. In light of these considerations, it is argued that those who reject AID on grounds that it destroys the biblical basis of parenthood (biological tie between parents and child) hold an untenable position. Moreover, Scripture contradicts this view of parenthood. For example, Joseph served genuinely as a parent/father to Jesus, despite no biological relation to him whatsoever. But, then, if one can serve as a parent without a genetic tie to a child, why cannot a man be a parent to a child who is genetically related to his wife and some sperm donor?[32]

A final ethical question receives less attention but is still significant. It focuses on the sperm donor himself. In essence, the sperm donor becomes merely a sperm salesman. He bears no responsibility for his actions, provides no support for his biological offspring, remains hidden from the mother and child, and may well have little or no concern for what is done with his sperm. For him it is purely a commercial matter. He has a commodity, there is demand, and he supplies the need for a price. Many find such commercializing of the most fundamental elements of life morally reprehensible.[33] We are often told that people are to be treated as subjects, not objects to be manipulated for our own ends. While sperm alone is not a person, it is part of the stuff of which persons are made. Buying and selling it strikes many as taking that which is potentially and partially personal and treating it as an object.

An Assessment of Artificial Insemination

From a moral standpoint, we have already explained why we find the objections that artificial insemination is unnatural and that it involves masturbation unconvincing. Most of the remaining issues relate solely to AID, and all of them deserve attention.

First, what about AID being used to promote single-parent families, encourage surrogate mothering, give children to lesbian couples, etc.? Given biblical commands against homosexuality, lesbianism, incest, and the like, we deplore the use of AID for such purposes. Likewise, there are serious problems with surrogate mothering and attempts to design a master race through the use of sperm banks or other means. In addition, we realize that sometimes God allows a parent to die while children are still in the home, thereby creating a single-parent home, but we see nothing in Scripture that allows a person who does not marry to *bear a child anyway*. It is permissible for a single aunt or uncle to become guardian of a niece or nephew whose parents have died, but that is quite a different matter from a person who decides not to marry reproducing anyway. Biblically, reproduction should occur within the bonds of marriage.

Does the preceding automatically make AID immoral? Not necessarily. One must always distinguish between the *existence of a thing* (object, act, technique) and its *use*. While using AID to give lesbians children, for example, is clearly an immoral use of this technique, that does not prove that AID itself or every use of it is immoral. If one must avoid contact with everything that might be used immorally, it would be difficult to function in the world, for many morally neutral things can be put to immoral use. For example, automobiles seem morally neutral in themselves, but they can be put to good or bad uses. They can be used to rush an injured person to a hospital for medical care, but they can also be used to escape quickly after a robbery. Do evil uses of automobiles make them evil and proscribe them from all use? Obviously not. Similarly, we conclude that AID may be used for evil purposes, and those practices should be avoided. However, none of those evil uses necessarily makes AID itself immoral. It may still be immoral, but if so, not because of evil uses that may be made of it.

A key moral issue with AID is whether it is adultery. If it is, AID is clearly ruled out. The best way to assess this matter is to consider what constitutes adultery. A marriage bond is constituted when a husband and wife commit their lives to one another before God. They promise to remain faithful in their love and devotion to one another beyond their love for any other person. That union of mind and will is symbolized outwardly by their physical sexual union. The Bible teaches that adultery is one way to break the marital commitment, for it involves giving oneself to someone other than one's spouse. Also, adultery usually involves an element of lust for the person with whom adultery is committed.

In light of this description of adultery, it is hard to call AID adultery. There is nothing sexually stimulating for a woman about being artificially inseminated. Moreover, since she does not normally know the donor, it is impossible to lust after him prior to or during the insemination. Likewise, there is no physical, emotional, or spiritual contact with the donor, so she can hardly be said to "give her body" or any other part of herself to him. Using artificial insemination does not mean the wife has forsaken her husband for another man. The point of this procedure is not unitive and does not involve commitment to some other man. It is purely procreative. In comparing adultery to AID, we think AID is not adulterous and should not be ruled out on that ground.[34]

In response, some agree that AID is not a matter of commitment to another man but is a purely procreative matter. But that is just the problem. God never intended the procreative aspect of human reproduction to be divided from its unitive aspect. Paul Ramsey objects to AID on just these grounds. He says sexual intercourse is an act of love and a procreative act at the same time. This does not mean it always nourishes love or always engenders a child, but that it tends toward those goals.[35] Though this apparently rules out contraception, Ramsey disagrees. He claims birth control can be practiced without separating personal love from procreation. Though contraception is used for particular acts of sexual intercourse, the sum total of all acts of sexual intercourse holds together its unitive and procreative functions. The person with whom the bond of love is nourished is still the same person with whom procreation is exercised.[36] In fact, Ramsey says that even if the couple decides to have no children, the unitive and procreative functions of sexual intercourse are upheld. This is so because husband and wife agree that if they have any children, they will be born "within their marriage-covenant, from their own one flesh unity and not apart from it."[37] Since God joined the unitive and procreative aspects of sexual intercourse, and since AID separates them, AID is immoral.

We find this objection more compelling than most, but not entirely convincing. Ramsey claims that the couple agrees that if they have any children, they will come within the one flesh unity and not apart from it, but is that so? Husband and wife do promise to forsake all others and cleave to one another, and that may be what Ramsey has in mind. However, as already argued, AID does not appear to break that commitment. On the other hand, if Ramsey means that the couple actually promises not to have children apart from their own acts of sexual intercourse (or at least their own sperm and egg), we find that hard to believe. Nothing of the sort is included in traditional wedding vows. Moreover, it is dubious that a couple would make such a promise because it rules out adopting a child if they decide to do so. Of course, if the couple has made this promise to one another, then they should not resort to AID, but we doubt that such a promise is made in most cases.

What about the broader issue? Is it immoral to separate the unitive and procreative aspects of sexual intercourse? Ramsey thinks so, but still thinks birth control is acceptable. We find this inconsistent. Ramsey says the totality of sexual acts by the couple holds together the unitive and procreative aspects of intercourse. But if that is so, the same is true for the couple that practices AID on *one* occasion. If it is acceptable to use birth control on *many* occasions and yet still hold together the unitive and procreative aspects of sex by the totality of sexual acts, why is only *one* instance of AID not permissible on the same grounds? Ramsey might reply that it is wrong because of that commitment to have children only within their own acts of sexual intercourse, but we have seen the problem with that reasoning. Moreover, if Ramsey's dictum that the unitive and procreative must be joined in sexual intercourse must be followed, then sexual intercourse for a couple after the wife goes through menopause is also ruled out. No act of sexual intercourse at that time of life even *tends* to engender children. If Ramsey were to reply that the sum total of sexual acts holds together the unitive and procreative aspects of sex, we agree if one looks at the whole of a couple's life together, but disagree if one considers only the whole of the couple's post-menopause life. And if *many* post-menopause acts of intercourse are acceptable in light of the whole sexual history of the couple, why is *one* instance of AID unacceptable, despite the general pattern of a couple's sex relationship?

For these reasons we think Ramsey's position is internally inconsistent and hold that if his logic were followed consistently, it would rule out all birth control and all sex after menopause.[38] On the other hand, if he allows these things, it is inconsistent to forbid one instance of AID when the couple's overall sex relation does hold together the unitive and procreative aspects of sexual intercourse.

Another point, however, must be made. It is hard to see how AID can overturn what happens in the couple's many acts of sexual intercourse or how it divides the unitive and procreative aspects of even one act of *sexual intercourse,* because AID involves no sexual intercourse! Of course, this is Ramsey's complaint, i.e., one can have procreation without sexual intercourse. But as argued above and in our chapter on birth control, Scripture and common sense argue that it is acceptable to have sexual intercourse without procreation. Scripture does not grant permission to have procreation without sexual intercourse, but it does not proscribe it either. It simply does not address the issue. None of the arguments considered seems to rule that out. Moreover, if procreation without intercourse is morally unacceptable, then even AIH is morally wrong. But even opponents of AID on this and other grounds find AIH to be acceptable. To be consistent, if they reject AID on this ground, they should reject AIH as well. We conclude, then, that if AID is immoral, it is not so because of disjoining unitive and procreative aspects of sexual intercourse.

What about the biblical view of parenthood, though? We agree that God's normal pattern for parenthood is that children be genetically related to a man and woman who are husband and wife. However, when necessary there are exceptions such as adoption or cases where a widow or widower with children marries. There are also cases of parenthood where the child is the genetic offspring of neither husband nor wife. Cases involving foster parents are an example, and so are situations where a child's parents both die and the child goes to live with his or her aunt and uncle. Unquestionably, there are exceptions to parenthood where children are biological descendants of both husband and wife. Is AID another exception? Nothing in Scripture sanctions or prohibits parenthood based on AID, for Scripture does not address that issue. The only other question, then, is whether on other grounds AID is immoral. If it is, then AID is wrong, regardless of one's views on parenthood. However, if it is not immoral on other grounds, we do not think it immoral on this ground. We see too many permissible exceptions to the general pattern of parenthood and no biblical or moral injunctions that prohibit *parenthood* by AID to conclude that AID contradicts moral concepts of parenthood.

Likewise, we also agree with those who say that more than genetic relation makes one a parent.

Despite the preceding, opponents might reject AID on other grounds. Some will reject AID because it allows man to play God (AIH is also wrong on these grounds).[39] If a couple cannot have a child through natural reproduction, then perhaps God wills the couple to remain childless. The use of artificial insemination too much takes matters into one's own hands and rejects what is apparently God's will for one's life.

We are sensitive to this argument, but do not find it as compelling as others do. For one thing, it is similar to the objection that AID is wrong because it is unnatural. But as already noted, medicine in general tampers with the natural order, as do many human endeavors. Likewise, if one rejects artificial insemination on grounds that it is playing God, then to be consistent one should reject any medical intervention into people's lives. Moreover, procedures in agriculture that enhance productivity and produce better strains of plants and animals could not be used. In fact, it would even be wrong to undertake means to protect ourselves from famine or flood, because that might thwart God's will to bring disaster (even punishment) through those means. Our point is man is constantly tampering with nature in order to subdue and rule it. Is all interference in the natural order outlawed on grounds that man is playing God? Even opponents of AID think not. Some instances of playing God are deemed permissible (they are not even thought of as cases of playing God). However, to be consistent with this line of argument, all intrusions into the natural order should be considered instances of playing God. How can one know which instances are acceptable and which not? Can that question be answered without begging it? What typically happens is that usual practices are not considered playing God, but new and unusual ones are. Obviously, this cannot be a consistent way of deciding what is or is not a case of playing God or whether it is permissible, for what is new now will soon be usual. Hence, we conclude that though this objection seems cogent, it is hard to make sense of it in a non-question begging way.

What about the claim that artificial insemination rejects God's will because God may want the couple to be childless, or God may choose without AID to give a barren woman children (as in the case of various women in the Bible)? The problem is that before trying these new technologies, a couple will not likely know God wants them to remain childless. Hence, there is no intent to thwart God's will, but to discern it and to discover the means to accomplish it, if his will is for them to have children. Likewise, in this situation it would not be immoral or attempting to thwart God's will to pray for children. God might answer by "opening the wife's womb" as he did in biblical times, but he might also lead them to seek adoption or even reveal that he will give them a child through a procedure like artificial insemination. If God really wants a couple to remain childless, he can keep them from having children regardless of what they do. But until God clearly closes all doors to having children, for someone to use artificial insemination is not necessarily resisting God's will or playing God. It may, instead, be a way of discerning whether God wants them to have a child.

Despite the preceding, we do think this objection has some merit. The fundamental problem with playing God is that man acts as if he controls these matters, rather than acknowledging that God ultimately controls childbearing as well as all else in life. In our pride we may use these techniques, because we think we know better than God what we need and when we need it. Thus, using this technology may indeed indicate a refusal to submit to God's control. Such attitudes are wrong, and if one uses artificial insemination or any other medical technology with these attitudes, he uses them immorally.[40] But that does not mean these attitudes always attach to these practices, nor that procedures such as artificial insemination *per se* are immoral.

A final moral issue is whether sperm donation is immoral. This is a hard issue that requires careful reflection. Initially we note that artificial insemination and sperm donating are not the same thing (here sperm donation refers to someone other than a woman's husband providing sperm either free or for a fee; in this sense AIH does not involve sperm donation). Because they are not the same thing, some might say that even if one is immoral (e.g., donating sperm), that doesn't make the other wrong. After all, users of a product cannot be held morally responsible for the morality or immorality of its makers.[41] The problem with this reasoning in regard to AID is that by definition it must involve both. When a woman decides to use AID, she knows this includes both. If any part of the procedure (donation or insemination) is immoral, the whole procedure should be refused.

Is sperm donation, then, moral? We believe that some objections to it are invalid. For example, some may argue that it is one thing to donate, buy or sell a car or a suit of clothes, but another to do that with sperm. Clothes and cars are objects, but sperm is at least a potential subject. We agree that sperm differs from clothes and cars, but not because it alone is a person or even a potential person. The union of sperm and egg is, we believe, a person with all the potential to develop into a baby able to exist outside its mother's womb. Hence, an embryo or fetus should be protected by law against practices such as abortion. However, to say sperm alone, or an egg by itself, is a person or potential person necessitates protecting all sperm and egg against loss. Loss of sperm or egg would be death and, depending on how they were lost, might be murder. Obviously, such notions are absurd, but then it is also wrong to think it immoral to donate or use sperm because one is treating a subject like an object.

Some may feel it is simply immoral to donate one's sperm or egg to another person because one should not donate parts of his/her body. Of course, without moral censure people donate blood, bone marrow, and even bodily organs to help others in need. Why is this donation for people in need of help to overcome infertility immoral?

Some may respond that it is immoral, because it is unnatural or because it involves masturbation, but we have already seen the problems with those objections. Others will argue that sperm donation is not like blood and organ donation, which clearly are moral. Those donations are made for people with a clear *medical* need. Without the donation the recipient might die. In contrast, infertility is not a disease, and it is surely not fatal. Bearing a child is something the infertile couple wants but does not need in order to stay alive and healthy. Hence, sperm donation, unlike blood and organ donation, is immoral because it addresses a want, not a need.

Though this sounds cogent, we believe it is not. We fully agree that infertility is not a disease, life-threatening or otherwise. We also grant that receiving donated sperm addresses a want rather than a need. However, we see no reason why that makes donating or receiving sperm *immoral*. Is one only moral when he donates what is needed and never what is merely wanted? Are recipients moral only when they take what is needed rather than what is wanted? We see no reason why these questions require affirmative answers.

Is sperm donation morally acceptable, then? We believe that sperm donation with an improper motive is wrong. If one perceives of sperm or eggs simply as commodities to be bought and sold, and if one's sole motive in donating is commercial gain, we think donation is wrong. It is wrong because it treats one's body and bodily products as objects to be used for sale. If buying and selling the use of one's body for sexual pleasure (i.e., prostitution) is wrong, then we believe that buying and selling one's body for reproductive purposes is also wrong. In both cases, a person is treated like an object, property to be bought and sold, and that is wrong. Here we add that we believe that blood donations and the like solely for financial gain are also immoral.

On the other hand, while many donors have no concern for childless couples but are only concerned to make money, that is not true of all. Some may donate sperm out of concern for those who cannot have children. Though anonymity is often maintained, sometimes a woman asks specific people to be donors, and they do so out of concern for the woman.[42] Unfortunately, these kinds of cases are the exception. However, we believe that when a donor gives sperm solely to help an infertile couple, and especially when payment for the sperm is refused, if the other conditions for morality already mentioned are met, then AID can be moral. What if the couple does not know the donor or his motivation in giving sperm? Since the couple should know that most who donate sperm anonymously for this purpose do so at least in part for financial gain, the morally safest procedure is to avoid using sperm from such sources. This means the couple should seek donation from acquaintances whose motives are not financial. This may create practical problems that do not arise with an unknown donor, but it seems the wisest way to guard against using sperm given immorally.

So far our assessment has focused on the morality of AIH and AID. From the preceding discussion we find that AIH is morally acceptable. Likewise, we conclude that though sperm can be donated from immoral motives and though AID may be put to immoral uses (such as giving lesbians children), when the sperm donor's intent is to help an infertile couple have a child, it need not break any moral dictum. However, this is not to suggest that we believe most cases of AID meet these moral guidelines. Nor does it mean that we would always recommend it, even when it could be used morally. In looking at the *practicality* of the procedure, we are concerned. The potential legal, social and psychological problems raised are serious and should be considered long and hard by couples before entering into this practice. From a practical standpoint, for example, it seems extremely unwise to use AID if one lives in a state or country where the question of legitimacy of AID children is not settled.

In sum, we conclude that there are neither moral problems nor other considerations which would prohibit AIH. As to AID, we believe there are limited instances where it is moral, but we think there are sufficient practical considerations to lead a couple to put it far down on the list of options for having a child. And for some couples, the psychological and social problems attached to AID will be so detrimental to the couple's marriage and/or personal well-being that AID should not be used.

IN VITRO FERTILIZATION AND FROZEN EMBRYOS

On July 25, 1978 Louise Brown, the world's first "test-tube" baby, was born in England. On December 28, 1981 Elizabeth Jordan Carr, the first American "test-tube" baby, was born. *In vitro* (literally, "in glass") rather than *in vivo* (literally, "in living") refers to the technique of fertilizing an egg in an artificial environment outside the body. As the procedure is practiced, it involves fertilization in a petri dish.

Though the first IVF baby was born in 1978, this was after many years of unsuccessful experiments. As early as 1878 in Germany there was an unsuccessful attempt to fertilize eggs in the laboratory. In 1934 the same experiment succeeded, but the eggs were not implanted. In 1944 John Rock of Harvard University reported success in fertilizing a human egg *in vitro*, as did Landrum Shettles of Columbia University in 1953. The first human pregnancy with IVF occurred in Melbourne, Australia in 1973, but lasted only nine days. Drs. Robert Edwards and Patrick Steptoe from England performed the procedure that led to Louise Brown's birth. They had developed the technique of laparoscopy, which allows a more successful retrieval of the woman's eggs. They also perfected the IVF procedure by injecting the woman with hormones that caused her to ovulate more than one egg per month. Of course, with more fertilized eggs available for transfer to the womb, the chance of success was enhanced.[43]

After the first test-tube babies were born, demand for IVF began to rise. By mid-1983 the number of IVF clinics in the U.S. and abroad was nearing one hundred, and the number of IVF babies was nearing two hundred.[44] It is estimated that by 1985 between seven hundred and one thousand babies had been produced by this technique.[45] By 1987, nearly a thousand IVF babies had been born in the U.S. alone.[46]

Though these statistics may encourage childless couples, they are a bit misleading. Despite the children born from IVF, there are far more failures than successes. For instance, estimates are that Steptoe and Edwards discarded 99.5 percent of all eggs fertilized in their laboratory over a twelve-year period because of various problems with the ova. By the mid-1980s the U.S.'s first IVF clinic in Norfolk, Virginia admitted that at best they expected a success rate of 25 percent, but had not yet reached that level.[47] Specifically, when only one embryo is transferred, the success rate has been 10 percent, whereas when three were used, the success rate rose to approximately 50 percent.[48] Of course, multiple transfers make multiple births possible, but since that is unlikely to happen and since multiple embryo transfers increase the likelihood of success, most couples are willing to undergo the "risks" of multiple transfers. As recent as 1987, statistics at one IVF clinic in the eastern U.S. showed a success rate of more like one in six couples (17 percent) achieving childbirth through IVF.[49]

Since statistics show that an infertile woman is more likely not to have a baby than to have one through IVF, why are so many women willing to consider it? The answer in part is the number of infertile women in our societies. Estimates again vary, but approximately 10 percent of U.S. couples, for example, are infertile, though some say the figure may be as high as 18 percent.[50] IVF especially addresses cases where a woman has blocked or diseased fallopian tubes. Corrective surgery might help some cases of blocked tubes (estimates run at the low end to at least 30 percent of these women), but not in all cases. This still leaves a sizable number of women whose only alternative for childbearing is apparently IVF.[51] Alvin Goldfarb, president of the American Fertility Foundation, estimated in the mid-1980s that some 650,000 married women in the U.S. were infertile because of some problem with their fallopian tubes.[52] Even if 30 percent of these women can be helped by surgery, that still leaves some 455,000 infertile women for whom IVF may be the only alternative for having children.

Though IVF is mainly used to overcome female infertility, it may also help in cases of male infertility. If the husband's sperm are abnormal in number, movement, or structure and fail to respond to treatment, IVF's controlled environment can solve many such problems.[53] Because infertile couples want children so badly, many are willing to try IVF despite no guarantee of success and despite how expensive IVF is.[54]

Interest in IVF worldwide has been phenomenal. A recent study surveyed fifteen committee statements on the new reproductive technologies formulated between 1979 and 1987. These statements came from various committees in the U.S., Australia, the United Kingdom, Canada (Ontario), Germany, Spain, the Netherlands, and France.[55] Findings are most revealing. For instance, all fifteen statements agreed in principle that *in vitro* fertilization is ethically acceptable. Likewise, all fifteen approved the use of IVF for married heterosexual couples, and eleven of fifteen supported it even for heterosexual unmarried couples living together in a stable relationship. Five of fifteen committees also sanctioned it for single women or members of lesbian couples. Finally, all committees approved IVF only for cases where some medical problem has caused infertility. They discouraged it for purely eugenic reasons like a desire to produce a superior baby.[56]

What exactly is this medical procedure? IVF may be performed using the gametes of both wife and husband, with donor semen or donor ova, or with donor embryo.[57] In preparation for collecting the eggs, a woman is given hormones for five to seven days to stimulate growth of the eggs in the follicles of her ovaries. Another hormone controls the exact time (thirty-two hours later) when the eggs are ready for removal. At that time a small incision in the woman's navel is made, and a laparoscope (a long, miniature microscope with a light which allows the doctor to view the woman's internal organs and the collection of eggs) is inserted. Through another incision forceps are used to hold the ovary in place, and a hollow needle is inserted to suck the egg from its follicle. If the egg is fully ripe and ejected before removal, or if it is not quite mature enough, it cannot be used. Once removed, the egg in follicular fluid is placed in a petri dish with a nutrient solution. After maturing for another five or six hours, it is exposed to about one hundred thousand sperm collected from the husband by masturbation. To increase the likelihood of success, several eggs are usually taken and fertilized in this fashion. The eggs develop into four, eight or sixteen cell embryos. At whatever stage the doctor considers most advantageous, the embryos are transferred in a tube or catheter through the cervix into the uterus. If implantation takes place, the baby begins to develop in a normal manner. In order to maximize chances that at least one embryo will implant, the woman should remain in bed for about eighteen hours.[58]

Practical Concerns

Despite interest in IVF, it raises some practical problems. In cases where a married couple resorts to IVF, but either the sperm or egg is donated by someone else, all the legal, social and psychological problems attendant to AID are potentially present, and there are others as well. Even when husband and wife donate sperm and ova, some practical problems still arise.

Sociological Concerns

A major sociological concern with IVF is its potential use to promote surrogate mothering. If the cause of infertility is the wife's eggs, another woman donates eggs and fertilizes the eggs *in vitro*, and they are then implanted in the wife, the donor, or even a third woman who is willing to serve as host of the embryos. All of this has implications both legally and socially for questions of parenthood, inheritance and the like. Those questions also arise with AID; the difference is that IVF merely proliferates the kinds of cases where surrogacy becomes possible.

Another sociological problem is IVF's expense. Prices vary from one clinic to another, but the cost is high. Moreover, there is no guarantee that medical insurance will pay for the procedure. In fact, with such a low success rate the procedure is still considered somewhat experimental, and since IVF does not treat a medical disease (infertility is hardly a life-threatening or even physically destructive disease), it is dubious how much insurance companies will pay for users of IVF.[59] Given the costs involved, it is likely that IVF will be only for the wealthy until costs come down and/or insurance companies pay for it.

There is another side to the financial issue. Only so much money is available for medical research and the treatment of disease. Should so much of it be allocated to IVF which does not treat a disease, when the same time and money could be used to research deadly diseases? The question of just allocation of resources is an ethical question, but it also has sociological import as it impacts the public policy of governmental and private health agencies.

Legal Concerns

Legal questions arise with IVF regardless of whether egg and sperm are donated by husband and wife or whether a third party is involved. For example, while the sperm donated and stored for AID clearly has no legal rights, what about a fertilized egg? Can an embryo inherit? The recent case of millionaire couple Mario and Elsa Rios shows that such questions are serious. The Rios couple wanted children, and in 1981 they went for help to Australia. Three of Mrs. Rios's eggs were fertilized *in vitro* with sperm from an anonymous donor. One was implanted, and the others were frozen. Ten days later the implanted embryo spontaneously aborted. Mrs. Rios was not emotionally ready to try again. Instead, she and her husband went to South America to adopt a child. In the spring of 1983, however, Mr. and Mrs. Rios and their adopted child were killed in a crash of their private airplane. Two questions arose. Who should inherit their estate, for they left no will? Could the frozen embryos inherit? Common law tradition in the U.S. and Australia permits those conceived but unborn to inherit, but inheriting is contingent on their being born. This might seem to clarify matters in the Rios case, but it didn't, since the "father" of the frozen embryos was not Mr. Rios. The other issue was who should decide the fate of the remaining embryos?[60]

Other legal questions arise as well. Are embryos persons legally, perhaps in the same way a corporation can be a person legally? How long are IVF clinics legally obliged to protect embryos? Does an embryo have a right to be implanted?[61] Suppose also that a doctor chooses an embryo which contains a genetic defect. The defect does not prohibit successful pregnancy, but later in life it will cause a serious disease. Could the doctor be sued for malpractice? Could a "wrongful life" case be brought against the doctor? Further, what if while handling the embryo the doctor damages it? Whether or not successful implantation and pregnancy occur, is the doctor liable to a malpractice suit?[62]

Then, there are legal questions about ownership of the embryos produced through IVF. Are the embryos the "property" of the parents, of the clinic, or are they no one's property? If they have status as persons, under American law they cannot also be property. These questions became extremely significant in the case of the Del Zios. In 1973 at Columbia Presbyterian Hospital in New York, Dr. Landrum Shields secretly fertilized Mrs. Del Zio's egg with sperm collected from her husband. Dr. Raymond Vande Wiele, director of obstetrics and gynecology at the hospital, deliberately destroyed the embryo without consent of the Del Zios. He did so on various grounds, including possible fetal abnormalities and belief that the fertilization had been done unethically (without consent of the parents). The Del Zios brought suit against the doctor and hospital, claiming that the contents of the test-tube were their property, and the doctor had no right to destroy it. A New York jury awarded them $50,000 for emotional distress over destruction of the embryo, but found the defendants innocent of wrongfully converting property.[63]

Finally, as noted, in IVF usually more than one egg is taken and fertilized. Often some of the embryos are frozen. In addition to questions of legal liability if freezing the embryos damages them, there are other potential legal ramifications. We have already noted two actual difficulties, the problem of the frozen embryos whose parents died, and Junior and Mary Sue Davis's custody fight over their frozen embryos.[64]

Moral Considerations

Many ethical questions arise with IVF. LeRoy Walters helps in sorting them out by distinguishing clinical from laboratory uses of IVF. The former are uses of IVF and embryo transfer to begin a pregnancy and produce a child. The latter uses are for research alone without any intent to transfer fertilized eggs to a woman so as to produce a child.[65] Most of what follows focuses on problems with clinical IVF.

Clinical IVF

Some ethical questions about clinical IVF also confront artificial insemination. Since we have already discussed them, we will just note them briefly now. First, IVF raises the question of masturbation. Second, there is also the issue of whether unitive and procreative aspects of sexual intercourse should be disjoined.[66] Third, IVF with donor sperm, donor egg, or a surrogate mother raises questions about moral notions of parenthood.[67] Fourth, some uses of IVF are morally questionable. As with artificial insemination, IVF can be used to give single women and lesbian couples children, and it offers more options leading to surrogate motherhood. It also leads to the morally questionable practice of freezing embryos.[68] Finally, as with artificial insemination, complaints abound that IVF is too much man's attempt to play God and tamper with nature. God never intended for man to resort to such unnatural techniques.[69]

In addition to these ethical issues, the major ethical issues with IVF involve the status and loss of embryos. With IVF there is significant wastage of embryos. This occurs not only because of the low success rate with IVF, but also because of how IVF is usually done. Most IVF clinics fertilize more than one egg and then choose the most likely candidates for successful implantation. It is assumed that any with detected genetic defects will be discarded, but other embryos may be destroyed as well. Likewise, many clinics use more than one egg in order to raise chances of a successful pregnancy. It is assumed (and hoped) that not all eggs inserted will implant. Of course, the body discards those that don't. In addition, IVF clinics typically require patients to agree to an abortion if at any time during the process any abnormality arises.[70] This wastage of life is deemed unacceptable by many.

Proponents of IVF argue that the loss of these embryos is not excessive, because even in natural reproduction many fertilized eggs are miscarried or not even implanted. Some doctors estimate that only 30 percent of natural fertilizations result in a baby, for the uterus aborts the other 70 percent, even when the embryo appears normal.[71] Hence, discarding defective embryos or those less likely to implant is not unique to IVF. The doctor simply does what the body would do in the case of a spontaneous abortion.[72]

Opponents are unconvinced. There is a major difference between losing an embryo with natural reproduction and the discarding and loss of embryos with IVF. In natural reproduction the element of willing the rejection of fertilized eggs is not present (often a women does not even know she is pregnant, so she cannot be volitionally responsible for an embryo's demise). With IVF, the deliberate fertilizing and selecting of embryos happens all the time. As Childs argues, "The fact that all eggs fertilized normally by sexual intercourse do not implant is morally irrelevant because there is no human volition involved."[73] As one ethicist says, the key here is "that death in the course of natural events is morally neutral but death at the hands of people is morally reprehensible."[74]

The loss and waste of fertilized embryos is a problem because of the issue of the embryo's status. Opinions differ, but there are generally two different opinions that parallel the discussion in the abortion debate. On the one hand, some think the early embryo either is or may be protectable humanity. Those who think humanness and personhood begin at conception view loss of embryonic life as tantamount to murder. Moreover, unlike the abortion argument in cases involving rape, incest, or unintended pregnancy that the baby's existence in these cases infringes the rights of the mother, no such argument will work here. These eggs are deliberately created.[75] There can be no question about whether a woman's right to privacy or freedom of choice supersedes the baby's right to life. The woman made her choice when she decided to fertilize the eggs through IVF.

The other view is that an embryo is not a human subject in any morally relevant sense. Factors such as twinning and mosaics are raised as evidence of a lack of human individuality. Moreover, as opposed to most abortions that occur later in pregnancy when one might say the developing baby qualifies as an individual, whatever is done with eggs fertilized by IVF happens so early in their development that one can hardly claim doctors are dealing with individual humans.[76] Those holding such views do not consider the loss of fertilized eggs a moral problem, nor would they think using fertilized eggs solely in laboratory research is a problem.

R. G. Edwards (the doctor, along with Steptoe, in Louise Brown's case) claims it is permissible not to protect these fertilized eggs for four reasons: 1) "fertilization is only incidental to the beginning of life," because "processes essential to development begin long before ovulation;" 2) nuclear transfer experiments show that "all nuclei can potentially sustain the development of an embryo;" 3) many people implicitly accept the abortion of early embryos by using IUDs; and 4) the fact that a developing child only gradually acquires personhood is underscored by the fact that many would sanction eugenic abortion but not infanticide in cases of genetic defects.[77]

This discussion about personhood and right to protection becomes even more significant when considered in light of the potential fate of a fertilized egg. There are at least five possible fates. First, it may be implanted in hope of producing a child and succeed at doing so. Second, it may die in one of several ways. It may be inserted in the woman's uterus, but not successfully attach to the uterine wall; it may never be inserted and just die by "natural" demise; or it may actively be destroyed. Third, it may be used in manipulative experimentation (embryonic, genetic, etc.). Fourth, there may be an attempt to perpetuate it *in vitro* beyond the blastocyst stage, even to viability and beyond (this has not yet been tried, but there is talk in the literature of the morality of using an artificial placenta outside the mother for gestation). Finally, the embryos may be frozen. If so, they may have one of several further fates. If a first embryo does not successfully attach to the uterus, twenty-eight days later when the uterus is ready again, a frozen embryo could be thawed for a second try. Even if the first egg successfully attaches to the uterus, a couple may store the extra embryos for several years until they are ready for another baby. This will avoid going through the first stages of the IVF process again. Another option is for a couple who succeeds with one embryo but doesn't want another child and doesn't want to destroy the other embryos to offer them to other infertile women. Of course, frozen embryos may also be thawed for experimental purposes or simply destroyed if no one wants to use them.[78]

What about the morality of these five fates of spare embryos? Those who believe the embryo at this stage is not a human person will probably find little objection to freezing these embryos and using them for future implantation, or to experimenting with them, or to destroying them. Likewise, there will probably be no objection to donating them to other infertile couples, unless one raises other objections that also beset AID.[79]

Those who think embryos qualify as persons will not agree. With the first option, if implantation succeeds, there will be no moral complaint *on the grounds of that fate.* If there are moral objections, they will arise over other aspects of IVF. As to the second fate, death by spontaneous abortion would be unacceptable to some, because it involves the death of a person, a death made possible by a technique they likely deem immoral on other grounds to be noted. On the other hand, others who consider the embryo a person might not think miscarriage immoral, because the intent was to produce a child and because the miscarriage occurs spontaneously and apparently beyond the control of the woman and her doctor. Of course, if the embryo is never used but is simply killed or allowed to die, that would be morally unacceptable.

As to the third and fourth options, those who believe the embryo is a person would radically object to the third fate and would probably frown on the fourth. As to freezing the embryos, if the frozen embryos were later used in experiments or simply discarded, that would be considered immoral. If instead the embryos were later used for implantation, some who believe embryos are persons might approve. Those who complain that IVF wastes embryonic life might believe that freezing the embryos for later use by husband and wife or some other infertile couple would dramatically relieve that problem. On the other hand, many would object regardless of the ultimate outcome on the grounds that there would be no frozen embryos if IVF used only one egg. The question of moral uses of spare embryos arises because of IVF, and IVF as usually practiced is immoral simply because it requires more eggs than doctors intend to implant, and that wrongfully wastes embryonic life. Still others would complain about freezing embryos, because science does not know enough at this time to guarantee that no damage will happen to an embryo by freezing it.[80]

A second objection to IVF views it as immoral even if an implanted egg successfully yields a baby. The problem is that IVF involves too much risk of damaging the embryo and thus the developing child. This objection has several aspects to it. On the one hand, there is risk of serious induced injury with IVF, and even if that risk is small, it is morally unacceptable.[81] Moreover, the risk is unacceptable also because IVF is undertaken without the informed consent of the child. Though some think this is really a non-issue because so many children have been born without defect,[82] opponents say such a response misses a very important point. The assumption is made that because of no ascertainable defect at birth or in the child's early development, there will be none. But we simply don't know that. At this point Louise Brown, the *oldest* test-tube baby, is just entering her teenage years. It is too soon yet to tell whether *most* IVF conceived babies will have any defect.[83]

Proponents of IVF respond in several ways. Some reply that all evidence thus far shows no reason for substantial fear of a defective baby. Others say this is not a problem, because IVF has proven to be as safe or safer than natural reproduction. Defective children are born through natural means, and natural generation involves both known and unknown risks. If we outlaw IVF because it poses risks to the unborn and because some defects have occurred, natural reproduction would also seem immoral on those same grounds.[84] One final response says that even if an IVF child is deformed, it is hard to see how the deformed child has been harmed. When IVF conception occurred, there was no child with rights to be violated. "The parents have not caused a child who would otherwise be normal to be born defective, for there is no child to be harmed aside from the very act creating the risk of harm."[85] The only other alternative to the action that supposedly violates the child's right not to be harmed is even less desirable, because it means no existence at all. "One does not respect a person's rights by refraining from an activity that prevents his existence altogether."[86]

A third and related concern, heard especially often before the first successes of IVF, is that IVF is wrong because it is still experimental.[87] Part of the complaint is that experiments with humans morally require informed consent, but obviously a blastocyst cannot give it. While its parents can give consent, some argue that parents are only morally allowed to do so when possible harm to the child is clearly balanced by possible benefit *to the child.*[88] Even if one uses this method to determine the morality of the procedure, prior to any successes with IVF it was dubious that possible benefits outweighed possible harm. Even today with limited success rates it is dubious that possible benefit can be shown to outweigh possible harm in *each* embryo's case.

Though such objections have largely subsided with the increasing successes of IVF, there is still an important point here. If one holds that with fertilization a human person results, the procedure of IVF really amounts to an experiment on a human being without his/her consent, and that is wrong. It does not matter that IVF has been successful before. It is still an experiment as to whether it will work with any given embryo. Even if success rates were high, it would still be an experiment without the informed consent of each embryo.

Fourth, some ethicists claim that those favoring IVF seem to believe every couple has a right to have a child. However, this is questioned. Moreover, IVF again uses medicine to treat a want, not a need. As such, it is deemed morally dubious, especially when other moral questions surround IVF. Donald DeMarco states the argument as forcefully as anyone. He says no one has a right to have a child since having a child involves the cooperation of two people, and one person has no right to take from another what is needed to produce a child. Moreover, it is wrong to think that even a married couple has a right to have a child, for a child is a person, not property, and no one has a right to another person. Children are not property but rather gifts conceived in a moment of self-surrender between husband and wife. DeMarco then argues that if a couple has no right to have a child, a doctor has no moral justification to produce one for them. While a doctor is morally justified in treating a disease which hinders the body from begetting children, IVF does not treat a disease but a desire. IVF still leaves the woman infertile. IVF does not treat the cause of her problem but the effect, her childlessness. He "is not practicing medicine as much as he is gratifying a desire, and the woman is not so much a patient as she is a consumer."[89] As a result, IVF is in no way therapeutic; it is "neither diagnostic, curative, alleviatory, or preventative."[90]

All of this raises a dilemma. On the one hand, IVF conflicts with traditional medical ethics, according to which medicine's purpose is to heal. On the other hand, if one thinks IVF treats a disease, he must depersonalize the child involved. Hence, "the only way to legitimize IVF therapeutically, from the point of view of the patient's health, entails the reduction of the child conceived to the status of a possession or property."[91] In sum, the desire to have a child is a worthy human desire, but it is not a right, nor can it legitimize medical intervention. As DeMarco says, "There is a crucial distinction between helping an infertile woman and helping a woman with her infertility."[92] IVF focuses on the former, not the latter. As such, it treats a desire, not a medical problem.

Fifth, other ethicists complain that IVF is an example of the growing encroachment of technology on our lives. Technology has brought many advances, but as applied in IVF, it tends too much to dehumanize man. Critics of IVF such as Ramsey and Kass complain that it invokes the specter of Aldous Huxley's *Brave New World* in which reproduction is handled totally artificially in the laboratory. The result, according to Kass, is likely to be the weakening of marriage and the family. Kass explains that for many, childbearing and childrearing are the best remaining justification for marriage and family, but with the new technology those institutions will be undercut.[93] We now have various ways of bringing a child into the world. Some are more human and some are less human, but the "laboratory production of human beings is no longer *human* procreation," for "making babies in laboratories—even 'perfect' babies—means a degradation of parenthood."[94]

In contrast, Joseph Fletcher thinks such control of human reproduction is very human. In fact, he believes laboratory control of reproduction is even more human than conception by ordinary sexual intercourse. Laboratory reproduction is willed, chosen, purposed and controlled, and these are qualities that distinguish humans from other creatures. On the other hand, ordinary sexual intercourse leaves everything to chance. The playing of this genetic roulette serves neither humanity nor morality. Hence, for Fletcher laboratory control of reproduction does not dehumanize man.[95]

A somewhat related argument is the wedge or slippery slope argument. Here the complaint is not just that technology dehumanizes, but that it is leading us down a slippery slope to Aldous Huxley's *Brave New World*. Early on there were fears this technology would lead to growing human embryos in the laboratory past blastocyst for the purpose of experimentation, to experimentation to alter the cellular and genetic composition of embryos, and to storing and banking embryos and eggs.[96] Others worry about the future, fearing that IVF technology will lead to practices like attempting eugenic improvement of the human species, cloning, and human-animal hybrids.[97] Obviously, as well, IVF encourages surrogate motherhood. For example, in March 1982 Dr. Alan Trounson of Melbourne, Australia claimed he would like to move to surrogate implantation, but neither law nor ethics allowed it. Later that year changes occurred in the law so that he could. Trounson also foresaw using embryos grown specifically for tissue repair, just as tissue from aborted fetuses is already used.[98]

The problem, of course, is not the inevitability of going all the way down the slope, but that once on it, it is easier to justify the next move and hard to argue with logical consistency against it. Some respond that common sense and ethics will keep us from going too far down the slope. But part of the problem with the slope of reproductive technologies is that there is disagreement over which foreseen practices are really immoral. That lack of agreement really worries those who raise the slippery slope/wedge argument.[99]

A seventh ethical issue concerns just allocation of resources and distributive justice generally. If the question is one of government funding, some argue that there are more basic health needs in society, especially in the area of preventive medicine. Anyway, funds for IVF research are available from private sources.[100] Moreover, even with funding from private sources, many still question if this is a just allocation of funds. Wouldn't it be better to apply this money to solve social problems such as poverty, pollution, urban decay, discrimination and poor education? Further, given IVF's costs and its low success rate, few insurance companies will pay for IVF procedures. But, then, this technology is primarily open to the rich, and it seems unjust that they alone should benefit from it.[101]

Finally, some oppose IVF because they see other alternatives for an infertile woman, alternatives with far fewer moral questions attached to them. Adoption is one possibility. Surgery to correct tubal blockage is another. Estimates vary as to how successful this surgery is, but some run as high as 50 percent, while others are as low as 5 percent of the surgeries performed.[102] Whatever the exact figures are, this shows that many women can be helped without IVF. Another option is low tubal ovum transfer. This involves moving the egg past the blockage and allowing it to continue naturally down the fallopian tubes for possible fertilization. A fourth option is the Estes method, which surgically makes a hole between the ovaries and the uterus. Fifth, if the problem is failure of the woman to ovulate, drugs to stimulate ovulation are available. Finally, a couple can remain childless. While children are a blessing from the Lord, it may be his will for some not to have them. It is no embarrassment or disgrace for a couple to remain childless.[103]

Proponents of IVF are unmoved by these alternatives. As to adoption, long waiting lists and heavy costs are problems, and the declining birth rate plus abortions plus single woman who keep their babies make it very difficult to succeed in adopting. Surgery to repair blocked tubes has some success rate, but still leaves many women unhelped. As to low tubal ovum transfer, it can only help women with slightly damaged tubes. If the tubes are severely damaged beyond repair, about the only hope for fertilization is if it happens outside the body. As to the Estes method, it was developed in the 1930s, but as of the early 1980s it had produced less than four pregnancies. Drug treatment is fine if the problem is lack of ovulation, but for women whose problem is something else, this is no solution. As for remaining childless, this is often offered by those with children who cannot fully understand and appreciate the pain of childlessness. Some can handle it emotionally, but not all.[104]

Laboratory IVF

Here we can be much briefer, because most of the relevant issues have already been raised. The key issue here is the status of the embryo. For those who think it is a human person (or even a potential human person), the creation of such embryos solely for experimentation is immoral and unacceptable.[105] On the other hand, those who think the embryo (especially in early stages) is less than a person see no problem with making embryos solely for experimentation.[106]

A second issue is the matter of informed consent by donors of sperm and ova. Before fertilization, there is no embryo's consent to get, and after it, informed consent of the embryo is still impossible. For those who view the embryo as a person, lack of its assent is morally problematic. On the other hand, some who don't think embryos are persons have still argued that it is wrong to use sperm and egg to produce embryos solely for experimental purposes without getting consent from sperm and egg donors.[107]

Third, there is a question about long term effects. Some point to benefits of increased knowledge for handling natural pregnancy and early development of babies. On the other side of the question, there is fear that laboratory IVF experiments might decrease respect for human life and lead to questionable experimentation such as cloning. Moreover, some fear that if experiments on early embryos are allowed, there will be a move to experiment on embryos that have developed past fourteen or sixteen days (the time some think critical in determining that an individual person is present and the time at which implantation normally occurs). Even some who support experimentation soon after fertilization are uncomfortable once this line of demarcation for personhood is reached.[108]

Assessment of In Vitro Fertilization

From an ethical standpoint, some of the issues that arise with artificial insemination (masturbation or tampering with nature, e.g.) also arise here, and we assess them the same way. As to IVF per se, the crucial issues from our perspective begin with the status of the embryo. As already argued in our abortion chapters, we believe the embryo is human and a person from conception onward. Hence, we believe it has the right to protection from harm.

Our views on the embryo's status lead to our greatest moral objection to IVF, namely, its waste and the loss of embryonic life. Given our views about the embryo as a person, fertilizing multiple eggs with the knowledge and even intent that some will not be implanted and others once implanted will be expelled by the body is morally wrong. Loss of these embryos is loss of human life.[109] In addition, we cannot sanction the need for a couple to agree to abortion if any abnormality develops in the IVF process.

We also think the claim that spontaneous loss of implanted eggs is not immoral because in natural reproduction fertilized eggs are lost is confused. This overlooks the fact that in natural reproduction no act of will produces the expulsion of the fertilized egg (we speak generally here, for we know some miscarriages are intentionally induced). IVF involves deliberately fertilizing eggs, some of which are expected (and even hoped) to abort after insertion in the woman because the couple does not want multiple births at one time. While the eggs expelled are not lost because of a specific act of will (i.e., there may be no more control over which expel than in natural reproduction), that still misses the point. The point is that none of these embryos would be in the position of possibly being aborted if not for a deliberate choice to fertilize and implant them (and deliberately to use more than are likely to result in pregnancy). Because of those intentional choices, we believe the couple and their doctor are morally responsible when IVF fertilized embryos spontaneously abort.

Some who agree wonder if these objections cannot be removed. Suppose a clinic takes only one egg at a time, and suppose the couple need not agree to abortion if any abnormality arises during the pregnancy.[110] Wouldn't IVF under those circumstances be moral, especially if all other alternatives have been tried? We reply that this would remove many of the moral questions surrounding it, but not necessarily all of them. Even if only one egg is taken and implanted, if it is expelled, that still follows a deliberate act of the couple and doctor to perform a procedure which put the embryo in a precarious position. Obviously, this is less objectionable than fertilizing many eggs and implanting several with the knowledge that several are unlikely to implant. However, given the small chance of success with only one egg, we think IVF even in these circumstances takes too much risk with human life.

Suppose the objection about wastage is handled by taking more than one egg, implanting only one at a time, and freezing the rest for further use. Would IVF under those conditions be morally acceptable? We have serious doubts. In addition to the question raised just above about using only one egg, there are other questions. If all eggs fertilized are equally good candidates for implantation as the one used, then there should be hope of success in the future when these eggs are thawed. But what if some are not good candidates (and that's why they weren't chosen for the first attempt)? Freezing them will not likely guarantee success at a later date. These are eggs which sooner or later are likely to be lost, but apart from IVF, they might never have been fertilized.

In addition, even if all embryos created are good candidates for implantation, the scenario envisioned assumes that freezing most of them would not damage them. At this stage in our knowledge, science does not know this. Since in our view those embryos are human persons, they have a right to protection from harm, but freezing them may harm them.

A second major moral concern for us is that IVF involves performing an experiment on a human being and doing so without his consent. IVF, in effect, experiments to see whether the egg so conceived can successfully be implanted in a woman so as to lead to the birth of a child. No matter how often this has been done before, it is still an experiment with each new egg, and it is done without the embryo's permission. This treats the embryo as an object to be manipulated, not as a subject. While some think the parents have a right to give consent on the basis of risk/benefit, we disagree that utilitarian concerns such as possible outcomes of this procedure determine what is ethical.

Some may respond that IVF is really no different than asking a family to decide on a medical procedure (even an experimental one) for a baby, for someone mentally retarded and unable to give informed consent, or for someone in a vegetative state and unable to give informed consent. In these cases no moral censure for making medical decisions falls on the family. Why should there be a problem in the case of the embryo?

We reply that the cases are not identical, and in circumstances where they would be identical, we have problems with others giving consent. Let us explain. It is crucial to remember that in the embryo's case we are talking about an experiment, whereas some of the medical procedures to be performed on a baby, the mentally retarded, or the vegetative person are not experiments. We know the likely outcome of these procedures and know they will not be harmful (even if unhelpful) to the person involved. Such is not the case with IVF. On the other hand, if anticipated procedures for a baby, the mentally retarded, or the vegetative are genuinely as experimental with as much chance of harmful results as in the case of IVF, then we think that for others to consent to such procedures for the person is also immoral.

Beyond all these considerations, there seems to be a crucial difference between the IVF case and the others. In the other cases, there is an existing person. The envisioned medical procedures for which we ask permission are necessary to treat a problem of an existing individual. Moreover, anticipated procedures have nothing to do with conceiving a non-existent person. In the case of IVF, no one treats a disease of any person (existing or potential). IVF involves the very bringing into existence (fertilization) and maintenance in existence (if implantation succeeds) of the one so produced. For us, the key questions are whether that kind of experimental procedure to bring into and sustain someone in existence is moral and whether the family has a right to give consent to such experiments. We believe that even if it is moral for a family to consent to an experimental procedure with potential harmful outcome in the case of a baby, the mentally retarded, and the vegetative, that would not justify the experiments in the case of IVF, because the cases are sufficiently different .

Some proponents of IVF further respond that even if IVF is an experiment, it is little more risky than natural reproduction where many fertilized eggs never implant. Surely, that doesn't make it immoral to try to have children by natural means. Again, we claim the situations are not identical. An egg fertilized in sexual intercourse may or may not implant in a mother's uterus, but whether it does or doesn't has nothing to do with an experimental procedure used to get it to implant. IVF does involve experiments to conceive and implant a baby. In addition, in natural childbirth no more eggs can be fertilized or implanted than those ovulated. With IVF more eggs are taken and fertilized than the doctor intends to use or even hopes will implant in the womb (the destruction of some is intended). None of this happens with natural reproduction. Hence, IVF is clearly not identical to normal reproduction. It is an experimental procedure manipulated by man, and programmed into it is the expectation and intention that some fertilized eggs will never produce a child. The objection still stands.

A related issue is the matter of damage to the developing child. We agree there is enough evidence that IVF is not likely to produce a baby with defects that will show up early in its development. However, the long-range effects of IVF are still not known. We understand that this concern may be answered by future evidence that as IVF babies get older they have no ascertainable defect attributable to IVF. But until that evidence is in, we think a moratorium on further IVF babies is in order.

On the basis of the preceding discussion, we believe there are enough moral questions associated with IVF to conclude that in general it is wrong. In some circumstances (e.g., only one egg taken, no requirement to abort if abnormalities arise) and as a last resort it might be considered, but even here we are dubious, because it is still an experiment on a human being without his/her consent. The same kinds of issues make it impossible for us to endorse IVF for laboratory research alone, though we discuss this more thoroughly in our chapters on abortion.[111]

In addition to moral problems with IVF, there are considerable practical questions. Foremost are that it is an expensive, tedious process, and one with few guarantees of success. On those grounds alone, we could not recommend it as anything more than a last resort. Though some of the alternatives (e.g., the Estes method) are not very helpful, there are other options for an infertile woman. For example, we are far less negative about adoption than are many proponents of IVF. It may take a long time, but some who won't even consider it may need to be more patient. Finally, we see no moral obligation to have a child. If after seeking every moral means of having children it becomes obvious that having a child is impossible, one should accept this as God's will. Surely, it cannot be his will to have a child by immoral means.

Assessment of Freezing Embryos

Closely associated with IVF is the practice of freezing embryos. From both a practical and ethical standpoint, it is worthy of reflection, as can be seen from the Davis and Rios cases already mentioned.

Both the Davis and Rios cases underscore two key moral questions about frozen embryos: 1) should the embryos have been frozen in the first place; and 2) what should be done with the embryos once frozen? The parents' death (the Rios case) or divorce (the Davis case) complicates the latter issue, but the question must be raised regardless of the parents' circumstances. Some may think both questions out of order, because it is wrong to use IVF to fertilize eggs in the first place. However, even if eggs should not be fertilized using IVF, and even if once fertilized they should not be frozen, still spare embryos (some frozen) from IVF do exist. What happens to them is not morally indifferent. Just as we must treat morally the baby conceived in an illicit sexual encounter, so there is an obligation to treat morally those conceived by IVF. The two questions raised are logically distinct from the issue of IVF's acceptability generally. Each must be addressed independently.[112]

What about that first issue? One's answer will rest heavily on one's views of the embryo's status. Those who believe the embryo is not a person are not likely to see anything immoral about fertilizing eggs *in vitro* or freezing them. Moreover, if they want a baby and do not want spare embryos used in experiments or simply discarded, freezing spare embryos for future tries at implantation surely seems moral.

What about those who believe the embryo is a person? If, like us, one believes IVF is wrong, because it performs an experiment on a person without informed consent, it will not suffice to address the frozen embryo question simply by saying it is a question which should not and would not arise if IVF were not performed. Even granting that IVF is wrong, some use it and fertilize many eggs. It is not inappropriate to ask opponents of IVF their moral evaluation of what should be done with spare embryos.

Given our view that the embryo is a person, we answer that what is morally proper is what is least wasteful of embryonic life and protects it the most. Obviously, this rules out simply discarding the extra embryos or using them for a procedure likely to end in their demise (experimentation, etc.). But if after implantation of one embryo the woman is unwilling to donate spare embryos to other infertile women (or no recipient is found), then, given the current state of technology, the most likely way to preserve the embryo's life is by freezing it with a view to implanting it as soon as possible. Though this does allow cases such as the Rios and Davis cases to arise, that possibility does not mean spare embryos should be discarded.

The lesson of those cases is that multiple embryos should not be produced in the first place. But if they are, freezing them is morally preferable to discarding them or using them in research, and it probably protects them better than implanting them all at once into the biological mother. If all are inserted, there will likely be much spontaneous loss, whereas using the eggs one by one may give each a better chance of survival.[113]

In sum, in answer to whether spare embryos should be frozen, we reply that if the goal is to protect embryonic life, then if spare embryos are produced (something we think should not happen to begin with) and no one uses them for implantation, the most morally acceptable alternative for the unused embryos is to freeze them, *but only for further use in producing a baby, not for experimentation.*[114]

The second question asks what to do with the embryos once they are frozen. For those who believe the embryo is neither a person nor has moral rights, what is done with the frozen embryos becomes a matter of the couple's and/or doctor's personal preference. Whatever is done will be morally indifferent.[115]

On the other hand, since we believe the embryo is a person, we believe it has a right to protection from harm. This means that thawing the embryos without placing them in an environment least likely to harm them is precluded. And that means that if the embryos are thawed, they should be inserted in a woman's womb. What makes this issue so tricky, however, is that while the right-to-life position entails that the embryo has a right not to be killed, "the moral right not to be killed does not automatically imply a right to the use of a womb."[116] Only by free choice of the womb's owner may the embryo be implanted in it. Some will respond that the genetic mother is obligated to give her womb for the baby's use. By bringing the embryo into being, she implicitly obligated herself to help it realize its full potential for human life. We agree but also note that the mother's obligation not only to protect the embryo but to do so by using her own womb (rather than protecting it in some other way) probably stems more from her freely undertaking to bring the embryo into being than from the fact that the embryo qualifies as a person.[117]

A further complication surrounding the question of what should be done with frozen embryos is that frozen embryos may likely deteriorate over time so that they will not likely survive implantation.[118] Since we believe the embryo has a right not to be killed, this complication means that as soon as possible the embryos should be thawed and implanted in the womb of their mother (by producing them she has obligated herself to give them the use of her womb). Since implantation all at once likely guarantees many will be lost, implantation *ad seriatim* in the mother seems necessary. If there are so many that using them *ad seriatim* gives little hope that those implanted later will survive, there should be an attempt to locate as soon as possible volunteers (perhaps infertile couples) willing to "adopt" the embryo. Likewise, if it is impossible for the genetic mother to use the embryos because she died (cf. the Rios case), then a right-to-life position seems to require seeking infertile couples to adopt the embryos as quickly as possible.

One must be careful not to misconstrue what we are saying. We are not suggesting IVF is acceptable as opposed to our original claims. Nor are we encouraging the reader to plan for IVF with a view to freezing spare embryos for future implantation. We are saying that if multiple eggs are fertilized using IVF (something we believe is wrong), what happens to them is not morally indifferent. If they are not all implanted when fertilized, the way to best protect these lives is probably to freeze them, and if they are frozen, the most moral way to handle them is to seek quickly their implantation in their biological mother or a volunteer mother.

None of the above means we generally sanction surrogate motherhood either (how we handle that topic will appear shortly). Our point is simply that once there is a person, one must seek the most morally acceptable means of preserving him or her from harm. When an unwed mother becomes pregnant she has sinned, but that does not mean what she does with the baby is morally indifferent. Having committed one wrong, she must take care not to commit another, and some things she could do with the baby are clearly immoral. In the same way, while we believe an IVF-conceived embryo has been produced by immoral means, once it exists, there is still an obligation to treat it morally. Killing it or allowing it to die is immoral. Freezing it and later implanting it makes it no less of an experiment than in other IVF cases, but at the current state of our technology, these procedures seem the most likely ways to protect the child, and that must be the overriding concern.[119]

SURROGATE MOTHERING

On February 6, 1985 for $10,000 Mary Beth Whitehead agreed to artificial insemination with William Stern's sperm in order to bear him and his wife a child. Mr. Stern and Mrs. Whitehead signed a contract to that effect. On March 27, 1986 Mrs. Whitehead gave birth to a girl in Long Branch, New Jersey. She called the girl Sara. On April 12, 1986 Mrs. Whitehead told the Sterns she would not give up the baby. The Sterns filed a custody suit. On May 6, faced with a court order to relinquish the child, the Whiteheads went to Florida, moving from one relative's home to another in an attempt to evade authorities. On July 31 authorities caught them and returned the baby to the Sterns. On January 5, 1987 the contract part of the trial began in Superior Court in Hackensack, New Jersey, and on February 2 the custody phase began. Though the judge wanted to separate the issues (contract and custody), the two issues were so entangled that he couldn't. On March 31 Superior Court Judge Harvey Sorkow gave his landmark ruling. He ruled the contract between William Stern and

Mary Beth Whitehead valid and awarded sole custody to the father, William Stern. Custody was granted to the Sterns because he concluded they would be better parents than the Whiteheads, given their respective socio-economic status and the relative stability of both homes. Hence, he thought granting the Sterns custody was in the child's best interests. This is the famous case of Baby M.[120]

In general, surrogate motherhood refers to the gestation of a baby by a woman who is not its biological mother.[121] Hence, a surrogate serves as a substitute mother. Though this sounds simple enough, actual surrogate cases involve many complexities not suggested by these definitions.

In dealing with surrogate motherhood several concepts should be distinguished. The terms "genetic motherhood" and "genetic fatherhood" refer to contribution and/or sale of one's ova or sperm. "Gestational motherhood" refers to carrying a fetus in one's womb. A genetic mother may also be the gestational mother, but a gestational mother may also be a third party who agrees to serve as surrogate for another. "Natural motherhood" is the combination of genetic and gestational motherhood wherein a woman carries her own fertilized ovum. "Nurturing motherhood" and "nurturing fatherhood" refer to those who actually raise the child. "Surrogate mothering," at least in theory, means being a substitute mother in *any* of the senses just mentioned.[122]

In general, a surrogate arrangement may be accomplished in one of three ways, though each allows for variations. First, artificial insemination may be the basis of a surrogate arrangement. If a wife is unable to conceive or carry a baby, or if she could conceive but does not want to (e.g., she fears she will pass on a genetic disease), the couple may seek out a surrogate mother. Her husband donates sperm to inseminate the surrogate. The surrogate then carries the baby to term and relinquishes it to its biological father and his wife. Other variations involving artificial insemination are also possible. A surrogate could be inseminated with anonymous donor semen to bear a child for a couple who cannot have children but will pay the surrogate for the resultant baby. In this case, neither husband nor wife would be genetic parents of the baby. Another variation is for a single male (homosexual or not) who wants children but not marriage to donate sperm to a woman who serves as gestational mother and then relinquishes the child. Through these means a homosexual couple might also acquire a baby genetically related to one of the men or perhaps to neither.[123]

Second, a surrogate relationship may involve *in vitro* fertilization. Here the options are about as broad as the imagination. A couple could arrange for IVF with either their own egg and sperm or anyone else's donated or bought egg and/or sperm. Then the embryo could incubate in the womb of any woman willing to take their money for the job.[124] These techniques and arrangements could also be used by single parents or by homosexual and lesbian couples (in this case, neither woman would carry the baby, so after donating their own egg or buying one from a donor, they would hire a surrogate). In addition, freezing embryos after IVF allows a number of options for surrogacy. For example, even if parents of frozen embryos die, a surrogate might be hired to gestate a thawed embryo for another couple who wants to buy/"adopt" it.

Finally, surrogacy is possible even when the baby is conceived using natural reproduction. For example, an infertile couple may hire another couple to conceive and bear a baby genetically their own and then give the baby to them at birth. Or a wife capable of conceiving a child but unable to undergo the strain of pregnancy and delivery might conceive a baby with her husband by normal means, but then transfer the embryo to a hired surrogate. Once born, the baby would be returned to its genetic parents.[125]

Yet another variation of surrogacy using natural reproduction follows the model of Abraham, Sarah and Hagar (Genesis 16). Sarah was barren, but God had promised a child. Sarah took matters into her own hands and gave her handmaid Hagar to Abraham. Abraham had sexual intercourse with her, and she conceived and bore him a son. This was not God's way to fulfill the promise of a son, but it suggests a possible surrogate relation using natural reproductive means.[126]

Further variations are possible depending on whether the surrogate donates her services *gratis* or whether she is to be paid, depending on whether or not the surrogate will have contact with the baby after his or her birth, and depending on whether the surrogate is someone the family knows or is chosen from a list of unknown applicants. Given these possible variations, the legal, social, etc. implications seem potentially endless. Undoubtedly, because of potential problems there has been much opposition. LeRoy Walters's study of committee reports on reproductive technologies (cited earlier) notes a generally negative attitude toward surrogate motherhood. Only three of fifteen statements (the Ontario Law Reform Commission, the American Fertility Society Ethics Committee, and the Dutch Health Council Committee) approved surrogate arrangements when a fee was involved, but all three strongly urged careful regulation of such arrangements. Even when surrogacy would be free, only four committees approved it.[127]

Surrogacy and Practical Concerns

The legal, social and psychological problems that confront AID and IVF arise when either of those techniques is used in a surrogacy arrangement. But beyond those problems there are others that attach specifically to the surrogacy aspect of the relationship.

The most obvious legal question is whether surrogacy contracts are binding. The judge in the Baby M case ruled that contract binding, but there is no guarantee the same will happen in other cases. In fact, in the *Doe v. Kelley* surrogacy case in Michigan (1981), the Supreme Court of Michigan said surrogate contracts were illegal and violated adoption rules of the state. However, in the surrogacy case of *Surrogate Parenting Associates v. Kentucky* (1986), the Kentucky Supreme Court said such contracts were valid since adoption played no role in them. The biological father signs the contract, so he need not think of adopting his own child. Once the father takes his child, his wife may adopt the child, but none of that is part of the surrogacy contract between her husband and the surrogate, nor need it be.[128]

Other legal matters can include custody fights (as in the Baby M case) and battles over the surrogate's visitation rights, if she decides not to remain anonymous. Other complications with surrogacy arrangements also have legal implications. For example, a surrogate might adopt a lifestyle likely to damage the embryo or fetus. If the baby were harmed, she could be sued. Even if the baby is unharmed, the contracting couple might bring legal pressure to curb her lifestyle. In addition, a contracting couple might require amniocentesis with the understanding that if there were any genetic abnormality in the baby, the surrogate would abort it. Suppose also that the surrogate, upon learning of defects, decided not to abort it. Moreover, if the baby is defective, who is legally liable? And what would happen if a child in a surrogacy arrangement had a physical or mental handicap and the contracting couple decided to refuse to accept it? Finally, might not poor women lacking similarly lucrative economic opportunities be coerced into surrogate motherhood to support themselves and their families?[129]

Some of the above-mentioned matters are also social problems, and there are others. From time immemorial women have sold their bodies for sexual use by men. Prostitution continues to be a problem in societies today. Surrogate motherhood (when the gestational mother is remunerated) amounts to selling one's body for procreative purposes. It is not identical to what is normally thought of as prostitution, but in a sense it is not far from it. The purpose is procreative, not sexual and lustful, but it still treats a woman as an object to be used to gratify the desires of others. Prostitution creates a social problem, and surrogacy for hire creates a similar one. In addition to what surrogacy does to the surrogate, there is also the matter of selling babies. Do we want societies in which babies are commodities to be bought and sold? Even if a surrogate volunteers her services, the baby still seems to be property to be attained.

Concerns that surrogacy might become a commercial enterprise are not imaginary. Karp and Donahue claim that some women call their offices ready to volunteer services if surrogate motherhood ventures become a reality. They say they love to be pregnant and would arrange always to be in that condition if it weren't for the matter of having to keep the babies.

Karp and Donahue conclude that it is inconsistent "to categorically deny such women this kind of livelihood while we permit and even encourage people to earn money by such dangerous means as coal mining, or racing little cars around a track at 200 miles per hour."[130]

Surrogacy and Ethical Concerns

Some legal and social problems mentioned also have moral overtones. For example, using surrogacy to give unwed mothers or homosexual and lesbian couples children has obvious moral implications. In addition, when surrogacy arrangements involve either AID or IVF, they involve the moral issues surrounding those techniques. Beyond those concerns, however, are others that specifically arise with surrogacy.

The first is the motivation for surrogacy. It is fairly uniformly agreed by ethicists that resorting to surrogacy solely for convenience sake is immoral. Some medical condition must necessitate it. Using it simply to avoid the pain and disruption of pregnancy and delivery is not moral.[131]

Second, surrogacy raises questions when a fee is involved. Two repeatedly surface. The first is whether a surrogacy arrangement is not simply selling one's body for profit. If so, it is not significantly different from prostitution. The prostitute sells the body for sexual pleasure, whereas the surrogate sells it for reproductive purposes. Since it is wrong to treat one's body as an object to be bought and sold, surrogacy for money is wrong.[132] The second question raised by the fee is whether or not this is baby selling. Most would say it is, and many find that objectionable because selling a baby treats a person like a piece of property. This degrades the baby and is immoral.[133]

Though one might think the preceding means ethicists believe surrogacy acceptable so long as it is done free, that is not so. Even without a fee Janet McDowell thinks surrogacy wrong for several reasons. For one thing, surrogacy arrangements usually do not involve a context of loving commitment between the surrogate and the child's father, nor does the surrogate have any intention of caring for the child. However, these elements are involved in the biblical notion of procreation and parenthood, according to McDowell. Without them human procreation is reduced to the mere biological production of babies. That is contrary to Scripture and thereby immoral.[134]

McDowell also claims that even if a surrogate performs her service free and out of sympathy, that does not make it right. There are limits even to behavior stemming from sympathy. We would not praise someone who shot himself in the head to provide a heart or other vital organ for someone in need. Likewise, someone who drained her child's education fund to support a worthy charity would be open to criticism, because she would be viewed as sacrificing one person's interests to show another compassion. McDowell says surrogate mothering may be analogous to the latter example, especially if the child may have some interest in knowing and being reared by its genetic mother. Hence, acting from compassion does not overturn other moral problems associated with surrogacy.[135]

Others complain that surrogacy is immoral because of its effects on the child beyond treating it like property. For one thing, the baby will likely have a confused or nonexistent relationship with its genetic mother, and that is potentially harmful to the child. Then, a child might be raised by a homosexual or by a single father who wants children but not marriage. It is one thing if a couple has a child and the mother dies; then the father must raise the baby. The problem with a surrogacy arrangement for a single father to raise a child is that it is deliberate. Few think being raised by only one parent is in the child's best interests. If that need arises through the death of one parent, one has no control over that. But with surrogacy one does have control, and one chooses deliberately to do what is not in the child's best interests.

Even if a couple arranges for a surrogate to bear a baby, this is not necessarily in the child's best interests. The couple will probably have no contact with the surrogate after the birth, but then the baby may never know its biological mother. Psychological problems for the child may arise if she or he learns of the surrogacy arrangement but can never contact the genetic mother. Likewise, it might be devastating to learn that one's genetic mother was paid to conceive and bear him or her; perhaps the genetic mother saw the whole thing as a business deal and didn't personally care about the baby. Moreover, this might also cut the child off from an important source of medical information about his or her genetic, etc. background. It hardly seems that any of this would be in the child's best interests, but then, it is argued, it is immoral to do things to the child which aren't in its best interests.[136]

A final ethical matter involves the rights of natural parents as opposed to surrogate parents. Here the Baby M case is the paradigm. The fundamental complaint is that genetic parents should have prior claims over surrogate parents, but in surrogacy cases that is not always so. In Baby M's case, for example, because of a contract, a surrogate parent (Mrs. Stern) had more claim to Baby M than did Mrs. Whitehead, the baby's genetic mother. Likewise, Mr. Stern's claim via the surrogacy contract took precedence even over his claim as the biological father. Traditionally, in law and morality it is assumed that genetic parents have rights over any potential adoptive or foster parents. Surrogacy arrangements of the Baby M kind say otherwise. Hence, they are objectionable.[137]

That does not end the matter, however, for surrogacy arrangements can produce situations that legally and morally seem odd. For example, in virtue of the surrogacy contract Mr. Stern, the genetic father, was required to buy his own baby. Though some may say he was merely renting womb space, more than that was happening. He purchased what was genetically his, and he asked the womb's owner to sell what was also genetically hers. Contracts in such cases are morally questionable, because "a mother cannot sell her baby (nor anyone else's for that matter), and because . . . a father (or anyone else) cannot buy it, but also because . . . in general, human beings have the very basic right not to be sold (or bought)."[138]

Assessment of Surrogate Motherhood

The potential legal, psychological and social problems associated with surrogate mothering make it inadvisable from a practical standpoint. From a moral perspective, we believe assessment must be made independently for each major kind of surrogacy arrangement (cases involving AID, cases involving IVF, and cases involving normal sexual intercourse). However, before addressing these individually, several points covering all forms are noteworthy.

First, we agree that surrogacy arrangements solely for convenience sake to avoid being bothered with pregnancy are prime examples of selfishness and as such are immoral. Second, surrogacy arrangements to give homosexuals and lesbians children are immoral uses of it because of the immorality of homosexuality and lesbianism. Likewise, the desire of single heterosexuals to have a child without marriage is unfair to the child and seems to violate the biblical ideal that children intentionally conceived should be born, if possible, to genetic parents married to one another.

Third, we cannot sanction any surrogacy arrangement involving a fee. We think it immoral for a woman to sell her body (and her egg as in the Baby M case) for procreative purposes, just as it is wrong to sell her body for purely sexual purposes. We also hold that the baby is a person, not property to be bought and sold. Treating him or her as a marketable object is immoral. We also believe surrogacy arrangements wrongly treat the surrogate like an object (a reproductive one) to be manipulated for the right price, not like a person.

Can surrogacy arrangements ever be moral? Let us examine each kind of surrogacy arrangement. As to those involving AID, we have argued that some limited cases of AID (apart from surrogacy) can be moral. AID without surrogacy, however, allows the wife to carry her own baby. No questions can arise about whether the gestational mother will create problems for the nurturing mother or the baby. AID with surrogacy (whether the wife is inseminated and the embryo transferred to a surrogate or whether the surrogate donates both her egg and womb), however, runs the risk of the kinds of problems that arose in the Baby M case. The problems that arose over custody of the child are hard to see as being in the child's best interests. If one foresees such problems and proceeds anyway, that seems immoral treatment of the baby. On the other hand, if none of those problems are anticipated, if a surrogate arrangement is medically necessary, and if compassion, not money, is the surrogate's and sperm donor's motive, surrogacy involving AID may in such instances be moral. The problem is that sometimes unexpected difficulties arise anyway. Surrogates, for example, after carrying a baby for nine months, get attached in unanticipated ways to the child, especially if the gestational mother is also the genetic mother. Hence, even if a surrogacy arrangement of this sort would be moral, we advise practically against it. Surely other moral options open to the couple are preferable.

What about surrogacy using IVF when no fee is involved and the surrogate's motivation is solely compassion? Here we still have problems, but they stem from our rejection of IVF as immorally wasteful of embryonic life and as an immoral experiment upon a human being. No matter how moral the intentions of the surrogate and the couple, and no matter how few practical complications there would be for the surrogate, the baby, and its nurturing parents, we cannot recommend surrogacy involving IVF, because we deem IVF morally objectionable.

What about surrogacy without fee when the motivation is purely compassion and the baby is conceived through natural sexual intercourse? Here the morality of the situation depends on the situation. For example, if an infertile wife contracts a woman to produce a baby with the wife's husband, that is immoral, because her husband commits adultery. Thinking the Abraham, Sarah, and Hagar arrangement was acceptable misreads Scripture. Though Abraham may have been within his legal rights to do this, it was still adultery.

Suppose, however, that a husband and wife conceive a baby intending for a surrogate to carry and deliver it. This decision is made because the couple wants its own genetic children, and the wife can conceive, but it would be unwise for her to carry the baby because of medical reasons. Suppose also the surrogate agrees out of love and compassion for the childless couple, not because of a fee (in the case imagined there is none). Suppose further that it is highly unlikely the gestational mother will want any rights to the child once born. Under those circumstances, could the surrogacy arrangement be moral?

In response, we think surrogacy under the conditions described is permissible, but we think several items are noteworthy. We note initially that the scenario described represents very few cases. We also think it wisest for the prospective surrogate to offer herself rather than for the couple to ask, for if the couple asks, the potential surrogate finds herself in a difficult position—she may not wish to serve as surrogate, but may feel obligated out of friendship. We also would advise considering this option for having a baby as a last resort, when no other options are possible. Potential unexpected problems can still arise and should keep this arrangement from having high priority.

Two other possible scenarios involving surrogacy and conception by natural means are worthy of comment. Suppose a healthy couple learns that the wife is pregnant. Suppose also that early in the pregnancy (when the developing baby could be transferred unharmed to a surrogate) the wife is in an automobile accident. The baby does not die, but after holding on, the mother does. A friend or relative of the couple knows that the mother's death will mean death to the baby, so out of compassion she offers to become the baby's surrogate mother. She agrees to this without fee and with the understanding that once born, the baby will go to its genetic father. In a case such as this where rejecting the offer means certain death to the baby, we think the surrogacy arrangement would be moral. We realize that transferring the baby may not result in successful implantation; the baby may die anyway. However, we believe there should be an effort to save the baby's life, and if a surrogacy arrangement is the only way to do that, we think an arrangement of the sort imagined would be morally permissible in these unusual circumstances.

A final scenario involves frozen embryos. Granting as we have argued that there should be no frozen embryos since they arise from a morally dubious practice, nevertheless, frozen embryos do exist. As already noted, one must decide what are morally correct ways to treat them. Think of the Rios case where Mr. and Mrs. Rios died before using their frozen embryos. We have argued that it is morally preferable to implant them in some woman as opposed to disposing of them or just letting them die. That woman (or women, if several eggs need to be implanted at the same time) would serve as a surrogate mother. In such circumstances, if the surrogate serves without pay out of compassion for the children, we think this would be morally permissible. Whether the surrogate decides to adopt the children or put them up for adoption, we believe she can do so without moral censure. If she agrees without pay to bear the child for another couple, and if there will be no legal wrangling over matters of custody, visitation rights, etc., then in this kind of case we think this arrangement can be moral. If only Mrs. Rios had died, would it be wrong for a surrogate to volunteer to bear the frozen embryos and give them to their genetic father free of charge? Under these circumstances, we think this arrangement would be morally acceptable and morally preferable to destroying the embryos without any attempt at gestation.

Though our discussion has focused heavily on unusual cases, it should be clear that we believe most cases of surrogate mothering are morally unacceptable. There are exceptional cases, but they only nullify the general rule in the exceptional cases.

CLONING

In 1978 David Rorvik's *In His Image: The Cloning of Man* was published. Though Rorvik's claim that an adult human being had been cloned was false, it stimulated a great deal of interest in cloning. Cloning (from the Greek *klon*, meaning "twig" or "offshoot") has been used for some time in horticulture, but only in this century has it been applied to the animal kingdom. Early work with animals was done by Robert Briggs and Thomas King. In 1952 they transplanted the nuclei of unfertilized cells with nuclei from blastula cells. In 1961 J.B. Gurdon cloned tadpoles from adult frogs. Most of this work with amphibians, however, did not lead to adult animals. In many cases defects arose in the developing organism, and it did not survive. In other cases the experiment ended before the adult stage was achieved simply because the scientists were interested in studying embryology, not cloning *per se*.[139] Though talk of cloning a human continues, scientists have not yet been able to apply this technology to humans.

Cloning as a procedure is the artificial reproduction of an organism which is the exact genetic copy of a living organism. The nucleus of a mature but unfertilized egg is removed by microsurgery or is incapacitated by radiation. Then, the cell is provided with a nucleus from a donor body cell, often taken from the intestine. While human eggs and sperm cells each have twenty-three chromosomes, when they are fused through natural or artificial reproduction, the product has forty-six chromosomes. The embryo begins to develop, and eventually the baby is born. However, each somatic cell (as opposed to germline cells, i.e., sperm or egg) in any living organism contains the complete genetic blueprint for the organism. When a body cell is transferred into the enucleated egg cell, the result is a cell with forty-six chromosomes, an exact genetic copy of the donor organism. The cell is stimulated to develop, and if all goes well, the donor nucleus controls the development of the egg, and the embryo begins to develop.[140] The developing embryo is then inserted into a host womb, and nine months later a baby is born, an exact genetic clone of the donor nucleus.

There are several potential benefits of using cloning in humans that make it attractive. For example, it offers another reproductive option. For those against artificial insemination or *in vitro* fertilization because they involve masturbation, cloning removes that objection. For those unable to have children by natural or other artificial means, cloning can give them a child, a child genetically identical to one of them. Second, individuals of great genius, beauty or talent could be replicated. Think of the benefits of continually replicating an Einstein or a Beethoven. Likewise, a country might produce a superior military by cloning its best soldiers. Third, cloning allows preservation of a given genotype that might be seen as a way to attain biological immortality. The chance of a recurring genotype (except with multiple births) is slim, but cloning guarantees it. Fourth, cloning lets a couple pick the sex and physical characteristics of their child. One would not have to clone oneself. One could produce an embryo with a transplanted nucleus from someone with desirable qualities. Fifth, cloning might be used to overcome genetic defects and diseases. Genetic defects could be avoided by cloning only healthy persons. Moreover, if both husband and wife carry a recessive gene for a disease, one of them could be cloned so the child would only carry the gene but not get the disease. Natural reproduction might pass the disease on. Finally, clones could provide a major source for organ donors and transplants. If the recipient were cloned for this purpose, given the genetic identity of the donor, fear of organ rejection would be greatly reduced.[141]

Cloning and Practical Concerns

Cloning presents some practical concerns, though some are not significant unless cloning becomes widespread. For example, some worry that wide use of cloning would cause deterioration of the gene pool, because it would limit variety and likely increase the frequency of genes that are defective. However, it is doubtful that those with known genetic defects would be cloned. As to gene pool depletion, this would probably not be a significant problem unless cloning became widespread and replaced other means of reproduction, neither of which is very likely.[142]

On the other hand, some concerns with cloning seem more serious. From a scientific standpoint, cloning could increase the incidence of some genetic diseases in a given population. As Anderson explains, clones of one person would be half-brothers and half-sisters of one another. Without careful record keeping and regulation of marriages, cloning could lead to an incestuous relationship. Genetically, this could result in marriages where genetic disorders depending on recessive genes would be expressed in offspring and then enter the human gene pool.[143] It is also noted that often cloning experiments have resulted in abnormalities in the developing organism. Just as such problems with IVF create both scientific and moral difficulties, so they create concerns about cloning.

There are also legal concerns. Errors which produce defective clones are possible, but then, are doctors open to malpractice suits? Moreover, are such creatures human, and do they have rights and protection as persons, or are they subhuman without any rights? What about inheritance questions? Can a clone of a wife inherit from the wife's husband? Would the clone's right to inherit supersede that of children born to the couple through natural reproduction? In case of divorce, is the husband in this imagined situation legally liable to pay child support to the clone of his wife? Would he have visitation rights?[144] And then, would a clone have to pay royalties to its genetic donor? Writers receive royalties for copies of their works; do persons who are copied deserve royalties?[145]

As to social difficulties, many that attach to AID and IVF with either donor egg or donor sperm also apply here. For example, the abuse of children not genetically related to oneself is possible. Single-parent families and homosexuals and lesbians having children are also possibilities.

Cloning also necessitates a host womb, and hence would contribute to surrogate motherhood.

Cloning and Ethical Concerns

Many objections against AID and IVF pertain here as well. Concerns that the process unduly tampers with the natural order, that it involves playing God, that it bypasses the traditional notion of parenthood, and that it wrongly disjoins the procreative and unitive aspects of sexual intercourse are frequently voiced.

There are also moral concerns about the *uses* of cloning. It could encourage surrogate motherhood, single-parent families, and gays and lesbians having children, all thought to be immoral uses. Likewise, clones produced solely for organ transplants raise the question of whether it is moral to use people in this way. The goal envisioned is admirable, but would the means be moral? Though many might not see the clone as a person, for those who do, it surely seems immoral to use persons as means to meet others' needs with little or no concern for the well-being of the clone. And would clones be forced to donate, or would their informed consent be required? Discussions of this topic give the impression that clones would have little say in this matter.

For those who believe life and personhood begin at conception, cloning seems wrong as well on grounds that make IVF objectionable. "Conception" for a clone, of course, occurs with insertion of the donor nucleus into the enucleated cell. At that point, all forty-six chromosomes are present, and the cell can divide and develop into a baby. But, as with IVF, here there will surely be concern over loss of embryonic life. Embryos produced by nuclear transfer solely for experimentation amount to murdered people. Likewise, even when the intent is to produce a baby, success rates are so low (currently zero) in humans, that the embryo is most likely to die. For those who believe that the embryo is a person made in God's image, this loss of life is unacceptable. And, as with IVF, cloning must be considered an experiment on a human being, an experiment without the consent of the person involved. Granted, the experiment is not identical to that in the case of IVF, but it is an experiment. Once the nucleus is transferred, one must wait and see how the embryo develops; and then, as with IVF, there is the further experiment as to whether the embryo (if apparently normal) can successfully implant into a womb. Those who believe the developing embryo is a person will find this morally unacceptable.

Assessment of Cloning

Here assessment can be made from several standpoints. Practically, the legal, social, and scientific concerns raised with cloning make it appear unwise to pursue it. Moreover, at current levels of knowledge and experiment, chances of successfully cloning a human being are indeed remote.

Hence, if an infertile couple wants to have a baby and is financially able to pursue some artificial means of reproduction, this method is an impractical one to try. Other options are much more likely to succeed than this.

From a purely conceptual standpoint, we suspect that some intrigued by cloning hold some faulty assumptions. For example, some may think cloning is a way to replicate someone with special abilities and personality. Think, for example, of a basketball team with clones of Michael Jordan. However, this kind of thinking rests on the faulty assumption that genetics and biology are all there is to personal development. Environment seems insignificant. But surely this oversimplifies things. A clone of Michael Jordan might be raised in an environment where his interests are purely intellectual, not physical at all. A clone of Beethoven could be bored with music. Just because a clone is genetically identical to the original doesn't mean all else about it will be identical, too.[146]

A related faulty assumption that may underlay cloning is the belief that all characteristics are genetically controlled. However, as we shall see in discussing recombinant DNA, characteristics such as personality traits and intelligence may depend on a number of different factors.

From an ethical standpoint, several comments are in order. As with the other procedures discussed in this chapter, we note the importance of distinguishing the technique from its uses. We agree, for example, that cloning to produce single-parent families and give children to gays and lesbians is immoral. Likewise, producing clones for organ transplants is immoral, for it treats persons as objects and quite possibly would bypass getting their consent to the transplant. However, none of this means the procedure *per se* is immoral. From our perspective, though, if cloning is at all moral, the only moral use of it would be to give infertile heterosexual married couples children.

As for cloning itself, we cannot endorse it morally. Believing that at conception a person is present, we believe that once the nucleus is transferred to the egg cell there is a person. Because of the likelihood of embryonic death either because of abnormality in the developing embryo or because embryo transfer is unlikely to succeed, we cannot see this practice as moral. Moreover, we believe cloning also involves an immoral experiment on a person and does so without his/her consent. Hence, we think cloning is both impractical and immoral. As LaBar says, "There is no need to put any nucleus in a human egg, except that of a sperm."[147]

CHAPTER TEN

Genetic Engineering and Genes

About four million Americans have Alzheimer's disease, a degenerative brain disorder characterized by a relentless loss of brain cells. It is accompanied by a gradual loss of memory and the ability to reason. Those who have the disease eventually become seriously disoriented and unable to care for themselves and die. What if this terrible disease were controlled by one's genetic makeup? What if it were possible to correct those genes so that those at risk would neither get the disease nor pass the defective genes to their children?

Early in 1991 researchers found a genetic defect that is related to Alzheimer's disease. In October of the same year, a second gene involved was reported, and researchers anticipated that a few weeks later a third gene would be found.[1] These discoveries are invaluable in providing information about the cause of the disease, and could well help in diagnosing it. They give hope for eventually finding a cure.[2]

The prospects for positive use of genetic research are indeed encouraging to those with a genetic disease or thought to be at risk. However, this research and the techniques that apply it allow manipulation of the basic building blocks of life. In so doing, they raise significant moral questions. This is the other side of genetic engineering, and in this chapter we want to discuss various technologies involved in gene manipulation and the issues related to them.

Before turning directly to those new technologies, a brief sketch of developments in understanding genetics is in order. Modern genetics is said to have begun with the work of the Austrian monk Gregor Mendel in the nineteenth century. Mendel studied inheritance by means of experiments with garden flowers. He concluded that there are "genes" which pass hereditary traits from one generation to another, based on ratios involving dominant and recessive traits. In 1902 Walter Sutton, as a result of studying grasshopper chromosomes, concluded that genes are located on the chromosomes. Not long after, Thomas Morgan discovered chromosomes that determine the sex of offspring.[3] In 1867 Friedrich Meischer discovered that cells contain a slightly acidic substance in their nuclei, and he called it nucleic acid. In the early 1900s the chemical composition of this material was determined, and it was called Deoxyribonucleic Acid (DNA). By the 1940s it was shown that genes within cell chromosomes are made of DNA.[4]

A crucial discovery occurred in 1953 when James Watson and Francis Crick determined the structure of DNA. They found that it "is a linear polymer of deoxy nucleotide repeating units, and is found in cells as two complementary strands forming a double helix."[5] One of the two strands contains regions of genes. These genes direct the synthesis of cellular products such as hormones or enzymes. Information transformation occurs as a given gene is transcribed into a messenger RNA (ribonucleic acid). That information is translated into the gene's product, which is typically a protein. "The protein product, such as an enzyme, is a linear polymer of amino acid repeating units, and the sequence of these amino acids is coded for by the particular sequence of nucleotides in the DNA."[6] DNA plays essential roles in processes that allow cells to reproduce and to maintain the life and function of the cell.[7]

In 1970 there was a major development that allowed scientists to change the genetic code of a given organism. Nathan and Smith discovered a new class of enzymes usable for transferring genetic material from one cell to another. This makes it possible to splice one DNA molecule to another in order to change the genetic code of the latter. At about the same time it was learned that "a bacterium called *E. coli* has closed circular pieces of DNA (plasmids) floating free in its cell liquid."[8] These plasmids proved to be usable in transferring genes from one cell to another. This technology can be used to repair or replace damaged or undesirable genes (a therapeutic use), but it can also be used to redesign offspring with genes and traits of one's choice (eugenic use),[9] or even create altogether new organisms for use in agriculture, industry and the like.

Once this technology was available, scientists held a conference at Asilomar, California in 1975. At that now famous conference, strict guidelines were established for the use of techniques to splice DNA from one species to another. As a result of that meeting, the National Institute of Health formed a committee (known as the RAC—Recombinant DNA Advisory Committee) to administer the guidelines developed at Asilomar. From 1975 to 1977 there was a moratorium on certain experiments involving various viruses and toxins until government scientists could test the risk factors involved in producing new organisms via recombinant DNA (rDNA) techniques. However, it was determined that risks were minimal, and the moratorium was lifted.[10]

One further development is noteworthy. Humans have twenty-three pairs of chromosomes. On those chromosomes there are some more than one hundred thousand genes.[11] Technologies described above offer tremendous opportunities for modifying man's genetic makeup. However, unless one knows what characteristic a given gene controls, one cannot use this technology to modify any given trait. For several decades scientists have been working to identify the various genes in human DNA. That project received a major boost in January 1989 when the Human Genome Project began. The human genome is "the complete set of instructions for making a human being."[12] The project is sponsored by the U.S. government, other countries and private organizations and was launched under the direction of James D. Watson. The goal is to discover and map every genetic chemical in human DNA. As of the late 1980s, only about 4,550 of the more than one hundred thousand genes had been identified, and only fifteen hundred of the 4,550 had been located on the various chromosomes.[13] While much of the work has been done by small groups of scientists working literally by hand, in more recent years scientists have been able to apply computer technology to the task. The project is expected to take years to complete, but computer technology is expected to speed up the process greatly.

GENETIC COUNSELING

In 1975 an Ad Hoc Committee on Genetic Counseling defined such counseling as "a communication process which deals with the human problems associated with the occurrence, or the risk of occurrence, of a genetic disorder in a family."[14] According to the committee, this counseling has five basic goals. Counselors want to help counselees

> 1) to understand the medical facts, which include diagnosis, probable course of the disorder, and available management; 2) to learn about the way heredity contributes to the disorder, and the risk of recurrence in other relatives; 3) to know the options for dealing with the risk of recurrence; 4) to choose the course of action which seems appropriate to them in view of their risk and their family goals, and act in accordance with that decision; and 5) to make the best possible adjustment to the disorder in an affected family member or to the risk of recurrence of that disorder.[15]

These are worthy goals. Moreover, availability of genetic information is significant in light of what is known about the magnitude and severity of genetic disease. By the mid-1980s scientists had identified more than three thousand different genetic disorders, and had concluded that one or more of those defects appear in more than two hundred thousand infants out of a total of three million born in the U.S. each year. By 1991 nearly four thousand genetic disorders had been identified, and it was estimated that "one out of 10 persons will be diagnosed with a genetic disorder sometime in their lifetime."[16]

Before directly addressing genetic counseling, we offer some basic facts about how genetic disease is transmitted. Genetic diseases are transmitted by one of four different types of inheritance. First, there is inheritance due to a *dominant* genetic trait possessed by one parent. With diseases controlled by a dominant trait, there is a 50 percent chance that each child will get the disease. If a parent suffers from a dominant disorder and the child does not, the child will not transmit the disease to his or her children, nor will the child be a carrier. If a child gets the disease not from his or her parents, but as a result of a new mutation in either the egg or sperm of the parents at the time of conception, there is little chance the disease will occur in the child's offspring. Examples of dominant gene disorders include achondroplasia (a form of dwarfism), glaucoma, hypercholesterolemia (high cholesterol levels with a tendency to heart disease), and Huntington's Chorea. Some dominant disorders can be mild, others lethal. Some such as Huntington's Chorea appear later in life.[17]

Second, some diseases stem from *recessive* genes. In such cases both parents must carry the defective gene, though often neither is affected by the disease. With recessive gene diseases, each child has a one in four chance of getting the disease (i.e., if one or the other parent or neither passes the gene, the child will not get the disease; only when both pass the gene does the child get the disorder). If a child does not get the disease, he or she still has a 50 percent chance of being a carrier of the gene and should, of course, be concerned about a future spouse also being a carrier. Examples of disorders caused by recessive genes include sickle-cell anemia (a blood disorder primarily affecting Blacks), Tay-Sachs disease (a condition involving brain deterioration most common among those of Eastern European Jewish ancestry), cystic fibrosis (affects the general U.S. white population and strikes one of every 2,500 births per year), and PKU syndrome (a deficiency of an essential liver enzyme resulting in mental retardation).[18]

Third, some inherited diseases are called *X-linked* or *sex-linked*. While males have an X and a Y chromosome, females have two X chromosomes. Typically, a clinically normal mother carries a faulty gene on one of the X chromosomes. When this happens, each son has a 50 percent risk of inheriting that gene and getting the disease that goes with it. Each daughter has an equal chance of being a carrier of the gene and transmitting it to her sons, though she is usually not affected by the disease herself. Fathers affected with an X-linked disorder cannot transmit it to a son, but when they have a recessive X-linked disorder, they pass the defective gene to daughters who will carry the gene but be unaffected. Well-known X-linked diseases include hemophilia and muscular dystrophy.[19]

A final kind of inherited disorder is due to *polygenic* or *multifactoral* inheritance. This means the disease results from many genes interacting with one another and sometimes with factors in the environment. With so many genes involved, the pattern of transmission of these diseases from parents is unclear. Hence, people with these diseases are often unaware of the hereditary basis of their disorder. One of the best-known examples of a disease thought to be polygenic is spina bifida.[20]

In addition to these four forms of inherited disorders, there are other genetically based diseases. In these cases birth defects result from a chromosomal abnormality. These abnormalities can occur when chromosomes are broken or rearranged. They also happen when there are extra or missing chromosomes. Down's syndrome is a condition resulting from chromosomal abnormality.

Detection of this last kind of genetic disorder requires a test but cannot be predicted before a child is conceived. However, in cases of inherited genetic disorders a genetic counselor who knows a patient's family's medical history can advise the patient of the likelihood that she or he will get a certain inherited disease or that his or her offspring will get it. This information is useful not only when a couple considers having children, but also in making decisions about whether to get married and in gaining a realistic assessment of the chance that children already conceived or born will get a particular disease. This information can help those involved to prepare emotionally, financially, etc. for what is coming or likely to come, but it can also be devastating and cause much mental and emotional anguish. Such information is also used as a basis for aborting an already conceived child.

ETHICAL CONCERNS AND GENETIC COUNSELING

Though some of the moral issues surrounding genetic counseling have practical implications, the concerns with genetic counseling are mainly moral in nature. An initial set of questions surrounds the use of information attained through genetic counseling. Counseling based either on amniocentesis or on knowledge of family medical and genetic history can lead to a series of options, depending on when in the reproductive process the counselee seeks advice. For example, the counselee may choose non-marriage, contraception, artificial insemination, abortion of a defective child already conceived, abortion of a child because of its gender, allowing defective newborns to die, treatment, or suicide because of what is learned about oneself.[21] Some of these options present ethical problems, and as a result, the morality of the whole procedure is questioned.

Another major issue is whether genetic counseling should be directive or non-directive. Non-directive counseling merely gives genetic information without evaluating (morally or otherwise) or suggesting what the counselee should do. Directive counseling makes such judgments and offers advice. At stake is individual autonomy versus paternalism. Some argue for non-directiveness in order to protect patient autonomy and because no one, professional or otherwise, can do more than imagine what he would do if in the counselee's shoes. Others, however, doubt that non-directiveness is either possible or preferable. Counselors clearly have moral preferences, and although the counselor wants to help the counselee come to a decision within his own value structure, if the counselor is asked for more than information, invariably his values creep in. Moreover, counselees seek advice because they know counselors have had experience with other cases, and they want the benefit of the counselor's expertise. And, then, sometimes a counselee (e.g., someone who is mentally retarded) is incompetent to make decisions with the information given. To maintain a totally non-directive stance in such a case leaves someone who needs help without an idea of where to get it and seems irresponsible on the part of the counselor.[22]

A third problem is the possibility of dysgenic (increased frequency of harmful genes) consequences from counseling. For example, two people detected as carriers of a harmful gene decide not to marry each other. Instead, they marry noncarriers. This removes the chance that selection would act against the homozygote. The end result is an increase in the gene frequency that can potentially harm future generations.[23]

A fourth concern is the conflict between the affected person's welfare and that of future generations. For example, there is no foolproof test to identify those with the gene for Huntington's disease, but there is a fairly accurate test to indicate probabilities. Since this disease has a late onset, is lethal, and at present has no known cure, should children at risk take the test? Some see no reason to take the test and then worry about possibilities that may never occur. But even if the test were completely accurate, should it be used? Such knowledge might be extremely detrimental to the well-being of the person involved. He might become so depressed that he commits suicide, or it might be impossible to find anyone to marry him. If married, a decision to forego the joy of children might follow once this news about his genetic condition is revealed.

On the other side of this issue is one's responsibility to others, especially future generations. While most think it immoral not to inform a prospective spouse that one can or will get the disease, there is also a question of whether it is fair and moral to saddle a prospective spouse with a husband or wife who is going to get this disease even if the prospective spouse knows and wants to shoulder this responsibility. Likewise, if one learned that his or her spouse would or might get the disease, would that not morally obligate them to consider long and hard foregoing children?[24]

These are hard questions, and these dilemmas can and do confront people as a result of information from genetic counseling.

Finally, there are the moral dilemmas of whether the counselor should tell the whole truth and whether either he or the counselee should divulge this information to other family members. As a result of this counseling, family secrets such as illegitimacy or previous abortions may come to light. Should that information be divulged to those involved? For example, suppose an illegitimate child is in line for a certain genetic disease. But suppose that to divulge that information to the child or its parents would mean divulging the secret of the child's illegitimacy. It is detrimental to the child's physical well-being not to pass on the information, but to pass it on might psychologically harm the child and the home in which a father, for example, learns that a child he thought was genetically his is not. Should the truth be told?[25] Moreover, suppose the disease a counselor detects is one for which other family members are likely at risk (either to get it or to be carriers). On the one hand, there is the principle of counselor/counselee confidentiality, but since the welfare of others is involved, should confidentiality be broken?[26] Such ethical dilemmas can arise because of and are associated with genetic counseling.

ASSESSMENT OF GENETIC COUNSELING

In assessing genetic counseling, we believe one must first distinguish *having* the information from *using* it. Nothing seems inherently immoral about methods used to gather genetic information on patients. Doctors frequently gather medical information about a patient from family medical history or tests performed on the patient, so we see nothing immoral about those procedures. Moreover, this information is essential in many cases for accurate diagnosis and treatment of the patient, and the information itself is neither moral or immoral; it is simply information.

On the other hand, it is clear that this information (like other medical information) may be put to immoral uses. Using genetic information to decide to abort a baby or to commit suicide rather than take the chance that one will get a genetic disease for which one is at risk are immoral uses of the information, for they involve intentionally taking innocent life. Of course, immoral uses of the information do not make the counseling or possession of the information immoral. Moreover, not all uses of the information are immoral. In fact, failure to inform people at risk for a disease (if one knows that) seems immoral, and if someone knows he will likely have a genetic disease and pass it on to offspring, it is at least irresponsible, if not immoral, to fail to take that information seriously when deciding whether to reproduce.

Our fundamental conclusion, then, is that genetic counseling is not immoral, though some uses are and should be avoided. As to the directive versus non-directive issue, we think making value judgments and offering advice need not abridge a patient's freedom of choice. Obviously, a counselor can be so overbearing that the counselee is psychologically in no position to decide contrary to the counselor's advice. On the other hand, a counselor can withhold judgment and advice until asked, and if asked can offer advice in the form of an opinion about prudent courses of action, can clarify several options open for the patient, and can stress that the choice is the patient's. Such an approach seems, on the one hand, to help the patient while still leaving the decision with the counselee. If the patient is incompetent to decide, the counselor should take this same approach with those who will decide for the patient. Of course, a counselor should never suggest an immoral course of action (e.g., "in view of what's ahead of you, you ought to consider suicide"), nor help a patient carry out an immoral decision (e.g., help an expectant mother attain an elective abortion).

As to whether one should tell a patient the whole truth about how she or he inherited the disease, we have several comments. If the genetic information is relevant to the patient's physical well-being and to that of future generations, it seems morally reprehensible to keep that information from the patient. If it is impossible to convey that information without divulging information about the exact parentage of the patient, or if treatment must involve contacting the genetic parents (e.g., to attain organ or blood donation from a near relative), then it is necessary to relate the information about biological parents. Failure to do so might entail an improper strategy for treatment, and if the doctor knows that, it seems immoral to proceed with that line of treatment just to safeguard the exact identity of biological parents. On the other hand, if information about the patient's genetic parents is not significant either to diagnosis or treatment, nor is it relevant to other genetic relatives who might be at risk, there is no need to divulge that information. That does not sanction lying if asked about genetic ancestry, but only removes the need to offer information unless asked.

In our opinion, the most difficult questions pertain to handling information about a degenerative disease for which there is no known cure. Having confronted many of these issues personally, we believe that some decisions must be left open to personal choice once one is in the concrete situation, whereas on other issues we can offer moral advice apart from specific situations. For example, if on the basis of a family's genetic history it is known that a given family member is at risk for a disease, it is immoral not to inform him or her. That information not only affects him or her, but has implications for anyone he or she might marry or consider marrying and implications for any children he or she might have. If one knows someone is in danger and could inform her of that fact, one is morally reprehensible for failing to do so and letting the harm befall her.

Some may reply that this is only so if the person at risk can do something to avoid the danger, but it is not so for diseases where nothing can be done to cure the disease even if one knows. Why, then, must the person at risk be informed, especially when doing so will only cause great mental and emotional pain long before the actual onset of the disease and may lead the person to suicide?

We disagree. For one thing, even when there is no known cure, that does not mean no treatment is available to minimize symptoms associated with the disease. One may need care, and help for coping with the disease may be available, but without knowing of one's condition, no help will be sought. Moreover, the person at risk needs to know the truth in order to make informed decisions about the future. And since choices that are made (e.g., marriage) affect other people and potential offspring, it is simply wrong to ignore the well-being of those others by refusing to inform the person at risk. We recognize that someone given this information may use it to justify committing suicide, and that would be immoral. We also agree that not all uses of this information are moral, but that doesn't make the information immoral, nor does it remove the obligation to inform persons at risk. Our obligation is to do whatever possible to help others avoid endangering themselves and others. If we know something that would accomplish that and fail to divulge it, we act immorally. Of course, those who receive the information must use it morally. But even if the recipient would use this information immorally, this does not remove the obligation for those who know it to reveal it.

Though some situations are easy to advise, not all are. For example, if someone knows she or he has or likely will have an incurable genetic disease, it is not clear if she or he should or shouldn't marry or have children. Not to consider the pros and cons carefully would be irresponsible, but what is decided must rest on personal preference and conviction in light of known facts. Let us illustrate. Suppose someone knows he has a disease controlled by a dominant gene, and he knows the chances are 50 percent that his offspring will get the disease. Does this degree of risk make it immoral to have a child? We doubt that a definitive answer is possible. Here each must make his own choice. Likewise, if someone considering marriage learns through a test that she has a 90 percent chance of getting a degenerative disease, she may think it immoral under such circumstances to saddle a prospective mate with this situation, even if he is willing to marry her. No easy answers to such cases are available.

What about the morality of taking a test to learn one's chances of getting a disease if other relatives have it? In response, if the test offers only probabilities, not exact answers, we see no moral obligation to take it, though taking it is morally permissible. If the test gives an exact answer, matters become more difficult. If the test is accurate but there is no known cure or treatment for the disease, it is hard to say the person at risk is morally obligated to take it just for his own information. If he considers marriage and/or children, then it seems at least irresponsible and imprudent, if not immoral, to refuse taking the test, since others' lives are involved. Of course, if the test is accurate and there is treatment to cure the disease or allow the person to cope with it, it is surely foolish, if not also immoral, not to take the test. While in this case we do not think refusing the test (and treatment) is committing suicide, we wonder what reason there could be for refusing the test.

Having said the preceding, we add that though we think taking the test is morally permissible (possibly obligatory in some cases), we must comment on the morality of various uses of the information. Using the information to justify suicide or abortion of an already conceived child is immoral. But there are moral uses of that information. The key point, though, is that whether the information is used morally or immorally must be separated from whether it is morally acceptable to take the test and have the information. We believe the test itself and the information it gives are morally neutral (hence, taking it is permissible), but we believe that taking it with intent to put the information to immoral use is wrong.

GENETIC SCREENING

Genetic counseling and genetic screening are related but not identical. With respect to genetic counseling, a counselor helps a patient learn about his genetic background and the likelihood of contracting a disease and passing it on to future offspring, and then offers counsel on various courses of action in light of the data.

With genetic screening, the point is actual detection of who is at risk for a disease so as to do whatever possible to prevent it. In particular, the point is to test a given population without symptoms of a disease, so as to discover people with a specific genotype that indicates they will develop a disease or are carriers of it.[27] The purpose of this detection is not merely to attain the information, but to put that information to various uses. For example, those identified as at risk can be advised to avoid certain conditions that would precipitate manifestations of the disease. Genetic screening is also used to detect latent or actual disease prior to making treatment available. In addition, genetic screening might be used to identify carriers of a recessive gene so as to help them make decisions about whether to have children. This information is also used for encouraging therapeutic abortion of children who through prenatal diagnosis are found to be genetically defective or likely to have genetically controlled diseases. Finally, genetic screening has been used to answer research questions about matters like selection, drift, frequency of a genetic marker, and natural history of a disorder.[28]

The value of genetic screening is easily illustrated. Sickle-cell anemia and Tay-Sachs disease are related to a recessive gene. The former disease is especially prevalent within Black communities, and the latter is most frequent in Ashkenazic Jewish communities. Screening members of those communities will help detect who carries the recessive gene. If a husband and wife both carry the recessive gene, that information will help them to make decisions about having children, given the likelihood that their offspring will have the disease. Another example of the value of screening involves phenylketonuria. Here screening is not done before a couple has children, but rather on the newborn. If PKU is detected, significant mental retardation can be prevented by putting the child on a low phenylalanine diet.[29]

ETHICAL CONCERNS

From the preceding description, one might wonder what possible moral objection there might be to genetic screening. Nonetheless, there are some ethical questions that arise in relation to it. Some practical problems also arise such as whether the cost of widespread screening is merited by the benefit derived from it. However, most of the practical concerns also have ethical implications, so our focus is the ethical concerns.[30]

Two initial problems go hand in hand. They are the problems of confidentiality and discrimination. Patient confidentiality is a major feature of medical ethics. However, when information from genetic screening has implications for relatives and is useful to interested third parties such as employers and insurers, there is a genuine temptation to divulge it. Informing relatives thought to be at risk raises potentially the problems noted in our discussion of genetic counseling. Not only are there questions about the wisdom of informing someone that he may get a lethal disease, but the issue of divulging paternity lines arises. As to interested third parties, an employer calculating who will likely be the best worker and least likely to contract life-threatening diseases might want to use this information when hiring. Likewise, if an insurance company knew the chances that a patient might get an incurable disease, the temptation to refuse insurance or at least raise premiums dramatically would be there. Hence, once this information goes to third parties, there is likely to be discrimination in the workplace and by insurance companies.[31] Since screening programs do not screen everyone for every kind of genetic disease, and yet many may have a gene that later results in a disease, it seems unjust to single out a particular group to screen, knowing that the screening may lead to placing their jobs in jeopardy or to running the risk of being uninsurable. Why should they suffer discrimination while others escape, not because others will not get a genetic disease, but because they are not part of a target community?

Another related problem with genetic screening is stigmatization. People who learn that they carry a defective gene or are likely to get a particular disease may be stigmatized. Stigmatization is "a complex social interaction that results in labeling, social distance, and lowered feelings of self-esteem."[32] The results of it can be a weakened self-image, difficulty in finding marriage partners, and supposed "proof" for the prejudice that a given ethnic group is worthy of discrimination.[33] Given these potential results, results that have actually followed genetic screening,[34] is it ethical to proceed with such screening?

A final question is whether screening should be mandatory or voluntary. Since those who require the screening will probably use it to discriminate in some way or other, many think screening should only be voluntary. As some note, if government mandates screening, there will be a tendency to pressure individuals about their choice of a mate and about reproductive decisions. Some favor this out of a desire to promote the public good and avoid the birth of those whose care will be a great financial and emotional strain on society. Others understand these potential values, but argue that interference in personal decisions such as choosing a mate is an invasion of privacy.[35]

Mandatory screening programs typically have been of two kinds. The first aims to detect affected individuals in order to begin treatment. The second attempts to identify carriers of recessive deleterious genes and inform them of the risk of having children if their spouse carries the same genes. Some support the former kind of screening plus treatment as a public health measure that tries to save public funds in the long run and tries to protect those who cannot protect themselves. PKU screening is the example often cited. On the other hand, using these same grounds to argue for compulsory screening of the second kind is much more controversial.[36] If genetic screening did not tend to lead to stigmatization and discrimination, it would be easier to convince those to be screened that it should be done on a mandatory basis. Voluntary screening is not a guarantee against stigmatization and discrimination, but at least the person screened can reject the testing.

ASSESSMENT OF GENETIC SCREENING

Our intent is not to assess this practice from the standpoint of public policy decisions. That enters the realm of social and political philosophy, which goes beyond the contours of this book. Moreover, we do not think genetic screening should be assessed on a cost/benefit basis,[37] for so doing presupposes a consequentialist approach to ethical decisions. While we think cost/benefit analyses are helpful prudentially, as non-consequentialists we do not believe such considerations should influence *moral* judgments and decisions.

In assessing genetic screening we begin, as with genetic counseling, by distinguishing the practice from its uses. Testing a person or group to determine the chances of acquiring a disease or to determine carriers of a recessive gene seems no more immoral *per se* than performing any diagnostic test to help with a patient's medical condition. Moreover, it is hard to argue that early detection of those who will get a disease so as to treat it or discovery of carriers of a recessive gene so that they may make informed decisions about marriage and reproduction are immoral uses of genetic screening.

There are, however, some intended uses that are clearly immoral. Prenatal screening so as to encourage, warrant, or even mandate abortion is immoral, since we believe abortion is immoral.[38] Screening to stigmatize people as of lesser worth, screening to withhold employment or insurance from those at risk, or even screening to mandate sterilization of carriers of a given gene seem to us immoral uses of screening. These uses of screening, we believe, invade privacy and abridge personal freedom of choice (when sterilization is mandated, e.g.). When the information is used to stigmatize and discriminate, this suggests too much that a person's worth is based on his or her genetic makeup and that the need for care of these people is secondary to the desire of insurance companies, hospitals, and doctors to have a positive financial balance. Such concerns of doctors, hospitals, etc. tend to treat patients not as persons with worth who deserve treatment and care regardless of physical condition, but rather as potential means to the end of making a living. Hence, those most able to pay or (in the case of insurance companies) likely to require the least payout are the most likely candidates for care and insurance. We believe this treatment of people as means to such financial ends is immoral. Hence, we conclude that genetic screening and the information gained from it are not immoral, but some uses of the information are.

As to confidentiality, we reply much as we did in regard to genetic counseling. This information should not be made public unless the patient wants it to be known. On the other hand, if genetic information has health implications for family members, it is only morally right to inform them. If paternity lines must be divulged to inform people at risk, then, as we have argued, it must be conveyed. However, we think in many cases that a person can be informed of being at risk without having to divulge the details of his or her genetic parents. In those cases, confidentiality should be maintained.

Finally, we think it immoral to abridge a person's freedom of choice in these matters. This may occur either because no choice is given or because someone is asked to consent without adequate information for making a decision. Hence, when screening is to be done, it is best done on a voluntary basis. In cases such as screening for PKU where the baby cannot give informed consent, mandatory screening is genuinely in the child's best interests and should be done. However, it is only fair that the child's parents be informed as to what will be done and why. In general, however, mandatory screening seems to abridge freedom of choice, and as such is not permissible.

SEX SELECTION

As a result of advances in medical technology, sex selection is being practiced and will likely become more prevalent in years to come. Currently
there are several different ways of choosing the sex of children.[39] One way
is to perform infanticide on children of unwanted sex or to offer them sub-
standard medical and nutritional care. Though these are radical ways of
selecting sex, in certain parts of the world it has been done.[40]

A second and much newer method for sex selection involves prenatal
diagnosis. By means of amniocentesis, it is possible to determine various
genetic information about a developing child, including its sex. While
requests for prenatal diagnosis are typically made on the basis of wanting
to discover whether the developing fetus has a genetic defect that will lead
to a serious disease, this can be used as a cover for gaining information
about the child's sex. If the child's sex is unwanted, the couple can simply
abort the child.

Wertz and Fletcher describe a case of a couple who had four daughters
and wanted a son. They requested prenatal diagnosis solely to determine
the fetus' sex, and they told the doctor that if the fetus were female, they
would abort it. They added that if the doctor would not do the diagnosis,
they would abort the baby rather than take the chance of having another
girl. According to Wertz and Fletcher, in a 1985 survey of 295 U.S. geneticists 62 percent of those surveyed said that in the case described they
would either perform prenatal diagnosis or refer the couple to someone
who would. Percentages in some other countries were not far behind. In
Hungary 60 percent, in Canada 47 percent, in Sweden 38 percent, in Israel
33 percent, in Brazil 30 percent, in Greece 29 percent, and in the United
Kingdom 24 percent said they would either do the diagnosis or refer the
couple.[41]

Another way to select the sex of one's child relates to *in vitro* fertilization. Once eggs are harvested from the mother and fertilized, the embryos
may be examined for various genetic information, including the baby's
sex. If the embryo is not the sex the parents want, a decision not to implant
the embryo is simple enough. If the embryo is of the desired sex and has
no detectable genetic problems, it can be implanted. This method of sex
selection is as easy, if not easier, to perform than amniocentesis. Many
would find it less objectionable, because if the embryo is of the unwanted
sex, it does not have to be aborted (in the usual sense of abortion).[42]

The preceding methods of sex selection involve already existing children (prior to or after birth), but other methods determine a child's sex
even before conception. One technique immobilizes sperm cells in a refrigeration unit. X chromosomes (girl producing) tend to be a bit heavier and
hence settle to the bottom of the mixture faster than Y (boy producing)
chromosomes. Y sperm cells also swim faster than X sperm cells. Hence,

if sperm are allowed to swim through a dense viscous fluid such as bovine albumin, X and Y sperm will likely separate, providing potentially up to 85 percent male sperm. When these two methods are used together (refrigeration and separation by swimming), the probability of success approaches 100 percent.[43]

Another means of sex selection before conception is through drug intervention. Some foresee a day when drugs that act to increase production and survival of particular sex-determining sperm cells (male or female) are available. Though the production and use of such drugs is not currently widespread, some expect it to happen in future years.[44]

One final method seems likely to be most successful in sex selection before conception. As recent as the summer of 1991, researchers in Chicago reported success in separating human X and Y sperm cells by means of a centrifuge. Once the sperm are separated, the couple chooses whether to have a boy or girl, picks the appropriate sperm, and conceives the desired child either through artificial insemination or *in vitro* fertilization. As research continues and this methodology becomes prevalent, it will likely become a widespread method of sex selection.

Though sex selection may seem an unnecessary tampering with the natural order, there are various reasons for a couple to consider it. Some think one benefit would be the prevention of much child neglect and abuse. It is often thought that some children are shunned because the parents wanted a child of the other sex. Though it is dubious that sex selection will end child abuse (many wanted children are also abused), at least when sex selection is practiced there should be no initial predisposition toward neglect or abuse just because the child was the "wrong sex."[45]

The most obvious reason for sex selection is family planning. If a couple could choose the sex of their children, they could plan the order in which children would be born. Some suggest that if that were done, family size would probably be smaller, since parents could be assured of having the exact desired number of children of each sex without having to continue bearing children until they get children of the desired sex.[46]

A further advantage of such family planning would especially be evident in countries where there is special emphasis on one sex or the other (usually males). For example, since male babies assure a family that its name will be carried on and in some countries assure the family of certain social and cultural advantages, there is typically a desire to have sons. Sex selection provides an efficient means of accomplishing these goals without necessarily having a large family. This becomes especially important in countries such as Red China where the government limits the size of families, and there is a great desire for male children.

A final reason for sex selection is to avoid a genetically transmitted disease. Some diseases are sex-linked. If a couple is thought to be at risk for passing on such a disease, they obviously would want to avoid having a child of the sex linked to the disease without foregoing having children altogether. If, for example, a given family has a history of hemophiliacs, rather than having no children at all, it would be a great advantage to be able to choose a girl and thereby remove the possibility of a hemophiliac.[47]

PRACTICAL CONSIDERATIONS

Many of the practical arguments favoring sex selection stem from the reasons listed above for wanting to do it. We need not repeat those considerations, but only note that in virtue of those advantages sex selection appears very positive to many.

On the other hand, some raise practical concerns against sex selection, most of which are social in nature. For example, some fear that widespread practice of sex selection would lead to an imbalance in the ratio of men to women. Since there is an apparent preference for males over females in many countries (especially in a one child family), it is feared that men would probably outnumber women. Some social scientists fear that this could lead to unwanted social developments like a more rugged, hostile society where women are in the minority. Others fear that an overbalance of men might also encourage homosexuality. Moreover, some social scientists argue that men are more likely to become criminals than women and are less likely to go to church and be involved in the moral instruction of children. The net result would be a society where violence is even more prevalent than it is now, a society not unlike a frontier setting.[48]

Those who favor sex selection think these fears are unfounded. Any imbalance in the sex ratio would probably be rectified in the following generation. As to whether an overbalance of men to women would create a more hostile society, it is argued that there is no guarantee that it would. It is just as likely that other social and environmental factors contribute to the kind of society created as it is that the sheer number of men to women is the only factor. Besides, in order to create the kinds of imbalanced scenarios mentioned, there would really need to be widespread use of the techniques of sex selection. Some say that unless these techniques become nearly universal (which is unlikely), sex ratios at least in Western countries are not likely to change significantly.[49]

ETHICAL CONSIDERATIONS

While many practical objections to sex selection seem outweighed by its practical advantages, one must also consider the ethics of sex selection. Here many voices object to it on one ethical ground or another. Some objections are raised on consequentialist grounds, whereas others are not.

Arguments in Favor

Various considerations favor sex selection as morally correct. An initial argument is that it allows parents to avoid having children where a sex-linked disease is involved. If it is moral to do whatever can be done to avoid pain and suffering, this is a noble and moral goal of sex selection.

Second, some say sex selection would increase the quality of life in several respects. Quality of life will be better for the child who is of "wanted" sex than if he or she had been unwanted. In addition, sex selection would result in a better quality of life for the family with the balance it wants. And it will also give a better quality of life to the mother, who will need fewer pregnancies to achieve the desired mix of boys and girls in the family.[50]

Third, some favor sex selection as a means to limit world population. Typically, families want a son, but with natural means of sex selection a family may have a series of girls before getting the son it desires. All of this contributes to overpopulation which presents various moral problems. Sex selection, on the other hand, allows a family to have just the number of boys and girls it wants without having "extra" children.[51]

Finally, sex selection is viewed as a possible way to fight sexism. Parents may want to balance the gender of their children as a basis for children to learn to respect sex-based differences and to treat members of the opposite sex fairly. Since sexism is undesirable and immoral, a strategy such as this would help to fight sexism, and that surely seems moral.[52]

Objections

Despite positive arguments, there are considerable moral objections to sex selection. An initial concern is that many sex selection techniques involve abortion or its equivalent (e.g., discarding embryos fertilized *in vitro*). While children selected by these methods are obviously not aborted, the fact that amniocentesis and sexing embryos even involves the potential of destroying human life if the child is the "wrong" sex troubles many greatly. In fact, even some who favor certain abortions see this practice as a needless waste of life.

Second, some doubt that sex selection would actually raise anyone's quality of life. Mary Anne Warren, for example, complains that the idea that sex selection will increase quality of life for the child, family and mother is based on the premise of a sexist society. According to Warren, the "better quality of life" argument is incomprehensible except against a background of preferential treatment of one sex. Thus, sex selection on those grounds only perpetuates a sexist society and is thereby immoral.[53] Others also worry that sex selection could even contribute to gender stereotyping before birth and perpetuate sexism in society. Neither of these results is morally acceptable.[54]

In addition, Warren says sex selection may actually have a negative impact on the quality of life of the family and of women in general. Sex selection could encourage better treatment of children whose sex was selected rather than chosen by nature. Moreover, it might produce marital conflict over the exact composition of the family, and it might also lead to foreclosing the opportunity of having a girl (in male dominated societies). While a family with children of one sex is not undesirable, there are many benefits of having children of both sexes. Deciding to rule out children of one sex or another deliberately does something not necessarily in the family's best interests, especially since sex selection could balance the family and bring the benefits of children of both sexes. As to better quality of life for women, Warren disagrees. She thinks sex selection would likely be used in most societies against women. Even in the U.S. there seems to be a preference for boys even if a family desires at least one child of each sex. But even if selection favored girls, Warren would not approve because she thinks sex selection is inherently sexist (regardless of which sex it favors) and rests on a belief in sexual inequality. Given these roots of the practice, it cannot be moral.[55]

As to claims that sex selection would help limit population, this is not necessarily true. As some writers note, there is no evidence that population trends result from a desire, for example, to have sons. Instead, most people have the number of children they feel they can afford to raise. Moreover, if there were some financial advantage to one sex and if that sex could be selected, that might even encourage a couple to have more children than they would have without sex selection. Hence, it is not clear that sex selection would solve any country's population problem.[56]

Some favor sex selection for the sake of a parent's companionship with a child of a particular sex, but opponents of sex selection reply that companionship is just as easily attained with a child of one sex as with one of the other. Most hobbies that involve a girl could also involve a boy. Moreover, even if there is greater companionship with a child of one sex, the basic motivations behind sex selection are sexist, and it also involves the other moral problems mentioned. The advantage of companionship is far overbalanced by these other moral considerations.[57]

A further objection to sex selection is that many might think it their right to select their child's sex. However, it is not at all clear that parents (or anyone else) have such rights in this matter. Scripture refers to children as gifts from God (Ps 127:3), but, then, it seems rather strange to think of manipulating the nature of the "gift" that is given, let alone to talk of having a right to do so. As Anderson argues, "At some point on the continuum children cease to be a gift from God (cf. Ps. 127:3) and begin to be a parental plaything."[58]

A final objection is the fear of where sex selection will lead. Once the Human Genome Project maps the genes on each chromosome, parents can choose not only the sex of their child but other characteristics as well. But *can* does not entail *should*. However, having set the precedent that one may choose one genetic feature of offspring (sex), by what logic can one then argue against choosing other (even all) characteristics? And if one can choose to produce "perfect children," what will this mean for those who do not meet such standards? One can easily envision all sorts of immoral uses of this kind of technology, and as a result it seems unwise, let alone immoral, even to begin down that path. Anderson's comment about the child as a plaything rather than a gift becomes especially poignant.[59]

ASSESSMENT OF SEX SELECTION

In assessing sex selection, some arguments do not strike us as particularly compelling. For example, we think sexism is wrong, but we are not convinced all sex selection is sexist-based or oriented. Likewise, as non-consequentialists we do not think results of sex selection such as limiting population (even if that happened) are *moral* reasons for favoring or rejecting it. Such results are significant prudentially, but we do not view them as *moral* justifications.

From our perspective, however, there are matters of moral significance that lead us to believe that generally (with some exceptions to be noted), sex selection is neither necessary nor morally right. Let us explain.

Initially, we must distinguish sex selection according to its various methods. Given our stance on the sanctity of life and its implications for abortion, we reject as immoral any form of sex selection involving infanticide or abortion (or procedures equivalent to it). Hence, sex selection by amniocentesis leading actually or even potentially to abortion is ruled out. Likewise, sexing embryos fertilized *in vitro* and discarding those of the unwanted sex is also wrong.

By logical implication, the preceding point entails that if sex selection is ever morally acceptable, it can only be in a case where the choice is made prior to conceiving the baby. However, before concluding that sex selection before conception is moral, we must ask if that method of sex selection involves any other practices that might be deemed immoral. We raise this question, because even if the sex is chosen before conception, the woman's egg must be fertilized by artificial insemination or, if her tubes are blocked, by *in vitro* fertilization. In the previous chapter, we argued that IVF is immoral in most cases, and that many cases of artificial insemination are immoral. Hence, if carrying out sex selection involves either IVF or artificial insemination (in cases where it would be immoral), such instances of sex selection cannot be sanctioned.

Where does this leave us? It means that basically the only cases of sex selection that *might* be morally permissible are those where the sex is selected before conception and AIH or AID (in acceptable cases) is the means of impregnating the wife. But are even these cases morally permissible? This is a difficult question, but we believe we can shed some light on it.

Initially, we note that even if a couple intends to attain family balance, etc. by sex selection, that does not mean any couple has a *right* to select a child in this manner. Though some societies guarantee a *legal right* to reproduce, we know of no instance of a legal right to choose the sex of one's offspring. Moreover, we know of no *moral* right that mandates or even allows sex selection. Likewise, there is no moral *command* to do this. Hence, if sex selection is moral, it is so because it is morally permissible, i.e., no moral principle forbids it, even if no moral rule commands it and no moral right demands it.

If a couple chooses a child's sex basically because they are afraid to leave sex selection up to chance, we think that is a wrong reason for sex selection. Our point is that we do not believe that when sex selection is left to natural reproduction, it is left to chance. In view of God's sovereign control of the universe and Scripture's teaching that God controls and guides our development even in our mother's womb (Ps 139:13-16), we believe God controls this matter, too.

Someone may reply, "I believe God controls these things, but I just want to be sure to have a boy," or "I just want to balance my family without having several children beyond what I can afford." These are acceptable goals, but the thinking behind them is flawed. The one who thinks this way seems to imply that he knows what is best for his family. Though God is in control, we must "help him out" to ensure that the right decision is made. But obviously this is wrong, if not in fact blasphemous. What troubles us especially here is an apparent unwillingness to believe that if this matter is left in God's hands he will do what is best for us. At some point one must remember that children are gifts from God, and one cannot always dictate the particulars of gifts given by anyone, let alone by God.

Suppose someone said, "But I have none of these improper attitudes toward God and myself. I simply want to guarantee a balanced family. If it is all right to regulate whether and when I have children at all via birth control, why can't I regulate this matter?" In response, it seems that the issues surrounding whether and when to have a child at all (birth control) are different kinds of issues than whether to have a boy or a girl. As argued in our chapter on birth control, we believe there are morally acceptable reasons for using birth control to preclude having children, but we fail to see that they apply to the question of having a boy as opposed to a girl or vice versa.[60]

Where does this leave us? Are there ever cases of sex selection that are morally permissible? We think so, but only in very specific kinds of situations. The situations envisioned are those where the sole reason for selection is to avoid having a child who will likely have a genetic disease linked to its sex. In this case, choosing the child's sex is not a matter of personal taste or preference, nor does it involve attempts to balance a family, nor does it need to involve any of the wrong ideas about God and ourselves mentioned above. Here we appeal to the principle that one should do what he can to prevent pain and evil, so long as so doing breaks no other moral rules in the process. While we don't believe this principle mandates sex selection in these cases, we believe it permits it. We must add, however, that sex selection in these cases is morally permissible only if done prior to conception and through a morally acceptable means such as AIH.

Someone might object, "But sanctioning sex selection to avoid disease contradicts what was said about letting God control these matters and recognizing that he knows what's best for us. If it is all right to intervene in these cases, why not in cases where we simply want a boy or a girl? Aren't the cases the same?" This is a significant objection, but it is answerable. We note initially that if the logic of this objection is carried out consistently, no medical intervention of any kind is warranted, for one should leave every medical situation in God's hands. But not fighting medical problems ignores the fact that diseases are present in our world because it is a fallen world. The divine mandate to subdue and rule the earth for God and to fight sin *and its effects* seems to us to warrant our intervention in a variety of medical situations, and we believe the prevention of disease is one of them. To intervene is not to presume to know better than God what should be done, nor must such intervention try to take control out of God's hands. God has already told us to fight sin and its consequences. When we intervene in such cases, we show that we recognize that God often uses our activities to accomplish his will in the world.[61] Hence, we can reasonably see our actions as under his control and furthering his ends.

Some may reply that if God can work through us to prevent disease, he can work through us to determine family composition. The cases are the same. However, the circumstances are not the same, and this is a crucial difference. If sex selection is practiced to avoid a disease, we show that we recognize this is a fallen world and we are to fight sin and its effects, one of which is disease.[62] If we don't, that does not mean, of course, that God is unable to bring good out of the evil situation. However, God's ability to bring good out of an evil situation is not warrant for allowing the occurrence of every evil, especially when we can do something to keep it from happening. So in cases of disease, we simply act in accord with God's desire that we do what we can to prevent evil. But consider cases of sex selection to balance a family or have a child for companionship sake. What disease or medical problem does this choice address? What evil are we trying to prevent? This kind of sex selection clearly addresses no disease or other evil. But, then, making the decision in no way fulfills the divine mandate to subdue the earth or fight evil. In such cases, letting God do the choosing through natural means in no way shirks our responsibility to fight sin or its consequences.

We conclude, then, that the two situations (sex selection to balance a family, etc. versus sex selection to avoid a genetically transmitted disease) are not the same. As a result, the warrants for sex selection in the latter cases do not sanction it in the former. The net result is that there are no cases where sex selection is mandated and very few where it is morally permissible.

RECOMBINANT DNA (GENE-SPLICING)

Prior to the early 1970s changes in an organism's genetic code were left to gene mutation. Those mutations were usually accomplished through the normal processes of cell replication and reproduction. Recombinant DNA technology, however, allows *scientists* to redesign the genetic makeup of an organism by deleting, adding, and/or changing the order of the genetic code. This technology involves three main phases. First, the desired DNA strand from the donor organism is isolated and cut. Then that material is transferred to a new organism. The third phase is expression by the receptor organism of the new characteristic. There are specific techniques for all three phases.[63] Below we describe in more detail techniques used in the first two stages.

THE TECHNIQUE

The first phase of isolating and cutting DNA from a given DNA molecule became possible in 1970 when Nathan and Smith discovered a class of enzymes that could be used to do this. These enzymes are called restriction enconucleases (or enzymes). "They bind to the double stranded DNA molecule and search for a specific nucleotide sequence in the DNA."[64] Once the enzyme finds the unique sequence, it makes a staggered cut of the two strands at this place in the DNA. There are many different kinds of restriction enzymes, and scientists have catalogued many of them so that they know the exact site where each will cut the DNA.[65] So long as the same restriction enzyme cuts the DNA from the cells of both the donor and the recipient organism, the same segment of DNA will be cut in both cases. Since DNA strands in a given cell contain complementary overlapping ends where the strands were cut by the restriction enzyme, they can each be easily rejoined by another enzyme called a ligase, or DNA from two separate organisms can be joined (scientists say recombined) to form a hybrid gene.[66]

Once scientists learned how to cut and splice genetic material, there were still questions about what could be done with it and how to do it. In particular, how could genetic material be transferred from the donor to the recipient cell? Some sort of vector (vehicle) was needed. The most frequently used vector is the bacterium *Escherichia coli* (*E. coli*), a very common bacterium which lives in the intestines of many animals and humans. This organism has been extremely well studied, having been grown and studied in laboratories for over fifty years.[67] Though most DNA is tangled in a large mass inside a cell's chromosomes, in the early 1970s scientists discovered that *E. coli* has closed circular pieces of DNA (called plasmids) that float free in the cell's liquid.[68] Scientists now saw a way to transfer genetic material cut from one cell to another cell.

Using a restriction enzyme, scientists cut a sequence from one DNA molecule. Using the same enzyme, the parallel segment is cut open in the plasmid of the bacterium. Then, the donor DNA is inserted in the plasmid and joins together (recombines) with the plasmid by means of the ligase. This technique of transferring genetic material from one organism into a plasmid is referred to as "cloning a gene." By this procedure, Berg cloned the first gene in 1973.[69] Once the gene is cloned, the recombined DNA begins to reproduce in the bacterium. Using *E. coli* as vector, the recombined DNA can then be introduced into the cell of another organism (using the techniques of gene cutting and splicing) in order to change that cell's genetic makeup. The cell with the newly recombined DNA will replicate, thereby changing the genetic code of the organism for the particular trait effected by the new DNA segment.

If there is no desire to introduce the cloned gene into another organism, the cloned gene may simply be allowed to replicate in the host bacterium. One of the best known examples of this is the production of human insulin (marketed as Humulin) by this procedure. By means of the gene cutting and splicing techniques described, scientists produced a gene that coded for human insulin, and they placed it into a bacterial cell. As the bacterium reproduces, it functions like a miniature factory to produce human insulin. Later the insulin is isolated from the bacterium and chemically split away from it. The result is human insulin, and in large quantities. The gene for human insulin reproduces whether located in the human pancreas or in a bacterial cell. However, in those suffering with diabetes, the pancreas does not produce the needed insulin, so it must come from somewhere else. Prior to producing human insulin by the techniques described, insulin had to be harvested from animals. However, it can only be harvested in small amounts from animal pancreas tissue, and some diabetics are allergic to animal insulin. By means of genetically engineered insulin, these problems are easily overcome. Humulin was the first gene-splicing product approved for human use by the U.S. FDA in 1982.[70]

USES

Recombinant DNA technology can be put to many uses, some beneficial and some harmful.[71] One use is the production of substances important in health care. Production of human insulin through rDNA technology has already been mentioned, and other substances are also noteworthy. For example, a human growth hormone has been developed that helps in treating dwarfism.[72] In addition, scientists have used rDNA to produce human interferon, which is used in treating cancer and viral diseases.

Other substances that have been made with this technology include factor VIII, a clotting protein which is lacking in hemophiliacs; thymosin, a hormone useful in treating immune defects; and tissue plasminogen activator (TPA), a circulatory system enzyme for dissolving blood clots associated with coronary heart disease.[73]

A second use of rDNA technology is in agriculture. Traditionally, when plant breeders cross one plant with another, all genetic characteristics of the one crop transfer to the other, regardless of whether the traits are wanted or unwanted. Using rDNA, if the breeder only wants to transfer one trait, it is now possible to do so. This technology can be used, for example, in developing plant strains which can resist viruses and are less likely to be damaged by herbicides. This technology, then, allows geneticists to combine genes in various ways to improve crops. It allows plant breeders to do what has been done for centuries, but with greater precision on the molecular level. Recombinant DNA can also be used in animal farming. Farmers breed cattle for certain desirable characteristics. Using rDNA technology, producing such cattle with greater precision is possible.[74]

Third, rDNA technology can also be used in industrial processes involving microorganisms. Immobilized enzymes and cells which carry out a variety of biosynthetic reactions useful in various manufacturing processes can be produced in this way. Previously, such processes had to be accomplished through expensive chemical reactions. As early as 1980, Genex, a firm active in this field, had identified over a hundred products which could probably be manufactured more easily through rDNA.[75] By 1986, genetically engineered enzymes were already in use in making compounds for artificial sweeteners used in diet soft drinks.[76] As one writer notes, industries involved in manufacturing drugs, plastics, industrial chemicals, vitamins, and cheese are likely to benefit from rDNA technology. Microorganisms that affect these processes are more easily and less expensively produced in larger quantities by this technology than by other means.[77]

A fourth use of this technology is environmental. Geneticists can design microorganisms to perform various environmental tasks. For example, genetically designed bacteria that feed on oil slicks have already been created, and other organisms that decompose the herbicide agent orange have been produced. Using these organisms to remove substances that pollute our soils and streams is tremendously beneficial in preserving the environment. Moreover, research has been done to create bacteria that can convert organic wastes into sugar, alcohol, and methane. Not only are these substances useful in industry, but producing them from waste material also helps the environment.[78]

Fifth, rDNA technology can help in treating people with genetic diseases. With the Human Genome Project, more will be known about which genes affect which traits. Using this information, scientists and doctors will be able to diagnose, treat, and even cure many genetically based diseases. If a particular gene is damaged or missing, rDNA technology may serve as the means for fixing and/or replacing it.

Whereas the preceding uses of rDNA would likely be considered beneficial, a final two uses are of dubious worth. If it is possible to find the genetic code for various human traits, and if genes can be spliced to correct genetic defects, genes can also be recombined to design "the perfect human." The intent would not be to cure any disease, but rather to enhance or include characteristics deemed desirable in a human being.

A final use of rDNA (also of dubious worth) is for biological warfare. If this technology can produce microorganisms that will benefit man, it can also create organisms which are harmful. In the earlier years of rDNA there was fear that scientists might create a deadly organism for which there was no antidote and that this organism might escape from the laboratory and endanger the lives of many. However, it goes without saying that if scientists can accidentally produce such organisms, they can use rDNA deliberately to produce harmful organisms for building biological weapons. Deadly microorganisms with no known antidote (since they are entirely new organisms) could be used in biological weapons that would appear to give one country a tremendous military advantage over others.[79]

PRACTICAL CONCERNS

There are obvious benefits from rDNA, as can easily be seen from our description of its possible uses. For some, the benefits are all that matter, and those benefits make rDNA morally acceptable in their eyes. Nonetheless, various concerns have been raised over rDNA. We note some of them in this section, and note also that some of them raise ethical questions as well as practical ones.

During the early years of rDNA technology, the most frequently heard concern was that this technology could accidentally produce new organisms dangerous to health and the environment. The concern was raised at several levels. On the one hand, it was feared that a new organism for which there was no antidote might accidentally escape into the environment.[80] Others complained that even if microorganisms were deliberately created to accomplish an environmental goal, no one could predict how they would interact with the environment. For example, a microorganism was created through rDNA technology that would clean up oil slicks. Before it had seen much use, concern was raised that after it slurped up the oil it might not die, but might destroy other hydrocarbons beyond oil.[81] Thankfully, to date such fears have proved unfounded, but no one can guarantee there will never be any accidents with other organisms created by rDNA technology.

There is another side to this issue of hazards. So far we have discussed potential disasters that happen accidentally. But harmful organisms can also be deliberately produced and released.[82] A particular part of the population could be targeted. Genetic diseases like sickle-cell anemia and Tay-Sachs strike only Blacks and Jews respectively. Hence, "it is conceivable that we could copy nature and create an organism to carry out a horrible genocide."[83]

Second, rDNA technology also raises legal problems. The obvious one is a potential flood of lawsuits in cases where organisms accidentally escape and harm the environment or individuals, or where organisms simply do not perform the function for which they were designed. In a society such as the U.S. that is so litigiously inclined anyway, there is genuine reason for concern over a procedure that could lead to an even heavier load on an already overloaded judicial system.

Another legal consideration concerns who owns newly created organisms. General Electric filed a patent application for an oil slick eating organism, *Pseudomonas*, which had been developed by Ananda Chakrabarty. The patent was originally denied, but the matter went to court and ultimately was argued before the Supreme Court. In 1980 the Supreme Court ruled in favor of General Electric, setting the precedent that living organisms produced by this technology were patentable. Once the decision on General Electric came down, many other patent applications were granted (e.g., six applications had been filed by Eli Lilly Company and Genentech for human insulin bacteria, and these patents were granted).[84] Obviously, patenting life has many legal and financial implications, but it also raises the moral question of whether anyone has a right to hold the patent on a living being.

The legal implications of this technology reach even further, however. Currently, children may legally seek a recovery for damages if they are born with a genetic defect that could have been avoided either by abortion or contraception.[85] Given that precedent, genetic engineers should use their techniques only if they produce offspring with fewer defects than those produced otherwise. Failure to work within this guideline could lead to a wrongful life suit. Beyond that, if rDNA technology progresses to a point where it can aid us in avoiding birth defects (not unlikely as gene mapping continues), then failure to use such technology might also be grounds for a wrongful life suit. Parents, especially those who know they might produce a genetically defective child, could be sued for failing to use available health care for their children.[86]

A third complaint with rDNA technology is that using it to remove so-called bad genes and replicate desirable genes dangerously tampers with and narrows the gene pool. It is not just that limiting diversity in humans, for example, might lead to a boring uniformity. The concern is also that such interference with natural selection has unforeseeable consequences.[87] Examples substantiate the concern. One author notes that by introducing a human growth hormone gene into a pig, there has resulted a leaner pig, but one also afflicted with strabismus and arthritis.[88] Another example is the genetic modification of wheat strains in the 1950s to produce bumper crops of "super wheat." When a new strain of disease hit the fields, the wheat was too delicate to resist, and within two years most of the crop was destroyed. Similarly, some fear that narrowing the human gene pool "might ultimately lead to the extinction of the human race."[89]

While the preceding concern focuses on unduly narrowing the gene pool, the next one emphasizes undue broadening. It is now possible in principle with rDNA to cross human with animal genes to produce human-animal hybrids that will be able to reproduce themselves. Some claim experimentation to do so is already under way *sub rosa* in some countries.[90] To some this is desirable. For example, Joseph Fletcher favors it on both medical and non-medical grounds. From a medical standpoint, Fletcher notes that herds of human-animal hybrids might be raised to provide organs for transplantation. From a social standpoint, such hybrids might be "created to do dangerous or demeaning jobs."[91] On the other hand, others see the idea as ethically questionable since the "human component would be condemned to a situation unworthy of it."[92] Moreover, some see Lev 19:19's prohibition of crossbreeding species as the basis for rejecting rDNA technology to produce human-animal hybrids.[93]

Fifth, for some the interest in rDNA technology is eugenics, the attempt to produce the "perfect baby." With this technology, it is possible to select genes that enhance particular traits. While this might seem desirable, it is not entirely clear even from a practical standpoint that eugenically enhanced traits would be better. For example, a super-strong sense of hearing might be more of a curse than a blessing. If every shuffle of paper sounded like a clap of thunder, it might be very hard to concentrate (let alone avoid a headache). Or, what about a super-strong sense of smell? We already know what it is like to walk into a locker room with athletes present after a ballgame. An extra-strength sense of smell might make walking into any room with any group of people a less than enthralling experience.[94] Moreover, it is not clear that we would want mental and physical abilities enhanced. What if everyone were an Einstein, a Mozart, a Michael Jordan? The possibilities sound attractive, but if everyone were a genius in these fields, accomplishments of any person would not have the value those achievements now have when genius is limited. "The sad truth is that the worth of human accomplishments is comparative. It is far from obvious that, if we were all that much brighter and more adept, we would be that much better off."[95]

A final practical consideration also has serious moral implications. It concerns the military use of this technology. Recombinant DNA can be used to build biological weapons for which there is no known antidote. Some think this would give the country with these weapons an incredible military advantage over its enemies. On the other hand, others argue that once biological weapons are used and new organisms released in the environment, there is no guarantee they will not invade and inflict disease upon those who used them. If a nuclear holocaust is a dreadful possibility, equally so is a biological holocaust.[96]

ETHICAL CONCERNS

Some ethical concerns with rDNA, such as one's views on technology and its interference with the natural order, beset other issues we have discussed.[97] Others are specific to this particular technology. Moreover, some of the practical concerns with rDNA also have moral implications. For example, if this technology deliberately or even accidentally produces harmful organisms, that harm would be immoral. In addition, rDNA raises other moral concerns.

Playing God

This issue is raised in regard to various ethical issues, but possibly has its greatest bite in regard to rDNA technology. Even Christian ethicists are divided on this matter. As Stroebel notes, those who view God as transcendent and totally other typically say the matter of creation is in God's hands since his knowledge exceeds ours. On the other hand, Stroebel argues for thinking of God in terms of closeness to his creation. Hence, knowledge of techniques such as rDNA does not usurp God's power or control, but helps man fulfill the biblical mandate to seek and know God and his creation. Moreover, it is crucial if man is to obey the biblical mandate to subdue, rule and serve the creation. The real question is not whether we should have this knowledge and use it, but how we should use it. According to Stroebel, the Incarnation is our model for this. The Incarnation shows that "advances in science and technology are God's way of sharing power and knowledge with humanity, not humanity's way of usurping God's power and knowledge. The power to manipulate genetic information is but the most recent in a long line of revelations of what it means to have power to subdue, to rule, and to serve."[98]

Many are unconvinced. They do not deny the biblical mandate to subdue and rule the earth, but they claim this mandate does not allow man to exploit nature for his own ends, but only to preserve and rule it for God so that it may fulfill his intentions. The problem is that man wants to decide on his own the intentions for life and creation and then use his own power to carry it out. This is an attempt to be like God, and this kind of "God-like" activity is wrong. The error stems from a mistaken belief that man's life and creation's life are at man's disposal to use for his selfish ends. Man neither owns life, nor decides the goals for the creation.[99]

Jeremy Rifkin finds especially deplorable using rDNA technology to produce new life forms that have never before existed in the living gene pool. In nature, few species can crossbreed. Even where it can happen, the offspring is neuter or asexual (e.g., the jackass). But this new technology makes it possible to "recombine all the forms of life one wants and make them sexually reproductive."[100] The problems with this are manifold, according to Rifkin, and should be clear to us. For one thing, such practices "reduce life to its physical components, mechanize it, and bring it under human control and design."[101] The result is that life is engineered in man's image, not God's. This control over nature and natural processes goes well beyond the typical uses of medicine to heal. This playing God, in the sense of trying to control life so it meets our ends without any concern for God's ends, is morally objectionable.

Patenting Life

Many argue that the arrogance they deplore when they raise the "playing God" objection is vividly illustrated in the U.S. Supreme Court's decision that new life forms may be patented. Moreover, in 1987 the U.S. Patent and Trademark Office also announced that all animal forms on earth, except man, should be considered patentable. Patent officials reasoned that all life can be regarded as a manufacture or composition of matter.[102] These decisions open the door to producing all sorts of microorganisms and animal life, and they give the impression that man owns and creates such life forms.

Opponents castigate the motive behind such practices (making a profit), but they also note that while man may manipulate, he cannot create the basic materials of life from which all things are made. Moreover, it is arrogant to think of man as owner (as patenting these life forms suggests) of anything in the natural order. Though these rulings do not give a right to patent new human beings, genetically speaking, and though they recognize a difference between man and the rest of the natural order, many reject the attitude that the natural order can be manipulated, owned and exploited in this way. Hence, they think the decisions to allow patenting of life are wrong.[103]

The Slippery Slope

In addition to fears about playing God, many ask where this will lead. This is the slippery slope argument. Put simply, the objection to rDNA says that once you design a new genetic makeup for human beings, there is no logical place to stop. Even if redesigning originally intends to correct genetic defects, once that is done, there is no logical reason to avoid using this technology for eugenic purposes. Moreover, while all would agree diabetes, cancer and sickle-cell anemia are disorders, where is the logic that keeps us from claiming that color blindness, left-handedness, and even skin color are "disorders" to be corrected by redesigning our genes?[104]

As Keith Boone notes, slippery slope arguments imply two principles, a principle of momentum and one of logic. The principle of momentum says that once x is done, it will be hard to refrain from doing y, even if x does not entail y. The logical principle states that "y will inevitably follow from x, since doing x contains the *principle of permission* for doing y."[105]

Boone thinks the principle most relevant to ethics is the logical one. He then says the slippery slope argument as applied to rDNA research is both a bad and good argument. It is bad because it assumes that if the principle of permission allows some kinds of intervention into man's genetic makeup, it allows all kinds. However, this is wrong, for the reasoning that justifies therapeutic uses of rDNA will not justify eugenic uses. Hence, there *is* a logical place to stop, namely, short of any eugenic measures.

On the other hand, the slippery slope argument is helpful, for it reminds us that once we move from therapy to eugenics, having justified one eugenic use of rDNA, logically we have granted permission for others. Even if some eugenic uses are permissible, others are wrong. So, we must avoid all because if we allow one, the logical principle in the slippery slope argument means we have granted permission for others.[106]

Here we should note that if rDNA is used in one case, there is no inevitability about its use in others. The principle of momentum may encourage the next step, but it guarantees nothing. As Boone says, the significant issue in the slippery slope argument is the principle of logic. Disagreements will arise, of course, over whether one can so clearly as Boone thinks distinguish between therapeutic and eugenic uses of rDNA.[107] Undoubtedly, all agree there is a major moral difference between treating leukemia and enhancing IQ, but that somewhat misses the point. Those who use the slippery slope argument might say the point is that once one justifies any tampering with the human genetic code (even if for therapy), logically it will be hard to restrict tampering with it for other purposes. Permission to tamper has been granted, and logic seems to demand it be grantable again.[108]

Who Controls It?

While rDNA technology is very powerful and raises hopes for dramatic benefits for mankind, it may also be put to diabolical uses. A crucial question is who will control this technology and make decisions about its use? Whom can we and whom should we trust to make these decisions? Should it be the scientific community, the government, the universities, medical and industrial corporations, or whom? There are no easy answers, but much is at stake. If this technology is used to redesign humans in an attempt at eugenics, to whom should we entrust "the authority to design the blueprints for the future of the human species?"[109] But, however the technology is used, who should control it?

These questions become especially significant in light of the Supreme Court decision to allow patenting of new life forms. In essence, "*a license*

*to manufacture and patent life has been delivered into the hands of cor-
porate America.*"[110] This is especially troublesome since all too often the
major concern of corporate America is the bottom line financially.
Moreover, even if those who control this power want to use it for humanitarian ends such as fighting disease, that does not mean that anything and
everything they do is acceptable. Experiments on the unborn or even the
born are questionable when there is uncertainty about the results. Even
when rDNA technology advances in its therapeutic capacities, who should
decide (and on what bases) how and when this technology should be
applied to individuals? These questions about the control and use of this
technology are significant morally, and they cause many hesitations about
further development and use of rDNA.[111]

Ecological Questions

Many note potential ecological implications of rDNA technology. They
ask who is responsible for ecological disasters and epidemics that result
when accidents occur. Insurance companies probably will not bear the
brunt, but who will? Until we know, it would be wise to go very slowly
with this technology.[112]

Beyond the practical issue, there is the moral question of whether man
has the right to tamper with the natural order in this way. God gave man
dominion over the created order, but that does not give him a right to
exploit it for his own gains. Our basic stance toward the created order
must be caretaking, not exploitation for selfish gains.[113]

Eugenics and Justice

The next concerns focus on what is often called positive eugenics, the
attempt to improve the genetic quality of the population. Is the use of
rDNA technology to "build a better human" moral? The issues are complex and involve various items. For example, how would proposed
changes affect the genetic composition of the population, even if they were
effective? Moreover, what constitutes a desirable gene or trait, and how
can one defend that judgment? And, what are the consequences of implementing such a program, and how would they be assessed from the perspective of social justice and human rights to liberty and equality?[114]

In addition to these initial questions, Twiss says there are really three
ethical dilemmas that accompany eugenics. One involves identifying and
appraising eugenic goals. Another involves specifying and justifying criteria for implementing eugenic policies. The third involves moral evaluation
of the case that can be built for eugenics.[115]

As to the first issue, the goals one chooses in large part depend upon
one's evaluation of the genetic condition of the population. Some argue
that if we don't purify the gene pool of deleterious genes (i.e., if we allow
the weak and deformed to live and propagate more of their kind), we are

headed for a genetic twilight. However, others deny any danger of genetic apocalypse. Moreover, some think genetic diversity is healthy since it represents evolutionary capability. Regardless of one's position on this issue, it is not abundantly clear what should be done. If the goal is to ensure survival of the species or even to improve it, it is not clear that without genetic engineering the species would either die or deteriorate. Moreover, what counts as genetic deterioration depends partly on what one considers an undesirable gene or trait, and that is no easy matter to resolve. For example, is left-handedness a defect? What about small height? And what about traits such as intelligence? If people could be genetically designed to have an IQ of 170, would an IQ of 140 be a defect? In virtue of the difficulty in assessing genetic pollution and determining eugenic goals, it is surely morally dubious to tamper with the gene pool for eugenic ends.[116]

The issue of articulating criteria for moral appraisal of eugenic policies is no easy matter either. In part the dilemma stems from not knowing the proper reference point to use in determining criteria. Should one develop criteria on the basis of obligations to future generations, or should one choose criteria that specify a conception of a just society? If the former perspective is adopted, care must be taken not to harm future generations and to provide for conditions that allow for survival and a full human life in the future. Unfortunately, these obligations do not clearly indicate what criteria ought to be used for moral assessment of eugenic possibility. For example, the need to provide for survival seems to rule in eugenic measures such as maintaining the quality of the gene pool and reducing the incidence of genetic disease. However, the need to avoid harm to future generations seems to rule out eugenic measures altogether.[117]

If one seeks criteria for moral assessment on the basis of social justice, other considerations become significant. In particular, matters of social justice stress moral principles that enjoin "nonmaleficence, mutual respect, equal treatment, and fairness,"[118] all of which are part of what it means to be just. As Twiss notes, this conception of social justice puts a premium on human individual rights. Hence, policies are preferred that uphold human rights such as the right to life with a self-determined destiny, the right to marry, and the right to have children.[119] A major problem is that criteria based on social justice may conflict with criteria based on obligations to future generations. For example, if a couple has genetic defects likely to lead to genetic diseases in offspring, should their right to procreate have precedence over obligations to future offspring and the quality of the gene pool in general? These sorts of questions are hard to answer and make it extremely difficult to determine the morally best eugenic policies.

As to the third set of problems, it is not abundantly clear how to assess the overall case for eugenic policies. Evaluation varies depending on whether one adopts a consequentialist or non-consequentialist approach to ethics. If one adopts the former, assessment will emphasize matters such as whether envisioned ends are acceptable. In addition, questions about allocation of resources to present and future generations become significant, as does cost/benefit analysis. On the other hand, a non-consequentialist will probably be more concerned about matters of individual freedom and personal rights. Hence, for example, compulsory eugenic policies that mandate sterilizing the genetically defective and behaviorally deviant may be applauded by those thinking in consequentialist terms of safeguarding the gene pool, but may be condemned by non-consequentialists concerned to safeguard basic human rights.

The net result of all these problems is that it is very difficult to assess the moral rightness of eugenic practices. But since that is so, it is wisest to avoid eugenics so as to avoid slipping into moral error.

Eugenics and Genetic "Have Nots"

One of the greatest fears raised about rDNA for eugenic purposes concerns the fate of those who do not "stack up," genetically speaking. Now that we can redesign humans genetically to avoid certain characteristics, will those with those characteristics be considered liabilities to society who must be eliminated? Will those with IQs below a certain level be expendable? Will they be refused permission to marry and/or procreate? And above all, who will decide? All of these possibilities are very disturbing from a moral point of view.

Though this sounds fanciful, it is already being practiced and encouraged to a certain degree. For example, such issues are raised in regard to the unborn. If an unborn child has a debilitating genetic defect, the mother is strongly encouraged to abort the child. Not only can pressure to abort be applied by the doctor and the family and friends of the pregnant woman, but social sanctions can be imposed to do the same. Hence, Allen Verhey wonders if health insurance plans in the future will refuse to pay for the care of a Down's syndrome child whose problems could have been predicted and prevented by abortion. Suggestions along this line are already being made.[120]

In support of such policies, hear the words of Sir Francis Crick, co-discoverer of DNA. Journalist David Rorvik claims that Crick said, "No newborn infant should be declared human until it has passed certain tests regarding its genetic endowment. . . . If it fails these tests, it forfeits the right to live."[121] Though rDNA technology may be able to do wonderful things, the nagging question of what happens to those who don't conform to the agreed genetic norm remains most troublesome to many ethicists.[122]

Dignity of Persons

A somewhat related issue concerns the dignity of persons. Genetic engineering generally (and rDNA in particular) involves experiments and procedures that can be detrimental to the integrity of persons. Hence, it is argued that any procedures that would violate the freedom, dignity or integrity of persons are wrong.

Examples of procedures that fall under this condemnation are the commercial use of embryos, the mixing of human and non-human genetic material, and cloning.[123] As Carl Henry says about appropriate uses of these technologies, "Whatever tends to overcome what would be a deterioration in the created order and seeks to restore what God purposed in Creation is on far safer grounds than all kinds of novel and experimental enterprise."[124] Moreover, any use of these procedures that tends to dehumanize man by reducing him to nothing more than a complex of chemicals is wrong. As Donald DeMarco warns, "The enthusiasm for genetically engineering Homo novus or Homo futurus betrays a profound misconception of genetics. Man is infinitely more than his genotype. Genetic engineering can do very little to improve him as a human being."[125] As he notes, many traits like intelligence are not governed by a single gene, but are polygenic, and beyond that, they rely also on a host of environmental factors. To reduce everything to genetic and chemical components is to misconstrue man's nature and oversimplify the complexity of human beings.[126]

Financial Issues

Initial financial concerns deal with distributive justice. Recombinant DNA technology is not cheap, and there are many other pressing social as well as medical problems. Some wonder if it is right to allocate resources for such an expensive process when resources are so scarce.[127] Not only is research expensive, but so are the techniques, even when the result is known and wanted. Thus, some ask whether any but the rich can afford this technology even when put to therapeutic use. Would being healed from a genetic disease depend on ability to pay? If so, it seems immoral for only the rich to have access to this technology.[128]

Another financial concern is that what ultimately motivates much of genetic engineering is not a desire to help mankind, but a desire for economic gain. Think, for example, of the marketing possibilities for human-animal hybrids that would do many menial tasks humans now do. Likewise, those who can produce a "super seed" that enhances the quality and quantity of a particular agricultural crop stand to make a healthy profit. Breakthroughs in medicines such as Humulin are tremendous in treating disease, but those who own the patents make quite a profit. Some ethicists claim that at times potential risks are ignored or minimized in light of financial profit to be gained from new substances. If so, that raises serious questions about the morality of technology so used.[129]

Risk/Benefit Analysis

Those inclined to make moral decisions on consequentialist bases like to discuss rDNA in risk/benefit terms. In the early years of rDNA technology, the risk of harmful organisms that would destroy large segments of the population was thought too great to overbalance any potential benefits. Hence, many urged restraint in using this technology.[130] Once scientists concluded that the risks were minimal on a risk/benefit analysis, benefits seemed to far outweigh risks.

Despite some ethicists' enthusiasm, others argue that the risk/benefit approach is in the end not particularly fruitful in determining what to do. The problem is not just that one favors non-consequentialism and risk/benefit analysis incorporates consequentialism. The problem is that risk/benefit arguments are beset with various limitations and ambiguities. For example, utility calculations invariably overlook questions of distributive justice. Hence, they do not always ask who bears the risk and who gets the benefit, nor do they ask if that distribution of risk and benefit is just. Moreover, risks and benefits are not parallel. Whereas risks compare with hopes, benefits compare with harms. The former deal with uncertainties and probabilities, while the latter deal with assured results. The tendency is to talk of hopes as if they are already benefits and to speak of harms as though they are only possible risks, but this tips the scales unfairly. Hence, some say it is more appropriate to evaluate not in terms of risks and benefits, but in terms of the old medical and moral principle "Do no harm."

Risk/benefit analysis is also problematic, because sometimes it is hard to know what the risks and benefits will be until the procedure has been performed. Even if risks and benefits are known ahead of time, that does not make evaluation of both a purely technical matter. Subjectivity enters the evaluation, and sometimes risk or benefit is more in the eye of the beholder than in the procedure itself.[131]

Freedom of Inquiry

A final ethical issue involves freedom of inquiry. Often when rDNA research is opposed, proponents protest that limiting the research limits freedom of inquiry. However, as Allen Verhey shows, more than simple freedom is at stake. Those who appeal to freedom of inquiry assume that everyone believes knowledge is intrinsically good. If one accepts that assumption, then to limit freedom of inquiry is certainly wrong.[132]

Verhey notes that there is even more to this issue. Ever since Francis Bacon, knowledge has been linked with power and benefit. As applied to rDNA research, this means that the research will lead to knowledge, knowledge will give us power, and power will allow us to do all sorts of beneficial things for the human race (e.g., make human insulin, clean up the environment, cure genetic diseases). Though knowledge, power and benefit appear to be all one piece, it is crucial to distinguish them. As Verhey argues, when researchers talk about benefits of DNA research, they like to link the three, but when opponents complain of dangers and risks with this technology, invariably proponents simply retreat to the argument that freedom of inquiry must be maintained (presumably because knowledge is good) and omit the link with power and benefit.[133]

The ultimate problem with this whole line of argument, as Verhey shows, is that rDNA actually does link knowledge with power. Engaging in this research does not merely exercise one's right to inquiry, but also exercises the freedom to create new life forms. Hence, to espouse rDNA research on grounds of freedom of inquiry accomplishes nothing unless it is linked with a claim about freedom to create new life forms. Likewise, limiting this research does not necessarily entail limiting freedom of inquiry; it may only express an awareness that freedom to know does not mean there is freedom to create.[134]

The net result is that there is pro and con on the freedom of inquiry issue. On the one hand, it is moral to allow freedom of inquiry and the advance of knowledge. On the other hand, knowledge, power, and benefit are not inextricably logically tied to one another. As for rDNA research, freedom of inquiry seems often to incorporate an alleged freedom to create. Since it is dubious that man has a right and freedom to create any organisms whatsoever, the freedom of inquiry argument can hardly justify everything that falls under rDNA research.[135]

ASSESSMENT OF RECOMBINANT DNA

In this section we assess rDNA in its uses other than gene therapy. We discuss gene therapy in the next section, though principles enunciated here also apply to that discussion.

Before evaluating arguments for and against rDNA, it would help to state several distinctions and principles usable in this discussion. Initially, as with other technologies, we distinguish the technology itself from the motivation for and uses of it. Obviously, biblical writers never foresaw this technology, so they neither commanded or forbade its use. Hence, whatever one says ethically about this technology (if Scripture is the basis of one's ethics) must be argued indirectly from other explicit or implicit moral principles taught in Scripture and by reason. We think some motivations behind rDNA and some uses of it are morally wrong, but that does not make the techniques immoral, nor does it make all motives and uses for it immoral.

Second, as this technology relates especially to human beings, one must distinguish eugenic (non-therapeutic) and therapeutic uses. Sometimes there is a fuzzy line between a genuine disorder and what is merely a preferred trait, but that is not so in all or even most cases. Left-handedness, black hair, and an IQ of 120, for example, are not diseases that will either kill or impair anyone's ability to function. Surely, it is possible to identify diseases as such and to distinguish them from these alleged "disorders."

We stress the distinction between therapeutic and eugenic uses of rDNA in part because of a fundamental theological principle. According to Scripture (Gen 3:16ff.; Rom 5:12), death entered the world as a result of sin. If people are to die, obviously they must die of something, and that something may be a genetically contracted disease. It seems clear, then, that in using rDNA to combat genetic defect and disease, we are simply fighting against sin and its consequences.[136] Surely, Scripture allows us to do this. On the other hand, there is no indication that if Adam and Eve had not sinned, everyone would have had identical traits of intelligence, skin color, hair color, height and the like. In other words, some differences among human beings seem in no way to result from the fall, and they in no way appear to lead to death. Other differences in humans (for example, defective genes) do seem related to the fact that we live in a sinful, fallen world.

The preceding leads us to propose that one must not only ask whether the envisioned use of rDNA is therapeutic or eugenic, but must also ask if the intent is to correct a problem resulting from the fall and sin or not. If one tries to correct a problem consequent upon the fall and sin, then his actions are proper in the sense that they fight the effects of sin, which God would want us to do. Of course, even in those cases motives and/or uses of this technology might be immoral, but that suggests another basis for moral evaluation.

Suppose the intent in using rDNA is not to correct a problem that stems from sin, but merely to alter traits which aren't results of sin so as to suit one's taste. Would that be immoral? We believe so. Since the trait in no way results from sin or its consequences, we think a desire to alter the trait in essence rejects God's original creative work. Scripture says God saw that what he had created was good, and it also says God considers man the crown of creation. Since there is no evidence that the diversity of human characteristics resulted from the fall, i.e., people would not be stereotypes of one another even if Adam hadn't sinned, God's evaluation of man as the crown of creation must include God's thinking of man in all of his diverse characteristics. Trying to change characteristics to create genetic uniformity (or even superiority) seems to claim implicitly that what God did in creating man may be good but not good enough. We think attitudes that reject God's appraisal of man as created in diversity and seek to "improve" on what God made are morally wrong. Hence, using rDNA to change human characteristics merely to fit personal taste is wrong.

Having set forth these initial distinctions and principles, we turn now to the argumentation in regard to rDNA.[137] As to playing God, one must be careful not to use this argument so as to rule out all medical intervention. The key seems to be the attitude with which one uses this technology. As stated above, we think the attitude behind eugenic uses is improper, because it wrongly rejects what God has created and tries to usurp God's role as creator and decision maker about man's basic genetic structure. As to other uses of this technology, some can be pursued without an improper arrogant attitude and without breaking other moral norms. So, we agree that man must be careful in using this technology not to try to usurp God's role, but we believe that guideline can be met so that rDNA technology can be used in many instances.

On the slippery slope issue, our intuitions are with Boone and against Rifkin. We see no logical inevitability of moving from rDNA in agriculture or industry, for example, to using it to redesign man for eugenic purposes. Moreover, we agree that once the door is opened for any tampering with the genetic code, logically it is open for other tampering. We further agree that if one once permits rDNA for any eugenic purpose, it will be difficult, logically speaking, to forbid it for other eugenic use. However, we agree with Boone that the distinction between therapeutic and eugenic uses of rDNA closes the door. We also think the distinction between attempting to correct effects of sin and the fall as opposed to making changes in traits that do not result from the fall is a valid way to close the door.

As to control of this technology and ownership of newly created life forms, we are concerned. We agree that God owns life and the materials from which it is made. Hence, though we understand why companies want to patent their newly created life forms, we are not convinced this is morally sound. This does not seem equivalent to getting a patent on an invention. Normally, inventions are not living things but inanimate objects. Living microorganisms seem to be in a different category. We are also troubled about who will control this technology and decide how to use it. From our discussion above, it is clear that we think using rDNA for eugenic purposes is morally wrong. These concerns, however, do not in themselves make rDNA technology immoral. They suggest a need to think carefully about its use and control, but that doesn't mean all use and control of it must be immoral.

As to eugenics and social justice, we agree with Twiss's analysis that even trying to evaluate the morality of eugenic policies in relation to social justice is fraught with problems. However, until those problems are solved to the satisfaction of consequentialists and non-consequentialists alike (if possible), it seems wisest to avoid eugenic uses.

We also agree that using rDNA as a basis for discriminating against those considered genetic "have nots" is immoral. This is so whether the object of discrimination is already born or unborn. We find deplorable Francis Crick's suggestion that only those who meet a certain genetic standard are human and have a right to live. Using this criterion, Down's syndrome babies not only could be but should be destroyed. But, on the contrary, we find no evidence that this child has forfeited the image of God or that it is unhuman. Hence, we see no moral justification to end its life just because of a certain genetic deficiency.

Likewise, we agree with those who deplore using this technology to dehumanize or depersonalize mankind or reduce its dignity. Man is indeed more than the sum total of his genetic code. He is not simply reducible to chemical and material components. Still, we see these as wrong attitudes that can arise with this technology. While using the technology with these attitudes and encouraging these attitudes is wrong, that does not mean rDNA *per se* is wrong or that users will of necessity incorporate these incorrect attitudes.

As to financial concerns about just allocation of resources for rDNA, we think such questions about distributive justice are important. However, we do not believe that questions of distributive justice tell us whether the practice *per se* is immoral or moral. These questions do suggest that even when all other moral rules are met, there may still be cases where on the basis of distributive justice alone it would be immoral to use rDNA.

Another financial matter raised concerns the profit motivation behind rDNA research. On the one hand, we do not think it immoral for businessmen to want or make a profit. On the other hand, we agree that if the sole or primary motivation for manipulating genes by rDNA to produce new medicines or aids for industry and agriculture, for example, is greed for financial gain, that is not a morally sufficient reason. It is especially deplorable for companies to take risks in using this technology just because the envisioned ends are financially rewarding. Moreover, we agree that man's basic stance toward the natural order should be that of caretaking, not exploitation for financial or other gain. God has told us to subdue and rule the earth. He did not grant permission to exploit it for selfish gains.

As to argumentation surrounding risk/benefit analysis, we find ourselves fundamentally unmoved. This is so because risk/benefit analysis is consequentialist in nature, and we are non-consequentialists. But we are also unmoved because of problems noted by those who say risk/benefit analysis in regard to rDNA is flawed.

Where does the preceding leave us in regard to the morality of rDNA? It suggests that some instances of its use may be moral and others immoral. The technology *per se* does not seem immoral. Though it is not commanded, it is not prohibited *per se* either. Hence, we consider it permissible, but not in all cases. When the motivation is improper (e.g., to usurp God's power as creator, to seek only financial gain regardless of risks involved, or to exploit nature for selfish gain), the use of rDNA cannot be morally sanctioned.

Moreover, we think some *uses* of this technology (apart from the motivation behind it) are not moral. For example, rDNA for either eugenic purposes or to create weapons of biological warfare seems clearly immoral. As to other uses of rDNA, we believe many can be moral so long as matters of distributive justice, one's attitudes toward the environment and God's control and authority over the created order, and the like are properly handled. For example, using rDNA in producing medicines for health care, in agriculture, in industry, and in environmental care seem moral, so long as adequate safety precautions are taken so that new organisms that would affect man and the environment negatively are not produced, or if produced, are not then allowed to escape from the laboratory. As to using rDNA to treat genetic diseases, we turn to that topic next.

GENE THERAPY

One of the uses of gene-splicing is therapeutic, the correction of defective genes. Because we think therapeutic use of this technology deserves evaluation independent of non-therapeutic use and because there are other methods of gene therapy than those involving rDNA, we think gene therapy warrants separate discussion.

In discussing gene therapy, one must distinguish somatic cell therapy from germline therapy. As to the former, in a tissue affected by some missing or defective gene, the requisite gene could be introduced through a variety of means. With gene-splicing in somatic cells, the results affect only the individual treated. Changes will not be passed on to future generations. On the other hand, germline alteration changes the genetic code in reproductive cells (sperm or ovum). Such changes will be transmitted to future generations, thereby precluding offspring from getting the disease, but germline changes do not cure the person who has the disease

To date gene therapy in humans has been limited to somatic cell therapy, and has only recently begun. The first experimental treatment was done by a team of NIH scientists, Steven Rosenberg, W. French Anderson, and R. Michael Blaese. It began in the early months of 1991, and by late July 1991 the team of doctors reported that the therapy was working beyond their expectations.[138]

This first experiment was performed on a five-year-old Cleveland girl with an incurable genetic disease called adenosine deaminase (ADA) deficiency. A second patient, a ten-year-old Cleveland girl with the same disease, began treatment shortly after the first. ADA is an enzyme "that rids the body of unwanted proteins, thereby avoiding toxic buildups of the proteins in the blood."[139] When the body cannot make ADA, toxins build up and form a lethal poison that destroys the body's immune system. The gene therapy experiment done on these two girls involved rDNA technology. Disease-fighting white blood cells (known as T cells) were removed from the girls and genetically redesigned so as to stimulate production of ADA. These corrective genes were introduced into the T cells through the use of genetically engineered retroviruses (the procedure for rDNA was discussed above).[140] By July 1991, the procedure was successful enough in the five-year-old that she was producing 40 percent of normal ADA levels (far better progress than when using only the genetically engineered drug PEG-ADA),[141] and doctors said the therapy had reconstituted her immune system. Still, not knowing the long range side effects of this technique (would the therapy stop working; might it as a side effect produce some other problem?), the doctors hesitated to call the therapy a success.

Gene therapy should be useful primarily for replacing "a defective or missing enzyme or protein that must function inside the cell that makes it, or of a deficient circulating protein whose level does not need to be exactly regulated."[142] Experiments on the ADA patients were of this sort. However, other methods of gene therapy are also possible. Specifically, in April 1992 another experiment in gene therapy was announced. This time a different method would be used. Rather than removing defective genes and redesigning them through rDNA technology, this experiment would use a more direct approach. The plan was to inject directly into malignant tumors new genes that would hopefully trick the human body into destroying the tumors. These genes have been engineered so that once injected they will produce a protein which invites attack from the body's T cells. The hope, then, is to destroy the tumors by inviting attack upon the protein produced by the injected genes. The experiment was to be performed in the late spring or early summer of 1992 on twelve volunteer patients dying from the most lethal form of skin cancer.[143] As of the writing of this section, reports about the success of the experiment had not been received.

ETHICAL CONCERNS

While all of this is exciting and promising for those afflicted with or at risk for a genetically controlled disease, we cannot simply accept it without considering the ethical implications of this technology. Since practical issues surrounding rDNA have already been discussed, there is no need to rehearse that discussion again. Our concern, therefore, is ethical questions that arise with gene therapy. Moreover, many ethical issues confronting gene therapy have been raised already in relation to rDNA in general. Hence, this section emphasizes issues which specifically arise in relation to gene therapy.

Though most ethical reservations about gene therapy object to germline therapy, there are also questions about somatic cell therapy.[144] Prior to attempts at any kind of gene therapy, a major concern often voiced was the safety of the people who would be the first recipients of this therapy. It was argued that unless safety could be assured, it was immoral to proceed with the therapy.[145]

As a result of widespread concern about safety, criteria were drawn up for experimental gene therapy that had to be met in animal tests prior to experiments on humans. Though the first human gene therapy experiment has already occurred, these criteria are still important, since so far there has been no gene therapy for most genetic diseases. Those who drew up the criteria said animal tests should show three things before the same test could be used on humans. First, there had to be evidence that the curative genes could be directed to specific cells and remain there long enough to be effective. Second, there needed to be evidence that the added genes would express their product in the target cells at a sufficient and appropriate level. Finally, no harm could result to the treated or surrounding cells, to the test animal, or to its children.[146] These three requirements are summarized as delivery, expression and safety.[147]

Not only was it argued that if these criteria were met, it would be moral to proceed with gene therapy in humans. Anderson claimed it would be unethical at that point to delay human trials. He reasoned that patients with serious genetic diseases have little other hope of cure or relief from their disease, and to withhold treatment (once criteria were met) would be an unnecessary and unethical refusal to use available means to ameliorate the suffering of patients with these diseases.[148]

Since one of the three doctors involved in the first gene therapy experiments was W. French Anderson, it is likely that those criteria have currently been met, at least for gene therapy for ADA deficiency. Moreover, so long as safety matters are taken care of, most ethicists agree that somatic cell gene therapy can be moral, especially if performed with the informed consent of the patient. However, not everyone agrees. In particular, Jeremy Rifkin has strongly opposed even somatic cell gene therapy. His argument is a slippery slope argument that once we begin genetically redesigning individuals, there is no logical place to stop. If diseases can be cured, why not other "disorders" such as color blindness, left-handedness, etc.? Moreover, if somatic cell therapy can be justified, then it is a small step to germline therapy.[149]

In turning to germline therapy, we note that to date this sort of therapy has not been tried in human beings, and development of methods which would be successful without harming the patient are still under discussion.[150] Despite potential advantages of germline therapy, typically ethicists condemn it. Some complain that it "runs a morally unacceptable risk of transmitting to future generations irreversible consequences of unintended but nonetheless disastrous mistakes."[151] For others, the problem at least in part is that it limits the genetic diversity of the species to which the species' strength is tied. Moreover, genes we may consider bad may actually have an unknown but indispensable role in humanity's ability to adapt genetically to its environment and continue to survive. Moreover, it also presumes humanity can be genetically perfected. However, "perfection" is typically defined in terms of mankind's perception of what is genetically perfect, and hence, involves a wish to re-create mankind in its own image.[152]

Yet others complain that germline intrusions (especially for eugenics, but it is noted that sometimes the line between eugenics and therapy is very blurry) are instances of playing God at its worst. These changes will affect future generations, but "the fact is, no individual, group, or set of institutions can legitimately claim the right or authority to make such decisions on behalf of the rest of the species alive today or for future generations."[153] Only God has the requisite knowledge and authority to do so.

For still others the critical ethical question is "should a treatment which produces an inherited change, and could therefore perpetuate in future generations any mistake or unanticipated problems resulting from the therapy, ever be undertaken?"[154] What complicates matters is the mechanism of genetics whereby harmful genes do not always express themselves in any given generation. Hence, genetic mistakes or problems incorporated in one's reproductive cells may not express themselves for several generations. Thus, to ascertain the safety of this procedure, several generations should be observed. Morally, use of these therapeutic procedures in humans should not begin until scientists are quite certain the process is safe.[155]

Given the problems that beset germline therapy, Anderson suggests three conditions that must be met before attempting such therapy in human beings. First, there must be considerable experience with somatic cell therapy that has shown it to be effective and safe. Until then, germline therapy should not be attempted. Second, there should be adequate study of germline therapy in animals to establish its reliability, reproducibility and safety. That study should use the same vectors and procedures that would be used in humans. Third, there should be public awareness and approval of the procedure before clinical trials on humans begin, because germline therapy has implications for unborn generations and thus affects more of society than just one person. According to Anderson, if these three criteria are met, germline therapy to correct genetic defects would be morally acceptable.[156]

In a similar vein, John Fletcher argues for germline therapy. He says once one distinguishes between curative or preventive uses and eugenic uses of germline alteration, one can determine which cases are morally acceptable. Fletcher believes the same kind of moral reasoning that supports somatic cell therapy also supports germline therapy. The major difference is that germline therapy has implications for future generations, whereas somatic cell therapy does not. However, so long as one takes adequate precaution to avoid passing on mistakes and harms that might arise in the therapy, the issues are the same as with somatic cell therapy.[157] And questions about the safety of future generations could be resolved by the procedures Anderson proposed.

Some may claim this does not allow future generations freedom to make informed consent to these genetic changes. However, no future generation makes decisions about its exact genetic makeup, nor does it even decide whether or not it will exist. Hence, it seems that no right they could exercise is taken from future generations. Moreover, it is true that a change is made without consent of the unborn, but it is clearly a beneficial change, not a detrimental or even neutral one. Who, given opportunity to make a choice that would remove the possibility of disease, would refuse? Hence, the loss of the right to choose in this case does not seem immoral. Moreover, we are obligated to do good to others when we can, regardless of whether they can make a choice about what we do. And such therapy would do good to future offspring.

ASSESSMENT OF GENE THERAPY

We begin by repeating the distinction between eugenic and therapeutic uses of this technology and the point that genetic defects and diseases occur ultimately because we live in a fallen world. Because we believe it is right to fight sin and its effects, and because we believe it is good to do what can be done to relieve pain and suffering, we conclude that in general gene therapy is moral. However, this general approval needs some nuancing.

First, we take seriously concerns about safety. We think the criteria enunciated by Anderson and Fletcher are imperative to ensure safety, but if the criteria are met and the patient gives informed consent, we see no problem with proceeding with somatic cell therapy. Moreover, we think gene therapy *for each genetic disease* should begin only after careful testing that meets the three criteria set forth.

Second, we recognize that while this use of technology is moral *per se*, motivation for using it may be flawed. If the major goal is to line the pockets of the medical profession with money, that is not a proper motivation. If desire for financial gain or desire for status in the medical community as a result of being a pioneer in this field causes one to take undue risks (e.g., using the therapy on humans before adequately testing it on animals), that would also be morally inappropriate. Hence, we urge that this technology be used with proper motivation. Likewise, we think it only appropriate to address matters of distributive justice as much as possible. If only the wealthy can afford this kind of care, that seems unfair. Poor people should not be left to die just because they cannot afford this therapy.

Third, as to concerns that this use of technology will lead to germline therapy and ultimately to eugenic uses, we note that this is the same old slippery slope argument. What we said about it when discussing rDNA generally applies here as well. We simply note here that while it is a helpful reminder to move cautiously, it is not a good enough reason to call this therapy immoral or to prohibit it.

Fourth, some may object that gene therapy is an extraordinary, heroic use of medical technology, and only ordinary, usual medicine should be practiced. However, any medical procedure when first introduced may seem extraordinary. That in itself should not preclude the advance of medicine in fighting disease. It should, however, warn of the need for adequate and careful testing and evaluation before using the procedure on human beings. If that is done, then the procedure at first will be unusual in that it has not been used on humans before, but it will not be unusual in the sense that little is known about it or that doctors have no idea of what to expect when it is used on humans. We think gene therapy, once adequately tested and monitored, need not be considered any more extraordinary than heart bypass surgery or even organ transplant surgery. In fact, in some ways gene therapy may be less dangerous than, for example, a heart transplant or bypass, for the patient will not likely die in the midst of gene therapy but might die during organ transplant or heart bypass surgery. That is, chances that the patient can survive the medical procedure of gene therapy itself are much greater than with other kinds of medical interventions.

Finally, as to somatic cell versus germline therapy, we believe both can be moral so long as appropriate safeguards are used in each case. We agree, for instance, with Anderson that germline therapy should come after a lengthy success record with somatic cell therapy and proper testing in animal subjects. However, once those criteria are met, we see no reason to think germline therapy any more immoral than somatic cell therapy. In fact, if it is possible to correct a gene so as to avoid a disease in future generations, we believe there is an obligation to tend to the welfare of the future in this way. And it is surely morally preferable to correct the problem before it is ever passed on, rather than to let a child be conceived only to abort it when one finds it has the genetic defect.

For those who fear that germline therapy runs the risk of passing on mistakes to future generations, mistakes that may not even show up for several generations, we have several replies. So long as proper testing and use according to the criteria set forth occur, we think this is very unlikely. However, because it might occur anyway, further precautions must be taken. Once therapy ends, there should be a thorough check of the patient's genetic makeup to ensure that no other genes were damaged in the process or that no other defective genes were passed on. Moreover, it would not be inappropriate to monitor the patient on these items periodically throughout his life. Even if a defective gene is passed on that will not express itself until future generations, it seems possible through the kind of periodic checking being suggested to detect the presence of that gene in the patient and correct it through further therapy. Given progress on the Human Genome Project, it seems possible in a few years to have a complete map of the genetic code so that scientists and doctors will know which genes control what and will be able to identify any abnormality in a person's genetic code. Moreover, if in spite of adequate testing before germline therapy is undertaken occasional slip-ups could occur, the prospective patient should be informed of that before consenting to the procedure. So long as these safety procedures are followed, we agree with Fletcher that germline therapy can be as morally acceptable as somatic cell therapy. The goal is surely moral, and the means, practiced under the restraints and cautions suggested, can be moral as well. We conclude that somatic cell and germline therapy can be moral and applaud the efforts of scientists who try to attack diseases that seem in no other way humanly attackable.

CHAPTER ELEVEN

Divorce and Remarriage

O ne of the most troublesome trends of our day is the increase in divorce, remarriage and broken homes. In the mid-1970s the U.S. Census Bureau estimated that approximately a third of first marriages end in divorce. Second and even third marriages fare worse, for two-thirds are unsuccessful.[1] Within recent years in the U.S. the divorce rate is approaching 50 percent, and in some states it is even higher.[2] In 1983 statisticians claimed that one in every four British marriages ends in divorce, and one in every three new marriages involves a divorced person. In both the U.S. and the United Kingdom about 80 percent of those divorced remarry.[3] The sheer number of divorces in a given year is staggering. In the U.S., for example, typically more than one million marriages a year end in a legal divorce. If one adds the number terminated through desertion (though not necessarily legally severed), figures go much higher.

Worldwide the figures are disturbing, though they vary from country to country. For example, in Arab countries divorces were relatively low. In Jordan in 1989 there were 8.1 marriages per 1000 and 1.21 divorces per 1000. In the same year in Syria there were 8.8 marriages per 1000 and only .73 divorces per 1000. In predominantly Catholic countries in Central and South America, marriages far exceeded divorces. In 1988 there were 5.3 marriages per 1000 but only .18 divorces per 1000 in Guatemala, in 1990 7.7 marriages per 1000 and .63 divorces per 1000 in Mexico, and in 1988 6.5 marriages per 1000 but only .43 divorces per 1000 in Ecuador. Other Latin American countries follow similar patterns. In Asia there also tends to be a proportionately higher marriage rate than divorce rate (e.g., in Japan in 1990 there were 5.8 marriages per 1000 and 1.27 divorces per 1000). Though these figures may sound encouraging, since they are measured per 1000, the actual number of divorces is quite substantial. Moreover, some countries have a divorce rate about half that of the marriage rate. For example, in the U.S. in 1990 there were 9.8 marriages per 1000 but 4.7 divorces per 1000 (though data are incomplete, the number of divorces already calculated for that year is 1,175,000). In the same year in Sweden there were 4.7 marriages and 2.22 divorces per 1000. In 1989 in Denmark there were 6 marriages but 2.95 divorces per 1000.[4] None of this is encouraging.

Divorce and remarriage are not merely societal problems, but also problems in the church. Not only must evangelical churches minister to so many non-believers who are divorced, but they must also cope with divorces among their own laity *and* clergy. Even theologically conservative denominations are confronted increasingly with questions about ordination of and ministry by divorced persons.

Societal attitudes do not help. In fact, they are part of the problem. Whereas there was once a stigma attached to divorce, divorce and remarriage are now considered ordinary facts of life. Many U.S. states have no fault divorce laws that make severance of a marriage relatively easy. Attitudes toward marriage show that many are prepared for failure. Prenuptial agreements to protect the parties in case the marriage does not work are becoming more common. Some couples pledge to keep wedding vows only "so long as they both shall love," not so long as they both live.

Despite societal attitudes, divorce and remarriage are problems in themselves and create other problems as well. A recent project studied children from sixty divorced families, spanning a variety of racial and economic backgrounds. Judith Wallerstein, a psychologist at UC Berkeley, conducted the study and was surprised at the results. She expected damage done by divorce to be over after the first year, but ten years after her study started she found damage to be acute. Thirty-seven percent of the children claimed to be "consciously and intensely unhappy and dissatisfied with their life in the post-divorce family."[5] Children felt intensely lonely, and in cases where there was remarriage, they felt abandoned or shunned by the newly married couple whose basic concern seemed to be their own privacy. Even many children who seemed to be coping well were lonely, unhappy or sorrowful about what had happened. Ten years after the divorce, they had vivid memories of their parents' breakup.[6]

Because divorce and remarriage create so many problems, one wishes the church would clearly enunciate biblical teaching on these topics. Instead, the church speaks words of confusion and adds to the level of confusion. Unfortunately, there is no consensus among evangelicals on the proper understanding of biblical teaching on this matter. Nor is there less disagreement among Roman Catholics. The Church allows no divorce on any grounds, but grants annulment for many causes. A Roman Catholic wishing release from a marriage need only show that the marriage was never valid in the first place. Needless to say, many Catholic marriages end in annulment.

Though it would be tremendously beneficial for the church to take a unified stance on divorce and remarriage, that is unlikely because of the complexity of the issues. Scripture says little on this issue, and what is said, especially in the teachings of Christ, is cryptic and ambiguous. It raises many questions. We cannot handle every question in these chapters (e.g., the question of whether a divorced person can serve as a pastor), but we want to address as many as necessary to elucidate biblical teaching on divorce and remarriage.

Our discussion begins with an analysis of biblical teaching on what constitutes marriage, for it seems foolish to talk about grounds for dissolution of a marriage without knowing if a marital bond was ever formed. After discussing marriage, we shall turn to the question of whether there are any grounds for divorce and remarriage. We shall investigate the biblical texts to see how they answer this question. Our concern is not to study this issue from the perspective of societal laws and customs, for those vary from age to age and society to society. Our concern is to discover God's perspective on these matters as revealed in Scripture.

MARRIAGE

In this section we want first to set forth the elements we believe are involved in creating a marital bond. Then, we shall consider whether any biblical teaching suggests that the bond is indissoluble. Of course, if Scripture teaches that the bond can be broken, we must still discover what would do so. That matter will be handled in later sections.

BIBLICALLY, WHAT CONSTITUTES A MARRIAGE?

Though Paul teaches about Christian marriage (Ephesians 5), he focuses more on how husbands and wives should relate to one another than on what forms a marriage. Thus, this question seems best answered by appeal to the creation ordinances in Genesis 2. Genesis 2 shows that marriage is God's idea (2:18). After God created the world and the first man, he decided man should not be alone. God created the animals, and Adam named them, but none was suitable as a helper for Adam (2:19-20). God then created Eve from Adam and brought her to him (2:21-22). Verse 23 records Adam's words of recognition that she was the one suitable to be his helper. The passage ends (v. 24) by setting forth the elements that go into making a marriage in God's eye.

Verse 24 states that because ("for this reason") a man recognizes a particular woman as suitable to be his mate, he leaves father and mother. The word for leave (*'azab*) is a very strong word that means more than simple departure. It means "to forsake, leave destitute, or refuse." The idea is not that a husband and wife no longer can have any relationship with their parents. Rather, they recognize that their relationship to one another must have priority over all other ties. It is in this sense that they forsake or leave their parents.

Marriage also involves a cleaving to one's mate. The word for cleave (dābaq) means "to cling to, remain close, adhere, be glued firmly." In this verse it means that once parents are forsaken, the man will not soon return to them. He will stay with his wife and direct his affection and attention to her. She will do the same to him. When the ideas of forsaking and clinging are taken together, it becomes clear that marriage amounts to each partner committing his/her life to the other. It is a pledge to emphasize one's mate as paramount beyond all other relations (forsaking) and to remain faithful to (cling to) him/her.

The verse concludes by saying they will become one flesh. This speaks of union. The point is not that now there is only one person. Eve still had her own body and mind, as did Adam. Likewise, the phrase is not merely a reference to the sexual union of the partners. Surely, the phrase refers to the sex act, but the context demands that it mean more. We believe the phrase is a metaphor meant to signify the bonding or uniting of the two as a married couple. The sex act outwardly and physically points to the bond that has been created. Some argue that the phrase also signifies the creation of kinship or blood relation (cf. Gen 29:12-14; 37:27; Judg 9:2; 2 Sam 19:13).[7]

How is this union brought about? It comes into being as a result of two factors. The first is the commitment of life to one another, signified by the forsaking and cleaving of the partners to one another. The second is an act of God constituting or uniting them together. Jesus' command in Matt 19:6 not to put asunder *those whom God has joined* emphasizes the divine element in establishing the bond. Some might think God unites only believers, but Matthew 19 and Genesis 1 and 2 suggest otherwise. Marriage is portrayed as a human institution for all mankind, not just for Christians. Unless the marriage involves those who should not marry because of some biblical prohibition (e.g., some unions are forbidden because they would involve incest—Lev 18:6ff.), God is involved in forming the union.

God constitutes the union, then, as the two partners make their commitment to one another. As long as this bond exists from God's perspective, the couple should not seek a legal divorce. Is the bond unbreakable? The notion of cleaving in Genesis 2 suggests permanence, but nothing inherent to the word's meaning tells how long the cleaving will last.[8] Jesus' commentary on Genesis in Matthew 19 makes it clear that God wants it to last throughout life on this earth, but there is no guarantee that it will. In the next section we discuss whether the bond is breakable. However, from what we have said heretofore, it should be clear that in determining whether there are grounds for divorce or remarriage in any given case, it is critical to determine the status of the marital bond in the first and any subsequent marriages.

IS THE MARRIAGE BOND TERMINABLE OR UNBREAKABLE?

We pose this question from a biblical and theological perspective, not a legal one. In God's eyes, can it be broken? The question is not whether it is permissible to break the bond but whether it is possible. By possibility, we mean logical possibility. Our question, then, is whether something in the very nature of the marital bond makes the notion of breaking it a contradiction.[9] That is, is the idea of a broken marriage bond like the idea of a round square, a flat contradiction?

Arguments for Indissolubility

Those who think the bond cannot be broken argue their position on several grounds. Some assert that marriage is like the biblical notion of a covenant, not like a contract. Contracts are witnessed by people with the state as guarantor, whereas covenants are witnessed by God with him as guarantor. Contracts can be broken; covenants cannot. Covenants always imply the expectation of permanence in a way contracts do not.[10]

Second, some maintain that biblical teaching about marriage suggests that the bond is indissoluble. Invariably the language of Gen 2:24 ("forsaking," "cleaving," "one flesh") and Jesus' command that no man put asunder what God has brought together (Matt 19:6) are cited as proof that God has created the bond, and it cannot be broken.[11]

Third, some appeal to Deut 24:1-4 and the OT concept of kinship as evidence against dissolubility. It is claimed that marriage establishes kinship (i.e., blood relations) between the husband and wife. Not only are there vertical lines of kinship with one's children, but horizontal lines with one's spouse. This is seen as the ultimate meaning of becoming one flesh (Gen 2:24). As to Deuteronomy 24, Moses says that if a woman is divorced and remarries, and if her second husband either divorces her or dies, she may not return to her first husband. To do so is an abomination before the Lord (Deut 24:4). The assumption, of course, is that if she loses her second husband, she may marry a third husband; the only prohibition is against going back to the first husband. But why? Is God against reconciliation between estranged spouses? According to this argument, the reason is that once the initial bond is established, it is permanent. With that bond comes kinship ties. Therefore, for the woman to return to her first husband after losing her second would be tantamount to committing incest, and Lev 18:6-18 clearly prohibits incest. In this view, then, the regulation in Deuteronomy 24 presupposes that even by divorce (a legal, societal procedure) one cannot actually break the marriage bond. It must be indissoluble.[12]

Finally, the indissolubility of the bond is argued from the nature of human sexuality. The sex act at its best in marriage is the most intimate and complete reciprocal self-giving of which two people are capable. Sexual union profoundly and permanently affects the married couple in the very core of their being. Sex relations, then, add another strand to the marriage bond. Even sex with a prostitute forms a personal bond, as Paul says, but that bond is not the marriage bond which involves several different strands. In addition, each person's identity involves his history, including his sexual history. Sex with one partner profoundly affects what one can give of himself to another potential partner. One's sexual history cannot be undone. The psychological and physical bonding sex produces in the married couple cannot be broken, no matter how many times one is married. All of this is seen as further evidence that the marriage bond cannot be broken.[13]

Arguments for Dissolubility

Despite the preceding arguments, we think it is possible to break the marital bond. As noted already, passages such as Gen 2:24 and Matt 19:6 do not say it is impossible to break the marriage bond. They only offer the pattern for marriage (Gen 2:24) and record God's command not to break the bond.

To say the bond cannot be broken because God makes it is to forget that Scripture nowhere says whether God makes an *indissoluble* bond. Commanding people not to break it is no proof that they cannot or will not, just as commanding them not to lie does not guarantee they will always tell the truth.

A further consideration which leads us to think the bond can be broken is the biblical teaching that the death of one of the partners breaks the bond. If the bond cannot be broken, one would expect a married couple to be married throughout eternity. Scripture teaches otherwise. Scripture allows widows and widowers to remarry (Rom 7:1-3; 1 Cor 7:39). Even those who think the marriage bond is indissoluble agree on that point. If widows and widowers can remarry even though their first marital bond is unbreakable, then Scripture in effect sanctions polygamy and polyandry—and for eternity! Evidence to the contrary comes from Matt 22:23-30. The Sadducees, the antisupernaturalists of the day, tried to catch Jesus on just this point. They did not believe in resurrections and thought they could pose a problem that would prove the notion of a resurrection problematic. They asked Jesus to whom a woman would be married in the resurrection if she had seven husbands while on earth. If the marriage bond really is indissoluble, Jesus should have said she would be married to all seven and that she would be polyandrous even if some husbands had died. Instead, Jesus corrects the Sadducees' error by noting that in resurrected bodies no one is married. Death breaks the marriage bond, despite how romantic thoughts to the contrary are. The underlying assumption behind the Sadducees' question is wrong.

The incident recorded in Matt 22:23-30 clearly teaches that the marriage bond can be broken, at least by death. The question before us in the next sections will be whether it can be broken by anything else. As to marriage as a covenant or contract, Scripture seems to describe it more in terms of a covenant than a contract. However, we disagree that permanence is intrinsic to the very notion of covenant. We agree that covenants such as the Abrahamic and Davidic are unbreakable and indissoluble. Nonetheless, that does not mean all biblical covenants are. For example, the Mosaic Covenant clearly was breakable, and Jeremiah says Israel broke it (Jer 31:32). In fact, they did so repeatedly. Moreover, as argued in the first chapter, the Mosaic Covenant and the Mosaic Code have been dissolved in the NT era in favor of the New Covenant and the Code of Christ.

The example of the Mosaic Covenant alone shows that nothing intrinsic to the biblical notion of covenant demands that it be unbreakable or indissoluble. Each covenant must be judged on its own terms. As to the marriage covenant, we have already shown it can be dissolved on at least one ground—death. Thus, covenantal language used to describe marriage does not prove the marriage bond is unbreakable.

All of these considerations lead us to think the marriage bond is breakable. Likewise, we do not think the Deuteronomy 24 and kinship argument proves indissolubility, but we shall explain why when we offer our interpretation of that passage.

IS IT PERMISSIBLE TO BREAK A MARRIAGE (DIVORCE) AND REMARRY?

STATEMENT OF POSITIONS

These issues have been heavily debated over the centuries of church history. In a sense the real culprit is the exception in Jesus' teaching on divorce as recorded in Matthew. In what follows we shall first state and explain the main views on divorce and remarriage. Then we shall turn to the interpretation of key OT and NT passages to see which view is best upheld by Scripture.

The many views on divorce and remarriage can be divided into three broad groups: 1) no divorce views; 2) divorce but no remarriage views; and 3) divorce and remarriage views.[14] The issue is further complicated by another consideration, namely, did Jesus ever utter the exception clauses, or are they Matthew's or someone else's editorial insertion?[15] Regardless of how one understands the origin of these clauses, this matter only increases the complexity of determining Jesus' and Scripture's teaching on divorce and remarriage.

No Divorce Views

No divorce views attempt to harmonize the exception clauses of Matt 5:31-32 and Matt 19:9 with Mark and Luke so as to allow no divorce on any ground. The first attempt is the *inclusivist view*. According to this view, the exception clause should be read as "not even in the case of *porneia*." On this view, Jesus is saying there is no divorce at all, not even in the case of *porneia*. No grounds, including *porneia*, warrant divorce.[16]

A second view is the *preteritive* or *"no comment" view*. This view sees *porneia* in the exception clauses as a reference to "something indecent" in Deut 24:1. The Pharisees asked Jesus whether "something indecent" (*porneia*) is any cause at all, i.e., was Moses allowing divorce for any reason whatsoever? According to this view, Jesus refused to comment on that issue. He responded, instead, that the Pharisees had misunderstood the basic point that God's intention was no divorce, and Moses never commanded divorce. Divorce is a concession because of the hardness of the people's hearts. Moreover, Jesus said that whoever divorces and remarries commits adultery. The exception clause is parenthetical and refers to the question Jesus will not comment on, the meaning of "something indecent."[17] On this view, Matt 19:9 can be paraphrased as: "if anyone divorces his wife—except in the case of *porneia* about which I shall make no comment—and remarries, he commits adultery." The preteritive view is obviously a no divorce position.

A third view focuses on Matt 5:32. That verse says: "but I say to you that every one who divorces his wife, except for the cause of unchastity, makes her commit adultery." On this view, Jesus offers no ground for divorce, but instead clarifies which action commits the offense. If the woman is an adulteress (she has committed *porneia* as this view interprets *porneia*), the divorce and remarriage do not make her an adulteress, because she already is one. Her offense is her adultery that led to the divorce, not her divorce or remarriage. On the other hand, if she is not an adulteress and her husband divorces her, she becomes an adulteress (presumably because she will remarry, and her sex relations with her new husband will be adulterous).[18] In this case the divorce is the offense, and it leads her to adultery (another offense). Clearly, none of this offers a ground for divorce.

The next three positions actually allow divorce in some cases, but the cases are so unusual that they do not cover most people. Each typically assumes that since Matthew wrote to a Jewish audience, the exception clause must be germane to them. The first position is the *betrothal view*. Jewish weddings involved three stages. The first was the betrothal period. Once betrothed, the couple was considered married, even though they did not live together and perhaps had not even met (parents arranged marriages for their children). After betrothal, the husband would take his bride from her parents' home to his home to live as husband and wife. The third stage of the ceremony was the wedding feast, held when the bride came to live with the groom. If the bride to be had sexual relations with some other man during the betrothal period, her act was considered adultery, and she was to be punished. If she was not stoned to death as the OT required, she was given a bill of divorce and the relationship was dissolved. According to the betrothal view, the exception clause refers to this point in Jewish law. As such, it did not refer even to all people of Jesus' day, let alone ours. Jesus' general teaching is no divorce. The exception pertains to another culture and another day.[19]

Another view appealing to the Jewishness of Matthew is the *mixed marriage view*. The incident recorded in Ezra 9–10 and passages such as Deut 7:3 (covenant people are forbidden to intermarry the heathen of the land) form the basis for this view. In Ezra's day the nation was trying to rebuild after the Babylonian Exile. In spite of the need for national and religious purity, Israelites, including priests and Levites, married heathen idolaters. Divorce was not only allowed but was mandated to purge the nation. The mixed marriage view comes in one of two forms. One claims that *porneia* in the exception clause refers to this incident in Ezra's time but nothing more. The other form of the view sees this exception as permitting believers in the newly forming church to divorce heathen spouses in order to ensure doctrinal purity in the early church. No other grounds at any other times were acceptable bases for divorce.[20]

A final no divorce view sees the exception clause as a reference to the prohibition of incestuous marriages (Leviticus 18). Marriages to blood relatives should never be contracted, so Jesus allows annulment of such marriages. On this view *porneia* refers to incest or incestuous marriage, not adultery. Matthew's normal word for adultery is *moicheia*, and in Matthew 15 a distinction is made between *moicheia* (adultery) and *porneia*. Moreover, *porneia* has the meaning of incest in passages such as 1 Cor 5:1 and Acts 15:20, 29. Aside from incestuous marriages, no others may end in divorce.[21]

Divorce but No Remarriage View

This view was the majority opinion of the early church fathers. Only Ambrosiaster among the Greek and Latin fathers held a different view.[22] On this view, only the death of a spouse can dissolve a marriage bond. Jesus' exception allows couples to separate in cases of *porneia* (normally understood as adultery). However, since *porneia* does not break the marriage bond, neither spouse can remarry. Hopefully, while remaining apart, the erring mate would be driven to repent and return to his or her spouse.[23] Moreover, the so-called Pauline Privilege (1 Cor 7:15) does not allow deserted believers to remarry. Thus, this view allows separation when there is *porneia* but never allows remarriage.

Heth and Wenham (*Jesus and Divorce*), relying heavily on Jacques Dupont's *Mariage et divorce dans l'evangile* (1959), defend this view in contemporary discussions. They hold that the marriage bond is indissoluble and appeal to the Deuteronomy 24 and kinship argument in support. Likewise, Mark 10 and Luke 16 allow no one to divorce, and Jesus' comments (Matthew 19) on creation ordinances and leaving intact what God has joined leave no room for divorce. In Matt 19:9 Jesus says: "And I say to you, whoever divorces his wife, *except for porneia*, and marries another, commits adultery." Who commits adultery, according to Jesus? The person who both divorces *and* remarries. Separation alone without remarriage is not adultery. How does the exception clause affect this basic teaching? The crucial point for Heth and Wenham is the placement of the clause *between* "divorces" and "marries." As such, it qualifies only "divorces" (not "marries another"). It gives a basis for divorce (*porneia*) but gives no basis for remarriage. Heth and Wenham see Matt 19:9 as an answer to the Pharisees' question in 19:3 ("is it lawful for a man to divorce his wife *for any cause at all?*"). Jesus responds that only *porneia* is just cause, but even then, one may not remarry without committing adultery.[24]

By combining this understanding of Matt 19:9 with the teaching of Matt 5:32a ("whoever divorces his wife, except for *porneia*, causes her to commit adultery"), Heth and Wenham derive a view that can be stated in four propositions: 1) divorce for any cause *plus* remarriage is adultery; 2) divorce because of *porneia* is acceptable, but no remarriage is allowed; 3) whoever divorces a woman forces her into adultery (i.e., once she remarries), unless the divorce resulted because of her *porneia* (adultery)— in that case she was already an adulteress before the divorce; and 4) whoever marries a divorcée commits adultery himself.[25]

Divorce and Remarriage Views

There are several divorce and remarriage views, most of which are variations of what many call the Erasmian view (named after Erasmus of Rotterdam). Those who hold some form of the Erasmian view consider the exception clauses in Matthew to allow a morally acceptable ground for divorce. Moreover, if divorce is permissible, then remarriage is as well.

Some variations in the Erasmian view stem from one's understanding of *porneia*. Many interpret it narrowly to refer only to adultery. On this view, Jesus is saying that if a wife commits adultery, her husband may divorce her and remarry without committing any sin himself. Others object that Matthew's usual word for adultery is *moicheia* and that in Matthew 15 he distinguishes between *porneia* and *moicheia*. Thus, *porneia* in Matt 5:32 and 19:9 should be understood in a more general way to refer to any kind of sexual impurity, including adultery, homosexuality, bestiality, and incest.

A further variation of the Erasmian view arises from interpreting Paul as allowing a second ground for divorce (1 Corinthians 7). Paul instructs converts to Christianity not to leave their unbelieving spouses just because they are non-believers. However, if the non-believer leaves the believer and seeks a divorce, the believer is told to let him depart (v. 15); the believer is not bound in such a case. Many understand this to mean that willful desertion of a believer by a non-believer is permissible grounds for divorce. The believer may not initiate divorce proceedings, but if the non-believing spouse does, the divorce is not a sin. Typically, those who think Paul allows divorce for willful desertion argue that if the divorce is morally permissible, so is remarriage.[26]

A complex divorce and remarriage position is found in William Luck's *Divorce and Remarriage: Recovering the Biblical View* (1987). Luck begins with the OT. When he turns to Deut 24:1-4, he says one must see it in the context that runs from Deut 23:15–24:7. All the other laws in the section attempt to protect a disadvantaged party from abuse by an advantaged one.[27] The function of Deut 24:1-4 is to protect a woman from a hard-hearted man who divorces her without cause. The passage prohibits her remarriage to such a man so that she would not be treated like a piece of chattel property that could be passed back and forth for the use of one man and then another.[28] As to OT teaching generally, adulterers were to be executed, but when that was not done, divorce was allowed as an act of discipline. If a husband was abusive to his wife, but no adultery was involved, the law allowed divorce in order to protect the woman.

As for remarriage, whether the husband was guilty or innocent for the divorce, he could remarry. Moreover, even when the divorce was groundless so that it did not break the marriage bond, the husband could remarry, for the OT permitted polygamy (actually, Luck says both the OT and NT agree that polygamy, but not polyandry, is morally acceptable).[29] As for women, if they were guilty for the divorce, they could not remarry but had to put away any subsequent partner and return to their former spouse. If they were not guilty of the divorce, they were allowed to remarry.[30] Luck believes Jesus basically repeats OT teaching, since he came to fulfill the law, not abolish it.[31] Matt 5:32 is seen as teaching that groundless divorce is treachery, and is, in fact, adultery. What about divorce when there are grounds (*porneia*)? Divorce is allowed as an act of disciplining the guilty party. *Remarriage* is permissible, except when someone groundlessly divorces just to get a new mate.[32]

Luck understands Matt 19:9 like Matt 5:32, but says more about remarriage on the basis of Matthew 19. The exception clause in Matthew 19 means that whoever divorces with grounds (the innocent party) is free to remarry without committing adultery, while those divorcing groundlessly just to get to a new mate commit adultery by remarrying.[33] As to the person groundlessly divorced (that innocent party), Luck says Matthew 19 does not discuss that person, but he thinks remarriage is allowed. For an innocent man groundlessly divorced, the morality of polygamy affirms his right to remarry. Deut 24:1-4 allows the woman wrongly divorced to remarry.[34]

Luck allows other grounds for divorce in accord with the following line of reasoning: 1) Scripture defines adultery as *porneia*; 2) *porneia* breaks the marriage covenant and is justifiable grounds for divorce and remarriage; 3) since lust without the sex act is adultery (Matt 5:27-28) and so is groundlessly divorcing someone, there is non-sexual adultery. The net result of points 1)–3) seems to be that anything one thinks is adultery (whether sexual or non-sexual) is *porneia* and thus an acceptable ground for divorce and remarriage. Luck does not quite say this, but his views seem to entail it. One thing is clear. He does think desertion (1 Corinthians 7) is non-sexual adultery and thereby a legitimate ground for divorce and remarriage.[35]

INTERPRETATION OF MAJOR TEXTS[36]

Deuteronomy 24:1–4

Though other OT passages are relevant to the divorce question, this passage is crucial, because it forms the background of Jesus' discussion with the Pharisees on divorce and remarriage. Most commentators see verses 1-4a as one continuous sentence. Verses 1-3 contain a series of "if" clauses, which, if *all* true, lead to the conclusion in verse 4 (the "punch line" of the legislation). This suggests that this law is meant to cover a very specific case; it is not a general rule covering all possible instances of divorce and remarriage.

In interpreting this passage, five major questions must be answered: 1) what is the major thrust of the legislation? 2) why was this legislation needed? 3) what has defiled the woman (v. 4)? 4) why is it an abomination for her to remarry her first husband (v. 4) under the circumstances outlined in verses 1-4? and 5) what does *'erwat dābār* ("something indecent") in verse 1 mean, and how does its meaning affect the teaching of the rest of the passage?

The first two questions can be handled together. Evidently, by the time of Jesus (as evidenced in the Pharisees' question—Matt 19:3) Deuteronomy 24 was understood as a basis for finding a ground to divorce one's wife. However, the thrust of the law is in verse 4, and it is not to offer a ground for divorce. Nor is it to legitimize divorce. Verses 1 and 3 assume divorce is being practiced, but neither says divorce is morally acceptable. Moses' legislation regulates divorce, but doing so does not even *tacitly* endorse divorce as morally acceptable.

We believe the purpose of the legislation was twofold. The initial purpose was to protect the rights of a divorced woman. In Jewish society women were considered men's property to be dispensed with as men chose. Moreover, marrying or having sexual relations with a woman already married was adultery, and adultery was punishable by death. So, if a woman was cast out of her husband's house but not divorced, no other man would dare touch her. Of course, if she could not remarry, in that society she had little chance to support herself except by prostitution. On the other hand, if she was duly divorced, she was free to remarry. But how would a prospective husband know if a woman was really divorced and free to remarry? Moses demanded the divorcing husband to give her a bill of divorce, so that everyone would know she was free to remarry. Thus, the legislation was meant in part to protect a woman from a husband who would merely throw her out without making it clear that she was divorced and so free to remarry.[37]

As to the second purpose of the legislation, commentators rightly argue that since divorce was occurring, there was concern that it might become customary for a woman to multiply divorces and remarriages.[38] The point of this legislation was to curtail that possibility, for the woman was forbidden (v. 4) to return to her first husband after a second marriage and divorce.

Luck thinks the law's point was to protect women from being treated as chattel property to be passed back and forth between husbands. However, he also seems to think this law would allow her to marry a third husband, even though she could not return to her first husband.[39] The problem here, though, is that if she could go to a third husband (and presumably a fourth and fifth), she would be handled like chattel property at least as much as if she were permitted to return to her first husband. Thus, while we think the law was meant to protect the woman and her rights, we do not think it warrants multiple marriages (more on this point shortly).

In turning to the last three problems, one finds great diversity of opinion. Some offer an explanation of the woman's defilement and then see it as the grounds of the abomination. However, most commentators have no explanation about what defiles the woman. For example, Heth and Wenham discuss the nature of the abomination involved in remarrying the first husband but offer no answer about why the woman is defiled.[40] Luck deals with the woman's defilement, but he makes it a statement against the husband, rather than against the woman's moral character (as does Moses). We agree that the husband causes the problem, but the *text* states that *she* is the one defiled.

Very few place much emphasis on the meaning of *'erwat dābār* ("something indecent," v. 1). Heth and Wenham even say the meaning of *'erwat dābār* is unimportant to the point of Deut 24:1-4 and dismiss the issue.[41]

On the contrary, we think the meaning of 'erwat dābār is extremely important, for without it one is hard pressed to explain why the woman is defiled by the sequence of events described and why it is abominable for her to remarry her first husband. Thus, we now turn directly to the meaning of 'erwat dābār.

Does 'erwat dābār refer to adultery? If so, Moses apparently contradicts himself, for in Deut 22:22 he explicitly says adulterers are to be *stoned to death*. Why, then, in 24:1-2 talk about a woman being divorced for adultery (understanding 'erwat dābār in 24:1 as adultery) *and then marrying a second husband?* Normally, one does not worry about regulations for remarriage of someone who is supposed to be dead! Some respond that this is true, but adulterers were not always executed, and Moses here makes a concession to that fact. In effect Moses would be saying here: "since you refuse to execute your adulterous wife, at least protect her rights by giving her a bill of divorcement so she can marry another man." However, we fail to see why Moses would grant a concession that would actually encourage people to continue ignoring the command to execute adulterers. Does God change his laws to accommodate man's failure to follow them? We find it hard to see how it makes sense for Moses to say this. Moreover, why would Moses cover adultery in chapter 24, when two chapters earlier he already stipulated how adultery was to be handled? Moses is not offering an accommodation to disobedience to that law; he is offering a further law which covers cases not involving adultery.

For similar reasons we believe 'erwat dābār does not refer to some other sexual offense such as homosexuality, bestiality, or even incest. The Holiness Code (Leviticus 18) lists offenses that defile those who do them. The Lord calls them abominable acts, and the key point that is often overlooked (especially in the case of incest) is that God says whoever does these abominations will be cut off from among his people (Lev 18:26-29, esp. v. 29). That is, the penalty for these offenses is death. Thus, it is unlikely that 'erwat dābār in Deut 24:1 refers to any of these sins, since each was punishable by death, not divorce.

What, then, does 'erwat dābār mean? This, of course, was the question on the minds of the Pharisees when they raised the question of Matt 19:3. In Jesus' day the Shammai interpreted the phrase narrowly to refer to some sexual impurity (usually adultery). We have seen that they were wrong. The Hillel understood it broadly to refer to anything a husband found disagreeable about his wife (even burning a meal, e.g.). The Hillel were probably closer to being right than were the Shammai, but they totally perverted Moses' overall teaching in Deut 24:1-4. The phrase probably referred to a variety of items a husband might find objectionable such as barrenness (which was frowned upon in Near Eastern culture) or some birth defect.[42] It is not clear whether it referred to burning a meal in Moses' day, but it surely was understood that way by Christ's time.

While the Hillel were on the right track in their understanding of *'erwat dabar*, they were wrong in thinking Moses permitted a man to divorce his wife for any cause whatsoever. It is here that their real perversion of the meaning of Deut 24:1-4 becomes clear. The Hillel understood Moses as granting permission or even commanding divorce on grounds of *'erwat dabar*. Moses said nothing of the sort. Moses merely *described* a situation where someone was divorced for *'erwat dabar*. The only explicit *prescription* in the passage comes in verse 4 ("do not let such a woman remarry her first husband"), not in verses 1-3. The Pharisees turned Moses' description into a prescription and perverted the true intent of the passage.

How does this understanding of *'erwat dabar* affect the overall meaning of Deut 24:1-4? We believe it means Moses says *implicitly* what Jesus makes very *explicit* in the Gospels when asked to comment on this passage. It also is the key as to why the woman in Deuteronomy 24 is defiled. Let us explain.

Moses describes a set of circumstances in verses 1-3, and verse 4 says the woman in question has been defiled. By what? By something in the sequence of events described in verses 1-3, i.e., by being divorced for *'erwat dabar*, remarried, and then divorced by the second husband (or he dies). Why would that defile her? We believe Jesus explains when he sets forth the rules that govern divorcing someone on flimsy, non-sexual grounds. In Matthew 5 (apart from the exception clause) Jesus says that whoever divorces his wife makes her an adulteress. In Matthew 19 (minus the exception clause) he says whoever divorces and remarries commits adultery. We suggest this happens for the exact same reason that the woman in Deuteronomy 24 has been defiled. When someone divorces a spouse for any cause at all (i.e., divorces for *'erwat dabar*) rather than for some sexual impropriety, in God's eyes they are still married. Consequently, if either mate remarries (and men and women in that society were quite likely to do so), sexual relations with the new spouse are adultery, since the marital bond with the first mate is not severed. This is precisely the substance of Jesus' general rule in Matt 5:32 and 19:9 (minus the exception clause) and in Mark 10:11-12 about divorce and remarriage.

If the woman of Deuteronomy 24 is defiled because she married a second husband after being divorced on inadequate grounds (for *'erwat dabar*), could she marry a second husband without defilement if she had been divorced on the grounds of adultery or some other sexual misdeed? In other words, is there really an exception clause implicit in Deuteronomy 24? The answer is no. The Mosaic Law prescribes that adulterers, homosexuals, etc. be stoned to death! Deut 24:1-4 does not even implicitly allow remarriage for someone who is to be executed for sexual misconduct. Whether and how this affects NT teaching on divorce for adultery and remarriage remains to be seen. Suffice it to say that Moses considers here only the case of a woman divorced on improper grounds, and then defiled by a second marriage.

In response, some might argue that if our interpretation is correct, the woman should have been stoned to death for adultery, not allowed to remarry. On the contrary, we respond that while she is made an adulteress, she winds up in that condition in ignorance of what she is doing and thus becomes an adulteress unintentionally. Moreover, she was forced into that situation by the actions of her first husband (and thus presumably against her will). But, then, it should be clear why it would be improper to execute her. Under Mosaic Law sins committed unintentionally were treated with greater leniency than sins done with premeditation. Moreover, as argued in the first chapter, moral praise or blame (and punishment) can only properly be assessed when an agent acts freely, but this woman was forced into this situation.

One issue still remains. Why is it an abomination if the woman in question remarries her first husband after her second husband divorces her or dies? Heth and Wenham, as already noted, think she would commit incest by remarriage,[43] but we disagree. Initially, we note that the passage makes no reference to incest. To see incest in this passage is to read it in from Leviticus 18, but nothing in Deut 24:1-4 indicates that incest is in view. Second, kinship is certainly involved in marriage, but if anything, the fact that Heth and Wenham think kinship ties with the first husband remain make it hard for us to see why it would be abominable for the woman to return to him. Moreover, if Heth and Wenham are right that the point of the legislation is that kinship lines must not be ignored, then why allow the second marriage (as verse 2 apparently does)? That marriage, too, would ignore kinship ties established in the first marriage. These problems lead us to conclude that a different interpretation of the passage is necessary.

A final point about incest is in order. The passage does not say remarrying her first husband would be abominable because it would defile her. Deut 24:4 says the woman cannot remarry "after" she has been defiled. That is, she is already defiled before any remarriage to her first husband. If incest caused that defilement, it must be that her second marriage was incestuous (that would surely defile her), but nothing in the passage teaches that she committed incest by marrying her second husband. Moreover, remarriage as abominable might *further* defile her, but as already argued, not because remarrying her first husband would be incest. We conclude that whatever is abominable about the woman returning to her first husband, it does not have anything to do with incest.

Why, then, is the remarriage an abomination? Once the reason for the woman's defilement is understood, the answer becomes clear. The reason the remarriage mentioned in Deut 24:4 is abominable is that it is abominable to marry an adulteress! Deuteronomy 24 does *not* say that if her first husband divorces her for *'erwat dābār* and *she remains unmarried*, then it is abominable for her to return to her first husband. Presumably, she could return to him under those circumstances, if he would have her back. Despite her harlotry, even Hosea's wife was allowed to return to him; God ordered him to take her back (Hosea 3).[44] If Gomer could return to Hosea, then surely the woman of Deuteronomy 24 could return to her first husband *if there had not been a subsequent marriage that defiled her.* Only the woman made an adulteress by a second marriage could not return to her first husband after a divorce from the second.

Some may respond that this makes no sense since the passage implies she could marry a third man; return to her first husband is all that is prohibited. However, assuming that marriage to a third man is allowed is merely an assumption. Moses says nothing about marrying a third man. In fact, if she is defiled because her second marriage made her an adulteress, she should marry no one. She should be executed. But as argued, we think OT law made this exception because she was "pushed" into adultery by a first husband who divorced her for *'erwat dābār* and put her on the street with nowhere to turn in that society but to another man.

Some will wonder why Moses did not make this explicit. That is, why prohibit remarriage to the first husband rather than forbid all remarriage to someone in her situation? This is a legitimate question, and we think the answer is that Moses is arguing from lesser to greater. If the woman is made an adulteress (defiled) by the second marriage, then would not marriage to a third man defile her more, especially if her second marriage also ended because of *'erwat dābār*? However, if Moses merely forbade marrying a third man, some in Israel would probably reason, "Well, at least a woman in that position could go back to her first husband, if he would take her back." In other words, they would reason that involving a third man would be a greater evil than returning to the first husband. We believe Moses made the regulation as he did as if to say, "If a woman winds up in this situation, she is not to marry *anyone else*. It is abominable for her to remarry even someone you might think would be acceptable for her. And if *that* is abominable, surely it is abominable to bring in a *third* party!" That is, if the apparently lesser problem (remarrying the first husband) is abominable, then the seemingly greater problem (marriage to a third man) is also prohibited.

Does this interpretation of Deuteronomy 24 too much read NT teaching back into the OT? Some will think so,[45] but we disagree. While we doubt the OT person understood all of this (as argued, even the Pharisees botched the fundamental point of the passage), that does not disprove our interpretation. What a passage means and/or implies should not be determined by what its readers understood.[46] Even OT believers did not understand every OT passage about a coming Messiah, but that does not negate the NT's interpretation of those passages.

Second, while one must be careful not to read NT ideas back into the OT without warrant, there is warrant in this case. Matthew 19 and Mark 10 are set in the framework of a discussion over the meaning of Deuteronomy 24. Matt 5:32 comes in the midst of a discussion on the proper meaning of the OT law, and Matt 5:32 is immediately preceded by Jesus' teaching on the law and adultery. Given the context of these discussions, Jesus does not evade the Pharisees' questions. He answers their questions about Deuteronomy 24, and thus, there is warrant to understand Deut 24:1-4 in light of Jesus' teaching. Of course, Jesus' answer is unexpected by his listeners, for he rejects the Pharisees' conceptual framework (the Hillel/Shammai debate) for this discussion. Christ reminds them that the point of OT teaching is not to find grounds for divorce but to recognize that God's desire is permanence in marriage.

Mark 10:2-12

In the NT we turn first to passages without the exception clause, and Mark 10 is the longest such passage. In comparing Mark 10 and Matthew 19, one notices differences beside the handling of the exception clause. In Mark the Lord's comments about divorce and remarriage are made to the disciples (10:10-12), whereas in Matthew 19 Jesus apparently speaks (v. 9) in the hearing of both the Pharisees and the disciples. In Mark the *Pharisees* say Moses permitted a man to give a bill of divorcement and send his wife away (v. 4), whereas in Matthew 19 *Jesus* says Moses permitted divorce.

While these differences could mean the passages refer to separate occasions, we think not. For example, it is possible to interpret Matt 19:9 as addressed only to the disciples since they alone respond (v. 10). Only Mark says the teaching was uttered privately, but Matthew's account does not rule out Jesus' *privately* saying 19:9 to the disciples. Moreover, in Mark 10:5 Jesus speaks about Moses' teaching on divorce (as he does in Matt 19:8), and in both passages Jesus links the Mosaic permission of divorce to the hardness of the people's heart. The major differences between the passages are the exception clause (included in Matthew) and the statement about a woman divorcing a husband and remarrying (in Mark alone). Undoubtedly, Matthew and Mark chose material appropriate to their audiences. However, in view of the many similarities between the two passages, we think they both record the same incident.[47]

Some see the discussion about divorce, as well as Jesus' reply to his disciples, as hardly imaginable in a Palestinian context. Nothing in OT law suggests that divorce is illegal, so the question does not make sense. Moreover, in Judaism a woman had no right to divorce her husband, so Mark 10:12 does not fit the Palestinian situation. On the other hand, if the story is transposed to the early Hellenistic church, everything fits perfectly. That is, the story arose somewhere else, but Mark adapted it into the Palestinian scene.[48]

We disagree for several reasons. Mark says the Pharisees asked Jesus this question, and a discussion ensued. This view says otherwise, so Mark either lied or was mistaken. The implications of this understanding for inerrancy are unacceptable. Moreover, the so-called Temple Scroll found at Qumran prohibits divorce. Thus, as Fitzmyer argues, the discussion does make sense in a first-century Palestinian context, for the Pharisees could be asking whether Jesus sided with the Pharisees or the Essenes on this issue.[49] Even apart from the Qumran material, there is ample reason to think the discussion appropriate. The Pharisees tried to trip Jesus up. Given the debates within Judaism between the Hillel and Shammai over the meaning of *'erwat dābār* in Deut 24:1, the discussion about divorce as set forth in both Mark 10 and Matthew 19 is thoroughly understandable. Jesus' unexpected answer is no proof the event never happened in Jesus' lifetime. In fact, it is in keeping with Jesus' habit of explaining clearly the full meaning of the law on a topic. We see no good reason to see the story as Mark's insertion for his own purposes.

As to the passage itself, some see it as following a typical rabbinic form. It begins with an insidious question followed by a counter question. Then, there is the expected reply followed by a public retort that is mysterious, if not misleading, but meant to silence the questioners. Once the opponents leave, the teacher's true followers demand an explanation, and he gives it.[50] While this is the basic format of the passage, Jesus did not try to deceive or mislead the Pharisees. In fact, Jesus pointed them away from their mishandling of Deuteronomy 24 to God's intention for marriage, and he explained that Moses' permission resulted because of the hardness of their heart. His response silenced them, and they may have misled themselves (though the passage does not say they were misled at all), but nothing in Christ's answer was deceptive.

The passage begins with the Pharisees' question (v. 2). Mark portrays it as a question about the legitimacy of divorce at all, whereas Matthew puts it in terms of lawful grounds for divorce ("for any cause at all"). Because the interchange of comments (vv. 3-5) refers back to Deuteronomy 24, Mark's account presupposes the whole debate about the meaning of *'erwat dābār*. Jesus asks the Pharisees what Moses commanded, and they respond in terms of what he permitted. Jesus then offers Moses' commandment.

How does this fit with Matt 19:8 where Jesus notes that Moses permitted but did not demand anything and with Deut 24:1-4 where the only clear command seems to be about remarrying the first husband? We answer as follows: in Mark 10:4 the Pharisees first mention writing a certificate of divorce and then speak of sending away the woman (the divorce). Is it not possible that in Mark 10:5 Jesus focuses more on what the Pharisees mentioned first, the bill of divorcement? If so, this explains why Jesus talks about commands, especially when one considers Deuteronomy 24. In Deuteronomy 24 Moses assumes that divorce is happening for *'erwat dabar*. Few commentators interpret Moses as commanding *divorce*. Instead, his teaching in effect commands that a bill of divorcement be given (even though his language about the bill is not prescriptive *per se*). This explanation fits with Matt 19:8 where Jesus takes pains to say Moses *permitted* (not commanded) divorce. He says nothing about a bill of divorcement (19:8), despite the fact that the Pharisees ask (19:7) about Moses' *command* to give a certificate *and* divorce the wife. This explanation harmonizes Mark 10 with Matthew 19 and Deuteronomy 24, for it sees Jesus as interpreting Moses as permitting divorce and commanding that when divorce occurs, a bill of divorce must be given to the divorced wife.

In Mark 10:6-8 Jesus next invokes the creation ordinances (Gen 1:27; 2:24) and commands (v. 9) that no man separate those whom God has joined together. This is Jesus' ultimate response to the Pharisees' question about whether it is lawful for a man to divorce his wife. Jesus' answer as recorded in Mark 10 is, "No; your line of questioning misses the whole point of God's creating man and woman and instituting marriage. You are asking if it is allowable to get out of marriage. God wanted marriage to be permanent, and I command that it be so."

The disciples were troubled by what they heard and later questioned Christ about it. Jesus' answer in private undoubtedly troubled them as much as had his public remarks to the Pharisees. Jesus said (Mark 10:11) that by divorcing and remarrying, a man commits adultery. The same rules apply when a woman does the same thing (v. 12). Some think the divorce is adultery, but Wenham correctly responds that Jesus says adultery is committed by the person who both divorces *and* remarries.[51] Divorce alone may involve adultery (though Heth and Wenham think not), but that is not the point of Jesus' remarks as recorded in Mark 10:11-12.

From Jesus' reply to the disciples, several things become clear that were not in the OT. As we argued in discussing Deuteronomy 24, by divorcing a woman for *'erwat dabar*, a man forces her into a position of defilement if she remarries (she winds up committing adultery). In Mark 10 that point becomes explicit. Moreover, Deuteronomy did not make explicit, but Jesus does, that the man who divorces his wife and himself remarries also commits adultery. If *'erwat dabar* does not break a marital bond and is improper grounds for divorce and remarriage, both the husband and wife who divorce and remarry under such conditions become defiled by committing adultery. This does not abolish the teaching of Deuteronomy 24. It merely makes explicit what is implicit there.

Second, Jesus teaches equality of the sexes on this issue. Traditional Jewish thinking allowed a husband to divorce his wife, but gave a wife no such right. Thus, the question of whether a wife would commit adultery by divorcing her husband and remarrying was not an issue. Nor could a woman "force" her husband to become an adulterer by groundlessly divorcing and forcing him into remarriage. However, in Greco-Roman culture women had the right to initiate divorce proceedings, even if they did so infrequently. Thus, Jesus' comments about a woman divorcing a husband would be relevant to Gentiles, and many think that is why Mark, writing basically to Gentiles, included this saying, whereas Matthew did not, given his Jewish audience. At any rate, Jesus' purpose is not to grant permission for women to divorce and remarry. His point is that if they do so groundlessly, they are just as guilty as the man who does the same. There is sexual equality on this matter.

A final point on Mark's account is in order. As Mark presents the story, Jesus encourages neither divorce nor remarriage. While verses 11-12 do not say "since this is adultery, I command you not to do it," since adultery is sin, it is safe to say that verses 11-12 were meant to prohibit divorce and remarriage. In effect, Jesus' comment in verse 9 already prohibited divorce even before he uttered the teaching of verses 11-12. Are there any exceptions to these rules? While exceptions to universal rules are possible (they apply only in the exceptional cases), no such exceptions appear in Mark.[52]

CHAPTER TWELVE

Divorce and Remarriage (II)

Luke 16:18

In comparison with Mark 10, this passage appears much simpler. Luke records nothing of the discussion with the Pharisees about grounds for divorce. Luke 16:18a omits the phrase "against her" but otherwise reiterates Mark 10:11a. For a man to divorce and remarry is to commit adultery. This highlights the Jewish concern over a man's rights. Luke omits the comment about a woman who divorces and remarries. What differs from Mark is Luke 16:18b, though Matt 5:32b says the same thing. The meaning of 16:18b is not hard to discern, but how 16:18 fits the context of Luke 16 is another matter.

As to 16:18b, Jesus says that whoever marries a divorced woman commits adultery. It is not just the first husband who divorces and remarries who commits adultery. Nor is it only the divorced woman who commits adultery by remarriage (Matt 5:32a—"makes her commit adultery"). A second husband of a divorced woman also becomes an adulterer by marrying her. Jesus never says whether this second husband was previously married and divorced. His only point is that the man commits adultery by marrying the divorced woman.

As to how this fits the context, that is more difficult. Chapter 16 begins with Jesus' teaching of the parable of the unrighteous steward. The unrighteous steward was caught squandering his master's possessions. Knowing he would be fired, he tried to prepare for "unemployment" by offering his master's debtors a cut rate. He reasoned that once he was dismissed, these debtors would care for him. Clearly, he cared nothing about his master. His own welfare was his only concern, and he was willing to do something wrong in order to ensure future position and wealth. He served position and money, though he tried to appear to serve his master. Jesus ends the parable by saying that one will either serve money or his master. In verse 13 Jesus applies the point by saying one cannot serve both God (the master) and money. Luke says (v. 14) that the Pharisees heard Jesus' teaching and scoffed, for they loved money. They supposedly served the master (God) by ostensibly keeping his law, but in reality their concern was their position in society.[1]

In verse 15 Jesus begins to address the Pharisees directly. After his teaching on divorce (v. 18), he tells the story of the rich man and Lazarus (this occupies the rest of the chapter). As chapter 17 begins, Jesus turns back to teaching his disciples. So, however verse 18 is understood, it must fit the context of Jesus' rebuke of the Pharisees. Jesus begins his explicit rebuke (v. 15) by noting that though the Pharisees justify themselves in men's eyes, God knows their hearts. What men think honorable, God hates. The story of the rich man and Lazarus (vv. 19-31) vividly illustrates this point and its converse. What man esteems (the rich man), God detests, and what men detest (the poor man, Lazarus), God esteems. The overall context for this teaching on divorce (v. 18) is, then, a rebuke of the Pharisees. They claimed to be righteous and to follow the law, but they were detestable in God's sight, because, like the unjust steward, they cared for position and possessions, not their master.

In verses 16-17 Jesus speaks of the law and prophets and of the imperishable nature of the law. Then, he comments about divorce and remarriage (v. 18). Commentators disagree about whether verses 14-18 form a related unit or represent separate scattered sayings.[2] We think the whole chapter forms a unit and that verses 16-31 illustrate Jesus' point that the Pharisees appear to serve their master but really only worry about themselves. In verses 16-18 specifically, Jesus offers two examples of the Pharisees' lack of concern for their master. They have generally ignored instructions on how to please God and be a member of his kingdom (vv. 16-17), and they have disregarded his law in the matter of divorce and remarriage (v. 18).

As to verses 16-17, one might think Jesus means that OT teaching was in force until the time of John, but that John's (and/or Jesus') message abrogates it. However, that would contradict verse 17. Instead, Jesus makes the historical point that with the appearance of John, both John and Jesus were preaching the gospel of the kingdom. The gospel neither abolishes nor contradicts the OT, for Christ fulfills OT promises. However, both the law and the prophets and John (as well as Jesus) demanded a change of heart in order to enter the kingdom ("Repent, for the kingdom of heaven is at hand," preached John). Rather than follow this teaching on how to get into the kingdom, Jesus says "everyone is forcing his way into it" (v. 16). How? Just as the Pharisees tried to do—not by a repentant heart, but by justifying themselves in the sight of men (v.

15). Rather than being good stewards of the law by obeying the command for an inward change of heart, they perverted the law for their own use in an attempt to "prove" their own righteousness. Despite their efforts to certify their purity, God was not fooled (v. 15).

The Pharisees also perverted OT teaching on divorce, and Jesus turns to that in verse 16. We have already seen how Deut 24:1-4 was twisted to justify divorce while ignoring the point of the creation ordinances. This is wicked stewardship of their master's teaching. They also remained silent in the midst of the Herod Antipas/Herodias affair so as not to upset the authorities. Herod and Herodias lusted after one another, but were married to other spouses (in fact, Herodias' husband was Herod's brother). Their solution was to divorce their mates so they could marry one another. John, as a good steward of his master's law, spoke against this and was beheaded. The mention of his name (v. 16) was probably meant to invoke the recent Herod/Herodias issue and thereby set the stage for Jesus' comments on divorce in verse 18.

Jesus stated God's basic outlook on divorce and remarriage, but did not include the exception clause. For Jesus to do so would unduly complicate the point of his attack on the Pharisees on this occasion. The implications of verse 18 for the Pharisees' stewardship of the law are clear. If the exception had been included, they might have retorted, "We *have* been good stewards of the law on divorce. We are following Moses when we allow divorce and remarriage. Even you understand Moses as we do, for you also allow exceptions to the general rule of no divorce." Jesus short circuited any such possible self-justification by excluding the exception.

The story of the rich man and Lazarus (vv. 19-31) vividly illustrates Jesus' point that those concerned for wealth and position rather than God ultimately lose. Verses 29-31 are Jesus' final sarcastic rebuke of the Pharisees. The rich man asks that Lazarus be sent to warn the rich man's brothers. Abraham replies that they have Moses and the prophets. They should listen to them. Of course, Jesus' point in chapter 16 is that the Pharisees have not listened to Moses and the prophets; they have perverted them (v. 29 is subtle sarcasm against the Pharisees). Lazarus then pleads for someone from the dead to be sent to warn his brothers so they will believe. The crushing blow comes in verse 31. If they ignore Moses and the prophets (which the Pharisees have done), they would not be persuaded if someone rose from the dead (which Jesus would do, and the Pharisees would still refuse to believe).

Understood in this light, chapter 16 hangs together very well, and the role of verse 18 is clear. Jesus' exclusion of the exception clause also makes sense. To include it would only deflect Jesus' listeners and Luke's readers from the point that anyone who tries to feather his own nest, rather than remain true to his master is detestable in God's eyes.

Matthew 19:3–12

Here the discussion is framed by the Pharisees' question (v. 3) which refers to Deuteronomy 24. We believe Jesus answered the Pharisees' question, so whatever Matt 19:3ff. means should fit with Moses' teaching.

At the outset, we must reject the view of some that Jesus never uttered the exception—that instead it is Matthew's or someone else's editorial insertion.[3] This is one way to harmonize this passage with Mark and Luke. Others see it as Matthew's insertion, for that removes the apparent contradiction between verse 6 (the prohibition of divorce) and verse 9 (a ground for divorce). Though we shall address these matters shortly, our basic problem with the idea that Jesus never uttered the exception is that it undermines the inerrancy of Scripture. Matthew claims Jesus spoke the exception. As argued elsewhere,[4] Matthew need not quote Jesus *verbatim* in order to uphold inerrancy, but Jesus must have uttered the sense of this exception. Moreover, as we shall show, proper understanding of the clause removes the need to harmonize it artificially by attributing it to Matthew.

Matthew, like Mark, begins with the Pharisees' question, "Is it lawful for a man to divorce his wife?" Matthew adds "for any cause at all," and that puts the issue directly into the context of the Hillel/Shammai debate over the meaning of *'erwat dābār* (Deut 24:1). Undoubtedly, the Pharisees tried to trap Jesus. If he sided with the Shammai, he would demand a harder rule than was practiced in his day. That would likely enrage the "libertarians" of the day. On the other hand, if he sided with the Hillel, Shammaites would complain that he rejected the stricter understanding of the Mosaic Law and was a libertarian himself. Either way Christ would apparently lose. Instead, Jesus rejected the categories of their debate. He refused to see OT teaching as a way to sanction escape from a marriage. He posed a question the answer to which invoked creation ordinances and God's original design for marriage. After appealing to creation ordinances (vv. 4-6a), Jesus demanded that marriages not be severed (v. 6b).

The Pharisees took the offensive again (v. 7) by asking why, if Jesus was right about no divorce, Moses gave the command to give a bill of divorce and divorce one's wife. Apparently Christ had contradicted Moses. In fact, it sounded like he had made Moses (Genesis 2—no divorce) contradict Moses (Deut 24:1-4—give a bill of divorce). Few note that Jesus responded in terms of Moses' *permission*, not *command*,[5] but the term "permission" is very important, for permission is not a command. Speaking of permission allowed Jesus to avoid contradicting Moses and making Moses contradict himself. God ordained permanence in marriage, and Christ commanded it (v. 6). Moses *permitted* divorce because the hearts of his people were stubborn (v. 8). However, Jesus never said Moses *commanded* divorce, nor did Christ command it. Even verse 9, regardless of what the exception clause means, does not *demand* divorce. As argued when we discussed Mark 10, Mosaic "permission" (not command) to divorce fits precisely the language of Deuteronomy 24, the passage invoked by the Pharisees' question (v. 7).

In verse 9 Matthew records Jesus' further teaching on divorce and remarriage. The basic teaching (minus the exception clause) makes explicit what was implicit in Deut 24:1-4 about committing adultery by remarriage after divorce. Unfortunately, the exception clause raises abundant problems. We agree with others that whatever the exception clause means here, it means the same in Matt 5:32.

In order to make progress, we must evaluate each understanding of the exception clause in light of the data of the text. Here is the key issue: does the phrase "except for *porneia*" 1) modify *only* the thought of the phrase "whoever divorces his wife," or does it 2) qualify (i.e., grant an exception to) the entire idea that "whoever divorces and marries commits adultery"? If 2) is correct, the exception clause is really shorthand for a complete sentence. Matt 19:9 is equivalent to: a) "whoever divorces his wife and marries another commits adultery;" and b) "whoever divorces his wife for *porneia* and marries another does not commit adultery."[6] Which understanding is correct—1) or 2)? Regardless of which is correct, the sentence could be written as is. The best way to discover what is meant is to see how each suggestion fits the context. Most no divorce positions and Heth and Wenham's divorce but no remarriage view understand the exception clauses as position 1) does. Divorce and remarriage positions hold view 2). First, we turn to the no divorce positions.

Inclusivist View

This view reads Matt 19:9a as: "whoever divorces his wife for any reason, even including *porneia*, and remarries, commits adultery." The basic problem with this view is grammatical. The Greek for the exception clause in Matt 19:9 is *mē epi porneia*. Grammarians note that when *epi* has an inclusivist or additive force (as it must in the inclusivist view), *epi* is not preceded by the word *mē*. *Mē* is a strong form of negation, not inclusion.[7] Thus, Jesus speaks of a genuine exception to the rule, not an addition or clarification of what is included in the rule.

Preteritive or No Comment View

According to this view, the Pharisees asked about the meaning of *'erwat dābār* (19:3). In verses 4-8 Jesus does not directly answer their question, but in verse 9 he speaks of *porneia*, which this view sees as a reference to *'erwat dābār* in Deut 24:1.[8] However, he refuses to comment on it. He talks about divorce and remarriage generally, but chooses not to comment on cases involving *porneia* (i.e., *'erwat dābār*).

Several objections are in order. On the basis of our understanding of

Deut 24:1 and the meaning of *porneia*, we conclude that *porneia* and *'erwat dabar* are not equivalent. Thus, the preteritive view is in trouble. As noted, some understand *porneia* as a reference to marriage to pagan idolaters, but most think it is refers to serious sexual sin. The major views on its meaning are: 1) illicit sexual relations during the betrothal period; 2) incestuous marriages; 3) adultery; 4) various forms of sexual impropriety including adultery, homosexuality and bestiality. We think it important to note that if *porneia* in Matt 5:32 and 19:9 refers either to sexual sin or to marriage to pagan idolaters, it does not refer to what we have argued is the best understanding of *'erwat dabar* in Deut 24:1. Thus, if the exception clause in Matt 19:9 is Jesus' way of refusing to comment on *porneia*, it cannot be seen as an unwillingness to comment on Deut 24:1 and *'erwat dabar*, since *porneia* should not be identified with *'erwat dabar*.

The same point can be made in a different way. If *porneia* is equivalent to *'erwat dabar*, we might expect the Septuagint (the Greek translation of the OT) of Deut 24:1 to render *'erwat dabar* as *porneia*, but it does not. *'erwat dabar* in Deut 24:1 is rendered in the Septuagint as *aschēmon pragma* ("something unseemly"). While this is not absolute proof that *porneia* in Matt 19:9 cannot possibly refer to *'erwat dabar*, it cannot be ignored either. If the Septuagint had used *porneia*, that would have helped tie together *porneia* and *'erwat dabar*.

Second, there are grammatical problems. Proponents of the preteritive view think that in the exception clause *mē* is a simple negative that nullifies *epi*. Thus, *mē* functions as it does in Matt 26:5 ("not during the festival," i.e., excluding the time of the festival). However, as Heth and Wenham note, *mē* by itself does not mean "except." Moreover, in 19:9 Matthew writes *hos an . . . mē*, not just *mē*. That means Matt 19:9 contains the conditional notion, "if someone . . . not," or "if someone . . . unless" (*ean mē* in Greek). Matt 26:5 contains only *mē*, not *ean mē*, and is not a conditional statement.[9] Matt 19:9 and 26:5 do not contain parallel constructions. The result of this grammatical point is that Jesus states a genuine exception to his rule about divorce and remarriage. He does not say, as the preteritive view claims, that he will comment on a variety of things but not on *porneia*.

Finally, the view is problematic because Jesus does comment on Moses' teaching and answers the Pharisees, even if indirectly. His first comment (vv. 4-6) in effect informs them that their emphasis on *'erwat dabar* mistakes the OT's fundamental perspective on marriage. Christ's second comment (v. 8) is that they have turned a permission into a prescription. Permission was granted for a particular reason, but God's original intentions included no permission for divorce ("from the beginning it was not so"). Verse 9 contains Christ's third comment. If *porneia* is some sort of sexual impropriety, as we shall argue shortly, and if *'erwat dabar* is some non-sexual problem, as we have argued, then verse 9 definitely answers their questions about Deut 24:1. The Pharisees ask (v. 3) if a man is allowed to divorce his wife for any cause at all. Jesus replies that if one does it for some non-sexual reason and then remarries, he commits adultery. Both Jesus and the Pharisees knew the Mosaic Law's penalty for adultery. By saying that groundless divorce (as would be the case if one divorced for *'erwat dābār*) and remarriage involves adultery, in effect Jesus was saying a man is not permitted to divorce his wife for just any cause at all. We doubt that the Pharisees understood him to mean anything else. We reject the preteritive view, then, because Jesus did answer the Pharisees' questions about Deuteronomy 24 and *'erwat dābār*. His only refusal to respond was a refusal to accept the Pharisees' incorrect general outlook on marriage and divorce.

Clarification of the Offense View

This position is built on Matt 5:32's exception clause, but it can be handled now since the exception clauses in both Matthew 5 and 19 make the same point. According to this view, the exception clause makes the point that the woman divorced for adultery cannot be *made* an adulteress by the divorce, because she already *is* an adulteress. That is why her husband divorced her. However, the problem is that this makes sense in Matt 5:32, but not in 19:9 where Jesus comments about the one who divorces (he commits adultery), not about the one divorced ("makes her commit adultery"). Since the exception clause in both passages means the same thing, one's interpretation of it should fit both passages. On this view, that is not the case.

In addition, on this view the exception clause in 5:32 becomes almost a meaningless tautology ("you cannot be made an adulteress if you already are one"). Why would Jesus make that point? If he were debating the Pharisees, it might make a neat debater's point, resting as it does on a point of logic. But Matthew 5 is part of the Sermon on the Mount spoken to the disciples, not a debate with the Pharisees. When Jesus does interact with the Pharisees (Matthew 19), he makes no such point. We conclude that this view is also untenable.

Mixed Marriages View

Nothing in Matthew 19 suggests that Jesus refers to the mixed marriage situation in Ezra's day. On the contrary, the discussion focuses on issues raised in Deuteronomy 24, and nothing in Deut 24:1-4 raises the matter of intermarrying with heathens. Many proponents of this view see this point and insist that the exception clause is Matthew's insertion to cover a problem prevalent in the days of the early church. However, nothing in Matthew 19 suggests Matthew addresses that situation either. In addition, this form of the mixed marriages view has the added disadvantage of undermining inerrancy. We conclude that this view has insurmountable problems.

Betrothal and Incest Views

Both of these views depend on a very narrow meaning of *porneia*, so we must ask what it actually means. We doubt that the word refers only to adultery. The more usual word for adultery is *moicheia*, and in 15:19 Matthew distinguishes *porneia* from *moicheia*. In fact, in Matthew *porneia* only occurs three times (5:32; 15:19; and 19:9). Two of the three are the cases in question, and the third (15:19) clearly distinguishes *moicheia* from *porneia*. Moreover, *porneuō* (the verb) never appears in Matthew, but *moichaō* (5:32; 19:9) and *moicheuō* (5:27, 28; 19:18) do occur and clearly refer to adultery. Matthean usage focuses on *moicheia* and its verbal forms for adultery, not *porneia* and *porneuō*.

Does *porneia*, then, mean only sex within the betrothal period or incest? As to the former view, some claim that premarital sex while engaged is the most usual meaning of *porneia*. In addition, the law had a specific punishment for an unfaithful betrothed wife (Deut 22:20-21).[10] Nonetheless, several items militate against this view. For example, even if premarital sex is the most common meaning of *porneia*, it is not the only possible meaning. In addition to Matthean uses, the word also appears in Mark 7:21; John 8:41; Acts 15:20, 29; 21:25; Rom 1:29; 1 Cor 5:1; 6:13, 18; 7:2; 2 Cor 12:21; Gal 5:19; Eph 5:3; Col 3:5; 1 Thess 4:3; Rev 2:21; 9:21; 14:8; 17:2, 4; 18:3, 9. It is dubious that all of these (especially all of the Corinthians, Acts and Revelation references) refer to premarital sex, and even more disputable that they all refer to premarital sex during an engagement period. Neither biblical use generally nor Matthean use in particular suggest that premarital sex is the only or even the most natural meaning for *porneia*.

Second, appeal to Deuteronomy 22 about premarital sex during the betrothal period actually seals the case against this meaning in Matthew 19. In Matthew 19, Deuteronomy 24 is under discussion, but Deuteronomy 24 does not address sex during the betrothal period. Nor need it do so, since that topic was already addressed two chapters earlier in Deuteronomy 22.

Finally, nothing in Matthew 19 suggests that Jesus speaks of sex during the betrothal period. When that is the topic, Matthew is quite capable of making it clear (cf. Matt 1:18). He could have done the same in Matthew 19 but did not. We conclude that the exception clause does not relate to illicit sex during the betrothal period.

Is *porneia* incest? That seems to be the meaning in 1 Cor 5:1, and many think it is the meaning in Acts 15:29 (cf. also Acts 21:25). In addition, some claim there is evidence from first-century Palestine (the Damascus Document from Qumran) that *porneia* means incest.[11] All of this evidence shows that *porneia* was commonly understood as incest in the time of Jesus and Matthew.[12]

Several responses are in order. As to Qumran and biblical usage generally, suffice it to say that cases where *porneia* means incest show that it *can* mean incest in Matt 19:9, but they do not prove it does. NT usage of *porneia* shows that it sometimes has other meanings. Thus, while *porneia* can mean incest, it can have a broader meaning. A decision about its meaning in Matt 19:9 must be made on the context of Matthew 19, not solely on the possible meanings for *porneia*, since there are various possibilities. In Matthew 19 itself, there is no explicit reference to incest. If one argues that *porneia* must refer to something in Jewish law, then why single out this item from the Holiness Code in Leviticus 18? That code mentions a series of sins. Why choose this one alone? If the answer is that biblical usage favors incest, we reply that it is not clear that incest is the predominant biblical meaning for *porneia*, and we note that the objection returns us to a discussion of possible meanings, not the specific meaning of *porneia* in Matthew 19.[13]

How, then, should one understand *porneia* in Matthew 19? Because it is not equivalent to *'erwat dābār*, and because nothing in Matthew 19 helps us identify some specific sexual sin, we think it best to understand *porneia in 19:9* as a general term referring to sexual impurities of various kinds. Could that include incest, adultery, homosexuality, bestiality and the like? We think so, and also hold that many NT uses of *porneia* use it in this general sense (cf. especially Pauline usage).[14]

The net result seems to be that the no divorce positions about the betrothal period and incest are unlikely on the grounds presented. In addition, as noted when discussing the inclusivist view, the language of the exception clause really does demand that Jesus is offering an exception to his general rule. These no divorce positions entail that there are no exceptions and are problematic in that respect as well.

Heth and Wenham's View

If the no divorce positions are unacceptable on the grounds presented, does a divorce and no remarriage view (Heth and Wenham's view) fare any better? Three fundamental arguments are used to support this view: 1) the historical argument; 2) the argument from the indissolubility of the marriage bond; and 3) the position of the exception clause in the protasis (the "if clause" of the sentence).

As to the historical argument, we do not quibble about whether this view was held by most of the early church fathers. However, their holding it does not make it right, especially if there is evidence against it. An initial problem is understanding the word for divorce in verse 9 (*apoluō*) to mean "separate without divorcing." The exact same word is used for divorce in verses 3, 7, and 8. Since those verses discuss Deuteronomy 24, and we know that passage speaks of divorce and remarriage, not just sep-aration, we doubt that *apoluō* in verses 3, 7, and 8 refers merely to sepa-ration and not full divorce. If that is so, it is quite unlikely that Jesus uses the same word in the next verse (v. 9) in a different sense—mere separa-tion. To think *apoluō* means separation in verse 9 requires clear contex-tual grounds, but they seem lacking.[15] Holding it because early church fathers did will not verify it.

As to the indissolubility matter, we have already shown the problems with Heth and Wenham's argument supporting the idea. Moreover, ear-lier we showed that it is possible to break the marriage bond. We are now considering whether in Matthew 19 Jesus gives a ground for doing so, but there seems little question that it is possible to break the bond.

The major support for Heth and Wenham's view is the position of the exception clause. According to Heth and Wenham, Matthew could have placed the exception clause in any of three positions in the sentence to try to convey Jesus' saying on divorce and remarriage. It could come after "whoever" and before "divorces" ("whoever, except for *porneia*, divorces his wife and marries another, commits adultery"). Heth and Wenham claim that this would make the sentence mean "whoever does not put away his wife for unchastity and does not marry another, commits adul-tery."[16] Of course, then divorce and remarriage would be mandatory if one's wife committed *porneia*. It is highly doubtful that Jesus says this, especially since it would *demand* not only divorce but remarriage when a wife commits *porneia*.

Second, Matthew could have placed the exception after "marries another" and before "commits adultery" ("whoever divorces his wife and marries another, except for *porneia*, commits adultery"). With this word order, Jesus says someone commits adultery if he divorces and remarries, unless he does so because of *porneia*. Heth and Wenham reject this word order, because they think it comes close to demanding the Erasmian view, which they reject.[17] In point of fact, this word order does not demand the Erasmian view, for written in this way the sentence could be taken to mean that *porneia* is the actual reason for *remarrying*. That is certainly not the Erasmian view.

The third possibility is the position Matthew gave the clause ("whoever divorces his wife, except for *porneia*, and marries another, commits adul-tery"). Heth and Wenham interpret this to mean that "whoever puts away his wife, if it is not for unchastity that he puts her away, and marries another, commits adultery." This means that divorce, except in cases of unchastity, is wrong, and remarriage after any divorce involves one in adultery.[18] This reading is Heth and Wenham's view.

Admittedly, the sentence would be ambiguous regardless of word order, and the word order Matthew chose does fit Heth and Wenham's view. However, the word order also fits other views. Heth and Wenham have concluded too much from Matthew's placement of the exception clause. They argue that the position of the exception clause makes it qualify only the first verb ("divorces") in the protasis (the "if" clause), but they overlook two very important facts. First, the apodosis (the "then" clause), "commits adultery," qualifies the whole "if" clause. Their interpretation seems to relate "commits adultery" only to the phrase "marries another." Second, they note that the "if" clause is compound ("divorces and remarries"), but they do not take that seriously enough. To say that Jesus sometimes allows divorce but never remarriage because it involves one in adultery is to ignore that "commits adultery" completes the thought of the whole "if" clause. That is, adultery results from *both* divorcing *and* remarrying, not just from one or the other. This seems the only way to take seriously the compound "if" clause and the fact that the "then" clause qualifies the whole "if" clause. Those facts of grammar fatally damage the Heth and Wenham proposal.

How does the exception clause relate to this? It grants an exception to the general rule that whoever divorces *and* remarries commits adultery. Granted, the exception clause follows only the word "divorces," but if it followed the word "remarries," it might give the impression that the way to avoid committing adultery when one divorces and remarries is to be sure that the reason for the remarriage is to commit *porneia* by remarrying ("whoever divorces and remarries, except when he remarries for the purpose of committing *porneia*, commits adultery"). Obviously, that is nonsensical, and it is good that Matthew avoided that potential misunderstanding by placing the exception clause elsewhere. It seems that the best way for Matthew and Jesus to make the exception a clear exception to the whole rule contained in the "if" and "then" clauses was to place the exception clause exactly where it is. As our discussion in the immediately preceding paragraph shows, however, the real issue of debate with Heth and Wenham is whether "commits adultery" relates to divorcing and remarrying (the whole "if" clause), or whether it applies only to cases of remarriage. Since Heth and Wenham lose that debate ("commits adultery" qualifies the whole "if" clause with or without the exception clause), we conclude that their view is untenable.

Luck's View

Luck's view is a divorce and remarriage position. We have noted problems with his understanding of Deuteronomy 24, and will shortly address the most problematic part of his position, his handling of Matthew 5.[19] As to Matthew 19, Luck agrees that the exception clause grants a legitimate ground for divorce. We agree that 19:9 teaches that groundless divorce and remarriage involve adultery; properly grounded divorce and remarriage do not. We also concur that Jesus makes this point about the divorc*er*. We *disagree* when Luck offers the implications of this verse for remarriage of the person divorced groundlessly ("treacherously," to use his term). Though the passage does not address this issue, Luck thinks remarriage for the *innocent* person divorced groundlessly is permissible. We disagree. Luck thinks the *woman* groundlessly divorced ("innocent party") is free to remarry, because he thinks the woman of Deut 24:1-4 incurs no moral stigma and can remarry. As we have seen, that interpretation is wrong. Moreover, we think Luke 16:18b ("he who marries one who is divorced from a husband commits adultery") also implicitly rules out remarriage for this woman. If a man commits adultery by marrying a woman groundlessly divorced (Luke 16:18b), is she not also guilty of adultery by that marriage? What could make her second husband an adulterer by marrying her other than the fact that she is still bound (in God's eyes) to her first husband (who divorced her groundlessly)? But if she is still bound to her first husband, marrying a second husband is adultery *for her too*, not just for her second husband! For this reason we cannot agree that the woman divorced groundlessly is free to remarry.

Luck says that a *man* groundlessly divorced ("innocent party") could always remarry, because polygamy is morally acceptable. We strongly disagree. We shall handle polygamy momentarily, but for now note that if a groundlessly divorced woman commits adultery by remarrying (the point inferred from Luke 16:18b), why would the same rule not apply to a groundlessly divorced husband who remarries? The only possible way this rule would not apply is if polygamy is acceptable, and we deny that it is. We conclude that neither the groundlessly divorced woman nor the groundlessly divorced man may remarry without moral censure.

Luck also considers whether the guilty party may remarry. If the man is guilty of groundlessly divorcing his wife, Luck believes he can remarry, since the Bible allows polygamy. On the other hand, what is outlawed as adultery is divorcing groundlessly just to get to the next wife. Remarriages that are not the goal of the divorce may be permissible (because polygamy is all right), but when one divorces with the intent of remarriage, that is unacceptable.[20] We disagree because we reject polygamy, but also because the general rule (Matt 19:9 minus the exception clause) is that whoever divorces groundlessly and remarries commits adultery, period!

As to someone guilty of *porneia*, Luck would probably say remarriage is not allowed, because the divorce was meant to discipline and drive the guilty spouse to repent and reconcile the marriage.[21] However, nowhere does Jesus or the apostles say this is the point of divorcing someone guilty of *porneia*. Moreover, if a husband divorces a wife for *porneia* and remarries another (he can do so without committing adultery, if *porneia* allows a genuine exception to the general rule in 19:9), surely the first wife should not try to break up her former husband's new marriage.

We conclude from the preceding that Luck's view inadequately handles Matt 19:9. However, before turning to the Erasmian view, we must address the issue of polygamy to refute Luck's views on Matthew 19 entirely. Space does not here permit a full-scale discussion of whether the OT sanctions polygamy, but we believe certain forms of polygamy are clearly repudiated in the NT by Jesus' teachings. That is, polygyny and polyandry that result from groundlessly divorcing one's spouse and contracting a second marriage are ruled out. Mark 10:11, Luke 16:18a, and Matt 19:9a (minus the exception clause) all say that the man who groundlessly divorces his wife and remarries commits adultery. As argued, adultery occurs because the marriage bond is still intact with the first wife. Jesus does not want people to commit adultery. If marrying a second wife while still married to a first (polygyny) involves a man in adultery, God must be displeased. That is, polygyny is outlawed! Moreover, Luke 16:18b (see the parallel saying in Matt 19:9b and 5:32b) implicitly prohibits polyandry. Anyone who marries a groundlessly divorced woman commits adultery. In God's eyes, such a woman is still married to her first husband. That means a second husband will commit adultery (Luke 16:18b), but it also means she will become polyandrous if a second man marries her. As argued already, if the second husband commits adultery by marrying her, she would also commit adultery by marrying him. Again, God does not want people to commit adultery. If marrying a second husband while still married to the first (polyandry) is adultery, polyandry must be unacceptable!

While Jesus' teaching rules out polygamy in cases where one obtains multiple wives by groundlessly divorcing and then marrying another, what about cases where one person simply marries many spouses without divorcing any of them (e.g., Solomon or David)? Is that kind of polygyny and polyandry acceptable? We think not for two fundamental reasons. First, we appeal to creation ordinances and our discussion of what constitutes marriage. It seems hard to square the language of Gen 2:24 ("forsaking," "cleaving to," "one flesh") with multiple spouses. Jesus' appeal to creation ordinances when the Pharisees asked about grounds for divorce and remarriage seems again to underscore the notion that monogamy is God's ideal. Polygamy was practiced by some, but that did not make it moral.

Second, by implication we believe Jesus' teaching in Matt 19:9, etc. rules out polygyny and polyandry. The point is this: if one divorces groundlessly and remarries, he commits adultery, since in God's eyes he is still married to the first spouse. When there is an existing bond with one spouse, one commits adultery when he tries to contract another bond with someone else. Of course, that principle is true whether one precedes the second marriage by formal divorce of the first spouse or whether one simply piles up spouses. Since we know God does not want adultery to be committed, and since accumulating multiple husbands or wives involves committing adultery with each new marriage, we conclude that monogamy alone is the morally acceptable pattern for marriage.

Erasmian View

According to this view, *porneia* is a legitimate ground for divorce (though it does not make divorce obligatory). In God's eyes *porneia* breaks the marital bond, so the one who divorces on this basis may constitute a new bond (remarry) without committing adultery against the first marriage. We hold this view, but recognize that several major objections to it must be answered.

The first objection is that if Jesus really does offer a ground for divorce in verse 9, he contradicts creation ordinances (vv.4-5) and his own demand (v. 6) not to divorce. It seems that Christ is saying, "God never wanted you to divorce (vv. 4-5), and I command you not to divorce (v. 6), but you can divorce on the ground of *porneia*" (v. 9).[22] Of course, Christ would never make such contradictory comments, so opponents of the Erasmian view conclude that the view must be wrong.

Several responses are in order. For reasons already offered, we believe the exception clause grants a genuine exemption from the no divorce rule. Moreover, we deny that Jesus contradicts himself, and we cannot believe that Matthew is such a poor thinker that he would not notice such a blatant contradiction and comment on it (or even try to remove it). These factors lead us to believe there is no contradiction and that the apparent difficulties can be explained. A way out of the dilemma begins to appear when one realizes verse 9 is not a command; it is an assessment of the sinfulness of certain actions. Had Jesus said, "I command you to divorce for *porneia*," his words would more clearly contradict verse 6. However, Jesus never *commanded* anyone to divorce for any reason. Verse 9 *allows* divorce and remarriage without moral censure when the divorce occurs because of *porneia*, but permission is not obligation. Moreover, in verse 8 Jesus is careful to say that Moses *permitted* divorce; he never says Moses demanded divorce. Thus, the exception clause does not command anything that contradicts Jesus' command in verse 6.

Having heard this explanation, one might reply that it does not remove the contradiction, because Jesus says it is morally obligatory to avoid divorce (v. 6). How can it be morally requisite to avoid divorce and then be morally permissible (v. 9) to divorce under certain circumstances? The answer stems from the way exceptions modify rules. Verse 6 gives the general rule (the *prima facie* duty), but general rules are only universally applicable if they have no exceptions. In verse 9 Jesus names the case that exempts one from the rule. Some think exceptions negate the rule, but that misunderstands the logic of exceptions to universal rules. Exceptions negate the rule *only in exceptional cases, not in all cases*. Once one understands how exceptions modify rules, the apparent contradiction between verses 6 and 9 disappears.

What we argue here is consistent with our handling of *prima facie* duties elsewhere in this book. "Thou shalt not kill" is a fundamental obligation. However, we think capital punishment, self-defense, and just wars are exceptions to that rule. None of those exceptions invalidate the duty in any cases other than the exceptional ones. Anyone who thinks capital punishment, self-defense, and just wars are legitimate exceptions to the general rule about killing, exceptions which invalidate the rule *only* in the exceptional cases, should not think the exception in Matt 19:9 negates altogether Jesus' general rule about divorce (Matt 19:6).

A second objection is that the Erasmian view necessitates two different senses for the word *apoluō* ("divorce") in verse 9. Jesus says divorce for *porneia* plus remarriage involves no adultery. But remarriage is adulterous if one divorces for reasons other than *porneia*. In the first proposition, divorce obviously dissolves the previous marriage and allows remarriage. In the second, "divorce" cannot have the same meaning, since remarriage involves adultery. It must mean simple separation. Of course, this means Jesus uses the same word in the same sentence equivocally.[23]

Actually, this objection is confused on several grounds. As argued previously, the exception clause is shorthand for a complete second sentence. Matt 19:9a really contains two sentences, one stating the general rule, and the other offering the exception. Since the two sentences refer to two different cases, there is no reason the same word cannot be used in two different senses to cover the two types of cases. In addition, this objection (raised by Heth and Wenham) is even more fundamentally flawed. The problem comes from failing to see the protasis (the "if" clause) as compound ("divorces" *and* "remarries") and from a subsequent failure to recognize that the apodosis ("commits adultery") qualifies the *whole* protasis. Those grammatical points mean that this sentence is not about the difference between a complete divorce and a mere separation. It is about the conditions under which divorce *and* remarriage involve adultery and the conditions under which they do not. Since that is the point of the verse, it is dubious that Jesus is thinking at all of divorce in the sense of separation. We conclude that the Erasmian view does not entail that Jesus equivocates in verse 9.

A third objection is that if the Erasmian view is correct, Jesus is not far from the Shammai in his views on divorce. If so, why are the disciples who hear his teaching so astonished (v. 10)? Surely, Jesus must be taking a stricter stand than the Shammai.[24] For the sake of argument, we grant that the disciples are truly astonished (especially in view of their evident perplexity as mentioned in Mark 10:10). Even so, there are several appropriate responses. Even if Jesus' position is not far from that of the Shammai, that does not mean the Shammai position was an easy one or that common practice in Jesus' day followed that rule. It was much stricter than the Hillel view, and as some note,[25] Jesus was stricter than the Shammai on who could remarry. However, our initial point is that this strict position fits very nicely with the disciples' cynical comment in 19:10. Our other point is that Jesus said something explicit which must have been rather astonishing. Jesus said that whoever divorces without grounds of *porneia* and remarries commits adultery. As we have shown, Moses talked about divorcing for *'erwat dābār* (something other than *porneia*), but he never said that to do so involved one in committing adultery. He merely said that someone who divorced for *'erwat dābār* and remarried was defiled. Jesus explicitly teaches the shocking truth that such cases involve the divorcer and the divorced in adultery. Moreover, when one adds to this astonishing truth the fact that these disciples knew that OT law said adulterers were to be executed, is it any wonder that they were astonished at Jesus' teaching? The Erasmian view leaves plenty of room for the disciples' astonishment.

A fourth objection is that the Erasmian view demands a loosening of God's ethical standards. In the OT, creation ordinances suggest permanence. Sins such as adultery and bestiality were grounds for execution, not divorce. Even when divorce and remarriage were allowed (Deuteronomy 24), Scripture says the woman was defiled. In the NT it appears that the rules are softened. Jesus allows a ground for divorce and remarriage and says the innocent party in such cases commits no sin. Is this not an easier standard than in the OT? How can God change ethical norms if they are grounded in his very person which does not change?

In response, we think something has changed, but we deny that God softened his ethical norms. The OT never commanded divorce, nor does Jesus, even when *porneia* has been committed. Moses said those divorced for *'erwat dābār* who remarry are defiled, but he did not say why. Neither did Moses say anything about the moral condition of the divorcer. Jesus says the woman groundlessly divorced is made to be an adulteress when she remarries (Matt 5:32). The divorcer in such cases also commits adultery if he remarries (Matt 19:9). The only change here from the OT is that Jesus blatantly labels as adultery the remarriage of the divorcer and the divorced. That does not loosen moral standards; it underscores the guilt and names the sin of those who divorce groundlessly and remarry. The one significant change we see is a change in the penalty for committing *porneia*. In the OT those guilty of *porneia* were to be executed (though they seldom were). Jesus does not demand that they be executed; he *allows* them to be divorced. While this is a different penalty, it is still a punishment and shows that *porneia* is not morally acceptable.[26] We conclude that nothing Jesus says softens moral rules (punishments are not moral norms; they specify penalties for breaking those rules). Nor does Jesus sanction as moral what the OT called immoral.

Finally, any view should try to explain why the exception clause appears in Matthew but not Mark, Luke, or 1 Corinthians. Opponents of the Erasmian view see this as a major problem since the Erasmian view teaches that Matthew's Gospel with the exception clause allows divorce, whereas Mark, Luke and Paul do not allow divorce on grounds of *porneia*.

Typically, no divorce positions hold that Matthew included the exception because he wrote to Jews and wanted to emphasize something from their law, whereas Mark and Luke wrote to Gentiles who would not be acquainted with Jewish law. The exception would mean little to them.[27] We think Matthew included the exception because of his Jewish audience, but we see no problem for the Erasmian view. We think Matthew's inclusion of the exception is explainable in light of the "changes" Jesus' teaching on divorce makes. Jesus makes explicit what is implicit in Deuteronomy 24. He teaches that whoever divorces for *'erwat dābār* and remarries commits adultery. Jews knew that OT law demanded the execution of adulterers. Now that Jesus reveals that those who remarry after divorce for *'erwat dābār* commit adultery, would he say they should be executed as adulterers? Jewish readers would also know the Shammai and Hillel debate over grounds for divorce and would wonder how the apparent permission and regulation of divorce (Deut 24:1-4) squared with Jesus' shocking teaching that remarrying after divorce for *'erwat dābār* involves one in adultery. Unless Matthew includes the exception clause, those questions that would undoubtedly be on the minds of Matthew's Jewish audience would be unanswered. By including the clause, Matthew made sure that those issues were addressed. Mark's and Paul's Gentile audiences would not key into these issues. Moreover, excluding the clause from Luke makes abundant sense, as we have argued, given the context of Luke 16.

By offering this explanation, we are not suggesting that the teaching of the exception clause is irrelevant to Gentiles. Ethical norms grounded in God's character apply to all people. Our only point is to attempt to explain why one writer includes the clause and the others do not. We see its inclusion in Matthew as his attempt to address issues that would be in the forefront of his readers' minds.[28]

In sum, we think the best understanding of the exception clause in Matthew 19 is that Jesus allows divorce on the ground of *porneia*. Those who divorce for that reason are allowed to remarry without committing any sin by the divorce or remarriage. Whether Jesus' teaching allows the person divorced for *porneia* to remarry, Jesus does not say here. The question is addressed, however, by what he says in Matt 5:32.

Matthew 5:31–32

This teaching of our Lord is part of the Sermon on the Mount. Verses 31-32 contain one of six antitheses (vv. 21-48) Jesus uses to correct the

Scribes' and Pharisees' misunderstanding of the Mosaic Law. Jesus first states the prevailing understanding and then adds his word of correction and/or amplification. Jesus makes a point about the commission of adultery (vv. 27-30, esp. vv. 27-28), and then he turns to the matter of divorce.

In verse 31 Jesus states the typical understanding of Deut 24:1. In verse 32 he counters that perception. Once one sees how verse 32 is antithetical to verse 31, Jesus' point in verse 32 becomes even stronger. We understand his point as follows: by following the letter of Mosaic legislation (give the wife a bill of divorcement), men think they care for the rights of the woman they divorce. They reason that with the bill of divorce she is free to remarry, so some other man will care for her. She need not beg on the streets or become a prostitute. No doubt, they conclude that their moral duties are satisfied and that they are righteous before God, even though they divorced for *'erwat dābār*. In verse 32 Jesus says otherwise. The bill of divorce does not make the husband morally blameless *when the reason for divorce is 'erwat dābār*. The husband has followed the letter of the law about a bill of divorcement and thus appears to show some concern for his wife's future. But actually, he has placed her in a horrible position. The divorce has put her in a position whereby she will commit adultery when she remarries, and in the society of that day it was unlikely that she would remain unmarried. Moreover, whoever marries her (v. 32b) will also commit adultery, despite the fact that the bill of divorcement will cause him to think that marrying her will involve no sin. The divorcing husband has really placed his wife and her future husband in a very precarious position. He is not to be congratulated for what he has done.

Understood this way, Matt 5:31-32 is a powerful indictment against those who meet the letter of the law while ignoring its underlying spirit. Moreover, the verses fit nicely the pattern of the other five antitheses. In each, Jesus begins by stating the prevailing opinion about what one must do to be righteous in the eyes of the law. Then Jesus offers his "but I say" teaching that shows a further dimension to the issue. If that further aspect of the law is not fulfilled, the individual who claims to keep the law is really evil, not righteous. Only when one obeys the whole of a law (whether the law is about adultery, divorce, anger, e.g.) will one be a member of the kingdom of heaven (v. 20).

With this understanding of the context of Matt 5:31-32, let us note a few particulars. In Matthew 19, Mark 10 and Luke 16, the emphasis is on how the divorcing person's actions affect *his own* moral condition. In Matthew 5 the emphasis is on what the divorcing husband does to the woman he divorces. Given the context already explained, one can see why Jesus would focus on that matter in Matthew 5. As to the exception clause (*parektos logou porneias*), it qualifies the general teaching, functioning as it does in Matt 19:9 as shorthand for a second sentence ("whoever divorces his wife for the cause of *porneia* does not cause her to commit adultery"). The word *parektos* means "outside of," "apart from," or "except for." It denotes something singled out from a large group—in this case an exception to a general rule. Linguistically, it is hard to see this as anything other than a genuine exception.[29]

What, then, does the passage mean? Note that in 5:32a Jesus says nothing about whether the divorcing husband remarries; he speaks merely about the effects on a wife when her husband divorces her.[30] The phrase *poiei autēn moicheuthēnai* (best translated "makes her to commit adultery")[31] explains what happens to the woman. How does he make her commit adultery by divorcing her? In that culture it was understood that a woman given a bill of divorcement (v. 31) would naturally remarry. But when a woman is divorced for *'erwat dābār*, the marriage bond with her first husband is not broken. Thus, when she marries a second husband, she commits adultery with him. Jesus' point is that the first husband is to blame for putting his wife in this untenable situation. Only if he divorces her for *porneia* does he avoid creating this situation. The situation does not arise, because it is morally permissible for the husband to divorce his wife for *porneia* (that is the force of the exception clause). The reason, we believe, is that *porneia* breaks the marriage bond, and if it is broken, divorce is permissible. Of course, if *porneia* broke the marital bond with the first spouse, remarriage will not break it again. Nor will it cause her to commit adultery against the first marriage, since that marriage was broken by the *porneia*. She is morally free to remarry. This does not excuse her *porneia*, but only notes that once *porneia* is committed, no further sin is committed by divorcing and remarrying.[32]

What happens to the first husband if he divorces without grounds of *porneia* and then remarries? Jesus addresses that issue in Matthew 19, Mark 10 and Luke 16, but not in Matthew 5. Those passages teach that whoever divorces groundlessly and then remarries also commits adultery!

Many objections to this understanding of the significance of the exception clause in Matt 5:31-32 were answered when Matthew 19 was treated. However, two other lines of objection are worthy of note. According to the first, on our interpretation, Jesus is really uttering a banality. He is saying nothing more than "he who divorces his wife, unless she is already an adulteress, now makes her liable to become an adulteress."[33] We respond that this is no banality. In fact, as argued, it makes explicit why the woman of Deuteronomy 24 is defiled by being divorced and then remarrying a second husband. Neither the reason for her defilement (she remarried after being divorced for *'erwat dābār*) nor the nature of it (she committed adultery by remarrying) seems to have been understood in Moses' day or even in the time of Christ. When the disciples heard this teaching, they were shocked (Matt 19:9-10). From our vantage point (which includes nearly two thousand years of interpreting these Gospel texts), this teaching might appear to some to be trite, but in the first century A.D., it is highly unlikely that these words were understood that way.

The second objection stems from Luck's interpretation of these verses. He says most commentators do not take seriously enough the fact that *moicheuthēnai* (the Greek for "commit adultery") is passive. They identify the form as passive but then translate it as active. To translate it as active focuses on the woman as though she is the sinner. Instead, the verse emphasizes what the divorcing husband does to his wife.

If the word is given its passive sense, how should it be translated? Luck rejects the translation "she becomes an adulteress," because it treats the verb like a noun. He also denies that the word simply means that the divorce unjustly stigmatizes the woman as an adulteress. The idea of stigmatization may be there, but only secondarily. Instead, Luck argues for "he makes her to be adulterized." Luck explains that to be adulterized is to have adultery committed against you. This clarifies that the husband is the offender. Luck grants that this amounts to what Mark 10:11 says— "whoever divorces his wife and marries another woman commits adultery against her."[34] He thinks the wording of Mark 10:11 would have made the point more easily, but sees a good reason for using the passive infinitive instead. Only with that construction, says Luck, could Matthew convey in a few words the ideas of both Mal 2:14-17 and Deut 22:19.[35] Malachi discusses those who treacherously divorce their wife just to devote themselves to another woman. Deuteronomy handles cases where a man wrongly accuses his new wife of not being a virgin on their wedding night.

In response, several problems are evident. First, though the infinitive is passive, it is usually interpreted in an active sense. What troubles us is that Luck seems to demand the passive understanding neither on grounds of word usage nor contextual considerations. The passive is necessitated because it makes the verse fit Luck's general understanding of the divorce and remarriage issue. Second, if Matthew really portrays Jesus as saying what Luck claims, it is a tortuously difficult way to make the point. Why not record what Mark does in 10:11? It is much less ambiguously stated, and Luck admits that. He also admits he holds his view because of Malachi 2 and Deut 22:19. However, there is no contextual evidence in Matthew 5 that Jesus is correcting anyone's understanding of those passages. Instead, Jesus' words (v. 32) are antithetical to the common understanding (mentioned in v. 31) of Deut 24:1, and Deut 24:1-4 does not cover the issue of Deut 22:19. Likewise, it is dubious that Malachi 2 relates to Deuteronomy 24.[36] Finally, Luck's interpretation does not meet the demands of the immediate context in Matthew 5. Luck rightly notes that Jesus emphasizes what the man does to the woman he divorces. However, Luck's view does not take seriously enough Jesus' point in citing the traditional understanding of Deut 24:1. We have already explained how Jesus' point in verse 32 is a powerful indictment of the man who thinks he is righteous because he has met the letter of the law by giving his wife a bill of divorcement. This action really puts her in a position of moral jeopardy. All of this is lost on Luck's understanding of the passage. Nothing is said about how verse 32 is antithetical to verse 31. Jesus merely says the man has done his wife wrong by committing adultery against her. Since we think there is much more to the passage than this, we conclude that Luck's interpretation does not do justice to the whole force of this passage.

1 Corinthians 7:1–24

The heart of this passage in regard to divorce and remarriage is verses 10-15. In verses 1-7 Paul speaks about sex relations among married couples. Verses 8-9 contain his advice to the unmarried and widows. Then he presents the Lord's teaching on whether marriage should be terminated by divorce (vv. 10-11). In verses 12-15 he offers his own teaching about divorce in cases where a believer and unbeliever are married.

Several questions arise in regard to this passage. First, is Paul speaking of genuine divorce in verses 10-15 or only about separation without divorce? Second, does Paul offer another morally acceptable basis for divorce, and if so, to whom is that option given? Finally, if a ground for divorce is taught, is permission to remarry included?

As to the first question, some think Paul speaks of separation, not divorce. They conclude this in part from a distinction between the Greek words *aphiēmi* and *chōrizomai*. The former means "divorce;" the latter means "separate." The former appears in verses 11, 12 and 13, whereas the latter is in verses 10, 11, and 15.[37] Some even suggest that *chōrizomai* relates to the woman, since under Jewish law women had no right to divorce. We disagree. Paul writes to Corinth, and in the Greco-Roman world women had the right to initiate divorce proceedings. Moreover, in verse 10 Paul says that his teaching is from the Lord and that wives should not divorce husbands. This must refer to the teaching we have seen in the Gospels. However, in Matt 19:6 and Mark 10:9 when Jesus prohibits divorce ("whom God has joined together, let no man put asunder"), the word for "put asunder" (divorce) is again *chōrizō*, not *aphiēmi*. All of this suggests that Paul is thinking of divorce, not separation, when he uses *chōrizō* in 1 Corinthians 7. Third, both *chōrizō* and *aphiēmi* appear in verse 11. Even though *chōrizō* is used of the woman, the verse tells her in the circumstances envisioned to remain *unmarried* or to reconcile. How could remaining unmarried be an option if she had not divorced (*chōrizō*)? Considerations such as these cause us to conclude that Paul speaks of divorce, not mere separation.

Is Paul, then, offering another ground for divorce? Verses 10-11 offer none, nor do verses 12-14. In verses 17-24 Paul instructs believers not to undo what happened before they accepted Christ. Paul says (vv. 12-13) that this newly found faith is not a ground for divorcing an unbelieving spouse. The advantage of staying married is seen in verses 14 and 16 (if verse 16 is taken with verse 14 instead of with verse 15). Verses 14 and 16 taken together teach the possibility of the unbelieving spouse being converted through the believing mate's testimony.

None of this permits divorce, but in verse 15 Paul addresses another situation. What if the *unbeliever* no longer wants to be married to a believer? Paul instructs the believer to let the unbeliever go. While many think the verse talks of desertion alone, we note that the same verb (*chōrizō*) is used both in verses 10-11 and 15. If it means divorce in the earlier verses, we doubt it means only departure (separation without divorce) in verse 15. Whether the idea of desertion in our modern sense is involved in *chōrizō* is moot. What is clear is that the unbeliever's actions involve divorcing the believing mate. Paul says the believer is not under bondage—presumably bondage to try to keep the marriage together at all costs—in such cases. God has called believers to peace. This seems to imply that trying to maintain the marriage in such cases would only create or continue a situation of strife. Let the unbeliever depart; God wants his people to be at peace.

Paul presents, then, a circumstance that allows a marriage to be terminated, but it is a very narrow kind of situation. Believers may not divorce unbelievers just because they are non-believers. However, if an unbeliever rejects a believer because of his faith, the believer is not to fight the divorce. In such cases, the non-believing spouse must initiate the divorce. Paul never allows believers to divorce unbelieving mates just because of their unbelief.

What about remarriage for a believer or unbeliever under the circumstance of verse 15? Even some who think Paul allows divorce in this special case think Paul prohibits remarriage.[38] However, even though Paul does not explicitly allow remarriage in such cases, he does not explicitly forbid it as he does in the case mentioned in verses 10-11. Actually, any argument about remarriage based on verse 15 is an argument from silence. On the other hand, what might one expect in this case? Suppose the unbeliever divorces the believer and then remarries. Even if the non-believer commits adultery by this remarriage, would not that act break the marriage bond with the believer and thereby release him or her to remarry as well? No one would expect the believer to attempt a reconciliation with the unbelieving spouse who remarried. Paul says the believer should let that unbeliever depart. We conclude that whenever divorce is morally acceptable, remarriage is permissible, and we think that rule covers this case.[39]

SUMMARY AND CONCLUSION

Had sin not entered our world, it is dubious that anyone would ever have grounds for divorce. Mankind would have lived in accord with the creator's original design for marriage. However, ours is a fallen world. From our study we conclude that when certain select sins are committed, divorce and remarriage are morally permissible. How can God allow divorce and remarriage once a marriage bond is constituted? As argued, it is possible to break that bond. Death breaks it. Moreover, when *porneia* occurs, it contradicts the commitment to remain faithful to ("cleave to") one's spouse and thereby breaks the bond. Likewise, in the case of 1 Cor 7:15, the non-believer's acts break the commitment to the believing spouse. If the bond is broken in God's eyes by *porneia* or the departure of the unbelieving spouse, divorce in the eyes of society with its laws governing divorce is permissible, and so is remarriage. Having said the preceding, however, we would be remiss if we did not end this discussion by emphasizing that divorce and/or remarriage are never morally obligatory. Reconciliation is the preferable response. May God grant that we shall seek ways to heal troubled marriages, not grounds for rending them asunder!

CHAPTER THIRTEEN

The Christian and War:
Christian Faith in a Nuclear Age

Mankind has always longed for peace, but more often than not has found it an elusive dream. Wars have been an important part of human history. From markings found in the caves of our earliest ancestors, it is not unreasonable to think that war is as old as human history.[1]

A BRIEF HISTORY OF CHRISTIAN ATTITUDES TOWARD WAR

Because of the frequency of armed conflict, the church from its very beginnings has been troubled by the question of war. Can one be a genuine follower of Jesus Christ, the Prince of Peace, and serve in a country's armed services? Christian thinking on this matter has developed over time. There is indisputable NT evidence that there were Christians in the Roman army. A centurion sent the elders of the Jews to Jesus to beseech him to heal his servant who was ill and about to die (Matt 8:5-13; Luke 7:1-10). Jesus healed the servant because he had not seen such faith even in Israel. A centurion who watched Jesus die said, "Surely he was the son of God" (Matt 27:54; Mark 15:39; Luke 23:47). Cornelius, a centurion in the Italian Regiment, and his household responded to the gospel as preached by Peter (Acts 10:1-48). And finally, Paul told the Philippians that his imprisonment had resulted in the salvation of some within the palace guard in Caesar's household (Phil 1:13; 4:22).

There is some disagreement about the period between the end of the NT and the end of the second century. Clouse holds that until 170 A.D. no known Christian was a Roman soldier. He adds that it would help if statements about war from this early period had been preserved, but because the Romans did not require universal conscription, there was no pressure to serve in the military, and we lack comments on that subject. Changes did occur about the end of the second century, and there is evidence of Christians in the imperial service, despite the protests of church leaders.[2]

The alternate view on this period claims that pacifism was an important view many Christians held in the early church. It was, however, not the only or even the dominant view of this time. There were Christians who served in the Roman army after the NT period. This view is based on three lines of reasoning. First, it is quite unlikely that Christians should have simply dropped out of the military. Second, information we have about this period is very limited. Clouse seems to concede this point. Third, a number of the persecutions directed against Christians in the third century were because they had become so numerous throughout the Roman army, and it was claimed that this was having a negative effect on the imperial service. Moreover, even if it could be shown there were no Christians in the Roman army, or that some or all Christians left military service, that would not settle the matter in favor of pacifism. This is so because soldiers were required to take a loyalty oath to the emperor that involved an idolatrous rite acknowledging him as God. Thus, it is entirely possible that Christians would refuse to join (or would leave) the Roman legions because they felt being in the army demanded idolatry, not because of any philosophical objection to war.[3]

About 170 A.D. there is clear evidence that Christians were in the army even though some theologians were condemning such service. The Canons of Hippolytus, a guide to church discipline written in the third century by a Roman Christian, states that a Christian soldier is not to be taught to kill, and if he is, he must refuse to do so if commanded. Tertullian and Lactantius even went so far as to condemn any military service.[4] What may seem to be a contradiction, being a soldier and not killing, is resolved by the fact that one could be in the Roman legions for a lifetime and never kill anyone, as the army performed many public services. That is, the Christian could serve in a non-combatant role.

During the fourth century a number of things happened that made Christians' service in the military acceptable. First, a number of pagans had criticized Christians for accepting the benefits of the Roman Empire without being willing to shoulder some of the responsibilities—for example, governmental and military service. Origen wrote a defense of these Christians. Initially, Origen's apology blunted complaints, but increasingly the pagan population found these Christians' position unacceptable. Second, Constantine became emperor and became a Christian. He no longer required the idolatrous oath of allegiance, so a major objection to military service was removed. Third, it appeared that the Empire was about to be overrun by destructive groups of barbarians. Christians could no longer enjoy the benefits of Roman citizenship and not shoulder some of the responsibilities. Fourth, by the end of the century, Augustine wrote that one could serve in the army and be a good Christian. He is responsible for what is called the "just war" theory.[5]

Augustine developed his theory in response to a Roman general who asked if he should lead his troops into battle or retire to a monastery. Augustine responded by bringing together the views of a number of classical thinkers such as Plato and Cicero and giving them a Christian emphasis. He argued that wars should be fought to reestablish peace and secure justice. War must be waged under a legitimate leader and be prompted by Christian love. Killing and love are not incompatible, as killing requires a bodily or external act, while loving is an inner emotion. Moreover, Augustine taught that a just war must be conducted in an upstanding way. There should be no unnecessary violence; destruction must be kept to a minimum. He also distinguished between those in government service and those in Christian service. Those in public office or the army could engage in a just war, but priests and monks were not allowed to fight.

During the early Middle Ages, pacifism and just war adherents dominated the views of the Christian community. There was no glorification of the Christian knight, and those forced to kill in war were made to do long terms of penance. However, by the eleventh century a new attitude toward war led to the Crusades. In 1095 Urban II preached a sermon at the Council of Clermont entreating his listeners to agree to an expedition under papal direction to free the Middle East from pagan control. Through explicit descriptions of how the Turks had disemboweled Christians, assaulted women, and desecrated churches, Urban sought to arouse the masses. He promised those who responded forgiveness for their sins, calling for unity in the face of such an enemy. The response was enthusiastic. Some historians claim that one of the reasons the Pope wanted the Crusades was to reduce violence in Western Europe. Knights were fighting one another. The Crusades provided opportunity to redirect their aggression against a new enemy.[6]

During the twelfth century a group called the Waldenses arose, condemning all wars and the taking of human life. However, ultimately they too were forced to defend themselves. Thus, it is not surprising that the just war theory was put in legal form by Gratian in the twelfth century and restated in scholastic form by Thomas Aquinas in the thirteenth century. Little time was spent discussing the morality of war. Aquinas has a single question on the topic in his massive theology in comparison with twenty-four on angels. He lays down three criteria for a war to be just. First, it must be declared by a legitimate authority and not some individual. Second, those attacked must be attacked for some just reason. Third, those who attack must do so with the right intention, the attainment of some good, and the avoidance of some evil.[7]

During the Renaissance and Reformation, certain factors made the relationship between Christianity and war an important topic. With the development of gunpowder and the cannon, the conduct of war changed. No longer were civilians safe behind walls or knights protected by armor. Moreover, Europe was in the process of being divided into dynastic monarchies from which the present national states would emerge. Rivalries arose between these kings, and wars followed. Whereas previous conflicts had pitted heathens against Christians, these wars were fought among Christians. Both the pacifist and just war traditions are represented during this period.

Some of the most vigorous voices raised against the new modes of warfare were those of Thomas More, Erasmus and John Colet. Erasmus is typical. He thought there was nothing more hostile to Christ's teachings than war. In his satire *In Praise of Folly*, he heaped scorn on theologians who justify participation in war from Jesus' counsel to the disciples to sell their clothes and buy swords. Whatever it meant, it did not mean to fight in wars. Moreover, he believed the church had accepted the idea of a just war along with the whole body of Roman civil law. The result was that wars not only became just but glorious. The church became the servant of the aspirations of the princes.[8]

This period also saw the birth of a number of pacifist groups. In the sixteenth century the Swiss Brethren and Mennonites practiced pacifism. The Quakers were formed by George Fox in 1668 and brought to Pennsylvania by William Penn in 1682.[9]

Defenders of the just war theory can be found as well. Luther taught that without arms, peace could not be kept. He thought that sometimes wars had to be waged to repel injustice and establish a firm peace. Wars were necessary in some cases to preserve the life and health of a people in the same way that a doctor sometimes finds it necessary to amputate a leg or arm to preserve the entire body. Such a work, Luther thought, could be a work of love.[10]

Calvin in his *Institutes of the Christian Religion* also defended the idea of a just war. He said princes by virtue of natural equity and the nature of their office have the right to be armed both to restrain the misdeeds of private individuals by judicial punishment and to defend by war the realms entrusted to their safekeeping.[11]

As with preceding periods, the modern period has had defenders of both pacifist and just war theories. The Russian novelist Leo Tolstoy and the Indian reformer Gandhi advocated pacifism, though the latter at least was not a Christian. The idea of international law binding on all nations was developed in the Hague Convention (1899), the Hague Court (1907), and the League of Nations Covenant (1920). The Kellogg-Briand Pact of 1928 attempted to obligate its sixty-three signatories to renounce war. Those who wrote on the just war side essentially refined the classical arguments for that position. The new element in the mix, however, was the view of Karl von Clausewitz (1780-1831) who defended the idea of total war.[12] He argued that the one who wages total war without regard to limitation would gain superiority over those who applied moderation to their actions. He said, "To introduce into a philosophy of war a principle of moderation would be an absurdity. War is an act of violence pushed to its utmost bounds."

APPROACHES TO THE WAR QUESTION

From the preceding, it is obvious that Christians have taken various views on the issue of war. We now turn to those views and their arguments.

PACIFISM

A pacifist is someone who is against killing and hence against war. However, there are many kinds of pacifists.

Varieties of Pacifism

There are, in fact, various forms of pacifism. Some even disagree with other forms. Therefore, it is important to identify and distinguish these various forms.

Though there is a form of pacifism that clearly does not represent a moral theory,[13] many forms do. In particular, four kinds are noteworthy. After describing those forms, we shall present arguments for and against pacifism in general. Then, because of pacifism's significance in Christian circles, we shall look more closely at two Christian pacifist positions.

Universal Pacifism

This is the view that killing or violence is *always* wrong. Universal pacifists reject violence in all relationships—personal, national and international. Killing and violence can never be justified. Albert Schweitzer, Mohandas Gandhi and Leo Tolstoy held this type of pacifism.[14]

Christian Pacifism

Christian pacifists distinguish between Christians and unbelievers. Christians are never allowed to use killing or violence, but unbelievers may justly resort to killing and violence in certain instances. A good example of one who holds this position is Herman Hoyt. He prefers to call his position nonresistance.[15]

Private Pacifism

This view is the least common and is associated with Augustine. He argued that personal violence is always wrong, but a nation may at times be justified in using force as in a just war.[16]

Antiwar Pacifism

Proponents of this position maintain that personal violence may be justified in some cases in defense of one's rights, but war is never morally justified. Individuals may defend their rights by resorting to violence, but nations are prohibited from such a course of action.[17]

Arguments for Pacifism

In this section, we shall examine arguments about pacifism in war. We shall not focus on arguments concerning personal self-defense. As we set forth the arguments, it will be clear that some relate more to one form of pacifism than another. The key question under consideration, however, is whether participation in a war, by a Christian in particular, is ever morally obligatory or permissible.

Non-biblical Arguments for Pacifism

Some defend pacifism on the basis of the *sacredness of life*. Almost anyone is awestruck when watching the birth and development of a baby or when studying living things in general. From the beauty and wonder of living things people come to believe in the sacredness of life.

From the idea of life as sacred, various forms of pacifism may be developed. In its most extreme form, the killing of any living thing is prohibited, as in the Jain religion in India. A more moderate form of pacifism derived from this principle forbids the killing of animals but allows the killing of plants. The most moderate position prohibits only the killing of human beings.[18]

A related argument appeals to the inherent *immorality of killing*. The heart of this argument is that all human beings have a right to life, and killing them denies them that right. If there is a right to life, then it will never be moral to kill people even to save a life, for it is never permissible to violate someone's right even to bring about a good. War necessarily involves killing enemy soldiers. It denies them their right to life and makes war immoral. Moreover, new and more destructive weapons, particularly those of the twentieth century, have increasingly threatened and killed civilians. This denial of their right to life also makes war immoral.[19]

A third argument is the *moral exemplar argument* drawn from Immanuel Kant. He argues that one's conduct should be such that it could serve as an example for all mankind. Pacifists such as Leo Tolstoy appeal to this Kantian notion by saying the world would be a better place if everyone were a pacifist and if there were no killing.[20]

A fourth argument comes from Gandhi's (1869-1948) thought. Gandhi, one of the leading twentieth century advocates of nonviolence, contended that violence is morally wrong because of its effect on the *condition of the soul*.[21] Man as an animal is violent, but his spirit is nonviolent. Thus, to use violence even in the service of good is to act in accord with our animal nature and pollute our soul. On the other hand, nonviolent acts (for Gandhi, nonviolence is not a passive posture but an active one) and even suffering in the cause of justice purify the soul from the contamination of man's animal nature. Thus, violence, including war, pollutes the soul and is ruled out, but nonviolent protest of injustice purifies the soul and is acceptable.

Scriptural Arguments for Pacifism

Christian pacifists believe an important argument for their position is found in the *ethical teachings of Jesus*. Though the Bible in its entirety is God's word, it is not a flat book. Divine revelation finds its culmination in Jesus Christ in the NT. This squares with the idea that there is progress in revelation (cf. Matt 5:17; Gal 4:4; Heb 1:2). Thus, a Christian attitude toward war should come from the NT, and particularly Jesus' teachings. But Jesus blessed the peacemakers (Matt 5:9) and told the disciple who sought to defend him by force, "Put your sword back in its place . . . for all who draw the sword will die by the sword" (Matt 26:52). In Luke 6:27-36, Jesus says we are to love our enemies and to do good to those who hate us.[22] The teaching of Jesus is confirmed throughout the NT (cf. Rom 12:17, 21; 13:10; 1 Pet 2:21). A pacifist interpretation of these and other texts leads to the conclusion that a Christian is precluded from military combat and certain offices within the government. Augsburger writes, "Thus, Christians should only serve at governmental levels where they can honestly carry out the functions of their office without compromising their fidelity to Jesus Christ as Lord. They should not consider holding positions where they could not both fulfill the obligations of the office and remain consistent with their membership in the kingdom of God."[23]

A closely related argument claims that the *Sermon on the Mount*, particularly Matt 5:38-48, is normative for Christian conduct today. This text does not simply express an *attitude* Christians should have in the face of opposition and persecution, but it literally prescribes appropriate *conduct* for Christians.[24]

A third argument appeals to the Christian's *citizenship in the kingdom of God*. That fact means the Christian's first loyalty is to Christ and his kingdom. Christians should never be guilty of nationalism, for the kingdom of God is transnational or global. Christians should respect the state, for it is ordained by God to order society. But since God ordains the powers that be, he is above them. It is faulty logic to assume that because God ordains governments, we are always obeying God by obeying them. We must be subject to our government, but Scripture does not say we should obey government blindly (cf. Romans 13, esp. v. 4). Thus, when duties to God and the king conflict, Christians must obey God.[25]

The *ethical implications of the cross* constitute a fourth argument. Christ must be our great example, and he died as an innocent victim in the face of the most outrageous injustice. We should be willing to do the same. Moreover, Christ came to redeem everyone and died on behalf of all people. How can we take the life of someone for whom Christ died, especially those who have not received him as savior? To kill people robs them of the opportunity to accept Christ and know the fullness of life he brings.[26]

A fifth argument grows out of the fact that *the church is a global community.* Since God's kingdom or the church is global and transcends national, racial, and cultural differences, it is entirely possible that one's nation will be at war with a country some of whose citizens are believers. How can Christians who claim to follow and worship Christ be at war with other believers?[27]

Finally, wars are fought by and large *to protect property.*[28] A Christian who refuses to participate in a war declared by his or her government is simply maintaining a consistent attitude toward material things. Jesus warns against valuing possessions above people. Material possessions are to be used to help others, not to be defended at the expense of other human lives.

Objections to Pacifism
Objections to Non-biblical Arguments
Each of the non-biblical arguments presented has been criticized. As to the argument from the *sacredness of life*, there is an obvious appeal of an argument that relates the immorality of taking life to its sacredness. It is hard to think of anything that violates life's sacredness more than killing, particularly when so much destruction of life seems unnecessary. Of course, the word "unnecessary" raises an important question. Does the principle that life is sacred mean nothing should ever be killed, or does it require us to preserve as much life as possible? Pacifists hold the former, nonpacifists the latter.[29]

One way to understand this argument is that it claims that killing is wrong because it diminishes the non-moral good in the world. Life is sacred and thus a good. Destroying life then lessens the non-moral good in the world, and is thereby wrong. Our problem with the argument understood this way is that it is based on a consequentialist approach to ethics (i.e., something is morally good that produces certain non-moral good) and is objectionable on that ground. In addition, there is a more general objection to this form of the argument. If the amount of non-moral good in the world is our goal, there might be situations where more lives overall would be saved by killing a specific group of people. In those situations the sacredness of human life, understood on a consequentialist understanding of ethics, appears to encourage rather than prevent killing.

Suppose someone understands the argument to mean that killing is inherently wrong, regardless of whether it diminishes non-moral good in the world or not. We think this argument still has problems. Is preserving life the highest value and to be accomplished at all costs? As noted in our first chapter, humans have a variety of *prima facie* obligations that may conflict. In such cases there is only one *actual* obligation. Take the case where Christians are required to recant their faith on pain of death. Here the conflict is between our duty to save or preserve life and our duty to obey and love God. Many Christians would say that in this case, one should forfeit one's life in order to obey God. Likewise, there may be other cases where the sacredness of life may acceptably be violated by a war in order to defend some moral or religious principle that could not be maintained with peace.

In response, the pacifist might say there is a difference between taking a life and getting oneself killed, and hold that only the former is immoral. No doubt the distinction is genuine, but that does not help the pacifist at this point. Whether one kills another or is killed, the result is destruction of life. Given the pacifist's rejection of all killing because life is sacred, neither kind of killing is morally acceptable. Hence, the distinction does not save his argument, because on his views, even getting oneself killed is wrong!

The argument from the *immorality of killing* is objectionable as well.[30] Killing does violate a person's right to life. However, possessing a right seems clearly to imply another right to defend the first right against loss. If not, of what value is that first right? If this reasoning is correct, notice how it applies to the right to life. It means that a right to life may be defended. But how can one's right to life be defended if one is attacked? Only by defending one's life against the aggressor, and in some cases that may necessitate killing the aggressor. But if this is so, a right to life *per se* will not necessarily exclude all killing. The net result is that the immorality of killing argument does not in fact rule out all killing. Some killing, including killing in self-defense which is often precisely what happens in war, can be morally acceptable, despite the immorality of killing in general.

What about the *moral exemplar argument*? It says the world would be a better place if everyone was a pacifist. Few would deny that, but does that make pacifism a moral obligation? Other rules would also make the world a better place. "Use violence only in self-defense" is an example. If everyone obeyed, the same consequence would result as would if everyone obeyed a rule such as "never use violence."

All of this is true, but does any of it make these rules our moral obligation? We think not.[31] However, assume for the sake of argument that "never use violence" is our moral obligation. Just as with other ethical obligations, there might be exceptions to this one. In fact, we believe there would have to be exceptions. Let us explain. Ethics says what ought to be the case, but what if "ought" does not match "is"? In fact, what happens if it is impossible to obey an "ought" such as "never use violence" unless everyone else does? The problem is that "never use violence" presupposes a world in which no one does use violence. Otherwise, I may have to use violence to defend myself in order to uphold another moral principle we all (pacifists included) hold dear, namely, preserve life (mine in this case). If everyone obeyed the rule "never use violence," it would be reasonable to expect there would never be any exceptions to that rule. But ours is a sinful and fallen world where people do resort to violence. And that just means that try as we might to obey that rule, there will be times when there must be exceptions in order to preserve life. But that is all that those who reject pacifism are saying (at least all that just war defenders are saying). They are not advocating indiscriminate violence. They are merely saying that since the moral exemplar must live in a sinful world, there are times when one who would be a moral exemplar must himself break the command against violence.

Gandhi's argument from the *condition of the soul* is also unsuccessful in establishing pacifism. At the heart of this argument is the belief that force corrupts or pollutes the soul. Few would deny that excessive, unwarranted force or violence is harmful to the soul. However, is limited force in pursuit of a just cause harmful to the soul? Pacifists think so; nonpacifists disagree.[32] Since just this point is at issue, to assume one position or the other begs the question. And that just means this argument cannot prove either position to be correct.

Objections to Scriptural Arguments

A first objection is related to the claim that moral theories must be *universalizable*. Pacifism defended on biblical grounds is open to criticism in that the Bible is authoritative for the Christian, but why should the Moslem or Buddhist accept its teaching? Scriptures may obligate Christians to pacifism but not Moslems or Buddhists. Thus, Christian pacifism fails the test of universalizability.

Though non-Christians will likely reject the Bible's authority as a ground for moral obligation, we do not think that frees them from doing what it commands. Regardless of whether non-Christians reject biblical authority, we believe the Scriptures are God's word, and therefore have the right to command all people everywhere and at all times about this and any other issue. If non-Christians reject some biblical command, they do so at their own peril. The real question for us is not whether Scripture is binding on non-believers, but whether Scripture actually mandates pacifism. We believe that when Scripture is properly understood, it does not demand pacifism.

A second objection to the claim that the Bible teaches pacifism is OT teaching on war.[33] There Israel is not only permitted but commanded by God to go to war, especially in regard to the conquest of the land of

Canaan in the time of Joshua and the judges. God is even said to have fought on the side of Israel in what has been called a "holy war." Moreover, the conquest of the land was not completed until the time of David, who himself was a great warrior. With the split of the kingdom into northern and southern kingdoms, both were constantly involved in conflict with hostile nations and were ultimately overrun by Assyria and Babylon.

Pacifists might respond in one of two ways to OT materials. The first is to claim that God did not command and did not fight on the side of the Israelites. They believed he had commanded them to destroy their enemies, and they thought he fought on their side, but they were mistaken. It is possible to show this from what is said about God and his character elsewhere in the Bible.[34] This argument is not very convincing, however. It is presumptuous to think we know better what God commanded and did for Israel than she did, especially since we are separated from the events by some three and a half millennia. Further, those who accept the inspiration and inerrancy of the text hold that the writers were protected from error, and thus what Scripture teaches is true.

A second more complicated response is that there are differences between what God commands and does in the two testaments.[35] In the OT, Israel was obeying God's command when she used physical force. However, it is wrong to think God permits the same thing in the NT, because there are important differences between OT and NT eras. For one thing, Israel was a nation among nations, and as such needed and was permitted to protect her territory with armies and carnal weapons. What set her apart from other nations of her day was God's choice of her as his people. The church, on the other hand, is not a nation but a spiritual organization. Christians are pilgrims and strangers in this world. While they own property, they are to possess it in a different way. Therefore, they do not need armies and carnal weapons. A second difference is that Israel was not a regenerate people, but the church is. Of course, there were regenerates in Israel, but even they were under OT law. The church has the indwelling Holy Spirit and is under a much higher standard than OT law. The church is called to nonresistance under this higher standard. A final difference is that Israel lived under the dispensation of law, while the church lives under the dispensation of grace. Therefore, we should not be surprised that each is governed by a different principle. There is no inconsistency in pacifism based on the NT.

This second response to Israel's practice of war in the OT raises two questions. First, how do the testaments relate on ethical matters? Is there continuity or discontinuity? As argued in our chapter on Christian decision-making, whatever is binding in the OT continues to apply to the NT era, *unless the NT either explicitly or implicitly abrogates it*. This leads to a second question this pacifist response raises. What is the NT teaching on war? Does it prohibit it, either entirely or at least for the Christian? Or does it permit it, at least in some cases? Augsburger and Hoyt take the former view, but are they correct?

It should be clear that much depends on what Jesus and the NT writers taught about using force. In turning to Jesus' general ethical teachings and his Sermon on the Mount in particular, we hear Jesus say certain things which indicate that he did not entirely eschew the use of force. Pacifists disagree, but a fundamental problem with pacifist interpretations of Jesus' teachings is the failure to distinguish between private and public duties, personal duties, and duties of a state. As a private individual I may turn the other cheek when unjustly attacked. However, my responsibilities are quite different when I stand in the position of a guardian of a third party as a civil magistrate or parent. Because I am responsible for their lives and welfare, I must resist, even with force, unjust aggression against them. Moreover, loving my neighbor or enemy does not mean I must stand idly by as my child is kidnapped and murdered. I am to use whatever force is necessary to protect his or her life and safety. The state stands in this third party relationship to its citizens. Texts that pacifists typically cite for nonresistance are verses that have to do with private or personal duties, not public duties. While Rom 13:1-7 is not uncontested in its meaning, it sets out the state's responsibility to its citizens.

Moreover, the interpretation of the Sermon on the Mount by pacifists is open to question. They typically advocate a quite literal approach to this text, but that hermeneutical approach is difficult to apply consistently because the Sermon on the Mount is given to hyperbolic speech in order to get the listener's attention and help him or her remember the saying. Certainly, Jesus is not literally advocating self-maiming when he says to cut off a hand or pluck out an eye (Matt 5:29, 30). If we take Jesus' command to hate one's relatives literally (Luke 14:26), we have a serious contradiction with the teaching of Paul that one who does not provide for his family has denied the faith and is worse than an unbeliever (1 Tim 5:8). Even Jesus (John 18:22, 23) and Paul (Acts 23:1-5) did not turn the other cheek on certain occasions when unjustly attacked. Rather, they challenged the injustice of their attackers.

Holmes makes this point powerfully in a slightly different way. He denies that different ethical principles govern the two testaments—justice in the OT and love in the NT. Justice and love operate in both testaments; there is no double standard. Justice is not superseded by love. The law of retaliation, *lex talionis*, has nothing to do with vengeance but with *retributive justice*. Retributive justice gives society a way to maintain a just and peaceful order and to punish those who disrupt that order. Both testaments permit retributive justice. That is why the state is granted the power of the sword (Rom 13:1-7).[36]

What about Christians as citizens of God's kingdom? Does that rule out their participation in war? While Christians are indeed citizens of God's kingdom, that does not mean they are not citizens of this world as well. Are the two kingdoms mutually exclusive? We think not. If the use of force is divinely entrusted to human governments, and if Christians receive benefits from the state, not the least of which is protection, it is unreasonable to think Christians should reject legitimate governmental use of force. Moreover, it does not seem inappropriate for government to expect Christians to participate in governmental action and to participate in the use of force to protect all members of the society. Responsibilities accompany benefits! If such Christian participation is ruled out, it seems that Christians would have to exclude themselves from the police force as well.[37] Moreover, if the two kingdoms are really mutually exclusive, then Christians, to be consistent, should have no relationship with worldly governments. That is, they should neither give nor receive anything from them. This, as Brown points out, is tantamount to refusing any responsibility for what society does.

Pacifists also claim that the ethical implications of the cross prevent Christians from participating in some wars, but this seems wrong. Surely, the cross does demonstrate God's patience in the face of unjust suffering. But that is not the only lesson the cross teaches. As Davis says, it is fundamentally a display of God's righteousness and justice. God must both punish sin so justice can be upheld in a moral universe, and provide the means to justify those who place their faith in Jesus. Thus, while the cross shows God's mercy, it also vindicates God's justice in punishing sin. The pacifist's use of the cross focuses on the exemplary character of Christ's actions and death but neglects the penal, substitutionary nature of his death.

Pacifists will still respond, "But how can we kill those for whom Christ died?" We respond, in the same way that God can and does send to a Christless eternity people for whom Christ died. That is, just as God must punish eternally some for whom Christ died, because they refuse to turn from sin to Christ, so evil and injustice on a national and international scale must be punished, even though that means killing people for whom Christ died. If Christ's death for the sins of all rules out any ultimate form of punishment, then not even God himself can justly send unrepentant sinners to eternal punishment.

Here as well we agree with Holmes in denying any inconsistency between loving one's enemies and civil justice. Love is captured in the law's justice. *Lex talionis* is both just and loving. When compared with many legal codes of the Middle East, the punishments prescribed in the OT were eminently fair. OT law insisted that there be a proportioned response to evil as well as setting limits on society's use of force. To love one's enemies, then, is to see that justice prevails.

The argument that the church is a global community and a war would mean that Christians would fight and kill Christians is also unconvincing. The argument assumes that a Christian might fight in any war. However, if the just war theory is defensible, one may not fight in just any war. To fight in a war the cause would have to be just, and also, one could only fight if attacked. Moreover, it seems that both sides cannot be just in a war, even if participants on both sides think they are just. One is *not*. But, then, it follows that Christians could only justifiably fight on one side, and if they do, there need not be any killing of Christians by other Christians. On the other hand, some Christians might fight on the side that is not just. If so, they may be killed (even by Christian opponents), but in this case their killing is not unjust. Being a Christian does not exempt one from punishment for wrongdoing, even if the instrument of punishment is another Christian!

As to arguments about wars being fought to defend private property, we respond that in modern wars this has not been the only or even primary reason for fighting. Wars have also been fought to prevent genocide and the loss of freedom that comes with attempts at world domination and colonial imperialism. Risking one's life to prevent these evils seems considerably more defensible than risking one's life to protect private property, unless one thinks human life is never to be risked because of its infinite worth. But we have already addressed that matter.

Christian Pacifism à la Hoyt and Augsburger

In Robert Clouse's *War: Four Views*, both Herman Hoyt and Myron Augsburger defend pacifism from a Christian perspective. There are two important differences in their views. First, while he appeals to biblical arguments regulating the actions of Christians, Augsburger thinks the pacifist ideal is obligatory on all people. However, he allows that there are levels of obedience to God's commands and that God meets men and women where they are. Since pacifism is a hard command, it is primarily the Christian who will obey. Hoyt, on the other hand, thinks the NT makes a clear distinction between the pacifism or nonresistance of the Christian and the access to force within limits for the non-Christian.

Second, Augsburger and Hoyt differ on the relationship of Christians to the military. Hoyt, after prohibiting Christians' use of force, says Christians are free to serve their country in the army or under civilian control in anything that is good. They may serve as noncombatants in the medical corps or as chaplains. Augsburger thinks this is inconsistent. A consistent pacifism requires Christians to object conscientiously to any identification with or support of the military enterprise. Noncombatant service prevents one from directly taking a life, but still supports the military.[38]

Since Hoyt consciously develops a position that obligates Christians only, we focus specifically on his views. He prefers calling his view biblical nonresistance. He thinks his position has positive benefits and does not simply react. His position can be summarized in six points. First, Scripture teaches Christians to be separate from the world and its ways (John 15:19; 17:16; Rom 12:2). Moreover, church and state are two separate kingdoms (John 3:3, 5; 18:36; Col 1:13). The Christian's citizenship is in heaven (Phil 3:20), and he or she is to be a pilgrim and stranger in this world (Heb 11:8-16). Consequently, involvement in war, one of the activities of the kingdom of this world, is ruled out for the Christian. Third, Scripture not only teaches two separate kingdoms, but says the weapons of the two kingdoms are different. Christ was very clear that his kingdom was not run on physical violence or with material weaponry (John 18:36). Instead, the Christian's weapons are spiritual in nature (2 Cor 10:4). Fourth, physical violence is forbidden for Christians (Matt 5:38-48). They are to follow the example of Christ who submitted to injustice rather than resort to force (1 Pet 2:21-24; 1 John 2:6). This means physical force is never justified in propagating the Christian faith. Power for expanding Christ's kingdom is purely spiritual in nature (Acts 1:8; 2 Cor 10:4). Fifth, when the church has united with the state, the inconsistencies in the methods used by each has led to criticism of the church by unbelievers. Finally, Christians have an obligation to use spiritual means to do good and bring blessing. Jesus taught this by example (1 Pet 2:21-24), word (Matt 5:38-48), and the instruction of the apostles (Rom 12:17-21; 13:8; Eph 6:10-13; Jas 4:7; 1 Pet 5:9).[39]

In elaborating his views on nonresistance, Hoyt argues that the key passages are Matt 5:38-48, Luke 6:27-36, Rom 12:19-21, 13:8, and 1 Pet 2:18-24. He says that while *lex talionis* was the rule in the OT (Exod 21:23-25), it is ruled out by NT teaching. Israel was unregenerate and a nation. The church is different and is under the dispensation of grace, not law. Hoyt admits that each of the four passages he cites addresses individual conduct of believers, but argues that this does not eliminate them from the argument about a country's going to war. It only shows that they do not exclude war for nations or governments, but they do exclude it for individual Christians. Of course, for Hoyt this also means nonresistance is only an obligation for believers, not for non-believers. But, then, such use of these passages of Scripture should not disturb us, because Scriptures were not "in any sense directed toward unsaved men."[40]

Hoyt further argues that Christ did not come to destroy lives but to save them (Luke 9:56). Thus, a Christian cannot take a life. Christ's methods differ from those of the world (2 Cor 10:3-4). The values of Christ and thus of Christians differ from the world's. This has implications for the meaning of life (Mark 8:35; John 12:25). Christ's protection of his own differs from the protection the world gives its own (Matt 26:53-54).

Finally, Hoyt also supports nonresistance on eschatological grounds. Scripture says men will wage war with one another during this age before the return of Christ (that is the course of the age). However, the believer knows that the ultimate resolution to all strife will come when Christ sets up his kingdom in justice. Consequently, the believer must not take vengeance on evildoers now, for God will take care of them when Christ returns. While Christians await God's resolution to earthly evil and injustice, they are to overcome physical evil with spiritual good (Eph 6:10-13; Jas 4:7; 1 Pet 5:9) and to live as citizens of the coming kingdom (Rom 13:11-12; 1 Pet 2:11). Moreover, God's plan for believers in this age is world evangelism (Acts 1:8; Matt 28:19-20). This simply leaves no time for war.

Hoyt concludes his presentation by saying that despite the above arguments, Christ tells us to render to Caesar what is Caesar's, and thus, we are to submit to government. Consequently, believers can perform various responsibilities to government, but in view of biblical teaching on nonviolence and the Christian's understanding of eschatology, Christians cannot serve their country by going to war. Noncombatant roles in war are allowable, but all else is ruled out.

Responses to Hoyt's Nonresistance Position

Some of the arguments Hoyt and Augsburger raise were already covered in our responses to pacifism in general. Hence, we need not repeat them here. However, several points about Hoyt's position seem in order. First, what about the matter of loving one's enemies and not seeking vengeance? Passages offered in support are the same ones typically used to rule out capital punishment. However, as noted in our discussion of capital punishment, those passages have to do with interpersonal relations, not with the role of government. Therefore, the verses have nothing to do with endorsing or forbidding Christian *or* non-Christian participation in war. Moreover, love of one's enemies does not supersede justice being meted out. If it did, there would be anarchy, since no government could ever punish any evildoer. And we also note that many verses cited speak of vengeance, but, as argued when discussing capital punishment, vengeance and retribution are not identical. As an agent of the government, one can punish retributively without vengeance as a motive at all.

As to Hoyt's claim that Scripture is addressed only to believers, so nonresistance is only for them, that is hard to swallow. If he is right, and if a theory must be universalizable to be taken as a serious moral theory, then that seems to eliminate his position as a serious moral theory. Moreover, his claim that Scripture is not addressed to the non-believer in any sense seems inconsistent with his call for believers to be witnesses. What should believers use in their witnessing? The Bible? How? If, as Hoyt says, the Bible is not addressed to non-believers in any sense, how is it then appropriate to use Scripture in witnessing to non-believers? Even if Hoyt is right about only believers being obligated to nonresistance, he is not right in arguing his view on the ground that Scripture is *in no sense* addressed to non-believers.

Third, Hoyt's claim that war is ruled out for the Christian because it is evil, but a noncombatant role is permissible seems thoroughly inconsistent. If war is evil and not for Christian participation, then *any* participation in the war effort seems to aid in evil. Thus, on Hoyt's grounds it should be forbidden.

Fourth, Hoyt argues against involvement in war because it takes us away from witnessing, but then says a noncombatant role is all right. But why doesn't a noncombatant role take up as much of our time as some other role in war? And one can witness in a foxhole as well as one can in an infirmary while binding soldiers' wounds. Hoyt's view here seems a bit inconsistent.

Finally, Hoyt argues that war is evil and open to grave moral abuse. Therefore, Christians, who should be the most principled, should not participate. The problem with this is that it leaves the conduct of war in the hands of unbelievers who, because they lack a Christian moral base, will likely try to win at *any* price. The notion that Christian protests might prevent immoral actions is unlikely. Having refused participation, why would governments listen to them?

THE JUST WAR THEORY

The just war theory recognizes that war is evil. The point at issue is not whether it is good, but whether it is unavoidable in all cases and whether it can be conducted in a just way.

Presuppositions of Just War Theory

Holmes thinks there are four presuppositions that underlie this theory. First, some evil cannot be avoided. Evil has pervaded human existence ever since the fall. In some cases any action, even the right action, may have evil consequences. This can even be true of inaction. Second, the just war position is normative for all, Christian and non-Christian alike. It does not describe how people have always acted, but prescribes how they should have acted in the past and should act in the present and future. Third, this theory does not try to justify war. Rather, it attempts to bring war within the limits of justice so that if everyone were guided by these principles, many wars would be eliminated. Its purpose is not to legitimize wars, but to limit them because sometimes evil cannot be avoided. Thus, while this is not pacifism, it is a peace position. Finally, the theory assumes that private citizens have no right to use force. Only governments have been given that right in order to keep peace and secure a just order. Thus, the key issue is not whether an individual can fight a war, but whether government has the right to engage in armed conflict and whether a citizen, Christian or not, should participate as an agent of that government.[41]

The Just War Theory Explained

We begin with the just war theory's understanding of duties. Some ethicists say duties are absolute, i.e, they can never be overridden. An example is the view of many pacifists about our duty not to harm another. Others think duties are relative. A duty is nothing more than a maxim or rule of thumb which illuminates but does not prescribe beforehand what one must do in any concrete situation. Just war theorists believe duties are *prima facie* duties. *Prima facie* duties, as advocated by W. D. Ross, are intrinsically binding, but do not necessarily determine one's actual obligation or duty in any concrete situation. There may be rule-governed exceptions to a *prima facie* duty. Non-maleficence, the duty not to harm or kill another, is such a duty. While it is intrinsically binding, there may be justification for overriding this *prima facie* duty.

If a *prima facie* duty is overridden in a concrete case, that should affect the agent's attitude and action in performing his or her actual duty. R. Niebuhr thinks overriding a *prima facie* duty should be done with remorse and repentance; Paul Ramsey only advocates regret.

As applied to war, this concept of duties means there are rule-governed exceptions to the duty not to harm or kill. These exceptions are governed by the criteria for a just war. Criteria are commonly divided into criteria for the right to go to war and criteria for the just conduct of a war. What follows are representative lists of such criteria.

There are a number of criteria for *the right to go to war*.[42] First, there must be a proper or legitimate authority who has responsibility for judging whether the other criteria are met. Second, war must be the last resort. Negotiations and compromise must have been tried and failed. Third, insofar as possible, a formal declaration of war is required. Since war is the prerogative of a government, not individuals, the declaration must come from the highest governmental authority. Fourth, there must also be reasonable hope of success. If not, it is generally unreasonable to sacrifice lives in a vain hope. Some think an exception to this criterion is allowable when the evil confronted is so outrageous that an attempt must be made as a protest, even if there is little or no hope of success. Fifth, there must be some proportionality between the objective hoped for and the price to achieve it. Sixth, there must be just cause. A war of aggression is condemned; only defensive wars are just. Finally, the war must be fought with the right intention, i.e., to secure a just and lasting peace. Revenge, conquest, economic gain, or ideological superiority must all be renounced.

Once a government has the right to go to war, the war must be conducted in a just way.[43] Criteria for *the right conduct of a war* are as follows: first, there must be a limited objective in waging the war, namely, the restoration of peace. This means that the collapse of a nation's economy and the destruction of its political institutions are unwarranted.

Second, the immediate object is not to kill or even injure people, but to incapacitate or restrain them. This means that if possible, enemy soldiers should be taken as prisoners of war rather than killed. Third, direct attack on noncombatants is illegitimate. They should be granted immunity. Fourth, one is obligated not to inflict unnecessary suffering. Hence, the smallest caliber bullet effective for the task must be used. Fifth, indirect effects upon civilians must be justified by the principle of proportionality, i.e., the evil averted or the good attained justifies the action. Actions must be limited to those that repel the enemy. Total or unlimited war is immoral. Destruction of crops and systems of transportation and communication must be defended on the principle of proportionality.[44]

Arguments for Just War Theory

Defense of the just war theory is twofold. It is justified on the basis of natural law, stretching back to Greco-Roman times, and on the basis of biblical teaching.

The natural law argument stretches back at least to Plato and Aristotle. In both his *Republic* and *Laws*, Plato urges limits, especially on Greeks fighting Greeks.[45] Peace is the only legitimate purpose for war. Aristotle insists that man's very nature calls for the rule of reason over passion, and thus war must be limited to what is needed to secure the peace.

It is Cicero, however, who first developed the just war theory in some detail.[46] Man naturally desires peace and order, and man's reason makes that possible in society. Right reason teaches true law which is universally valid and unchanging. It prohibits treachery, even to our enemies, and demands that war be governed by moral law. Cicero was the first to state explicit rules for a just war. His rules had two differences from Christian versions. First, the defense of honor, as well as peace and justice, was a just cause for war. He did not rule out revenge either. Christian versions limit just cause to defending and securing peace. Second, Cicero advocated humane treatment of the enemy. Christian writers go beyond him and demand merciful treatment of one's enemies. These differences are attributable to the differences between actions ruled by reason and natural law and those ruled by Christian love.

Just war theory has been defended within the Christian tradition by Augustine, Aquinas, Luther, Calvin, Vitoria, and Suarez. In modern times Pius XII, James Childress, Dietrich Bonhoeffer, Reinhold Niebuhr and Paul Ramsey have espoused it.[47]

Another line of argument draws upon biblical teaching. Four theological considerations support the just war theory.[48] There is the biblical view of *man*. Man was created in God's image, and as such, has intrinsic worth and dignity (Gen 1:26-28; Ps 8:3-9; Matt 10:29-31; Luke 12:6; Jas 3:9, 10). But man has sinned and is a rebel (Ps 51:5; Jer 17:9; Rom 3:10-18, 23; Jas 4:1-3). Human depravity extends even to those who are part of the redeemed community. It touches every area of human life (Rom 7:14-25; Jas 4:1-3; 1 John 1:8-10).

There is also the biblical view of the *state*. Human government or the state is ordained by God (Dan 5:21; Rom 13:1, 2; 1 Pet 2:13, 14). The NT says the state is created to maintain justice and equity, and is thus granted the right of force to maintain such. This includes the right to use force in self-defense (Rom 13:3, 4; 1 Pet 2:13, 14; cf. Exod 22:2, 3). This last point is admittedly controversial. We discuss it below.

The biblical view of the *church* supports the just war theory, too. While the NT does not advocate establishing a theocracy, it teaches that the church in general (and believers in particular) has a positive responsibility to participate in building a more just and peaceful human society. To use the language of Vatican II, although the church has no specific political mission since its ministry is spiritual, it is to contribute to the protection of human rights, the promotion of human dignity, and the unity of the human family (Matt 5:13-16; Rom 13:1-7; 1 Pet 2:13, 14).

A final theological matter is Scripture's view of *history and eschatology*. God's ideal is subjection of the earth to peace, righteousness and justice (Gen 1:28-30; Isa 2:1-4; 11:3-9; Rev 21:1–22:5). Because of man's sin, human history includes evil and war (Matt 24:6, 7; John 16:33; 2 Thess 2:3-7; 2 Tim 3:1-9). Human effort does *not* bring in God's kingdom. God's ideal will be realized through his intervention into human history at the second coming of Jesus Christ to this earth to set up his kingdom and establish peace, righteousness and justice (Isa 2:1-4; 9:7; 11:3-9; Rev 21:1–22:5).

A second line of argument drawn from Scripture is that not all killing is prohibited. That is, the command not to kill is not absolute. At the very time the Sixth Commandment of the Decalogue was given, Israel was on its God-ordained journey of conquest from Egypt to Canaan. The history of this period shows that war was a harsh reality of life. In addition, the Mosaic Law prescribes the death penalty for a number of crimes and permits killing in certain cases of self-defense. Thus, it seems that not all killing is prohibited by this commandment. Hence, it cannot be used as a blanket prohibition of war.

The rest of the OT is consistent with the understanding of the prohibition against killing just stated. Some of the most godly OT saints engaged in military action. Abraham rescued his nephew by military action (Gen 14:13-16). Joshua, the judges and David spent a good deal of their administrations in military conflict, and there is no hint that their actions met with divine disapproval. In fact, the writer of Hebrews says that by *faith* they "conquered kingdoms, enforced justice . . . became mighty in war, put foreign armies to flight" (Heb 11:33, 34).

In spite of the OT's recognition of war as a fact of human existence, war is not glorified. Rather, OT figures tried to control its conduct and lamented its destruction. When Israel was poised to take Canaan by military conquest, the people were instructed to limit destruction and violence (Deuteronomy 2). David was not allowed to build a house for the Lord because he was a man of war and had shed blood (1 Chron 22:8, 9; 28:3). The Psalms contain laments over the violence of war and petitions to God to make war cease and to destroy its weapons (Psalms 46, 120). Moreover, the prophets looked forward to a day when peace and justice would be united in Messiah's reign (Isa 2:1-4; 9:1-7; 11:1-9; 65:19-25). They condemned those who kill their brothers, decry unrestrained violence (Amos 1, 2), and weep over the destruction of Jerusalem (Lamentations).

When we turn to the NT, we find less about warfare. Holmes thinks this is because the NT is directed to individuals, whereas the OT is addressed to nations.[49] Still, the NT is not silent on this matter. Soldiers came to John the Baptist and asked how kingdom citizens should act. He did not say they had to leave the army, but said they should conduct themselves in a principled way, robbing no one and being content with their wages (Luke 3:14). Moreover, Jesus praised a Roman centurion for having exemplary faith. Nowhere is there any suggestion that he should resign from military service (Luke 7:9). Peter's actions in Acts are in keeping with those of John the Baptist and Jesus. He went to preach the gospel to a Roman soldier, Cornelius. Cornelius is described as one who was devout and feared God (Acts 10:2). He had a good reputation among the Jews, although he was a representative of an occupying power (10:22). Cornelius responded to the preaching of Peter, was saved, and received the Holy Spirit. Peter did not tell Cornelius that his newfound faith required him to leave service in the Roman army.

The key NT passage, however, is Rom 13:4. This text, we think, demonstrates ethical continuity between the OT and NT on the matter of war. This text has been and will be discussed in our chapters on capital punishment and the Christian and the secular state. Hence, only a brief summary is needed here. Paul tells believers to submit to civil authorities since God ordains them (v. 1). To resist the civil authority in fact resists God (v. 2). The civil magistrate is not a terror to those who do good, but to evildoers (v. 3; cf. 1 Pet 2:13, 14). It is in this regard that human governments are granted the right to "bear the sword," i.e., to use lethal force. Though this right is explicitly granted for matters of *civil* justice and order and relates only by application to a state's right to defend itself against an outside aggressor, this passage clearly shows that at least for some purposes, the state does have the right to use lethal force. This right is given amidst a context of repudiating vengeance, showing concern for one's enemies and for those who suffer, and pursuing peace. The context also sets the limits on the use of force. It must not be motivated by vengeance, and it must seek peace as its goal.

Those who think the sword only *symbolizes* authority and the right to use force do not do justice to the context or the fact that the word for sword here is *machaira*. This is not a ceremonial sword, but in the Greek OT, the Septuagint, this word is used for a lethal weapon (Gen 34:26; Judg 3:16).

Objections to Just War Theory

Certain arguments for pacifism also function as objections to the just war theory. For instance, the arguments that a NT ethic of love supersedes an OT ethic of justice and that Jesus' ethical teachings require nonresistance are objections to the just war theory. We have already explained why we find these arguments unconvincing. Hence, we do not think they refute this position.

There are, however, further objections to the just war theory which must be examined. First, some might object that the just war theory is too optimistic in believing that human beings, particularly sinful human beings, will *do* right because they *know* what is right.[50] Thinkers such as Thomas Aquinas and John Locke were much more confident than modern thinkers about establishing a just war theory on the basis of reason alone. They believed that from man's nature it is possible through reason to reach universal and certain moral principles that would govern the conduct of war. However, the metaphysics of morals is no longer considered a demonstrative science. Ideas of justice and their application to war differ markedly, making agreement even on the content of just war theory difficult, if not impossible. But that is not the most troubling matter. The just war theory is overly optimistic about the ability of reason and law to control human emotions and passions. Human beings can be self-deceived, and in some instances, even when they know what is just, they do what they know is wrong anyway for personal or national advantage. Thus, the just war theory has problems at its core. It admits that human beings and war are evil, but says people will do what is right anyway when they know what it is.

This is a serious objection and should not be dismissed too easily. Just examining twentieth-century history shows that the principles of just war theory have been violated. However, ethical norms stipulate what *ought* to be done regardless of what *is* being done. If a certain course of action is morally obligated, it does not cease to be obligated just because people disobey. Surely one would not sanction discarding biblical commandments against lust, stealing, lying, and murder, for example, just because they are frequently broken. Likewise, if the just war theory is the correct standard for moral conduct of war (and we believe the evidence offered shows that it is), it does not cease to be the standard just because nations disobey it. Moreover, nations that fail to meet the standard need to know that, and need to experience pressure from other nations to conform.[51]

Second, some object that nuclear arms as a part of modern warfare make a just war impossible. Nuclear weapons make a limited objective, noncombatant immunity, and proportionality impossible criteria to meet in the conduct of a just war. Thus, the theory must be abandoned. Because of the seriousness of this objection, we shall treat it at some length after we discuss the crusade or preventive war theory. However, at this point we simply note that at most the objection rules out wars involving nuclear weapons. It does not rule out all wars. And we should add that the possession of nuclear weapons does not guarantee that they will be used (cf. Operation Desert Storm).

THE CRUSADE OR PREVENTIVE WAR THEORY

According to this theory, the fundamental tenets of just war theory are correct. However, they are not enough. In particular, the just war theory sanctions defensive wars, but there are other kinds of wars, crusades and preventive wars, that may also be just. This position in its most convincing form is presented by Harold O. J. Brown in Robert Clouse's *War: Four Christian Views*.

The Theory Explained and Defended

This theory rests on the assumption that war is justified under some conditions. If not, then it is useless to discuss special wars. Thinking that war can be just, Brown tries to extend what is meant by just cause.[52] In the just war theory this is limited to a nation's right to defend itself against an aggressor. Brown thinks modern wars are so complex that they fail to fit traditional categories, and he argues that "just cause" must be extended to include two special cases, the crusade and the preventive war. A crusade is a "war that is begun not in response to a present act of aggression, but as the attempt to set right a past act." Its goal is not conquest but reconquest.[53] Crusades are wars fought to undo something that never should have been done. Brown offers two examples of what he means. He includes in this class "wars of liberation." He also thinks that efforts, had they existed, to prevent the Pol Pot government's attempts at genocide in Cambodia would have fallen in this class.

Brown's defense of crusades is twofold. First, he likens a crusade to police intervention to prevent an atrocity. Suppose your next-door neighbor was in the process of mutilating and killing your children. Would you not expect police to intervene if they knew about it (let alone what you might do)? If police intervention is morally justified in this case, then it should be on an international scale, too. Second, the crusade is justified on the lesser evil principle. That is, the crusade, though not provoked by any direct act of aggression against those who mount the crusade, is justified because it prevents a greater evil than a crusade would be either from occurring or continuing.

A preventive war is one begun in *anticipation* of, not in *response* to, an act of aggression. It is an attempt to prevent an evil that has not yet taken place. The most striking example of preventive war in recent times is the Six Day War of 1967. Brown argues that Israel's action to preempt a strike by her Arab neighbors was morally justified. Israel acted in self-defense, and if self-defense is legitimate (Brown thinks it is), it justifies responding in anticipation of a lethal or crippling first blow. A person does not have to wait until struck with a crippling first attack before response is justified, and the same is true for a nation. If one nation threatens another's security, a preventive response is in order.

Objections

Brown's position points up the complexity and vagaries of modern warfare. It shows that recent conflicts do not fit neatly the traditional moral categories for determining what is just and unjust. It also reminds us that governments often deceive their citizens, making determination to participate very difficult. However, three objections make us think Holmes's attempt to bring these special cases under the just war theory is preferable.

First, extending "just cause" to include crusades and preventive wars broadens its meaning so that almost any side in any war could justify involvement.[54] This is easiest to see with a preventive war. All that is needed to permit a first strike is that one's enemy act menacingly towards you. Has any nation that went to war in recent times failed to say its enemy did that?

Second, this position depends heavily on the lesser evil principle. That is, failure to act will result in greater evil. This principle is at the heart of utilitarian or consequentialist ethics. Holmes correctly cautions, ". . . utilitarianism does not guarantee the rights of minorities, does not define good and evil, and might allow the use of perverse means to good ends."[55]

Third, the lesser evil principle, at least as developed by Brown, seems incomplete as an ethical decision-making principle. While one certainly wants to avoid greater evils, the Christian's primary obligation is to do good. Functioning on the basis of the lesser evil principle would sanction a horrendous evil, so long as it was less evil than a worse evil that might occur if one did not act. Surely, the desire to do the lesser evil must be supplemented at least by principles of justice and beneficence or love. Otherwise, the lesser evil principle alone might sanction atrocity.

Despite these objections, we think the problems Brown raises are both difficult and important. But we think the just war theory can account for Brown's concerns. For example, Holmes suggests that instead of starting a crusade, recognize that international law has been violated. If there were some international law-keeping force, that violation would be within their jurisdiction and would constitute aggression. It would then be possible to redress the evil. On the matter of preventive war, just war theorists have discussed what "aggression" means. It does not require allowing a first strike, but does require, among other considerations, limitations on the timing and extent of the response. This approach seems to address Brown's legitimate concerns, but brings them under the limitations of the just war theory. Our fear is that Brown's approach would fail sufficiently to limit wars and participation in them.

NUCLEAR WEAPONS

The atomic bomb that exploded over Hiroshima had the force of about twelve thousand tons of TNT. Modern nuclear warheads on the American Minuteman II missile are a hundred times more powerful, having the explosive force of about 1.2 million tons of TNT. The United States has 450 of these missiles. Moreover, various nations are thought to possess nuclear weapons, including republics in the former Soviet Union, Great Britain, France, China, India, and probably Israel and South Africa.

The world's nuclear arsenal is estimated to be more than sixty thousand weapons. This is large enough to destroy all the cities of the world many times over. Moreover, there are various delivery systems for these weapons. These include strategic bombers, strategic fighter bombers, land-based intercontinental missiles, submarine-launched intercontinental missiles, air-, land-, and sea-based cruise missiles, shorter-range rockets, nuclear cannons, and even hand-planted nuclear mines. With these systems, any city in the world could become a Hiroshima in thirty minutes. It is also frightening to realize that present technology makes it impossible to recall a nuclear device once it has been launched.

Given the unprecedented threat that nuclear weapons constitute, some think these weapons and their likely use in any war make the just war theory unworkable in the modern world. Moreover, a number of positions on the morality of these weapons have developed. We shall examine four and then address whether any of these positions can still render the just war theory usable. The positions are: nuclear pacifism, finite deterrence, strategic defense, and countervailing defense.[56]

NUCLEAR PACIFISM

Nuclear pacifists differ from pacifists in that they do not think all forms of military combat are immoral. The point of agreement among nuclear pacifists is that it is always immoral to use nuclear weapons.[57] For some this means that a nation may possess nuclear weapons in hopes of deterring an attack, but they must never use these weapons. Others are for unilateral nuclear disarmament, and still others are for multilateral disarmament. Given this diversity, some arguments support all views, while others are specific to a given form of nuclear pacifism.

Arguments for Nuclear Pacifism

Arguments for nuclear pacifism are both moral and practical. A common argument used by various positions stresses that nuclear devices are not ordinary bombs.[58] Since the bombing of Hiroshima, most people have sensed that there is something special and terrible about a nuclear bomb. The blinding flash, enormous heat, great mushroom cloud and firestorm all support the sense that nuclear destruction is not the "normal" destruction that accompanies war. Nuclear pacifists contend that these are not really weapons at all but are rather instruments of mass destruction, and that they have no rational use on the battlefield.

This claim is defended by various considerations. Because of the destructive power of nuclear bombs, they have unusual effects on civilization as a whole. If a full-scale nuclear war broke out, it could easily destroy life on earth as we know it. Even if their use did not totally destroy all life, radiation and radioactive fallout from these weapons could poison the earth and harm nations that had no part in the war, resulting in changes in the genes of future generations. Furthermore, one group of scientists claim that large-scale use of nuclear weapons would result in smoke and dust that would blot out the warmth of the sun and lower the earth's temperature. Such a change would have both short and long range consequences for the earth's climate. These changes would bring a "nuclear winter" that would kill many people from exposure and starvation.[59] Further, it is argued that nuclear weapons have a unique characteristic that sets them apart from anything else in military history. When nuclear bombs are delivered by large missiles, they increase greatly the offensive capabilities of the user without any gain in defensive potential. Clearly, a war fought with nuclear weapons would *have no winners*.

A second argument says that disarmament, even unilateral disarmament, would decrease the possibility of nuclear war. This may sound outrageous, but proponents defend it as follows.[60] If two nations possess nuclear weapons and one unilaterally disarms, the nation keeping its weapons must double its potential for war for the possibility of a nuclear war to remain the same. As long as two nations have nuclear weapons, the potential for starting a nuclear war either by choice or by chance exists with both nations. When one disarms, that potential is reduced. While the nation that retains its weapons may be more likely to use them, that likelihood will not double. Moreover, one of the major reasons for using nuclear weapons, namely, to preempt nuclear attack from an enemy, will be removed in regard to the disarming nation. Thus, though the disarming nation's vulnerability to nuclear attack might increase, the *overall* potential of such attack is reduced. Such disarmament is in the best interests of the international community, even if it is not serving the interests of a specific country. Chances of a large scale nuclear war that would kill billions of people and possibly destroy the human race would be significantly reduced.

Third, it is claimed that unilateral disarmament would also be in the best interests of the *disarming nation*.[61] If two nations with nuclear weapons keep them and one decides to use them against the other, the first use would have to be massive so as to prevent counterattack. But such an attack could result in widespread loss of life and the contamination of the earth and its atmosphere. On the other hand, if one of the nations disarmed and the other decided to use nuclear weapons against it, the attacking nation would probably not launch such a massive attack because victory could be assured through smaller-scale use, and because prudence dictates not endangering oneself through radioactive pollution. The result, as well, would be less destruction for the nation attacked.

Fourth, disarmament, unilateral and multilateral, or weapons reduction is in the best interests of any nation, because nuclear weapons and the modern technology to deliver them are so expensive.[62] To build and modernize these weapons takes a heavy toll on even the wealthiest of nations. That money would be better used to help the poor and raise the standard of living of a nation.

Fifth, though it may seem that having nuclear weapons is an advantage for a nation, it actually is not. To possess a nuclear bomb only encourages other nations to try to develop similar or better weapons. Once they do, the first nation must try to outdo them. The result is an ever escalating arms race where the world becomes a more dangerous place to live and the desire for security becomes an elusive dream. Any advantage one might have lasts only until one's opponent builds a better and/or more powerful system. This is an example of what game theorists call "the prisoner's dilemma."

Sixth, nuclear war is most often condemned on the grounds that it violates the rights of noncombatants in a participant nation and more generally the rights of people in nonparticipating nations.[63] Just war theory requires that noncombatants be protected as much as possible, but that is not possible when nuclear weapons are introduced into battle. Strategic nuclear weapons like the bombs dropped over Hiroshima have only one purpose, mass destruction. Since there cannot be noncombatant immunity from these weapons, just war theory condemns their use as immoral.

Finally, though a fundamental reason for having nuclear weapons is their deterrent value,[64] deterrence is an immoral reason to have them. Having them may deter their use by other nations, but to lack them opens one to nuclear blackmail. To those who would retain a few devices to prevent blackmail but never actually use them, the response is that as soon as an opponent realized that one would never use the weapons, the weapons would cease to have any deterrent value. Moreover, deterrence can never be a morally adequate reason for having nuclear weapons, because it holds civilians of another nation hostage. Deterrence requires another nation to have weapons for its protection that it does not wish to have.[65]

Objections to Nuclear Pacifism

Probably the most common objection is that nuclear pacifism is hopelessly utopian.[66] It is an attempt to put the genie back in the bottle *after* she has escaped. This position fails to deal with the world as it really is. It seeks a return to a pre-nuclear era, and that is no longer possible. Moreover, even if the nations of the world accepted this position and agreed to destroy all nuclear weapons, there would still be the problem of verification. How could one be sure some nations would not cheat? How could one be sure that in the event of a war, some nation would not build nuclear devices more quickly than the rest and thus have an advantage? Some suggest on the spot inspections, but even that cannot guarantee stopping nations bent on cheating. The international community's experience with Saddam Hussein's weapons vividly illustrates these problems.

Second, though unilateral disarmament may reduce *overall* risk to the international community, it does not for the disarming nation. In fact, it rather dramatically increases their risk. Nations with nuclear weapons need only threaten the cities of disarmed nations and their blackmail will succeed, because any threat could be carried out with impunity.[67]

Third, rather than decreasing the risk of nuclear war, disarmament might actually increase it, because allies of a disarming nation might feel threatened. Suppose the U.S. disarmed its nuclear arsenal. What would allies like Germany do? For the U.S. to disarm its nuclear arsenal would potentially jeopardize the defense of Germany. This could lead Germany to try to build or obtain their own nuclear weapons. The end result if other allies did the same would be nuclear proliferation, not disarmament or pacifism.

Fourth, unilateral nuclear disarmament is inconsistent. Its supporters say nuclear weapons and the concomitant risk of nuclear war are so great that one's own nation should disarm regardless of what other nations do. However, any argument that applies to one nation can be formulated as a good argument for other nations to disarm. Yet, unilateral disarmament does not require other nations to disarm. In fact, it may remove the most important incentive for another nation's disarmament, the possession of nuclear weapons by other nations.[68]

Moreover, supporters of unilateral nuclear disarmament make much of the threat that possessing nuclear arms poses for nonaligned or non-nuclear nations. However, if there is not multilateral disarmament, any nation that disarms ends up subjecting itself (as well as other non-nuclear nations) to the threat and injustice of the nuclear powers. Thus, the only consistent position on disarmament is one that commits a nation to disarm *if and only if* all other nations agree similarly.

Fifth, though nuclear bombs are not "ordinary bombs," some at least are no more destructive than conventional weapons. Many do not realize that more people died in the bombing of Dresden in February 1945 and the bombing of Tokyo in March 1945 than died in Hiroshima or Nagasaki. As a matter of fact, the explosive charges on our smallest nuclear bombs are smaller than the explosive charges on the conventional "blockbuster" bombs of World War II. The essential element of a nuclear bomb is an explosive device, but explosives have been the main components of bombs since the Middle Ages. While it is true that modern nuclear weapons are more powerful than those used in World War II, it is unnecessary to use the large, strategic weapons and to drop them on cities.[69]

Sixth, protecting noncombatants as required by the just war theory is not impossible with all nuclear weapon use. Two things make it possible. One is the dramatic advance in computer and radar technology that aids missile accuracy. Early ICBMs were relatively inaccurate, landing within a mile of the target. This required a larger warhead to be carried by the missile. The new Pershing II missile has radar on board that can "see" the topography on the final approach and make corrections based on a map stored in its computer so it can deliver the warhead within thirty yards of the intended target. Improved accuracy makes it possible for this missile to be militarily effective with a much smaller payload.[70]

A second matter that improves noncombatant immunity is a recognition that targets of nuclear weapons must be military. For instance, the primary targets of U.S. nuclear weapons are Russian strategic and theater nuclear forces, conventional forces, political and military command and control centers, and war supporting industries. These targets all fall within the guidelines of traditional just war theory criteria. Moreover, claims that any use of nuclear weapons would of necessity escalate into a nuclear holocaust are hypothetical projections. As such, they ought to be taken with great seriousness, but they should not be accepted as fact. To assume a holocaust assumes that leaders of nations, field commanders, and armies could not act rationally.

Seventh, a war that included the use of nuclear weapons would not necessarily produce a "nuclear winter" on the earth. Some claim that the dust and smoke of a nuclear explosion in the upper atmosphere would not produce a nuclear winter but a "nuclear summer." Obviously, nuclear summers are no more desirable than nuclear winters, but the argument is that the effect would be temporary. There would be a temporary warming of the atmosphere similar to the "greenhouse effect," since pollution in the atmosphere would not only block the sun's rays from reaching the earth, but would also make it more difficult for the earth's heat to escape into space. Of course, both scenarios (nuclear summer or winter) assume that the dust and smoke would spread uniformly over the earth's atmosphere, but that may or may not be the case.

For the sake of argument, assume that a nuclear winter would occur if any large-scale nuclear war were waged. Even Carl Sagan admits that this might lead nations to develop low-yield and highly accurate weapons. Already under development is technology that will make possible the delivery of a nuclear warhead within thirty-five meters of its target even when launched over intercontinental distances. Moreover, technology is underway that will allow a warhead to burrow into the ground on impact and explode closer to its target. Again, Sagan concedes that nuclear weapons within the one to ten kiloton range would be able, with high degree of accuracy, to strike and penetrate even hardened silos. Such weapons would result in less collateral damage than the larger weapons of today, less smoke and dust would be thrown into the upper atmosphere, and the likelihood of a nuclear winter would be greatly reduced.[71]

Finally, the relationship between the development and deployment of nuclear weapons and social programs for the poor is more complex than the nuclear pacifist makes it. It is true that any money spent on defense *could* be used for social programs for the poor. In a perfect world that would be the case. But this is not a perfect world. Any nation, therefore, needs to spend some money on defense. The question becomes whether the spending is reasonable and moral. Those who object to nuclear pacifism claim that in the U.S. spending has been reasonable and moral. Proponents of nuclear pacifism claim otherwise. We doubt there is an objective way to answer this debate to everyone's satisfaction. But then, the argument, while an important reminder to take care of domestic needs, cannot be conclusive.[72]

FINITE DETERRENCE

Finite deterrence is a nuclear strategy that permits the use of nuclear weapons as a last resort *after* a nation has sustained a nuclear attack from another.[73] Nuclear weapons should not be available for general use on the battlefield. Much of the world's nuclear arsenal could be disarmed and nations that have these weapons could retain just enough to survive a nuclear attack and retaliate.

Arguments for Finite Deterrence

Supporters of finite deterrence defend their position with various arguments, most of which focus on pragmatic concerns, not moral issues. An initial argument claims that while various fighting forces have nuclear weapons, authorization to use them can only be made by a President or his special delegate. This makes their use very unlikely, because anyone with the power to authorize their use would likely hesitate for fear of nuclear retaliation or for psychological or moral reasons, because their use might constitute a greater danger to allies than to enemies, or because battlefield commanders or troops might refuse to obey orders to use them.

Second, structuring military strategy primarily upon nuclear weapons that may never be used may lead to an army inadequately trained in conventional methods of combat. It is better to focus on conventional warfare, and maintain only enough nuclear weapons to repel a nuclear attack.[74]

Third, finite deterrence is not a *first* use or *early second* use policy. That should be clearly seen in the actions of nations that adopt it. Nuclear weapons that are retained should be protected so they would survive a first strike. But defensive systems that would prevent enemy missiles from reaching their targets should be abandoned. Such defensive systems are destabilizing as they shield a nation, giving the appearance that a first strike could be launched with impunity. Moreover, missiles that have "hard kill" capabilities (e.g., the ability to strike hidden enemy silos with accuracy) should be destroyed. Most importantly, all delivery systems should be single, not multiple, warhead systems.

Would these changes weaken a country's defenses? The answer is yes if the intent is to attack and destroy another nation, but no if the goal is survival. Once weapons with first strike capability are removed from a nation's arsenal, every effort should be made to make the remaining nuclear arsenal as invulnerable as possible. Weapons should be placed on submarines and the submarines hidden and dispersed. Strategic bombers should be developed with ability to penetrate enemy defenses so that shorter-range missiles can be used. Land-based missiles should be smaller and more mobile so they could sustain an attack. And finally, to end all interservice rivalry, control of nuclear weapons should be placed under the direct command of such people as the President or Secretary of Defense. That is, the use of such weapons should be under civilian and not military control.

Objections to Finite Deterrence

Just as most of the support for this view focuses on pragmatic concerns, so do the objections. The underlying assumption seems to be that while the all out use of nuclear weapons cannot be moral, limited use could fit within just war guidelines. The key, then, is to ask about the practicality of such a limited use policy as finite deterrence, and here there are questions.

Opponents of finite deterrence note first that any attempt to deter an enemy depends as much on what he thinks you will do as what you will actually do. Because nuclear weapons are feared, they have value regardless of how they would actually be employed. To remove them, except as a last resort, invites attack with conventional weapons. But if an aggressor with a large nuclear arsenal sees that he is losing the battle, he would likely escalate the conflict to the nuclear level, realizing that his opponent is in no position to respond. Thus, rather than reducing chances of nuclear war, finite deterrence increases it.[75]

Second, finite deterrence strategy requires strong command and control links between those who use the nuclear weapons and those who must authorize their use. A crafty opponent could either kill those who must authorize use or destroy the communications link to the forces. This could happen under any strategy, but it is most troublesome here, because so much authority is centralized in so few individuals.[76]

Third, some object to this approach to nuclear weapons because they claim it would never be rational to respond with a second strike. If another country attacks yours, either your country will be devastated by that assault or it will not be. If it is, then it would be irrational to respond with nuclear bombs because there is nothing to save. On the other hand, if you survive the attack with very little damage, it would still be irrational to respond with a nuclear second attack, because the enemy would likely retaliate with a third strike that would destroy your cities. Either way there is no rationale for a second strike, and thus, a first strike may be launched without fear of retaliation.[77]

Fourth, finite deterrence policy leads to a strange and unwelcome consequence. It mandates that nuclear weapons cannot be used unless one's country is attacked with such weapons and survives. Suppose, though, that an evil dictator is about to conquer the world, but he only uses conventional weapons. The only way to stop him is nuclear attack, but a country with finite deterrence strategy could never justify launching that attack.

A final and very important objection is based on this strategy's morality depending on the threat that a second strike would deter a first strike. But once a first strike is launched, this strategy has failed. The only point in launching a second strike would be to kill millions of people, and that is immoral.[78]

Defenders of this approach respond in three ways. Some reply that no threats are made using this strategy. A nation only holds the option to use nuclear weapons; there is no threat that it will actually do so. Since there are no threats, they cannot be immoral. Second, others grant that the actual use of nuclear weapons in a second strike would be immoral, but the threat to use them, a nuclear bluff, is not. The threat to use and the actual use of nuclear weapons are distinct acts. The threat would be moral even if use is not. Finally, some have argued the moral acceptability of a second strike from the morality of making the threat. To defend oneself, it is morally permissible to threaten the use of nuclear weapons in a second strike, and from the moral permissibility of the threat, it follows that it is morally permissible actually to follow through on that threat.[79]

Critics of finite deterrence are unconvinced by these responses. For a nuclear bluff to succeed, there must be a genuine threat to use nuclear weapons. If there is no threat, there is no bluff. Moreover, if there really is a threat, its morality depends on the intended action. In each case the action intended is a nuclear response. But those who raise this objection usually think a nuclear strike even in retaliation is immoral. Hence, they conclude the threat is also immoral, and they opt for nuclear pacifism.

STRATEGIC DEFENSE

A third strategy allows for the more general use of nuclear weapons and is called the strategic defense strategy or strategic defense initiative (SDI).[80] Today it is better known as the "star wars" theory. Strategic defenses are systems for intercepting and destroying enemy missiles before they land. Such systems were proposed as early as the 1950s. Anti-bomber surface to air missiles were actually deployed, and work on an anti-ballistic missile system (ABM) was started. Both the U.S. and the then existing Soviet Union developed partially effective ABM systems by the end of the 1960s. However, in 1972 both countries agreed to stop work on these systems. By the late 1970s the vulnerability of ICBMs, the development of new methods of tracking missiles, advances in computer technology, and new approaches to attacking missiles were responsible for renewed interest in anti-ballistic missile systems. In 1983 President Reagan inaugurated research to deploy a strategic defense system by the end of the 1990s. This system would attack enemy missiles throughout their flight. This would involve laser attacks during the boost or ascent phase, a variety of attacks while in midcourse, and more attacks in the descent phase, possibly even from solid projectiles that would crash into the missile.

Arguments for Strategic Defense Strategy

Though there are not many arguments for SDI, those used are significant.[81] By far the most important consideration is that this strategy does not threaten people, only nuclear weapons. This system is purely defensive. It constitutes a true system of defense, not deterrence, and is therefore justified by the right of self-defense. Whatever else one thinks of this strategy, one must agree that a system that destroys missiles on their way to their targets is not morally bad.

Second, even if the strategic defense system is not entirely effective, it would guarantee the survival of nuclear weapons for retaliation. Suppose the defensive system can protect only 50 percent of a country's missiles. Fifty percent of a country's nuclear weapons would survive for counterattack on the enemy. Such an eventuality should serve to deter an opponent.

Objections to Strategic Defense Strategy

An initial question arises with respect to the development and effectiveness of the strategic defense system.[82] Some question whether we presently possess technology to build an effective system. Suppose an enemy launched one thousand to two thousand missiles, each with ten thousand separable warheads and mixed in with thousands of decoys. Could a defensive system sort out and destroy the genuine missiles in about thirty minutes? This would be no easy task.

Moreover, a strategic defense system would be called into action without ever being tested under wartime conditions. Thus, no one really knows how much confidence should be placed in the system. Defenders of SDI claim this does not harm their approach, because the enemy also does not know how effective it will be.

Second, it is reasonable to think the presence of an SDI system would influence the size of a missile attack by an enemy. If they thought 50 percent of their missiles would be destroyed and never reach their target, they would likely double the size of the launch. While it would cost the launcher more money, it would cost the defender more as well. And if the defense system was not as good as thought, the enormity of the attack would wreak havoc many times over.

Moreover, suppose it was possible to build a strategic defense system that was 100 percent effective against a missile attack. Would that protect a nation against nuclear attack? No! The reason is that not all nuclear devices are delivered on missiles. A bomber, cruise missile or small boat could still deliver a nuclear explosive. Even a piece of luggage could conceal a nuclear device. Thus, the best one could hope for is reduced vulnerability, not invulnerability.

Third, if one superpower builds a strategic defense system, all will have to. When all nations have such defensive systems, then all will be deprived of second strike capability and forced into first strike use to assure victory.

Finally, ever since nuclear weapons were developed, their main purpose has not been to fight war, but to make threats. Because the threat of retaliation has been so great, no one has carried out any of these threats. However, if a strategic defense system were developed, it is not inconceivable that threats, at least by the nation with a star wars system, would be carried out. This would, of course, increase the likelihood of nuclear attack and thereby increase tension, not reduce it.

COUNTERVAILING OR MUTUAL ASSURED DESTRUCTION STRATEGY

A final strategy is called by two names, the countervailing or mutual assured destruction (MAD) strategy. This is presently the nuclear policy of the United States of America. It was first adopted in 1974 by President Gerald Ford and was revised in 1980 by President Jimmy Carter.[83]

The primary aim of this strategy is to deter another nation from a nuclear attack. This is done by showing an aggressor that any gains it might get from a first strike would be more than offset by losses it would sustain in a retaliatory attack.

For this strategy to be effective, the nation that uses it must be prepared to survive a first attack and be capable of a second strike that would inflict unacceptable losses on an enemy. This requires the nuclear arsenal to be hidden and spread out over land and sea. Nuclear weapons must be delivered by bombers, land missiles and submarines. This policy recognizes that the tendency will be to escalate responses. Therefore, it is necessary to have an escalating response that will win at each level without destroying humanity. This is called "escalating dominance."

To gain dominance at each new level it will be necessary not only to survive a first attack, but also to destroy as many of the enemy's weapons as possible before they are used and to cut its communication systems as completely as possible to limit its ability to wage war. This requires a variety of nuclear weapons that are highly accurate. Finally, the countervailing strategy does not renounce first use of nuclear weapons either. That may be necessary for certain kinds of defense for oneself or an ally. An underlying assumption of this view is that one achieves "peace through nuclear strength."

Arguments for Countervailing Strategy[84]

Proponents of this strategy claim it has worked for about forty-five years. While not every element in this strategy has been in place for forty-five years, nevertheless, the basic idea of deterring an enemy from widespread aggression has been a central element of U.S. policy, and it has been successful in preventing any world wars. Moreover, since nuclear war would be bad for humanity, whatever prevents it serves both a country's national interest and the interests of the international community.

A second argument is that nations have the right of self-defense. Since nuclear weapons cannot be recalled after launched, this right includes the right to threaten counterattacks in hopes of deterring an enemy. Moreover, the right of self-defense is conceded to other nations as well. In the case of the U.S. and the former Soviet Union, agreement was reached in 1972 to stop development and deployment of ABMs. This guaranteed both nations survival from first use and retaliation in acceptable terms.

Finally, proponents think this strategy morally superior to the alternatives. SDI denies the right of self-defense to other nations. It allows the nation with the defense to inflict risks on other nations that it will not accept itself. Finite deterrence strategy does not provide for conventional conflict. Moreover, since one's stockpile of nuclear weapons is so small, they must be directed at the cities of another nation, holding them hostage. And nuclear pacifism is worst of all, since it opens one to nuclear blackmail by anyone with such weapons. Countervailing or mutual assured destruction strategy is a tough approach, but this is a tough world, and this policy has demonstrated that it can prevent nuclear conflict.

Objections to Countervailing Strategy

Critics of this policy can be found on the left and the right.[85] Those on the left are mainly concerned about the risks it poses for international peace, and those on the right are disturbed by the risk it imposes on the nation adopting it.

As to the latter issue, critics on the right say this strategy leaves nations that adopt it defenseless. The strategy operates through a series of threats to counterattack an enemy in hopes that the threats will deter him from attacking. Thus, this is a strategy of nuclear *deterrence*, not of nuclear *defense*. This poses at least two problems. A really determined enemy might not be deterred by threats of counterattack. Moreover, if nations do have the right to self-defense, deterrence and self-defense are not the same, making a strategy of nuclear deterrence morally questionable, for a nation unprepared or unwilling to defend its people is reprehensible.

Second, escalating dominance will only work against an enemy whose responses are measured and who at some point refuses to accept the destruction further response would require. Escalating dominance provides no protection against an enemy so bent on your destruction that he risks his as well. Moreover, the point where risk no longer deters can be reached anywhere in a conflict. It is even conceivable that an enemy would launch everything it had in a first strike in hopes of instant victory. Furthermore, these strategies are developed in terms of superpowers who have a lot to lose in any war. In the 1990s and beyond, it is not unlikely that nuclear weapons will fall into the hands of and be used by terrorist groups who feel they have nothing to lose by their use. In other words, this strategy rests on the assumption that those who have these weapons will act rationally in times of war. That is open to question.

Third, escalating dominance leads to an arms race. If a nation must have superiority at every level of conflict, then it must develop weapons that are better than its opponent's at each level. The result is a costly arms race.

Fourth, the countervailing strategy is primarily a tactic of retaliation. This leaves the initiative in the hands of the enemy, but if there were a large-scale war, a good many military men think it is better to have the initiative, particularly if a first strike could mean annihilation in a nuclear war. An essential element of this strategy is "damage limitation," ending the conflict on favorable terms. This, however, is best achieved by a first preemptive strike against an enemy. It is necessary to take out his hardest targets—hidden and hardened underground silos and mobile weapons systems.

Fifth, while deterrence, not defense, is the goal of this strategy, some think it cannot even guarantee that. Deterrence depends on a balance of weapons between two opponents. If one has dominance, the deterrent value of the other's weapons is greatly reduced.

Sixth, a nuclear strategy where nuclear weapons are employed throughout and not just as a last resort lowers the nuclear threshold. History since 1945 shows that nations are very reluctant to use nuclear weapons. There have been threats to use these weapons, but none have ever actually been exploded. To adopt a plan such as MAD that encourages wide distribution of these weapons is to lower the nuclear threshold, and that places the world at greater risk of nuclear conflict should a war break out.

Seventh, some say that if the time ever came to use weapons according to this strategy, field commanders and armed forces would refuse. When Japan was bombed, everyone followed orders. But we now know better the destructive power of nuclear weapons, so that if their use were ever ordered, many might disobey orders. For example, if a command came to use tactical nuclear weapons on the crowded plains of Europe where devastation of cities would be assured, it is likely that many would refuse to obey orders.

Eighth, a common argument for a policy such as MAD is that it has worked for nearly forty-five years. But is this true? Would there have been war if this strategy of deterrence had not been followed? Any answer is a guess. The forty-five years of nuclear peace since Hiroshima could be attributed to various factors (e.g., fear of conventional war, internally developing countries did not want external conflict, or a decline in nationalism).

Finally, though the argument for the countervailing strategy is put in terms of self-defense, one may question whether the use of nuclear weapons is a genuine case of self-defense. Self-defense is a right for those attacked, but it allows the nation to defend itself, not destroy the enemy for what it did. The latter sounds more like punishment than self-defense. Furthermore, self-defense gives the right to stop an attack. The countervailing approach stops the attacker but also kills many innocent bystanders.

CONCLUSION

In this chapter we have tried to present fairly arguments and objections for a number of positions on war and the use of nuclear arms. As we close, we need to state our conclusions.

No sane person, regardless of their position, wants war. But is war totally avoidable? We do not think it is. Ours is a fallen world, a world under Satan's power. This means there will likely be wars no matter how hard we try to avoid them. History and common sense bear this out, and so does Scripture.[86]

Given these facts about human nature and the apparent unavoidability of war, we cannot see pacifism as a realistic position on war. As argued in our discussion of the biblical basis for pacifism, we do not believe Scripture mandates pacifism for all or even just for believers. Moreover, while we greatly value life, we believe there are religious and human values worth fighting for and even dying for, not least of which is protecting others and ourselves from genocide and from the enslaving regime of a totalitarian dictator.

Despite our rejection of pacifism, we do think it is important to limit the wars in which Christians may participate and how they may conduct themselves in those wars. Thus, we hold the just war theory in spite of the difficulties complex modern warfare presents it. We must add, however, that we would always uphold the right of conscientious objection for those who could not in good conscience participate in any war.

As to nuclear weapons, we pray they will never be used again, but no one can predict the future. In evaluating the four nuclear strategies presented, we find none of them completely convincing. Objections raised against each position seem to be compelling to one degree or another. But even apart from these theories we doubt whether the use of strategic nuclear weapons whose sole purpose is the widespread and indiscriminate destruction of life and property could possibly meet the demands of just war theory. As to tactical nuclear weapons whose destructive power would be much less, a judgment on their use would have to be made in a concrete situation. With advancing technology that allows for greater accuracy and less overall destruction, perhaps they could meet just war criteria such as noncombatant immunity and proportionality. In sum, though we could not preclude all use of nuclear weapons in advance of a concrete situation, our adherence to the just war theory and our skepticism about whether nuclear weapons could meet its criteria pushes us toward a position which is not far *in practice* (even though very far *in theory*) from nuclear pacifism.

In closing, we must add that we do not believe that what we have said is grounds for despair, especially not for the Christian.[87] History is still under God's sovereign control. Thus, nothing will happen without his permission or beyond his control. Of course, this does not remove responsibility from nations or individuals to do what is possible to avoid armed conflict. War is one of many expressions of the sinfulness of the human heart. God has called his children to fight this sin by being peacemakers. Perhaps through our actions and prayers God will see fit to grant peace in our time to the furtherance of his glory and his kingdom's cause.

CHAPTER FOURTEEN

The Christian and the Secular State

In his Templeton Prize address Alexander Solzhenitsyn said: "Over half a century ago, while I was still a child, I recall hearing a number of older people offer the following explanation for the great disasters that had befallen Russia: 'Men have forgotten God; that's why all this has happened.' Since then I have spent well-nigh 50 years working on the history of our revolution; in the process I have read hundreds of books, collected hundreds of personal testimonies, and have already contributed eight volumes of my own toward the effort of clearing away the rubble left by the upheaval. But if I were asked today to formulate as concisely as possible the main cause of the ruinous revolution that swallowed up some 60 million of our people, I could not put it more accurately than to repeat: 'Men have forgotten God; that's why all this has happened.'"[1]

If totalitarianism and slavery rule where men forget God, how should Christians respond? Should Christians work to wed church and state to try to guarantee that men will not forget God? Or should they merely proclaim the gospel and let the Lord use that preaching to bring to Christ those who run the social and political processes? Jesus calls us to be light and salt (Matt 5:13-16) in society, but how should we do that? In the 1980s especially, Christians of conservative political bent tried to influence American political processes in an organized way. Some complain that the methods and rhetoric are too strident, while others say politics is just too dirty for Christian involvement at all.

Unquestionably, government has great legal and judicial control over matters like abortion, euthanasia and capital punishment. Many U.S. Christians, dissatisfied with their government's direction in these areas,

have felt compelled to enter the political process to try to make a difference. Here again, the question constantly arises about the appropriate
means of protesting and redressing wrongs in society. Should any single
religious group have a right to legislate its morality on others, especially
in a pluralistic society? Should Christians effect change only by voting
their conscience, or should they also engage in acts of civil disobedience
when their viewpoint on moral questions is not enacted? In fact, can one
justify violent and even revolutionary tactics in order to establish a more
just and moral (by Christian standards) order? Christians disagree on
these important issues.

While we could address many issues, of necessity we must be selective.
In this chapter we propose to handle the following: 1) should a Christian
participate in affairs of the state, or should he withdraw in favor of preaching the gospel? 2) how should the corporate church relate to the political
process? 3) is there a "Christian position" on each of the social and political issues that confront society? 4) is it ever morally permissible for a
Christian to disobey the state or even use violence to accomplish social
goals? Though each issue is relevant to Christians generally, some have a
slightly different nuance, depending on the form of government in each
country.[2]

In order to set the stage for discussion, we shall begin with a summary
of biblical teaching on government and the believer's relation to it. Many
issues for which one might wish guidance are not addressed in Scripture.
Consequently, for some issues there may be any number of social and
political solutions compatible with the general tenor of Scripture.

SUMMARY OF SCRIPTURAL TEACHING

In discussing relevant biblical data, two words of caution must be remembered. First, the distinction between description and prescription must
curb the tendency to absolutize everything one sees. Descriptions of governmental practices and believers' actions in relation to the state do not
prescribe moral obligations. Unfortunately, this means there is little direct
biblical instruction on many of the matters before us.

Second, one must not make timeless absolutes out of OT Israel's experience under the theocracy, for that was an unusual situation. God literally was the ruler in Israel. God was directly in charge of both spiritual
and political matters. The OT nowhere teaches that this was to be the
arrangement for Gentile nations, nor does the NT show that this is the format for saved or unsaved after the time of Christ.

OT TEACHING

Gen 1:26-28 is the first passage with relevance to government, for it
records the creation of man and the divine mandate that man subdue and

rule the earth. Nothing is said about the form of such rule or how man should relate to man in this process. Man is both instructed and permitted by God to rule over the earth and the animal kingdom.[3]

Many consider Gen 9:1-7 to be the first clear teaching to mandate some form of government. After the flood, God tells Noah to subdue and rule the earth. In addition, capital punishment is sanctioned when life is taken. This alone does not institute any particular form of government, but it does establish the right of retributive justice when life is taken. That right is foundational to government's ability to maintain order and dispense justice.

Probably the most formal and thorough ordering of society in the OT comes through the Mosaic Law. Not only the civil and ceremonial laws, but also the Decalogue itself relates to social order. Many of the Ten Commandments regulate interpersonal relationships. Commandments against murder, stealing, adultery, etc. are later amplified in the Mosaic Code, where penalties are prescribed for breaking those laws, and rules are presented which govern various situations involving those laws (cf., e.g., Deuteronomy 22–24 with all its specific laws and punishments relating to human sexuality). The result of Mosaic legislation was to establish Israel as a theocracy ruled directly by God. Even though Israel opted in favor of a king, God was to select the king, and the king was to submit to God. To disobey the king was to disobey God.

None of this guaranteed that the king would always follow God. Kings in Israel were often ungodly and oppressive toward the people. Prophets arose who attacked the evils of society. For a prophet to criticize the king was technically an act of treason and disloyalty to the state (e.g., Amos 7:10-13), and sometimes the prophet paid with his life. Of course, the prophet had to speak for God anyway.[4] The prophets called the people to repentance, and if the people complied, there would be changes in social practices. Nonetheless, the prophets did not *per se* stir up social and political revolution against the state. God had chosen the king, however bad he might be. The prophet's role was simply to call the king and his people back to righteousness.

Two further comments about the OT are appropriate. First, once Israel came under foreign rule, there was no indication that God wanted them to institute a theocracy in the lands of their captors or to try to overthrow those governments. On the contrary, the pagan kings served as God's instruments of judgment upon his people, and he used Gentile rule to accomplish various purposes among the Israelites. Moreover, Jews in foreign lands were submissive to political leaders insofar as their conscience would allow (cf. Daniel and Joseph), and they were involved in the affairs of state when given opportunity (cf. Daniel, Esther, and Joseph). Total separation from pagan governments was not the order of the day.

The other comment relates to OT revelation about the coming world ruler and his government. Though there is much debate over the particulars of these prophecies, Daniel 2 and 7 put the whole matter of governmental rule in perspective. According to those passages, God has given the rule of mankind to Gentile powers until the Son of Man becomes king. Dan 7:14 shows that his kingdom will be worldwide and everlasting. Isa 11:1-11 describes the qualifications of this coming ruler and the nature of his rule. That passage shows that he will rule both Israel and the Gentiles. As premillennialists, we believe that all of these passages and others like them show that the ultimate form of government will be an absolute monarchy with Christ as the monarch. Regardless of one's understanding of the millennial kingdom, all sides in the debate agree that someday all human rule will cease, and God will be absolute monarch. So, the OT begins with God's command for man to rule the earth for God, but in the end portrays God directly ruling over all.

NT TEACHING

In this summary of NT teaching, we want to look at Jesus' and apostolic teaching. Of special interest is Pauline and Petrine thought.

Jesus and the State

In assessing Christ's teaching, one must distinguish between explicit instructions and actions that suggest underlying attitudes. As to explicit statements, there are three main passages that apparently speak of the Christian's role in society and relation to government. Those passages are Matt 5:13-16, 17:24-27, and 22:15-22 (cf. parallels in Mark 12:13-17 and Luke 20:19-26), though it is debatable that the second is relevant to the topic.

In Matt 5:13-16 (part of the Sermon on the Mount) Jesus says that believers are light and salt in the world and should function as such. Light offers guidance and direction, and salt preserves. Jesus instructs believers to live in such a way that men will see their good works and glorify God in heaven (v. 16). Of course, the passage does not say exactly what good works in society the Christian should do to serve as light and salt. That is, should Christians start programs to feed the hungry and house the homeless? That would be appropriate, but Jesus is not that specific. Consequently, there has always been uncertainty as to how the Christian should fulfill this obligation.

As to Matt 17:24-27, traditional interpretation sees the didrachma as a temple tax. This tax was required of all Jewish males above the age of nineteen for the upkeep of temple services. As such, it was not a tax to support the government (Rome) but the current Jewish religious "establishment." The assumption that the temple tax is in view is based in part on Josephus' comment that the temple tax was about two drachmas.[5]

According to Matthew 17, tax collectors asked Peter if Jesus paid the tax, and Peter replied affirmatively. That settled the matter for the collectors, but not for Jesus. Jesus asked Peter if the kings of the earth collect taxes from their sons or from others. Peter replied that taxes come from others. Jesus reasoned that the sons, then, are exempt. Still, so as not to offend, Jesus said they should pay the tax. Peter caught a fish with a stater (a four drachma piece) in its mouth and paid the tax for Jesus and himself. On the traditional interpretation, Jesus' point is that he really did not owe a temple tax because his Father owned the temple. In fact, all properly related to God are sons of the owner and are thus exempt. However, for the sake of those who do not understand who Jesus really is, he paid the tax so as to offend no one.[6]

Though we think the traditional interpretation of Matthew 17 is most likely,[7] we question use of the passage in discussing the Christian's relation to civil authority. Jesus claimed exemption from a religious tax, but paid it so as not to offend. That does not mean Jesus is teaching that believers in every age should pay religious taxes, and it says nothing about civil taxes. It suggests that this passage really teaches little from which one can generalize to a Christian's relation to civil authority. In fact, it is even difficult to ascertain any *application* relevant to a believer today in relation to his government. Perhaps one might reason from the passage that there are some occasions when it is better not to challenge authorities but to comply, even if we are exempt from their specific demand. This is surely sound prudential advice, but hardly *prescription* from Matthew 17 on how Christians should relate to their government or to any other authority figure.

Matt 22:15-22 does relate to the issues of this chapter, but it must be understood in its context. The Pharisees and Herodians tried to trap Christ by asking if he thought taxes should be paid to Caesar. A negative answer would bring trouble with the Roman government but keep peace with Jewish nationalistic tendencies. Answering affirmatively would not oppose the Romans (nor the Herodians, who supported the ruling house in Palestine), but it would anger Jewish nationalists opposed to the Roman yoke. Something further was also at issue. Roman coinage normally bore Caesar's image and had an inscription that referred to Caesar as divine. Jewish law forbade the use of icons in any form, so Jewish coinage typically was minted without any icons.[8] In 26 A.D. when Pontius Pilate posted some Roman icons around Jerusalem, massive civil disobedience ensued. Pilate was forced to remove the icons.[9] Jesus knew his opponents were trying to trap him, so he asked for a coin. They brought him a denarius (a Roman coin minted in Gaul). It was an unusual coin for common people to have, but it was used by the high priests (the ruling nobility in Israel), the Herodians, and other members of the tax-exempt upper classes.[10] Moreover, the coin bore the image of Caesar and the inscription. The fact that Jesus' opponents had access to the coin suggests their hypocrisy. The

Pharisees, for example, supposedly concerned with strict adherence to Mosaic Law, should not have had coinage bearing Caesar's image, but they did. The hypocrisy, however, extends further. By possessing a Roman coin, they were benefiting from the economic privileges of the Roman Empire, and yet their question asked whether one had to fulfill a key matter of civil financial responsibility to that government. That is hypocrisy.

Jesus asked whose image the coin bore. When they replied that Caesar's image was on the coin, Jesus told them to render to Caesar what was Caesar's and to God what belonged to him. There are various ways to understand Christ's comments. One way is to say that Jesus was merely saying in an offhanded way, "Well, if it has Caesar's image on it, it belongs to him, so give it back."[11] This would suggest that Christ really did not care about the coin; it bore Caesar's image, so give it to him. The whole matter is indifferent. On the other hand, we think the most common understanding of Christ's answer is correct. Jesus is saying that some things rightfully belong to Caesar and should be given to him. Jesus does not specify everything in that group, but context demands that it includes tax money. In addition, Jesus says some things belong to God and should be given to him. Jesus' answer affirms both the right of a government to demand that its people fulfill certain responsibilities and the legitimacy of God to require allegiance in things pertaining to himself. In effect, Jesus is commanding that Caesar be given what has his image on it (the coin) and that God be given what has his image on it (man).[12] In sum, Jesus affirms two fundamental points in regard to government: 1) human government has a legitimate right to demand that its people fulfill certain responsibilities; 2) it is appropriate to distinguish between the things of the state and the things of God (many appeal to this passage as support for the two kingdoms idea).

Jesus' attitude and actions are also instructive. Some call Christ's attitude respectful disregard.[13] While he did not want to incite rebellion against prevailing powers, he made it clear that his mission was not simply to fit within existing structures. Thus, he spoke on the divorce issue (Mark 10:1-12), knowing that his words were a rebuke of the Herod/Herodias affair. John the Baptist lost his life for such criticism, but that did not deter Jesus. His task was to speak spiritual truth and call men to a higher plane of living. Moreover, Jesus said that his kingdom is not of this world (John 18:36), but he also clarified that those who brought him to trial had authority over him only because God had given them power to rule (John 19:8-11).

As to national prejudices, Jesus avoided them. Tax collectors (who collected taxes for Rome) and soldiers were considered enemies of the Jewish people and thus traitors to God. Nonetheless, Jesus overlooked such nationalistic concerns in that he received tax collectors (cf. Luke 19:1-10), healed the servant of a centurion, and dealt with the hated Samaritans.

Jesus focused on individuals with their spiritual and physical needs and refused to be identified with partisan political issues of the day. When it was appropriate, he also criticized and rebuked the authorities, regardless of whether they were leaders of the Jewish religious establishment or of the secular government. Matthew 23 records his indictment of the Pharisees, while Mark 10:1-12 and Luke 13:32ff. present his rebuke of governmental rulers. In Luke 22:25ff. we hear his indictment of rulers who claim to benefit the people but only care for themselves.

In sum, Jesus refused to absolutize the state, but he would not wage war against it either. To those who would absolutize the state, he reminds them to render to God what is God's. To those who want the overthrow of the state, he demands that they render to Caesar what belongs to him.[14] Jesus acted as both subject to the general authority of the state while above it in his mission and ministry. Christ's career and the ongoing of the state intersected at those points where Jesus' moral teachings served to indict those in power, at points where he mingled with political and social untouchables in order to meet individual needs, and at the point where the King of Kings submitted to the ignominy of trial at the hands of human potentates in order to accomplish his spiritual program for the whole world.

Apostolic Teaching

Here again we must distinguish between direct teaching and apostolic practice. The two most explicit passages are Rom 13:1-7 and 1 Pet 2:13-17. In many ways the Petrine passage is less controversial. In verse 11 Peter reminds readers that they are aliens and strangers in the world. Because believers' citizenship is in heaven, some may think they can live as they please in the world. But Peter urges his readers (v. 12) to live good lives on earth in order to avoid offending non-believers. In verse 13 Peter explains further how to witness in a world where one is really an alien. As a child of God and his kingdom, believers are actually free from obligation to earthly institutions. Peter encourages them to use that freedom to serve God in society, and he commands them to do so by submitting to the powers that be. Verses 13-14 and 17 enjoin submission to governmental authorities. Submission will silence the foolish accusations of the ungodly (v. 15) who might think Christians are subversive of the government (as many in Peter's day thought). Verse 14 offers Peter's only comments about government's function. God has instituted governors to mete out justice. Christians should submit to government for the Lord's sake (v. 13), recognizing its positive function in society.[15]

As to Pauline thinking, commentators note that Romans 13 must be understood in its overall context. Beginning in chapter 12 Paul offers a series of imperatives regarding relationships. The passage just prior to Romans 13 speaks of love and living in harmony with one another. Believers must not seek revenge against enemies, but rather must do them good. The passage immediately following 13:1-7 again focuses on the need for love (13:8-10). How 13:1-7 precisely fits this context is much debated,[16] and space prohibits detailing that debate here. Suffice it to say that we do believe Paul is addressing the believer's relation to government in this passage and that his message is not inappropriate in a context devoted to the way a believer ought to respond to others. In this passage Paul broadens the focus from the treatment of individuals to one's response to his government.

In this passage Paul makes four main points. First, Christians must submit to government, because God has established all governmental authorities. Rebellion against the government is rebellion against God (vv. 1-2). This does not mean God is happy with every ruling official, but only that government itself is instituted by God and under his authority. Second, in verses 3-4 Paul notes one of the functions of the state, namely, dispensing justice to evildoers and the law-abiding alike. This is the same function Peter mentioned in 1 Peter 2. Verse 5 raises a third point. Christians should submit not only from a negative motive (fear of punishment if they disobey) but from a positive one (conscience). Conscience should remind the believer that rulers are established by God as his ministers, and thus, disobeying the ruler disobeys God. Finally, in verses 6-7 Paul states a practical outcome of this teaching. Rulers serve God and are to be remunerated. The means is through the payment of taxes, and Paul enjoins Christians to pay their share. Refusing to pay taxes while claiming to be submissive to the state is inconsistent. Believers must not take away with their hand (support through taxes) what they pledge with their mouth (submission).

A final element in Paul's explicit comments on the Christian and government is his command in 1 Tim 2:1-4 to pray for kings and all in authority. Believers should pray so that we may live peaceful and quiet lives. The reason for desiring such a life is implied in verses 3-4. God wants all men to be saved, and Paul knows that during a time of peace the gospel is more likely to be given free rein. Thus, more people will likely hear the gospel, and that should result in many responding to Christ. Prayer for rulers also asks God to give them wisdom in handling national and international problems. In essence, it asks God to prosper the ruler's efforts to do things that will bring peace and thereby create a climate in which the gospel can be proclaimed.

A final question remains. Do Peter and Paul, then, require unqualified obedience to government regardless of what it asks? The practice of Peter and Paul suggests not.[17] More on this when we discuss civil disobedience, but suffice it now to note Peter's comments in Acts 4:19 and 5:29 when told not to preach the gospel and Paul's answers to the Philippian magistrates (Acts 16:11-40).

Apostolic teaching, like that of Jesus and the OT, basically enjoins submission to ruling powers in order to accomplish certain goals in society (for example, order and peace) that will benefit Christians' efforts to achieve spiritual goals (for example, evangelism). Underlying this attitude of submission is the awareness that rulers have power only because God allows them to rule. Moreover, submission does not force one to ignore God-given tasks or divine principles of morality, nor does it remove the believer's right and responsibility to speak on the moral and spiritual issues confronting society.[18]

From this general summary of biblical teaching two things become rather clear. First, despite the obvious differences between an OT theocracy and the NT era, both the OT and NT take the same basic approach on the believer's relation to government. Second, Scripture, while presenting the general contours of church/state relations, leaves much unsaid. Consequently, many of the issues treated in this chapter are not directly touched in Scripture. For many of these issues, the only scriptural help will come inferentially from general biblical principles whose applications to concrete problems are not spelled out.

To Participate or Not Participate

If the fundamental task of Christians is to fulfill the Great Commission, does this mean individual Christians should refuse to participate in the social and political process? Some have thought so. Of course, in some countries about the only participation allowed is payment of taxes to the government. Regardless of how little participation a country allows its people, the question of the Christian's participation or withdrawal from society should be asked. Some who favor withdrawal are not merely pacifists. They may also refuse to serve on juries, vote, support political activities and organizations, serve as public officials, or even pay taxes.

ARGUMENTS AGAINST PARTICIPATION

In arguing against involvement, some appeal to the concept of the two kingdoms. Scripture seems to distinguish between the kingdom of God and the kingdom of this world. Jesus said his kingdom was not of this world (John 18:36), and Paul said believers are citizens of heaven (Phil 3:19, 20). Christians must decide which kingdom they will support; loyalty cannot be divided. Allegiance to worldly rulers or kingdoms and their goals is tantamount to being an enemy of God (John 15:19; 17:16; Rom 12:2; Gal 1:4; Jas 4:4; 1 John 2:15). Though Christians must submit to the government in power, they can never defend or support the programs and goals of earthly potentates. Allegiance must go to Christ and his kingdom.

Second, it is often argued that the believer's chief responsibility is evangelism (Prov 11:30; Matt 28:18-20). Obedience to the Great Commission leaves no time for involvement in political activity. Moreover, political activism does not strike at the core of man's sinful condition. The best way to change society is to lead people to Christ, and anyway, the essential thrust of the gospel is spiritual, not social and political. As 2 Tim 2:4 states, believers must avoid entanglement with the world's affairs if they are to be good soldiers of Christ. The example of Peter and John in response to the man crippled from birth is instructive. Rather than responding to the man's needs with various social and economic answers, Peter offered a spiritual solution (Acts 3:6).[19]

According to a third argument, Christian ethics are for Christians and do not apply well to the world of political power. Secular society cares little about our standards, and we are not likely to succeed in legislating our morality. Moreover, it is difficult to square our ethics with secular society. For example, how do the ethics of the Sermon on the Mount square with a nation's call to its citizens to go to war? Or, how can one opposed to abortion justify paying taxes when some of that money may pay for federally funded abortions? Is it not better, then, for the Christian to withdraw from society?

Fourth, many complain that politics is a dirty business. It is simply impossible to get involved in the political process without being tainted by compromise, corruption and unprincipled behavior. Compromising ethical standards in order to "get along" in politics is unacceptable for a follower of Christ. The Christian life allows no compromise. One must either be for God or against him (Matt 12:30).[20]

Fifth, some think the only way to have any genuine hope of affecting the political process is to act in a block with other believers. However, this raises several issues. Should Christians join those with different doctrinal commitments just to attain a particular goal in society? Some on the extreme right wing criticized the Moral Majority for such compromise. In addition, cooperation with believers of other denominations (and even with non-believers) raises the question of whether there is "the Christian position" on some of these social and political issues. If not, how does the church agree on what policies and programs to support or oppose? Further, this matter of cooperation *en masse* raises the question of whether the church has a right to attempt to impose its morality and its will on the state. Even Christians disagree here. For example, many who think Christians should uphold their viewpoint in society think the proper way to implement Christian ethics is to preach the gospel, not to try to affect the political process.

Finally, some have argued for non-involvement on the ground that Christ will return soon, and then social problems will be rectified. The force of this argument is especially felt by those who are premillennial in their eschatology. However, even amillennialists have no delusions about the course of this age. If one's view of human history is basically pessimistic so that the only hope for resolution of social, political and economic problems is the return of Christ, the need for involvement in society may seem less urgent. Those to whom this line of argument appeals feel that a Christian's time is best invested in living a godly life and evangelizing the unsaved. This is the way to prepare for the new age. Moreover, for those who think Christ's return is quite near, there may be a feeling that any long range planning to effect social change is futile.[21]

ARGUMENTS FOR INVOLVEMENT

Despite these arguments, there are good reasons for Christians to participate in the social and political process. In what follows, we shall respond to the preceding arguments and offer other supports for participation.

As to the matter of the two kingdoms, it is true that our allegiance must be to Christ first. John's command (1 John 2:15) not to love the world means that believers are not to set their highest affections on the things of this world, nor should they adopt its philosophies and values. However, that does not mean we have no role to play in our society for Christ. In his high priestly prayer for his disciples, Jesus did not ask his Father to take believers out of the world, but asked that while they are in it God would protect them from the evil one (John 17:15). Moreover, Christ tells us to love our neighbors as ourselves (Matt 22:39), and John says (1 John 4:20-21) that we cannot claim to love God at the same time we are hating our brother or sister. Since people have needs that are physical, social and material as well as spiritual, we cannot fulfill the command to love our neighbor solely by preaching the gospel. In fact, the only way to care for some of our neighbors' needs may be to get involved in the political process to bring changes that will help them. For example, many have concluded that helping the unborn (those neighbors) involves more than just preaching the gospel. So, while Christ's kingdom and the world's kingdom are separate, Christ has a task for his people to perform in society. Participating in social and political processes is not disloyalty to Christ. So long as one keeps his affections on Jesus Christ first, and so long as his goals are always in keeping with Christ's desires for mankind, Christian involvement in the social process is not only acceptable but necessary.

As to preaching the gospel, this is a priority, but the gospel is preached not only in word but in deed. If we really love mankind as Jesus did, that love will be demonstrated through our concern for all their needs. Jesus' example, even if not prescriptive, is most instructive. Christ's ultimate concern was the spiritual needs of mankind, but he also ministered to the physical and material needs of those he met. In Jesus' day there were four basic models of interaction with the world that he might have adopted, but he adopted none of them. The Sadducean option totally subordinated the things of God to the state. The Roman government appointed and controlled the Jewish high priest at will. Second, there was the Essene approach of withdrawal from society to await messianic intervention. A third approach was that of the Zealots who openly revolted against Rome. They relied on the sword and expected divine intervention on their behalf. Finally, there was the Pharisaic option. They lived in the world but tried to be separate from it by adhering to rules that covered externals. Jesus rejected all of these options.[22] Instead, he was in the world but not of it. Unlike the Pharisees, his separation was not merely external. He rejected the philosophies and values of the world in favor of heavenly principles, but that kept him neither from proclaiming the gospel nor from meeting people's needs.

Third, we reject the idea that Christian ethics is only for Christians. God is sovereign over both believers and non-believers. Moreover, if ethical norms flow ultimately from his character, as we have argued, different (even conflicting) ethical principles will not stem from his one unchanging nature. God wants the same standard of holiness for non-believers as for believers. The decreased ability of non-believers to obey his standards does not excuse them from it any more than their inability to accept Christ excuses them from that demand.

In addition, claiming that Christian ethics do not work well in the arena of politics is an empirical judgment, not a statement of what ought to be the case. If it were not for the sinfulness of man, Christian ethics would work quite well in society. The fact of man's sinfulness, however, does not warrant changing the standards to meet the level of man's depravity. As to the bromide that one cannot legislate morality, it is just that—a bromide. Somebody's morality (and in some cases, immorality) is being legislated all the time. The Supreme Court's decision legalizing abortion on demand is surely an example of legalizing someone's morality. In fact, it is evidence that in America, despite all the talk about separation of church and state, religion/ethics and politics are not separate. Since someone's morality is always being legislated, why should the Christian be apologetic about a social and political agenda in accord with his morality?[23] If Christians refuse to work for programs and policies that reflect their morality, they may find themselves legally forced to live under the immorality of the non-believing!

Fourth, the notion that involvement is unnecessary because of the soon return of Christ is a *non sequitor*. In the days of the apostles there was vivid anticipation of the Lord's return, but that did not cause the apostles to urge withdrawal from the world. No one knows exactly when Jesus will return, but we do know that he has called believers to be light and salt to society until he does. Because of the imminence of Christ's return, we must be active in proclaiming the gospel, but as noted in our biblical survey of Peter and Paul, if there is not a social and political climate congenial to Christianity and the proclamation of the gospel, we may not be able to proclaim that message. Moreover, the changes to be wrought in society when Christ returns are not only spiritual; they will transform all of society. God cares about the needs of the whole person, and we must, too, if we want to represent him properly in our world.

In addition to answering opposing arguments, there are some positive reasons for involvement. For example, one cannot say God does not want to use believers to impact the political realm. In fact, sometimes God places his people in positions of governmental authority to minister to the needs of the godly and the ungodly. The examples of Daniel, Mordecai, Esther and Joseph are well-known. In addition, in the NT Jesus commended the faith of a Roman official (Matt 8:10) and did not ask him to leave his post. Likewise, when Zacchaeus was saved, Christ did not demand that he relinquish his job as a local tax official; Christ only required that he amend past injustices and henceforth perform his duty in a godly way.

When one considers the question of involvement further, common sense suggests that one cannot completely withdraw from social and political participation. Even the advocate of complete non-involvement depends on governmental protection of his freedom to live that way. Moreover, one may dislike governmental intrusion into certain areas of life, but he depends on it in other areas such as mail service, police protection and maintenance of roads. To be completely consistent, if one rejects all interaction with the social and political process, he ought also to reject the benefits of living in a society.

Finally, the form of government in one's country does seem to make a difference. Those who live in a democracy are the government and can effect greater change than those living in a totalitarian state. The privileges of living in a democratic society seem to warrant greater responsibility to work within the system to bring about changes for good. The complaint that involvement is futile because it will not make any difference is not always true, even in a totalitarian state; it is even less convincing in a democracy.

THE CORPORATE CHURCH AND THE POLITICAL AND SOCIAL PROCESS

What should the corporate (and even the individual) church do in society? Approaches to this question usually fall within one of three categories: 1) complete disengagement of the church from social and political matters; 2) complete engagement of the church in social and political issues (a kind of social gospel); and 3) a combination of engagement and disengagement. Unfortunately, there is no direct scriptural teaching on this issue.

Typically, those who argue for total or near total disengagement note that the primary mission of the church as a whole is the proclamation of the gospel and edification of the saints. Neglecting these duties in favor of preoccupation with social concerns is considered by some to be a form of escapism from the church's primary mission.[24] Some claim that when Christ was asked about the restoration of the kingdom to Israel, he rebuked his disciples for asking this question about nationalistic concerns and reminded them of their task to proclaim the gospel.[25] The description in Acts 2 of elders in the early church devoting themselves to prayer and preparation to proclaim the word of God is taken as the role model for ministers. Even within the church, elders were not asked to care for the concrete material needs of their people. All the less should they become involved in social concerns.

Those who argue for heavy involvement of the church in social problems usually justify their position from Scripture as well. Contemporary proponents of this position often claim that God's action in our world creates an ongoing process of social change, and if we are to be God's faithful followers, we must be involved in this process of change at the cutting edge.[26] This view involves perceiving "history as the arena of a messianic struggle for the liberation of man in a new social order."[27] Christ is seen as Redeemer, but his redemption affects all areas of life, and sin is understood largely in terms of the oppressiveness of existing social and political orders. This kind of approach characterizes much of what today is called political theology. The basic views are as old as the old social gospel and as contemporary as Liberation Theology.

The third approach is a mixture of the previous two, and we think it is the best. The church's mission is to make disciples, but part of that process involves being salt and light to society. Nevertheless, many of the biblical injunctions about the Christian's role in society relate to individual believers as citizens, not to the church as a whole. It seems, then, that the fundamental mission of the corporate church must be spiritual.

On the other hand, the church collectively can have a role in social issues. The gospel makes a difference to individual holiness, but it should affect all of life. Unfortunately, not everyone responds to the gospel, many leaders in society remain unbelievers, and the social, economic and political problems continue. Should the church's response to these features of society be only the proclamation of the gospel? Many church leaders have concluded that the corporate church must take a more active role in the social and political process in order to bring about change. We believe the church can and should have at least three significant roles in effecting change.

The first may be seen as a negative role, but we believe it has a positive function. The church should play what can be called a prophetic role in society. This involves dissociating itself from the ideologies and crusades of the state. This means that while the church must obey the state (and even be patriotic), it must be careful not to see its major role as legitimizing the state. When the church becomes too wrapped up in defending the state, it loses its ability to speak for God against the evils of the state.[28] The church should, then, function prophetically to point out evils when they arise and call the state back to God. In American history the role of the church in combating slavery is a prime example of the church playing this prophetic role.

Second, if the corporate church resides in a country where change can come through the social and political process, and if the social issues cannot be addressed successfully by individuals, but a corporate group could make a difference, it would be appropriate for the church to enter the fray. We are not suggesting involvement on every problem, because that would not leave time for fulfillment of the church's commission to preach the gospel, and because there is no consensus among Christians on all issues. However, when the issue is significant and there is a general consensus among Christians (e.g., the abortion issue), surely it is proper for the corporate church to exert social and political influence. On the other hand, questions like whether there should be a tax increase to support public schools seem to lack moral urgency, and it is dubious that in a given community there would be a "Christian consensus" on such an issue.

Third, the church can offer practical alternatives for people caught in the midst of moral dilemmas. For example, the church must preach against the evils of abortion, but it should also present viable alternatives to abortion to women who are financially incapable of supporting the child. The church can offer financial aid for the birth of the child, but can also organize members of the local church to provide day care so single parents can earn a living to support their child. Likewise, it is one thing to decry the plight of the hungry and homeless and also to speak against the "evils" of granting indiscriminate governmental welfare to these people. It is another to make the church's resources available so that, for example, church facilities may be used to provide food and shelter for the homeless. Church members might even donate time to teach these people a trade or teach them to read so they can support themselves. We are not suggesting that every local church must implement these programs. We are only saying that churches need to consider how they can minister to people's needs so as to provide genuine alternatives for those facing difficult problems. We think these kinds of programs can function without deflecting the church from its primary task of preaching the gospel.

In sum, neither complete disengagement nor complete involvement with social problems should characterize the corporate role of the church. The church must primarily speak for God in society. Of course, what God has to say to society speaks to spiritual needs, but it goes beyond that. We see no reason why churches individually and collectively cannot and should not both proclaim the gospel and meet social needs in the ways mentioned. Nothing scriptural mandates the kinds of involvement we have set forth, but nothing prohibits them either. Such involvement seems to be a logical and reasonable application of the Christian's obligation to be light and salt in society.

IS THERE A "CHRISTIAN POSITION" ON SOCIAL AND POLITICAL ISSUES?

In recent years some have claimed that a proper understanding of Scripture mandates a certain approach to such matters as the size of the defense budget, ratification of the Panama Canal treaty, the kind of economic system implemented in a society, and voluntary school prayers. If there is a Christian position on these issues, all Christians should support it. Others wonder if the Bible can be used to teach specific positions on such issues. Even more fundamentally, this whole discussion raises the question of the proper use of the Bible in contemporary social and political discussions.

We believe progress can be made in this discussion if one bears in mind three distinctions: 1) prescriptive versus descriptive language; 2) ethical principles versus prudential advice; and 3) universal general norms versus contextualized specific applications of principles. The distinction between descriptive and prescriptive language has already been addressed in the first chapter and need not detain us any longer than to note that patterns and practices are not mandates. According to the second distinction, when trying to decide on a course of action, one must determine whether his sense of obligation stems from some ethical norm (a moral absolute) or from a sense that a certain course of action is wisest to accomplish a given end. For example, disagreement over whether abortions are right is a moral debate ultimately stemming from the commandment not to commit murder. On the other hand, disagreement among opponents of abortion about the best way to fight abortion (e.g., picket abortion clinics, seek a constitutional amendment, or encourage the selection of Supreme Court justices who will overturn the 1972 *Roe v. Wade* decision) is a pragmatic debate about the most effective way to influence the political process.[29] Scripture gives help on the moral questions (though we may disagree about what Scripture says), but it does not answer the prudential questions. Answers to ethical questions should be "the Christian position," but answers to prudential questions are not. Real difficulties arise when prudential answers are treated as ethical ones and then absolutized for all Christians.

The third distinction is very important to the use of Scripture in this discussion. "Universal" principles are applicable for all people at all times. "General" means that the norm does not state how to handle each specific case that arises or how to implement the norm. "Love your neighbor" is a general norm, whereas "if your friend is hungry and has no money to buy food, give him something to eat" is a specific norm. The former explains no specific course of action to demonstrate love; the latter does.

As opposed to universal norms, there are contextualized specific applications of principles. "Contextualized" means that what was done or mandated related to a specific context; it is not universalizable. The difference between specific and general is explained above. By referring to an application of a principle, we mean that what was done in one situation recorded in Scripture was nothing other than the most prudent way to obey a more general principle. This third distinction suggests that one must be careful not to pull a rule out of context without asking whether it is universalizable or only germane to a particular time. Needless to say, the discussion in the first chapter about the relation of OT law to NT law is also relevant for determining what parts of Scripture (whether ethical principle, application of principle, or mere prudence) could properly be applied today.

In relating these distinctions to the question of a "Christian position" on social and political issues, several points are noteworthy. First, many questions under debate in modern society are not directly addressed by Scripture. Therefore, it is difficult to talk of a "Christian position" on those matters. Second, we are convinced that many items debated within the church are not matters of scriptural ethics, but are rather matters of prudential policy. Even legislation about voluntary school prayer seems to fall within this category. There is no question that the worship of God is mandated in Scripture. Whether it is morally right or wrong to pray to God should not be a matter of debate among Christians. However, whether one's right to pray requires legislation of a mandatory moment of silence so that those who want to pray can do so *at that moment* is hardly a moral issue. It is a question of which public policy will best recognize a student's right to pray when he chooses. Likewise, Scripture clearly enjoins us to be wise stewards of the financial resources God has given us individually and collectively as a church. However, that does not mean Scripture morally dictates (implicitly or explicitly) capitalism over socialism as *the* way to be wise stewards.

Finally, in speaking of a biblical position on an issue (even a genuinely ethical rather than prudential question), we must distinguish between biblical prescription and description and between universally true principles and contextually applicable demands. When one takes these items into account, he finds, we suggest, no "Christian position" on many of the specific social and political issues that arise in each country. Instead, a variety of positions could be consistent with Christian teaching.

THE CHRISTIAN AND CIVIL DISOBEDIENCE

This is really a three-pronged issue. One aspect deals with disobeying the law (non-violently); a second focuses on the use of violence by Christians; and the third treats Christian participation in the revolutionary overthrow of a government. Revolutions are difficult to assess even under just war theory. However, they ultimately involve questions of social and political justice that invoke matters of social and political philosophy. Since such issues go beyond the scope of this book, we shall not discuss the question of revolution. However, in this chapter we shall address the other issues.

LAWBREAKING

Defining civil disobedience is no easy task. Nonetheless, for many, civil disobedience is the "deliberate attempt to coerce the legal order; it is not merely dissent, where a person differs with the legal order in speech, in the press, by petition, or in an assembly. It involves deliberate and punishable breach of a legal duty."[30] Disobedience may either be direct (breaking a law that is the object of protest) or indirect (breaking a different law than the one protested).[31] What drives one to commit an act of civil disobedience is a decision based on the following: "(a) a moral decision or judgment that a law or activity is unjust, (b) after normal channels of addressing the injustice have proven fruitless, (c) the moral objections to this injustice of the law outweigh the moral reasons in favor of obedience."[32] Of course, those who engage in civil disobedience have no legal right to break the law, but they claim a moral justification. Since they have no legal right to break the law, they should expect to be punished.

Within a Christian context, arguments against civil disobedience usually rest on scriptural principles as well as practical concerns. The fundamental scriptural point comes from biblical commands in passages such as 1 Peter 2 and Romans 13 for Christians to obey government as God's agent. Practical arguments often suggested include the ideas that civil disobedience implies contempt for the law, it supposes that personal interests are superior to concerns of society as a whole, it allows people to take the law into their own hands and thereby encourages social chaos, it is self-defeating, for it creates a feeling of resentment and anger toward those who disobey the law and thereby engenders a negative reaction to the advocated cause, and it ignores the lawful channels always open under a constitutional government.[33]

Those favoring civil disobedience typically point to biblical incidents when believers non-violently refused to obey the law. Examples often mentioned are Esther (Esther 4), Daniel (Daniel 1, 6), Shadrach, Meshach, and Abed-nego (Daniel 3), and Peter and John's refusal to stop preaching (Acts 5:29). These people were asked to do something contrary to the revealed will of God, and they refused. Scripture records no moral censure of any of them; on the contrary, in most of these cases Scripture records the Lord's great blessing upon them.

Some carry the matter even further. The preceding are all cases where people were asked to do something God forbade. Some Christian thinkers argue that believers should not only refuse when asked to disobey God, but should also protest ungodly practices (like abortion) by civil disobedience even when they are not asked to participate in ungodliness. For example, some argue that Christians ought to protest legalized abortion (even if never asked to have an abortion themselves) by doing whatever is necessary to change the laws.[34] In response to a buildup in nuclear arms, Christian pacifists not only encourage conscientious objection from military service (a legal right in countries such as the U.S.) but also support withholding a portion of their income taxes that might go to the defense budget. Of course, refusing to pay taxes is against the law and an act of civil disobedience.[35]

By way of assessment, we think on some occasions civil disobedience is not only morally permissible but even obligatory. Specifically, it is proper when a Christian is asked to do something directly contrary to the revealed will of God and thus contrary to the dictates of moral conscience. Of course, this needs amplification. We think living in a democratic society makes a difference. In such a society, individuals have more rights in formulating the laws and more opportunities for legal and political redress of unjust laws. So, when someone living in a democracy sees immoral laws but is not asked to do something immoral, he should at least initially seek redress through legal and political channels. For example, if I am not told to consent to an abortion, I still have a right to protest legalized abortion, and on moral grounds I should do so, but within the law. There is only a moral obligation to act outside the law if I am directly required to do something contrary to Scripture.

As argued in Chapter 3, it is here that advocates of bombing abortion clinics and breaking other laws to protest legalized abortion go too far. No one forces them to have an abortion; they need not break a law. Even if so forced, it is dubious that bombing an abortion clinic is the morally mandated response. Could they not simply refuse and go to jail? Here the question of resorting to violence to accomplish ends enters the discussion, and that issue will be handled shortly. However, we see no reason to justify destroying property and even injuring people in the clinic when refusing to undergo abortion would avoid committing an immoral act without bringing about consequences harmful to others.[36]

Several further points should be made. First, granted that disobeying a societal law when asked to break God's law leaves one open to societal punishment, does it also entail *moral* censure? We think not. In such cases, the individual cannot obey both the human law and God's law conjointly. Of course, as argued throughout this book, no one is morally culpable for failing to do what he could not do. If one cannot obey both God and man, he is not morally guilty for failing to do so. The only remaining question is whether the choice made (obeying God and not man) was the correct choice. We think biblical example is helpful here. Specifically, we agree with Peter and John (Acts 5:29). Moral obligations to God take precedence over the demands of human authority figures when the two conflict. Moreover, in cases where there are two *divine* commands (consider, for example, Shadrach, Meshach, and Abed-nego's case: worship God alone and obey the king), those two commands need never conflict so long as the powers of government never require citizens to contradict anything God demands.[37] When the human authority figure forces those commands to conflict by demanding that we disobey something God has ordered, one must obey God's command to worship him, preserve life, etc. rather than God's command to obey the ruler. Failure to obey both commands when one could not do both entails no moral censure.

Second, asserting a moral obligation to refuse when commanded to disobey God does not specify which means of disobedience are morally permissible or prudentially advisable. For example, many Europeans during World War II refused when told to turn over Jews to the authorities. That decision *per se* did not determine *how* they should disobey. They could have started a revolt, they could have simply said no and tried to protect the Jews by personally fighting the soldiers, they might have tried (like Bonhoeffer) to assassinate Hitler, or they could do what many did—hide the Jewish people in their homes. Morality dictated disobeying the government. Prudence suggested various ways.

Finally, claiming a believer must disobey when asked to break a moral norm does not indicate which cases involve contradicting a moral norm. For example, the pacifist who thinks Scripture forbids all Christian participation in war will likely consider a demand to pay taxes or serve in the military a violation of God's law. But someone holding a just war theory will not always interpret such requests negatively. Fortunately, for many ethical questions scriptural teaching is clear enough for Christians to agree on what would count as a request to disobey God. Since this is not so with all moral issues, it becomes very difficult in some instances to decide whether one is actually being asked to break a divine command.

VIOLENCE

Is the use of violence in accomplishing Christian goals in society morally acceptable? In favor of using violence, some argue that violence of some sort is endemic to human relationships. Even representatives of the Lord do not always refrain from violence in accomplishing their ends (cf. American missionary efforts at times). In addition, some countries are born out of violent revolutions, so violence is not entirely foreign to our experience.

Second, it is commonly argued that societal institutions are often structured so as to favor certain groups above others. Those oppressed by such structures at times experience both psychological and physical violence. The powerful are not likely to relinquish their power. Thus, the only hope for escaping the injustice of these institutions is to meet violence with violence.

Third, some claim that in a democratic society one can always redress grievances without violence, but government moves very slowly in rectifying injustice. Often the only way to get government's attention is mass confrontation of existing structures. Unfortunately, confrontation often involves violence, but without confrontation it would be difficult to bring needed changes.

What seems to us the strongest line of argument stems from an understanding of the function of society and government. Generally, it is agreed that any society needs both order and justice to survive. Often demands for justice are modified or overlooked in favor of demands for order. Proponents of order fear that without order there will be great societal upheaval. Consequently, various forms of oppression can be justified in the name of order. On the contrary, proponents of using violence think the real issue is not between order and disorder, for there will always be some sort of order. The question is whether that order will be just or not. Those who argue this line claim that the end justifies the means—i.e., the end is justice; any form of government or order is justified insofar as it accomplishes that end.[38]

According to this line of thinking, justice is clearly more valuable than order. In fact, it is claimed that it is wrong to say in a particular case that an appeal to justice must be modified, delayed or denied out of regard for order. "What justifies any order is the degree of justice it embodies, or makes possible."[39] Consequently, the use of direct action to rectify a wrong does not necessarily show disrespect or rejection of order; it merely demands a different order.[40] All of this means that when there is injustice in society and all other means of redress have been attempted, as a last resort violence may be justified. The argument does not end here, for further appeal is made to the analogy of the just war. Just war theorists hold that it is morally right in certain situations for nations to wage war to rectify an international injustice. If it is morally acceptable to use violence to right an international wrong, why not to address a domestic wrong?[41]

Opponents of Christians' using violence answer the first argument by admitting that while violence is endemic to human relations, that hardly suggests the ideal or justifies the retributive use of violence by individuals. One cannot move to an "ought" from an "is." Moreover, we should note that the first three arguments favoring violence are based on the utilitarian notion that the end justifies the means. Anyone rejecting that ethic should not be convinced by those arguments.

The line of argument about government and the functioning of society is more challenging but inconclusive. Though Romans 13 and 1 Peter 2 command believers to obey governments, that does not preclude protesting injustice or trying to work within the law to rectify an injustice. Only if the Christian is directly asked to disobey a command of God may he disobey the government. Moreover, even when disobedience is permissible, nothing scriptural justifies disobedience in the form of *violent disruption* of the state. One might respond that nothing *explicit* prohibits it, and that is probably true. However, we contend that the overarching obligation to submit to government and the fact that God has instituted even the worst government to maintain order at least indirectly suggest that if one must disobey, he should try to create as little disruption as possible to the state's general right to maintain order. Thus, even if violence is permissible, it seems preferable to protest in a more peaceful way.

From a non-scriptural standpoint, we also find this line of argument unconvincing. One should always strive for justice, but violence tends to produce anarchy, not order, in society, and we see little justice in times of anarchy. Some may respond that one or two people using violence will not eliminate all order, but once the precedent of getting one's way by using violence is set, the temptation for others to try the same thing increases, and that can lead to anarchy. At any rate, we find it odd to think that justice can only be *legally* accomplished and guaranteed by means (violence) which go outside the law. At some point that strategy will return to haunt us in the form of anarchy.

Another problem with favoring violence to bring justice is that it is not always clear which policies, programs or actions would be just. The initial difficulty is agreeing on the notion of justice that should operate in society. Should government implement egalitarian justice (everyone receives an equal amount) or compensative justice (rendering each his exact due even if that differs from person to person)? If I opt for egalitarian justice and also believe in using violence to procure justice, I then should encourage violence to ensure that everyone in society (including myself) has an equal income; pure egalitarian justice demands that. If you favor compensative justice, you will disagree that I should make as much money as you, regardless of my skills and how hard I work, and you will see my use of violence to inaugurate egalitarianism as unjust.

Our point is that since there are conflicting notions of justice, before one encourages confronting order with violence in the name of justice, there must be agreement on what justice is. Moreover, even if everyone understood justice in the same way (which is most unlikely), that would not guarantee that in any given situation it would be clear that circumstances are unjust. Nor is it always easy to calculate when the point comes that all non-violent means to overturn injustice are exhausted so that the only recourse is violence.

As to the analogy with the just war theory, we are unconvinced. There is a major difference between trying to right a wrong within a society as opposed to trying to correct injustice in the international setting. Within a country there are legally and politically established means for redressing injustices, especially in a democratic society, and the government has power to enforce any changes in laws that would be enacted. However, on the international scene there is no organization with either authority or power to enact or enforce justice among nations. Since there is none, the only recourse for an *individual nation* to protect itself against unjust attack is the use of violence. The just war theory allows a nation to protect itself in self-defense. Within a society, then, the situation is not analogous to international relations. Since that is so, appeals to just war theory to justify domestic use of violence are improper.

One final word against using violence to accomplish societal goals. The basic biblical approach is that believers, rather than retaliating against those who persecute them, should follow Christ's example (cf. 1 Pet 2:21-23; 3:10-12). The oft-quoted comment of Jesus about bringing a sword (Matt 10:34-36) has nothing to do with Jesus' relation to the political structure; it emphasizes the dramatic impact discipleship has on personal relationships. Moreover, biblical examples of people disobeying civil authority in order to obey God do not include the use of violence in defying the authorities. While examples are not prescriptive, they do suggest that one can protest and even disobey governmental policy without violence and still make an impact on the social order. We conclude, then, that the basic biblical perspective excludes violence as the way for Christians to effect social change.

SUMMARY AND CONCLUSION

From our discussion it should be clear that Scripture does not answer all questions about the Christian's relation to society. Nor does it present a comprehensive Christian social and political philosophy. Christians should be salt and light in society, and as a result there will be times when they must speak and act in protest. Perhaps there will be occasions when they must even break the law. When those decisions arise, believers should seek the direction of the Holy Spirit as to whether to disobey and as to the appropriate means for registering displeasure. They should also remember that they are members not only of a secular community but also of a religious, spiritual community, the church. Counsel and prayer with other members of the body of Christ are advisable not only when planning strategy for representing God in society, but also when the option of acting beyond the law presents itself.

NOTES

PREFACE

1. William Shakespeare, "The Tempest," in *The Complete Plays and Poems of William Shakespeare*, ed. William A. Neilson and Charles J. Hill (Cambridge, MA: Houghton Mifflin Company, 1942), Act V, Scene I, 181-184, p. 563.

CHAPTER 1: *Moral Decision-making and the Christian*

1. William Frankena, *Ethics* (Englewood Cliffs, NJ: Prentice-Hall, 1963), p. 5. See also William Frankena, "Ethics," *Dictionary of Philosophy*, ed. Dagobert D. Runes (Patterson, NJ: Littlefield, Adams & Co., 1962). Our discussion illustrates (but does not exhaust) the many ways terms such as "ethics," "morals," etc. may be used. Sometimes the terms are used interchangeably, but at other times they are used in distinct ways. Frankena's book and the *Dictionary of Philosophy* give a good indication of the terms' many uses. In addition, though many never discuss this, we think it proper to indicate how moral and non-moral matters are distinguished. As with most issues in ethics, this is open to much debate. Nonetheless, we think the moral can be distinguished from the non-moral by at least four characteristics. All four requirements must be met to qualify an act, principle, etc. as moral. First is *universalizability*. This involves several things. For a moral principle to be universal, it must be stated in a universal form, i.e., it must apply to all, not just some. A universal principle must not lead to inconsistency. This means that if everyone acts in accord with the principle, one person's so acting will not prohibit others from obeying the rule. Here see Charles E. Harris's helpful discussion in "Can Agape Be Universalized?" *J Relig Ethics* 6 (1978): 20-21. An example clarifies the notion of universalizability. Some might think universalizability rules out the following as a *moral* principle: "If confronted by Germans asking if you are hiding Jews in the attic, lie in order to protect the Jews." Since the axiom allows lying on some occasions, one might think it is not universalizable (and thus not moral), for it permits exceptions. However, this misunderstands universalizability as well as the commands in question. Universalizability refers not to whether the norm has any *occasions* when it does not apply. It relates rather to whether there are any *people* to whom the rule does not apply. The *norm itself* may be stated so as to cover all situations of a particular kind or only some (i.e., there may be exceptions to the general rule) and still be universalizable so long as the rule applies to all people who face the situation. Hence, the command to lie to the Germans is an exception to the general rule of telling the truth, but it is still universalizable (and thus relevant to *morals*), because presumably it would apply to everyone confronted with the decision of handing over the Jews or telling a lie. In comparison, a decision to use a red towel after bathing is in itself not a moral decision, for it is not reasonably universalizable. A second characteristic of the moral is its *concern with human well-being*. Though some talk of animal rights

and the morality of treatment of animals, traditionally moral concerns have focused on humans and their welfare. Moreover, persons are the subject matter of morality; objects or things pertain to the non-moral (see Frankena, *Ethics*, pp. 47-48). Manicuring one's toenails is relevant to a human being (perhaps even to one's welfare), but a decision to use scissors instead of clippers is inconsequential to well-being, and hence, is a non-moral decision. Likewise, taking a neighbor's property is a moral matter, because doing so impacts his welfare, but deciding to step on a dirt clod is non-moral unless so doing impacts someone's welfare. Third, matters of morality involve *prescription*. The prescriber may be an individual or a group. In light of the first quality of the moral, matters of morality are universally prescriptive. It makes little sense to prescribe for all or even a few a decision to have steak instead of chicken. One might recommend such a choice as a personal preference, but recommendations and commands are not the same. On the other hand, it makes sense to prescribe a rule against murder and to prescribe it universally. Finally, morality concerns the *supremely authoritative*. This means the matter in question must be of serious import, and the individual must consider it as having supreme control over him. Judging that one car functions better than another is normally not a matter of supreme importance to most. Thus, while it is a value judgment, it is not a moral value judgment. On the other hand, the judgment that preserving life is significant does involve an important matter, and those who make that judgment think it has implications that are supremely authoritative for their thinking and action. Of course, as noted, one may make value judgments and statements of obligation in matters that are non-moral. Such claims may, for example, merely suggest a wise course of action for achieving a certain end (i.e., they may merely be judgments and duties of prudence).

2. For example, G. E. Moore (*Principia Ethica*) emphasizes the concept of good. For Moore, good is an indefinable property inherent in various objects, actions, etc. To say someone, something or some act is good means it has this property in its very nature. Though Moore focuses on good and value, he also stresses that one's understanding of what is good should lead to norms for conduct (moral obligations). That is, if a certain state of affairs, for example, has this quality of good, it is right to do, and our obligation is to do whatever brings about such states of affairs. While Moore speaks both of good and obligation, not every theory explicitly has this dual emphasis. Theories that clarify duty may or may not explicitly state what is valued. For example, some theories hold that one is obliged to do certain actions because it is one's duty to do so, irrespective of any value that may be produced when one obeys. On the other hand, other theories (e.g., various forms of utilitarianism) state that one must do certain things because so doing will produce some valuable object, state of affairs, etc.

3. See W. D. Hudson, ed., *The Is/Ought Question* (London: Macmillan, 1972), and W. D. Hudson, "Fact and Moral Value," *Relig Stud* 5 (December 1969) on this matter.

4. Some believe indeterministic free will is the only kind of freedom there is. Some determinists also speak of a legitimate sense of freedom. Our intent is not to solve that debate, but only to note that regardless of how one defines freedom, both determinists and indeterminists agree on the principle that moral praise and blame cannot be assessed to an individual unless he acted freely. For discussion of various kinds of free will see Randall and David Basinger, eds., *Predestination and Free Will* (Downers Grove, IL: InterVarsity Press, 1986).

5. Immanuel Kant, *Foundations of the Metaphysics of Morals* (Indianapolis: Bobbs-Merrill, 1959), pp. 13-14 with slight adaptation on our part.

6. *Ibid.*, pp. 13-18, especially p. 16. For Kant, coordinate with the notions of prudence and morality are hypothetical and categorical imperatives (*ibid.*, p. 31). Hypothetical imperatives state (advise) what one ought to do to achieve a certain end. They have the form "if you want to accomplish x, then you must do y as a means to x." Categorical imperatives command actions as necessary in themselves apart from any

end that might be accomplished by obeying. They have the form "you must do *x*." Hypothetical imperatives are imperatives of prudence; categorical imperatives are demands of morality. Kant also distinguishes a heteronomous and an autonomous will (*ibid.*, pp. 59-60). A heteronomous will is always determined by matters outside itself that deal with ends to be accomplished. An autonomous will operates independent of any ends external to it that it might wish to accomplish. The autonomous will functions solely for duty's sake, and is thus essential to morality. The heteronomous will operates to achieve ends the agent hopes to attain, and thus is essential to prudence, but has nothing to do with morality.

7. We are not saying that these three books cover no other ethical questions or that they explicitly claim to address these three respective questions. Our point is only that the main categories they use for organizing their description of ethical theories tend to reflect answers to the questions raised more than answers to other ethical questions.

8. Frankena, *Ethics*, pp. 80-81.

9. *Ibid.*, p. 86.

10. See *ibid.*, pp. 88-89 for a description of non-cognitivist theories.

11. Kant, p. 39.

12. Ruth Caspar, "Natural Law: Before and Beyond Bifurcation," *Thought* 60 (March 1985): 67 and Alan Johnson, "Is There a Biblical Warrant for Natural-Law Theories?" *JETS* 25 (June 1982): 198-199.

13. Johnson, p. 186.

14. Compare Henry Stob's critical appraisal of natural law ethics in Henry Stob, "Natural Law Ethics: An Appraisal," *CTJ* 20 (April 1985). Stob offers various complaints about natural law ethics, but many seem to miss the mark since he apparently overlooks the difference between knowing and doing the law. Natural law ethics says everyone, believer or non-believer, can know moral law through the natural order; that in itself, however, gives no one the ability to obey.

15. See Roderick Firth, "Ethical Absolutism and the Ideal Observer," *Phil Phenomenal Res* 12 (1952) and Roderick Firth and Richard Brandt, "Discussion: The Definition of an 'Ideal Observer' Theory in Ethics," *Phil Phenomenal Res* 15 (1955). See also discussion of this theory in Charles Reynolds, "The Place of Reason in Christian Ethics," *J Rel* 50 (April 1970): 159-161. Another prescriptive system in which God is not the prescriber is proposed by John Rawls (*A Theory of Justice* [Cambridge, MA: Harvard Press, 1971]). He says the way to determine proper ethical norms is to imagine a group of people in an ideal position, i.e., a position prior to entering a society with the advantage of knowing how various actions affect well-being. Suppose those people draw up an ideal contract containing norms for society to follow. Whatever norms that group would include in an ideal contract should become commands for us.

16. See the discussion of Ockham in John S. Feinberg, *Theologies and Evil* (Washington, D.C.: University Press of America, 1979), p. 15.

17. *Ibid.* According to Ockham (*ibid.*, pp. 15-16), the unchanging standard of morality is God's will. No set of intrinsically good or evil actions defines the standard of morality. Saving a drowning person is no better or worse morally than pouring gasoline on a baby and striking a match. The morality of these acts depends entirely on what God says about them. Hence, Ockham thought God could just as easily order men to obey the opposite of the Ten Commandments, and if they did, God would give them merit. All of this amounts to saying there is really only one unchanging moral rule: obey whatever God commands.

18. Robert M. Adams, "A Modified Divine Command Theory of Ethical Wrongness," in Paul Helm, ed., *Divine Commands and Morality* (Oxford: Oxford University Press, 1981), p. 87.

19. *Ibid.*

20. *Ibid.*, p. 88. Suppose, though, that God did command such a thing. Would it be morally right to disobey God? Adams's basic answer is that our whole notion of

moral right and wrong resting on the will of God presupposes our notion of God as loving. If God commands the unthinkable, we should disobey, but a major reason for disobeying is that such a divine command would totally shatter our ideas about God and moral right and wrong. For a defense of divine command theories in general, see Janine M. Idziak, "In Search of 'Good Positive Reasons' for an Ethics of Divine Commands: A Catalogue of Arguments," *Faith Phil* 6 (January 1989). For further discussion of arguments pro and con on divine command theories see Wyle Tan, "The Euthyphro Puzzle," *Asia J Th* 3 (1989).

21. Richard Brandt, "The Real & Alleged Problems of Utilitarianism," *Hast Center Rep* 13 (April 1983): 37; John Harsanyi, "Does Reason Tell Us What Moral Code to Follow and, Indeed, to Follow Any Moral Code at All?" *Ethics* 96 (October 1985): 44-45; and Frankena, *Ethics*, pp. 30-32. Rule utilitarianism leads to much less relativism than act utilitarianism. Moreover, many refutations of utilitarianism are actually attacks on act utilitarianism alone. In the Christian camp, Joseph Fletcher's situation ethics is an act utilitarian theory. It has only one basic rule (do the most loving thing), but how that rule applies varies with the situation. Even similar situations may be handled differently on Fletcher's theory. It is also noteworthy that some Christian ethicists claim that Christianity really does not fit with consequentialist ethics. For an interesting interchange on this question, see Gilbert Meilander, "*Eritis Sicut Deus*: Moral Theory and the Sin of Pride," *Faith Phil* 3 (October 1986), and James A. Keller, "Christianity and Consequentialism: A Reply to Meilander," *Faith Phil* 6 (April 1989). Meilander argues against Christian ethics as consequentialist, while Keller claims that R. M. Hare's consequentialism answers Meilander's objections.

22. Frankena, *Ethics*, pp. 13-45 not only describes teleological and deontological theories, but critiques them as inadequate for determining moral obligation and moral assessment of the rightness or wrongness of individual acts. All of this leads him to offer (p. 35ff.) his theory, which he calls a mixed deontological theory. Another example of a theory that mixes both concerns is found in John Finnis, *Fundamentals of Ethics* (Washington, D.C.: Georgetown University Press, 1983). Finnis says about the distinction between teleological and deontological ethics:

> That dichotomy, however, fails to accommodate Platonic, Aristotelian, Thomistic and any other substantially reasonable ethics. For the moral terms, "right" and "wrong," "duty," "obligation," "vice" and "virtue," and so forth, express the *requirements* of practical reasonableness, but those requirements are nothing but the implications of an integral pursuit of the basic forms of human good (including the good of practical reasonableness itself) which constitute the basic *ends* of all rational decision and action. . . . Ethics is thoroughly deontological; the basic practical principles which express the basic forms of human good are not, in themselves, moral or ethical principles. But ethics is also thoroughly teleological; all specific moral norms identifying duties, etc., are derived . . . from the basic practical principles identifying intelligible objects (ends) of human pursuit. (p. 84)

See also Benedict Ashley, "The Methodology of Moral Theology" and Germain Grisez, "Legalism, Moral Truth, and Pastoral Practice," paper for a symposium on the Catholic Priest as Moral Teacher and Guide, held at St. Charles Borromeo Seminary, Philadelphia, in January 1990.

23. *Ibid.*, p. 42.
24. *Ibid.*, p. 35.
25. Norman Geisler, *Ethics: Issues and Alternatives* (Grand Rapids, MI: Zondervan, 1971).
26. Frankena, *Ethics*, p. 81.

27. Some will still probably think our view is a mixed theory. We disagree, but do not think it is a point worth quibbling over. So long as our claim about what element in the equation (justice, benevolence, or God's command) makes the act morally right is understood, we are surely willing to live with either the deontology or mixed deontology label.

28. W. D. Ross, "The Right and the Good: What Makes Right Acts Right?" in Richard B. Brandt, ed., *Value and Obligation: Systematic Readings in Ethics* (New York: Harcourt, Brace & World, 1961), p. 221. Other *prima facie* duties Ross lists are those that arise in a situation where one can distribute pleasure and happiness and must decide how much will go to each person (the duty to act justly), cases where one can help himself (the duty of self-improvement), and cases where one can avoid hurting others (the duty of non-maleficence).

29. For example, Ross (*ibid.*, p. 223) argues that sometimes it is morally justified to tell a lie or break a promise, as in cases where to do so would allow one to relieve someone else's stress.

30. *Ibid.*, pp. 219-220.

31. Geisler, p. 112.

32. One final point about ethical systems, viz., their relation to relativism and absolutism. Theories based on reason usually are not relativistic. If an action is rationally compelling, reasons commending it will not likely change. Prescriptive systems may or may not be relativistic, depending on how likely the prescriber is to change the commands. If laws are prescribed arbitrarily, they may be changed with equal capriciousness. On the other hand, if there is a rationale behind the demands, rules will not likely change unless the rationale changes. Undoubtedly, relation-based systems are most open to relativism, for few systems of this sort have a set of rules to tell exactly what to do in each situation. Even "do what Christ would do" is open to differing interpretations about how it applies to concrete situations. In evaluating the relativism of deontological versus teleological systems, on the whole one can say deontological theories are less relativistic than teleological ones. Teleological systems typically determine right and wrong based on consequences, and obviously, calculating consequences varies with the situation. Of course, deontological systems can be relativistic, though most are not. For example, a theory which determines right and wrong on the basis of God's commands might be very relativistic if, according to the theory, God frequently changes his prescriptions (hence relativism). As to the relativism of systems in Geisler's schema, theories such as antinomianism and situationism are very relativistic. On the other hand, systems such as non-conflicting absolutism and ideal absolutism are not very relativistic. For a very stimulating article on the issue of moral conflicts and relativism, see Judith W. DeCew, "Moral Conflicts and Ethical Relativism," *Ethics* 101 (October 1990). DeCew argues that typically those who reject ethical relativism think conflicts in moral norms are resolvable. Likewise, ethical relativism is usually thought to go with views denying that conflicts of ethical norms can be resolved. DeCew presents Stuart Hampshire's case for genuinely unresolvable conflicts of moral norms as well as his arguments that such views about moral conflicts do not necessitate commitment to ethical relativism.

33. See such discussions and claims in works such as C. F. Evans, "Difficulties in Using the Bible for Christian Ethics," *Mod Ch* 26 (1984), Robin Scroggs, "The New Testament and Ethics: How Do We Get from There to Here?" *Per Rel St* 11 (Winter 1984), and James F. Childress, "Scripture and Christian Ethics," *Interp* 34 (October 1980). Others say NT ethics must be understood in light of a perception that the readers and writers were living in the final generation. That is, NT ethics cannot be divorced from its eschatological perspective, a perspective that, we are told, is wrong since that generation was not the final one. Evangelicals would say that first century Christians did not err in taking Scripture at face value when it speaks of Christians living in the last times. Many surely misjudged how long those times would last, but

they were not wrong about living in the last times and needing to adopt an ethic fit for the times.

34. Childress, p. 376.
35. Scroggs, p. 91.
36. Some argue that cultures where the situation is similar to the biblical culture may apply the same principle. This in itself, however, does not entail that rules that are only cultural are universally applicable. Hence, one must first look for theological grounds for justifying a principle's universal application.
37. Greg Bahnsen, *By This Standard* (Tyler, TX: Institute for Christian Economics, 1985) and *Theonomy in Christian Ethics* (Phillipsburg, NJ: Presbyterian & Reformed, 1977) takes this position.
38. Bahnsen, *By This Standard*, p. 152.
39. *Ibid.*, pp. 137-138.
40. Bahnsen, *Theonomy in Christian Ethics*, p. 210.
41. Bahnsen, *By This Standard*, pp. 200-209.
42. *Ibid.*, p. 247, but see also pp. 210-269 for Bahnsen's discussion of the political use of the law.
43. Knox Chamblin, "The Law of Moses and the Law of Christ," in John S. Feinberg, ed., *Continuity and Discontinuity* (Wheaton, IL: Crossway Books, 1988).
44. This is the basic stance taken by Douglas Moo in "The Law of Moses or the Law of Christ," John S. Feinberg, ed., *Continuity and Discontinuity* and in "Jesus and the Mosaic Law," *JSNT* 20 (1984).
45. Cf. Chamblin's position ("The Law of Moses and the Law of Christ") as typical of this problem. No clear indication is forthcoming in his essay on which hermeneutical principles tell which items are carried over as is and which are transformed.
46. Verne H. Fletcher, "The Shape of Old Testament Ethics," *SJT* 24 (Fall 1971): 68 and *passim*.
47. Moo, "The Law of Moses or the Law of Christ," pp. 205-206.
48. See further "The Law of Moses or the Law of Christ" and "Jesus and the Mosaic Law" for Moo's fine discussion of Matt 5:17-19 and other Matthean passages as to how they suggest that other parts of the OT law are not for today.
49. For an excellent discussion of the latter three passages that sets forth why these passages are best understood as teaching an end to Mosaic Law, see Moo, "The Law of Moses or the Law of Christ," pp. 212-217.
50. Cf. Robert Badenas, *Christ the End of the law: JSNTSupp* 10 (Sheffield: JSOT, 1985).
51. Moo, "The Law of Moses or the Law of Christ," pp. 206-208 on Rom 10:4.
52. James Gustafson, "The Place of Scripture in Christian Ethics: A Methodological Study," *Interp* 24 (October 1970): 439-444.
53. Richard Mouw, "The Status of God's Moral Judgments," *Can J Theol* 16 (1970): 62 makes this point about the distinction between the source and justification of ethical norms.
54. See discussions of this issue in articles such as John Bishop, "Theism, Morality and the 'Why should I Be Moral?' Question," *Int J Phil Relig* 17 (1985).
55. For a fine discussion of cultural relativism, see Arthur F. Holmes, *Ethics: Approaching Moral Decisions* (Downers Grove, IL: InterVarsity Press, 1984), Chapter 2.
56. See Frankena, *Ethics*, pp. 86-88 for a discussion of intuitionism and some of its problems.
57. That is, statements of obligation rest on factual matters. The facts on which these value judgments rest may be empirical facts (ethical naturalism) or metaphysical or theological facts (metaphysical moralism).
58. Frankena, *Ethics*, p. 81.
59. G. E. Moore, *Principia Ethica* (Cambridge: Cambridge University Press, repr. 1968), pp. 13-16 (especially pp. 15-16).
60. See, for example, Frankena's discussion of the naturalistic fallacy and answers to it in *Ethics*, p. 82.

61. A further issue about definist theories based on theological claims is noteworthy. Proponents of such theories often say morality and ethics logically rest on religion. Thus, the only hope of justifying morality is by appeal to God. Objections to this idea are abundant but, we think, answerable. The interested reader can pursue this line of debate in works such as William Frankena, "Is Morality Logically Dependent on Religion?" in Paul Helm, ed., *Divine Commands and Morality* (Oxford: Oxford University Press, 1981), Kai Nielsen, "God and the Basis of Morality," *J Relig Ethics* 10 (Fall 1982) and *Ethics Without God* (London: Pemberton Books, 1973). If objectors simply mean that one can structure and logically tie an ethical system to something other than theology, we agree. However, doing so does not prove the system is right any more than tying a system to a theology automatically confirms it as right. Here again one must be able to show the viability of the worldview undergirding an ethical system.

CHAPTER TWO: *Abortion*

1. J. Carl Laney, "A Biblical Appraisal of the Abortion Epidemic," *Living Ethically in the 90's*, ed. J. Kerby Anderson (Wheaton: Victor Books, 1990), p. 204. These figures are corroborated in a recent article by Ted Gest, Mary Lord, Constance Johnson, Matthew Cooper and Steven Roberts in *U.S. News & World Report*. In this article, "Sound and Fury Signifying Little," July 13, 1992, p. 32, the authors state that during the 1980s abortions averaged about 1.6 million a year in the U.S.
2. These statistics are taken from *The World Almanac and Book of Facts: 1992* (New York: World Almanac, 1991), p. 947.
3. As an example, the Alan Guttmacher Institute reported that in 1980 there were 6,043,000 pregnancies, of which 3,349,000 were unwanted. Of the unwanted pregnancies, half, or 1.6 million, ended in abortion. This amounts to one in four pregnancies. Statistics are reported in Joan Beck, "Women, Sex and Contraception," *Chi Trib*, October 10, 1983.
4. "Abortions in the U.S." *Chi Trib*, July 4, 1989. The source for the figures was the Alan Guttmacher Institute.
5. For details of the policy in China, see Michael Weisskopf's two articles from the *Chicago Sun-Times*, February 18, 1985 and February 19, 1985. Those articles are respectively, "Birth Curb Resisted: Peking Relies on Coercion, Abortion to Enforce One-child Rule" and "Population Policy Leads to Killing of Infant Girls."
6. Linda P. Campbell, "Abortion-Foreign Aid Policy OKd," *Chi Trib*, June 4, 1991.
7. Gest, Lord, *et al.*, "Sound and Fury Signifying Little," claim that before 1973 the number of legal abortions was nearing six hundred thousand a year. They also note that more than a century ago several hundred thousand woman a year were having abortions. For details, see p. 32.
8. For details of the *Roe* decision and its implications, see Harold O. J. Brown, *Death Before Birth* (Nashville: Thomas Nelson, 1977), Chapter 4; C. Everett Koop, "The Right to Live," in Jeff L. Hensley, ed., *The Zero People: Essays on Life* (Ann Arbor, MI: Servant Books, 1983), p. 54ff.; Steve Daley and Charles M. Madigan, "Top Court OKs Abortion Limits: Rancorous Battle Heads to the States," *Chi Trib*, July 4, 1989; and the editorial "Wise Middle Course on Abortion," *Chi Trib*, July 4, 1989.
9. "The Abortion Decisions: At a Glance," *Chi Trib*, July 4, 1989.
10. "Wise Middle Course."
11. Glen Elsasser and Ray Moseley, "Top Court OKs Abortion Limits: Doctors Must Conduct Fetus Viability Tests," *Chi Trib*, July 4, 1989. For further details of the *Webster* decision, see "Text of U.S. Supreme Court Decision: *Webster v. Reproductive Health Services*," *J Ch St* 32 (Winter 1990); and George J. Annas, "At Law: *Webster* and the Politics of Abortion," *Hast Center Rep* 19 (March/April 1989).
12. Elsasser and Moseley.

13. For example, a very restrictive anti-abortion law in the state of Louisiana was passed but vetoed by the governor in 1990 and has gone nowhere. In 1992 the Supreme Court voted in *Planned Parenthood v. Casey* to uphold a set of Pennsylvania laws that restrict access to abortion, but in essence all those laws do is make a woman get an "informed consent lecture" and return on another day for the abortion or simply travel out of state where such regulations don't exist. Both sides on the abortion question agree that *Casey* will not make much practical difference. For further details on the *Casey* ruling see Gest, Lord, *et al.*, pp. 32-33.

14. Linda P. Campbell, "Abortion Counseling Ban Upheld," *Chi Trib*, May 24, 1991.

15. For details, see "Abortion Gag Rule Survives Override Try," *Chi Trib*, October 3, 1992.

16. This way of classifying abortions is quite common. For example, see Laney, p. 205.

17. J. N. D. Anderson, *Issues of Life and Death* (Downers Grove, IL: InterVarsity Press, 1977), p. 78. Anderson cites as authority for these figures G. R. Dunston's work as part of the Ciba Foundation Symposium entitled *Law and Ethics of A.I.D. and Embryo Transfer* (Elsevier, Excerpta Medica, North Holland, 1973), pp. 68, 69.

18. The number of ectopic pregnancies has increased fourfold over the last twenty years and now accounts for about 11 percent of maternal deaths. The reasons include: the rise in sexually transmitted diseases, particularly chlamydia trachomatis; a retained IUD; a tubal ligation; and tuboplasty. *Chi Trib*, January 30, 1987 and *The Waukegan News-Sun*, June 6, 1990.

19. For a description of amniocentesis and alternative procedures, see Nigel M. de S. Cameron and Pamela F. Sims, *Abortion: The Crisis in Morals and Medicine* (Leicester, England: Inter-Varsity, 1986), pp. 53-56.

20. Laney, pp. 206-207. See also Cameron and Sims, p. 49.

21. Laney, p. 206.

22. *Ibid.* See also Cameron and Sims, p. 50.

23. Laney, p. 206. Again, see Cameron and Sims, p. 50.

24. Laney, p. 206. See also Cameron and Sims, p. 48.

25. Cameron and Sims, p. 56.

26. John Willke, *Handbook on Abortion* (Cincinnati: Hayes, 1975), p. 83.

27. Cameron and Sims, p. 59.

28. *Ibid.*, pp. 57-59, 64-66. See also Laney, p. 207; and Edward H. Fehskens, "Post-Abortion Syndrome: 'I Couldn't Shake the Nightmares,'" *Luth Wit* (January 1988): 2-4.

29. Descriptions of the physiology of human development are widely available. A detailed one can be found in Cameron and Sims, pp. 71-84.

30. Vincent J. Collins, Steven R. Zielinski, and Thomas J. Marzen, *Fetal Pain and Abortion: The Medical Evidence*, Studies in Law and Medicine, No. 18 (Chicago: Americans United For Life, Inc., 1984), p. 5. See also Stephen Schwarz, *The Moral Question of Abortion* (Chicago: Loyola Press, 1990), Chapter 3; and John T. Noonan, Jr., "The Experience of Pain by the Newborn," in Jeff Hensley, ed., *The Zero People: Essays on Life*.

31. J. C. Willke, *Abortion: How It Is* (Cincinnati: Hayes, 1972), pp. 6, 7.

32. See Laurence H. Tribe, *Abortion: The Clash of Values* (New York: W. W. Norton & Co., 1990), pp. 113-120 for a fine discussion of the issues. For an argument that it is a religious question, see Justice John Paul Stevens's separate opinion in the *Webster* case.

33. Norman Ford, "When Does Human Life Begin?" *Pacif* 1 (1988): 304.

34. *Ibid.*

35. For details as to why *human* life begins at syngamy, not at sperm penetration of the egg, see *ibid.*, pp. 316-324.

36. This is certainly true in regard to IUDs and morning after pills. Likewise, as we shall explain in the next chapter, it is also the case with RU-486. If these means of abortion are used after sexual intercourse, they are not likely to work prior to twenty-four

hours. On the other hand, it is conceivable that someone would take an abortion pill in anticipation of sexual intercourse. However, the exact timing with which these abortifacients work is not known, nor can the exact timing of fertilization be predicted. Hence, it is still not clear that the abortion would occur prior to syngamy. One further point should be raised here, because it has relevance to attempts to prevent fertilization after rape and incest. That point is that even fertilization of an egg does not occur immediately upon sexual intercourse. Fertilization of the egg occurs about two hours after insemination *in a case of in vitro fertilization.* Fertilization (the first entrance of the sperm into the egg) in natural reproduction takes longer. For example, if the egg is in the fallopian tubes, it takes from five to sixty-eight minutes after coitus for the sperm to reach the ampulla of the fallopian tubes and another few hours before it actually begins to penetrate the egg (see Ford, p. 303). All of this makes it exceedingly possible to prevent fertilization after rape and incest for several hours. We discuss this matter further in the next chapter.

37. Brown, p. 93.
38. Paul Ramsey, "Abortion: A Review Article," *Thomist* 37 (1973): 184-185. See also Paul B. Fowler, *Abortion: Toward an Evangelical Consensus* (Portland: Multnomah, 1987), Chapter 2. Fowler's treatment of this issue is excellent and shows that this is indeed what has happened.
39. Paul D. Feinberg, "The Morality of Abortion," in Richard L. Ganz, ed., *Thou Shalt Not Kill* (New Rochelle, NY: Arlington House Publishers, 1978), pp. 129-130.
40. Tribe, pp. 116-117.
41. Charles A. Gardner, "Is an Embryo a Person?" *Nation* (November 13, 1989): 557-558.
42. See Schwarz, pp. 42-56 for an excellent discussion of this issue.
43. Robert Wennberg, *Life in the Balance: Exploring the Abortion Controversy* (Grand Rapids, MI: Eerdmans, 1985), pp. 31-36.
44. See *ibid.*, pp. 54-79 for a variety of arguments.
45. Fowler, pp. 144-145; Wennberg, p. 66ff.
46. As noted, not even Ramsey can claim that it refutes the genetic concept of personhood altogether. If one accepts the argument, it refutes it for only about the first fourteen days of pregnancy. But after that there is no question about whether there is a person or how many persons there are if one uses genetic criteria to answer those questions. Hence, though the facts of twinning and mosaics raise significant questions about the genetic view of personhood, we see no reason that they should warrant dropping the genetic notion of personhood in favor of views whose criteria are far more subjective to interpret and apply.
47. Mary Anne Warren, "On the Moral and Legal Status of Abortion," *Monist* 57 (1973). Perhaps the most detailed set of criteria in the contemporary debate is offered by Joseph Fletcher in his *Humanhood: Essays in Biomedical Ethics*. He lists fifteen positive and five negative criteria of personhood. Included in his list are minimum intelligence, a degree of self-awareness, capacity for self-control, a sense of the passage of time and of futurity, conscious recall of the past, the capability to relate to others, a capacity of concern for others, communication with others, a responsible control of existence, curiosity, being open to change and creativity in his life, a right balance of rationality and feeling, being idiosyncratic in the sense of having a recognizable individuality, and having a functioning cerebral cortex. On the negative side, a person is "not non- or anti-artificial" (i.e., persons are characterized by techniques and should welcome technology), persons are not essentially parental, not essentially sexual, not a bundle of rights, and not a worshiper (New York: Prometheus, 1979), pp. 7-19, cited in Atkinson, "Causing Death and Allowing to Die," *Tyndale Bul* 34 (1983): 221.
48. We note here as well that sometimes this issue is stated in the form of a corollary point, namely, the difference between a sanctity of life ethic and a quality of life ethic. A quality of life ethic says that only those possessing certain capacities (such as those

outlined by Warren) can enjoy a quality of life that is genuinely human. So long as there is that quality of life, life should be preserved. Without it, there is no obligation to protect life, for the mere possession of life is not a value so sacred as to warrant protection. Obviously, no developing fetus has a quality of life worth protecting; hence, it may be aborted.

49. This is the interpretation set forth and defended by John Frame in "Abortion from a Biblical Perspective," in Richard Ganz, ed., *Thou Shalt Not Kill*, pp. 52-57.

50. Meredith Kline (Interp: "Lex Talionis and the Human Fetus," *JETS* 20 [September 1977]: 194ff.) offers a different premature birth understanding of this passage. He thinks neither verse 22 nor verses 23-25 refer to the mother's injury. The blow that strikes her kills her. Verse 22, on this view, teaches that if an uninjured, premature child is delivered, the penalty required is only the fine. However, verses 23-25 teach that if there is some injury to the child as well, then *lex talionis* is to be invoked. We prefer Frame's interpretation for these reasons: the lack of an indirect object for the word "harm" in both verses 22 and 23, and the lack of a more severe penalty for death of the mother that, on Kline's view, is presupposed but not stated in either of the cases. However, even if one adopts Kline's interpretation, the value of the fetus is not lessened but heightened.

51. Judith Jarvis Thompson, "A Defense of Abortion," *Phil Pub Affairs* 1 (1971): 47-66.

52. *Ibid.*, p. 56.

53. Wennberg, p. 159. Wennberg, of course, wrote this before the advent of RU-486.

54. *Ibid.*, pp. 159-164.

55. This is particularly true, given the special relationship existing between mother and child. In fact, most would say that the greater the dependence, the greater the responsibility not to harm. Hence, it is more wrong to mistreat a two-year-old than a fifteen-year-old (though it is wrong to mistreat either) precisely because the two-year-old is more dependent and thus more vulnerable to harm.

56. Baruch Brody, "Thomson on Abortion," *Phil Pub Affairs* 1 (1972).

57. Feinberg, p. 145.

CHAPTER THREE: *Abortion and Special Problems*

1. Arthur F. Holmes, "Some Ethical Questions," in *A Christian Understanding and Response*, ed. James K. Hoffmeier (Grand Rapids, MI: Baker, 1987), pp. 103-113.

2. Paul B. Fowler, *Abortion: Toward an Evangelical Consensus* (Portland: Multnomah Press, 1987), pp. 169-170.

3. Nigel M. de S. Cameron and Pamela F. Sims, *Abortion: The Crisis in Morals and Medicine* (Leicester, England: Inter-Varsity, 1986), pp. 98-99. See also Fowler, *Abortion: Toward an Evangelical Consensus*, p. 170, and J. Carl Laney, "A Biblical Appraisal of the Abortion Epidemic," *Living Ethically in the 90's*, ed. J. Kerby Anderson (Wheaton, IL: Victor Books, 1990).

4. Cameron and Sims, pp. 100-102.

5. *Ibid.*, pp. 88, 101ff. See also Laney, pp. 216-217, and Fowler, pp. 170-171.

6. The no duty-nonforcing principle says it is wrong to force someone to do something for which they have no duty. As applied to abortion in a case of rape or incest, this means it is wrong to force the baby to forfeit its life to make a mother happy or to relieve her pain. The baby has no such duty, so it is wrong to force it to give up its life. See Stephen Schwarz, *The Moral Question of Abortion* (Chicago: Loyola Press, 1990), pp. 146-147 for the definition of this principle and p. 172 for its application to abortion.

7. *Ibid.*, pp. 145-147. See also Cameron and Sims, pp. 102-104; Fowler, pp. 171-173; Laney, pp. 215-216; and Laurence H. Tribe, *Abortion: The Clash of Values* (New York: W. W. Norton, 1990), p. 233.

8. Schwarz, pp. 147-149.

9. David Reardon, *Aborted Women: Silent No More* (Chicago/Wheaton, IL: Loyola/Crossway Books, 1987).

10. Fowler, p. 173.

11. "Zero Pregnancies in 3500 Rapes," *Educ* (September 1970); B. M. Sims, "A District Attorney Looks at Abortion," *Child Fam* (Spring 1969): 176-180; and David Granfield, *The Abortion Decision* (Garden City, NY: Doubleday, 1971), pp. 107-108. We are not so insensitive as to ignore the fact that some rape and incest victims are so physically brutalized that they may be unconscious and unable to get to a doctor soon enough to get help in preventing conception. Nor do we underestimate the feeling of shame and helplessness that makes it difficult for victims to admit what has happened and seek help. Our point is that something can be done to lower substantially the number of cases where rape and incest result in pregnancy. In those cases, despite the embarrassment, etc. involved, victims should seek this help.

12. *DH*, April 22, 1987.

13. *Ibid.*

14. Robert Cross, "The Other Pill: An Abortion-Rights Activist's Fight Over RU-486," *Chi Trib*, April 28, 1991; Kenneth Vaux and Tom Maggio, "RU-486: Abortion Revisited," *Chi Trib*, December 17, 1988.

15. See Cross, "The Other Pill: An Abortion-Rights Activist's Fight Over RU-486"; and *Chicago Sun Times*, July 18, 1992 for earlier figures. See also "France's View of Abortion Pill: Putting Women in Charge," *Int Her Trib*, August 24, 1992.

16. *Chicago Sun Times*, July 8, 15, 18, 1992.

17. *NY Times*, April 25, 1982.

18. Cross, "The Other Pill: An Abortion-Rights Activist's Fight Over RU-486"; "France's View of Abortion Pill: Putting Women in Charge."

19. Susan Duffy, "The RU-486 Question," *Am Drug* (August 1991): 31.

20. See *ibid.*, p. 28; "France's View of Abortion Pill: Putting Women in Charge"; Vaux and Maggio, "RU-486: Abortion Revisited"; Cross, "The Other Pill"; *DH*, April 22, 1987; Cal Thomas, "We Need to Debate Abortion Issue," *DH*, January 7, 1987; *USAT*, December 18, 1986; *NY Times*, April 25, 1982; and Ellen Goodman, "New Drug Could End Abortion Debate," *Chi Trib*, March 1, 1986.

21. We well remember how some argued before *Roe* that the legalization of abortion in the U.S. would not increase abortions but only ensure the safety of mothers who would have had abortions anyway. Statistics belie those claims, and we suspect that widespread availability of RU-486 would over time increase the number of abortions.

22. Duffy, pp. 29-32.

23. Dave Andrusko, "Fetal Tissue Transplants Suggest Pregnancy for Hire," *E/SA* 40 (July/August 1988): 31.

24. *Ibid.*

25. *Ibid.* See also *DH*, February 2, 1990 and Doug Waymire, "News: National Institute of Health Sanctions Research Involving Fetal Tissue Transplant," *FuJo* 8 (February 1989): 60.

26. Waymire, p. 59. Consideration of the ethical and medical issues involved in this kind of research was going on for some time. For a list and some discussion of the questions considered, see "The National Commission and Fetal Research," *Hast Center Rep* 5 (July 1975): 11-46; and "Fetal Research: Response to the Recommendations," *Hast Center Rep* 5 (October 1975): 9-17.

27. *Ibid.*

28. *Ibid.*, p. 60, and Andrusko, p. 31.

29. James T. Burtchaell, "Case Study: University Policy on Experimental Use of Aborted Fetal Tissue," *IBR* 10:4 (July/August 1988): 7.

30. John A. Robertson, "Rights, Symbolism, and Public Policy in Fetal Tissue Transplants," *Hast Center Rep* 18 (December 1988): 5.

31. Here it goes without saying that we think conceiving fetuses for the sole purposes of abortion in order to harvest fetal tissue for use in experimentation or treatment of

disease is immoral. We believe the fetus to be a person, and we agree with those ethicists who claim that persons are ends in themselves, not means to ends. Conceiving fetuses only to abort them and use their tissue treats them as means, not as ends, and is thus immoral.

32. Robertson, pp. 5-13. See also Waymire, pp. 59-60; Andrusko, pp. 30-32.
33. Robertson, pp. 5-6.
34. *Ibid.*, pp. 6-11.
35. *Ibid.*, p. 5; and Andrusko, p. 32.
36. Burtchaell, pp. 7-11.
37. *Ibid.*, pp. 8, 9.
38. *Ibid.*, p. 9.
39. *Ibid.*, p. 10.
40. *Ibid.*, p. 6.
41. Needless to say, in the case of the homicide victim, though intervention was made to save his life, if his organs are taken apart from consent prior to his death or even against prior refusal to donate, such use of his organs would be wrong. In other words, we believe the analogy between the homicide victim and the aborted baby breaks down, but that does not mean we think under *all* circumstances use of the homicide victim's organs would be moral. Despite the differences in the cases we have mentioned, use of the homicide victim's organs might still be immoral on the ground that he never gave permission to use them.
42. Burtchaell, p. 8.
43. Robertson, p. 9.
44. Donald DeMarco, "Health Care Ethics: Fetal Research and Experimentation," in *Human Life and Health Care Ethics*, ed. James Bopp, Jr. (Frederick, MD: University Press of America, 1985), pp. 155-156. This is a brief but very helpful discussion on many of the issues discussed in this section.
45. Burtchaell, p. 10.
46. For a discussion of this group and its thinking, see Randall A. Terry, *Operation Rescue* (Springdale, PA: Whitaker House, 1988). See also, on civil disobedience, Paul Bechtel, "Civil Disobedience: A Necessary Option?" *Chr Life* (February 1982): 16; John Jefferson Davis, *Evangelical Ethics* (Phillipsburg, NJ: Presbyterian and Reformed, 1985); Daniel Stenick, *Civil Disobedience and the Christian* (New York: Seabury Press, 1969), p. 85.
47. Terry, pp. 77-95. See also Randy Alcorn, *Is Rescuing Right?: Breaking the law to Save the Unborn* (Downers Grove, IL: InterVarsity Press, 1990).
48. Terry, pp. 47-48.
49. Joseph Scheidler, *Closed, 99 Ways to Stop Abortion* (Wheaton, IL: Crossway Books, 1982), p. 132.
50. Terry, p. 123, and also used widely throughout his book.
51. For the details of how we would argue for the acceptability of civil disobedience, see our chapter on the Christian and the secular state. We note here, however, that those who were tried at Nuremburg used the defense that they were simply following what their governments demanded of them. This defense was rejected as inadequate, and the accused were convicted of crimes against humanity. Hence, it was recognized by the court in the Nuremburg trials that under certain circumstances one must disobey one's government.
52. Philip Meade, "Civil Disobedience as a Pro-life Tactic: A Consensus Approach to Its Justification and Parameters as Drawn from Three Contemporary Thinkers," unpublished M.A. thesis, Trinity Evangelical Divinity School, 1988, pp. 24-26.
53. Norman L. Geisler, "A Premillennial View of Law and Government," *Bib Sac* 142 (1985): 262.
54. This must not be misunderstood. We do believe that one has a moral obligation to prevent others where possible from doing evil. But we are arguing that one has no obligation or right to prevent others from wrongdoing *by breaking the law oneself!*

55. For a critical analysis of the biblical argument, see William F. Luck, "Abortion Update: Operation Rescue's Biblical Rationale," *Lode R* 4 (1989): 8.

56. We would also point out that if the Proverbs passage obligates one to civil disobedience and intervention, there probably would have been at least some small godly minority in that day who would have taken such action. However, there is no evidence (scriptural or otherwise) that there was any action that approximates the activities of Operation Rescue. Granted, that might be because we simply don't have access to such evidence, and it might be because the passage demands such action, but the people were too immoral to obey. However, when one takes seriously the evidence we present in our text, it seems more likely that there is no evidence of Operation Rescue-like activities in response to this passage, because the passage simply placed no such requirements on the people.

CHAPTER FOUR: *Euthanasia*

1. Bonnie Steinbock, "The Removal of Mr. Herbert's Feeding Tube," *Hast Center Rep* 13 (October 1983): 13.

2. Martin Mawyer, "Court Decision Paving the Way for Euthanasia," *FuJo* 3 (July-August 1984): 60.

3. For the details of this case see Sharman Stein, "Physician Aids in Suicide," *Chi Trib*, June 6, 1990; Stephen Chapman, "Assisting Suicide: Whose Painful Life Is It, Anyway?" *Chi Trib*, June 7, 1990; Michael Hirsley and Karen Thomas, "'Doctor Death' Puts New Focus on Right-to-Die Debate," *Chi Trib*, October 25, 1991. For discussion of these cases see George J. Annas, "Killing Machines," *Hast Center Rep* 21 (March-April 1991). For discussion of another case of doctor assisted suicide, see the report of Dr. Timothy E. Quill in the March 1991 *NEJM*.

4. Hirsley and Thomas, "'Doctor Death' Puts New Focus on Right-to-Die Debate."

5. Consider also the case of Ida Rollin who was dying of cancer. She underwent repeated chemotherapy to no avail. She would die soon, but not an easy death. Wracked with unremitting pain, she asked her daughter and son-in-law to find out what dosage of sleeping pills would kill her. Seeing absolutely no hope for relief or recovery, they reluctantly agreed. Betty Rollin recounts how her mother unflinchingly carried out her own suicide, and she tells how friends and family alike applauded the bravery and "wisdom" of this act when they heard how her death occurred. Is suicide under such conditions morally justifiable? Are Ida Rollin's family members accessories to a murder, or should they be applauded for their compassion in granting their dying mother's last wish? See Betty Rollin, "My Mother's Last Wish," *GH* (October 1985) for details of this story.

6. Examples of articles that discuss various details of this case include Tabitha M. Powledge and Peter Steinfels, "Following the News on Karen Quinlan," *Hast Center Rep* 5 (December 1975); Richard McCormick and Robert Veatch, "The Preservation of Life and Self-determination," *ThSt* 41(June 1980); and Kenneth L. Woodward, "To Live and Let Die," *Newsweek* 96 (July 7, 1980): 80.

7. Alan L. Otten, "The Oldest Old," *The WSJ* (March 30, 1984): 1.

8. Sid Macaulay, "Euthanasia: Can Death Be Friendly?" *ChrT* 20 (November 21, 1975): 37. Macaulay reviews various books on euthanasia.

9. Otten, p. 1.

10. *Ibid.* It is estimated that dementing illnesses roughly double every five years after sixty-five: 1 percent show it at sixty-five, 2.5 percent at seventy, 5 percent at seventy-five, 12 percent at eighty, between 20 and 30 percent at eighty-five, and 40 percent to 50 percent in the nineties. Other diseases that strike with increasing frequency and severity as old age progresses are arthritis, limiting heart conditions, hypertension, and problems with hearing and vision.

11. *Ibid.*, p. 2. As of 1984, the U.S. government estimated that only 6.4 percent of the seventy-five to eighty-four-year-olds are in nursing homes, while 21.6 percent of the eighty-five-or-over group are.

12. Teodoro Dagi, "The Paradox of Euthanasia," *Judaism* 24 (Spring 1975): 157.

13. Plato, *Republic*, III: 405.

14. D. Ch. Overduin, "Euthanasia," *Luth Th J* 14 (December 1980): 114. Overduin (pp. 115-116) notes that in Thomas More's fictional utopian society, euthanasia was encouraged for the terminally ill who granted their permission. The English philosopher Francis Bacon (1561-1626) in *Advancement of Learning* claimed that a physician should use medicine not only to restore health, "but to mitigate pain and dolors; and not only when such mitigation may conduce to recovery, but when it may serve to make a fair and easy passage." In addition, many have advocated certain forms of euthanasia for religious purposes. For example, the Papal Bull *Summi desiderantes* of December 5, 1484 introduced the practice of witch finding and witch burning. Some claimed there were women who cohabited with the devil. As a result, they would be pregnant with monsters who were thought by people like Luther not to have a soul. These women were killed to prevent the birth of such monsters. The practice was permitted in some countries until the first half of the nineteenth century. Self-induced euthanasia and suicide were also supported by such philosophers as Voltaire and Rousseau, though rejected by Kant.

15. *Ibid.*, p. 114.

16. *Ibid.*, p. 117. Some claim that the modern debate over voluntary euthanasia really began in 1873 with the publication of L. A. Tollemache's "The New Cure for Incurables," *Fort R*. Moreover, the real medical debate is said to have begun when Dr. Killick Millard gave his Presidential Address on euthanasia to the Society of Medical Officers of Health in 1931.

17. *Ibid.*, pp. 117-118.

18. This came as a result of a case involving an Amsterdam barmaid who was so shamed by her pregnancy that she hired a man to kill her. He complied, but he not only slit her throat; he also chopped off her fingers in order to steal her rings. As a result of this case, a law was passed against euthanasia, and the penalty was twelve years in prison. For details see Tim Harper, "Dutch Accept, Regulate Suicides Aided by Doctors," *Chi Trib*, November 3, 1991.

19. Overduin, pp. 117-118.

20. Reported on a "Nightline" program on euthanasia on the U.S. network ABC in January 1987. See also Harper, "Dutch Accept, Regulate Suicides Aided by Doctors," who lists slightly different conditions, though ones that are consistent with those reported on "Nightline." He says doctors are not prosecuted "if the patient repeatedly and consistently requests death; the doctor has extensive consultations with the patient, the patient's family and at least one other doctor; the patient's suffering cannot be averted by any accepted medical treatment; and the illness is terminal, even if death is not 'imminent.'"

21. Harper, "Dutch Accept, Regulate Suicides Aided by Doctors." In the "Nightline" interview in 1987, Dr. Pieter Admiraal of Holland, when asked about euthanasia for those in a coma who had not requested it, stated emphatically that it would not be performed in such a case. Even if the family asked, that would not matter. Admiraal, who admitted performing euthanasia on many occasions, urged its legalization. He argued that without legalization, the government will not be able to regulate it, and it will be abused.

22. The Karen Quinlan case, in which her parents went to court and won the right to remove her comatose body from the respirator, is quite famous, but it is hardly the only such case. Moreover, in 1983 the Virginia Senate passed a bill that would allow terminally ill people to order the discontinuance of life-support systems. According to the bill, when "a reasonable degree of medical certainty" exists regarding a patient's imminent death, a previously signed document allows the physician (with

one concurring opinion) to stop life-preserving procedures. One doctor noted that though there was debate over the bill's wording, the bill was really unnecessary, for doctors all the time do what the bill proposed to make legal. Taken from "Natural Death Act Passes Virginia Senate," *FuJo* 2 (May 1983): 62.

23. Robert C. F. Cassidy, "Euthanasia: Passive *and* Active?" *St Luke J* 20 (December 1976): 7. It is safe to say that attitudes have changed even more since that poll in 1973, especially in view of the Karen Ann Quinlan case. In 1980 Donald Granberg ("What Does it Mean to Be 'Pro-life?'" *Chr Cent* 99 [May 12, 1982]: 566) surveyed almost nine hundred members of the National Right to Life Committee and the National Abortion Rights Action League. He asked not only about abortion but about a series of other "pro-life" issues, including various forms of euthanasia. When asked if a doctor should be allowed to end a patient's life in cases of incurable disease if the patient and family so request, 97 percent of the NRLC people polled said no, whereas only 11 percent of the NARAL people responded negatively. When asked if a person with an incurable disease had a right to end his or her own life (suicide), 94 percent of NRLC respondents said no, while only 6 percent of NARAL members polled said no.

24. Stephen Wise, "The Last Word—Whose?" *Chr Cent* 98 (September 16, 1981): 895. Wise notes that although Catholic pronouncements tend to be more conservative than Protestant viewpoints, in 1957 Pope Pius XII ("The Prolongation of Life") stated that neither the doctor nor patient is bound to use anything other than "ordinary" means of prolonging life. Thus, a doctor may properly remove artificial respiration apparatus before blood circulation completely stops. In 1980 Pope John Paul II essentially reiterated this position when he said: "When inevitable death is imminent in spite of the means used, it is permitted in conscience to take the decision to refuse forms of treatment that would only secure a precarious and burdensome prolongation of life, so long as the normal care due to a sick person in similar cases is not interrupted."

25. Interestingly, at about the same time the Cruzan case was decided before the Supreme Court, Belle Greenspan was granted permission by the Cook County (Illinois) Circuit Court to withdraw the feeding tube from her husband Sidney, who had been in a persistent vegetative state since 1984. Her request was approved because she was able to bring the judge conclusive evidence that her husband would not have wanted to remain in that state. For details, see Barbara Brotman, "Man's Life Is Put on Display So He May Be Allowed to Die," *Chi Trib*, September 27, 1990; and "Six Years of 'Living Hell,'" editorial in the *Chi Trib*, October 5, 1990.

26. For details of this case, see the following: Glen Elsasser, "Justices Will Decide on Right to Die of Long-comatose Woman," *Chi Trib*, July 4, 1989 and "Court Blocks 'Right-to-Die' Bid," *Chi Trib*, June 26, 1990; Ronald Kotulak, "Doctors Rip 'Right-to-Die' Edict, Say More Suicides Could Result," *Chi Trib*, June 26, 1990; Michael Tackett, "Judge OKs Removing Comatose Woman's Feeding Tube," *Chi Trib*, December 15, 1990. As Elsasser reported in his June 26 article, this case was watched closely by both medical and religious groups especially because an "estimated 10,000 Americans are being maintained in a persistent vegetative state in care centers around the country."

27. Elsasser, "Court Blocks 'Right-to-Die' Bid." Despite the enthusiasm of many for living wills, not everyone is convinced. For an interesting discussion of some of the problems with living wills, see Richard Hughes, "Ethical Problems in Living Will Legislation," *J Rel Aging* 5 (1988).

28. Paul D. Simmons, "Death with Dignity," *Per Rel St* 4 (Summer 1977): 140-141.

29. Elsasser, "Court Blocks 'Right-to-Die' Bid." The Illinois power of attorney form for health care "grants the designated person power to make all decisions on personal care, medical treatment, hospitalization and health care including withdrawal of treatment, even if death could result" (see Jean L. Griffin, "Hospitals Confronting the 'Right-to-Die' Issue," *Chi Trib*, July 26, 1990). In addition, the Cruzan case and

others like it have occasioned much debate over whether food and water should be administered to the person in the persistently vegetative state. For interesting discussions of this topic, see Thomas A. Shannon and James J. Walter, "The PVS Patient and the Forgoing/Withdrawing of Medical Nutrition and Hydration," *Th St* 49 (1988); Thomas D. Kennedy, "Eating, Drinking, and Dying Well," *Chr Sch R* 20 (1991); and Lisa Cahill, "Bioethical Decisions to End Life," *Th St* 52 (March 1991).

30. Hugh Dellios, "Edgar Signs Law Giving Patients a 'Right To Die,'" *Chi Trib*, September 27, 1991.

31. *Ibid.*

32. "Nightline," March 1988, quoting from the proposed bill.

33. In a phone conversation with the law office of Robert Risely (in Los Angeles), author of the bill, I learned that approximately 370,000 signatures were needed to get the measure on the ballot. Sponsors had only 150 days to get the signatures and got approximately 150,000. However, he claimed that polls showed about a 58 percent approval of the measure.

34. For an excellent treatment of medicine in the Hippocratic mold and the history of the move away from that paradigm, see Nigel M. de S. Cameron, *The New Medicine* (Wheaton, IL: Crossway Books, 1991).

35. Jonas Robitscher, "Living and Dying: A Delicate Balance," *E/SA* 1 (October 1973): 42.

36. Douglas K. Stuart, "'Mercy Killing'—Is it Biblical?" *ChrT* 20 (February 27, 1976): 9.

37. Dagi, "The Paradox of Euthanasia," p. 161.

38. Thomas St. Martin, "Euthanasia: The Three-in-One Issue," in Dennis Horan and David Mall, eds., *Death, Dying and Euthanasia* (Frederick, MD: University Publications of America, 1980), pp. 596-597.

39. *Ibid.*, p. 596.

40. *Ibid.*, pp. 596-597. Though it is imaginable that someone might request this kind of euthanasia, this form is usually involuntary.

41. See our chapters on abortion.

42. Robert Wennberg, "Euthanasia: A Sympathetic Appraisal," *Chr Sch R* 6 (1977): 297-298.

43. James Childs, "Euthanasia: An Introduction to a Moral Dilemma," *Curr Th Miss* 3 (April 1976): 69.

44. For further discussion of recent literature on the matter of quality of life considerations, see James J. Walter, "Termination of Medical Treatment: The Setting of Moral Limits from Infancy to Old Age," *Rel St R* 16 (October 1990): 303-306; and Shannon and Walter, "The PVS Patient and the Forgoing/Withdrawing of Medical Nutrition and Hydration," pp. 634-637.

45. Humanist Manifesto II, as discussed in Joseph R. Stanton, "From Feticide to Infanticide," in Jeff Hensley, ed., *The Zero People: Essays on Life* (Ann Arbor, MI: Servant Books, 1983), pp.188-189.

46. Greville Norburn, "Euthanasia," *Mod Ch* 16 (April 1973): 179.

47. Joseph Fletcher, "Ethics and Euthanasia," in Dennis Horan and David Mall, eds., *Death, Dying and Euthanasia*, p. 296.

48. *Ibid.*

49. *Ibid.*

50. *Ibid.*, pp. 300-301.

51. *Ibid.*, p. 301.

52. Paul Brand's comment in an interview with three other scholars. The article reporting the interview is "Biomedical Decision Making: The Blessings and Curses of Modern Technology," *Chr TI* (March 21 1986): 8.

53. Joseph Fletcher, *Morals and Medicine* (Boston: Beacon Press, 1960), pp. 213-215.

54. Childs, pp. 68-69. The same point is also made in Anthony Flew, "The Principle of Euthanasia," in A. B. Downing, ed., *Euthanasia and the Right to Death* (Los Angeles:

Nash Publishing, 1970), p. 33. See also Eike-Henner Kluge, *The Practice of Death* (New Haven/London: Yale University Press, 1975), pp. 178-179, who argues that euthanasia is allowable in all cases where the individual asks to be killed or allowed to die because he finds life physically or psychologically unbearable, and there is no other way to relieve the pain. Of course, the person must be fully aware of what he is doing. Kluge notes that murder involves infringement of rights, but in the cases he mentions the individual gives up his right to live.

55. Flew, p. 33.

56. *Ibid.*, pp. 33-34.

57. Arthur Dyck, "Beneficent Euthanasia and Benemortasia: Alternative Views of Mercy," in Dennis Horan and David Mall, eds., *Death, Dying and Euthanasia,* summarizes Kohl's point on pp. 353-354.

58. Fletcher, "Ethics and Euthanasia," p. 297.

59. P. F. Baelz, "Voluntary Euthanasia," *Th* 75 (May 1972): 250-251.

60. While the distinction seems intuitively correct, as Milton Sernett shows ("The 'Death With Dignity' Debate: Why We Care," *Springf* 38 [March 1975]: 270), difficulty can arise in trying to specify the difference between ordinary and extraordinary means of treatment. He says physicians define ordinary means as the standard, recognized, orthodox or established medicines and procedures of that time-period at that level of practice and within limits of availability. On the other hand, many moralists define it to include not only normal food, drink and rest, but also all medicines, treatments and operations that offer reasonable hope of patient benefit and which can be obtained and used without excessive expense, pain or other inconvenience. Obviously, words such as "reasonable hope" and "excessive" are ambiguous. As to extraordinary means, Sernett explains that many physicians include any medicine or procedure that might be fanciful, bizarre, experimental, incompletely established, unorthodox or not recognized. He claims that for many moralists, extraordinary means are all medicines, treatments and operations that are excessively painful and expensive or produce other inconveniences for the patient and others and/or are treatments that offer no reasonable hope of benefit to the patient.

61. *Ibid.* Those who use the distinction agree with Pope Pius XI's 1957 statement to anesthesiologists that it is ethically correct not to employ such extraordinary means. For further discussion of this issue, see Shannon and Walter, "The PVS Patient and the Forgoing/Withdrawing of Medical Nutrition and Hydration," pp. 643-645.

62. Dyck, p. 356.

63. Cassidy, p. 8. For further discussion of the principle of double effect, see A. Van Den Beld, "Killing and the Principle of Double Effect," *SJT* 41 (1988). As Van Den Beld shows, the principle of double effect states that the bad effect must not be the means to the good effect. The good effect must be logically (if not also chronologically) prior, even though it leads to a bad effect, and the good effect must be what the agent intends. In other words, if one does evil to do good, that is not moral by the principle of double effect. Nor is it moral to do good to accomplish evil. One must do good for its own sake, even though the doing of good also eventuates in an evil.

64. Somen Das and Hunter Mabry, "Human Rights and the 'Mercy-Killing Bill,'" *Rel Soc* 29 (June 1982): 18-19. (The authors cite Matt 5:4, which says nothing about giving alms. Matt 6:2-4 deals with alms, but doesn't quite say what they claim. Their more general claim, though, is clear, apart from reference to specific verses.)

65. Millard Erickson and Ines Bowers, "Euthanasia and Christian Ethics," *JETS* 19 (Winter 1976): 17.

66. Simmons, pp. 142, 153.

67. Flew, p. 46.

68. Wennberg, pp. 299-300.

69. Das and Mabry, p. 20.

70. *Ibid.*, p. 28.

71. *Ibid.*

72. Glenn Graber (cited in Donald S. Klinefelter, "The Morality of Suicide," *Sound* 67 [Fall 1984]: 338) defines suicide as doing "something that results in one's death in the way that was planned, either from the intention of ending one's life or the intention to bring about some state of affairs (such as relief from pain) that one thinks it certain or highly probable can be achieved only by means of death."

73. Klinefelter, pp. 340-342.

74. See Baelz's citation (p. 241) of David Hume's "On Suicide."

75. Erickson and Bowers, p. 19. For further argumentation to the effect that Christians who oppose suicide really do not have a very good case, see Kenneth Boyd, "Terminal Care, Euthanasia and Suicide," *Mod Ch* NS 30 (1988): 12-14. See also Walter, p. 306.

76. James Rachels, "Active and Passive Euthanasia," in Tom Beauchamp and Seymour Perlin, eds., *Ethical Issues in Death and Dying* (Englewood Cliffs, NJ: Prentice-Hall, 1978), pp. 241-242.

77. *Ibid.*, p. 243.

78. Gilbert Meilander, "The Distinction Between Killing and Allowing to Die," *Th St* 37 (September 1976): 467. Wennberg (pp. 284-285) speaks of the supposed difference between withholding treatment (at the patient's request) and stopping treatment begun (at the patient's request). Generally, the former is less objectionable than the latter, because the latter involves "doing something," whereas the former involves refraining from doing something. Wennberg thinks there is no difference. If it was wrong to start treatment, the error is compounded by refusing to stop it. He says (p. 285), "The decision to unplug a life-support system is no more serious a decision—though every bit serious as—the decision not to plug it in to begin with."

79. McCormick and Veatch, pp. 390-395.

80. Erickson and Bowers, pp. 21-22.

81. See our section on personhood in Chapter 2.

82. J. Kerby Anderson, "Euthanasia: A Biblical Approach," *Bib Sac* 144 (April-June 1987): 215.

83. See Klinefelter on Aquinas, p. 340 and Robert Nelson, "Euthanasia: A Dilemma for Christians," *E/SA* 13 (April 1985): 33-34.

84. In an interesting article, Leon Kass argues that despite what some claim, it is possible to uphold the sanctity of life principle and at the same time favor death with dignity. See Leon R. Kass, "Death with Dignity & the Sanctity of Life," *Commentary* 89 (March 1990).

85. David J. Atkinson, "Causing Death and Allowing to Die," *Tyndale Bul* 34 (1983): 207-208. This does not mean God does not care about what happens to us or that consequences of actions are irrelevant to him. It only means that for those committed to biblical ethics, the moral justification of an action has traditionally been understood along non-consequentialist lines.

86. *Ibid.*

87. Dyck, p. 351.

88. *Ibid.*, p. 352.

89. M. Pabst Battin, "The Least Worse Death," *Hast Center Rep* 13 (April 1983): 14 and Nelson, p. 37. See also Battin's argument that those who desire a natural and peaceful death cannot guarantee it even with euthanasia.

90. "Nightline," March 1988. Because of this fact, even some with AIDS who consider suicide choose to live on with pain-killing medication. See also Erickson and Bowers, p. 23.

91. Robitscher, p. 44.

92. Paul Ramsey, "The Indignity of Death with Dignity," in Dennis Horan and David Mall, eds., *Death, Dying and Euthanasia, passim.*

93. Stuart, p. 10.

94. *Ibid.*, p. 11. Stuart also argues that in view of biblical teaching on the resurrection, "the events of this life, whether miserable or joyful, are placed in a very different

perspective. This life is seen as by definition temporary and transitory (Jas 4:13), and its miseries are not ends in themselves but are potentially beneficial."

95. *Ibid*. Here the case of Jackie Cole is a beautiful example of what God can do. Her husband relates how she was in a coma as a result of a massive stroke. He sought legal permission to remove her life-support systems but was denied. Six days after permission was denied, Jackie miraculously opened her eyes and has been on the road to rehabilitation since then. Though this case is extraordinary and one cannot expect a miracle in every situation, this case does underscore the need to be patient enough to allow the Lord to do what he chooses. For details of this compelling story see Harry A. Cole, "Deciding on a Time to Die," *Sec Opin* 7 (March 1988).

96. Anderson, p. 217.

97. *Ibid.*, p. 216.

98. Baelz, pp. 241-242.

99. *Ibid.*, p. 242.

100. *Ibid.*, pp. 242-243.

101. Stanley Hauerwas and Richard Bondi, "Memory, Community and the Reasons for Living: Theological and Ethical Reflections on Suicide and Euthanasia," *JAAR* 44 (1976): 449-450.

102. *Ibid.*, pp.450-451.

103. James Childs, Jr. makes this point nicely in citing Joseph Fletcher's belief that there is no moral difference between active and passive euthanasia. See James M. Childs, Jr., "Ethics at the End of Life," *Curr Th Miss* 15 (April 1988): 168-170.

104. Because of the different kinds of cases that can arise in regard to killing and letting die, Michael Philips ("Are 'Killing' and 'Letting Die' Adequately Specified Moral Categories?" *Phil Stud* 47 [1985]) thinks this proves that the categories of killing and letting die are not adequately specified. Philippa Foot ("Commentary," *Hast Center Rep* 9 [October 1979]: 20) thinks the distinction between active and passive is relevant in cases where rights are in question. A person's right to noninterference usually extends farther than his right to receive care. Thus, even if we may not interfere to bring a certain result (active), it does not follow that we may not allow it to come about (passive). On the other hand, in some cases active and passive make no difference. She states that if someone grants permission to kill a person for his own good, it makes no moral difference whether we kill him or let him die. If one is moral, so is the other; and if one is immoral, so is the other. In other words, *voluntary* active and passive euthanasia are morally the same. Only when euthanasia is *involuntary* is there any moral difference between active and passive. Here we disagree, for if it is wrong to kill or let die, it is wrong to do either, regardless of whether the patient requests it or not. Moreover, we have also shown cases where there is a moral difference between killing and letting die, and those differences remain regardless of whether the patient does or does not give permission for killing or letting die. See also Michael Wreen, "Breathing a Little Life into a Distinction," *Phil Stud* 46 (1984): 400-401; and J. P. Moreland, "James Rachels and the Active Euthanasia Debate," *JETS* 31 (March 1988) for further discussion of this issue.

105. Here the emphasis is not on what makes the agent moral in doing the act, because the voluntary/involuntary distinction focuses not on the one who does the act but on the one who requests the act. Therefore, the key category for moral assessment is the act itself.

106. We note here that our point is also true for those whose theory of moral obligation mixes deontological and teleological concerns.

107. See, for example, comments in the *Chr TI* (March 21, 1986), p. 7, on biomedical decision-making.

108. "A Definition of Irreversible Coma: Report of the Ad Hoc Committee of the Harvard Medical School to Examine the Definition of Brain Death," *The Journal of the American Medical Association* 205 (August 5, 1968): 337-340.

109. Here the obligations might be stated as duties to relieve pain and not to take a life. From scriptural injunctions against murder, one can see that there is a duty not to take a life. One might wonder, however, if there is also a positive duty to preserve life. We believe there is and that it stems from the principle of benevolence. It is commonly agreed upon by ethicists that if one is in a position to do benefit to others without exposing oneself to harm, one is morally obliged to do so. In a case where someone is in danger of losing life, the moral principle just stated translates into an obligation to preserve that life, unless our life would be endangered by doing so. The point about the double effect principle can be equally made in the case mentioned in the text, regardless of whether one focuses on the duty to preserve life or the duty not to take a life.

110. James Mathers, "'Brain Death' or 'Heart Death'? Reflections on an Ethical Dilemma," *ExposT* 87 (1976): 328.

111. *Ibid.*

112. *Ibid.*, pp. 328-329.

113. *Ibid.*, p. 329.

114. Some might think this means that in cases where a person is comatose but hooked up to a machine, life will last indefinitely. This is not so. Even someone hooked up to a machine can die while on the machine.

CHAPTER FIVE: *Capital Punishment*

1. Kay Isaly, "In a Discriminatory and Arbitrary Manner," *E/SA* 8 (January 1980): A14.

2. Data from Amnesty International.

3. Susan Agrest, Lucy Howard, and George Raine, "To Die or Not to Die," *Newsweek* 102 (October 17, 1983): 45.

4. Hilary Shelton, "Racial Justice Requires Review of Death Penalty," *Chr Soc Action* 3 (February 1990): 27.

5. Opponents of the amendment say it claims that statistics would not be allowed in determining whether a given state's death statute was being applied discriminatorily. Those who favor the Racial Justice Act note that this really undercuts the force of the Racial Justice Act, for that act allows decisions about whether a given state is discriminatory to be based on statistics. Hence, the amendment in effect overturns the Racial Justice Act.

6. For a review of developments since 1940 in the U.S. with regard to the death penalty, see Hugo A. Bedau, "Death Penalty in America: Yesterday, Today, and Tomorrow," *Iliff R* 45 (Spring 1988).

7. *USAT*, 1983.

8. Nicholas C. Ulmer, "Doctors & the Death Penalty: Hippocratic or Hypocritical?" *Chr Cris* 41 (April 13, 1981): 109.

9. See Amnesty International Report, "The Ultimate Cruel, Inhuman and Degrading Punishment," *E/SA* 8 (January 1980): A6ff. for these statistics.

10. 1992 data from Amnesty International.

11. Amnesty International Report, "The Ultimate Cruel . . . Punishment," pp. A5-A7. For an excellent historical survey of capital punishment, see M. B. Crowe, "Theology and Capital Punishment," *Ir Theol Q* 31 (1964): 24-61, 99-131. See Eric E. Hobbs and Walter C. Hobbs, "Contemporary Capital Punishment: Biblical Difficulties with the Biblically Permissible," *Chr Sch R* 11 (1982): 250-262 for a brief historical survey of the issue in America.

12. Hobbs & Hobbs, p. 254.

13. Norman Dake, "Who Deserves to Live? Who Deserves to Die? Reflections on Capital Punishment," *Curr Th Miss* 10 (April 1983): 74.

14. Hugo A. Bedau, "The Death Penalty as a Deterrent: Argument and Evidence," *Ethics* 80 (1969-1970): 209.

15. Crowe, pp. 110-111.

16. Dake, p. 74.
17. Bedau, "The Death Penalty as a Deterrent," p. 210.
18. Robert Wennberg, "Legal Punishment and Its Justification," *Chr Sch R* 3 (1973): 104.
19. See Herbert A. Deane, *The Political and Social Ideas of St. Augustine* (New York: Columbia University Press, 1963), p. 134.
20. Chana K. Poupko, "The Religious Basis of the Retributive Approach to Punishment," *Thomist* 39 (1975): 535.
21. L. Harold DeWolf, "The Death Penalty: Cruel, Unusual, Unethical, and Futile," *Rel in Life* 42 (1975): 37-38.
22. Thomas A. Long, "Capital Punishment—'Cruel and Unusual'?" *Ethics* 83 (1972-1973): 217-218. Long offers an excellent discussion of the whole matter of cruel and unusual punishment.
23. Hobbs & Hobbs, p. 253.
24. Isaly, p. A10.
25. Hobbs & Hobbs, p. 253. See also James Barber, "Never Say Die!" *Other Side* 132 (September 1982): 11, and Shelton, "Racial Justice Requires Review of Death Penalty," pp. 26-27 for further statistics that support the discriminatory way in which the death penalty has been applied in the U.S. In addition, others note that racial discrimination is not the only way in which the death penalty is arbitrarily applied. For example, juries and prosecutors usually distinguish three categories of murders: bad ones, really bad murders, and horrendous murders. The death penalty is usually imposed in the third case, seldom in the first, and sometimes in the second. What winds up looking arbitrary is when a given state's death penalty statutes do not protect from execution people who fall in the first category. For amplification of this point as well as further discussion of arbitrary application of the death penalty, see Mark Tushnet, "Reflections on Capital Punishment: One Side of an Uncompleted Discussion," *J Law Rel* 7 (1989), esp. pp. 27-30.
26. Morton Enslin, "Capital Punishment—'Cruel and Unusual'?" *Rel in Life* 41 (1972): 256-258.
27. Steven Goldberg, "On Capital Punishment," *Ethics* 85 (1974-1975): 68.
28. *Ibid.*
29. Jeffrey Murphy, "Three Mistakes About Retributivism," *Analysis* 31 (April 1971): 166.
30. See Poupko, p. 535.
31. See Atkinson's discussion of three ideas of fairness that are often used in retributive discussions, in Max Atkinson, "Interpreting Retributive Claims," *Ethics* 85 (1974-1975): 83-86.
32. Long, pp. 216-218.
33. *Ibid.*, p. 221.
34. *Ibid.*, pp. 221-222.
35. John Yoder, "Capital Punishment and the Bible," *ChrT* 4 (February 1, 1960): 348. See also Charles Milligan, "Capital Punishment and the Bible," *ChrT* 4 (February 1, 1960): 350-351 for examples of other OT commands that defenders of capital punishment ignore.
36. Yoder, p. 348.
37. *Ibid.*, pp. 348-349.
38. Milligan, p. 351. See also John Dear, "Seventy Times Seven," *Sojourners* 18 (August-September 1989).
39. *Ibid.*, p. 351. See also p. 352 where Milligan discusses the case of Onesimus as another example of granting mercy in a capital case.
40. David Llewellyn, "Restoring the Death Penalty: Proceed with Caution," *ChrT* 19 (1974-1975): 10-11.
41. L. B. Smedes, "Is the Death Penalty Necessary?" *Un Ev Action* 23 (December 1964): 18.

42. Hobbs & Hobbs, p. 256. See also James J. Megivern, "Biblical Argument in the Capital Punishment Debate," *Per Rel St* 8 (Summer 1981): 147.
43. Smedes, p. 18. As already noted, some say the point of shedding blood is for expiation, but with Christ's death all expiatory sacrifices are ended. Thus capital punishment, meant as it was to expiate the sin of the criminal, is ended.
44. Hobbs & Hobbs, p. 258.
45. Jim Stentzel, "No-Mercy Killing," *Sojourners* 8 (July 1979): 4.
46. Dake, pp. 68-69.
47. Milligan, p. 351.
48. Yoder, p. 349.
49. Stephen James, "The Adulteress and the Death Penalty," *JETS* 22 (March 1979): 47-48.
50. *Ibid.*, p. 48.
51. *Ibid.*, pp. 49-51.
52. *Ibid.*, p. 52.
53. Hobbs & Hobbs, p. 256.
54. Smedes, p. 13.
55. For a treatment of the debate over different senses of freedom and divine sovereignty, see Randall and David Basinger, eds., *Predestination and Free Will* (Downers Grove, IL: InterVarsity Press, 1986).
56. For further helpful reading on the subject of capital punishment, see William Baker, *On Capital Punishment* (Chicago: Moody Press, 1985) and C. S. Lewis, "Humanitarian Theory of Punishment," *God in the Dock*, ed. Walter Hooper (Grand Rapids, MI: Wm. B. Eerdmans, 1970).
57. That this issue of consistency is indeed a matter on the minds of many is evident from a recent article by Stephen D. Johnson and Joseph B. Tamney. In their article they take the findings from 1983 and 1984 nationwide NORC surveys and try to determine a "profile" of the kind of person who holds what they believe to be inconsistent life-views (i.e., rejection of abortion while approving capital punishment). They conclude that people holding this view are most likely to be members of rather conservative, fundamentalist, Protestant churches, are more concerned with the sexual morality of younger adults than with preserving life of the unborn, believe that physical force is needed to solve problems, and believe that hard work leads to success and that racial intermarriage is wrong. Needless to say, such conclusions use highly emotive language and carry with them a particular evident bias. What is also interesting is that the authors nowhere attempt a similar analysis of people who hold a pro-abortion but anti-capital punishment stance, another apparently inconsistent position. One suspects that these people would likely be portrayed as rather moderate and sane in their views. See Stephen D. Johnson and Joseph B. Tamney, "Factors Related to Inconsistent Life-Views," *R Rel Res* 30 (September 1988).

CHAPTER SIX: *Sexual Morality*

1. Sey Chassler, "What Teen Boys Think About Sex," *Par Mag* (December 18, 1988): 8.
2. *Ibid.*, pp. 8-9.
3. Tim Stafford, "Intimacy: Our Latest Sexual Fantasy," *ChrT* 31 (January 16, 1987): 21-22.
4. "Great Sex: Reclaiming a Christian Sexual Ethic," *ChrT* 31 (October 2, 1987): 25-27.
5. "Morality," *USNWR* (December 9, 1989): 52.
6. Chassler, pp. 8-9.
7. Lloyd Shearer, "*Parade's* Special Intelligence Report," *Par Mag* (August 6, 1989): 12.
8. "My Generation," *Sev Mag* (October 1989): 103-104.

9. Victor Grassian, *Moral Reasoning: Ethical Theory and Some Contemporary Moral Problems* (Englewood Cliffs, NJ: Prentice-Hall, 1981), pp. 195-196. See also Stafford, "Intimacy: Our Latest Sexual Fantasy," p. 22, and "Great Sex," pp. 32-33.
10. Stafford, p. 22.
11. *Ibid*. See also Grassian, pp. 194-195.
12. Grassian, p. 194.
13. Stafford, p. 22.
14 Grassian, p. 196.
15. Carl Wellman, *Morals and Ethics* (New York: Scott, Foresman, 1975), p. 124.
16. *Sev Mag*, p. 103. See also Deborah W. Huff, "What Price Promiscuity?" *FuJo* 1 (November 1982): 50-51, 62. Obviously, a promiscuous approach to extramarital sex opens one up to the same consequences. The case of Magic Johnson vividly illustrates that fact. What is frustrating and disturbing about such cases is that those who reflect on them seldom advise abstinence (or faithfulness to one's wife/husband in the case of married people), but rather taking precaution to protect oneself with condoms. It is seldom assumed that premarital or extramarital sex is morally wrong and in need of curtailment. It is only portrayed as foolish if you get caught without protection.
17. Wellman, p. 124.
18. See the following articles which make this point at some length: Brendan Byrne, S. J., "Sinning Against One's Own Body: Paul's Understanding of the Sexual Relationship in 1 Corinthians 6:18," *CBQ* 45 (1983): 608-616; Joseph C. Weber, "Human Sexuality: The Biblical Witness," *Rel in Life* 49 (Fall 1980): 336-348; Peter S. Zaas, "Cast out the Evil Man from Your Midst," *JBL* 103 (June 1984): 259-261.
19. "Great Sex," p. 32.
20. For good treatments of the biblical and theological arguments, see John F. Dedek, "Premarital Sex: The Theological Argument from Peter Lombard to Durand," *Th St* 41 (December 1980): 643-667 and John Goldingay, "The Bible and Sexuality," *SJT* 39 (1986): 175-188.
21. Stafford, p. 22.
22. *Ibid*., p. 23.
23. *Ibid*.
24. *Ibid*.
25. *Ibid*.
26. *Ibid*.
27. *Ibid*.
28. *Ibid*. See also Chassler, p. 8.
29. Stafford, p. 24.
30. *Ibid*.
31. Wellman, p. 125.
32. *Ibid*., pp. 125-126.
33. *Ibid*., p. 126.
34. C. S. Lewis, *Mere Christianity* (New York: Macmillan, 1943), p. 89.
35. Grassian, pp. 194-195.
36. *Ibid*., pp. 198-199.
37. *Ibid*., p. 198.
38. "Great Sex," p. 44.
39. *Ibid*., p. 31.
40. *Ibid*., p. 32.
41. Grassian, p. 200ff.
42. "Great Sex," p. 33.
43. Michael S. Patton, "Masturbation from Judaism to Victorianism," *J Rel Health* 24 (Summer 1985): 133-146.
44. Herbert S. Miles, *Sexual Understanding Before Marriage* (Grand Rapids, MI: Zondervan, 1957), pp. 137-162.

45. Tim Stafford, "Love, Sex and the Whole Person," *CL* 35 (May 1977): 74-78.
46. This is precisely how the term is defined, for example, in James F. Childress, "Masturbation," in James F. Childress and John MacQuarrie, eds., *Westminster Dictionary of Christian Ethics* (Philadelphia: Westminster, 1986), pp. 372-373.
47. For further discussion of ways in which sperm may be collected if one disapproves of masturbation in any form (self-stimulation or mate stimulation), see our discussion of artificial insemination in our Chapter 9 on genetic engineering.

CHAPTER SEVEN: Birth Control

1. See, for example, Herman Kahn and Julian Simon, eds. *The Resourceful Earth: A Response to Global 2000* (New York: Basil Blackwell, 1984); Jacqueline Kasun, *The War Against Population* (San Francisco: Ignatius, 1988); Julian Simon, *The Ultimate Resource* (Princeton, NJ: Princeton University Press, 1982); and Ben Wattenberg, *The Birth Dearth* (New York: Pharos Books, 1987).
2. Charles Birch, "Three Facts, Eight Fallacies and Three Axioms About Population and Environment," *Ec R* 25 (January 1973): 29.
3. Statistics taken from the *1990 Demographic Yearbook* (New York: United Nations, 1992), p. 141.
4. *Ibid.*, p. 33.
5. Statistics were taken from *1985 Demographic Yearbook* (New York: United Nations, 1987) and the *1990 Demographic Yearbook*.
6. Charles E. Curran, "The Contraceptive Revolution and the Human Condition," *Amer J Theol Phil* 3 (May 1982): 42-43.
7. For example, Florence Widutis ("The Parenthood Time Bomb," *E/SA* 10 [November 1982]: 42), writing in 1982, indicated that since 1978, population growth in Mexico had dropped from 3.4 percent to 2.5 percent. Mexico's goal is 1 percent growth by the year 2000. To those who are concerned about overpopulation this is only somewhat encouraging. This is not zero population growth; it is growth. In 1980 the population of Mexico was 66,846,833. Even a 1 percent increase a year over 1980 figures would mean an increase of more than 668,000 people for 1981. Continuous growth of 1 percent per year would result in a population close to 74,000,000 by 1990 for Mexico. As a matter of fact, the annual rate of increase in Mexico between 1985 and 1990 was 2 percent. The population of Mexico in 1990 was already around 86,154,000, not 74,000,000 (see *1990 Demographic Yearbook*, p. 145). In addition, between 1985 and 1990 the average rate of population growth in Latin America was 2.1 percent, 1.9 percent in all of Eastern, Southern, Southeast, and Western Asia, and 3.0 percent in Africa (*1990 Demographic Yearbook*, p. 141).
8. Alan F. Guttmacher, "Population and Pollution," *Rv Ex* 69 (Winter 1972): 59.
9. *1990 Demographic Yearbook*, p. 379.
10. *Ibid.*
11. Statistics taken from *1985 Demographic Yearbook*.
12. *1990 Demographic Yearbook*, p. 141.
13. Birch, p. 30.
14. *Ibid.*, p. 31.
15. Curran, p. 43.
16. "Morality," *USNWR* 99 (December 9, 1985): 52.
17. *Ibid.*
18. For example, see "Should Parents Be Told When Teens Get Contraceptives?" *ChrT* 27 (March 18, 1983): 22 about a case in New York, and Kenneth Slack, " The Underage Girl: A Surprising Judgment," *Chr Cent* 102 (November 20, 1985): 1054-1056, about a case in Great Britain.
19. Curran, p. 45.
20. *Ibid.*, p. 44.

21. Kenneth W. Eckhardt and Gerry E. Hendershot, "Religious Preference, Religious Participation, and Sterilization Decisions: Findings From the National Survey of Family Growth, Cycle II," *R Rel Res* 25 (March 1984): 245.

22. See also John T. Noonan, *Contraception: A History of Its Treatment by the Catholic Theologians and Canonists* (Cambridge, MA: Harvard University Press, 1966), pp. 87-160, and Garth L. Hallett, "Contraception and Prescriptive Infallibility," *Th St* 43 (1982): 638.

23. Noonan, p. 165.

24. *Ibid.*, Chapter 8.

25. John Peel, "Birth Control and Catholic Doctrine," *Lon Q & Hol Rev* 190 (October 1965): 315-316.

26. *Ibid.*, pp. 316-317.

27. *Ibid.*, pp. 320-321.

28. For a slightly different interpretation of *Humanae Vitae*, see Richard Malone, "*Humanae Vitae* Revisited," *Com* 15 (Winter 1988). According to Malone, the key issue in this document was not the rejection of contraception, but rather the affirmation of the absolute value of conjugal love.

29. Thomas W. Hilgers, "Human Reproduction: Three Issues for the Moral Theologian," *Th St* 38 (March 1977): 137-138.

30. Charles G. Chakerian, "The Population Crisis, Conception Control, and Christian Response," *McC Q* 20 (January 1967): 152-153.

31. C. E. Cerling, "Abortion and Contraception in Scripture," *Chr Sch R* 2 (1971): 49.

32. Alan Guttmacher, "Traditional Judaism and Birth Control," *Judaism* 16 (Spring 1967): 159.

33. Chrysostom Zaphiris, "The Morality of Contraception: An Eastern Orthodox Opinion," *JES* 11 (Fall 1974): 686.

34. Curran, pp. 45-46.

35. *Ibid.*, p. 47.

36. Lawrence B. Porter, "Notes and Comments: Intimacy and Human Sexuality: A Challenge to the Consensus on Contraception," *Com* 7 (August 1980): 271-275.

37. Noonan, pp. 33-36. See also Bruce K. Waltke, "The Old Testament and Birth Control," *ChrT* 13 (November 8, 1968): 5.

38. For a different view see Diane Payette-Bucci, "Voluntary Childlessness," *Direction* 17 (Fall 1988). Payette-Bucci explores Paul's teaching in 1 Cor 7:25-40 about remaining unmarried and celibate. She notes that Paul offers principles that sanction such a state as morally acceptable. She then argues that the case of remaining single and celibate is analogous to the case of a married couple that decides to remain childless. She argues that the same reasoning Paul used to justify the former is applicable to justifying voluntary childlessness. We are inclined to disagree. For example, one of the reasons offered for staying single is that one might more effectively serve the Lord. Payette-Bucci says the same reasoning can apply to choosing not to have children. However, it seems that once one accepts the responsibility of marriage, there are other things that normally come with it, such as children. Moreover, if one is so concerned to be free of responsibility so as to serve the Lord, then why bother getting married? Once having married, it seems that the argument that one has to forego children in order to be free of responsibilities so as to serve the Lord loses its force.

39. Rosalind P. Petchesky, "Reproduction, Ethics, and Public Policy: The Federal Sterilization Regulations," *Hast Center Rep* 9 (October 1979): 30.

40. George J. Annas, "Sterilization of the Mentally Retarded: A Decision for the Courts," *Hast Center Rep* 11 (August 1981): 18.

41. Whether the third group refers to people who have been castrated or instead to people who for the sake of the kingdom of heaven abstain from sexual relations and marriage in order to devote themselves exclusively to serving the Lord so that they are like eunuchs is debated by commentators. We need not, however, make an

interpretive decision on that matter in order to judge whether the passage sanctions
or eliminates sterilization.

CHAPTER EIGHT: Homosexuality

1. Tom and Nancy Biracree, *Almanac of the American People* (New York: Facts on File, 1988), pp. 180-182.
2. Robert E. Fay, Charles F. Turner, Albert D. Klassen, and John H. Gagnon, "Prevalence and Patterns of Same-Gender Sexual Contact Among Men," *Science* 243 (January 20, 1989): 338-348. See also the *Chicago Sun Times*, January 20, 1989. Here we would add that a further complicating factor in determining how many homosexuals there are is the distinction between having homosexual tendencies and acting on those tendencies. It is likely that there are people who have those feelings at one time or another but have never engaged in homosexual activities. Do the feelings make them homosexuals, does acting on those tendencies make them homosexuals, or what?
3. Nikki Meredith, "The Gay Dilemma," *Physch T* (January 1984): 56-57.
4. Maria Barinaga, "Is Homosexuality Biological?" *Science* 253 (August 1991): 956.
5. D. F. Swaab and M. A. Hofman, "An Enlarged Suprachiasmatic Nucleus in Homosexual Men," *Br Res* 537 (1990): 141-148.
6. Simon LeVay, "A Difference in Hypothalamic Structure Between Heterosexual and Homosexual Men," *Science* 235 (August 30, 1991): 1034-1037.
7. Swaab and Hofman, pp. 141, 143.
8. *Ibid.*, p. 141.
9. LeVay, p. 1034.
10. *Ibid.*, pp. 1035-1036.
11. Cal Thomas, "Sexual Preference Is Not Determined by Genetic Factors," *DH*, September 6, 1991.
12. Barinaga, p. 957.
13. Swaab and Hofman, p. 143.
14. LeVay, p. 1035.
15. Swaab and Hofman, p. 141.
16. LeVay, p. 1035.
17. Barinaga, pp. 956-957; LeVay, p. 1036.
18. Barinaga, p. 956.
19. *Ibid.*, pp. 956-957.
20. Cf. G. Timothy Johnson, "Studies Link Homosexuality to Genetics," *Chi Trib*, November 8, 1985.
21. For a rather thorough discussion of this matter from a Christian perspective, see the works of Elizabeth R. Moberly: *Homosexuality: A New Christian Ethic* (Cambridge: James Clarke & Co., 1983); *Psychogenesis: The Early Development of Gender Identity* (London: Routledge & Kegan Paul, 1983); and *The Psychology of Self and Other* (London: Tavistock, 1985).
22. Garfield Tourney, "Hormones and Homosexuality," in Judd Marmor, ed., *Homosexual Behavior: A Modern Reappraisal* (New York: Basic Books), p. 42.
23. *Ibid.*
24. *Ibid.*, p. 55.
25. Those who support the learned behavior thesis include Klaus Bockmuhl, "Homosexuality in Biblical Perspective," *ChrT* 17 (February 16, 1973): 13ff.; Kenneth O. Gangel, *The Gospel and the Gay* (New York: Thomas Nelson, 1978), pp. 125-135; and William P. Wilson, "Biology, Psychology and Homosexuality," in *What You Should Know About Homosexuality*, ed. Charles W. Keysor (Grand Rapids, MI: Zondervan, 1979), pp. 147-167.
26. Evelyn Hooker, "Sexual Behavior: Homosexuality," *International Encyclopedia of the Social Sciences*, ed. David L. Sills (New York: Macmillan, 1968), 14: 224.

27. For recent discussions of the biblical materials that go beyond the direct references that follow, see Fred Craddock, "How Does the New Testament Deal With the Issue of Homosexuality?" *Encount* 40 (1969): 197-208; David Field, *The Homosexual Way—A Christian Option* (Leicester, England: Inter-Varsity, 1979); Michael Green, David Holloway and David Watson, *The Church and Homosexuality* (London: Hodder & Stoughton, 1980); Roger Moss, *Christians and Homosexuality* (Exeter, England: Paternoster Press, 1977); Kent Philpott, *The Gay Theology* (Plainfield, NJ: Logos, 1977); John White, *Eros Defiled* (Leicester, England: Inter-Varsity, 1978); and Malcolm Macourt, ed., *Towards a Theology of Gay Liberation* (London: SCM Press, 1977).

28. Walter Barnett, "Homosexuality and the Bible," in *Pendle Hill Pamphlets* (Wallingford, PA: Pendle Hill Publications, 1979), p. 3.

29. John J. McNeill, "Homosexuality: Challenging the Church to Grow," *Chr Cent* (March 11, 1987): 246.

30. Barnett, p. 8.

31. *Ibid.*

32. This view has been defended by a whole host of writers. Barnett, pp. 7-10; D. Sherwin Bailey, *Homosexuality and the Western Christian Tradition* (Hamden, CT: Archon Books, 1975), pp.1-28; John Boswell, *Christianity, Social Tolerance, and Homosexuality* (Chicago: University of Chicago Press, 1980), pp. 91-100; James B. Nelson, "Homosexuality and the Church," *SLJT* 22 (June 1979): 199; McNeill, pp. 244-245; John McNeill, *The Church and the Homosexual* (Kansas City: Sheed, Andrews, and McNeel, 1976), pp. 42-50; Harry A. Woggon, "A Biblical and Historical Study of Homosexuality," *J Rel Health* 20 (Summer 1981): 158-159.

33. Bailey, p. 4.

34. *Ibid.*, pp. 2-5.

35. *Ibid.*, p. 6.

36. See Barnett, p. 8ff.; Boswell, p. 94; and McNeill, *The Church*, pp. 47, 48.

37. Bailey, pp. 9, 10; Barnett, p. 9; Boswell, pp. 94-95; McNeill, *The Church*, pp. 46-47.

38. Bailey, pp. 10-28; Barnett, p. 9; Boswell, p. 94; McNeill, *The Church*, pp. 46-47.

39. Bailey, p. 7 relates this to such legends as that of Philemon and Baucis; Barnett, p. 9 finds antecedents in rabbinical literature; Boswell, p. 96 associates this with the legend that Zeus is the protector of visitors; McNeill, *The Church*, pp. 48-49 relates this to the Yahwist tradition. See also S. R. Driver, *The Book of Genesis* (London: Methuen, 1906), p. 203, note 1; and T. K. Cheyne, "Sodom and Gomorrah," in *Encyclopedia Biblica* (New York: Macmillan, 1914), IV: 4670-4671.

40. P. Michael Ukleja, "Homosexuality and the Old Testament," *Bib Sac* 140 (July-September 1983): 261.

41. See Bailey, p. 2; Barnett, p. 8; Derek Kidner, *Genesis: An Introduction and Commentary*, in *Tyndale Old Testament Commentaries* (Chicago: InterVarsity Press, 1963), p. 137; or Ukleja, p. 261.

42. Paul D. Feinberg, "Homosexuality and the Bible," *FuJo* 4 (March 1985): 17-18.

43. *Ibid.*, p. 18.

44. Richard Lovelace, *Homosexuality and the Church* (Old Tappan, NJ: Revell, 1979), pp. 100-101.

45. Virginia Mollenkott and Letha Scanzoni, *Is the Homosexual My Neighbor? Another View* (San Francisco: Harper & Row, 1978), pp. 55-59.

46. Lovelace, p. 101.

47. Ukleja, p. 262.

48. *Ibid.*, pp. 262-263.

49. Bailey, pp. 29-37.

50. *Ibid.*, p. 37.

51. For an opinion that is unrelated to the question of the morality of the practice, see John Bright, *A History of Israel*, 2nd ed. (Philadelphia: Westminster, 1972), p. 118 and 3rd ed. (Philadelphia: Westminster, 1981), p. 239.

52. Boswell, pp. 100-102; Barnett, p. 12. Here we note, however, that in Leviticus 18 the prohibitions against idolatrous sexuality and homosexuality are juxtaposed in vv. 21 and 22, whereas in chapter 20 the prohibitions are substantially separated from one another (vv. 1-5 as opposed to v. 13). Therefore, while it might be reasonable to think that in chapter 18 the two practices are being joined together (i.e., homosexuality in ritual worship is what is condemned), it is much harder to draw that conclusion in chapter 20.

53. Lovelace, pp. 88-89.

54. Mollenkott and Scanzoni, pp. 60-61.

55. Boswell, pp. 100-101.

56. Barnett, pp. 12-13 is a clear example of this kind of argument.

57. Ibid., p. 13.

58. McNeill, The Church, pp. 42, 54ff.; Boswell, p. 108.

59. Boswell, p. 108.

60. Bailey, pp. 40-41.

61. See Boswell, p. 108ff. and McNeill, The Church, p. 54ff. as examples of important advocates of pro-homosexual interpretations of Scripture who follow this line.

62. P. Michael Ukleja, "Homosexuality in the NT," Bib Sac 140 (October-December 1983): 352-353.

63. See Bailey, pp. 40-41; Barnett, pp. 21-26; Boswell, p. 109ff.; McNeill, The Church, pp. 54-56.

64. Barnett, pp. 21-22.

65. Boswell, p. 109. For a critique of Boswell's views, see Richard B. Hays, "Relations Natural and Unnatural: A Response to John Boswell's Exegesis of Romans 1," J Relig Ethics 14 (Spring 1986): 184-215.

66. We find it significant that those favoring homosexuality seldom discuss Genesis 1 and 2. However, those chapters recount God's creation of man as male and female, not male and male or female and female. God then explicitly tells Adam and Eve that they are to reproduce. Does this not clearly imply that God's desired order for human sexuality is that men and women will have sexual relations with one another, not with members of the same sex? We think so. Some may object that God created man as male and female only because that was the only way to propagate the race; other than reproduction, homosexual and lesbian relationships are fine. However, this overlooks two very important facts. First, Adam named the animals, but none of them was suitable as a helpmate for him. God then created the appropriate mate for Adam, and it was not another man, but a woman (Gen 2:18-25). The suitable mate (not only sexually but emotionally, etc.) for man is woman, not man. Second, for those who think God had to create a man and woman because no other way would allow the race to multiply, this is not so. The same God who created Adam from the dust of the ground could have produced the rest of the race by special creation, and the rest of that race could have been male only. God created woman not because there was no other way to produce the race, but because woman is the proper helpmate for man.

67. Ukleja, "Homosexuality in the NT," p. 355 and Lovelace, pp. 92-93.

68. Barnett, pp. 17-21.

69. We also note that Barnett's views misunderstand the significance of the divine inspiration of Scripture. Even if Paul says the views originate with him, the fact of inspiration entails that so long as Scripture includes them and does not reject them, they express not only the human author's views, but God's as well.

70. Barnett, pp. 26-27. See also Boswell, p. 108 and Lovelace, pp. 94-95.

71. Lovelace, pp. 95-96.

72. Ibid, p. 96.

73. Ukleja, "Homosexuality in the NT," pp. 350-352.

74. Mollenkott and Scanzoni, p. 70; David L. Tiede, "Will Idolaters, Sodomizers, or the Greedy Inherit the Kingdom of God?" Word World 10 (Spring 1990): 147-169.

75. Lovelace, pp. 96-97.

76. See Barnett, pp. 14-15; Boswell, pp. 106-107; McNeill, *The Church*, pp. 50-53.
77. William F. Arndt and F. Wilbur Gingrich, *A Greek-English Lexicon of the New Testament and Other Early Christian Literature*, 4th ed. (Chicago: University of Chicago Press, 1957), s.v. *"malakos,"* pp. 489-490.
78. Dionysius, *Roman Antiquities* 8.2.4. See also Ukleja, "Homosexuality in the NT," p. 351.
79. Aristotle, *Problems* 4.26. See also Ukleja, "Homosexuality in the NT," p. 351.
80. See David F. Wright, "Homosexuals or Prostitutes?: The Meaning of *Arsenokoitai* (1 Cor. 6:9; 1 Tim. 1:10)," *VigChr* 38 (1984): 125-153; William L. Peterson, "Can *Arsenokoitai* Be Translated by 'Homosexual?' (1 Cor. 6:9; 1 Tim. 1:10)," *VigChr* 40 (1986): 187-191; David F. Wright, "Translating *Arsenokoitai* (1 Cor. 6:9, 1 Tim. 1:10)," *VigChr* 41 (1987): 396-398.
81. Boswell, pp. 341-342.
82. Ukleja, "Homosexuality in the NT," p. 352.
83. Don Williams, *The Bond That Breaks: Will Homosexuality Split the Church?* (Los Angeles: BIM, 1978), p. 83. See also D. J. Atkinson, *Homosexuals in the Christian Fellowship* (Grand Rapids, MI: Eerdmans, 1979), p. 91; Peter Zaas, "1 Corinthians 6:9ff: Was Homosexuality Condoned in the Corinthian Church?" *SBL Seminar Papers*, Vol. 2, ed. Paul J. Achtemeier (Missoula, MT: Scholars Press, 1979), pp. 206-210; Harold J. Greenlee, "The New Testament and Homosexuality," in *What You Should Know About Homosexuality*, ed. Charles W. Keysor, pp. 97-106; David Field, *The Homosexual Way—A Christian Option?* (Downers Grove, IL: InterVarsity Press, 1979), p. 16.
84. Williams, p. 84.
85. Centers for Disease Control, "Pneumocystis Pneumonia-Los Angeles," *Morb Mort W Rep* 30 (1981): 250-252.
86. Mathilde Krim, "AIDS: The Challenge to Science and Medicine," *Hast Center Rep* 15 (August 1985): 3.
87. *Ibid.*
88. Kathleen McCleary, "Sex, Morals and AIDS," *USA Weekend* (December 27-29, 1991): 5.
89. See D. A. Carson, *How Long, O Lord?: Reflections on Suffering & Evil* (Grand Rapids, MI: Baker, 1990), pp. 258-264.
90. For example, the adulterer can trust Christ and be forgiven, but that does not mean his relationship with his wife will automatically be repaired. She may still find it hard to trust him. And if through his adulterous relationship he contracted a sexually transmitted disease, his repentance of sin will not guarantee healing from the disease. Earthly consequences of sin can continue long after our relationship with God is repaired!
91. Carson, p. 263.

CHAPTER NINE: *Genetic Engineering—Reproductive Technologies*

1. Michael Fitzgerald, "Embryo Trial Goes to Judge," *USAT*, August 11, 1989.
2. "Court Sides with Man on Frozen Embryos," *Chi Trib*, June 2, 1992. The article notes that the judges called the frozen embryos "preembryos" and said they were neither persons nor property. In this way, the court removed the need to consider the embryos' rights independent of the rights of the donors of the egg and sperm, and solely focused on the individual procreative rights of the biological parents. This court decision settled whether Junior Davis would be forced to become a father, but it did not settle the question of what to do with the embryos. Should they continue to be stored, or should they be destroyed?
3. News report on NBC 10 o'clock news (WMAQ, Chicago), August 9, 1991.
4. Some practices, such as fetal and embryonic research and fetal and embryonic tissue transplants, are covered in our chapters on abortion.

5. Samuel A. Ramirez, "Advances in Genetic Engineering: Great Promises or Great Dangers?" *E/SA* 11 (November 1983): 19. See also J. Kerby Anderson, *Genetic Engineering* (Grand Rapids, MI: Zondervan, 1982), p. 27.
6. Edward D. Schneider, "Artificial Insemination," in Edward D. Schneider, ed., *Questions About the Beginning of Life* (Minneapolis: Augsburg Publishing House, 1985), p. 10. Schneider also cites data to the effect that as of 1979 approximately one million children worldwide had been born using artificial insemination by donor.
7. Anderson, pp. 27-28.
8. Linda Delloff, "The Noblest Baby of Them All," *Chr Cent* 99 (July 7-14, 1982), details the creation of a sperm bank in California that stores the sperm of Nobel prize science winners.
9. Fred Rosner, "In Vitro Fertilization and Surrogate Motherhood: The Jewish View," *J Rel Health* 22 (Summer 1983): 150. As Rosner shows, in Jewish thought masturbation is to be avoided if at all possible. The three means noted are ways of doing so.
10. John Breck, "Bio-medical Technology: Of the Kingdom or of the Cosmos?" *St Vlad Th Q* 32 (1988): 11. Breck cites from the document produced in the 1980s and translated into English and published by the Daughters of St. Paul, Boston, 1987.
11. Schneider, pp. 20-26 discusses this issue at great length, especially as it relates to AID. We shall refer further to his discussion when we come to AID.
12. Anderson, p. 29; and Schneider, p. 10.
13. Ruth Macklin, "Artificial Means of Reproduction and Our Understanding of the Family," *Hast Center Rep* 21 (1991): 6.
14. Schneider, p. 13, citing Jeffrey M. Shaman, "Legal Aspects of Artificial Insemination," *J Fam Law* 18 (1979-1980): 336-337; Laurelle H. Kinney, "Legal Issues of the New Reproductive Technologies," *Cal St Bar J* 52 (November-December 1977): 515; and John B. Gordon, "Some Legal Considerations," *Sound* 54 (Fall 1971): 312.
15. See Anderson, pp. 30-31; and Schneider, pp. 11-12.
16. Schneider, p. 11; and Anderson, p. 31.
17. Schneider, pp. 12-13.
18. *Ibid.*, p. 14.
19. *Ibid.*, p. 15; and Kenneth Frerking, "Biomedical Ethics: A Sociological Response," *Acad* 36 (1979): 74.
20. Anderson, p. 33.
21. Schneider, p. 18.
22. *Ibid.*, pp. 18-19.
23. See Lesley Northup, "On Having an Ethical Baby," *Witness* 70 (October 1987), about a female Episcopal priest who had no desire to marry but wanted a baby. She chose artificial insemination by chosen donors.
24. Anderson, pp. 33-35.
25. George J. Annas, "Artificial Insemination: Beyond the Best Interests of the Donor," *Hast Center Rep* 9 (August 1979): 15.
26. *Ibid.*
27. *Ibid.*, p. 14.
28. See Schneider, p. 26, who quotes Pope Pius XII's condemnation in 1949 of artificial insemination. Though Pius did not state matters in terms of adultery, he linked procreation to the marital bond and argued that AID allows entrance into the bond between husband and wife of someone with whom there is no bond of origin, no moral bond, nor any juridical bond of conjugal procreation. Given such considerations, some would say AID must constitute adultery.
29. Anderson, p. 40.
30. Some such as Anderson say that in particular cases as a last-resort measure AID may be allowable in principle for married couples (*ibid.*, pp. 40, 41), but he does not clarify how to determine from one case to another which are moral.

31. Northup, p. 8.
32. For an excellent discussion of the whole question of what constitutes a family, see Macklin's "Artificial Means of Reproduction and Our Understanding of the Family." Though Macklin discusses this issue largely in relation to surrogate motherhood, she relates it also to cases of artificial insemination and *in vitro* fertilization. As Macklin shows, the designation "biological mother" is not a very useful term anymore, for both the genetic mother (the one donating the egg) and the gestational mother (the one whose womb is used) contribute biologically to the child. Hence, it is better to distinguish between the genetic mother and the gestational mother. In some cases (even of surrogacy) the same woman may serve both functions, while in others different women may be involved (p. 6). Macklin then discusses who has legal and who has moral right to the child if disputes arise in surrogacy cases. She notes that some argue for gestation as the primary criterion, others for genetics, and still others for both as having the greatest precedence (pp. 8-10). Clearly, this is no easy issue, but it does show how complex legally and morally matters have become as a result of advances in reproductive technology.
33. Schneider, p. 27.
34. Obviously, we believe a woman should not use AID without informing her husband or getting his agreement. But it does not make AID adultery if mutual consent is not given.
35. Paul Ramsey, *Fabricated Man: The Ethics of Genetic Control* (New Haven, CT/London: Yale University Press, 1970), p. 32, as cited in Schneider, "Artificial Insemination," p. 22.
36. Ramsey's views as cited in Schneider, p. 23.
37. Ramsey, p. 41. For a similar position see Schneider's further explication (pp. 24-26) of the views of Helmut Thielecke, Harmon Smith, and Karl Rahner.
38. It would also seem to eliminate sex for the couple who found that one or the other partner was sterile or infertile to the point that a baby could not be conceived under conditions of normal sexual intercourse.
39. This issue impacts many of the practices discussed in these chapters on genetic engineering and many of the issues discussed in this book as a whole. We think it important and choose to address it here, though we mention it in other parts of the book as well.
40. See Keith Boone's helpful discussion on this issue in his article "Bad Axioms in Genetic Engineering," *Hast Center Rep* 18 (August/September 1988): 10.
41. To illustrate this point, suppose a clothing manufacturer makes the best suit of clothes he can, not because he cares about his customers' appearance, nor because he wants to give them their money's worth, but only because he knows that making an excellent product will increase his volume of sales. Being greedy, he wants to make as much money as possible. Following Kantian ethics, one concludes that he did not act morally but prudentially. One might even think his motivation immoral. However, that does not make us immoral if we buy one of his suits.
42. From Northup's discussion (p. 6) of what she did, this is precisely what happened. She chose the donors because of their characteristics, and as friends they agreed to help her.
43. Paul Jersild, "On Having Children: A Theological and Moral Analysis of *In Vitro* Fertilization," in Edward Schneider, ed., *Questions About the Beginning of Life*, p. 31. See also John Buuck, "Biomedical Ethics: Are We Playing God?" *Acad* 36 (1979): 41-42 for further details of the history of the development of this procedure.
44. Jersild, p. 32.
45. Charles Meyer, "A Question of Ethics: *In Vitro* Fertilization," *Witness* 68 (1985): 7.
46. S. J. Ludwig, "IVF, Cautions and Cheers," *Luth F* 21 (1987): 14.
47. Donald DeMarco, "Health Care Ethics: *In Vitro* Fertilization and Implantation," in James Bopp, Jr., ed., *Human Life and Health Care Ethics* (Frederick, MD: University Press of America, 1985), p. 139.

48. Jersild, p. 35.

49. Ludwig, p. 13.

50. DeMarco, p. 139.

51. Though advances in surgery to repair blocked oviducts continue, the number of women who cannot be helped by such surgery is likely to increase because of several current trends. Those trends are: 1) the increase in venereal disease with accompanying increase in pelvic inflammatory diseases; 2) an increase in late childbearing; 3) tubal diseases stemming from the use of intrauterine devices; and 4) tubal ligations for sterilization that cannot be reversed through surgery. For details see *ibid.*, p. 139.

52. *Ibid.*

53. Jersild, p. 34.

54. Donald DeMarco (p. 140) notes that in 1980 the Norfolk IVF clinic received requests from five thousand women seeking IVF, even though the clinic had been open only a few months, had not had any successes, and charged a minimum of $4000 for the first *in vitro* attempt. This shows the intense desire of many women to have a child and a perception that IVF may be a way to achieve their goal. Meyer, writing in 1985 (p. 8), said the success rate of IVF is generally between 10 percent and 20 percent, and the cost factor is from $5000 to $7000 per attempt.

55. LeRoy Walters, director of the Center for Bioethics at the Kennedy Institute of Ethics, Georgetown University, did the study. Though there were at least eighty-five committee statements, Walters chose the fifteen that covered multiple topics in greater depth.

56. LeRoy Walters, "Ethics and New Reproductive Technologies: An International Review of Committee Statements," *Hast Center Rep* 17 (June 1987): 3-6. For a discussion of how some countries have tried to regulate the use of IVF, see also Peter Singer, "Making Laws on Making Babies," *Hast Center Rep* 15 (August 1985) and Helen B. Holmes, "And in the Netherlands, Guidelines for IVF," *Hast Center Rep* 15 (August 1985). For further discussion of the international debate over IVF and other new reproductive technologies, see the following articles in *Hast Center Rep* 17 (June 1987): Anne Fagot-Largeault, "In France, Debate and Indecision," pp. 10-12; Amos Shapira, "In Israel, Law, Religious Orthodoxy, and Reproductive Technologies," pp. 12-14; Maurice A. M. de Wachter and Guido M. W. R. de Wert, "In the Netherlands, Tolerance and Debate," pp. 15-16; Raanan Gillon, "In Britain, the Debate After the Warnock Report," pp. 16-18; Koichi Bai, Yasuko Shirai, and Michiko Ishii, "In Japan, Consensus Has Limits," pp. 18-20; Louis Waller, "In Australia, the Debate Moves to Embryo Experimentation," pp. 21-22.

57. Daniel Overduin, "IVF-related Technology: An Ethical and Legislative Proposal," *Luth Th J* 19 (1985): 142.

58. See Jersild, pp. 34-35; DeMarco, p. 138; Anderson, pp. 53-54. For a detailed description of the step by step procedure see Walter S. Ross, "Inside America's First Test-Tube Baby Clinic," *RD* (July 1980).

59. See Anderson, p. 60; David and Renee Sanford, "'Test-Tube' Babies," *Other Side* 19 (November 1983): 23; Jersild, p. 47; and Ludwig, p. 15 for comments about the financial dimensions of this procedure.

60. David T. Ozar, "The Case Against Thawing Unused Frozen Embryos," *Hast Center Rep* 15 (August 1985): 7.

61. Sharon Curtin, "New Reproductive Technology: Who Will Be in Control?" *Witness* 68 (1985): 11, 19.

62. Anderson, p. 61.

63. Warren T. Reich, "In Vitro Fertilization and Embryo Transfer: Public Policy and Ethics," in Doris Teichler-Zellen and Colleen D. Clements, eds., *Science & Morality: New Directions in Bioethics* (Lexington, MA: Lexington Books, 1982), p. 102. See also Anderson, *Genetic Engineering*, p. 62.

64. For further discussion of the legal and moral implications of this case, see George J. Annas, "Crazy Making: Embryos and Gestational Mothers," *Hast Center Rep* 21 (January-February 1991).

65. LeRoy Walters, "Human In Vitro Fertilization: A Review of the Ethical Literature," *Hast Center Rep* 9 (August 1979): 23.

66. See, for example, the discussions of this topic in relation to IVF in Anderson, p. 72; Reich, p. 113ff.; DeMarco, pp. 145-146; and William B. and Priscilla W. Neaves, "Moral Dimensions of *In Vitro* Fertilization," *Perkins J* 39 (1986): 13-14.

67. See discussions of this issue in relation to IVF in Jersild, pp. 37-38; Reich, pp. 110-113; DeMarco, pp. 144-145; and Neaves and Neaves, pp. 14-15.

68. For discussion of some of these issues as they relate to IVF see, for example, Anderson, pp. 63-64; Sanford and Sanford, p. 23; and Walters, "Human In Vitro Fertilization," pp. 30, 32.

69. For discussions of this issue as it relates to IVF, see, for example, Jersild, pp. 37-39, 40-42; Sanford and Sanford, pp. 22-23; Colin Honey, "The Ethics of *In Vitro* Fertilization and Embryo Transfer," *Mod Ch* 26 (1984): 8; and Neaves and Neaves, pp. 12-13. Because IVF involves a greater amount of manipulating the various elements of the reproductive process, this argument is heard even more vehemently than with artificial insemination.

70. Anderson, p. 71; Jersild, p. 44; and James M. Childs, Jr., "In Vitro Fertilization: Ethical Aspects and Theological Concerns," *Acad* 36 (1979): 9.

71. Sanford and Sanford, p. 22, citing the estimate of John D. Biggers of Harvard Medical School.

72. Jersild, p. 45.

73. Childs, pp. 9-10.

74. Neaves and Neaves, p. 20. Even if a couple has sex with the intent to abort if a child is conceived, that does not strengthen the moral case for IVF, for the procedures are so different. About the only other procedure generally analogous to IVF is the use of an intrauterine device for birth control (Childs, p. 10). Of course, those who reject abortion typically think use of an IUD and engaging in sex with intent to abort a conceived embryo are immoral, too.

75. Leon Kass, "Making Babies—The New Biology and the 'Old' Morality," *Pub Int* 26 (Winter 1972): 32-33. A slight variation of the view that the embryo possesses personhood says that while the blastocyst is not fully a human being or a person, it is not humanly nothing either. It ought to be treated with respect, and that means at least to avoid doing it harm. This means also that no noxious or harmful drugs be administered to it and that no one should produce a human blastocyst with intent to abandon or extinguish it (Reich, pp. 116-117).

76. See Clifford Grobstein, "The Moral Uses of 'Spare' Embryos," *Hast Center Rep* 12 (July 1982): 6 for such views.

77. R. G. Edwards, "Fertilization of Human Eggs In Vitro: Morals, Ethics and the law," *Q Rev Biol* 49 (March 1974): 13-14, as cited in DeMarco, p. 143 and Walters, "Human In Vitro Fertilization," p. 24. For others holding the view that the fertilized egg is less than human and has no claim to rights of protection, see John Harris, "*In Vitro* Fertilization: The Ethical Issues," *Phil Quart* 33 (July 1983): 222ff.

78. Here the discussion has been adapted and amplified from the ideas of Kass, "'Making Babies'—Revisited," in Thomas A. Shannon, ed., *Bioethics* (Ramsey, NJ: Paulist Press, 1981), p. 452ff., and Grobstein, pp. 5-6.

79. For further discussion of the fate of the embryo and the morality thereof, see Kass, "'Making Babies'—Revisited," pp. 452-454. Though what he says most directly addresses the first three options in our schema, how and what he says is also applicable to the question of the fate of frozen embryos.

80. Grobstein, pp. 5-6.

81. Paul Ramsey, "Manufacturing Our Offspring: Weighing the Risks," *Hast Center Rep* 8 (October 1978): 8. Ramsey also argued that in addition to the potential risks of the

procedure, damage may also be done to IVF children through all the publicity they and their family receive. This fear may have been realized with some of the earlier IVF babies, but now that is not a substantial problem since IVF is common enough not to draw special attention to a specific baby born by the procedure.

82. Neaves and Neaves, p. 15 note that "among the 590 babies conceived by IVF and born between 1978 and January 1984, only one was afflicted with chromosomal abnormalities"; but considering the age of the mothers involved, this is really a low incidence of abnormality and is no higher than the rate for natural conception. Sanford and Sanford, p. 22 say that "from July 1978 to July 1983, approximately one hundred and fifty children, including a set of twins and triplets, were conceived through IVF. The only birth defect found among these children was one heart condition that was corrected. So the rate of defects for IVF to date is actually less than the 2 to 3 percent found among children born of normal pregnancies."

83. See Ludwig, p. 14.

84. Reich, p. 121; Neaves and Neaves, p. 15.

85. John A. Robertson, "In Vitro Conception and Harm to the Unborn," *Hast Center Rep* 8 (October 1978): 14.

86. *Ibid.*

87. There were those in particular who argued that not enough research using IVF on laboratory animals had been conducted to warrant its use on humans. See Walters's summary of this issue in his "Human In Vitro Fertilization," pp. 26-27. See also Sanford and Sanford, p. 22.

88. Childs, p. 9, citing Verhey's article in *Ref J* 28 (September 1978). See also Kass, "'Making Babies'—Revisited," pp. 454-455.

89. DeMarco, p. 141.

90. *Ibid.*

91. *Ibid.*

92. *Ibid.*, pp. 141-142. See pages 140-142 for DeMarco's whole discussion. For discussions making the same basic points, see also Honey, pp. 5-6; and Kass, "'Making Babies'—Revisited," pp. 464-465.

93. Leon R. Kass, "The New Biology: What Price Relieving Man's Estate?" in Thomas A. Shannon, ed., *Bioethics*, p. 394. See also Ramsey's discussion of the disturbing direction in which reproductive technology is going in Ramsey, pp. 8-9, as cited and discussed in Childs, pp. 11-12. Likewise, Kass offered his fears about what likely will happen with IVF technology, and some of his fears have already been realized. See Leon Kass, "'Making Babies'—Revisited," pp. 458-460. See also Walters, "Human In Vitro Fertilization," p. 25. See also Childs's discussion of this issue on pp. 16-17ff.

94. Leon Kass, "Making Babies—The New Biology and the 'Old' Morality," p. 49 as cited in Walters, "Human In Vitro Fertilization," p. 25.

95. Joseph Fletcher, "Ethical Aspects of Genetic Controls," *NEJM* 285 (1971): 781, as cited in Childs, "In Vitro Fertilization: Ethical Aspects and Theological Concerns," p. 13.

96. Kass, "'Making Babies'—Revisited," pp. 458-459.

97. Neaves and Neaves, pp. 17-19 discuss these and other possible eventualities from IVF technology. See also Meyer, p. 9; and Harris, pp. 232-233.

98. Honey, p. 10.

99. For further discussion of the slippery slope argument and variations thereof, see Stephen Toulmin, "In Vitro Fertilization: Answering the Ethical Objections," *Hast Center Rep* 8 (October 1978): 10-11; Harris, pp. 232-236; and Anderson, pp. 63-65.

100. Reich, pp. 121-122.

101. *Ibid.*, pp. 387-388. Reich speaks about distributive justice in terms of all advances in genetic engineering, not just IVF, but his points are surely applicable to IVF.

102. Anderson, who is very cautious about IVF, says (p. 68) that from 20 to 50 percent are successful, while Sanford and Sanford, who are more positive to IVF, estimate only a 5 to 25 percent success rate.

103. These six options were constructed from those discussed by Anderson, pp. 68-69 and Sanford and Sanford, p. 23.

104. See Sanford and Sanford, p. 23 for many of these objections. Another objection emphasizes potential health hazards to the woman with IVF. For example, the drug therapy used to stimulate growth of eggs needs careful regulation. Moreover, care must be taken with laparoscopy not to damage the woman's uterus. Techniques to monitor and assess the pregnancy can put both mother and child at some risk (Ludwig, p. 14). Though the procedure is now fairly routine, some may think these risks still remain. If they do, they raise questions about the ethics of IVF.

105. Walters, "Human In Vitro Fertilization," p. 33.

106. *Ibid.*, citing Rahner's position. See also Mitchell's discussion of the British Warnock Report. As he reports, the majority position took this view. The minority view held that before the embryo reaches the status of personhood, it has a special status because of its potential for development into full humanity. Hence, the minority view said it is wrong to create something with the potential for becoming human and then deliberately destroy it. The majority position accepted these principles but claimed that the principles could be overridden in the interests of research, so long as the embryo was at a sufficiently early stage of development. See Basil Mitchell, "Review-Article: Warnock," *Mod Ch* 27 (1985): 47-48.

107. Walters, "Human In Vitro Fertilization," p. 34.

108. *Ibid.*, pp. 35, 37-38. Other issues involved in IVF laboratory research include how much laboratory IVF is really needed, whether it constitutes appropriate allocation of resources, and how to balance the need for freedom of inquiry with other moral considerations involved in such research (see *ibid.*, pp. 34-35).

109. Here Norman Ford's discussion of when human life begins is helpful, but does not refute our point. Ford argues on biological grounds that it is best to believe that human life begins not when sperm penetrates an egg but at syngamy, the point in fertilization when the male and female pronuclei begin to break down and allow the male and female chromosomes to mingle. This mingling gives rise to a single cell with forty-six chromosomes that is ready to replicate itself. Syngamy occurs about twenty-two hours after insemination. Even if one agrees with Ford's analysis that human life does not begin until twenty-two hours after insemination, this would still not refute our point about loss of life with IVF. The point is that eggs fertilized with IVF are neither inserted in a womb, frozen or even discarded until they become four, eight or sixteen-cell embryos. But since syngamy occurs about a day after fertilization, and since at syngamy there is only one cell, it is obvious that by the time the embryo is ready to be inserted, the process has gone well past syngamy. Hence, if one accepts Ford's reasoning, the only way with IVF to avoid the immoral loss of embryonic life is to discard them before the first twenty-four hours after insemination. Since that simply is not the procedure in IVF, we maintain that our objection to IVF on the grounds that it wastes human life is not refuted by matters Ford raises. See Norman Ford, "When Does Human Life Begin? Science, Government, Church," *Pacif* 1 (1988).

110. From conversations with couples investigating the possibility of IVF and from some published reports, we have learned that some IVF clinics are willing to operate on this basis.

111. As to the other moral issues raised, we find the arguments less convincing. As to the technology question, we note that it need not dehumanize man, and much of it has not. We agree, however, that vigilance is needed. As to the wedge/slippery slope argument, there is no guarantee that one will go all the way down the slope, but we do agree that some stages on the slope are immoral and must be avoided. Some will reply that once the wedge is allowed, there is no rational way to rule out other procedures. We disagree, for we think it is possible to state the moral principles that apply to one technique and rule it out but do not apply to others. Compare our discussions on artificial insemination and IVF. Having argued that one procedure

could be moral in some instances, we were not logically bound to accept the other. The right to a child issue intrigues us. We agree that no one has a right to a child in the sense of owning it as property. We also concur that IVF treats a desire, not a need. However, we are not convinced that all of this *per se* makes IVF immoral. Even if the couple has no right to a child, that in itself does not prohibit having one any more than it prohibits adopting one. Nor does it prohibit using IVF or other means to have one. Objections to IVF must rest on other grounds. Finally, we find the argument about just allocation of resources unconvincing. Governments should carefully consider the fairest use of funds, but we don't see this as ruling out all funding for IVF. Moreover, claiming private foundations should not use money for this purpose or arguing that the rich should not have sole access to IVF seems misguided. It seems to suggest that those with money may never use it to fulfill anything but their own or others' needs, not wants. But since the money belongs to them (not to everybody), so long as their needs are provided, we fail to see why using their money to meet a desire is immoral. As argued, we think IVF to satisfy this desire is wrong, but not because using one's own money to fill a desire is wrong.

112. Ozar, p. 8. Though initial intuitions might disagree with Ozar, on further reflection we think he is right. His point is a rather simple one, viz., having committed one error, that does not automatically make one immoral for what one does as a result of that first sin, nor does it mean that what one does next is morally neutral.

113. Currently, to our knowledge the only other possible fate for spare embryos is to require that each be implanted in an artificial placenta, brought to birth, if possible, and then given up for adoption. However, the technology of artificial wombs is not well established, so the embryo will have a better chance for survival if it is frozen and implanted later than if it is used in experiments with artificial wombs. For further argumentation favoring the freezing of multiple embryos, see Ozar, pp. 11-12, though the arguments there do not stem so much from belief that the embryo is human nor from deontological considerations. Many of the arguments offered are utilitarian in nature.

114. Here we must add one further note in light of our discussion in our chapter on abortion and special cases. In that chapter it was argued that the one who uses fetal tissue from aborted babies for research or transplantation is guilty of complicity. The fetus never should have been aborted, and on top of that, fetal tissue is used for some sort of personal benefit. Some may think the same is true in the case of freezing spare embryos. We disagree, because the two cases are different. As Burtchaell argues, in the case of using fetal tissue, there is complicity because there seems to be approval of the act that produced the tissue (abortion), and there is certainly benefit from it (the use of fetal tissue). In fact, that benefit seems to underscore the apparent approval of the one benefiting. On the other hand, in the case of freezing embryos there is no approval of the act that produced them, and there is no particular benefit in view when they are frozen. The motivation for freezing them is to protect life. But there is another even more fundamental difference between the two cases. In the case of freezing embryos, an initial immoral act (IVF) *produced* a person. In the case of fetal tissue use, an initial act (abortion) *killed* a person. In the latter case, since the person is dead, there are no further obligations to protect that person. Hence, use of the aborted fetus' tissue is not for the benefit of the fetus but of the tissue user. Benefit from his/her death in this case surely seems complicitous. In the former case, once a person is produced, there are moral obligations to that person that must be met. Hence, one has no choice but to do whatever is possible to protect that person, and in this case, that means freezing the spare embryos. If one receives some benefit from helping the embryo, that is secondary so long as the aid is given to protect life rather than benefit oneself. Hence, we believe the two cases are not identical. Once life exists, there is a duty to protect it. That obligation takes precedence. To attempt to meet that obligation by freezing spare embryos no more shows approval of and complicity in

creating the embryos than adopting a child from an unwed mother suggests that one approves the act of premarital sex that produced the child.

115. In this respect, it is very interesting to see how some would resolve cases where there are disputes over frozen embryos (as in the Davis case). The only rights taken into consideration are the procreative and parental rights of the genetic parents. No rights are attributed to the embryo, and its welfare is the least of considerations. For such analysis see John A. Robertson, "Resolving Disputes over Frozen Embryos," *Hast Center Rep* 19 (November/December 1989). In contrast to this view, Ozar builds a case that even if one believes the embryo has no moral rights, one could still argue for not thawing the embryos and using them for just anything. Instead, one could argue for seeking out recipients and thawing and implanting the eggs as soon as possible. His arguments heavily rest on utilitarian concerns, but do show that a case can be built against prematurely thawing the frozen embryos. See Ozar, pp. 9-11.

116. Ozar, p. 9.

117. *Ibid.*

118. *Ibid.*, pp. 9, 10.

119. What we suggest here is an exception to the general rule that IVF is wrong. We do not sanction the use of IVF, but if it is used, our point is that there are consequences (lives are conceived), and those lives must be protected. Since the best way at this time to do that seems to be further use of IVF techniques and technology, that should be done. However, these exceptional cases do not nullify the general prohibition against IVF and its related technology. Likewise, we do not generally favor surrogate motherhood, but this may be an exceptional case where one could endorse its use (more on that matter below).

120. For more specifics of the details in this case, see Philip Lentz, "Surrogate Baby Contract Upheld," *Chi Trib*, April 1, 1987; and Henry M. Butzel, "The Essential Facts of the Baby M Case," in Herbert Richardson, ed., *On the Problem of Surrogate Parenthood: Analyzing the Baby M Case* (Lewiston, NY: The Edwin Mellen Press, 1987).

121. Arnold Voth, "Christian Principles in Medical/Ethical Dilemmas," *Conrad Grebel R* 6 (1988): 35-36 offers this general definition, but then notes that the surrogate arrangement may take many forms.

122. Patricia H. Werhane, "Against the Legitimacy of Surrogate Contracts," in Richardson, ed., *On the Problem of Surrogate Parenthood: Analyzing the Baby M Case*, pp. 21-22. See also Judith L. Bellow Khazoum, "The Ethics of Surrogate Motherhood," *Dialog* 28 (Summer 1989) on this matter of definition.

123. See Voth, p. 36 for a discussion of some of these options with artificial insemination. See also Janet D. McDowell, "Surrogate Motherhood," in Edward Schneider, ed. *Questions About the Beginning of Life*, pp. 50-56.

124. Voth, p. 36.

125. For further variations on the surrogacy theme see McDowell, pp. 50-56.

126. For an interesting historical survey of the practice of surrogacy, see Ignacio L. Gotz, "Surrogate Motherhood," *Th Today* 45 (July 1989). Interestingly, Gotz notes that Mary's giving birth to Jesus is also an example of surrogacy. Moreover, he writes (pp. 18-19):

> In the entire body of literature on the incarnation and the virgin birth, there isn't a single voice that even raises the question of the appropriateness of Mary's decision to be a surrogate. Endless discussions center around her virginity, the reality of Jesus' body, the kind of marriage Mary and Joseph had, and whether or not it was properly a marriage, since sexual intercourse was supposedly excluded before if not after the birth of Jesus. There are questions about the relationship of motherhood to virginity, of virginity to marriage, of marriage to sin. There are profound inquisitions into the nature of the symbolism of the virgin birth. But never is there even the slightest hint of disapproval of Mary's

decision to be a surrogate. The contemporary disapproval of surrogacy is the more surprising given this implicit acceptance of Mary's surrogacy as the right thing to do.

127. Walters, "Ethics and New Reproductive Technologies," p. 8.
128. Butzel, p. 13.
129. Walters, "Human In Vitro Fertilization," p. 32. See also Khazoum, pp. 196-197.
130. Laurence E. Karp and Roger P. Donahue, "Preimplantational Ectogenesis: Science and the Speculation Concerning *In Vitro* Fertilization and Related Procedures," *WJ Med* 124 (April 1976): 295, as cited in Walters, "Human In Vitro Fertilization," p. 32. Likewise, Joseph Fletcher argues in favor of surrogate arrangements as follows: "If a wet nurse can supply another woman's child with her milk, and if we can give our blood to others, then how could there be any moral barriers to donating even some basic gifts, such as . . . placental sustenance, in hostess gestation?"*The Ethics of Genetic Control: Ending Reproductive Roulette* (Garden City, NY: Anchor Press/Doubleday, 1974), p. 163, as cited in Walters, "Human In Vitro Fertilization," p. 32.
131. De Wachter and de Wert, p. 16; Walters, "Ethics and New Reproductive Technologies," p. 8; Dennis Fields, "The Immorality of Surrogate Mothering," *FuJo* 2 (1983): 22.
132. Voth, pp. 36-37; McDowell, pp. 65-66.
133. Werhane, p. 26. See also Khazoum, pp. 193-194; and George J. Annas, "The Baby Broker Boom," *Hast Center Rep* 16 (June 1986). For a contrary view that selling babies is acceptable see H. E. Baber, "For the Legitimacy of Surrogate Contracts," in Richardson, ed., *On the Problem of Surrogate Parenthood: Analyzing the Baby M Case*, pp. 34-35. Baber says many reject baby selling because it is meant to further some ends, and thus the baby is not seen as an end in itself. However, Baber notes that babies are typically conceived to accomplish some end the parents have in view. They are conceived to demonstrate a man's masculinity, to give parents someone to comfort and care for them in old age, etc. If such ends are not immoral, then conceiving a baby and buying it through a surrogacy arrangement is not immoral on the grounds that it is meant to accomplish some further ends of the parents.
134. McDowell, p. 66. See also Janice G. Raymond, "Reproductive Gifts and Gift Giving: The Altruistic Woman," *Hast Center Rep* 20 (December 1990) for a further objection to surrogacy arrangements done free. Raymond argues that even in such cases surrogacy is wrong, because the altruism of the woman only serves to uphold a picture of women which exploits them, i.e., that they are present on the earth to meet the needs of others, and in this case to serve as donors of their time, energy, and body. This view of women continues to uphold the notion of their inequality with men and hence is sexist and immoral.
135. McDowell, pp. 66-67.
136. *Ibid.*, pp. 68-69.
137. Werhane, p. 26. See also Annas, "Crazy Making: Embryos and Gestational Mothers" for a discussion of legal decisions in a recent surrogacy case involving Crispina and Mark Calvert, on the one hand, and Anna Johnson, on the other. We note also that the Uniform Parentage Act maintains that a husband who consents to AID of his wife is the legal father of the child, even though there is no genetic tie. Moreover, a surrogate such as Mrs. Whitehead who is both genetic and gestational mother loses her rights to the baby in virtue of the contract she made with a man (genetic father or not) to bear him a child. Hence, legal precedents in regard to both AID and surrogacy have favored contracted agreements more than the rights of genetic fathers and mothers. As noted, some think this is morally wrong. Others note that it raises the moral question of whether genetics, gestation or combinations of both should give *moral* precedence in determining who has a right to a given child. See Macklin's discussion of the various criteria (gestation, genetics, etc.) for determining this issue

("Artificial Means of Reproduction and Our Understanding of the Family," pp. 8-11). For an example of someone who argues that gestation should give precedence to the child, see George J. Annas, "Baby M: Babies (and Justice) for Sale," *Hast Center Rep* 17 (June 1987); and George J. Annas, "The Baby Broker Boom."
138. Werhane, pp. 26-27.
139. Anderson, p. 102. See also Martin LaBar, "The Pros and Cons of Human Cloning," *Thought* 59 (1984): 320-321.
140. John A. Hammes, "Psychological, Philosophical, and Moral Aspects of Biogenetic Engineering," *Com* 5 (Summer 1978): 162-163; LaBar, p. 320; and Buuck, pp. 45-49.
141. Anderson, pp. 105-106; Hammes, p. 163; LaBar, p. 322; and Kenneth Frerking, "Biomedical Ethics: A Sociological Response," *Acad* 36 (1979): 43.
142. Some also worry that clones would lose individuality, but this overlooks several important facts. Not only the nucleus but also the cytoplasm of an egg cell likely affects development, so a cloned person may resemble his/her forebear less than identical twins resemble one another. Moreover, the concern emphasizes only heredity and ignores environment's role in personality development. In addition, a clone is usually a generation younger than the person from whom the nucleus was taken. The older person might even be dead. Whether dead or alive, it is dubious that the clone would lose individuality (see LaBar, pp. 324-325).
143. Anderson, p. 107. Anderson also notes that Gurdon found that cloned frogs had a higher incidence of sterility than did those raised in the laboratory, and those raised in the lab had a higher incidence of sterility than those raised in the wild. Anderson speculates that similar problems might accrue to cloned humans.
144. See LaBar, p. 328 for a discussion of some of these legal matters.
145. Anderson, pp. 108-109.
146. Frerking, p. 43 makes this point nicely.
147. LaBar, p. 333. LaBar's overall assessment is:

> If it is possible, cloning might give some persons control over the genotype of their offspring, and they might consider it beneficent on those grounds. On the other hand, there are potential risks to the unborn, to children derived from such a procedure, and to society in general. The only clear benefit to be gained from cloning *per se* is allowing a couple to select the genotype of their offspring. This benefit is slight, and would be gained at the risk of injustice and maleficence to the clones, and of not treating them, or perhaps the source of the nucleus from which they are derived, with the respect due to them as persons. We do not need this procedure. There is no need to put any nucleus in a human egg, except that of a sperm.

CHAPTER TEN: *Genetic Engineering and Genes*

1. Reported in "Studies Link Genetic Defects to Alzheimer's," *Chi Trib*, October 4, 1991.
2. *Ibid.*
3. Gerald Roller, "'What's in Your Genes?' Medical Genetic Engineering," *Breth Life* 31 (Autumn 1986): 237.
4. Monsanto Company, "Genetic Engineering Is Beneficial," in William Dudley, ed., *Genetic Engineering: Opposing Viewpoints* (San Diego: Greenhaven Press, 1990), p. 19.
5. Dale L. Oxender, "The Biotechnology Revolution," *Breth Life* 31 (Autumn 1986): 224. See also Roller, "'What's in Your Genes?' Medical Genetic Engineering," pp. 237-238 for a detailed description of the contents of DNA molecules; and Leon

Jaroff, "Mapping the Genetic Makeup of Humans Would Improve Health," in Dudley, ed., *Genetic Engineering: Opposing Viewpoints*, pp. 96-98.

6. Oxender, p. 224.
7. See Monsanto Company, p. 20ff. for a description of these processes and DNA's role in them.
8. *Ibid.*, p. 22. The procedures for gene-splicing and transfer will be described in more detail when we discuss recombinant DNA.
9. Here the terminology differs from one writer to another. W. French Anderson, "Human Gene Therapy: Scientific and Ethical Considerations," *J Med Phil* 10 (1985) calls the attempt "to alter or 'improve' complex human traits, each of which is coded by a large number of genes" (p. 277) *eugenic* genetic engineering, whereas he refers to attempts to repair a genetic defect either in the body cells or in reproductive tissues of the patient as *therapy* (p. 275). Donald DeMarco, "Health Care Ethics: Genetic Engineering," in James Bopp, Jr., ed., *Human Life and Health Care Ethics* (Frederick, MD: University Publications of America, 1985) uses *genetic engineering* in a strict sense to refer to "various direct attempts to change genes in order to correct or eliminate gene disorders or add new traits with a view to engineering a more desirable or more desired human being" (p. 128). He distinguishes (pp. 128-129) this from *eugenic engineering* (the manipulation of a genotype by directed control of conception) and *euphenic engineering* ("the effort to compensate for a genetic defect by controlling the phenotype rather than the genotype, such as a diabetic taking insulin as a compensatory measure"). Finally, Samuel A. Ramirez, "Advances in Genetic Engineering: Great Promises or Great Dangers?" *E/SA* 11 (November 1983) distinguishes what he calls *therapeutic eugenics* and *preventive eugenics*. Therapeutic eugenics (which he also labels *euphenics*) aims at correcting already existing genetic defects. Preventive eugenics refers to preventing the birth of individuals affected by genetic diseases (p. 17). Ramirez further distinguishes (p. 18) between *positive eugenics* (improving the human race and gene pool by selective breeding, encouraging those with desirable characteristics to mate) and *negative eugenics* (improving the genetic stock by preventing transmission of defective genes). In our discussion, we simply distinguish between therapeutic uses (where someone has a genetic defect and there is some attempt to correct it) and eugenic uses (where no defect or disease is involved, but genetic structure is manipulated for some other purpose than therapy) of this technology. We also use "non-therapeutic" to refer either to eugenic uses of technology in humans or the use of this technology in agriculture, industry, and the like.
10. Oxender, p. 227. For more information on the history of regulating recombinant DNA research, see Leland Wilson, "Toward Regulating Genetic Engineering," *Breth Life* 31 (Autumn 1986); Key Dismukes, "Recombinant DNA: A Proposal for Regulation," in Thomas A. Shannon, ed. *Bioethics* (Ramsey, NJ: Paulist Press, 1981); and Tabitha M. Powledge, "You Shall Be As Gods," *Worldview* 20 (1977).
11. Jaroff, p. 97.
12. *Ibid.*, p. 95, quoting biochemist Robert Sinsheimer of the University of California at Santa Barbara.
13. *Ibid.*, p. 97.
14. Ad Hoc Committee on Genetic Counseling, "Genetic Counseling," *Am J Hum Genet* 27 (1975): 240-242. This information was reported in John C. Fletcher, "Ethical Issues in Genetic Screening, Prenatal Diagnosis, and Counseling," in William B. Weil, Jr. and Martin Benjamin, eds., *Contemporary Issues in Fetal and Neonatal Medicine: Ethical Issues at the Outset of Life* (Boston: Blackwell Scientific Publications, 1987), p. 87.
15. Fletcher, p. 87. For a discussion of the history of genetic counseling and other related genetic topics, see Arthur Caplan, "Genetic Counseling, Medical Genetics and Theoretical Genetics: An Historical Overview," *Birth Defects: Original Article Series* 15 (1979): 21-31.

16. E. Virginia Lapham, "Living With Disabilities," *Chr Soc Action* (January 1991): 5. James M. Childs, Jr. cites a 1981 article in *Newsweek* that estimated that genetic disorders account for 30 percent of children and 10 percent of adults in our hospitals. In light of increasing knowledge about genetic diseases, it is likely the *Newsweek* estimates will prove to be conservative. See James Childs, "Genetic Screening and Counseling," in Edward D. Schneider, ed., *Questions About the Beginning of Life* (Minneapolis: Augsburg Publishing House, 1985), pp. 99-100. Childs cites an article in the May 18, 1981 edition (p. 120) of *Newsweek*.

17. Childs, pp. 100-101.

18. *Ibid.*, pp. 101-102.

19. *Ibid.*, p. 102.

20. *Ibid.*, p. 103.

21. James Childress and Kenneth Casebeer, "Public Policy Issues in Genetic Counseling," *Birth Defects: Original Article Series* 15 (1979): 282-283. This whole article is very helpful on the broader issue of governmental policies in regard to genetic counseling. That broader issue moves the discussion into matters of social and political philosophy, which goes beyond our purpose in this book.

22. Fletcher, pp. 88-89. See also Childs, pp. 111-112.

23. John C. Fletcher, "Moral Problems and Ethical Issues in Applied Human Genetics," in Doris Teichler-Zallen and Colleen D. Clements, eds., *Science and Morality: New Directions in Bioethics* (Lexington, MA: Lexington Books, 1982), p. 64.

24. *Ibid.* Childs, pp. 112-115 also handles this problem but slightly differently. He asks if the potential counselee should avail himself/herself of the information at all. It is easy simply to leave matters in God's hands, but though we should do that, God still wants us to take responsibility for caring for our own lives. Hence, Childs argues that "we have an obligation to seek the knowledge we need if we have reason to suspect problems with our genetic heritage. Such knowledge can enable us to prevent pregnancies that could lead to the birth of a child who will suffer or maybe even die a painful death" (pp. 112-113). In essence, Childs says the welfare of future generations should outweigh any problems that knowing this genetic information might create for the counselee.

25. *Ibid.*, pp. 64, 66.

26. Childs, p. 110. Childs notes that in such situations there is the rule that one should not break a promise or betray a trust, but on the other hand, there is also the rule that one should do no harm and should guard the neighbor's well-being. In this situation, those two sets of rules conflict. Childs opts in favor of breaking confidentiality so as to guard the well-being of others, but notes that however one chooses, it is not an easy decision.

27. John Fletcher, "Ethical Issues in Genetic Screening," p. 64. See also Robert H. Blank, "Public Policy Implications of Human Genetic Technology: Genetic Screening," *J Med Phil* 7 (1982): 356.

28. Blank, p. 357; Fletcher, "Moral Problems and Ethical Issues in Applied Human Genetics," p. 63; and Fletcher, "Ethical Issues in Genetic Screening," p. 64.

29. Fletcher, "Ethical Issues in Genetic Screening," p. 65. As Fletcher notes, many newborns are also tested for hypothyroidism, which can be treated by thyroid hormone replacement.

30. There are also important ethical considerations associated with prenatal diagnosis, but we handle that topic in the abortion chapters.

31. *Ibid.*, pp. 66-67, 69-70. See also Marc Lappe, "The Predictive Power of the New Genetics," *Hast Center Rep* 14 (October 1984): 20-21; Fletcher, "Moral Problems and Ethical Issues in Applied Human Genetics," p. 64; and Childs, p. 104. In addition, Paul Billings lists examples of discrimination on the basis of screening that he has heard about. See his "Screened Out," *Chr Soc Action* (January 1991): 33.

32. *Ibid.*, p. 67.

33. *Ibid.* See also Childs, pp. 104-106; Fletcher, "Moral Problems and Ethical Issues in Applied Human Genetics," p. 63; and Blank, pp. 364-365, who notes that economically and logistically, screening for high-risk groups is most practical, while screening the entire population would not be; but it is just those groups who tend to be stigmatized as inferior and discriminated against anyway, and disclosure of a further disease associated with the ethnic group will only serve to stigmatize them and raise the likelihood of discrimination.

34. See accounts in Fletcher, "Ethical Issues in Genetic Screening," pp. 67-68 and Childs, pp. 104-106, for example.

35. Childs, pp. 107-108. See also Fletcher, "Ethical Issues in Genetic Screening," p. 66 for similar points.

36. Blank, pp. 366-367.

37. See Blank's cost/benefit analysis (pp. 361-366) as an example of such thinking.

38. Here we note as well Troy Duster's caveat. Duster notes that with some genetic diseases such as sickle-cell anemia, some people can live reasonably well into their fifties and sixties. As a result, a prenatal diagnosis that someone has this disease is not always a good indicator of what should be done. Duster says, "Since there is no cure for most genetic disorders, and since *the manifestation of their variability cannot be known at the point of human decision-making about whether to prevent conception or birth*, we are in a situation of knowing too much of one important part of the equation but not knowing enough about the other part. Yet, with prenatal information at hand, a decision will be made" (italics ours). See Troy Duster, "Assessing the Quality of Life," *Chr Soc Action* (January 1991): 9.

39. Our concern here is artificial methods of sex selection, not so-called natural methods. There are "old wives' tales" and folklore about ways to enhance through natural means the likelihood of having a boy or a girl. For a brief discussion of such methods, see Kerby Anderson, *Genetic Engineering* (Grand Rapids, MI: Zondervan, 1982), p. 45.

40. For example, reportedly in India there is significant preference for males over females. In parts of northern India the preference is so strong that the ratio of men to women reached a low of 935 women to 1000 men in 1981. This imbalance occurred by means of preferential medical treatment and nutrition to male children, coupled with an occasional infanticide. See Dorothy C. Wertz and John C. Fletcher, "Sex Selection in India," *Hast Center Rep* 19 (May/June 1989): 25.

41. Dorothy C. Wertz and John C. Fletcher, "Fatal Knowledge? Prenatal Diagnosis and Sex Selection," *Hast Center Rep* 19 (May/June 1989): 21.

42. LeRoy Walters, "Human *In Vitro* Fertilization: A Review of the Ethical Literature," *Hast Center Rep* 9 (August 1979): 38.

43. Anderson, pp. 45-46.

44. *Ibid.*, p. 46. John Buuck, "Biomedical Ethics: Are We Playing God?" *Acad* 36 (1979): 41 reports that German scientists have already discovered antibodies that will attach to Y sperm, inhibiting it from fertilizing the egg. This ensures that X sperm will fertilize the egg so the child will be female.

45. Anderson, p. 47.

46. *Ibid.*, p. 46.

47. *Ibid.*, p. 47.

48. *Ibid.*, pp. 47-49.

49. *Ibid.*, pp. 48-49.

50. Wertz and Fletcher, "Fatal Knowledge?" p. 22.

51. *Ibid.*

52. *Ibid.*, p. 23.

53. *Ibid.*, p. 22. For a thorough examination of this and other issues surrounding sex selection from a feminist perspective, see Mary Anne Warren, *Gendercide: The Implications of Sex Selection* (Totowa, NJ: Rowman & Allanheld, 1985); Christine Overall, *Ethics and Human Reproduction: A Feminist Analysis* (Boston: Allen &

Unwin, 1987), pp. 17-39; and Helen B. Holmes, "Review of *Gendercide*," *Bioethics* 1 (1987): 100-110.

54. Wertz and Fletcher, "Fatal Knowledge?" p. 23. See also Anderson, p. 50.
55. Wertz and Fletcher, "Fatal Knowledge?" p. 22.
56. *Ibid.*
57. *Ibid.*, pp. 22-23.
58. Anderson, p. 50.
59. Wertz and Fletcher, "Fatal Knowledge?" p. 24; and Anderson, pp. 50-51.
60. Here we must add, too, that if the underlying reason for wanting a child of one sex or the other is really preference for one sex over the other, that decision does smack of sexism and is wrong.
61. We grant that even if a couple has children who will be diseased, God can perform a miracle to prevent the gene from passing to the child or can simply heal the child. However, God has not guaranteed that he will do either of these things. That he can does not obligate him to do so, nor does it release us from the responsibility to use common sense in such cases.
62. Scripture says there is death because of sin. But if people die, they must die of something. Hence, there are diseases. If there were no death, there would be no disease, at least no life-threatening ones.
63. Henry W. Strobel, "Recombinant DNA Technology and the Relationship of Humanity to God: A Plea for Thought About the Effects of Developments in Modern Molecular Biology on Theological Considerations," *St Luke J* 30 (1987): 266.
64. Oxender, p. 225.
65. Monsanto Company, p. 22.
66. See Oxender, pp. 224-225, Monsanto Company, p. 22, and James H. Burtness, "Genetic Manipulation," in Schneider, *Questions About the Beginning of Life*, pp. 80-81 for explanation and diagrams that illustrate how this works.
67. Burtness, p. 80.
68. Monsanto Company, p. 22.
69. Oxender, pp. 225-226; and Monsanto Company, p. 22.
70. Oxender, p. 229; Monsanto Company, pp. 22-23; and Dennis Chamberland, "Genetic Engineering: Promise & Threat," *ChrT* (February 7, 1986): 25.
71. For an excellent, detailed analysis of the "state of the art" in genetic technology as it relates to genetic manipulation, see Darryl Macer, "Genetic Engineering in 1990," *Sci Chr Belief* 2 (1990): 25-40.
72. Anderson, p. 83 notes that it is a basic hormone that regulates a variety of body functions, and thus, it can be used in treating problems such as obesity, severe burns, bleeding ulcers and broken bones.
73. For further discussion of these medically significant substances that have been synthesized through recombinant DNA, see Anderson, pp. 82-84; Chamberland, pp. 24-25; and Harvey F. Good, "Life with Genetic Engineering," *Breth Life* 31 (Autumn 1986): 249-250.
74. For further discussion of agricultural uses of rDNA, see Anderson, pp. 84-85; and Monsanto Company, p. 23. Though many are positive about the use of rDNA in agriculture, others note some dangers. See, for example, Jack Doyle, "The End of Nature?" *Chr Soc Action* (January 1991): 29-30.
75. "New Life Forms: A Clear Road Ahead?" *USNWR* 30 (June 30, 1980): 34, as reported in Anderson, p. 85.
76. Oxender, p. 234.
77. For further discussion of industrial uses of rDNA technology, see Anderson, p. 85, and Oxender, p. 234.
78. For further discussion of this use of rDNA technology. see Anderson, pp. 85-86; and Monsanto Company, p. 24. For an interesting and helpful interchange on the effect of genetic engineering *per se* on the environment, see "Genetic Engineering Is Environmentally Safe" (by the National Acad of Sciences), and Frances E. Sharples,

"Genetic Engineering Raises Environmental Concerns." Both articles appear in William Dudley, ed., *Genetic Engineering: Opposing Viewpoints.*

79. The matter of biological warfare is most interesting. Here we note that some say the building of genetically engineered organisms for use in biological weapons is not as much a bargain for the country using them as might be suspected. The assumption is that these weapons would harm the enemy, and no one else would be affected. However, though these weapons might destroy the enemy, if there is no antidote to these new bacteria and viruses, they will not necessarily die after killing the enemy. Once released into the atmosphere, there is no guarantee that the country (let alone the army) using the weapons will escape their effect. Hence, critics of these weapons argue that they shouldn't be built, since there is no guarantee that the weapon user could escape being killed by his own weapon. As to the morality of these weapons, we think they are immoral. In our chapter on war we shall argue for support of the just war theory. One of the principles of that theory is that a just war must exempt noncombatants from harm. In view of what has been said about biological weapons, it is clear there can be no guarantees of noncombatant immunity. For an interesting interchange on this whole matter of genetic engineering as it relates to biological warfare, see Charles Piller and Keith R. Yamamoto, "Genetic Engineering Will Lead to a Biological Arms Race"; William Bains, "Genetic Engineering Will Not Lead to a Biological Arms Race"; Joseph D. Douglass, Jr., "Biological Weapons Research Should Continue"; Jay A. Jacobson, "Biological Weapons Research Should End"; H. Allen Holmes, "The Biological Weapons Convention Can End Proliferation"; and Douglas J. Feith, "The Biological Weapons Convention Is Useless," all of which appear in William Dudley, ed., *Genetic Engineering: Opposing Viewpoints.*

80. Arnold Voth, "Christian Principles in Medical/Ethical Dilemmas," *Conrad Grebel R* 6 (1988): 37; Anderson, p. 89; H. Tristram Engelhardt, Jr., "Persons and Humans: Refashioning Ourselves in a Better Image and Likeness," *Zy* 19 (September 1984): 286; Wes Granberg-Michaelson, "A Biblical Look at Genetic Engineering," *Sojourners* 12 (June-July 1983): 21; Fred Rosner, "Test Tube Babies, Host Mothers and Genetic Engineering in Judaism," *Tradition* 19 (Summer 1981): 146.

81. Jeremy Rifkin, "Playing God," *Sojourners* 9 (August 1980): 9; see also Anderson, p. 90.

82. Susan Wright, "Genetic Engineering: The Risks Are Real," *Chr Cris* 14 (1983): 330.

83. Chamberland, p. 26.

84. Anderson, pp. 92-93. For further discussion of patenting life, see Lee Ehrman and Joe Grossfield, "What Is Natural, What Is Not?"; Key Dismukes, "Life Is Patently Not Human-Made"; Harold P. Green, "Chakrabarty: Tempest in a Test Tube"; Norton D. Zinder, "The Berg Letter: A Statement of Conscience, Not of Conviction"; and David Baltimore, "The Berg Letter: Certainly Necessary, Possibly Good," all part of a symposium, "The Supreme Court and Patenting Life," *Hast Center Rep* 10 (October 1980): 10-15. See also Rifkin, pp. 9-10.

85. See Angela Holder, "Is Existence Ever an Injury?: The Wrongful Life Cases," in Stuart F. Spicker, Joseph M. Healey, Jr., and H. Tristram Engelhardt, Jr., eds., *The Law-Medicine Relation: A Philosophical Exploration* (Dordrecht, Holland: D. Reidel, 1981), pp. 225-239; and the discussion of this in Engelhardt, p. 286.

86. Engelhardt, pp. 286-287.

87. John Breck, "Bio-medical Technology: Of the Kingdom or of the Cosmos?" *St Vlad Th Q* 32 (1988): 17. See also Rifkin, "Playing God," *Other Side* 19 (April 1983): 16.

88. Breck, p. 17.

89. Rifkin, "Playing God," *Other Side*, p. 16. For his further discussion of this matter see pp. 16-17. See also Engelhardt, pp. 287-288 for an interesting discussion of this problem and what might be done to alleviate this problem of undue uniformity without also having to include defective disease-producing genes.

90. Breck, p. 17.

91. Joseph Fletcher, *The Ethics of Genetic Control: Ending Reproductive Roulette* (Garden City, NY: Anchor/Doubleday, 1974), pp. 172-173, as cited in Leroy Walters, "Human *In Vitro* Fertilization," *Hast Center Rep* 9 (August 1979): 39.

92. R. G. Edwards, "Fertilization of Human Eggs In Vitro: Morals, Ethics, and the law," *Q Rev Biol* 49 (March 1974): 15, as cited in Walters, "Human *In Vitro* Fertilization," p. 39.

93. Benjamin Freedman, "Leviticus and DNA: A Very Old Look at a Very New Problem," *J Relig Ethics* 8 (1980): 106-108, 111-112. Freedman concludes that this prohibition does not exclude all uses of rDNA technology, for it is still appropriate for therapeutic use. However, he claims that Lev 19:19 definitely forbids use of this technology to produce hybrid life forms.

94. Michael Ruse, "Genesis Revisited: Can We Do Better Than God?" *Zy* 19 (September 1984): 306-309.

95. *Ibid.*, pp. 311-312.

96. Wright, pp. 332-333. See also the articles in section 5 ("Will Genetic Engineering Lead to a Biological Arms Race?") of William Dudley, ed., *Genetic Engineering: Opposing Viewpoints.*

97. While some find objectionable the use of technology to interfere with the established order in nature and see it as all too easily used to deemphasize and dehumanize persons, others think of it as society's "toolbox." On this latter view, the more technology, the better, for it gives society more tools to conquer man's environment and someday possibly construct utopia. For an excellent discussion of this whole issue of technology and its relation to the natural order, especially in relation to rDNA research, see Allen Verhey, "The Morality of Genetic Engineering," *Chr Sch R* 14 (1984-1985): 133-136.

98. Strobel, p. 270. See also more generally his discussion of this issue on pages 267-271. See also Lewis P. Bird, "Universal Principles of Biomedical Ethics and Their Application to Gene-Splicing," *Per Sci Chr Faith* 41 (June 1989): 82-83 for a discussion of this matter of playing God. He concludes that using this technology is not necessarily playing God but can be seen as part of our task of subduing and transforming God's creation. Similarly, Ronald S. Cole-Turner, "Is Genetic Engineering Co-creation?" *Th Today* 44 (1987): 346-347 argues that man is not trying to take God's place, but to work with him as co-creator. Of course, one can hardly co-create without knowing God's intent in creation. Cole-Turner says it is best to view God as a transcendent creator who works through natural processes, but whose creative intention transcends natural processes. God works through the evolutionary process, according to this view, and we are his co-creators. The key is not to withdraw from genetic engineering so as to avoid playing God. The key as God's co-creators is to see this technology as "power *within* nature for creation's aims," not as "power *over* nature for our aims" (Cole-Turner, p. 349). True co-creators work as partners with God toward the former end and avoid the latter goals.

99. Granberg-Michaelson, p. 20.

100. Rifkin, "Playing God," *Sojourners*, p. 10.

101. *Ibid.* See also Donald DeMarco's discussion of this matter (pp. 130-132).

102. Dick Russell, "Genetic Engineering Is Dangerous," in William Dudley, ed., *Genetic Engineering: Opposing Viewpoints*, p. 26. See also Jaydee Hanson's discussion of animal patenting in "Congress Sees Biotechnology Problems on the Horizon," *Chr Soc Action* (January 1991): 42.

103. For discussion of this matter of patenting life forms, see Russell, pp. 26-28; Verhey, pp. 135-136; Breck, p. 22; Anderson, pp. 91-95; and the symposium in *Hast Center Rep* 10 (October 1980) on "The Supreme Court and Patenting Life."

104. Jeremy Rifkin, "Whom Do We Designate to Play God?" *E/SA* 11 (November 1983): 23 uses this illustration of what might be done as an example of the slippery slope we are on with genetic engineering. He argues, in agreement with the *NY Times* editorial of July 22, 1982, that once you begin these procedures, there is no logical

way to distinguish between repairing inheritable genetic defects and improving the species.

105. Keith Boone, "Bad Axioms in Genetic Engineering," *Hast Center Rep* 18 (August/September 1988): 11.

106. *Ibid.*

107. In fairness, Boone does admit there are some gray areas in what counts as eugenics, but he does not think most things are in the gray areas.

108. At this point we are not suggesting that we agree either with Boone's assessment of the slippery slope argument or with this alternate formulation of it. We simply note that there is more than one way to make the argument. As to the success of either way, see our assessment of rDNA research.

109. Rifkin, "Whom Do We Designate to Play God?" p. 27. See also Wright, p. 329; Breck, p. 19; Buuck, pp. 11-12; Rifkin, "Playing God," *Sojourners*, p. 10; and Rifkin, "Playing God," *Other Side*, p. 18.

110. Breck, p. 19.

111. See Leon Kass, "The New Biology: What Price Relieving Man's Estate?" in Thomas A. Shannon, ed. *Bioethics*, pp. 388-391 for a discussion of the issues surrounding the possible uses and abuses of this power.

112. Breck, p. 20. Despite the many years of testing genetically engineered organisms, there is still fear that there are decided risks to the environment through these newly created organisms. For discussion of such concerns see Margaret Mellon, "Engineering the Environment," *Chr Soc Action* (January 1991) and Doyle, "The End of Nature?"

113. Granberg-Michaelson, p. 21; and Anderson, pp. 98-100. For an interesting interchange about the environmental implications of rDNA technology, see The National Acad of Sciences, "Genetic Engineering Is Environmentally Safe," and Frances E. Sharples, "Genetic Engineering Raises Environmental Concerns," both in William Dudley, ed., *Genetic Engineering*.

114. Sumner B. Twiss, "Problems of Social Justice in Applied Human Genetics," in Alexander M. Capron, ed., *Genetic Counseling: Facts, Values and Norms* (New York: Alan R. Liss, Inc., 1979), p. 257.

115. *Ibid.*

116. *Ibid.*, pp. 257-264 offers an excellent discussion of the different views on these issues and shows that much fallacious thinking often enters into eugenic thinking. Twiss notes further how difficult it really is to determine specific goals for eugenic programs and to know how to assess those goals as moral or immoral, worthy or unworthy.

117. *Ibid.*, pp. 264-265.

118. *Ibid.*, p. 265.

119. *Ibid.*

120. Verhey, p. 137.

121. Crick, as cited in Chamberland, p. 28.

122. This issue is raised not only by Chamberland and Verhey, but is discussed by many others, including Engelhardt, p. 289ff. and Buuck, pp. 11-12. See also the interesting interchange on this and other issues in the articles by Brian Stableford ("Humans Should Be Genetically Redesigned") and Jeremy Rifkin ("Humans Should Not Be Genetically Redesigned") in William Dudley, ed., *Genetic Engineering: Opposing Viewpoints*, pp. 65-78.

123. Breck, p. 21.

124. Martin Mawyer, "Genetic Engineering Raises Moral Questions," *FuJo* 4 (1985): 63.

125. DeMarco, p. 132.

126. *Ibid.* See also his further discussion of the nature of man on p. 133ff. In a similar vein Leon Kass warns against reproductive technologies such as *in vitro* fertilization, saying that they increasingly take a human activity and consign it to the laboratory. In so doing, they depersonalize and dehumanize the process of human reproduction. See Kass, "The New Biology: What Price Relieving Man's Estate?" p. 393.

127. Breck, p. 18 and Ramirez, p. 21, for example, raise this question. See also Leon R. Kass, "The New Biology," pp. 387-388.
128. Breck, pp. 18-19. For an excellent lengthy discussion of the whole matter of distributive justice as it relates to genetic engineering, see Twiss, pp. 265-266, 269-274.
129. See Granberg-Michaelson, p. 21; Jonathan King, "Prospects and Hazards of New Genetic Technologies," *Chr Cris* 39 (1979): 250; and Russell, pp. 28-30.
130. Dismukes, pp. 434-436. On p. 436 he cites various comments made by scientists, philosophers and lawyers in the mid-1970s. Depending on one's perspective and who was taking the risk, they evaluated differently whether the risk was worth it. However, at that time there were thought to be some considerable risks. See also Verhey, pp. 126-127.
131. Verhey, pp. 130-131. See also Twiss, p. 274 for further discussion of why what he calls cost/benefit analysis is often not very helpful and overlooks key ethical concerns.
132. Verhey, p. 129.
133. *Ibid.*, pp. 129-130. See also Leon Kass's discussion of the link between knowledge and power in his "The New Biology," pp. 397-398.
134. *Ibid.*, p. 130.
135. Lewis Bird offers seven principles (p. 78) that he calls universal principles of medical ethics. The first six he believes are relevant to gene-splicing. They are: *primum, non nocere* ("first of all, do no harm"), the sanctity of human life, the alleviation of human suffering, the confidentiality of the physician-patient relationship, the right to truth, and the right to informed consent. He evaluates rDNA in light of these principles and concludes that it fits with these principles and is thus morally acceptable. For his reasoning on these matters, see pp. 78-82.
136. Though it can be debated, what we suggest here assumes that there would be no disease, life-threatening or otherwise, if the race had not fallen into sin.
137. Various legal implications of rDNA were also raised. We think those considerations urge prudence in using this technology. However, we do not think those potential legal pitfalls make rDNA immoral *per se*. Of course, in some cases where legal problems arise, rDNA might be both immoral as well as imprudent. Our point here is only that as non-consequentialists, we do not see the legal problems that might result from rDNA as an adequate basis for thinking rDNA immoral.
138. Peter Gorner, "Early Gene Therapy Gets Rave Reviews," *Chi Trib* (July 28, 1991): 1, 6 (sec. 1). See also the original announcement that the experiment was to be undertaken, in Ronald Kotulak, "Scientists Find Ways to Give Patients Genes," *Chi Trib* (February 24, 1991): 21, 25 (sec. 1).
139. Gorner, p. 6.
140. *Ibid.*
141. Previously, sufferers from the disease were given the genetically engineered drug PEG-ADA, which replaces the missing enzyme in the patient's blood. However, it does not cure the disease, and its long term effects are unknown.
142. W. French Anderson, "Human Gene Therapy," p. 276.
143. Peter Gorner, "Direct Gene-to-Cancer Injection OKd for Test," *Chi Trib* (April 14, 1992): 2 (sec. 1).
144. At the outset, we note that there is discussion about whether gene therapy of any kind will actually work. For an interesting interchange on the pros and cons of this issue, see Jim Merritt, "Genetic Engineering Can Cure Inherited Diseases" and Stuart Newman, "Genetic Engineering Cannot Cure Inherited Diseases," both in William Dudley, ed., *Genetic Engineering: Opposing Viewpoints*. Both articles were originally published in 1989. Though this is a question of great interest to scientists, it is not the focus of our discussion. We believe questions of whether such therapies can succeed are of import to the ethicist, but our intent is to distinguish and address the question of whether these therapies should (morally should) be used. That is a moral question which must be addressed whether or not gene therapy accomplishes its end.

While this question is likely to be answered by consequentialists in light of whether successful gene therapy can be done (i.e., the end, if attainable, would clearly seem to justify the means), for non-consequentialists such as ourselves, the "can" and "should" questions must be asked separately.

145. DeMarco, pp. 129-130.
146. John C. Fletcher, "Ethical Issues in and Beyond Prospective Clinical Trials of Human Gene Therapy," *J Med Phil* 10 (1985): 294. These criteria were first presented in 1980 in W. F. Anderson and J. C. Fletcher, "Gene Therapy in Human Beings: When Is It Ethical to Begin?" *NEJM* 303 (1980): 1293-1297.
147. W. French Anderson, p. 278. On pp. 278-282 Anderson then outlined the scientific state of affairs at the time he wrote with respect to the three criteria. At that point, he argued that delivery and expression systems were being developed that would meet the criteria for successful gene therapy. Safety was still the biggest unknown.
148. *Ibid.*, pp. 282-283.
149. Jeremy Rifkin, *Algeny* (New York: Viking Press, 1983), p. 232. Cited and discussed in Fletcher, "Ethical Issues in and Beyond Prospective Clinical Trials of Human Gene Therapy," p. 299ff. See also the articles cited earlier by Rifkin that express the same point of view. Fletcher (pp. 302-303) thinks Rifkin's views contain a number of logical errors. Among them is the implicit assumption that once we begin engineering genes, there will be no logical way to stop, because it will be impossible to distinguish uses of this technology that are moral from those that are not. On the contrary, Fletcher thinks there are ways to make distinctions. He sees the most fundamental distinction as the difference between uses that may relieve real suffering as opposed to uses that may alter characteristics that have little or nothing to do with disease. This is basically the therapeutic/eugenic distinction we have already noted.
150. See W. French Anderson, pp. 283-285 for a discussion of the method of microinjection of a fertilized egg. He explains how this has been done in animals and why he believed it to be inappropriate for use in humans at the time of his writing of the article.
151. Breck, p. 21.
152. For these objections, see Granberg-Michaelson, p. 22. Though it may seem like he is saying the problem is that we are usurping God's role, that is not exactly his point. His point is that we think we know the consequences of what we are doing, but there is no guarantee that we do. To proceed in such a case is morally objectionable.
153. Rifkin, "Whom Do We Designate to Play God?" p. 28. See also his "Playing God," *Other Side*, p. 18, where he makes it very clear that his concern is over germline gene-splicing. See as well for the same point that no one should be trusted with such decisions except God his "Playing God," *Sojourners*, p. 10.
154. W. French Anderson, p. 285.
155. *Ibid.*
156. *Ibid.*, pp. 285-287.
157. Fletcher, "Ethical Issues in and Beyond Prospective Clinical Trials of Human Gene Therapy," p. 304.

CHAPTER ELEVEN: *Divorce and Remarriage*

1. William Oglesby, "Divorce and Remarriage in Christian Perspective," *Past Psych* 25 (Summer 1977): 290.
2. David E. Garland, "A Biblical View of Divorce," *Rv Ex* 84 (Summer 1987): 419.
3. David Field, "Talking Points: The Divorce Debate—Where Are We Now?" *Them* 8 NS (April 1983): 26.
4. Statistics are taken from the *1990 Demographic Yearbook*, 42nd edition (New York: United Nations, 1992), pp. 520-533, 744-757. These are the most current statistics available (as listed in the yearbook) at the time of the writing of this chapter.

5. Lloyd Billingsley, "Bad News About the Effects of Divorce," *ChrT* 26 (November 12, 1982): 84.
6. *Ibid.*
7. A. Isaksson, *Marriage and Ministry in the New Temple*, as cited in William F. Luck, *Divorce and Remarriage: Recovering the Biblical View* (San Francisco: Harper & Row, 1987), p. 17.
8. Compare Luck's discussion (*Divorce and Remarriage: Recovering the Biblical View*) on pp. 8-16 to the effect that there is nothing inherent in the biblical words that demands permanence. Moreover, Genesis 2 focuses on marriage, not on divorce, so the issue of terminating marriage and the question of how long the bond will last are not really entertained.
9. John Macquarrie, "The Nature of the Marriage Bond," *Th* 78 (1975): 230-231. Before directly addressing the question of possibility, one should distinguish between a moral and a metaphysical or ontological bond. In the former sense, marriage is a "life commitment," a moral obligation that ought not to be broken. In the latter sense the marital bond is considered a real union brought into existence, a thing that *cannot* be destroyed. Those who raise this distinction usually do so to note that a moral bond can be broken, though it should not be, whereas an ontological bond cannot be broken regardless of what happens. Others correctly note that even if the marital bond is ontological, that does not prove it is ontologically indissoluble. From our perspective, the concepts of marriage as a moral and ontological bond are not mutually exclusive. Though the kind of entity created in the ontological sense has a rather strange ontological status (it is not some material object), this is an issue better left to metaphysicians. The question of import is whether the bond (ontological or not) can be broken. As noted, if one thinks not, his reasons ought to be different than merely pointing to the bond as ontological in nature. For further discussion of this issue, see Helen Oppenheimer, "Is the Marriage Bond an Indissoluble 'Vinculum'?" *Th* 78 (1975).
10. Paul F. Palmer, "Needed: A Theology of Marriage," *Com* 1 (Fall 1974): 253; see also Eugene F. Roop, "Two Become One Become Two," *Breth Life* 21 (Summer 1976): 135, and Gordon Wenham, "May Divorced Christians Remarry?" *Chmn* 95 (1981): 153. See Field, p. 27 for comparison of the biblical notion of covenant and marriage.
11. Paul Steele and Charles Ryrie, "Are Divorce and Remarriage Ever Permissible?" *FuJo* 3 (June 1984): 17. See also Macquarie, p. 232; and J. Carl Laney, *The Divorce Myth* (Minneapolis: Bethany House, 1981), pp. 20-22.
12. William A. Heth and Gordon J. Wenham, *Jesus and Divorce* (Nashville: Thomas Nelson, 1984), pp. 106-111.
13. Macquarrie, pp. 234-235. See also pp. 232-234 for further arguments that seem of lesser import to us.
14. For organization of divorce and remarriage positions on the basis of whether they are deontologically or teleologically oriented, see Bruce M. Haight, "Ethical Considerations on Divorce and Remarriage," *Cov Q* 47 (May 1989).
15. For examples of views on divorce that presuppose that the exception clause was not said by Jesus, see Stanley B. Marrow, "Marriage and Divorce in the New Testament," *Angl Th R* 70 (January 1988), and Don T. Smith, "The Matthean Exception Clauses in the Light of Matthew's Theology and Community," *Stud Bib Theol* 17 (April 1989). For further argumentation that Jesus did not utter the exception clause, see Garland, p. 424.
16. Heth and Wenham, p. 179.
17. *Ibid.*, pp. 179-181.
18. Described by Luck, p. 93. Though one could use this understanding of the exception clause and still say on other grounds that divorce for *porneia* is acceptable (though the divorce does not make the woman an adulteress), this understanding of the exception clause could be used in the way explained to support a no divorce position.

19. Isaksson, *Marriage and Ministry in the New Temple*, is one of the best-known scholars holding this view. See also Heth and Wenham, pp. 169-171 for a description of the view. This is precisely the situation that confronted Joseph when he learned during his betrothal to Mary that she was pregnant.
20. Luck, p. 96ff. Some have also understood Mal 2:10-16 to relate to this issue. They have interpreted the passage to suggest that Jewish people in Malachi's day were divorcing their wives and marrying foreigners. God says he hates divorce (2:16), and some take this to mean the divorce of Jewish women in favor of marrying foreign women. In such a circumstance, it might be argued, God would allow divorce of the foreign woman. Others claim that God's real complaint is that his people have apostasized from their covenant with him and have gone after foreign gods. That kind of divorce is what he hates. Still others see a blending of the two ideas in Malachi; i.e., Judah has apostasized from the Lord, and one of the signs of that is the divorcing of Jewish wives in order to marry foreign women whose allegiance is to another God. For interesting discussions of Malachi 2 see Beth Glazier-McDonald, "Intermarriage, Divorce, and the *BAT-'EL NEKAR*: Insights into Mal 2:10-16," *JBL* 106 (1987), and David Clyde Jones, "Malachi on Divorce," *Presbyterion* 15 (Spring 1989).
21. Laney, Steele and Ryrie, F. F. Bruce, *Commentary on the Book of Acts*, and J. A. Fitzmyer, "The Matthean Divorce Texts and Some New Palestinian Evidence," *Th St* 37 (June 1976) are examples of those who hold this view.
22. Heth and Wenham, pp. 22, 38.
23. *Ibid.*, pp. 35-36. They show this to have been Tertullian's view.
24. *Ibid.*, p. 52.
25. *Ibid.* See their summary of the whole position.
26. Variations of the Erasmian position are ably described in Heth and Wenham, Luck, and Ryrie and Steele.
27. Luck, p. 59.
28. *Ibid.*, p. 66.
29. *Ibid.*, pp. 228-243.
30. *Ibid.*, pp. 84-85.
31. *Ibid.*, p. 88.
32. *Ibid.*, pp. 122-123.
33. *Ibid.*, pp. 144-146.
34. *Ibid.*, p. 145. However, he also claims (p. 145) that to say that a husband who groundlessly puts away his wife could not remarry is to deny the OT doctrine of morally permissible polygamy. His position is not clear here.
35. *Ibid.*, pp. 247-251.
36. For an interesting discussion of laws and customs in regard to marriage and divorce in the ancient Near East as well as in the Roman Empire and the OT, see Gordon Wenham, "Marriage and Divorce in the Old Testament," *Didaskalia* 1 (November 1989).
37. Garland, p. 419.
38. C. F. Keil and F. Delitzsch, *Biblical Commentary on the Old Testament*, Vol. III (Grand Rapids, MI: Eerdmans, 1968) and D. A. Carson, *The Expositor's Bible Commentary: Matthew*, Vol. 8 (Grand Rapids, MI: Zondervan, 1984) suggest this purpose of the legislation.
39. See Luck, pp. 57-67 for his discussion of this passage.
40. Heth and Wenham, pp. 106-110.
41. *Ibid.*, p. 107.
42. See, e.g., Wilhelm Schroeder, *Deuteronomy*, in *Commentary on the Holy Scriptures*, Vol. 2, ed. J. P. Lange (Grand Rapids, MI: Zondervan, 1969) on Deut 24:1.
43. Heth and Wenham, pp. 106-110. See also Wenham, "May Divorced Christians Remarry?" pp. 154-155 and William Heth, "The Meaning of Divorce in Matthew 19:3-9," *Chmn* 98 (1984): 143-145.

44. See Dwight H. Small, "The Prophet Hosea: God's Alternative to Divorce for the Reason of Infidelity," *J Psych Th* 7 (Summer 1979) for ten good reasons why it is best to believe Hosea never divorced Gomer. Moreover, if Gomer returned to Hosea after marrying and being divorced by another man, the commandment in Deut 24:4 would have been broken (and because God ordered it). This leads us to believe Gomer was never divorced from Hosea.

45. P. C. Craigie outlines a view that begins to approach what we have suggested, but Heth and Wenham reject it because they say he relies too heavily on NT ideas. See Heth and Wenham, p. 108.

46. See Paul D. Feinberg, "Hermeneutics of Discontinuity," in *Continuity and Discontinuity*, ed. John S. Feinberg (Wheaton, IL: Crossway Books, 1988), p. 113.

47. See also Bruce Vawter, "Divorce and the New Testament," *CBQ* 39 (1977): 532-533. See Robert Stein, "Is it Lawful for a Man to Divorce His Wife?" *JETS* 22 (June 1979): 16 for an analysis of the items that are similar in the two passages. He notes seven similarities. Note also that while Matthew 19 records the Pharisees' question about the bill of divorce, from the way the question is posed, it is clearly a veiled assertion (v. 7).

48. D. L. Dungan, *The Sayings of Jesus in the Churches of Paul: The Use of the Synoptic Tradition in the Regulation of Early Church Life* (Philadelphia: Fortress, 1971), pp. 111-112, as cited in Fitzmyer, p. 222.

49. Fitzmyer, pp. 216, 222-224.

50. Thomas Thompson, "A Catholic View on Divorce," *JES* 6 (1969): 60, and Augustine Stock,"Matthean Divorce Texts," *Bib Th Bul* 8 (February 1978): 29.

51. Wenham, "May Divorced Christians Remarry?" pp. 156-157. There is some question in verse 11 as to whether the adultery is committed against the divorced wife or the remarried one. Grammatically, the phrase *epi auten* could refer to either. How one interprets that phrase seems beside the point. In verse 12 the phrase "against him" is not even included. Jesus' point is that the husband commits adultery by divorcing and remarrying.

52. For an interesting, though somewhat strange, alternate interpretation of this passage, see Barbara Green, "Jesus' Teaching on Divorce in the Gospel of Mark," *JSNT* 38 (1990). According to Green, the point of Jesus' teaching is not to explain grounds for divorce, but to show that we must love another (the spouse) to the full and to the end.

CHAPTER TWELVE: *Divorce and Remarriage (II)*

1. William F. Luck, *Divorce and Remarriage: Recovering the Biblical View* (San Francisco: Harper & Row, 1987), pp. 124-125 nicely makes this point, though we do not agree with all of his contextual interpretations or the way he uses this passage in the divorce debate.

2. For an explanation of the two views on this matter, see J. J. Van Oosterzee, *The Gospel According to Luke*, in *Commentary on the Holy Scriptures*, ed. J.P. Lange (Grand Rapids, MI: Zondervan, 1969), pp. 251-252.

3. Robert H. Stein, "Is It Lawful for a Man to Divorce His Wife?" *JETS* 22 (June 1979): 117-118; and Thomas Thompson, "A Catholic View on Divorce," *JES* 6 (1969): 55. See also Don T. Smith, "The Matthean Exception Clauses in the Light of Matthew's Theology and Community," *Stud Bib Theol* 17 (April 1989).

4. See Paul Feinberg, "The Meaning of Inerrancy," in *Inerrancy*, ed. Norman Geisler (Grand Rapids, MI: Zondervan, 1980) on the distinction between *ipssissima verba* and *ipssissimus vox*.

5. They probably do not mention it, because in Mark 10 Jesus talks about what Moses *commanded*, and commentators probably think that undercuts the use of *permission* in Matthew 19. We disagree. Though both passages relate the same incident, Matthew and Mark give a slightly different slant on the issue, and in that different

perspective, the difference between "command" and "permit" is very important. As to how both passages harmonize with one another, see our discussion on Mark 10.

6. For a similar suggestion with explanation of how this point relates specifically to Heth and Wenham's view, see Phillip H. Wiebe, "Jesus' Divorce Exception," *JETS* 32 (September 1989): 327-333. Wiebe's paper was published after we had written our original draft of this current chapter. Hence, we both came to this point independently of one another, though he elaborates it in much greater detail than we do in this chapter.

7. D. A. Carson, *The Expositor's Bible Commentary: Matthew*, Vol. 8 (Grand Rapids, MI: Zondervan, 1984), pp. 414-415.

8. Bruce Vawter, "The Divorce Clauses in Mt 5, 32 and 19,9," *CBQ* 16 (1954): 155-167 and "Divorce and the New Testament," *CBQ* 39 (1977): 528-548.

9. William A. Heth and Gordon J. Wenham, *Jesus and Divorce* (Nashville: Thomas Nelson, 1984), p. 188.

10. Mark Geldard, "Jesus' Teaching on Divorce," *Chmn* 92 (1978): 140.

11. See J. A. Fitzmyer, "The Matthean Divorce Texts and Some New Palestinian Evidence," *Th St* 37 (June 1976): 216-221.

12. For further argumentation favoring this view, see David E. Garland, "A Biblical View of Divorce," *Rv Ex* 84 (Summer 1987): 425; Smith, pp. 66-73; and David Clyde Jones, "The Westminster Confession on Divorce and Remarriage," *Presbyterion* 16 (1990): 31-32.

13. We note as well that some such as Smith (p. 63ff.) argue for the incestuous marriage view on the grounds that this was a problem facing the church in Matthew's day. Many Gentile Christians who were coming to Christ had incestuous marriages. This created tension with their Hebrew-Christian brothers and sisters. Matthew inserted the exception clause (which Jesus never really uttered) as a way to address this issue. Though Smith may be right about Matthew's *Sitz-im-Leben*, we cannot agree that Jesus never said this. And if Jesus said it, it was not to address the problem Smith thinks Matthew was addressing (in Jesus' lifetime there weren't Gentiles coming to the church and creating this kind of tension among their Jewish-Christian brothers—the church simply wasn't that far developed). Thus, if the incest view is correct, it is surely not correct because of Matthew putting it into Jesus' mouth to address a problem in the early church.

14. Here it is interesting to see how some commentators try to broaden the meaning of *porneia*. David Clyde Jones (p. 38), for example, says, "Though *porneia* in the exceptive clause in Matthew may refer in the first instance to the specifically sexual sin of adultery, its pervasive use in the Old Testament for Israel's covenant breaking creates the possibility that it is used here as a synecdoche, that is, as a part (adultery) for the whole (gross violation of the marriage covenant)." As to what those other sins designated by *porneia* might be, Jones says, "it is clear that some violations of the marriage covenant are the moral equivalent of adultery: a husband who forces his wife to have an abortion; a wife who has an abortion without the knowledge of her husband; a husband who habitually beats his wife or children. All these actions strike at the heart of the marriage relationship. The adulterer, the deserter, and the inveterate abuser are alike guilty of gross betrayal of their marriage companion. By their actions they willfully repudiate the one flesh relationship of the marriage covenant and so provide just cause for the dissolution of the marriage bond" (*ibid.*).

15. Carson, p. 416 makes this point, though he only notes the use of *apoluo* in vv. 3 and 9.

16. Heth and Wenham, p. 115.

17. *Ibid.*

18. *Ibid.*

19. As to the assumption that Jesus only repeats OT law, we have already addressed this issue in our first chapter on moral decision-making. Luck's understanding of Matt 5:17 is deficient. Moreover, since Jesus by the Holy Spirit speaks through the NT

writers (cf. John 14:25-26; 15:26-27; 16:12-15), they had better say nothing that abrogates any part of the law, if Luck is right. But they do. For example, they do not demand blood sacrifice for sin, nor do they enjoin obedience to OT dietary and ceremonial laws generally. Christianity and Judaism are distinct (though related) religions. Luck's attempt to harmonize the OT with all NT passages is admirable but misguided.

20. Luck, pp. 146-147.
21. This is probably what Luck would say if the woman is the one guilty of *porneia*. If it is the man, it is not clear what Luck would say. If the man committed *porneia* and then sought a divorce just to get to the new wife, Luck would probably argue against it. However, this is speculation about Luck's views since he is unclear on this point.
22. Heth and Wenham, pp. 126-129; and Geldard, pp. 135-137.
23. Heth and Wenham, p. 134.
24. Geldard, p. 138.
25. Carson, p. 411.
26. Actually, Jesus takes an even harder stance on adultery (Matt 5:27-28) than the OT, and through his apostles' writings in the NT condemns other forms of *porneia*. The various forms of *porneia* are still morally wrong. We also note that while ethical rules are rooted in God's nature, specific punishments for breaking laws are not necessarily so rooted. Obviously, since God is just, the punishment must be just, but there may be several different punishments that could be just for a particular crime. Moreover, God is also a merciful God. If he functions in mercy rather than strict justice, that is surely acceptable. What is inadmissible is for him to abandon both mercy and justice. Lightening the penalty for adultery upholds both God's mercy and justice. Justice is served, for there is a punishment for wrongdoing. Mercy is also exhibited by exacting a lesser penalty. Even though this may be less than exact retribution, all that is demanded is that it not be an unjust penalty, and as merciful, it is not.
27. Luck's answer is basically that Matthew includes it when Mark does not for the sake of completeness. Matthew tends to be more complete than Mark anyway. This may sound good, but it is unconvincing when one recognizes that Luke, who is most prone to detail, excludes it as well and only devotes one verse to the matter of Jesus' teaching on divorce and remarriage. Luck never bothers to consider Luke in the discussion of why the exception appears in Matthew alone.
28. Having offered this explanation, one further word is in order. It is unthinkable that Matthew thought no Gentile would ever read his Gospel or that Mark and Luke thought no Jew would read theirs. Moreover, the Holy Spirit who inspired these books knew who would read them. That is, we do not want to give the impression that we think only Jews would read Matthew and only Gentiles would read Mark and Luke. The point is only to note the initial readers of the Gospels, their levels of knowledge, and their concerns as helpful in explaining what the Gospel writers did with the clause.
29. Ben Witherington, "Matthew 5.32 and 19.9—Exception or Exceptional Situation?" *NTSt* 31 (1985): 571.
30. Augustine Stock, "Matthean Divorce Texts," *Bib Th Bul* 8 (February 1978): 24-25 notes this important difference between Matthew 5 and the other Gospel passages, but one should not make more of this than to recognize its purpose in the immediate context.
31. The infinitive *moicheuthēnai* from *moicheuō*, though passive in form, seems to have an active force, as does *moichatai*—also passive or middle in form—later in the same verse.
32. Here one must be careful not to draw the wrong conclusion. If a woman commits *porneia* and is divorced, she is free to remarry without committing adultery. This does not mean that if she is divorced for *porneia* and stays unmarried she is free to have sex relations with whomever she pleases. God makes very clear that sex is reserved for marriage. See our chapter on sexual morality.

33. Vawter, p. 531.
34. Luck, pp. 103-110.
35. *Ibid.*, p. 108.
36. See, for example, Glazier-McDonald's helpful article on Malachi 2. Given her discussion, it is surely dubious that Malachi refers to Deuteronomy 24. See Beth Glazier-McDonald, "Intermarriage, Divorce, and the *BAT-'EL NEKAR*: Insights into Mal 2:10-16," *JBL* 106 (1987).
37. J. K. Elliott, "Paul's Teaching on Marriage in 1 Corinthians: Some Problems Considered," *NTSt* 19 (January 1973): 223-225.
38. See, for example, Gordon Wenham, "May Divorced Christians Remarry?" *Chmn* 95 (1981): 158-159. Others such as Charles C. Ryrie, "Biblical Teaching on Divorce and Remarriage," *GTJ* 3.2 (1982): 189-190 are not even sure Paul allows divorce.
39. For an interesting handling of Paul's teaching on marriage, divorce, and remarriage in 1 Corinthians 7, see Stanley B. Marrow, "Marriage and Divorce in the New Testament," *Angl Th R* 70 (January 1988).

CHAPTER: THIRTEEN: *The Christian and War: Christian Faith in a Nuclear Age*

1. For a brief history of war and the development of warfare, see the excellent discussion in John J. Davis, *Evangelical Ethics* (Phillipsburg, NJ: Presbyterian & Reformed, 1985), pp. 227-229.
2. Robert Clouse, "Introduction," in *War: Four Christian Views*, ed. Robert Clouse (Downers Grove, IL: InterVarsity Press, 1981), pp. 11-14.
3. Davis, pp. 228, 230. See also L. L. McReavy, "Pacifism," in *New Catholic Encyclopedia* (New York: McGraw-Hill, 1967), 10: 855; and Edward A. Ryan, "The Rejection of Military Service by the Early Christians," *Th St* 13 (1952): 1-32.
4. McReavy, p. 855.
5. Clouse, pp. 14-15.
6. *Ibid.*, pp. 16-18.
7. Thomas Aquinas, *Summa Theologica*, Pt. II-II, Q. 40, Art. 1, trans. Fathers of the English Dominican Province (New York: Benziger Brothers, 1947).
8. Clouse, pp. 19-22.
9. For a typical statement of pacifist sentiment, see John C. Wenger, "The Schleitheim Confession of Faith," *MenQR* 19 (1945): 243-253.
10. Ewald M. Plass, compiler, *What Luther Says* (St. Louis: Concordia, 1959) 3: 1428-1429.
11. John Calvin, *Institutes of the Christian Religion*, IV.xx.11, "On the Right of the Government to Wage War," trans. Ford Lewis Battles (Philadelphia: Westminster, 1960).
12. Karl von Clausewitz, "On War," in Alfred Vagts, *A History of Militarism* (Cleveland: Meridian Books, 1959), p. 182.
13. This view is more of a lifestyle. It is a "live and let live" personal philosophy. People who hold this view will say, "I myself am absolutely opposed to killing and violence, but I do not try to impose my personal views on anyone else. If someone else disagrees with me and thinks that violence or killing may be justified in certain instances, so be it. That is their view. They have their values, and I have mine." While people who espouse this personal philosophy are undoubtedly sincere and desire to live in accord with their beliefs, a moral theory must be universalizable.
14. Douglas P. Lackey, *The Ethics of War and Peace* (Englewood Cliffs, NJ: Prentice-Hall, 1989), pp. 11-16.
15. Herman A. Hoyt, "Nonresistance," in Clouse, ed., *War: Four Christian Views*, pp. 29-57.
16. Lackey, pp. 16-18.
17. *Ibid.*, pp. 18-24.

18. *Ibid.*, pp. 9-10. See also Mohandas Gandhi, *Nonviolence in Peace and War*, ed. Mahadev Desai, 2 vols. (Ahmedabad, India: Navajivan Press, 1945).

19. *Ibid.*, pp. 10-11.

20. Leo Tolstoy, *My Religion*, in *The Collected Works of Leo N. Tolstoy*, trans. Leo Wiener (New York: John Wanamaker, 1904), Chapters 4-6.

21. Gandhi, II: 8.

22. Hoyt, pp. 34-44; and Myron S. Augsburger, "Christian Pacifism," in Clouse, ed., *War: Four Christian Views*, pp. 86-87.

23. Augsburger, p. 89.

24. Hoyt, pp. 35-36; Augsburger, p. 82; and Lackey, pp. 11-12.

25. Hoyt, pp. 55-57, and Augsburger, pp. 87-97.

26. Augsburger, pp. 91-92.

27. *Ibid.*, pp. 87-92.

28. *Ibid.*, pp. 88-89.

29. For a good, clear discussion of the objections to this argument, see Lackey, pp. 9-10.

30. *Ibid.*, pp. 10-11.

31. In fact, many things would make our world a better place, but that doesn't mean we are obligated to do those things. For example, sharing all wealth equally would likely make the world a better place. But that does not make "distribute all wealth equally" our moral obligation. Likewise, just because the world would be a better place if no one used violence, that does not make "never use violence" our moral obligation. See *ibid.*, pp. 12-13.

32. *Ibid.*, pp. 15-16.

33. Peter C. Craigie, *The Problem of War in the Old Testament* (Grand Rapids, MI: Eerdmans, 1978).

34. While he is not dealing with the question of war, this seems to be the approach of Stephen T. Davis, *The Debate About the Bible* (Philadelphia: Westminster, 1977), pp. 96-98, where he claims that God could not have commanded the slaughter of the Canaanites because that would have included those who were innocent.

35. Hoyt, pp. 50-53, and Augsburger, p. 86.

36. Arthur F. Holmes, "A Just War Response to Nonresistance," in Clouse, ed., *War: Four Christian Views*, pp. 65-67.

37. *Ibid.*, pp. 68-69, and Harold O. J. Brown, "A Preventive War Response to Christian Pacifism," in Clouse, ed., *War: Four Christian Views*, pp. 111-112. Here we note that some pacifists believe this is right and practice it. That is, they believe that since all force is ruled out, not even service on the police force is allowed. Of course, if everyone followed that rule, how could order be maintained in society? Someone must use government authorized force or government will be unable to fulfill its God-given duty to punish evildoers and maintain order (Rom 13:4).

38. Hoyt, pp. 48-49.

39. *Ibid.*, pp. 31-44.

40. *Ibid.*, p. 37.

41. Arthur F. Holmes, "The Just War Theory," in Clouse, ed., *War: Four Christian Views*, pp. 118-120.

42. See *ibid.*, pp. 120-22; Lackey, pp. 28-57; Arthur F. Holmes, ed., *War and Christian Ethics* (Grand Rapids, MI: Baker, 1975).

43. See Holmes, "Just War," pp. 120-122; and Lackey, pp. 58-97.

44. In assessing these criteria for a just war, it seems possible to make a case for and against participating in a revolution against one's own government. On the one hand, it might appear just, for example, because there is just cause, and revolution is a last resort. On the other hand, it may appear unjust because there is no duly appointed official to declare war for the rebels, and in a revolution it is often difficult to ensure non-combatant immunity. So, the issue is complex, and adding further to its complexity is the fact that revolutions typically involve considerations about social and political justice internal to a country. Hence, we do not believe one can decide

on the moral propriety of a revolution simply by appealing to standard moral theories about war. Given our concern in this book to avoid matters that involve social and political philosophy, we cannot pursue the question of whether wars of revolution are just. As to whether individuals should participate in them, we believe they must make that judgment at least in part on the basis of their commitment to pacifism, just war theory, or the crusade or preventive war theory.

45. See Holmes, *War and Christian Ethics*, pp. 13-23 for the readings from Plato.
46. See *ibid.*, pp. 24-31 for the Cicero readings.
47. Again, Holmes, *War and Christian Ethics,* is a good source for primary readings on this matter.
48. Holmes, "Just War," pp. 122-125.
49. *Ibid.*
50. Myron S. Augsburger, "Response to the Just War Theory," in Clouse, ed., *War: Four Christian Views*, pp. 144-145.
51. Here we would add a similar point about pacifism. If we believed evidence supported pacifism as the correct theory of war, then we would hold that it specified moral obligation, even though we know that few nations have obeyed pacifist principles. Our rejection of pacifism is not based on the fact that nations don't play by those rules, but on a belief that pacifism is not mandated by scriptural or non-scriptural teaching.
52. Harold O. J. Brown, "The Crusade or Preventive War," in Clouse, ed., *War: Four Christian Views*, pp. 153-168.
53. Sometimes Brown talks as if a crusade involves a relationship to religion in general or Christendom in particular, other times not. For this discussion, we shall divorce crusades from any relationship to religion.
54. See Herman Hoyt, "A Nonresistance Response to the Crusade or Preventive War," in Clouse, ed., *War: Four Christian Views*, pp. 172-174; and Arthur F. Holmes, "A Just War Theory Response to the Crusade or Preventive War," in Clouse, ed., *War: Four Christian Views*, p. 185.
55. Holmes, "Response to Crusade," p. 182.
56. Here we follow the classification of Lackey, pp. 98-138.
57. See Daniel A. Dombrowski, *Christian Pacifism* (Philadelphia: Temple University Press, 1991), especially Chapters 2, 5, and 6; Norman C. Freund, "The Just War: Viable Theory or Moral Anachronism?" *Amer J Theol Phil* 3 (September 1982): 71-79; and Ronald J. Sider, *Completely Pro-life* (Downers Grove, IL: InterVarsity Press, 1987), pp. 155-186.
58. Lackey, pp. 111-113.
59. See "Letters to the Editor: Nuclear Winter Remains a Chilling Prospect," *WSJ* (December 12, 1986).
60. Lackey, pp. 121-123.
61. *Ibid.*
62. Richard H. Ullman, "Nuclear Arms: How Big a Cut?" *NY Times Mag* (November 16, 1986), pp. 70-75.
63. Sider, pp. 155-168; and Lackey, pp. 122-123.
64. Lackey, pp. 113-121; and Davis, pp. 248-250. Interestingly, one form of nuclear pacifism depends on deterrence. It allows the possession of nuclear devices and even the threat of their use to deter other nations from using them. However, actual use is prohibited.
65. We find it interesting that superpowers do not want every nation to develop nuclear weapons for their own security. Rather, they want to limit their spread. But this is unfair to many nations that are vulnerable to attack from those that possess the weapons.
66. Davis, pp. 244-246.
67. Lackey, p. 124.
68. *Ibid.*, pp. 123-124.

69. *Ibid.*, pp. 111-113.
70. Davis, pp. 244-250. Albert Wohlstetter, a leading nuclear strategist, says that improvements in midcourse guidance systems on cruise missiles make it possible to attain accuracies as close as two hundred feet in comparison to the twelve thousand to thirty thousand feet misses with the ICBMs of the late 1950s. He argues that with the improved terminal guidance systems that will be developed within the next few years, collateral damage from both nuclear and non-nuclear explosions will be reduced to about one-thousandth of a square mile, a significant improvement over the Second World War.
71. *Ibid.* Sagan, however, thinks there is an important reason not to develop and employ such weapons. He thinks the accuracy of these weapons would force nations into preemptive first strikes to prevent destruction of their weapons, and this would result in destabilizing international relations. But as Davis says, Sagan forgets that these modern weapons are mobile, and it is reasonable to think that at least some would survive a first attack. Hence, temptation to mount a first strike would be reduced. The result would not necessarily be destabilized international relationships but rather a stable deterrent.
72. Though statistics can be marshaled on either side of the issue, we offer a few that are encouraging. Since 1967 the U.S. has withdrawn from the arms race. The number of land-based and submarine-launched missiles was unilaterally and voluntarily frozen in that year. The nuclear arsenal has been reduced by at least eight thousand. Changes in the former Soviet Union and Eastern Europe led President Bush to announce further cuts. The total throwweight of U.S. nuclear warheads has decreased by more than half. The average destructive power of these weapons was ten times as great in 1957 as today. The total destructive power of U.S. nuclear weapons was four times greater in 1960. A comparison between defense and social programs over the years yields some interesting results. For example, in 1955 payments to individuals constituted around 20 percent of the U.S. budget, while defense spending took 50 percent of that budget. In 1982, 49 percent of the budget went to social programs, while defense spending had dropped to 23 percent of the budget in 1980. Obviously, figures vary with the relative emphases of each President, but the general trend has been encouraging.
73. Lackey, pp. 113-117.
74. A corollary to this argument is that including nuclear weapons as an *integral* part of military strategy tends to lessen conventional preparedness for *defense*. If a nation emphasizes nuclear weapons but is attacked with conventional weapons, lack of non-nuclear preparedness will increase one's chances of defeat. Hence, emphasis should be on non-nuclear weapons, while keeping only enough nuclear weapons for finite deterrence.
75. Lackey, pp. 117-118.
76. *Ibid.*
77. *Ibid.*
78. *Ibid.*, pp. 119-121.
79. *Ibid.*
80. *Ibid.*, pp. 103-104.
81. As with finite deterrence, most arguments pro and con in regard to SDI are practical in nature, not moral. The assumption is that a nation surely has the right to self-defense. Since this strategy is a defensive posture, there can be little moral objection to it. Most considerations, then, should be about the practicality of the system.
82. Lackey, pp. 104-106.
83. *Ibid.*, pp. 99-101.
84. As with the other views, again arguments and objections focus on both moral and prudential concerns, though the major emphasis tends to fall on the latter.
85. Lackey, pp. 102-103, 106-111.

86. Even when Christ reigns on earth, there will be some who rebel. Destruction will be swift and certain, but nonetheless, some will try (see, e.g., Rev 20:7-10; cf. Zech 14:16-19 for an example of what will happen to nations that refuse to obey the Lord during his earthly reign).

87. We do not even despair over nuclear arms. We could wish they never were invented and that we, our children, and our grandchildren wouldn't live under the threat of nuclear destruction. But God is still in control. Scripture teaches there will be people alive when Christ returns to this earth. From this we conclude that though there may be wars fought with nuclear weapons, God will not allow humanity to annihilate itself before he comes. From this we take hope.

CHAPTER FOURTEEN: *The Christian and the Secular State*

1. Remarks made by Alexander Solzhenitsyn when he received the Templeton Prize at Buckingham Palace, London, on May 10, 1983.
2. Though we might also profit by considering how the First Amendment to the U.S. Constitution relates to the Christian and the state, that issue is not handled here because we want to treat issues that affect Christians everywhere.
3. W. Robert Cook, "Biblical Light on the Christian's Civil Responsibility," *Bib Sac* 127 (January-March 1970): 45.
4. Peter H. Davids, "God and Caesar," *Sojourners* 10 (April 1981): 12, 14.
5. John P. Lange, *The Gospel According to Matthew*, Vol. 8, *Commentary on the Holy Scriptures*, ed. J. P. Lange (Grand Rapids, MI: Zondervan, 1969), p. 318. See also Richard Cassidy, "Matthew 17:24-27—A Word on Civil Taxes," *CBQ* 41 (1979): 572.
6. Lange, p. 319. See also R. V. G. Tasker, *The Gospel According to St. Matthew*, Vol. 1, *Tyndale New Testament Commentaries*, series ed. R. V. G. Tasker (Grand Rapids, MI: Eerdmans, 1983), pp. 169-171.
7. Some suggest an alternate interpretation. They claim that the language of Matt 17:24-27 uses typical words for civil taxes. The only reason the didrachma is assumed to be the temple tax is the information Josephus gives on the amount of that tax. However, Jesus makes his point in terms of kings and their taxation procedures. This suggests that Jesus' point is about paying civil taxes, not religious taxes. Anyway, archaeological data show that there were a number of civil taxes levied by the Roman government at that time that cost approximately two drachma (Cassidy, pp. 571-580). On this interpretation, Jesus' point is that God rules all, and his sons are exempt from civil taxes. Jesus is the King's son, but so are the disciples, so they are all exempt. Still, so as not to upset the authorities, the tax will be paid. We have several problems with this view, because we doubt that civil taxes are under discussion. Even those holding the view admit that it is unclear whether the tax structure for Judea included several taxes (or any taxes) worth two drachma. (Cassidy, p. 577ff., admits this problem, but argues it by analogy from what is known of Roman taxes in Egypt.) This means there is no concrete evidence there was such a tax in Judea. In addition, if Jesus is talking about freedom from governmental taxes, it is dubious that this teaching coincides with that in Matthew 22 (or with Rom 13:6-7). We shall address those passages in more detail, but nothing in either passage suggests that believers are exempt from civil taxes. On this interpretation of Matthew 17, that is precisely what Jesus is saying, so we reject that interpretation.
8. Arthur Bud Ogle, "What Is Left for Caesar?" *Th Today* 35 (October 1978): 256.
9. *Ibid.*, pp. 256-257.
10. *Ibid.*, p. 256.
11. Davids, p. 15.
12. Cook, p. 50, citing Tertullian.
13. Davids, p. 15.

14. Oscar Cullmann, *The State in the New Testament* (New York: Scribners, 1956), pp. 52-53.

15. John A. T. Robinson, *Redating the New Testament* (Philadelphia: Westminster, 1976), p. 140ff. Peter writes to people undergoing persecution for their stand for Christ. We do not believe governmental persecution had begun at the time of Peter's writing. Some think Peter wrote during the Neronian persecutions, but those persecutions were confined to Rome. Peter's readers were scattered throughout the Roman Empire (cf. 1 Pet 1:1) and did not experience those persecutions. The only official persecutions that spread throughout the Roman Empire occurred both later than the time of Nero and after Peter's death. Nonetheless, Peter's readers were being persecuted for their faith, and many think passages such as 1 Pet 4:12ff. intimate that more was coming.

16. See Cullmann for a lengthy exposition and defense of these views. Given the emphasis on love in Romans 12 and 13, some think 13:1-7 is parenthetical and out of place. Others think it fits the context but cannot refer to a Christian's relation to government, for that moves too far from interpersonal relationships. Instead, they think the authorities are rulers in the local church and see Paul urging his readers to submit to them. (Ogle, pp. 258ff. elaborates this strange hypothesis.) That interpretation is hard to sustain, especially in light of the command to pay taxes to these authorities (vv. 6-7). Still others think the passage is about government, but see the authorities as the ultimate angelic powers that stand behind governments. Since God controls these spirit beings, by obeying these authorities, one ultimately submits to God (v. 2). A major support for this view is that the word used for "authorities" is Paul's typical word for angelic and demonic powers. In our opinion human rulers are in view, regardless of whether angelic beings are as well, and the passage clearly speaks to believers' obligations to governments. Moreover, we think this passage fits the context. Having urged Christians to love and live in harmony with one another, Paul turns to obligations to one's rulers. It is especially proper for Paul to address this matter when writing to people living at the center of government for the Western World.

17. See also James Moulder, "Romans 13 and Conscientious Disobedience," *J Th So Africa* 21 (December 1977): 13-23 for a lengthy discussion of why Romans should not be understood as teaching absolute and unqualified obedience to the state.

18. Some claim that the final word on NT teaching about the state comes from Revelation 13, where the state is likened to a beast. Those who argue this line interpret the passage as a reference to some Roman Emperor (perhaps Nero or a later emperor). Regardless of when one sees the fulfillment of Revelation 13, it is surely dubious that the passage gives a political philosophy about all governments. The passage refers to a particular regime and predicts its activities; no generalizations about all governments are offered. Thus, we see the passage as of negligible value for determining biblical teaching on the nature of the state or on the relation of the believer to government.

19. John Eidsmoe, *God & Caesar: Christian Faith & Political Action* (Wheaton, IL: Crossway, 1984), pp. 55-56.

20. *Ibid.*, pp. 56-57.

21. *Ibid.*, pp. 57-59.

22. Frank Stagg, "Rendering to Caesar What Belongs to Caesar: Christian Engagement with the World," *J Ch St* 18 (Winter 1978): 97-102.

23. See Glenn W. Olsen, "You Can't Legislate Morality: Reflections on a Bromide," *Com* 2 (Summer 1975).

24. Thomas B. McDormand, "Church and Government," *ChrT* 9 (April 23, 1965): 14-15.

25. *Ibid.*, p. 14.

26. Richard Shaull, "Does Religion Demand Social Change?" *Th Today* 26 (April 14, 1969): 7.

27. *Ibid.*, p. 9.
28. Frank Stagg, "Rendering to God What Belongs to God: Christian Disengagement from the World," *J Ch St* 18 (Spring 1976): 217-218.
29. James P. Hanigan, "Militant Nonviolence: A Spirituality for the Pursuit of Social Justice," *Horizons* 9 (1982): 21.
30. Gerald Coleman, "Civil Disobedience: A Moral Critique," *Th St* 46 (1985): 29.
31. *Ibid.*
32. *Ibid.*, p. 32.
33. *Ibid.*, p. 34.
34. Francis Schaeffer, *A Christian Manifesto* (Wheaton, IL: Crossway, 1982).
35. Dale Brown, "Some Possibilities for a Biblical Case for Tax Refusal," *Breth Life* 19 (Spring 1974).
36. For further discussion of the whole question of abortion and civil disobedience, see our handling of that matter in Chapter 3.
37. We contend that when the two commands are made to conflict, it is because man creates a situation which brings the two into conflict. This seems, for example, to be the way to interpret dilemmas such as whether one should lie about hiding Jews in the attic or tell the truth about their whereabouts. The only reason the demands not to lie and to preserve life conflict is the situation man has created, namely, the soldiers demanded that the Jews be handed over to be killed; in order to obey God on preserving life, those protecting Jews had to disobey the command to tell the truth. However, *prima facie*, nothing in the commands themselves necessitates that they ever conflict with one another.
38. Walter Wiest, "Can There Be a Christian Ethic of Violence?" *Perspective* 10 (Fall 1969): 131-135.
39. *Ibid.*, p. 140.
40. *Ibid.*, p. 141.
41. *Ibid.*, p. 143ff.

GENERAL INDEX

DNA (deoxyribonucleic acid), 254
DNA plasmids, 275
DNA strands, 60-61, 274
Doe v. Bolton, 48
Doe v. Kelley, 243
Donahue, Roger P., 243-44
Dorner, G., 188
Double effect doctrine, 110, 123, 124, 168
Dresden, 373
Dupont, Jacques, 308
Dyck, Arthur, 116

E. coli (*Escherichia coli*), 254, 274-75
Edwards, R. G., 228
Edwards, Robert, 222-23
Eighth Amendment (to the Constitution), 127, 132, 135
Embryos, 220, 225-229, 234-36, 238-39, 251, 286
Embryos, frozen, 226, 229-30, 239-40, 248
Emotivism, 24
Erasmian view (divorce and remarriage), 308, 330, 334-37
Erasmus, Desiderius, 348
Erickson, Millard, 110, 112-13
Estes method, 233, 237
Escalating dominance, 379, 380
Eschatology, 359-60, 364, 392-93, 394-95
Essenes, 394
Ethics, xiv, 17-43
Ethics (Frankena), 23
Ethics: Alternatives and Issues (Geisler), 23
Eugenics, 213-14, 232, 279, 281-85, 288-90
Eunuchs, 176, 180-81
Euthanasia, 105, 106-25
Euthanasia Society of America, 101
Euthanasia Society of England, 101
Euthyphro (Plato), 26
Evangelism, 391-92, 393-94
Exception clause, 323, 325, 326, 334, 337
in Matt. 5, 338-39
position of, in Matt. 19:3-12, 330-31
overview of, 305-10
Execution, 128
Existential schizophrenia, 151

Factor VIII, 276
Fairness in Death Sentencing Act, 128
Family composition, 267, 271-72, 273
Fatherhood, 241
Fetal tissue, 84-91, 232
Final Exit, 100
First Amendment (to the Constitution), 49-50
First use (nuclear weapons), 371, 375, 378, 380
Firth, Roderick, 25-26
Fitzmyer, J. A., 317

Fletcher, John C., 266, 295, 296, 298
Fletcher, Joseph, 107-8, 109, 232, 279
Flew, Anthony, 109, 111
Food and Drug Administration (FDA), 80-81, 170
Ford, Gerald, 378
Ford, Norman, 57-58
Fowler, Paul B., 62
Fox, George, 348
Fox, Joseph, 114
Frankena, William, 23, 29, 30, 42
Free choice, right to, 69-71
Free love. See Natural impulse view
Freud, Sigmund, 151
Furman v. Georgia, 127

"Gag rule," 49-50
Gallup Poll, 102, 152, 166
Gandhi, Mohandas, 348, 349, 350-1
Gardner, Charles A., 59
Geisler, Norman, 23, 29-30, 32, 93
Gene mapping, 278
General Electric, 278
Generalism, 29
Gene-splicing. See rDNA
Genetic disease, 255-62, 267-68, 272-74, 276-77
Genetic "have nots," 285, 290
Genetic pollution, 284
Genetics: counseling in, 255-62
engineering in, and human reproduction, 208-52
mixing of human and non-human materials in, 286
history of engineering in, 253-55
homosexuality and, 186-88
tampering with gene pool in, 278-79, 283-84
therapeutic uses of, 292-98
Genetic screening, 262-65
Genex, 276
Genome, 255
Germline therapy, 292, 294-96, 297-98
Goldberg, Steven, 133
Goldfarb, Alvin, 223
Gonorrhea, 173
Good Samaritan principle (abortion), 92
Government, 37, 365, 384-89, 391-95, 403, 404
Gratian, 347
Great Commission, 391
"Greenhouse effect," 373
Gurdon, J. B., 249
Gustafson, James, 39

Hague Convention, 348
Hague Court, 348
Hammurabi, Code of, 193

SCRIPTURE INDEX

ETHICS FOR A BRAVE NEW WORLD